The Reading and Preaching of the Scriptures
in the
Worship of the Christian Church

Volume 5

MODERATISM, PIETISM, AND AWAKENING

The Reading and Preaching
of the Scriptures
in the
Worship of the Christian Church

Volume 5

MODERATISM, PIETISM,
AND AWAKENING

Hughes Oliphant Old

WILLIAM B. EERDMANS PUBLISHING COMPANY
GRAND RAPIDS, MICHIGAN / CAMBRIDGE, U.K.

Wm. B. Eerdmans Publishing Co.

255 Jefferson Ave. S.E., Grand Rapids, Michigan 49503 /
P.O. Box 163, Cambridge CB3 9PU U.K.

Printed in the United States of America

09 08 07 06 05 04   7 6 5 4 3 2 1

Library of Congress Cataloging-in-Publication Data

Old, Hughes Oliphant.

The reading and preaching of the Scriptures in the worship of the Christian church /
Hughes Oliphant Old.

p.   cm.

Includes bibliographical references and index.

Contents: v. 5. Moderatism, pietism, and awakening.

ISBN 0-8028-2232-0 (alk. paper)

1. Preaching — History.   2. Public worship — History.
3. Bible — Homiletical use.   4. Bible — Liturgical use.

I. Title.

BV4207.O43   2004

264'.34 — dc21

97-30624
CIP

www.eerdmans.com

Contents

CHAPTER II
The Awakenings of Eighteenth-Century Pietism   69

Preface

This fifth volume takes as its focus the eighteenth century, commonly thought of as the century of enlightenment on one hand and pietism on the other. One thing that becomes clear as we go along is that the stories we must tell are hardly limited to a single century. To tell the story of Russian preaching, for example, we have to begin in the tenth century and continue into the nineteenth. To tell the story of Scottish preaching we have to begin with John Knox. The same way with the preaching of New England. We have to start with John Cotton, Thomas Hooker, and Thomas Shepard early in the seventeenth century.

While the eighteenth century was the century of the Enlightenment for secular humanism, for Christians much more important things happened during this century. There was the Great Awakening here in America and the Evangelical Revival in England. Neither was quite the same thing as pietism. A number of the stories we want to hear continue long into the nineteenth century. Evangelicalism, for instance, reached its height in the early nineteenth century, and much of this story we will have to leave to volume VI, although its beginnings will be clearly seen in the volume before us.

Secular thought has much to say about the Enlightenment. In Europe and the European colonies in America, the Enlightenment saw itself as a movement away from religion. It was an age in which many people became preoccupied with other than religious concerns. For many, revelation lost its fascination. In their attempts to understand their existence, they began to lose interest in the Christian Scriptures and to try to explain life on the basis of human reason and the natural sciences. If they were going to have religion, it was going to stay within the limits of reason alone. The Reformation had stressed faith in God; the Enlightenment put the emphasis on human reason and little more.

There were, of course, preachers who tried to satisfy the demands of the Enlightenment, and found themselves taken far afield from Christian worship. We might have written a chapter on the preaching of Ralph Waldo Emerson, Charles Chauncy, or the German Johann Joachim Spalding, but we have restricted our inquiry to preaching explicitly in the context of Christian worship.

For Christian history awakening has been much more important than enlightenment. In many ways the two are similar. One could, I am sure, say that awakening is but a religious approach to enlightenment, or that enlightenment is a secularized awakening. Often awakening came as a response to enlightenment, either positively or negatively. The Enlightenment did rather shake up the saints at times. Certainly it is important to see the similarities between the two. At several points in this volume we will study preachers who exemplify both movements: John Howe in England, Jacques Saurin in the Netherlands, and to be sure, Jonathan Edwards in New England. They all have in common deep piety and consecrated rationality.

Particularly important for the understanding of Christian preaching in this period is moderatism. Moderatism was firmly established by the end of the seventeenth century, especially among the heirs of English Puritanism. We mentioned Howe, a prominent Presbyterian preacher in London, as well as Saurin, the Huguenot preacher at The Hague. In addition we should name Franz Volkmar Reinhard, court preacher in Dresden, and Johann Kaspar Lavater, pastor in Zürich. Many dismiss moderatism too quickly. Moderatism, as I understand it, carefully maintained its commitment to Christian orthodoxy while at the same time cultivating a reasonable faith and a generous concern for the needs of this world. It was especially careful to support Christian society and Christian culture. In the moderatist school we must include John Tillotson, the archbishop of Canterbury, although he might be called more precisely a latitudinarian. It has to be admitted that he gives moderatism a bad name, and yet he is a big part of the picture. We have also included Matthew Henry, a preacher of such stature that he transcends any of the usual categories. He seems to have been what moderatism aimed at being but too often failed to attain.

Even more important than moderatism was pietism. The word is often used to speak very specifically of German pietism as found in Spener, Francke, Zinzendorf, and Bengel. But the American Great Awakening shared many of its approaches, so in our chapter on pietism we include Gilbert Tennent and Samuel Davies, two thoroughly turned-on American Presbyterians. Like moderatism, pietism began to take shape before the end of the seventeenth century. It continued throughout the eighteenth century and well into the nineteenth. Although it can be distinguished from Evangelicalism, the latter might also be understood as a later development of pietism. But then, too, Evangelicalism is a lineal descendant of Puritanism. Surely pietism took different forms in different countries. In France the pietism of Archbishop Fénelon, whom we treated in volume IV, took a very different form from that of Spener and Francke in Germany. As closely related as German pietism may have been to the Wesleys and Whitefield, there were distinct differences between German pietism and English Evangelicalism. Pietism was an international religious movement which may have reached its high tide in the eighteenth century but had begun long before and would last long after.

Pietism, like the natural sciences, was concerned to sound the depths of human experience. Blaise Pascal, a pioneer physicist, was a devout pietist as well, describing in detail the phenomena of religious experience. Pascal was a French Catholic who saw Christianity very differently from either his sovereign, Louis XIV, or the Jesuits. (The Jesuits, we must be sure to remember, had no monopoly on Catholicism.) Pascal was a Catholic for whom absolutism had little appeal. Sad to say, he was never a preacher. In a very similar way Jonathan Edwards helped us understand the religious affections. Like Pascal, he began to bring out the empirical and experiential nature of the Christian faith. To be sure, this had an influence on the pulpit, although it worked its way in rather slowly.

A good part of this volume is given over to the study of certain national, or denominational, schools of preaching. Up to this point Christian preaching was largely exercised in the Mediterranean world and western Europe. But now we must look more carefully at Christianity in the American colonies and then in eastern Europe. First we take a long look at New England Puritan preaching. It is a heritage in which we can delight. Never has preaching been taken so seriously or cultivated so carefully. Far more material was available to me than is usually the case. Here the library at Princeton Theological Seminary was at its best!

Some will find the appearance of a chapter on the preaching of the

Romanian Orthodox Church a bit exotic, but I have come to admire the traditions of this church through a friend of many years, Joan Alexandru, who introduced me to a very lively circle of monks and theologians both in Paris, where we were students at the time, and in his homeland. Appreciation is expressed to Calinic, bishop of Arges, as well as to Father Maxim Nica, who one summer read for me the sermons of Antim of Iveria line by line, translating as he went. This chapter has been written on the principle of *pars pro toto*. A chapter on Serbian preaching could have been written just as well, or Christian preaching in Alexandria, Smyrna, or Crete, for that matter. There is supposed to have been some superb Greek preaching in the eighteenth century, but the study of Romanian preaching was the opportunity which presented itself. The need for a chapter on the preaching of the Russian Orthodox Church was obvious enough. It was the Russian Orthodox who first suggested to me that awakening and enlightenment for a Christian are much the same thing. Philaret of Moscow, in my opinion at least, has given us the last word on the subject of enlightenment and awakening.

Another national preaching culture is that of Scotland. We have given much space to Scottish preaching simply because it is so solid. We follow it from John Knox down to Thomas Chalmers, almost three hundred years. That is the way the story goes. There is a real continuity to the history of Scottish preaching. We could have brought the story on for at least another century, but the chapter is long enough as it is.

After the brilliant court preachers of Louis XIV, Catholic preaching became a long succession of attempts to imitate Bossuet, Bourdaloue, and Massillon. It continued that way until well after the French Revolution. The famous Curé d'Ars, for example, beloved as a preacher, did little more than memorize the sermons of Bourdaloue, incredible as that may sound. It would take the cataclysmic eruptions of the 1790s to shake French Catholicism free of the old homiletical molds. That story we will leave to volume VI. Beyond France, however, Catholic Europe continued to imitate the imposing French pulpit orators of the court of Louis XIV for generations, with ever decreasing success.

It was my intention to write a chapter on preaching at the court of Maria Theresa just to balance out the story, but digging around the library, I discovered a dark underside to preaching in the Austro-Hungarian Empire. Much of it was determinedly anti-Protestant. Adam Kravařský in Bohemia and Péter Pázmány in Hungary were among the chief examples. The concerns of the Hapsburg dynasty and the Jesuit Order had far too great an influence on preaching in the Catholic Church in eastern Europe. There was, however, a strong tradition of Protestant preaching in Hungary which even in the face of martyrdom maintained itself down to our own day.

Again, to give balance, we have tried to learn what we could about the preaching of the Spanish missionaries in California. We discovered more than one might expect, which was enough to make an interesting chapter. It was, at least, interesting for me! Having spent several years of my childhood in California, I was familiar with the story of Father Junípero Serra. What kind of preacher he was I was determined to discover.

We bring this volume to a close with a chapter on the Evangelical Anglicans. They furthered the cause of true Christian faith in England when conventional religion had chilled the devotional life of the common people almost out of existence. The Evangelical awakening in the Church of England, from a numerical standpoint, has had considerable significance. The English may have a reputation for being stuffy, especially in the theological world, but from time to time they surprise us with a burst of irrepressible vitality. The Evangelical Anglicans make the point.

As the rains of mid-September begin to suggest the end of another year, we should note the retirement of William Harris, who has done so much to organize the archives of Princeton Theological Seminary. We have been friends since at least 1957. He was a graduate student then, having completed a tour of duty as a Navy chaplain. He was old enough and wise enough to command a sort of younger brother devotion. He has always been one of those people who make Princeton Princeton. How often he has pointed out preachers I should be sure to include. Another friend who has recently become a most helpful confidant in evaluating some of the preachers discussed in this volume is Jim O'Brien, pastor in Locktown, New Jersey. It was shortly after the death of Ford Lewis Battles, his beloved teacher, that we first met, and it was from Jim that I came to know so much about that eminent Calvin scholar.

It would probably be appropriate in this preface to volume V to recognize in print what most of my colleagues have long known. Ever since my volume on the Reformed baptismal rite, it has been my wife, Mary Old, who has put my handwritten manuscripts on the computer; corrected my spelling, grammar, and punctuation; and made my written work appear literate. She has a way of making my scribbled notations at least look intelligent. It has to be said: without her constant editorial work my writing career would never have been possible.

For those who have found my literary productivity a bit intimidating, the explanation is simple: my wife's gifts are the perfect complement to my own.

September 2002

CHAPTER I

Moderatism

Moderatism has been a very creative force in the Protestant pulpit even if it all too often has been misunderstood by church historians. Much more attention has been given to the more extreme movements of the eighteenth century, Deism and pietism. One is usually content to read the more moderate preachers of the period and discover premonitions of the Enlightenment or the first intimations of pietism. All too many who have studied the preaching of the eighteenth century figure it was a century when the Church got badly off the track, wandering either into rationalism or emotionalism. A more careful look shows us that not everyone went off to the extremes. Some very strong voices held the middle ground and steadfastly refused to go off with either movement. Pietism was a well-defined movement; Deism even more so. Moderatism, on the other hand, distinguishes itself more subtly. Perhaps it was not so much a movement as a refusal to go off to extremes. It was just mainline Protestantism with no particular flag of its own. It is only in looking back at it that we find a term for it, much less a definition. This can be seen quite quickly when we look at some of the leading representatives of the school.

Moderatism was a response to certain widely felt needs the Church began to feel toward the end of the seventeenth century. By that time Protestantism had lost its novelty. It was a permanent feature of European Christianity. No longer did it have to prove its right to exist. Even if Louis XIV revoked the Edict of Nantes, even if James II ascended the throne of England, Protestantism was going to survive. It had won the hearts of a significant portion of the population of Christendom.

1

Yet as much as devout Protestants were convinced of the evangelical message, it was beginning to be an old story that every one had heard again and again. We have seen this before. We noticed how a major school of preaching comes into existence, reaches its zenith, and then declines. These schools last about 150 years, sometimes as many as 200, but often not more than a century. Some of the most brilliant schools of preaching have lasted only for a single generation.

Moderatism began to appear when the various schools of preaching which the Reformation had inspired began to play out. Methods and techniques which had once been new and exciting were now tired, overused, and shabby. Truths which were once fresh and sharp sounded a bit stale and dull when preached three, four, or five generations later. Passages of Scripture which had once caught fire in the pulpit now seemed trite and flaccid. Moderatism was the response of the more perceptive young Protestant preachers to an older generation of Protestantism which had lost its freshness and become stale.

Moderatism had several characteristics. Of first importance was the appreciation of a growing number of Protestants for the rationality of the Christian faith. While the classical Protestant Reformers had been highly educated men, and while their intellectual brilliance was formidable, they had not put any emphasis on the rationality or even the reasonableness of the faith they preached. That was not their message, and yet, unlike their contemporaries, the Anabaptists, they were not anti-intellectual. They emphasized faith rather than reason, but they never deprecated the intellectual dimension of the Christian life. They assumed the reasonableness of the faith, even if they never made a particular point of preaching it. With preachers like John Howe and Jacques Saurin things begin to change. Both of these preachers still understood that the Christian faith was based on revelation rather than reason and that preaching was first of all the exposition of Scripture, but they were careful to show that the Christian faith was reasonable as well. We will have to leave to the historians of Christian doctrine a more precise account of just why this change of attitude occurred. All we can do here is note that the reasonableness of faith becomes an increasingly important theme with preachers such as Howe, Saurin, and Jean-Frédéric Ostervald. These preachers in one way or another were intellectually engaged with Descartes, Leibniz, Spinoza, Hobbes, and Locke. Some they liked and some they did not like, but their intellectual world was increasingly defined by such philosophers in a way the intellectual world of the Reformers had not been.

A second characteristic of moderatism was a growing acceptance of the diversity of Christianity, and with it a growth of tolerance. By the end of the seventeenth century there was a noticeable cooling of the confessional passions set loose by the Reformation and Counter-Reformation during the previous century. In the work of Howe, Matthew Henry, and Johann Kaspar Lavater this came from a deepening perception of the breadth of Christian love and a more profound sense of humility about our human capacity. There were other sources, of course. While for some this growing appreciation of the breadth and variety of the Christian faith came from a deeper commitment to Christian love, for others it was more a matter of weariness. Some people just got tired of squabbling over issues that seemed beyond solution. The question of the real presence at the Lord's Supper and the dispute between free will and predestination eluded any kind of settlement, and the arguments became more and more far-fetched. For those who had only a minimal commitment to the Christian faith, disputes over these same old themes had become a scandal, if not simply an excuse to ridicule those of more earnest faith. Moderatism tended to back away from polemical theology.

A third characteristic was a certain disillusionment with the state and its supposed sponsorship of the Church. Politicians had profited greatly from the passions stirred up by the Reformation. They had learned the art of fishing in troubled waters. Christians had come to suspect that the support of the state often came at a very high price. Neither Charles II nor Louis XIV could be regarded as a genuine Christian leader. They presided over notoriously dissolute courts which contradicted the most fundamental principles of Christian morality. Both monarchs insisted on strict religious uniformity out of political self-interest. The religious establishment was reduced to a sham in both of these kingdoms. During the reign of Charles I in England, Protestants began to question the divine right of kings. Oliver Cromwell tried to establish a Protestant commonwealth, but it was a failure. Even the most convinced Puritans decided they didn't want a state-sponsored Protestant uniformity. When the Catholic House of Bavaria inherited the Protestant Palatinate and when the Catholic James II inherited the throne of England, it became patent that *cuius regio eius religio* was a principle long out of date. The revocation of the Edict of Nantes finally convinced many that the state did not have the right to force people to practice a religion against their will. In 1688 when James II fled England, *cuius regio eius religio* was dealt a hard blow. It became clear that things just didn't work that way any more.

3

A fourth concern of moderatism was to develop a well-ordered life. From the beginning Protestantism produced a distinct form of morality. This became clear almost immediately. It differed from the morality of the Christian Middle Ages in that it was less ascetic, less otherworldly. Protestantism encouraged Christians to regard their life in this world positively. The classical Reformers were pioneers in this, and yet the Protestant approach to life was an implication of basic theological affirmations. Neither Luther, Zwingli, nor Calvin spent too much time with moral catechism. It was different with moderatism. As we will see, preachers like John Tillotson, Saurin, and Hugh Blair gave much time to moral catechism.

The fifth characteristic is moderatism's careful cultivation of the literary arts. The classical Reformers were naturally endowed with the literary gifts necessary to get across their message. Luther, Zwingli, Calvin, and Knox had great natural ability as orators. They did not have to spend a lot of time cultivating their literary talent. Two centuries later Protestant preachers, at least those of the moderatist school, seem to have relied less on native ability than on the formal cultivating of those gifts. A number of them were highly regarded by their contemporaries for their literary ability, and quite rightly so. The preachers of the period did much to shape their respective languages. The religion of moderatism was well considered. It was thought out, reasoned, and meditated upon, and the literary arts were part of that process of carefully thinking things over and expressing them clearly. In the pulpit Hugh Blair and George Whitefield, almost exact contemporaries, were about as antithetical as two preachers could be. Whitefield is the perfect example of the pietist preacher while Blair is the consummate example of moderatism. In formal theology the two were probably not all that far from each other. They were both Calvinists, but Whitefield was the fiery, born-again evangelist while Blair was the child of the covenant, born and brought up in the covenant of grace. Somehow the Church is not quite complete unless there are both. These two perennial types of Christians produce very different kinds of pulpit rhetoric. Whitefield preached without notes while Blair carefully prepared a full manuscript and then read it to the congregation.

Moderatism in its earlier days had a spiritual vitality it had largely lost by the end of the eighteenth century. Howe and Henry were moderate in a much more profound way than the latitudinarian Anglicans or the Scottish moderatist Blair. There is a dark side to moderatism, a sort of liberal conformism. As the awakenings of both pietism and Evangelicalism began to appear, the old moderatism began to harden into a rigid intolerance. Alas, only too often the word "moderatism" conjures up those who closed the Church to Wesley, Whitefield, and the Evangelicals of the early nineteenth century.

One more thing before we look at the leading representatives of the moderatist school. Moderatism was committed to being both orthodox and enlightened. This may sound a bit strange, but that was its genius. It distinguished itself very carefully from Deism. It emphatically defended the doctrine of the Trinity, the deity of Christ, and the inspiration of Scripture, and yet it felt inspired by the spirit of the Enlightenment. It is true, sometimes moderatism crumbled into Arianism, particularly among English Presbyterians, with the result that Presbyterianism virtually disappeared in England toward the end of the eighteenth century. But when moderatism lost its orthodoxy, it was no longer moderatism.

I. John Howe (1630-1705)

The first preacher we want to study is John Howe.[1] He gives us a good picture of moderatism in its earliest stages.

As the seventeenth century came to its end, one begins to notice an increasing number of Puritans who sought a form of Christianity enlightened enough to engage the intellect and moral enough to encourage a simple, honest Christian life. Through adversity the Puritan vision was coming to maturity. Like many Puritans of his time, Howe believed in the reasonableness of faith. The more elaborate ceremonies proposed for the worship of the Church of England held little interest for many Englishmen. In fact, they fled the sacramentalism and sacerdotalism of the Restoration. The religion of King Charles II was not very attractive to the serious-minded. It insisted on conformity and therefore encouraged in-

---

1. For biographical material on John Howe, see the memoir of Edmund Calamy prefaced to the 1724 edition of *The Works of the Late Reverend and Learned John Howe, M.A.,* 2 vols. (London: Printed for John Clark and Richard Hett, John and Benjamin Sprint, Daniel Midwinter, Ranew Robinson, Richard Ford, Aaron Ward, L. Jackson, and Samuel Chandler, 1724), 1:1-88, hereafter Howe, *Works* (1724); A. Gordon, "Howe, John," in *Dictionary of National Biography,* 22 vols. (London: Oxford University Press, 1885-1973), 10 (1891): 85-88; Robert Forman Horton, *John Howe* (London: Methuen, 1895); and Henry Rogers, *The Life and Character of John Howe, M.A.: With an Analysis of His Writings* (London: William Ball, 1836).

sincerity. There were many in England for whom a liturgy imposed by the throne, just as dogma drawn up by ecclesiastical politicians, suffocated both Christian thought and Christian devotion. As the Puritans understood it, if Christian worship was to avoid sinking into superstition, it must put the emphasis not on outward rites but on the insights of the mind and the affections of the heart. What Puritans wanted was a sermon which gave them solid doctrinal teaching as well as fundamental ethical instruction. They wanted more from the sacraments than a routine ritual. They wanted from the Lord's Table a foretaste of transcendent reality. They expected a learned and sincere minister who could preach intelligently and pray devoutly. John Howe was just that sort of minister.

Howe had all the Puritan credentials. He was the son of a respected minister of the Church of England who during the reign of Charles I had been turned out of his church by Archbishop Laud. For a few years his father was able to find employment as a minister in Ireland, but then as the forces of Parliament gained power, the family returned to England. By the time young Howe was ready to attend the university, Laud himself had been turned out and Howe was able to begin his studies at Christ College in Cambridge. Henry More and Ralph Cudworth, the famous Cambridge Platonists, were influential at the time of the Puritan ascendancy at Cambridge.

The influence of the Cambridge Platonists on the unfolding of Protestantism needs to be more fully appreciated. It is an important strand of Protestant thought, and needs to be distinguished from the classical Protestantism of the sixteenth century. Neither Luther, Zwingli, Calvin, nor Cranmer was interested in the Greek philosopher, but toward the end of the seventeenth century a significant group of philosophers and theologians began to discover Plato as a proponent of a more "spiritual" religion. Plato seemed a good antidote to the highly institutionalized forms of Christianity advocated by both the English and French monarchies. The Cambridge Platonists opposed the kind of High Church dogmatism advocated by Laud and the Stuart dynasty as much as they opposed the kind of secular totalitarianism propounded by Thomas Hobbes. They were among the first to make a convincing case for religious toleration. They advocated a rational theology and yet insisted on the necessity of revelation. As Christian Platonists before them, they were convinced of the reality of the transcendent.[2] Howe

2. Cambridge Platonism turned out to have some rather disastrous side effects for

was a good student of these men and remained a lifelong friend especially of More.

In those days it was the mark of the inquiring mind to study in different universities. Having received his bachelor's degree in Cambridge, Howe went to Oxford and took a second bachelor's degree in 1649. There he was elected fellow of Magdalen College. Thomas Goodwin was president of the college during the Puritan ascendancy, and Howe could hardly have studied under a greater example of solid Christian preaching. It is interesting that John Locke studied in Oxford during the same years. Nothing, of course, could lead more in the opposite direction from Platonism than the philosophy of Locke. Be that as it may, Locke was a Puritan of much the same temper as Howe, sharing many of the same ideas, such as the reasonableness of Christianity and the necessity of toleration. Locke was warmly regarded by most Puritans. Howe seems to have studied his *Essay on Human Understanding* soon after it was published.[3]

Between his years at Cambridge and his years at Oxford Howe gained a broad theological education, the foundation of which was the study of Scripture as the revelation of transcendent reality. This is the basis, as the great Puritans taught, of both our understanding of God and our understanding of ourselves. In the tradition of the Christian university ever since the Middle Ages, Howe thoroughly studied the Greek philosophers and those who interpreted them down through the ages. The ideas of Thomas Hobbes, René Descartes, and Benedict de Spinoza, who were leading philosophers of the day, were thoroughly discussed in the English universities at the time, and Howe was well familiar with these discussions. This is evident from Howe's work on Christian philosophy, *The Living Temple*. He seems to have worked on it over a number of years. It shows a wide knowledge of Spinoza, Descartes, Hobbes, and Locke. The Schoolmen of the Middle Ages were still studied at Oxford and Cambridge, and we know that Howe included these thinkers in his study. He read the works of a number of the classical Protestant Reformers and the divines who followed them. A lot of theology was written by the generation which followed the Reformers, and Howe seems to have read a considerable amount of it. Ames and Perkins would have headed the list.

Anglo-Saxon Protestantism. Just as Platonism encouraged Arianism in the fourth century, so it encouraged the same error in eighteenth-century Protestantism.

3. John Locke's *Essay on Human Understanding,* published in 1690, was an attack on Plato's concept of innate ideas.

One is impressed by the breadth of Howe's theological education. In 1652 he received his master's degree, giving formal sanction to his obvious mastery of academic theology.

The call to preach was very strong for John Howe. Bringing his studies to an end, he was presbyterially ordained and began his ministry at Great Torrington in Devon. He had hardly begun his ministry there when Oliver Cromwell appointed him his house chaplain, a position he accepted with hesitation. Howe was not always completely in accord with Cromwell. The position did, however, give him the opportunity to preach to those who were presiding over the affairs of England, and Howe took the responsibility seriously. As chaplain to the Lord Protector, he often used his influence to protect sincere Anglicans who may have offended Puritan politics but who had nevertheless exercised a devout ministry. Already, when he was in a position of some power, Howe began to win a reputation for his tolerance.

A. Dissent and Toleration

With the restoration of the monarchy and the reestablishment of episcopacy, Howe was ejected from the ministry. He was a latitudinarian, to use the term popular at the time.[4] The establishment considered him too broad-minded to fit in. He could accept episcopacy as a pragmatic solution to the problem of how to govern the Church, but he could not accept it when presented in the form of the doctrine of apostolic succession and when it implied that his presbyterial ordination was thereby invalid. Willing to suffer the consequences of his convictions, he retired from an active ministry though still a young man. Through the generosity of a few prosperous friends he was able to pursue his studies, work out his basic theological perceptions, and prepare several manuscripts for publication. In the meantime the officially established Anglicanism was having increasing difficulty suppressing Puritan worship. Even in London, Presbyterian and Congregational churches were gathering together in spite of official opposition. In 1676 Howe was called to be pastor of a Presbyterian church in London, and for the next ten years he was able to exercise his ministry with little interference.

In 1683, at the end of the reign of Charles II, Howe published a

4. A generation or two later, the term meant something quite different.

sermon entitled "Concerning Union among Protestants."[5] He tells us at the beginning of the sermon that he had been asked to preach specifically on this subject.[6] He chose as his text Colossians 2:2, "That their hearts might be comforted, being knit together in love, and unto all riches of the full assurance of understanding, to the acknowledgement of the mystery of God, and of the Father and of Christ." Our preacher carefully analyzes the text before beginning to apply it. He divides it to show us how unity might be achieved among Protestants: first, by mutual love to one another; second, by a clear, certain, and efficacious faith in the essential tenets of the gospel.[7] Howe addresses himself to the spiritual problem of tolerant dissent. Adroitly keeping himself out of politics, he disclaims any interest in changing the law of the land. From a spiritual standpoint, however, a genuine unity can arise from a mutual love and respect for each other and a deeper devotion to the essentials of the Christian faith. Those who led the Church of England during the Restoration had insisted on a ceremonial uniformity as a means of assuring the unity of the English church and state. The Puritans thought that was about the last way to accomplish a genuine spiritual unity. As a matter of fact, it worked against a true unity because it put the emphasis on externals.

One notices that Howe does not identify these ceremonies. Very carefully they are not mentioned. Once a particular ceremony was mentioned, then the preacher was liable for opposing a particular rite established by law. What Howe and the Presbyterians and Congregationalists found so burdensome were such things as the use of more elaborate ministerial vestments, especially the stole and surplice; the use of the sign of the cross; candles on the altar and the ceremonial lighting of those candles; an elaborate use of the liturgical calendar with the observance of seasons of fasting such as Lent and Advent; a celebration of the ordinary Sunday service without a sermon; and a mechanical reading through of the services of the *Book of Common Prayer*. All this made worship seem too superstitious, too magical, too hocus-pocus to the Puritans. They were wise enough to realize that government regulations to discontinue these practices as well as royal decrees to observe them would never get

---

5. Howe, *Works* (1724), 2:225-47. Concerning the occasion of the sermon, see Edmund Calamy's memoir at 1:26.

6. Howe, *Works* (1724), 2:225.

7. Howe, *Works* (1724), 2:228.

them beyond a religion of outward conformity. That was why they were so disillusioned with Cromwell. Even if Howe had been very close to Cromwell, he still had his reservations. Having gone through the restrictions of Cromwell and the regulations of Charles II, a growing number of Englishmen were looking for a new approach to church unity.

Very cautiously, and yet quite unmistakably, Howe is suggesting that the Church allow for a variety of liturgical celebrations and doctrinal formulations.[8] Certain basic fundamentals should be maintained, but in the working out of these there could be considerable latitude.

This whole idea of tolerant dissent was beginning to develop throughout Christendom at this time. More and more Christians were beginning to weary of a politically sponsored uniformity in religion. Charles I and Archbishop Laud had provoked a revolution by trying to impose High Church Anglicanism. Cromwell tried to do the same thing in the name of Puritanism. While the Puritans revolted against an Anglicanism imposed by the state, even the staunchest among them soon realized they did not want a Puritanism imposed by the state either. Presbyterians were almost unanimous in their disapproval of the execution of Charles I. In France the religious policy of Louis XIV was even more disastrous. In 1685 he revoked the Edict of Nantes, chasing three hundred thousand of his most industrious subjects from his domain and achieving religious uniformity for France. The loss suffered by French Protestants was minor compared to that suffered by Catholics. The sort of Catholicism he fostered forged an alliance between Catholicism and totalitarianism from which it is only now recovering.

Howe was a good enough historian to be able to show that the Church had good reasons to be very suspicious of a uniformity imposed on it by the state. As much as uniformity may be desired by the civil authority, enforcing unity may not be the most desirable policy. He showed that from the beginning the Saxons and the Helvetians had different interpretations of the meaning of Protestantism.[9] Certain of the participants in these discussions set a fine example of tolerance. The tolerance and patience of Heinrich Bullinger, Zwingli's successor in Zürich, is mentioned particularly.[10] Early in the English Reformation there were differences of opinion between Bishop Ridley and Bishop Hooper, but they re-

---

8. Howe, *Works* (1724), 2:239.
9. Howe, *Works* (1724), 2:234.
10. Howe, *Works* (1724), 2:243.

fused to let those differences break the bond of love.[11] One precursor of religious tolerance whom Howe frequently quotes is John Davenant, the Cambridge New Testament scholar.[12] As time went on, toleration became a major feature of moderatism. It was a toleration built not on indifference to Christian doctrine but on a more solid devotion to fundamental Christian teaching, and most important of all, a more ardent Christian love.[13]

With the accession of James II in 1685 the political situation changed. Lord Wharton took Howe under his protection and established him with a number of other ministerial exiles in the Netherlands. Two years later, in 1687, Howe was able to return and continue his ministry in London. With the accession of William of Orange in 1688, the latitudinarian position received strong support from the throne. Side by side with his friend John Tillotson, who soon became archbishop of Canterbury, Howe became one of the most influential preachers in London.

It was during the reign of William and Mary, 1688-1702, that moderatism first flowered in England. At this time Howe began to preach an outstanding series of doctrinal sermons which was exceptionally well received.

B. Doctrinal Preaching as Worship

As we will see during the course of the eighteenth century, more and more theologians began to think out their theology in sermons. In fact, a number of the major religious thinkers of the century left their theology to us as series of sermons. It was not for presentation in the classroom that theologians thought out their ideas, but for the service of worship. We will notice this preeminently with John Wesley. What he has left us is his standard sermons, or in more popular terms, a barrel of sermons, not a volume of theology. His theology was meant to be preached to a congre-

---

11. Howe, *Works* (1724), 2:241.

12. Howe, *Works* (1724), 2:232. John Davenant (1572-1641) later became bishop of Salisbury. His two-volume commentary on Colossians is considered even to this day one of the classic commentaries on the book. A comparison of Howe's sermon with Davenant's commentary on the text shows that Howe's interpretation in several important lines could well have been suggested by Davenant. There is no question, however, but that Howe had advanced considerably on the ideas of Davenant.

13. Howe, *Works* (1724), 2:246.

gation. The same is true of Gilbert Tennent, Samuel Davies, Jacques Saurin, John Tillotson, and Hugh Blair. Whether these preachers represent pietism or moderatism, it is the sermon which shapes their theology.

Not all were Sunday morning sermons. The tradition of the weekday morning lecture was vigorously cultivated by the Puritans. It was a favorite time for the preacher to unroll a series of sermons, especially a series of doctrinal sermons. These weekday morning lectures did not differ from the Lord's Day sermon in any particular way. It is true that they tended to draw those who were free to be away from their work on a weekday morning. Other ministers would be found in the congregation as well as the most interested members. While on the Continent they were held at an hour early enough for people to attend before work, the Puritan lectureships, as they were called, seem to have been held in the middle of the morning. They were very well attended — obviously plenty of people considered it important to attend — and were complemented with generous amounts of prayer and praise, just as the Sunday sermon. Although the word "lecture" to us implies an academic lecture without any liturgical setting, that was not what the Puritans meant.

Starting in November of 1690, Howe preached a long series of doctrinal sermons evidently intended as a full systematic theology. Only the first seventy sermons have survived.[14] The series, insofar as we have it, includes sermons on the following topics:

First Part
1. The necessity of doctrinal preaching (two sermons)[15]
2. The existence of God, manifest from the creation (four sermons)
3. The divine authority of the Scripture (five sermons)
4. The unity of the Godhead
5. The doctrine of the Trinity (four sermons)
6. The divine attributes (nine sermons)

Second Part
1. The decrees of God (eight sermons)
2. The work of creation (seven sermons)

14. It was well over a century later when these manuscript sermons were published as *The Whole Works of the Rev. John Howe, M.A.,* ed. John Hunt, 8 vols. (London: F. Westley, 1822), hereafter Howe, *Works* (1822).
15. The volume containing these sermons refers to these works as "lectures."

12

3. The creation of man (five sermons)
4. The fall of man (four sermons)
5. The justice of God vindicated (eight sermons)
6. The general and special grace of God in order to recover apostate souls (three sermons)

Several other shorter series of sermons, likewise edited by Hunt, may well have fit into this larger series, for example:

The gospel commending itself to every man's conscience (seven sermons)
On hope (fourteen sermons)
On friendship with God (ten sermons)
On regeneration (thirteen sermons)

The title Howe gave to this series was *The Principles of the Oracles of God.* He says it comes from Hebrews 5:12, in which the writer tells his readers they need instruction in basic theology. This, Howe tells us, is something all Christians need. He reminds his congregation of the long history of catechetical preaching and insists on its abiding importance. He speaks at length of the catechetical ministry of Origen and the catechetical discipline of the ancient Church. Howe is completely aware that his vigorous doctrinal teaching is one of the fundamental dimensions of the ministry of the Word, and that in his performing this ministry he is following a time-honored tradition.

Among the many excellent qualities of this outstanding series of doctrinal sermons, we would like to point first of all to their sobriety. They assume an intelligent, thinking congregation. Howe counts on convincing them with a clear and well-thought-out explanation of the relevant passages of Scripture. Rhetorical fireworks are hardly necessary when a preacher is convinced that those to whom he is preaching are intelligent and sincere people. That such sermons could be preached in London during the reign of William and Mary is really quite complimentary to the age.

A second quality of these sermons is the attempt to refocus on some of the theological problems which had vexed the seventeenth century but were still unsolved at the end of that century. Howe is trying to find a way out of some of the old dilemmas. One is surprised how rarely he quotes the classical theologians of the past. It is quite clear he has studied their works, but they are not often quoted. For Howe doctrinal preaching is not a matter of reinterpreting Augustine, or Bernard, or Calvin for his own time.

Howe's series on regeneration is interesting because it bypasses the classical Protestant discussion of justification and sanctification and considers how we become Christian under the heading "regeneration." Obviously he wants to avoid the split which had developed between justification and sanctification in Protestant orthodoxy. Apparently he is just as intent on avoiding Arminianism as were some of the older Puritan theologians. Howe's old friend John Tillotson had done a series on regeneration that seemed much too Arminian for many. Perhaps Howe's series is an attempt to answer Tillotson with a more Calvinistic interpretation. Tillotson died in 1694 while Howe's series was in progress. A more detailed study might find this refocusing on the doctrine of regeneration to be one of the origins of evangelicalism.

A third point to be noticed in these sermons is their irenic tone. Much doctrinal preaching adopted the invective style of classical rhetoric. Invective may be excusable when writing theology, and one can argue that it makes polemical preaching more exciting, but in the long run it produces more heat than light. By admiring the great orators of classical antiquity, the sixteenth-century Reformers were seduced into using it far more widely than is appropriate for Christian preaching. At the court of Charles II invective was thought to be high wit by the king and his courtiers, but the more serious-minded found it less than Christian. Howe showed his contemporaries that serious doctrinal preaching could be filled with light and peace. The soul of moderatism was profoundly irenic.

Finally we notice that Howe has a very clear idea of how his serious doctrinal preaching is worship. The preachers of the moderatist school usually understood their preaching much the same way. As Howe explains in the introductory sermon of his series, doctrinal preaching serves God because God is by his very nature a teacher. Appealing to John 6:45, our preacher insists that we shall all be taught by God.[16] This is quite consistent with the Wisdom theology of the Gospel of John, which understands Christ as the Word. It is of the nature of God to teach. Jesus as Son of God demonstrated this in his own teaching ministry as recorded in the Gospels. The true disciple is one who learns from his master. Luther

16. Howe, *Works* (1822), 6:381.

14

made the same point, although Howe develops it a bit differently. Learning the teaching of the master is fundamental to the service the disciple performs for him. We find the same thing at the end of the Gospel of Matthew. As Howe points out, it was Jesus himself who sent the apostles out to teach all nations those things he had taught them. Teaching is of the essence of the apostolic ministry,[17] and therefore so is learning of God and his ways an important dimension of the service God has asked of his people.

Teaching is an important part of worship because God is of his very nature a teacher. This is a fundamental insight of the moderatist school. Moderatism developed in an age when there was a profound appreciation for the rational nature of human beings. We are by nature thinking creatures. Descartes summed it all up with his famous motto, *Cogito ergo sum,* "I think, therefore I am." But if this were true of us, it is even more true of God. God is a God of truth, and we, if we are restored in the image of God, should reflect the rational nature of God himself.[18] In the sermons on the doctrine of regeneration, Howe takes another Johannine text, "God is light and in him is no darkness at all" (I John 1:5).[19] Howe well understands Johannine Wisdom theology: holiness and truth are closely connected. The light that is God's glory is in the first instance holiness, but it is also truth and purity.[20] Christian worship takes place when we are regenerated, and as children of God reflect the nature of our Father. This glorifies God. When the divine truth is both proclaimed and received by God's people, then God is glorified.

One often discounts Protestant worship of this period as obsessively influenced by rationalism. A lot of eighteenth-century rationalism was non-Christian and even anti-Christian, but the rationality of the moderatist school was completely Christian. It was Christian in its inspiration, and it was kept in balance by the totality of Christian theology so that it refused to go to the excesses of Deism. Howe, as did the other leading representatives of the school, continued to affirm the doctrine of revelation, the reality of the fall, and the sovereignty of grace, yet Christianity was a rational religion for him and he expected Christian worship to be quite rational.

17. Howe, *Works* (1822), 6:382.
18. Howe, *Works* (1822), 8:567.
19. Howe, *Works* (1822), 8:563ff.
20. Howe, *Works* (1822), 8:566.

For many of us John Howe maintained a very attractive stance, the sort we would like to claim for American Protestantism today. It is interesting for us as Americans to reflect on the reaction to Howe's preaching reported by Benjamin Colman, a young American theologian who heard him preach in London about the time these doctrinal sermons were delivered. Colman had finished his studies at Harvard and had been given the opportunity of finishing his preparation for the ministry by a trip abroad. Of all the preachers young Colman heard abroad, Howe impressed him most. And when Colman eventually returned to Boston and began his long and notable ministry in the spiritual capital of America, the temper of Howe entered into the mainstream of American Christianity.

II. John Tillotson (1630-94)

Once again we must speak of John Tillotson, the archbishop of Canterbury during the reign of William and Mary.[21] It has been rather difficult to decide where we should treat this giant. He certainly had to be treated in the chapter on Anglican preaching in volume IV, but one could hardly write a chapter on moderatism and leave him out. His preaching was pivotal for the eighteenth century, especially in the English-speaking world.[22] As we said above, he was a man who caught the spirit of the age. He was a preacher, sad to say, who had lost the intensity of the Reformation. He was very Protestant, to be sure, but it was a sort of dumbed-down Protestantism.

A. A More Relaxed Spirituality

Tillotson shows moderatism at its most ineffectual. He never had the theological depth of John Howe nor the insights into the meaning of the

---

21. See our study of Tillotson in Hughes Oliphant Old, *The Reading and Preaching of the Scriptures in the Worship of the Christian Church,* vol. 4, *The Age of the Reformation* (Grand Rapids: Wm. B. Eerdmans Publishing Co., 2002), pp. 365-68.

22. For biographical material on Tillotson, see A. Gordon, "Tillotson, John," in *Dictionary of National Biography,* 19:872f.; Louis Glenn Locke, *Tillotson: A Study in Seventeenth-Century Literature* (Copenhagen: Rosenkilde and Bagger, 1954); and Irène Simon, *Three Restoration Divines: Barrow, South, Tillotson: Selected Sermons,* 2 vols. (Paris: Société l'Editions "Les Belles Lettres," 1976).

Scriptures that we find in Matthew Henry. And yet, all three men were re-
acting to the same religious problem. By the end of the seventeenth century, Christians all over Europe were suffering from a sort of spiritual
burnout. For over 150 years the same issues had been argued with ever increasing acrimony and ever decreasing insight. We see this happening
again and again in history. The same old thing, round and round, just
gets tiring. Howe, Henry, and Tillotson each reacted in a different way.

Cromwell's interpretation of Puritanism was very much at odds
with that of many Puritans themselves. It was too political, too secular.
That was not the problem for Tillotson. He lacked the devotional intensity of Puritanism. He wanted a more relaxed sort of spirituality.

From a literary standpoint Tillotson was a pioneer. He left the baroque prose of the seventeenth century far behind and led the way to
what today we call Augustan prose. Somehow that name never seemed
quite right. It was a sort of secularized Protestant plain style. There was
nothing stirring about it, nothing that intimated the heavenly. It was a
dispassionate, matter-of-fact sort of prose. Yes, it was rational, but sort of
mundane. Its primary grace was that it was polite.

B. Moderatism Becomes Civil Religion

Tillotson was a preacher of civil religion. A typical example of this is his
sermon "The Advantages of Religion to Society." The text is Proverbs
14:34, "Righteousness exalteth a nation; but sin is the reproach of any
people."[23] The purpose of his sermon is "to shew how advantageous religion and virtue are to the public prosperity of a nation." There is no question but that he has chosen the right text for the point he wants to make.
He comments, "And here I shall not restrain righteousness to the particular virtue of justice (though in this sense also this saying is most true) but
enlarge it according to the genius and strain of this book of the Proverbs,
in which the words wisdom and righteousness are commonly used very
comprehensively, so as to signify all religion and virtue."[24] There is no
question that the Wisdom tradition of ancient Israel which is so funda-

---

23. *The Works of Dr. John Tillotson*, 10 vols. (London: Richard Priestley, 1820),
1:409, hereafter Tillotson, *Works*. While this study started out in vol. IV using the edition
of 1700, it proved too fragile, and therefore it seemed more practical to continue the study
with the edition of 1820.

24. Tillotson, *Works*, 1:410.

mental to the book of Proverbs is quite congenial to the civil religion Tillotson preached. Our preacher has indeed chosen the right text.

That religion makes for a better society has been maintained fairly consistently down through the years, but since the fashion of his day was to question everything, Tillotson will try to prove his point. The moral judgment of history seems self-evident to him. While for individuals immorality may not be punished, for nations punishment is inevitable. Immorality destroys the foundation of society, whereas morality builds it up. Saint Augustine makes this point about the Roman Empire. It prospered as long as it maintained the temperance and justice in which its leaders took such pride. Although their leaders were not yet converted to Christianity, God rewarded them for their virtue.[25] We find this specifically taught in the prophecy of Daniel.[26]

It is only reasonable that the virtues taught by religion should have a good influence on society. "For religion in general, and every particular virtue, doth in its own nature conduce to the public interest. . . . Chastity, and temperance, and industry, do in their own nature tend to health and plenty. Truth and fidelity in all our dealings do create mutual love, and goodwill, and confidence among men, which are the great bands of peace." Surely this is only reasonable!

The rationality of it is even more obvious when one argues from the negative side. "[W]ickedness doth in its own nature produce many public mischiefs. For as sins are linked together, and draw on one another, so almost every vice hath some temporal inconvenience annexed to it, and naturally following it." Tillotson makes a strong case for public morality and civil religion. "Intemperance and lust breed infirmities and diseases, which being propagated spoil the strain of a nation. Idleness and luxury bring forth poverty and want; and this tempts men to injustice, and that causeth enmity and animosities, and these bring on strife and confusion and every evil work." Here our preacher brings out a proof text to clinch his point: "'Whence come wars and fightings among you? Are they not hence, even from your lusts that war in your members?' [James 4:1]."[27]

Tillotson wants to show the value of religion to society because it has a good influence upon both the magistrates and their subjects. Religion teaches the magistrates to rule over their subjects in the fear of God.

25. Tillotson, *Works,* 1:411.
26. Tillotson, *Works,* 1:413.
27. Tillotson, *Works,* 1:414.

Religion in the magistrates strengthens their authority. When the general population recognizes piety in their rulers, they receive them with reverence and respect. But even more importantly, "Religion hath a good influence upon the people; to make them obedient to government, and peaceable one towards another." Tillotson's argument was no doubt significant at the time, but it soon became a reproach to established religion as the social revolutions of the nineteenth and twentieth centuries developed. Here, however, it is very clearly used as an argument in favor of civil religion. The state should support religion because "He that hath entertained the true principles of Christianity is not to be tempted from his obedience and subjection by any worldly considerations, because he believes that whosoever resisteth authority resisteth the ordinance of God, and that 'they who resist shall receive to themselves damnation.'"[28] As Tillotson argues the case, Christianity is a good means of keeping the common people under control. He insists, moreover, that this is the teaching of the Savior and his apostles!

Tillotson sees religion as a means of healing the divisions and passions of society. "Now if this be the design of religion to bring us to this temper, thus to heal the natures of men, and to sweeten their spirits, to correct their passions, and to mortify all those lusts which are the cause of enmity and division, — then it is evident, that in its own nature it tends to the peace and happiness of human society."[29]

Tillotson is indeed presenting this sermon as a Christian apologetic to those in his day who wanted to minimalize the influence of religion on society. Its conclusion is an open argument against "the insinuations and pretences of atheistical persons."[30] According to Tillotson, atheists claim good government can be maintained without belief in God or a system of rewards and punishments in the afterlife. Not only do they argue that government is quite possible without religion, they also maintain that what is considered virtue and vice is quite arbitrary. By the end of the seventeenth century all standards of morality were coming under question. Tillotson takes up the arguments of Hobbes. Although he does not mention him by name, Tillotson makes very clear his disagreement with "the ingenious author of a very bad book, — I mean the Leviathan."[31]

28. Tillotson, *Works,* 1:415.
29. Tillotson, *Works,* 1:416.
30. Tillotson, *Works,* 1:417.
31. Tillotson, *Works,* 1:418.

There is nothing obscure about Tillotson's gospel. For him a sincere practice of the traditional Christian virtues promotes public happiness and prosperity. In this we honor God and show a pious devotion and reverence toward the divine majesty.[32] This sermon is about as good an expression of civil religion as one could find.

C. The Rewards of Religion

Let us look now at another sermon, one intended to complement the one we just studied. Here the Arminianism of the Anglican party comes clearly to expression. The text is taken from Psalm 19, which begins by praising God for the magnificence of his creation and ends by marveling at the perfections of God's Law. It is in this context that the psalm tells us, "and in the keeping of them there is great reward" (Ps. 19:11). The sermon, then, aims at showing the benefits and advantages which come from the observance of the divine Law.

Tillotson has already given us a sermon which shows "how much religion tends to the public welfare of mankind; to the support of government, and to the peace and happiness of human societies." He now turns to showing that "religion and obedience to the laws of God do likewise conduce to the happiness of particular persons, both in respect to this world and the other."[33]

The intellectual rewards of being religious claim our preacher's first attention. "First, I shall endeavor to shew how religion conduceth to the happiness of this life; and that both in respect of the inward and outward man. . . . As to the mind; to be pious and religious brings a double advantage to the mind of man. (1) It tends to the improvement of our understandings. (2) It brings peace and pleasure to our minds." Tillotson brings out a number of passages from the Wisdom psalms to make the point that religion helps us understand our human existence. Psalm 19:8 teaches us, "The commandment of the Lord is pure, enlightening the eyes." Then from Psalm 111:10 we learn: "The fear of the Lord is the beginning of wisdom; a good understanding have all they that keep his commandments." From Psalm 119:104 he quotes, "Through thy precepts I get understanding," and again from verse 130, "The entrance of thy word giveth light; it

---

32. Tillotson, *Works,* 1:422.
33. Tillotson, *Works,* 1:424.

giveth understanding to the simple."[34] The temper of Tillotson's piety is obviously of a more intellectual sort. "Now, religion doth purify our minds, and refine our spirits, by quenching the fire of lust, and suppressing the fumes and vapours of it, and by scattering the clouds and mists of passion. And the more any man's soul is cleansed from the filth and dregs of sensual lusts, the more nimble and expedite it will be in its operations."[35]

Tillotson seems to be inclined toward a rather abstract moralistic sort of spirituality, for he goes on in this way at some length. Then, in a magnificent sentence of the most refined English prose, he assures us, "Religion tends to the ease and pleasure, the peace and tranquillity of our minds; wherein happiness chiefly consists, and which all the wisdom and philosophy of the world did always aim at, as the utmost felicity of this life."[36] The very sentence, so stylistically refined, is a tip-off to his reflective piety. One gets the impression that here is a preacher who enjoys nothing quite so much as sitting in his study and writing out his sermon.

There are, of course, advantages to the religious life beyond our intellectual dimension. "Religion does likewise tend to the happiness of the outward man," Tillotson continues. Again the good archbishop turns to the Wisdom literature of the Old Testament and brings out a generous selection of appropriate sayings. Wisdom exhorts any who would be wise, "My son, forget not my law, but let thy heart keep my commandments; for length of days and long life shall they add to thee" (Prov. 3:1-2).[37] The practice of religion, we are assured, brings prosperity. It stimulates industry. Religion encourages honesty, and this, too, tends to bring success in business. All these points our preacher supports with quotations from Proverbs. No Scholastic proof-text artist could have surpassed Tillotson at this point. Integrity makes for good business, and that can be proved from the Bible. Civil religion and business ethics go hand in hand. And yet religion does not always make us prosperous. Sometimes by reason of difficult circumstances we do not prosper in material wealth, "yet religion makes a compensation for this, by teaching men to be content with that moderate and competent fortune which God hath given them."[38] This our preacher tacks down with a Latin quotation from Seneca.

One point Tillotson makes at particular length is that a sincere and

34. Tillotson, *Works,* 1:425.
35. Tillotson, *Works,* 1:426-27.
36. Tillotson, *Works,* 1:427.
37. Tillotson, *Works,* 1:430.
38. Tillotson, *Works,* 1:433.

disciplined religious life tends to be a blessing to one's children. The temperance and industry of parents are often rewarded in the prosperity of their children.

The final point of this sermon is that the consistent practice of religion is rewarded in the blessings of eternal life. "Religion and virtue do likewise most certainly and directly tend to the eternal happiness and salvation of men in the other world."[39] The whole point, as Tillotson sees it, is to prepare us for the blessings of the world to come. That is why in this life we begin to live in the peace, and order, and tranquillity of the world to come. "The greatest part of our work is a present reward to itself. . . . And if men did but truly and wisely love themselves, they would upon this very ground, if there were no other, become religious. For when all is done there is no man can serve his own interest better, than by serving God."

For many in his day Tillotson's apologetic for personal religion was appealing. The question is, was it the gospel? In the end the Christian faith was an offer of God-given rewards for our obedience to divine law. To be sure, it was a good and wise law which God had given, but its reward was in itself; it was not grace, but it was reasonable. In the conclusion of the sermon Tillotson says, "God requires of men, in order to their eternal happiness, that they should do those things which tend to their temporal welfare; that is, in plainer words, he promises to make us happy for ever, upon condition, that we will but do that which is best for ourselves in this world."[40]

D. "His Commandments Are Not Grievous"

This sermon, taking its title from I John 5:3, has always been the most famous of Tillotson's sermons. It expresses the spirituality of a whole age, roughly the first half of the eighteenth century. It is moderatism which has lost its balance, if you will, and fallen into latitudinarianism.

The introduction presents the problem. "One of the great prejudices which men have entertained against the Christian religion is this — that it lays upon men 'heavy burdens and grievous to be born,' that the laws of it are very strict and severe, difficult to be kept, and yet dangerous to be broken." Moving from the general to the very specific, our preacher piles up a

39. Tillotson, *Works*, 1:436.
40. Tillotson, *Works*, 1:442.

number of the hard sayings of the gospel. We are taught to keep our passions under control, "to contradict many times our strongest inclinations and desires, 'to cut off our right hand,' and 'to pluck out our right eye,' to 'love our enemies' . . . 'to do good to them that hate us,' . . . to sacrifice our dearest interest in the world, and even our very lives, in the cause of God . . . all these seem to be hard sayings and grievous commandments."[41] And yet, our text tells us, "His commandments are not grievous."

Our preacher, ever the apologist, wants to show that this prejudice is unreasonable. It is, however, necessary to take "some pains to satisfy the reason of men concerning this truth; and, if it be possible, to make it so evident, that those who are unwilling to own it, may yet be ashamed to deny it."[42] First, Tillotson wants to show that the laws God has given us are suitable to those to whom they are given. Second, he wants to maintain that they are within the capability of Christians to obey, and to insist that those who keep them will reap great rewards.

The laws of God are reasonable, the good archbishop maintains. They are "suitable to our nature and advantageous to our interest." He has commanded nothing which goes against the grain of our nature. To make his point he quotes the famous line from the prophet Micah, "'He sheweth thee, O man, what is good; and what doth the Lord thy God require of thee, but to do justly, and to love mercy, and to walk humbly with thy God?' This is the sum of the natural law, that we should behave ourselves reverently and obediently toward the Divine Majesty, and justly and charitably toward men."[43] There is nothing here which is unreasonable or against our nature. He elaborates the several parts of worship, "prayer and thanksgiving, hearing and reading the word of God, and receiving of the sacrament."[44] Nothing unreasonable or against our nature here. In fact, if one enters into them in the proper spirit, they can even be enjoyable. As to our service to our neighbors, there is nothing unreasonable there either. The divine commandments all concern the building up of a good society. If all these things are considered carefully, even such things as self-denial, humility, and repentance, which at first may seem distasteful, have great advantage.

The next point Tillotson makes is that "We are not destitute of suf-

---

41. Tillotson, *Works,* 1:466.
42. Tillotson, *Works,* 1:467.
43. Tillotson, *Works,* 1:468.
44. Tillotson, *Works,* 1:469.

ficient power and strength for the performing of God's commands." If God had given us laws that we could not possibly obey, then one could claim that his commandments are indeed grievous. Quite to the contrary, the grace we are offered in the gospel is sufficient for us. For the apostle, after giving us our text, continues by saying, "'for whosoever is born of God, overcometh the world.' Therefore the commandments of God are not grievous; because every child of God, that is, every Christian, is endued with a power, whereby he is enabled to resist and conquer the temptations of the world."[45] Again our preacher takes up the text of I John to show that the Christian has the power to resist the temptations of the world, for the Christian has the gift of the Holy Spirit, and as the apostle John points out, "Greater is he that is in you, than he that is in the world" (I John 4:4).[46] The Christian can and must resist the temptations of the world. Then, with one of the best biblical similes I have heard from any preacher, he warns Christians against laying ourselves open to temptation, lest loving any lust we "with Sampson lay our head in Delilah's lap."

The third point the good archbishop makes is that we are encouraged to keep God's commandments because of the pleasure it gives us in this world and the rewards it gives us in the world to come.[47] One gets the impression that this is the constant theme of Tillotson's pulpit: there are great rewards in being religious. Being a Christian seems to be a matter of propriety.

While Tillotson spends much time answering objections to his proposition, we need not follow it all out here. The conclusion underlines his point very clearly. "There is no man that is a servant of sin, and a slave to any base lust, but might if he pleased get to heaven with less trouble than he goes to hell."[48] The prose is magnificent, but the theology rather prosaic.

III. Matthew Henry (1662-1714)

Matthew Henry is one of those figures who transcended his age.[49] There is something classic about his interpretations of Scripture. One of the fore-

---

45. Tillotson, *Works,* 1:473.
46. Tillotson, *Works,* 1:474.
47. Tillotson, *Works,* 1:475.
48. Tillotson, *Works,* 1:486.
49. See my article on Matthew Henry in *Historical Handbook of Major Biblical Interpreters,* ed. Donald J. McKim (Downers Grove, Ill.: InterVarsity, 1998), pp. 195-98.

most teachers of the Christian life, he presents us with an admirable approach to a Protestant spirituality. Yet it is hard to categorize him. Surely there will be objections to including him in a chapter on moderatism, and yet he represents moderatism at its best. He brought to flower the teaching of John Howe. He learned much from Howe, and communicated the best of Howe's insights to the next generation. Still, there was much more to Henry. He summed up the Puritanism of his father, Philip Henry. He made public the underground faith of a whole generation of Puritans who had been ejected from their pulpits. He was the essence of the old school. He represented classic Protestantism in all its depth. With Henry *sola fides, sola Scriptura,* and *sola gratia* are solidly in place. One is tempted to put him in a chapter of old school preachers, but that might fragment our study in a way he himself would never have liked. He was a generous and irenic preacher who brought harmony to an age of discord.

Matthew Henry was born in 1662, the year those of Presbyterian or Congregational persuasion were ejected from the ministry of the Church of England.[50] Matthew's father, Philip Henry, was among that impressive company that stood fast in their faith and lost their jobs. Providentially his mother owned a substantial estate in the country not too far from the church where his father had been the minister. When the Henry family was forced to move from the parsonage, they took up residence at Broad Oak, the rather ample farmhouse on his mother's estate. Not being allowed to earn his living as a minister of the gospel, Philip settled down to being a country squire.

In good Puritan tradition family prayers were maintained in the Henry household both morning and evening. This was an impressive feature of life on the Henry estate. Matthew tells us about it at length in the biography he has left of his father.[51] When the family gathered together for worship, it was apparently no small group. There were the members of the family, a number of servants, perhaps even field hands or others employed on the farm. In addition there were theology students who came to stay with the Henry family for longer or shorter periods of time. As one reads the story Matthew has left us, one gets the impression that it ran as a sort of retreat house. Broad Oak was equipped with an ample library. His

50. For more information on the life of Matthew Henry, see William Tong, *An Account of the Life and Death of . . . Matthew Henry* (London, 1716), and John Bickerton Williams, *The Lives of Philip and Matthew Henry,* 2 vols. in 1 (Edinburgh and Carlisle, Pa.: Banner of Truth Trust, 1974).

51. Matthew Henry, *The Life of the Rev. Philip Henry, A.M.,* first published 1698, found in Williams, *The Lives of Philip and Matthew Henry.*

father, renowned for both his piety and his learning, was sought out by many, and those who came to the respected former pastor would stay for supper and prayers. They might stay for several days — even for several weeks or months.

Today we would say that Matthew was homeschooled. He could not, of course, have had a better teacher than his own father. Philip had attended Westminster School in London, which since the Reformation had excelled at teaching Latin and Greek in the best Christian humanist tradition. To go through such a school would have been to absorb thoroughly the classical languages, to learn the history and the philosophy of ancient Greece and Rome, and to have developed an impressive command of the language both as it was to be spoken and as it was to be written. All this Philip communicated to his son Matthew, and Matthew's complete command of it is found all through his sizable literary legacy.

Philip's education did not stop with his studies at Westminster School. From there he went to Oxford and was admitted to Christ Church College in 1647. Shortly after his entrance Parliament reorganized the universities, giving the Puritans a larger influence than had been allowed previously. Some of the great Puritan theologians such as John Owen, Edward Reynolds, and Thomas Goodwin were teaching at Oxford when Philip was a student. Dr. Henry Hammond, a moderate Anglican, still remembered as an outstanding biblical scholar, was one of the elder Henry's most beloved teachers. Philip had an excellent education, and at Broad Oak he passed it all on to son Matthew.

The time came for young Matthew to leave home. At first he was sent to the academy of Mr. Thomas Doolittle at Islington. This was regarded as a Puritan seminary for a time, but it was soon dissolved and Matthew returned to Broad Oak where, surrounded by his father's extensive library, he continued his studies.

In 1685 he left Broad Oak again, this time to study the law in London at Gray's Inn. It was not that he intended to become a lawyer; it was simply that the formal study of theology at Oxford or Cambridge was open only to those who would conform to the government-sponsored church. The law schools were in London rather than Oxford or Cambridge. They were open to Puritans as well as Anglicans. The law was a learned profession open to a thoroughly committed Puritan. Just to live in London was an education in itself. Young Matthew, having an inquiring mind, heard all kinds of preachers in London, Conformist as well as Nonconformist. With real appreciation, apparently, he went to hear both

Tillotson and Stillingfleet. John Howe, however, he heard most frequently. He even went to visit Richard Baxter in prison.

In 1685 James II ascended the throne, throwing the Restoration's religious settlement, under which Matthew had grown up, into complete confusion. For good reason many Protestants feared that the new king was bent on imposing Roman Catholicism on England. He intended to do this by offering increased liberties to the Protestant Dissenters as well as Roman Catholics, hoping to build an alliance between them which would then defeat the Anglicans. It was just at this point in English history, when the Anglican hegemony was tottering, that young Matthew was completing his education and thinking of ordination. The vanity of the Restoration's religious establishment had been unmasked when the king who imposed it, Charles II, embraced Catholicism on his deathbed. Once more many Englishmen were beginning to yearn for an uncompromised Protestant faith free from the duplicities of government control. The free churches, both Presbyterian and Congregational, were beginning to recover, and were organizing congregations all over England. In the spring of 1687 Matthew was offered the pastorate of the Presbyterian church in Chester, a city very close to Worthenbury where his father had been the minister when the Puritans had been ejected in 1662.

Young Henry accepted the call and was ordained by a presbytery. It was done very modestly, if not secretly, because the politics of the day were very uncertain. They would remain uncertain until 1688 when James II fled England and William and Mary took his place. With their accession the old restrictions were largely lifted, and Henry was able to begin his ministry unmolested. His preaching in Chester was well received. His congregation grew and became strong enough in a few years to build their own building. Although often encouraged to accept other calls, he continued in Chester until 1712, when he did finally accept a call to Hackney in the outskirts of London. Two years later, in 1714, he died at the height of his ministry.

Only a few of Henry's sermons have come down to us, and yet he has left a number of very important historical documents which tell us much about the preaching and especially the worship of his day. His writings on public prayer as well as the discipline of family prayer are particularly rich. Equally important for the period are his works on the Lord's Supper. His exposition of the whole Bible gives us an important insight into how the Puritans exercised the ministry of the Word. These are only the most obvious contributions of his work. As we will see, there is much more. This study of Henry comes relatively late in my research on preaching, although he has been an important figure in other aspects of my studies in the worship of the Reformed churches for well over twenty years. No one gives us a better picture of English-speaking Reformed worship for the early eighteenth century. Finally, it has become clear to me that the writings of Matthew Henry throw more light on our subject than do any other available sources.

A. *The Westminster Directory for Public Worship and the Double Sermon*

For Matthew Henry and many like him in England, Scotland, and America, the *Westminster Directory for Public Worship* was a precious heirloom. It had been adopted by Parliament forty years before Henry began his ministry, but in England at least, it had been little used for a generation. With the new age of toleration brought in by William and Mary, it was regarded as a key to recovering a simple, sincere, and unpretentious form of worship which was faithful to Scripture and edifying for the congregation. For the Presbyterian, Baptist, and Congregational churches which were beginning to appear all over Great Britain, the *Directory* had considerable authority although it was relatively untried. There were not too many congregations in England where it was actually followed during the twenty-five-year reign of Charles II.

The *Directory* was never an actual liturgy in the sense of a description of how worship was in fact conducted. It was rather a prescription of how things ought to be done. At many important junctures it was a compromise between what some people thought ought to be done and what other people thought ought to be done. Whether it would actually work was still unknown. But it had most admirable objectives. The Westminster divines were concerned that public worship not become a perfunctory routine. They were concerned that preaching be at the center of public worship rather than an occasional supplement as it had become under the mendicant orders in the Middle Ages. They were concerned that prayer be formulated in a fresh and thoughtful way, mindful of the times and the needs of the congregation. The *Directory* is of value for these insights, but it was never as comprehensive a statement of what worship should be as the *Genevan Psalter*.

Although formulated in the mid-1640s, in England at least it did not begin to have much effect until the 1690s. It had been written for fifty years before Presbyterian and Congregational churches had free reign in organizing their own churches. We do not yet have a thorough study of the sources of the *Directory*. What seems to have happened is that in the ministry of the Word, two very different approaches to the reading and preaching of Scripture had been acknowledged in such a way that there was a double sermon. The first and older tradition was to read and expound a chapter of the Scriptures. This was the tradition emphasized by the Continental Reformers, in South Germany, Switzerland, the Rhineland, and Geneva. It was a very ancient tradition that went back to the patristic age and eventually to the synagogue.

The second tradition goes back to the preaching orders of the High Middle Ages, which developed their sermons apart from the saying of the Mass, after the Mass was over or on Sunday afternoon. Very much under the influence of Scholasticism, they tended to preach on a text, dividing it analytically and applying it to different doctrinal or moral questions. While the Continental Reformers made a sharp distinction between medieval preaching and Reformed preaching, English preachers did not. Edward Dering, Thomas Cartwright, and Richard Rogers followed the method of the Continental Reformers, while Hugh Latimer and many others followed the traditional medieval homiletical methods. Most preachers, of course, employed a mixture of these two methods.

That the Westminster divines allowed for both was no doubt quite unconscious, but the result was the double sermon that we begin to find at the end of the seventeenth century. There were the reading of the lesson and commentary on it rather early in the service, and then a sermon on a text toward the end. The former was called the exposition while the latter was what was usually meant by the sermon. In effect, one ended up with the Reformed expository sermon based on the lesson preached early in the service followed at the end of the service with a sermon on some point of moral or theological catechism. The second sermon followed the tradition of the preaching orders of the Middle Ages while the first followed the tradition of the Continental Reformers.

This is advanced as a hypothesis. Much more work needs to be done on the *Westminster Directory for Public Worship* before one can claim this as an established fact, but it certainly does explain what we know about the preaching of Matthew Henry and a number of his contemporaries. This may not have been what the Westminster divines actually decided or even what they intended so much as what Henry and his colleagues understood the *Directory* to recommend. However this may be, let us look at how this worked out in Henry's preaching ministry.

B. The Exposition of Scripture

Today Matthew Henry is best known for his six-volume *Exposition of the Bible*. That it is available in several editions even in our day, almost three hundred years after he wrote it, is witness to the fact that it is a classic. For generations it has been the old standby among biblical commentaries found in the libraries of both theologians and nontheologians alike. What few people realize is that it is the fruit of years of the expositions which accompanied the readings from the Old Testament and New Testament at the regular Lord's Day services held each Sunday morning and afternoon. The normal procedure was to read through the Old Testament in the morning and the New Testament in the afternoon.

Henry began to write out these expositions in 1704.[52] He did not write them out each week for a particular service. His diary makes clear that they were written for publication on the basis of his preparation of these expositions over his entire ministry.[53] As we have often seen, the *lectio continua* sermons of many a preacher have come down to us in published commentaries rather than in published sermons. This is apparently the case here. His diary records that he began work on volume III of his expositions on 1 June 1708,[54] and at the end of May in 1712 he finished the Old Testament and began work on volume V, which contained the Gospels and Acts.[55] He had done some work on Romans before his sudden death, but the remainder of the New Testament commentary was done by several of his colleagues.

These expositions in the form they have come down to us do not tell us everything we would like to know, but we can learn some important things from them. First, they tell us how edifying simple biblical exposition can be. They are so transparent that one hardly needs to have an application spelled out. When Henry explains the text, there is a certain

---

52. John Bickerton Williams, *The Life of Matthew Henry,* first published 1828, found in Williams, *Lives,* pp. 301-9. Williams's *Life of Matthew Henry* and Henry's *Life of the Rev. Philip Henry, A.M.,* are separately paginated.

53. Williams, *Life of Matthew Henry,* pp. 301-9.

54. Williams, *Life of Matthew Henry,* p. 305.

55. Williams, *Life of Matthew Henry,* p. 307.

poetry about it. Here was a preacher who had the soul of a poet. One immediately sees the point of the passage without a lot of explanation about how it applies to the Christian life.

Another thing which is especially remarkable about these expositions is the strong sense of continuity between the Old Testament and the New Testament. Henry sees the New Testament as the fulfillment of the Old Testament. The Hebrew Bible is filled with intimations of the Christ and is to be understood as pointing the way to the coming of the Savior.

Again, especially worthy of notice is Henry's great respect for the authority of Scripture. The Scriptures have authority because they are the Word of God. They are necessary for a true knowledge of God, of how we are to serve him and worship him, and they are sufficient to show us the way of salvation. The Scriptures are clear in and of themselves. Scripture is to be explained by Scripture. The interpretation of Scripture is established by no human authority or private interpretation. Neither church councils, schools of philosophy, nor government decrees establish the truth of the Holy Scriptures. Their truth is recognized by the inner testimony of the Holy Spirit. God alone presides over the effectiveness of his Word. God alone fulfills his promises in the time he has appointed and brings it to fruit and finally to an abundant harvest.

C. The Preaching of Christian Doctrine

This exposition of the Scripture lesson could easily have taken twenty minutes or half an hour — at least that seems to have been the case in Henry's day. The second sermon came toward the end of the service, unless of course Communion was to be celebrated. This sermon tended to be a discourse on Christian doctrine. That, at least, was Henry's practice. We know this because a full list of his sermons for his entire ministry at Chester has come down to us.[56] We will look at this list in some detail because few preachers have left us such a complete record and because it probably gives us a good idea of how a conscientious Reformed preacher mapped out his preaching ministry at the beginning of the eighteenth century.

---

56. According to Tong, Henry himself wrote out this list of the subjects of his sermons at the close of his twenty-five-year ministry at Chester. It is found in an appendix to Williams, *Life of Matthew Henry,* pp. 273-93.

The first thing Henry records is that he began his ministry at Chester by preaching on the First Psalm at a lecture on a Thursday. He continued to preach on the Psalms at the Thursday lecture, going through the entire book five times in the course of his twenty-five-year ministry at Chester. This alone would explain the richness of his commentary on the Psalms in his famous *Exposition of the Whole Bible.* These commentaries on the Psalms have at times been published separately. Henry's writings on prayer also show an uncommon mastery of the significance of the Psalms as Christian prayer.

Henry began his Lord's Day sermons with a series of evangelistic sermons on the misery of the sinful state. This opened up the subject of conversion, and on this subject he continued for some two years, until the summer of 1689. These sermons were intended to show the way of salvation.[57] This was followed by a series on the covenant of grace. This was developed in a trinitarian arrangement, showing the role of God the Father, God the Son, and God the Holy Spirit.[58] Henry took up the following subjects in regard to the role of the Christ: Christ is our righteousness, our life, our peace, our hope, our redeemer, our high priest, our captain, our forerunner, and our friend. He devoted one or more sermons to each theme.

The list Henry drew up gives us the text in each case.[59] Sometimes more than one text was used to make each point, and the subject thus continued through several sermons. This series took our preacher something like a year and a half, until the summer of 1692. For the next two years he treated sanctification. Then in the spring of 1694 he turned to the subject of worship, preaching on the various ordinances of worship — word, prayer, praise, and sacraments — followed by sermons on the occasions of worship, and finally by sermons on the manner of worship.[60] Each sermon was based on a text that Henry selected, and sometimes the text demanded several sermons. This was followed by a set of sermons on our duty to our neighbors.[61]

In June of 1698 Henry began an ambitious project. He set himself to preach a long series of sermons which would be in effect a systematic theology. It was, to use the parlance of the time, a body of divinity. This

57. Williams, *Life of Matthew Henry,* pp. 274-75.
58. Williams, *Life of Matthew Henry,* pp. 275-76.
59. Williams, *Life of Matthew Henry,* p. 276.
60. Williams, *Life of Matthew Henry,* p. 277.
61. Williams, *Life of Matthew Henry,* p. 278.

sort of thing was often done in that day. We have large portions of a similar project from John Howe as well as from the American Gilbert Tennent. Thomas Watson's *A Body of Divinity* we have already spoken about. Such series were not thought of so much as evangelistic sermons as they were catechetical sermons.

The first series concerns the doctrine of God.[62] One notices from the subjects listed that our preacher is following the order of the *Westminster Catechisms* and the Confession of Faith, although it is largely amplified. We find, for example, that God is presented as a spirit, infinite, eternal, and unchangeable in his being, wisdom, power, holiness, justice, goodness, and truth, but these attributes mentioned in the *Westminster Shorter Catechism* are expanded by a large number of sermons treating each of the names of God. He is El Shaddai, God Most High, the Living God, Everlasting King, God of Love, God of Peace, and finally Father.[63] This series on the nature, attributes, and titles of God was followed by one on the Word of God, and by another on the works of God. Here the doctrine of creation is elaborated at length, as is the doctrine of providence.[64] This leads to a string of sermons on the creation of the angels and the creation of Adam and Eve. On the doctrine of anthropology Henry seems to have dwelt at special length, speaking of the perfections of human nature which God intended as well as the realities of the fallen state.

With this our preacher's systematic theology preached from the pulpit takes another turn, focusing on the doctrine of our redemption in Jesus Christ.[65] Henry begins by pointing out that the prime author of our redemption is God; his wisdom contrived it, and his patience left room for it. The manifold elaboration at this point of the theme of redemption is admirable. With a rich fullness the doctrines of the person and work of Christ are unfolded. Nothing is neglected as sermon after sermon testifies to the fullness of God's love for us in the sending of his Son for our salvation. Our preacher explores the traditional theme of the three offices of Christ, again following the *Westminster Shorter Catechism*. Once more we find the evangelistic concerns brought to the forefront.

Our evangelist becomes increasingly practical, preaching a long se-

62. Williams, *Life of Matthew Henry*, p. 279.
63. Williams, *Life of Matthew Henry*, p. 280.
64. Williams, *Life of Matthew Henry*, pp. 280-81.
65. Williams, *Life of Matthew Henry*, p. 282.

ries on the application of the redemption purchased by Christ. Sermons on the divine Law follow, showing the Christian interpretation of the Law as found in the New Testament.[66] This is followed by an equally detailed series of sermons concerning the gospel rule of faith and repentance. This then leads into the subject of the doctrine of the Church and the doctrine of the last things. Here, with characteristic thoroughness, our preacher unfolds his theology, sermon after sermon, Lord's Day after Lord's Day.[67]

William Tong, Henry's colleague and biographer, after sharing with us this list of ten years of sermons, comments that we must remember that "while he was pursuing this method, abundance of occasional discourses were mixed with it." Henry was convinced that this kind of systematic theological preaching was most helpful in teaching the Christian congregation, and yet, in shepherding the flock, it was also important to observe the acts of divine providence and bring the Scriptures to them, interpreting them for the edification of the Church.[68] This we take to mean that frequently, on fast days or days of thanksgiving, and apparently from time to time on the Lord's Day, Henry preached occasional sermons.[69]

One cannot help but lament that this preached theology never got to the printing press, but it is significant that Henry's six volumes of expositions of the Bible did get to the printer. Perhaps this says that for Henry, as for many other preachers, the exposition of the Bible was the foundation for the reading and preaching of the Scriptures. For Henry the most important part of the ministry of the Word was the systematic reading and preaching of the Holy Scriptures.

IV. Jean-Frédéric Ostervald (1663-1747)

Neuchâtel is one of the most beautiful towns in the world. Built of mellow gold-colored sandstone, it sits beside the tranquil, blue Lake of Neuchâtel and looks over to the snow-covered Alps on the other side. Its

---

66. Williams, *Life of Matthew Henry,* pp. 284-85.
67. Williams, *Life of Matthew Henry,* pp. 287-88.
68. Williams, *Life of Matthew Henry,* p. 288.
69. Several examples of Henry's occasional sermons are found in *The Complete Works of Matthew Henry,* 2 vols. (1855; reprint, Grand Rapids: Baker, 1978). Especially notable among these are sermons for weddings, funerals, and ordinations.

château, its Romanesque Collegial Church, the Hôtel du Payrou, and several other neoclassical town houses give it an air of sophistication to match its natural beauty. Neuchâtel had for centuries been an independent principality ruled by the counts of Neuchâtel. In the sixteenth century Guillaume Farel, having finished his work in Geneva, became the reformer of Neuchâtel, spending the last years of his long life in this pleasant little city.

It was as pastor of Neuchâtel that Jean-Frédéric Ostervald exercised his remarkable ministry.[70] What is of special interest about him is his blend of orthodoxy, enlightenment, and pietism. His orthodoxy was enlightened and warmly pietistic. He was one of the most beloved pastors a church could ever have. When he died, the whole city turned out for the funeral. People came streaming in from the other towns of the canton, the villages up in the Jura Mountains, and the towns along the lake. Neuchâtel had a population of thirty-five hundred at the time, and five thousand people accompanied their preacher to his grave, celebrating with high seriousness the hope of the resurrection. After the funeral the city council ordered that a monument be inscribed to Ostervald and set beside the monument of Farel, recognizing him as the second reformer of the church of Neuchâtel.

Ostervald was born in the parsonage of the Collegial Church, his father, Jean-Rodolphe de Ostervald, being the principal pastor of the city. Young Jean-Frédéric received the education of a patrician. When he was only thirteen years old, he was sent to Zürich that he might learn German and study the Greek and Latin classics. Two years later, in 1678, he was sent to the Academy of Saumur to sit under the leading Huguenot theologians of the day. He defended a thesis there in 1681, then moved on to Paris, where he attended the theater, cultivated his French style, and listened to the sermons of Jean Claude. In those days, spending some time in Paris was part of a good education. Finally in 1683 he sat at the feet of the theologians of Geneva. This was the way a French-speaking Protestant theologian got his education in the years just before the revocation of the Edict of Nantes, which, alas, would take place in 1685, only two years after Ostervald completed his academic pilgrimages.

Essentially, Ostervald never left Neuchâtel again. He was ordained

---

70. On the ministry of Jean-Frédéric Ostervald, see Jean-Jacques von Allmen, *L'Église et ses fonctions d'après Jean-Frédéric Ostervald* (Neuchâtel: Imprimerie Delachaux et Niestlé, 1947).

and spent the rest of his life in his native city occupied with different aspects of the sacred ministry.

His catechetical ministry was of special importance.[71] While it has not come down to us as published sermons, it has come down as an extensive catechism. Not only is it much longer than the usual catechism, but it contains much material not usually covered by a catechism. Questions raised by the Enlightenment are treated in a sympathetic way, and yet orthodoxy is carefully maintained. The concerns of pietism are considered as well. This catechism was widely distributed. In America it was particularly in use among the Huguenot churches in South Carolina and New York. It was translated into English and recommended for use by the Presbyterian General Assembly in 1812. Samuel Miller was among those who had examined and approved it.

Ostervald was most well known for his Bible.[72] For several generations this was the standard Bible in French-speaking Switzerland. The translation from the Hebrew and Greek had been the work of the theological faculty of Geneva, but it was Ostervald's annotations which made it popular. In many ways it was the French Protestant version of the Bible commentary of Matthew Henry, who had been born the year before Ostervald. The summaries of each chapter of the Bible as well as the frequent annotations show a profound piety as well as an awareness of the problems the Enlightenment had raised with the accuracy of Scripture. This popular home-study Bible was pastorally sensitive to the spiritual needs of nontheologians and was in common use for well over 150 years.

Ostervald was chosen pastor of the city in 1699. He was an engaging preacher and drew large crowds. Neuchâtel was a popular refuge for the French Huguenots, who took up residence in the city and attended worship with particular devotion. Soon it was necessary to build a larger church building to accommodate these crowds. The Temple du Bas was

---

71. Jean-Frédéric Ostervald, *Catéchisme ou instruction dans la religion chrestienne* (Geneva: Compagnie des Libraires, 1702). An English translation was published in 1812: Jean-Frédéric Ostervald, *A Catechism for Youth, Containing a Brief but Comprehensive Summary of the Doctrines and Duties of Christianity*, trans. Samuel Bayard (New York: Published by Whiting and Watson for the New Jersey Bible Society, 1812).

72. *La Sainte Bible qui contient le Vieux et le Nouveau Testament, Revuë & corrigée sur le text Hébreu & Grec par les pasteurs & les Professeurs de l'Eglise de Genève,* Avec les *Argumens et les Réflections* sur les chapitres de l'Ecriture Sainte & des Notes par Jean-Frédéric Ostervald, nouvelle edition, revuë, corrigée & augmentée (Neuchâtel: Imprimerie d'Abraham Boyve et Compagnie, 1744).

dedicated in 1702 and is to this day a remarkable example of Protestant church architecture of the period. The most interesting feature of this building is the way the congregation is gathered around three sides of the pulpit to afford better hearing and a more intimate sense of participation in the sacraments. In accordance with Protestant plain style, the building is neither luxurious nor ornate, but simple and functional.

As popular a preacher as Ostervald was, he has left us only one small collection of sermons, *Douze sermons sur divers textes de l'écriture sainte,* published in Geneva in 1722.[73] In homiletical form these sermons are a good example of Protestant scholasticism. They take a text of Scripture and analyze it; in fact, this is quite clear from the title of the collection. Ostervald follows the preaching manual of Jean Claude rather than the example of John Calvin or Jean Daillé and the older generation of French Protestant preachers. The older system of a running commentary on a somewhat longer passage of Scripture had been replaced by a minute analysis of a text or a single verse. Even at that, Ostervald's sermons are clearly expository. Characteristic of them is that they stick very closely to the text. His preaching is strongly biblical in that it is rich in parallel texts and biblical examples.

The range of concerns which occupied his pulpit is indicated quite clearly by the titles of these twelve sermons:

1. "That Religion Is a Most Serious Matter"
2. "The Divinity and the Excellence of the Christian Religion"
3. "That It Is Necessary and Easy to Keep the Commandments of God"
4. "On the Purpose of God in Sending His Son into the World"
5. "A Picture of the True Christian"
6. "On the Security of the Christian in the Faith"
7. "On St. Paul's Desire for the Thessalonians"
8. "The Glory of Jesus Christ Revealed in the Eyes of Men"
9. "On the Hope of the Resurrection"
10. "Concerning Those Who Reject God and the Knowledge of God"
11. "That Which Men Value Is Often What God Rejects"
12. "The Judgments of God on Guilty Nations"

---

73. Jean-Frédéric Ostervald, *Douze sermons sur divers textes de l'écriture sainte* (Geneva: Chez Fabri & Barrillot, 1722).

Jean-Frédéric Ostervald was the perfect example of true moderatism. He was fervently orthodox and had the passion of pietism and the common good sense of the Enlightenment.

V. Jacques Saurin (1677-1730)

Jacques Saurin had a wide influence on the history of Protestant preaching. He was the single Protestant among the great French pulpit orators of the Age of Louis XIV. In many respects he belongs to the school of Bossuet, Bourdaloue, and Massillon because of his general approach to pulpit eloquence and because he mediated this approach to Protestantism. During the eighteenth century he was widely read by Protestant preachers in Germany, the Netherlands, and Great Britain. He brought to the Protestant pulpit that aura of French culture which was so much admired in that day. French literature had conquered more of Europe by the beginning of the eighteenth century than the armies of Louis XIV ever laid eyes on. There were many Europeans who, although Protestant, wanted to emulate the literary and intellectual refinement of France. Saurin showed them the way.

Saurin was born to a genteel professional family of Nîmes.[74] The family had produced a number of distinguished soldiers, lawyers, and scientists. Nîmes was a southern city. It had prospered in Roman times and was still filled with monuments of Roman architecture. It had always been one of the leading cities of Provence. With the coming of the Reformation it became a center of French Protestantism. Saurin's father was a lawyer. With the revocation of the Edict of Nantes, Protestants, unless they were willing to convert to Catholicism, were denied the practice of learned professions. The Saurin family left France and settled in Geneva. Jacques was nine years old when he left his native France, and therefore received most of his education in Geneva. As a young man he spent a couple years as a soldier and then returned to Geneva to study theology. In 1701 he was ordained to the ministry and was sent to London to serve the French-speaking congregation there. He soon became known as an outstanding preacher.

74. For biographical information on Jacques Saurin, see Alexandre Rodolphe Vinet, *Histoire de la prédication: parmi les réformés de France au dix-septième siècle* (Paris: Chez les éditeurs, 1860).

In 1705, while traveling in the Netherlands, Saurin was called to preach in the Hague. The city had a large colony of Huguenot refugees who had organized a French-speaking congregation and had been allowed to hold services in the palace chapel. Effectively Saurin became preacher to the court of the House of Orange, a family still proud of its Provençal origins. It was there that he won an international reputation as the most eloquent Protestant preacher of his generation.

At the beginning of the eighteenth century the Hague was not the largest city of the Netherlands. It was in fact a small city, but the court resided there. It was a city of considerable sophistication, and Saurin drew all kinds of people to his sermons, not just French Huguenot refugees. Although he often preached for more than two hours at a time, he preached to a crowded church. His rich voice and his striking appearance added to his popularity, but his appeal was above all his intellectual brilliance, his rich imagination, and his refined French eloquence.

Saurin had a tremendous appeal to the intelligentsia of the Netherlands. He introduced a new spirit to the religious life of the day. The Netherlands was a center of enlightenment and tolerance in the seventeenth century. Its prosperous merchants had an optimistic view of life. Being a republic, the Netherlands was free from the absolutism of France. It was a merchant republic, and the middle class had a prominent place in society generally, but especially in the Church did it play an important role. Protestantism and the middle class had established a firm alliance. The hardworking artisans, businessmen, and professional people were especially attracted to Protestantism.

While Saurin was quite orthodox, he appealed to the enlightened leadership of society. The Enlightenment was beginning to make its appearance, and Saurin emphasized those elements of Christianity which appealed to those who had been attracted to this movement. Still, he was often critical of the Enlightenment. He made it quite clear that there were limits to the popular ideology of mercantile society. Saurin had no sympathy for Deism, although the upper middle class often found it attractive. Nevertheless, he was sympathetic to the aspirations of the age, and his interpretation of Protestant Christianity was congenial to that spirit. Some of his most memorable sermons defended such subjects as the divinity of Christ and the Christian doctrine of revelation, yet his defense was addressed to those who had been influenced by Descartes, Locke, and the prophets of the Enlightenment whose voices were already being heard.

His sermons were addressed to the problems of the day. He followed neither the lectionary nor the *lectio continua* but was the champion of the topical sermon, and his example contributed largely to its spread. He preached sermons for the feast days of the Reformed church as well as for the special fast days called by the civil authority. One of his greatest sermons was what today we would call a stewardship sermon. Not only is "On Almsgiving" a great piece of oratory, it seems to have raised an amazing amount of money for refugees. Saurin took special interest in charitable causes and in the support of the various benevolent institutions which were so characteristic of the Netherlands. He also, interestingly enough, was one of the first Protestant preachers to raise his voice for foreign missions. Yet the topics that seem to have interested him most were the questions that bothered the progressive, thoughtful Christians of his day. We find sermons, for instance, with such titles as:

"On Conversion"
"The Deep Mysteries of God"
"The Sufficiency of Revelation"
"Assurance of Salvation"
"The Immensity of God"
"The Devotion of Pilgrims"
"The Divinity of Jesus Christ"
"On the Mystical Transport of St. Paul"
"On the Pains of Death"
"The Problems of Europe"
"The Necessity of Progress"
"The Accord of Religion and Politics"
"The Most Sublime Devotion"
"The Difficulties of the Christian Religion"
"Seeking the Truth"
"The Advantages of Revelation"
"On the Manner of Studying Religion"
"On Love for One's Native Land"
"Holiness"
"On the Beatific Vision"
"On the Universal Devotion to the Divine Laws"

One notices in this list both an interest in the questions of the day and a concern to defend or reinterpret historic Christian orthodoxy.

One cannot resist the temptation to compare Saurin to the great triumvirate of Bossuet, Bourdaloue, and Massillon. There are many similarities and many differences. About French eloquence opinion seems to be divided, but that is not our primary interest, and we leave discussion of that subject to others. There is one point at which Saurin is to be preferred to the great three. Whereas they were so obsequious to the absolutism of Louis XIV, Saurin was not. He supported the intellectuals of the Netherlands in their attempt to build a Dutch republic that was progressive, enlightened, and orthodox. Saurin was more like Fénelon than Bossuet. He had his eyes more on the transcendent glory of God than did the favorites of the French court. As exiles from France, the Huguenots knew what it was to be pilgrims in the world and to search for the glory that is beyond the pomp and ceremonials of this transient life.

A. The Grandeur of God

In reading through Saurin's sermons one cannot help but notice how forcefully he draws our attention to the grandeur of God. Again and again one gets a sense of how the majesty of God pervades his thinking. This is no doubt the secret of his eloquence. He has a profound sense of the grandeur of God. We notice the same thing in the organ works of his contemporary Johann Sebastian Bach (1685-1750). Saurin's sense of the grandeur of God is found throughout the standard collection of his works which has come down to us, but a number of his sermons are devoted particularly to this subject. Let us look at three sermons on the perfections of God. Such subjects seem especially to excite Saurin's sense of God's glory.

Sermon II, "The Eternity of God," was preached on the first Lord's Day of 1724.[75] The text is taken from II Peter 3:8, "With the Lord one day is as a thousand years, and a thousand years as one day." These words

75. My first reading of his sermons was from the French edition: Jacques Saurin, *Sermons sur divers textes de l'Escriture Sainte,* 10 vols. (La Haye: Abraham Troyel, 1708-49). My quotations are from an English translation of his sermons published in Princeton in 1827: *Sermons of the Rev. James Saurin, late Pastor of the French Church at The Hague,* trans. R. Robertson, H. Hunter, and J. Sutcliff, 2 vols. (Princeton: D. A. Borrenstein, 1827), hereafter Saurin, *Sermons.* That two volumes of his sermons were published in Princeton, soon after the founding of Princeton Theological Seminary, would suggest that those who were shaping American preaching thought well of him and were very influenced by him. This was almost a century after his death.

41

are constantly repeated through the course of the sermon almost like a big bell chiming out the cardinal points of the sermon. Saurin introduces his sermon by telling of the rabbinic tradition about the pillar of cloud which led the children of Israel through the wilderness by day and which at night became a pillar of fire. As the rabbis understood it, this was in reality the Shekinah, or the presence of the divine majesty. The pillar that marched before Israel was both the most radiant light and the most impenetrable darkness. Let the skeptical philosopher search the mystery of the presence of God, Saurin remarks, and it is beyond finding out, but let the simple soul in need of consolation direct itself to God, then the presence of God is light and peace. As the psalmist puts it, "Does he look to him? he shall be lightened" (Ps. 34:5).[76]

For Saurin the eternity of God is self-evident. Any reasonable person must conclude that human life is mortal, and if mortal, then finite. It is just as reasonable that behind the finite creation there is an infinite Creator who is immortal and infinite and therefore eternal. We notice that Saurin is confidently arguing natural theology. As we read this sermon, we are struck by the fact that his thoughts on the reasonableness of belief in God sound very much like the ideas of René Descartes (1596-1650). Descartes was another Frenchman who spent the productive years of his life in the Netherlands. Saurin admired Descartes, and certainly his philosophy was well known to the members of Saurin's congregation. His confidence that the basic truth of the existence of God and the perfection of his attributes were self-evident was shared by many intellectuals of the day.

At the beginning of the eighteenth century it was common for Christians to regard their faith as being all quite rational. Very typically they understood themselves to be both rational and orthodox, and they understood Descartes to encourage them in this direction. These matters on which all reasonable men could agree Saurin preached with particular fervor. He tells us that even if the psalmist had not taught the eternity of God, even if we did not learn from revelation that God is the Alpha and the Omega, the beginning and the end, that God was and is and is to come, still we could believe in the eternity of God because it is a reasonable belief.[77] The biblical authorities Saurin cites are rich and imaginative. One gets the impression that he has carefully worked with the bibli-

---

76. Saurin, *Sermons,* 1:55.
77. Saurin, *Sermons,* 1:56.

cal passages. They seem to have fired his imagination, but then, so do the topics of natural theology to which he addresses himself in these three sermons.

One of the topics he treats in this sermon is the supreme felicity of God. He finds the reasons for believing in it self-evident. "Every intelligent being is capable of happiness, nor can he regard happiness with indifference; he is inclined by his very nature to render himself happy."[78] Saurin admits that this line of reasoning may not be regarded as completely conclusive, but since the witness of Scripture tells us that God is blessed (I Tim. 1:11), we can be well assured that our philosophy does not lead us astray.[79] Finally, Saurin's meditation leads him to conclude that Scripture represents God to us as

> a Being who is approved by intelligences, skilful in virtues, in grandeurs, in objects worthy of praise; a Being who loves only order, and who has power to maintain it; a Being who is at the summit of felicity, and who knows that he shall be so for ever. O ages! O millions of ages! O thousands of millions of ages! O duration, the longest that can be imagined by an intelligence composed (if I may speak so) of all intelligences, how short must ye appear to so happy a Being! There is no time with him; there is no measure of time. One thousand years, ten thousand years, one quarter of an hour, one instant, is almost the same. "A thousand years are with him as one day, and one day as a thousand years."[80]

Here is a beautiful example of classical French pulpit oratory worthy of any of the preachers of the court of Louis XIV.

Sermon III, "The Omnipresence of God," is rich with theological insights. It perfectly illustrates the facility of the moderatist preachers to communicate a sense of God's grandeur. The sermon takes as its text Psalm 139:7-12 (RSV):

> Whither shall I go from thy Spirit?
>> Or whither shall I flee from thy presence?
> If I ascend to heaven, thou art there!
>> If I make my bed in Sheol, thou art there!
> If I take the wings of the morning

78. Saurin, *Sermons,* 1:57.
79. Saurin, *Sermons,* 1:58. The footnotes give us both the Greek and Latin texts, both of which support his assertion much more than the traditional translation.
80. Saurin, *Sermons,* 1:59.

and dwell in the uttermost parts of the sea,
even there thy hand shall lead me,
and thy right hand shall hold me.
If I say, "Let only darkness cover me,
and the light about me be night,"
even the darkness is not dark to thee,
the night is bright as the day;
for darkness is as light with thee.

This is, to be sure, one of the classic texts on the omnipresence of God. Our preacher sets up the text with consummate art. He exhorts his hearers to let the veil of flesh over their eyes fall away and perceive the presence of God in the worshiping assembly, for God, as Jesus teaches us in the Gospel of John, is Spirit and we must therefore worship him in spirit and in truth. As in the previous sermon, one quickly recognizes that Saurin has in the back of his mind the thoughts of the philosophers who were popular at the time.

In this case the philosopher is Benedict de Spinoza (1632-77), a Dutch Jewish thinker who, while born in Amsterdam of Portuguese parents, finally settled in the Hague. Spinoza's ideas would have been well known to Saurin's congregation, even if only at second hand. To the philosophically inclined, Saurin wants to make it clear that when we speak of the omnipresence of God, we do not mean that God is extended to every place so as to be contained in it. God is a spirit and cannot therefore be contained in a place. While Saurin carefully distances himself from Spinoza, he nevertheless gives us a most interesting interpretation of his thought. Just as I can call my body all that I can move by an act of my will, so God, who can move all creation simply by the impulse of his will, can legitimately call all of creation his body. It is because of such ideas that Spinoza is called a pantheist, and apparently Saurin, while he had no interest in slipping into anything as foreign to Christianity as pantheism, finds Spinoza's ideas engaging nevertheless.[81]

From Spinoza our preacher moves to Plato. He is reminded of a passage where the famous Greek philosopher says divinity cannot be conceived of except by the understanding, by leaving behind sensible objects. In order to contemplate the divinity, terrestrial ideas must be surmounted. The human eye cannot see God, nor can the human ear hear

81. Saurin, *Sermons,* 1:64.

him. Just as the Cambridge Platonists had found the ancient Greek philosopher an ally of Christian rationality, so Saurin seems to approach Plato the same way. Again and again Christian thinkers have called Plato, Aristotle, Cicero, and Seneca to their aid. Saurin is doing the same thing. Even the reason of pagan philosophers can recognize that God is a spirit. For Saurin this is a strong argument for regarding the Christian faith as rational.

One of Saurin's most interesting thoughts is that we should not regard the omnipresence of God as simply one of the attributes of God but rather as the extent of his attributes. Omnipresence is the universal quality by which God communicates himself to all, diffuses himself to all, and is the great director of all. God is everywhere because he sees all that comes to pass. His omnipresence is omniscience. God is present everywhere because his influence is over all. His omnipresence is omnipotence.

Saurin has a very strong doctrine of providence, and he is quick to defend it against the proponents of the Enlightenment who were beginning to make it one of their primary targets of attack. At some length Saurin refutes the argument that the doctrine of providence makes God the author of evil. The knowledge of God is not a bare knowledge, as Saurin explains it, nor is his presence an idle presence. It is an active knowledge; it is a presence accompanied with motion and direction. "When God communicates himself to all, when he thus acts on all, when he diffuseth himself thus through the whole, he relates all to his own designs, and makes all serve his own counsels: and this is our third idea of his immensity and omnipresence. God is present with all, because he *directs* all."[82]

With this our preacher launches into a superb rhetorical passage extolling the wisdom of divine providence. It is a perfect example of the principle of classical rhetoric that the most eloquent expressions must issue from the most noble ideas. Great rhetoric, as we have so often seen, has a way of assuming that beauty is a strong evidence of truth.

Sermon IV, "The Grandeur of God," takes as its text that beautiful passage from the center of Isaiah 40 which begins:

> Who has measured the waters in the hollow of his hand
> and marked off the heavens with a span,
> enclosed the dust of the earth in a measure

---

82. Saurin, *Sermons,* 1:68.

> and weighed the mountains in scales
> and the hills in a balance?
> Who has directed the Spirit of the LORD,
> or as his counselor has instructed him?
> Whom did he consult for his enlightenment,
> and who taught him the path of justice,
> and taught him knowledge,
> and showed him the way of understanding?

The passage goes on to speak of the vanity of the nations of the earth and the foolishness of idolatry, and then concludes:

> Have you not known? Have you not heard?
> The LORD is the everlasting God,
> the Creator of the ends of the earth.
> He does not faint or grow weary,
> his understanding is unsearchable. (Isa. 40:12-14, 28 RSV)

One would have to look far to find a passage of literature where beauty of expression is so clearly an intimation of truth. From the very beginning of this sermon one is aware that this has captured Saurin's imagination. The sheer beauty of his text assures him of its truth. Saurin, by way of excursus, cannot help making a few remarks on pulpit eloquence which we will look at more thoroughly further along. But getting down to his subject, he proposes to treat four points: the sublimity of God's essence, the immensity of his works, the efficacy of his will, and the magnificence of his mighty acts. On the first point Saurin delivers these lines:

> When we attempt to measure the duration of God, by tracing it beyond the first periods of this universe, we lose ourselves in the unfathomable depths of eternity: we heap ages upon ages, millions of years upon millions of years; but no beginning of his existence can we find. And when we endeavour to stretch our thoughts, and to penetrate the most remote futurity, again we heap ages upon ages, millions of years upon millions of years, and lose ourselves again in the same abyss, perceiving that he can have no end, as he had no beginning. He is "the ancient of days, the alpha and omega, the first and the last," Dan. vii.9. "He is, he was, he is to come," Rev. i.8. "Before the mountains were brought forth, before the earth and the world were formed, even from everlasting to everlasting he is God," Ps. xc.2. And, when the moun-

46

tains shall be dissolved, when the foundations of the earth shall be destroyed, when all sensible objects shall be *folded up like a vesture,* he will be *the everlasting God,* Heb. i.12. He will be, when they exist no more, as he was before they existed at all.[83]

A bit further on, treating the immensity of God's work, Saurin follows the lead of his text and lifts his eyes to contemplate the evening sky. It is God who led out the host of heaven and called them all by name. For Saurin the wonders revealed by astronomers were only a confirmation of the grandeur of God, and yet even a novice is astounded.

A novice is frightened at hearing what astronomers assert; that the sun is a million times bigger than the earth: that the naked eye discovers more than a thousand fixed stars, which are so many suns to enlighten unknown systems: that with the help of glasses we may discover an almost infinite number: that two thousand have been reckoned in one constellation; and that, without exaggerating, they may be numbered at more than two millions: that what are called nebulous stars, of which there is an innumerable multitude, that appear to us as if they were involved in little misty clouds, are all assemblages of stars.

A novice is frightened, when he is told, that there is such a prodigious distance between the earth and the sun, that a body, moving with the greatest rapidity that art could produce, would take up twenty-five years in passing from the one to the other: that it would take up seven hundred and fifty thousand to pass from the earth to the nearest of the fixed stars: and to the most distant more than a hundred millions of years. . . .

A novice is frightened, when he is assured, that although the stars, which form a constellation, seem to touch one another, yet the distances of those that are nearest together can be ascertained, and that even words are wanting to express the spaces which separate those that are the greatest distances from each other. . . . All this startles a novice: and yet, what are these bodies, countless in their number, and enormous in their size? What are these unmeasurable spaces, which absorb our senses and imaginations? What are all these in comparison of what reason discovers? Shall we be puerile enough to persuade ourselves that there is nothing beyond what we see? Have we not reason to think that there are spaces far, far beyond, full of the Creator's wonders, and affording matter of contemplation to *the thousand thousands,*

83. Saurin, *Sermons,* 1:75.

to the *ten thousand times ten thousand* intelligences that he has made? Dan. vii.10.[84]

The lens makers of the Netherlands were just beginning to employ their art in the service of astronomy. The modern science of astronomy was just beginning to astound the intellectuals of the day, and our preacher marvels at the discoveries being made. For Saurin the natural sciences only confirm the Christian understanding of the glory of God. He makes a very interesting remark in introducing this superb period. He says that even to narrate the wonders of the heavens is to move us to simulate the most sublime of rhetoric. But if the contemplation of nature is a motivation to great oratory, it is also a motivation to worship, devotion, and piety. That the natural sciences should become the chief artillery of atheism for several generations to come would no doubt appear as a most curious perversion to Saurin and his friends. As they saw it, the order, and especially the beauty, of the creation led most reasonably to an appreciation of the grandeur of God.

B. The Eloquence of Preaching

Jacques Saurin had a wide reputation for eloquence. He lived in an age when eloquence was highly prized. It was the golden age of French literature. The memory of Bossuet, Racine, and Pascal was still fresh, and Voltaire and Rousseau were beginning to appear on the scene. In the French-speaking world one was very conscious of the art of speaking well. Belles lettres was cultivated in the best schools. Saurin's father, as a Huguenot refugee in Geneva, was highly respected for the purity of his diction. It was only natural for a preacher with such a background to attend closely to his use of language.

Considering when he lived, Saurin was rather reticent in his estimation of the importance of eloquence. He understood it as a gift of grace which God pours out from time to time according to the council of his will. A bit like the gift of signs and wonders which sometimes accompanies the preaching of the gospel, eloquence can make preaching especially effective. Why God pours out this gift or why he does not is beyond our understanding, just as it is beyond our understanding why he blesses

---

84. Saurin, *Sermons*, 1:75.

some Christians with prosperity and denies it to others.[85] The truths of the Christian faith are too interesting and too profound to require ornamentation. In fact, Saurin reminds us that the apostle Paul teaches that we have these treasures in earthen vessels to make clear that the transcendent power belongs to God (II Cor. 4:7). Richly ornamental oratory often draws our attention away from the message a preacher is charged with proclaiming. Saurin admits that the Corinthian church experienced great difficulties because some had been carried away by the eloquence of one of their preachers. Saurin was too Protestant to be completely captivated by the grandeurs of baroque style. It bore the mark of the Jesuits through and through. It was far too contrived, but like Bach, Saurin transformed the baroque into something weighty and profound.

In his sermon on the methods of preachers, Saurin makes the point that purity of doctrine is the highest virtue of the preacher.[86] The purpose of preaching is edification. Those preachers who are true to the basic teachings of the faith and teach these doctrines to their congregations are building up the Church with gold, silver, and precious stones, to use the figure of Paul (I Cor. 3:11-15). Their work will endure. The most precious teaching the faithful Christian preacher can communicate to his congregation is the teaching about the person and work of Christ. At the heart of Christian preaching is the saving passion and resurrection of Jesus. This is why Paul tells the Corinthians that he is determined to know nothing among them except Jesus Christ and him crucified (I Cor. 2:2).[87]

While Saurin recognizes that vain eloquence can be nothing more than trying to build the faith of Christians with wood, hay, and stubble, he recognizes that often the Scriptures themselves provide models of eloquence which are unsurpassable.[88] All the different genres of literature are exemplified in the Holy Writings. In Genesis we find a variety of superb examples of literary form: the creation narrative, the story of Abraham's sacrifice, and the story of Joseph are choice passages which rival any of the historians. What could be found more tender, what more elegiac, than the poetry of Jeremiah? Who could have a greater power to sober the thoughts of his hearers than Ezekiel? When it comes to nobility of expres-

85. Saurin, *Sermons,* 1:72-73.
86. Saurin, *Sermons,* 2:97f.
87. Saurin, *Sermons,* 2:99.
88. Saurin, *Sermons,* 1:73.

sion, none can surpass Isaiah. In the New Testament we discover the Epistle to the Hebrews to be eloquent Greek. The Christian preacher need not take Demosthenes or Cicero as his guides to pulpit eloquence. Far more important it is for him to "investigate the ideas, and appropriate the language of the inspired writers. — Heat thine imagination at the fire which inflamed them, and with them, endeavour to elevate the mind to the mansions of God." Then, with a particularly eloquent quotation from Paul, he drives home his point. It is to the light unto which no man can approach that the preacher must point (I Tim. 6:16). It is from the sacred writers that the preacher learns best to handle the sword of the Spirit.[89] As Paul himself, Saurin is capable of the greatest eloquence and at the same time is fully aware of its limitations.

Today we read Saurin, and unless we have a full appreciation of what was considered good French oratorical style at the beginning of the eighteenth century, we find his work a bit overblown. He fits very well into his age, but the age into which he fits so well is hard for us to appreciate. As true as this may be, we cannot help but be grateful that indeed his considerable eloquence is a witness to the truth. Beauty of expression can be a powerful testimony to the truth.

VI. Johann Kaspar Lavater (1741-1801)

Johann Kaspar Lavater was one of the most widely admired preachers of his time.[90] He was regarded as a man of the Enlightenment, open to new ideas, conversant with the leading thinkers of the day, and sensitive to the artistic taste of his time. Still, he was a completely orthodox Christian who lived a simple, honest, and devout life. Lavater has a secure place among the writers of that golden age of German literature. Of particular interest are his poetry and his diaries. A good number of his hymns are

89. Saurin, *Sermons,* 1:73.
90. My first acquaintance with the preaching of Lavater came from the collection of his works by Ernst Staehelin, whom I remember so fondly from my student days at Basel: *Johann Caspar Lavaters ausgewählte Werke,* ed. Ernst Staehelin, 4 vols. (Zürich: Zwingli-Verlag, 1943), hereafter Lavater, *Werke.* Only recently have I discovered the extraordinary study of Klaus Martin Sauer, *Die Predigttätigkeit Johann Kaspar Lavaters (1741-1801)* (Zürich: Theologischer Verlag Zürich, 1988). This work tells us all we need to know about Lavater in its over seven hundred pages, and yet anything Staehelin has to say on any subject is golden.

still included in the standard German hymnbooks of our day. He published two epic poems, *Jesus Messias* and *Joseph von Arimathia*, which are good representatives of the Sturm und Drang period of German literature. True to that period, he left posterity a particularly engaging diary, *Aussichten in die Ewigkeit*. Maintaining a wide correspondence with the intellectuals of his day throughout Europe, he was respected at home as both pastor and preacher. Lavater belonged to the age of genius and has appropriately been called "the genius of the heart."

But it is as a preacher where his greatness is best appreciated. Born to one of the distinguished patrician families of Zürich and educated for the pastorate in his native city, he was a legitimate heir to a distinct religious tradition. Led by Ulrich Zwingli and Heinrich Bullinger, Zürich had developed a particular approach to Reformed Protestantism. This tradition Lavater sought to maintain with a loving and mystical fervor. In the well-established manner of the Reformed church of Zürich, he began his ministry at a diaconal post, being chaplain at an orphanage from 1769 to 1778. It was his preaching in the evening at the orphanage chapel which first brought his gifts to the attention of his native city. In the course of time he became pastor of Saint Peter's Church in the center of Zürich. One can say of Lavater, as one can say of Francis of Assisi, that he was preeminently a preacher of the love of God. Typical of moderatism in the Reformed pulpit, he combined the themes of classical Protestantism, evangelical pietism, and the Enlightenment. What put his preaching over was above all his enthusiasm and deep piety.

A. Worship in Zürich, 1750-1800

It had been more than two centuries since Zwingli had reformed the worship of the church of Zürich. The form of worship he laid down had been essentially maintained up through the time of Lavater.[91] The service was still very simple. It began with the singing of a hymn, followed by an invocation read from the official liturgy of the church of Zürich. This invocation was concluded by the recitation of the Lord's Prayer.[92] The lesson followed, upon which the sermon was based. Following the sermon came

---

91. For a detailed study of the worship in the church of Zürich at the time of Lavater, see Sauer, *Predigttätigkeit*, pp. 64-88.

92. Sauer, *Predigttätigkeit*, p. 68.

the prayers of intercession, the giving of alms, a benediction, and a final hymn.[93] The one important modification which had been made was the introduction of psalmody and then hymnody. It has never been clear why Zwingli did not follow the lead of other Protestant churches in this matter. He clearly approved of congregational singing on general principles. One supposes there was some practical hindrance of a purely local nature, but we cannot say for sure.

Long before Lavater began writing his hymns, the church of Zürich was singing as regularly as any other Protestant church of the day. Even at that, the sermon was still the core of the service, except for the four times a year that Communion was celebrated. The sermons were well thought out and well delivered by learned and conscientious ministers.[94] They normally lasted an hour and were well attended, at least until about the end of the eighteenth century, when there was a marked cooling of Christian conviction and devotion, a phenomenon experienced throughout Europe regardless of confession.

The church of Zürich held a full schedule of services. Both in the city and the countryside there were morning and evening worship on Sunday, and for the city churches at least, morning services on most weekdays.[95] In addition to vespers on Sunday, there were evening services on Wednesday and Saturday.[96] Toward the end of the century attendance at weekday services dwindled somewhat and a number of them were discontinued. They tended to be of a more popular nature. More attention was given to reading larger passages of Scripture following the *lectio continua* and explaining the passages.[97] On Saturday afternoon and in the middle of the day on Sunday there were catechetical services.[98] While originally designed to explain the catechism to children, they often drew a good number of adults. Some preachers were better at addressing themselves to children than others, but a serious attempt to engage even younger children was made by some of the pastors and especially by the deacons. On the other hand, in some of the catechetical services the catechism was simply preached through question by question, aiming primarily at adults. Serious doctrinal preaching based on the catechism and

93. Sauer, *Predigttätigkeit*, p. 69.
94. Sauer, *Predigttätigkeit*, p. 79.
95. Sauer, *Predigttätigkeit*, p. 68.
96. Sauer, *Predigttätigkeit*, p. 69.
97. Sauer, *Predigttätigkeit*, p. 71.
98. Sauer, *Predigttätigkeit*, p. 85.

addressed primarily to adults was quite popular in Reformed churches on the Continent until fairly recent times.

The Sunday morning service, as Klaus Martin Sauer puts it, had an official, or civic, character, and most citizens of Zürich felt an obligation to be present.[99] Before the service began, announcements of a public character were made. In connection with the prayers of intercession, banns of marriage were read and the passing away of the faithful was reverently remembered. The pastor of each congregation normally preached at the morning service, where he was expected to preach through one of the Gospels; at the evening service he or his assistant would preach through an epistle. The *lectio continua* was followed, but, at the discretion of the ministers, it was often interrupted. Sacramental occasions regularly interrupted it. This was especially the case because three of the four celebrations of the Lord's Supper were connected to the celebration of the three major evangelical feasts, Christmas, Easter, and Pentecost.[100] There needed to be a sermon for the feast day and a preparatory sermon the Sunday before. We will say more about this further on.

Occasional days of prayer and repentance or days of praise and thanksgiving established by the civil authority also demanded sermons appropriate to the occasion. Any public disaster or cause of celebration might call for a sermon of this sort. In September, however, a national day of prayer was observed throughout the Swiss Confederation. In Zürich this called for a special sermon on that day as well as on the Sunday preceding. As in New England, these sermons afforded the preacher an opportunity to give a sort of state of the nation address. As had the jeremiads preached by our ancestors, these sermons received the special attention of both the preacher and the congregation. It was not at all uncommon for the city council to order the publication of a sermon it felt had been notably prophetic. Apparently the minister was always free to depart from his *lectio continua* when he felt it important to address some problem or issue of the time. The registry of Lavater's sermons suggests this happened six or eight times a year.

Let us look at these different types of sermons as preached by the best known of Zürich's preachers at the end of the eighteenth century.

99. Sauer, *Predigttätigkeit,* p. 78.
100. Sauer, *Predigttätigkeit,* pp. 74f.

B. Expository Sermons

The foundation of Lavater's preaching ministry was in his expository preaching. As we have seen, expository preaching has been an honored tradition from most-ancient times. We found this to be true to a large measure during the patristic age, and especially during the Reformation. Indeed, Zwingli had introduced the Reformation in Zürich with a systematic exposition of the Gospel of Matthew. In January of 1519 he began his ministry at the Greatminster by preaching through Matthew using the *lectio continua.* In January of 1789, 270 years later, Lavater was still honoring the tradition by beginning a series on the Gospel of John.[101] This series would occupy him on and off for the remaining eleven years of his ministry. We have manuscripts or outlines for over two hundred of these sermons, but there were, no doubt, considerably more for which we have no record.[102] Even at that, Lavater had not yet begun the twelfth chapter of the Gospel. It was indeed a very slow *lectio continua.*

One of the reasons it went so slowly is that, following the taste of the day, Lavater turned his expository sermons into theme sermons. In the register of his sermons so carefully drawn up by Sauer, we see how this was done.[103] Sauer lists the first ten sermons of the series as follows:

1. January 4, 1789 — John 1:1-3
   John and his Gospel
2. January 11, 1789 — John 1:1-3
   Jesus, the Word of God
3. January 18, 1789 — John 1:1-2
   The divine nature of Christ
4. January 25, 1789 — John 1:1-3
   Jesus Christ, the Creator of all things
5. February 1, 1789 — John 1:4
   Jesus Christ, the Source of Life

101. Two years earlier, on the Sunday following his taking up his ministry as pastor of Saint Peter's, he began a series of thirty-five sermons on the eleventh chapter of John.

102. There are a good number of sermons on the fourth, fifth, and sixth chapters of John which are not dated, but which show every evidence of fitting into the series. The last year of his ministry records no sermons for the series.

103. Sauer, *Predigttätigkeit,* pp. 591-94. This exemplary study makes it possible to get a much clearer picture of Lavater's preaching ministry than we have been able to get for any other preacher of the period.

6. February 8, 1789 — John 1:4-11
   Jesus Christ, the True Light of Men
7. March 1, 1789 — John 1:4-11
   The behavior of darkness toward the Light
8. March 8, 1789 — John 1:4-11
   The foolishness of rejecting the Light
9. March 15, 1789 — John 1:10-11
   The sin of rejecting Jesus
10. March 22, 1789 — John 1:6-8
    The trustworthiness of John the Baptist

Up to this point Lavater is averaging close to a sermon per verse. It would be hard to argue that the prologue to the Gospel of John is not worth ten sermons, but on the other hand, one can well imagine how long it would take to cover the whole Gospel.

The Gospel of John offered Lavater a colorful bouquet of subjects.[104] Its high Christology is a subject to which he constantly returns. The divinity of Jesus, denied by so many Deists of the time, our preacher confidently affirms. While Lavater is certainly not a systematic theologian, and the reasons he advances for believing in the full divinity and full humanity of Jesus lack theological precision from an academic standpoint, from a more popular standpoint he makes a good case of the reasonableness of the teaching that Christ is truly God and truly man. The simple meaning of the text of John shows quite clearly that Christ is to be received as the divine Word of God. He is to be adored as Savior of the world and obeyed as the revelation of divine wisdom. This message Lavater finds repeatedly in the Fourth Gospel. He is convinced of the trustworthiness of John's report, as becomes quite clear in his treatment of the miracle stories in the Gospel.

While Lavater gives full attention to the Christology of John, he frequently treats the devotional and moral aspects of the Gospel. This is manifestly the case when he gets to the story of the wedding of Cana, where he gives a Protestant interpretation of the virgin Mary.[105] The mother of Jesus is presented as an example of Christian piety.[106] Her hu-

---

104. For a more thorough analysis of this series on the Gospel of John, see Sauer, *Predigttätigkeit*, pp. 273-92.

105. Sauer, *Predigttätigkeit*, pp. 605-6.

106. Sauer, *Predigttätigkeit*, p. 277.

mility, her maternal love, her trust in God, and her helpfulness to others should inspire all Christians. Far from polemicizing against Catholic views, the sermon is filled with a tolerant and enlightened spirit.

Lavater was particularly fond of John 11, the story of the raising of Lazarus.[107] This was a good chapter for him to develop many of his ideas on the life of devotion. The spiritual meaning of illness and death was a frequent topic in his preaching ministry. Pietism encouraged Christians to take such matters to heart. It made the writing of a journal a spiritual discipline. It cultivated introspection. Illness or the death of a friend or relative was a favorite focal point for this introspection. The story of Lazarus brought this subject to discussion. As we have already noted, in the age of genius Lavater has been called "the genius of the heart." It is easy to understand why he devoted so much attention to the Gospel of John, which has so often been called the Gospel of love.

Lavater's approach to expository preaching could vary considerably depending on which service during the week he had been assigned. While on Sunday morning he preached thematically and went very slowly through John, the sermons he preached at vespers on weekday evenings were quite different. He preached a series of forty-four sermons on Revelation from May to October of 1779.[108] As Lavater understood it, these services were basically *abendgebet*, that is, evening prayer, and he therefore emphasized the prayers rather than the sermon.[109] That left him only half an hour or so for a sermon. By long-established tradition in Zürich, the Scripture lesson at vespers was supposed to be read from the New Testament, going on through the whole New Testament on the basis of the *lectio continua*, half a chapter at a time.[110] That meant a rather rapid use of the *lectio continua*. To develop only a single theme from half a chapter does not adequately treat the whole passage. As Lavater recognized, the patristic method of giving a running commentary on the passage was a better way of handling a longer text.

At the end of the century of the Enlightenment, Lavater's approach to the interpretation of Revelation, this most enigmatic of books, is par-

---

107. Sauer, *Predigttätigkeit*, p. 292.
108. Sauer, *Predigttätigkeit*, p. 220.
109. Sauer, *Predigttätigkeit*, p. 218.
110. Seven years later the cycle brought Lavater to Revelation again. For that year we have record of him preaching through the Catholic Epistles before he reached Revelation, and then beginning the cycle over again with Matthew when he had completed Revelation. Cf. Sauer, *Predigttätigkeit*, pp. 552-58.

ticularly interesting. One wonders if he was familiar with the series of sermons his predecessor Heinrich Bullinger had preached on this book in
the middle of the Renaissance. In England the Elizabethan divines held it
in high respect. It was translated into English, and by the authority of the
queen was distributed to every parish church in the realm. Lavater had evidently studied enough commentaries to know that there were a good
number of approaches to the interpretation of the book. He assures his
congregation that he wants to treat the book with reverence and that he
has a feeling of humility before the interpreters of the past. For him, however, the key to interpretation is to see how Christ sustained John during a
time of persecution by the visions he granted him.[111] For Lavater this is a
book of the Bible which encourages us. It teaches us that God always supports us in time of need with visions of eternity. God may well give us
other visions to support us in our own time, but Lavater wants to bring us
as close as possible to the historical situation in which John lived and in
which he was ministered to by Christ through these visions. For many of
us this interpretation is a bit too simplistic. The pietism of this approach
is striking! It is the sort of pietism, however, that would not be offensive
to the Enlightenment.

C. Festal Sermons

The church of Zürich had a calendar of feast days very similar to those of
other Reformed churches on the Continent.[112] Basically it came down to
the observance of Christmas, Easter, and Pentecost, and the days closely
associated with these three primary evangelical feast days, such as
Maundy Thursday, Good Friday, and Ascension. Each feast was observed
for two days, Easter and Easter Monday, Pentecost and Pentecost Monday, Christmas and the day following. Advent and Lent were not observed, but Holy Week was. It was by intention a very simple calendar.
The feasts which were celebrated, however, were celebrated conscientiously. The high point of the celebration of Christmas, Easter, and Pentecost was the observance of the Lord's Supper. This meant that the preaching served the purpose of preparing the congregation to participate in the
Sacrament and to make the covenant vows which receiving the sacred

111. Sauer, *Predigttätigkeit,* p. 220.
112. Sauer, *Predigttätigkeit,* p. 74.

meal implied. Sacramental preaching and festal preaching went hand in hand. Preparatory services were taken very seriously by Reformed churches in the eighteenth century. We will see this in both Scotland and America. It is a most important observation for us to make.

Let us look, then, at the festal sermons preached by Lavater between Easter and Pentecost in 1799, the last year of the eighteenth century. They give us a good view of the way a Reformed church observed Christian feasts about midway between the Reformation and our own time:

Fourth Sunday before Easter (24 February)
    Matthew 25:1-13 (Wise and Foolish Virgins)
Third Sunday before Easter (3 March)
    [no record]
Second Sunday before Easter (10 March)
    Matthew 25:1-6 (Wise and Foolish Virgins)
Palm Sunday (17 March)
    Mark 14:1-14 (Passion Narrative)
Monday of Holy Week (18 March)
    Mark 14:32-40 (Passion Narrative)
Wednesday of Holy Week (20 March)
    Mark 15:1-6 (Passion Narrative)
Maundy Thursday (21 March)
    Mark 15:6-20 (Passion Narrative)
Good Friday (22 March)
    Mark 15:33-40 (Passion Narrative)
Easter (24 March)
    Romans 10:9 (Professing Faith in Christ)
Easter Monday (25 March)
    Romans 10:9-10 (Professing Faith in Christ)
Sunday after Easter (31 March)
    [no record]
Second Sunday after Easter (7 April)
    [series interrupted]
Third Sunday after Easter (14 April)
    Matthew 25:1-9 (Wise and Foolish Virgins)
Fourth Sunday after Easter (21 April)
    Matthew 25:8-10 (Wise and Foolish Virgins)
Fifth Sunday after Easter (28 April)
    Matthew 25:8-10 (Wise and Foolish Virgins)

Ascension (2 May)
  John 14:1-4 (The Promise of the Spirit)
Sixth Sunday after Easter (5 May)
  Matthew 25:13 (Wise and Foolish Virgins)
Pentecost (12 May)
  I Corinthians 12:3-11 (Gifts of the Spirit)
Pentecost Monday (13 May)
  I Corinthians 12:3-11 (Gifts of the Spirit)

The first thing which captures our attention is the way Lavater has set the observance of the whole Easter cycle in the context of the parable of the wise and foolish virgins. Six sermons on this parable have been preserved, but for two Sundays we have no record. There could have been eight sermons in the series. There is obvious theological significance in this arrangement. Today we might say that he put the celebration in an eschatological light. The Church is waiting for the wedding feast. Again and again we find that Reformed piety in the eighteenth century interprets the Lord's Supper in terms of the wedding feast.[113]

Into this interpretation of the parable is set a series of five sermons on the passion narrative from the Gospel of Mark. Again, it was typical of Reformed churches at the time to preach through the passion narrative of a different Gospel each year during Holy Week. The third thing which interests us is that Lavater chooses to preach on Mark 14:1-14 on the Sunday before Easter. Obviously this service is not celebrating Palm Sunday, but is rather a preparatory service for the receiving of the Sacrament at Easter. The lesson starts out, "It was now two days before the Passover and the feast of Unleavened Bread. . . ." It goes on to tell of Christ's anointing at Bethany and the sending of the disciples out to prepare for the eating of the Passover. It then concludes, "Where is my guest room, where I am to eat the passover with my disciples?" The theme implied by the selection of the Scripture passage is preparation for the sacred meal.

There is another thing to be noticed, and it is the most interesting of all. For Easter Sunday and Monday Lavater does not use Mark 16, which would have been the logical way to finish the series. Rather he chooses to preach on Romans 10:9-10 (RSV), "Because, if you confess

113. Cf. my article on Gilbert Tennent: "Gilbert Tennent and the Preaching of Piety in Colonial America," *Princeton Seminary Bulletin*, n.s., 10 (1989): 132-37.

with your lips that Jesus is Lord and believe in your heart that God raised him from the dead, you will be saved. For man believes with his heart and so is justified, and he confesses with his lips and so is saved." This might seem an unlikely text for an Easter Sunday sermon unless one is aware that it is a Communion Sunday and that from the standpoint of covenantal theology, at the heart of the communion service is the renewing of the covenantal vows, that is, a profession of faith in Jesus Christ, crucified and risen.

Fifth, one notices that the texts for Ascension Day and Pentecost Sunday and Monday are equally appropriate for handling the themes of these feasts — the transcendent fellowship which Christ has ascended into heaven to prepare for us (John 14:1-4) and the ministry the Holy Spirit has been poured out upon us to perform here on earth, respectively — in the eschatological context of the parable of the wise and foolish virgins. The way Lavater has linked the celebration of Christ's passion, resurrection, and ascension and the giving of the Spirit by interpreting them in the context of this parable shows a tremendous grasp of the significance of the central themes of Christian worship.

At this point something important needs to be said. One should not imagine that the striking insights of this series of festal sermons were an example of the eccentricity of an individual genius. A comparison of the themes of this communion service with the typical Scottish communion season as we find, for example, in the sacramental sermons of John Willison, with the communion sermons of Jodocus van Lodenstein in the Netherlands, and with Gilbert Tennent in New Jersey, shows that this was typical of eighteenth-century Reformed eucharistic piety.

The celebration of Christmas was also built around the celebration of the Sacrament. There was no observance of Advent, any more than there was of Lent. Discontinuing the penitential seasons of preparation for Christmas and Easter was one of the first reforms of Reformed Protestantism. This may seem a bit radical to some, but it is at the heart of the Reformed approach to worship. The whole history of these seasons of fasting had been marked by a legalistic asceticism which is far removed from Christian piety as taught in the New Testament. While specifically Reformed churches have been characterized by their avoidance of Lent and Advent, few Protestants find the kind of asceticism implied by these observances consistent with the teaching of Jesus. Most Protestants have found the old observances of Lent and Advent terribly reminiscent of the piety of the Pharisees which Jesus so explicitly condemned. The objection to Lent and Advent is that they overemphasize the penitential dimension of Christian devotion.

The celebration of Christmas in 1789 involved the following services:[114]

1. Sunday before Christmas (December 20, 1789)
   John 1:31-32 (John the Baptist points to Christ as the Lamb of God)
2. Christmas Day (December 25, 1789)
   Luke 2:6-14 (The Angels and Shepherds)
3. Day after Christmas (December 26, 1789)
   Luke 2:15-16 (The Shepherds are our example in seeking and finding Christ)
4. Sunday after Christmas (December 27, 1789)
   Luke 2:17-20 (The Shepherds find the Christ Child)
5. New Year's Day (January 1, 1790)
   Luke 2:21 (The naming of Jesus)

All year Lavater had been doing a thorough study of John 1. For several months he had been focusing on the ministry of John the Baptist and his witness to the coming of the Messiah. The transition to the traditional themes of Christmas was very easy. Normally the first pastor of a church was to preach through one of the nativity narratives at the main services during the Christmas season. The second pastor or the deacon, if the church had more than one preacher, might take up an appropriate psalm or some other passage for the daily prayer services. But the pastor was not bound to the nativity narratives. For the Christmas season in 1798, for example, Lavater chose the apostle Paul's christological hymn in Philippians 2:6-11 as the text for some very theological sermons.[115] As first pastor in 1789, he took the nativity narrative in Luke.[116] As the outline above shows, he developed a set of sermons from it which handle the theme of seeking and finding the Messiah. The shepherds are our example. Then, after the first of the year, Lavater returns to John 1 and continues on the same theme of seeking and finding the Messiah. The conclusion of John 1 lends itself to this theme because it tells how a number of

114. Sauer, *Predigttätigkeit*, p. 601.
115. Sauer, *Predigttätigkeit*, p. 644.
116. Sauer, *Predigttätigkeit*, p. 601.

disciples discovered Jesus to be the Savior of the world. Here is another series of festal sermons that is amazingly well thought out.

D. Sermons on Current Affairs

It was at the height of Lavater's career, in 1789, that the French Revolution broke out. Only slowly was the magnitude of the event realized, and that this signaled the passing of the old regime was not recognized at first. During the last decade of his ministry, however, our preacher found it necessary to preach more and more frequently on the meaning of these changes for the life and faith of the Christians of Zürich. As so often happens, he found ample opportunity in the course of his *lectio continua* of the Gospel of John to comment extensively on current events. Some of the most prophetic preaching in history has been exercised well within the most exacting disciplines of expository preaching. Lavater, as Chrysostom, Augustine, and Zwingli before him, did not hesitate to apply the text providence had put before him to current affairs. He did not, however, limit himself to expository preaching but frequently chose texts which were appropriate to the unusual events of the day.

On one occasion he developed a series of six sermons on the Revolution, taking as his text for all six Luke 21:9-10 (RSV): "'And when you hear of wars and tumults, do not be terrified; for this must first take place, but the end will not be at once.' Then he said to them, 'Nation will rise against nation, and kingdom against kingdom.'" The sermon was Lavater's response to a battle between the troops of the Swiss canton of Unterwald and the French. This battle was one more event which brought Switzerland into the wars the French Revolution was spawning all over Europe. The sermons were delivered in September and October of 1798.[117]

The church of Zürich, typical of eighteenth-century Reformed churches, gave the conscientious preacher ample opportunity to address the problems of society. On several dozen occasions during the year the minister was encouraged to preach on current events. First, two Sundays a year were set aside for elections, a Sunday early in June and a Sunday early in December. The election and inauguration of the masters of the guilds, city councilmen, and the mayor had a strong religious flavor and de-

117. Sauer, *Predigttätigkeit*, pp. 642-43.

manded something similar to what our ancestors in colonial New England called an election sermon. Also, a Sunday early in May was set aside for the reading of the mandates of the city council on the behavior of the citizenry. This Sunday called for a sermon on Christian citizenship. Finally, as we mentioned above, a national prayer day was held on a Thursday early in September. The observance claimed eleven days and included a celebration of Communion and a preparatory service on the two Sundays before prayer day. A proclamation was read setting forth the needs of the Swiss Confederation, a special prayer was published for the occasion, and a series of Scripture lessons was drawn up on which the sermons were to be based. Even the hymns were selected. As we have often said, the prophetic dimension of Christian preaching can never be institutionalized. That is of its very nature. On the other hand, ever since the strongly prophetic ministry of Zwingli, the church of Zürich has recognized the need for a prophetic ministry and given its ministers every opportunity to exercise that prophetic ministry.

Sauer has given us a detailed study of Lavater's preaching on public affairs from the outbreak of the French Revolution to the end of his ministry, a bit more than ten years later.[118] At first Lavater showed a certain sympathy for the Revolution, the sort one would expect a loyal citizen of a democratic republic to have for a land which had finally revolted against one of the most totalitarian monarchies Europe had ever produced. The heirs of Louis XIV had a royal court that was as antithetical to the spirit of Swiss Protestant democracy as one could imagine. One might, therefore, expect the Swiss to be sympathetic. At first there was some sympathy, but things changed. When it had been learned that almost a thousand Swiss mercenary soldiers had been killed by the mob at the Tuileries, when news came that the king had been guillotined, and when it became clear that France had turned itself over to anarchy, Lavater grew more and more critical. He began to see events taking place as the natural result of what happens when a nation preens its enlightenment to the point of giving up its faith in God. Before long he was regarded as an enemy of the Revolution. How could it have gone any differently? Bit by bit the French Revolution had revealed that the new egalitarianism could be as despotic as the old aristocracy. As Lavater saw it, the Enlightenment was now mocking Christian love as it had mocked Christian doctrine.

---

118. Sauer, *Predigttätigkeit,* pp. 271-337.

E. Preaching the Love of God

Lavater is remembered above all as one who preached the love of God. That is quite a distinction! One could hardly imagine a greater tribute. Beyond Bonaventure the Franciscan theologian, Bernardino da Siena the Italian evangelist, and Richard Sibbes the Puritan preacher of London, few have gained such a reputation. The distinguished Swiss church historian Ernst Staehelin, in his four-volume selection of Lavater's works, gives us a sermon which typifies Lavater's message on this theme.[119] The sermon concluded in his *lectio continua* series on the book of Jonah held on Sunday evenings in the chapel of the orphanage. This chapel was at one time a Dominican priory, and as one would expect, it was built for preaching and could hold a good number of worshipers. It had no regular congregation, but services were open to those who lived in the neighborhood, and a good number of people attended them as a matter of convenience. During Lavater's chaplaincy the attendance at vespers grew considerably. The fourteen sermons on Jonah were published in 1773 under the title *Predigten über das Buch Jonas*.[120]

As Lavater interprets it, the book tells us about the love of God. The book makes as its central point that the love of God is universal.[121] It extends to all kinds of people over the whole wide earth. He takes as his text the last two verses of the book, "And the LORD said, 'You pity the plant, for which you did not labor, nor did you make it grow, which came into being in a night, and perished in a night. And should not I pity Nineveh, that great city, in which there are more than a hundred and twenty thousand persons who do not know their right hand from their left, and also much cattle?'" (Jon. 4:10-11 RSV).

Having announced his text, our preacher introduces his sermon by reminding us that love is the fundamental principle of the Christian life. He quotes I John 4:16, "God is love," as that which unlocks the message of Jonah. This is the theme of all Scripture; this is what is behind God's creation; this is the basis of God's providence. He quotes at length from Psalm 103 and Isaiah 57, two beautiful passages on the love of God.[122] Lavater's ability to quote Scripture from memory is one of his more effec-

---

119. Lavater, *Werke*, 2:8-29.
120. Lavater, *Werke*, 2:9.
121. Lavater, *Werke*, 2:12.
122. Lavater, *Werke*, 2:13.

64

tive homiletical techniques. These two passages certainly make clear that the love of God is not something we find only in the New Testament. Love is the fundamental principle of the book of Jonah, and Lavater reviews the whole story to demonstrate it.[123] Love sent the prophet out to Nineveh in the first place. Love frustrated his attempt to run away. Love prepared the great fish which preserved him in the sea and spat him up on the shore and again sent him on his way to Nineveh. What else but love brought the people of Nineveh to repentance? Finally, was it not the love of God which saw the repentance of Nineveh and spared the city? We notice the consummate artistry with which Lavater reviews his fourteen-sermon series, the point of which was to show that the divine truth revealed in the book of Jonah is the universality of God's love. The introduction to the sermon is a review of the whole series.

The first point our preacher wants to make is how unspeakable is the love of God in regard to his paternal care for our natural needs.[124] He invites us to review our own lives and think of how we have experienced the love of God in his acts of providence. Have we never been sick and recovered our good health? Have we never experienced poverty and yet been provided with food and drink, clothing and shelter? Have we ever experienced the support of friends and family? Do we not enjoy all kinds of strength, all kinds of abilities, hearing and eyesight, the power to get around, to come here and to go home again? In all these we experience God's fatherly love. Lavater is, to be sure, quite aware that the Enlightenment attacked the whole concept of providence. His response to this attack is very simple: the God revealed to us in Jesus Christ is our Father.[125] He is our Father in heaven, as the Lord's Prayer puts it. If God is Father, he is a true father, not an absentee father who figures that with our procreation his work is done. A true father sees to the daily well-being of his children, and so it is with God. Lavater's constant insistence on the fatherly love of God has polemical significance.

The second point in Lavater's sermon is that God shows his love for us in caring for our spiritual needs. Continually and in all kinds of ways God works on our enlightenment and improvement. He reveals himself through the beauties of nature. He makes our hearts glad through the enjoyable things of life. He has put in our own hands his divine precepts

---

123. Lavater, *Werke*, 2:14.
124. Lavater, *Werke*, 2:17.
125. Lavater, *Werke*, 2:19.

and the story of his mighty acts. He has given us examples of virtue and provided teachers, both in an official way and in a more personal way. He has set true friends at our side to encourage us, to cheer us with the bond of friendship, and to make easier the way of life. He speaks to us through our understanding, through our hearts, and through our conscience.[126] He shows us the way to immortality through death, the path of blessedness through suffering. Richly and freely he gives us everything which serves for life and the divine blessing of life. Of all this the story of Jonah is the perfect example, as Lavater's congregation has seen through the whole series of sermons.

Much of what Lavater has said up to this point demonstrates an attempt to engage the thoughts of a congregation that had been affected by the claims of the Enlightenment. One notices how in the thoughts just expressed Lavater has plucked the chords of understanding, of heart, and of conscience. In the eighteenth century there were those who would appeal alone to reason, those who would appeal to the heart as the primary guide in life, and those who would appeal above all to conscience. Lavater talks about all three. He was a man of the Enlightenment, but he was also a pietist.

Above all he was a Christian, and so now he begins to speak of how we experience the love of God in Christ. The eternally loving God leads us not only through the ordinary works of providence; he has made himself visible in the person of Jesus Christ.[127] He has presented himself in bodily form and entered fully into our humanity. He came to us the only begotten Son of the Father, full of grace and truth, the immediate, the complete image of eternal love. He was Love itself in his ministry and in his passion. He breathed love and prayed love and spoke love. To every man he gave himself up a servant, and for every man he offered himself up to the Father. Following the will of the Father rather than his own will, he took upon himself all our illnesses, all our suffering, and all our sin. It was unsurpassable love that poured out its lifeblood for us all.

For Lavater it was clear that whatever enlightenment the eighteenth century may have discovered, the Christian faith had something beyond it. In the cross of Christ the love of God is revealed, and that, we would want to admit, is the Christian gospel at the beginning of the twenty-first century as well as at the end of the eighteenth.

126. Lavater, *Werke*, 2:20.
127. Lavater, *Werke*, 2:21.

The third point our preacher wants to make is the universality of God's love for all his creatures. That is, of course, the point made so forcefully in the last two verses of the book of Jonah. It sums up the point of the book, and so in his sermon on these two verses Lavater is able to sum up his whole series of fourteen sermons. There were 120,000 people in Nineveh, and God out of his love wanted to show them mercy. Lavater also notes that the text tells us there were many cattle. While he does not develop this theme, he hints that one can well speak about God's mercy to animals as well as to humans.[128] And if God even includes cattle in his care, how much more, Lavater asks, are we included. He nails in his point with an effective bit of classical rhetoric. Oh, man, whoever you are, from whatever nation you may come, however much you may have forgotten God, yes, even you who have been careless of the things of God, even you who have been hard-hearted, God has the same patience and long-suffering toward you that he had toward the people of Nineveh.[129]

The fourth point Lavater wants to make is that the goodness and mercy of God is especially full toward those who turn to him in repentance. Our preacher challenges his congregation to name any repentant sinner in the holy history who did not receive the mercy of God. Beginning with Adam and going through the apostles, he reminds them of the many examples Scripture gives of repentant sinners who discovered God's mercy.[130] Lavater, as so many effective preachers, uses biblical illustration with particular ability. In this sermon he illustrates the meaning of God's reproach of Jonah for murmuring against his mercy toward the people of Nineveh with the story of the prodigal son.[131] When the younger son repented and came home to the father, the elder son grew angry. The father has to reproach him, reminding him that he had a special blessing because he had always been with him, had never gone away, and all he had was his. He should rejoice that the younger son had come home. God's mercy is surprising to the righteous, but the righteousness of God is above and beyond the righteousness of men. God's love is beyond our love. His mercy, the Scriptures tell us, is everlasting. That truth found in one of the most profound of Jesus' parables is the central message of the book of Jonah.

The final point Lavater wants to emphasize is God's love toward those

---

128. Lavater, *Werke,* 2:22.
129. Lavater, *Werke,* 2:23.
130. Lavater, *Werke,* 2:24.
131. Lavater, *Werke,* 2:25.

who know him to be their Father, those who trust him as their Father.[132] Unspeakable is the divine goodness toward the godly. Those who are open to God, those who are of one mind with him, those who believe and love God in their innermost hearts stand in fellowship with God and in that enjoy his abiding love. They discover that part of that blessing is that they see things differently. They see things others do not see. The whole of life is changed because it looks different. Oh, my beloved congregation, Lavater exhorts us, does it not give great strength to know that the Creator of all is our own Father![133] With this Lavater begins to quote a whole anthology of great passages of Scripture on the love of God; most are from the Gospel of John.[134] Again we see how effectively Lavater quotes Scripture. He ends with the words of the High Priestly Prayer from John 17:21f., praying that the world might know the Father's love. In good Reformed tradition the service of the Word leads to the service of prayer. Lavater leads his congregation into prayer with this beautiful invocation:

> Oh unspeakable mercy!
> Oh love without end!
> Oh how good you are, my Father!
>> How full of grace,
>>> you heavenly goodness![135]

---

132. Lavater, *Werke,* 2:26.
133. Lavater, *Werke,* 2:27.
134. Lavater, *Werke,* 2:28.
135. "O Erbarmen ohne Namen! / O Liebe ohne Gränzen! / O wie bist du so gut, mein Vater! / Wie gnadenvoll, / du himmlische Güte!" Lavater, *Werke,* 2:29.

CHAPTER II

The Awakenings of Eighteenth-Century Pietism

The appearance of pietism as an international program of church reform had a tremendous effect on Christian worship.[1] It demanded a complete reorientation of preaching as well as the disciplines of prayer. The coming of pietism brought a more informal, private approach to worship. It emphasized the element of personal fellowship and gave great attention to spontaneous prayer and inspirational hymnody. While devotional prayer and devotional Bible study became important to the pietists, they tended to ignore the sacraments and relegated them to formal worship, which might or might not be important. Pietism was an international movement which found different expressions in the various national churches of Europe and America. While it reached its high tide in the eighteenth

---

1. On pietism in general see Martin Brecht, Klaus Deppermann, Ulrich Gäbler, and Hartmut Lehmann, *Geschichte des Pietismus,* 2 vols. (Göttingen: Vandenhoeck & Ruprecht, 1995); Dale W. Brown, *Understanding Pietism* (Grand Rapids: Wm. B. Eerdmans Publishing Co., 1978); Heinrich Heppe, *Geschichte des Pietismus und der Mystik in der reformierten Kirche* (Leiden: Brill, 1879); John Charles Hoffman, "Pietism," in *New Catholic Encyclopedia,* 17 vols. (Washington, D.C.: Catholic University of America Press, 1968), 11:355; Ronald A. Knox, *Enthusiasm: A Chapter in the History of Religion* (London: Oxford University Press, 1950); Albrecht Ritschl, *Die Geschichte des Pietismus,* 3 vols. (Bonn: A. Marcus, 1880-86); M. Schmidt, "Pietismus," in *Die Religion in Geschichte und Gegenwart,* 3rd ed., 6 vols. (Tübingen: J. C. B. Mohr [Paul Siebeck], 1957-65), 5:370-81; and F. Ernest Stoeffler, *Continental Pietism and Early American Christianity* (Grand Rapids: Wm. B. Eerdmans Publishing Co., 1976).

century, it began to appear well before the end of the seventeenth. We find its spirit in the Jansenist movement in France, in the work of Spener and Francke in Germany, in Dutch Calvinism, in the Evangelical Revival led by Wesley and Whitefield in England, and in the Great Awakening in America. In each place it brought new life and a profound quickening of religious devotion.

This new devotion was not limited to any one class of people. The countess of Huntingdon, Nikolaus Ludwig von Zinzendorf, King Christian IV of Denmark, and King Frederick I of Prussia were among its strongest supporters, yet the lower classes embraced it passionately. In England the Evangelical Revival brought faith to mill workers and coal miners. The Wesleys did much to return the Christian faith to the common people who were being so abused by the Industrial Revolution. The utopian Christian communities Zinzendorf set up for the Moravians did much to ennoble the life of the farmer and artisan. It was the Moravians who took the gospel to the slaves of the sugar plantations in the West Indies. In North America the Great Awakening first gave the colonists a sense of a common religious identity. Pietism expressed itself differently in each place, and yet the basic unity of the movement is clearly discernible.

Eighteenth-century pietism as a program of spiritual reform had many forerunners. We have spoken of Byzantine pietism as well as the nominalist pietism of the late Middle Ages in a metaphorical sort of way. Strictly speaking, the pietism we want to speak about is a clearly discernible movement led by very specific figures, at a very distinct period of history, namely, the late seventeenth through the eighteenth century. One can speak of late medieval pietism, but properly speaking the term belongs to the eighteenth century. The pietism of the late Middle Ages as expressed in the Brethren of the Common Life certainly had its effect on the pietism of the eighteenth century. Thomas à Kempis, John Tauler, and the *Theologia Germanica* were read and admired by Spener, Francke, Zinzendorf, Wesley, and Whitefield. Some scholars would insist that pietism was founded by Johann Arndt, who at the end of the sixteenth century called German Lutherans to a renewed emphasis on the devotional life and the daily practice of Christian piety. Arndt's call was heard by a significant segment of German Protestantism. Almost all the great preachers of Lutheran orthodoxy during the seventeenth century had been influenced by his writings. As we have seen, Johann Gerhard, Heinrich Müller, and Christian Scriver were all shaped by his work. Orthodox Lutheranism was much more interested in the inner life than is so often claimed. Luther himself was, after all, warmly pious. Lutheran orthodoxy never really lost this piety, as the hymnody of the late sixteenth and early seventeenth centuries so clearly shows. Arndt belongs to the age of Lutheran orthodoxy even if he was a powerful inspiration to the pietists.

Others have traced the beginnings of pietism to the English Puritans or the Dutch Calvinists. To be sure, common elements can be found in each. The Puritans were very much interested in the practical concerns of living the Christian life, maintaining family worship, and the pastoral care of individuals. Certain Puritans put a strong emphasis on the necessity of conversion, particularly William Ames, who taught for many years in the Netherlands. Calvinists generally, whether in Great Britain or the Netherlands, were very interested in the doctrine of sanctification. Teellinck and van Lodenstein can well be considered forerunners of pietism, but they belong much more clearly to the age of Calvinist orthodoxy.[2] Both Puritanism and Dutch Calvinism had a great interest in practical piety and the inner life, but pietism was more than simply an emphasis on these things.[3] It was a very distinct configuration of these concerns.

The mainstream of pietism as expressed in the awakenings of the eighteenth century flows above all from the work of Philipp Jakob Spener (1635-1705).[4] Born into a very devout home in the Alsatian town of Rappoldsweiler, Spener from his youth had come to know Arndt's *True Christianity.* He began his theological studies in Strasbourg where the influence of Martin Bucer was still significant, even though the teaching of Luther was predominant. From Strasbourg he went to Basel and then Geneva, where he came under the influence of Jean de Labadie, who, although schooled by the Jesuits, embraced Jansenism, then Calvinism, and finally started his own religious community. Spener was attracted by the rigorism of this Protestant Jansenist as well as his communitarianism, which had strongly monastic tendencies.

It was Jansenism, not Calvinism, which Spener took with him when he left Geneva. He spent some time in Tübingen, where he apparently inspired several who later became the leaders of Swabian pietism; he had

---

2. For more information on Teellinck and van Lodenstein, see F. Ernest Stoeffler, *The Rise of Evangelical Pietism* (Leiden: Brill, 1971), pp. 127-48.

3. Cf. Stoeffler, *Rise of Evangelical Pietism,* pp. 109-79.

4. For the most recent evaluation of Spener's place in the history of pietism, see Martin Brecht, "Philipp Jakob Spener, sein Programm und dessen Auswirkungen," in Brecht et al., *Geschichte des Pietismus,* 1:281-389.

particular influence on Johann Andreas Frommann and Johann Andreas Hochstetler, younger members of the faculty of theology at Tübingen. While there Spener started two conventicles of the type that became so significant in the spreading of pietism. This circle of devout Swabians continued to follow Spener's teachings as they developed and eventually produced the famous New Testament scholar Bengel. Having returned to Strasbourg, Spener received his doctorate from the Alsatian university. He was called to Frankfurt am Main, where he began a whole series of pastoral reforms which made him one of the most respected pastors in Germany. He put a strong emphasis on the catechizing of children as well as on their confirmation. Even more significant was his institution of conventicles for members of the Church who wanted to cultivate a more intense devotion. In Frankfurt Joachim Neander came under his influence. Neander was to become an important figure in the spread of pietism in the Reformed churches of the Rhineland. In 1675, while still at Frankfurt, Spener published his *Pia Desideria,* which soon became one of the classics of pietism. In fact, one might call it the manifesto of pietism.

Spener's *Pia Desideria,* originally written as a preface to an edition of Arndt's sermons, called for a thorough reform of German Protestantism. The Lutheran churches of Germany, he believed, had failed to accomplish the goals of the Reformation and had misunderstood Luther. As Spener saw it, the Church needed to recover personal piety. Far too much emphasis had been put on doctrinal purity. To be sure, Spener recognized the importance of sound doctrine, but its importance was that it ought to promote the Christian life. Furthermore, the churches of Germany had depended far too much on the state. The princes too often lived drunken, scandalous lives, and their political concerns hindered the Church from doing its work. The theologians were also responsible for the sad plight of the Church. They had reduced Christian theology to philosophy. That Protestant theology had become head knowledge rather than heart knowledge was a major pietistic concern. Another criticism of Spener's was that too many Protestants had settled for an *ex opere operato* approach to baptism, which gave people the impression they could be saved without living a holy life. Interestingly enough, Spener does not directly attack the traditional Lutheran doctrine of baptismal regeneration; he simply claims that the baptismal practice of the day nullified God's intention in establishing the sacrament.

Having made these criticisms, Spener makes a number of very specific suggestions on how the situation could be improved. First, it is through a more extensive use of the Word of God that the Church should be reformed. It is not enough simply to preach the lessons appointed in the lectionary. The whole Bible needs to be preached from the pulpit as well as read in the home. It would be helpful if pastors would hold informal Bible study groups in an informal atmosphere of fellowship. In these groups the Scriptures could be discussed and the people encouraged in their Christian walk. In these meetings psalms, hymns, and spiritual songs should be used to praise God and inspire the participants. Spener's program of reform was not to rest on the princes but on the pastors and the people. He very specifically invokes Luther's doctrine of the priesthood of all believers. Both pastors and people must study the Bible. Spener thought the study of Scripture needed to be changed. It should not put the emphasis on theological knowledge but on the practicing of the Christian life. Love for God and the neighbor must be its aim. Theological disputes do not edify the Christian and therefore should be avoided. The study of Scripture should not lead to disputes, but to repentance and holiness. Even when dealing with non-Christians, Christians would get much further if they would love and pray for those they wished to convert rather than arguing with them and insulting them. If the divisions of Christianity are ever to be healed, it will be through brotherly love.

One of Spener's great concerns was the conversion of the ministry. Those going into the ministry should be true Christians and trained not only in theology but in piety. Particularly they should study such devotional works as the sermons of Tauler, Arndt's *True Christianity,* the *Theologia Germanica,* and the *Imitation of Christ* by Thomas à Kempis. To this end theological faculties should organize small groups to encourage pious practices among students for the ministry. Finally Spener suggests that sermons follow the example of Arndt's sermons. They should not attempt to be works of art. Sermons should above all edify. They should inspire faith and the fruits of faith. The true sermon should be directed to the inner man. It is not enough to hear the Word with the outward ear. The Word must penetrate the heart, so that the Holy Spirit speaks to us and we feel the emotion and power of it. The pious hopes put forth in this introduction to Arndt's sermons stimulated great enthusiasm and considerable criticism. This pietist manifesto was heard throughout Germany. While the *Pia Desideria* offended many, it inspired many as well.

One thing should be noticed here that had an effect on preaching and the way it was understood. Many of the reforms Spener advocated concerned small groups rather than the regular service of worship. For pietism formal sermons took second place behind devotional meditations presented in the fellowship of the small group. This was not always the case, to be sure. There were certainly exceptions, but pietism did not produce great preachers the way classical Protestantism or Puritanism did.

In 1686 Spener became court preacher at Dresden, but his short ministry there had little effect at the Saxon court. But it was while in Dresden that he came in contact with August Hermann Francke, a young theologian at the University of Leipzig who was to become his most effective disciple. In 1691 Spener was called to Saint Nicholas Church in Berlin, where through the support of Frederick the elector of Brandenburg he began to influence the Prussian church. Frederick saw in pietism a means of spiritually uniting the Lutherans and the Reformed in his widespread domains, which ten years after the arrival of Spener became the Kingdom of Prussia. Frederick himself was Reformed, and he had brought to his kingdom a considerable number of French Huguenots who had fled France at the revocation of the Edict of Nantes in 1685. He saw in pietism, with its de-emphasis of doctrine, a means of overcoming the rivalry of the two Protestant confessions. He saw in the Huguenots a source of economic stability for his lands, and was eager to ease their acceptance. Frederick was of a devout frame of mind and receptive to Spener's views. Spener developed quite a following in Berlin, and it was there that his followers were first called pietists. When the University of Halle was founded, Frederick gave Spener much influence in the selection of the faculty. At Spener's suggestion, his disciple Francke was appointed to the theological faculty. Under Francke's leadership at Halle, a host of young pietist ministers were produced, who through Spener's influence at court were sent to important ecclesiastical posts throughout the rapidly growing Prussian domains. By 1705, the year Spener died, he was already able to see the firstfruits of the great harvest his ministry was to bear in the new century.

Spener's influence was largely confined to Germany during his lifetime. But with the founding of the University of Halle and the work of his disciple Francke, the influence of pietism began to take on an international character. Particularly significant for this was Nikolaus Ludwig von Zinzendorf, the son of a prominent noble family who attended Francke's Paedigogicum in Halle between 1710 and 1716. Zinzendorf, who was born in 1700, was very significantly Spener's godson. Although his family intended him for service at the Saxon court in Dresden, he soon became the diplomat of pietism, making important contacts for the movement in Copenhagen, Paris, and London. In Paris he developed a friendship with the Jansenist cardinal archbishop, Louis de Doailles. Through contacts at the Danish court he was instrumental in sending graduates of Halle as missionaries to the Danish colonies in India, Greenland, and the West Indies. Perhaps even more significant was the influence his disciples had on the conversion of John Wesley. A few months after he was converted, the budding genius of the Evangelical Revival visited Zinzendorf's religious communities in Germany as well as the pietist foundations at Halle.

The impetus of Spener's thought was still strong when it passed into the English-speaking world. Wesley and Whitefield were influenced not only by the Moravians, but by the writings of Francke, Bengel, and other German pietists as well. Even though Wesley eventually turned away from the Moravian fellowship in London, German pietism continued to influence him strongly. Pietism came to America by a number of routes. Theodorus Jacobus Frelinghuysen, who had come under pietist influences in the Netherlands, sparked the Great Awakening among the Dutch Calvinists in the Raritan Valley of New Jersey. Frelinghuysen had a strong influence on the Scotch-Irish Presbyterian Gilbert Tennent, one of the early leaders of the Great Awakening. Henry Melchior Mühlenburg, who organized the first Lutheran synod in America, had studied theology at Halle and was active in Francke's foundation. Philipp W. Ottinger, the founder of the Evangelical United Brethren Church, had also received his theological training under the pietists. Even Count Zinzendorf himself helped bring pietism to America. Each of these had been profoundly influenced by Spener either directly or indirectly. The American Great Awakening was, in fact, largely a pietist phenomenon. If Puritanism was its mother, pietism was its father. Many of its most important features were inherited from Spener.

To be sure, neither the Evangelical Revival in England nor the Great Awakening in America would have caught fire so rapidly if someone had not set the wood in place. In England Puritanism with its strong concern for personal piety had never died out. Many were very uneasy about the tepid devotional life and conventional morality fostered by Anglicanism. The works of the great Puritans such as Richard Baxter were still being read. Although John and Charles Wesley were brought up in a home firmly committed to Anglicanism, their ancestors on both sides of the family had been staunch Puritans, and the passion for inward devotion and purity of life had obviously not been quenched by the established Church. The Wesleys were deep thinking, and they quickly adapted Continental pietism to their native land.

In America, particularly in New England, the situation was quite different. Puritanism was still strong. There had been a number of developments in the religious life of the colonies. Solomon Stoddard and his grandson Jonathan Edwards had witnessed the beginnings of a revival in the Connecticut Valley. Edwards began to work out a theology of experiential religion which had many points of contact with pietism, although his approach was clearly Calvinistic. A concern for conversion which had developed in certain strands of Puritan thought had been encouraged in New England, so that when Whitefield made his first evangelistic tour of New England his words caught fire even more readily than they had in England.

In the middle colonies the situation was somewhat similar among the Presbyterians of New Jersey and Pennsylvania. William Tennent came to Pennsylvania from Ulster and established his famous Log College at Neshaminy. There he trained a significant number of young ministers, imparting to them a concern for personal piety and inward devotion together with a traditional Calvinist theology. Among his students was his son Gilbert, who during a pastorate at New Brunswick came under the influence of Frelinghuysen, pastor of the Dutch Reformed church in New Brunswick. The pastoral concerns instilled in him by his father led him to have a great respect for his Dutch colleague, who was well along the road to instituting the typical reforms of pietism among the Dutch-speaking congregations under his care. With Gilbert Tennent and the other young ministers trained by his father, it was much the same when George Whitefield began to itinerate through the middle colonies. These young Presbyterians were open to Whitefield's message and eager to learn his rather novel techniques. The Great Awakening, sparked by pietism, fed on the traditional concerns of New England Puritanism and both Dutch and Scotch-Irish Calvinism.

The Great Awakening began to go its own way. It quickly became a particularly American religious movement which united its adherents from New England to Georgia. In the beginning it had attacked the unconverted ministry in much the same way Spener had, and this was not well received by the more established and conservative ministers in such places as Boston, New York, and Philadelphia, any more than Spener's criticisms were in Germany. Gilbert Tennent was the most vocal critic of the unconverted ministry, and his indiscretion did much to precipitate a split in the Presbyterian church. Edwards took a much more irenic approach, and it was well known that he did not completely approve of Whitefield's methods. Eventually Tennent began to mellow. His strong Calvinist doctrine of the Church began to move him toward attempting to heal the split in the Presbyterian church. When Count Zinzendorf arrived with his rather amorphous theology, Tennent began to see the virtues of a theological system. When he took up his pastorate in Philadelphia, he began to preach in a much more traditional fashion. Samuel Davies grew up in the Great Awakening and offers an example of the tradition at its most mature. He was a student at the Presbyterian academy at Faggs Manor in 1740 when Whitefield preached there. When he was ordained in 1747, he was sent to be pastor of a Presbyterian church in Hanover, Virginia. There he soon became the prominent voice of the Great Awakening in that most important colony. As a preacher Davies was outstanding. Sent to England and Scotland in 1759 to raise money for the establishing of Princeton University, he not only succeeded in his mission but won an international reputation as a preacher and spokesman of the Great Awakening.

I. Philipp Jakob Spener (1635-1705)

Let us return to Spener, and having already spoken of his vision, take a look at his preaching.[5] How pivotal he was for the whole pietist movement![6] A good number of his sermons have been preserved, including a traditional series based on the Lutheran liturgical calendar.[7] These sermons, however, do not attract our attention. They tend to be rather per-

5. In addition to the recent work of Brecht, "Philipp Jakob Spener, sein Programm und dessen Auswirkungen," a number of other works are helpful, particularly Johannes Wallmann, *Philipp Jakob Spener und die Anfänge des Pietismus* (Tübingen: J. C. B. Mohr [Paul Siebeck], 1986), and K. James Stein, *Philipp Jakob Spener: Pietist Patriarch* (Chicago: Covenant Press, 1986).

6. For a recent evaluation of the place of Spener in pietism, see Brecht, "Philipp Jakob Spener, sein Programm und dessen Auswirkungen."

7. Philipp Jakob Spener, *Die Evangelische Glaubens-Lehre 1688, Predigten über die Evangelien*, photolithographic reproduction with introduction by Dietrich Blaufuss and Erich Beyreuther, vol. 3, *Philipp Jakob Spener, Schriften* (Hildesheim, Zürich, and New York: Georg Olms Verlag, 1986).

functory, going through once more the liturgical Gospels and Epistles.[8] Much more indicative of Spener's place in the history of preaching is his long series of sermons on the new birth, *Der hochwichtige Articul von der Wiedergeburt,* preached in Berlin in the last decade of the seventeenth century.[9] While the great body of these sermons describes the life of born-again Christians, the three introductory sermons give a good summary of basic pietist teaching.

A. The Born-Again Experience

Spener preached these sermons on the new birth upon taking up his duties as pastor of Saint Nicholas Church in Berlin. The call to Saint Nicholas had been supported by Frederick III, prince elector of Brandenburg, whose backing gave Spener a tremendous advantage. Within a few years he would become Frederick I, king of Prussia, which during the eighteenth century would become the dominant principality of Germany. Frederick was a devout man, unlike his grandson, Frederick the Great. In Dresden, at the Saxon court, Spener's ministry had not been received with much enthusiasm. Orthodox Lutherans had been very critical of him. When he arrived in Berlin in June of 1691,[10] he was sixty-seven years old and had already influenced the faith of Protestant Germany profoundly, even if he had drawn out the opposition of the orthodox Lutheran theologians of the University of Leipzig, a leading Saxon university. The invitation to become pastor of Saint Nicholas put him safely out of the reach of his opposition. As critical as he had been of the role of the princes in the ecclesiastical affairs of Germany, in the end it was a prince who bestowed on him the opportunity he needed. Just as Frederick the Wise gave Luther a safe pulpit, so Frederick III gave Spener a prestigious pulpit.

---

8. For a recent evaluation of these sermons, see the introduction by Dietrich Blaufuss in Spener, *Die Evangelische Glaubens-Lehre 1688, Predigten über die Evangelien,* pp. 10-89.

9. Philipp Jakob Spener, *Der hochwichtige Articul von der Wiedergeburt (1696) 1715,* vol. 7, *Philipp Jakob Spener, Schriften* (Hildesheim, Zürich, and New York: Georg Olms Verlag, 1994), hereafter Spener, *von der Wiedergeburt.*

10. Jan Olaf Rüttgardt, "Zur Entstehung und Bedeutung der Berliner Wiedergeburtspredigten Philipp Jakob Speners," in *Philipp Jakob Spener, Schriften,* ed. Erich Bayreuther, 16 vols. (Hildesheim, Zürich, and New York: Georg Olms Verlag, 1994), 7/I: 1-112.

Spener did not preach his sermons on the born-again experience on Sunday mornings or Sunday evenings, but rather on weekday mornings. He tells us in the introduction to the first sermon that he cannot say very well what he wants to say in these sermons if he follows the traditional Gospels of the lectionary. The key passage of Scripture for the doctrine of the new birth is John 3:1-15, which appears only once in the lectionary, on Trinity Sunday. Because Trinity Sunday demands a sermon on the Trinity, the preacher rarely gets around to teaching the doctrine of the new birth.[11] That was why he preached these sermons at the midweek service.

This is a typical pietist approach. The old ecclesiastical forms are in no way attacked; they are simply bypassed. Spener will go on preaching the traditional Gospels and Epistles of the lectionary, but that will not be where his creative energies are invested. It will be in the intimate circles of the small-group fellowship that the real action will take place. The traditional Sunday morning sermon will become a formality.

Spener's sermons usually have very distinct conclusions in which he admonishes the congregation on the matters he treated in the sermon. His sermons always have an introduction, ending with a brief bidding prayer or prayer for illumination. Then at the conclusion there are several admonitions, concluding with a somewhat longer prayer. In between there is first an explanation of the text and then a setting forth of the doctrine to be drawn from it. In homiletical form these sermons are not unlike the Puritan arrangement of text, doctrine, and use.

One of the most admirable features of the German Lutheran sermon of this period, whether pietist or orthodox, is the careful attention given to the explanation of the text. For this first sermon the text is John 3:3, "Jesus answered and said to him: truly, truly, I say to you: unless one is born anew, he will never see the kingdom of God."[12] Spener begins his sermon with a rigorous examination of this text.

The first thing he wants to point out is that the teaching on the new birth found in John 3 is the teaching of Jesus, for the text specifically tells us, "Jesus answered Nicodemus, saying to him . . ." This doctrine is the teaching of Jesus himself.[13] Furthermore, Jesus gave special weight to his

11. Spener, *von der Wiedergeburt*, p. 2.

12. The preacher quotes the German text as "Jesus antwortete / und sprach zu ihn: Warlich, warlich ich sage dir: Es sen denn / dass iemand von neuem gebohren werde / kan er das reich Gottes nicht sehen." Spener, *von der Wiedergeburt*, p. 1. For Spener's sermons we will quote Scripture as he quotes it, but in the form of a free translation into English.

13. Spener, *von der Wiedergeburt*, p. 3.

words here by saying, "Truly, truly, I say to you."[14] The importance of the new birth is then made even more explicit when Jesus tells us we cannot be saved without it.[15]

Spener duly notes that one can translate the Greek text in two ways. One can read either "unless one is born anew" or "unless one is born from above."[16] Spener, who always wants to appear the good Lutheran, admits that our beloved Luther reads "anew" rather than "from above," but there are good reasons for taking it the other way, "born from above." Such a translation makes it clear that this new birth is a gracious act of God.

But what is this new birth? Spener wants to make it very clear that it is not something like recovering from an illness, but rather a total transformation. That is why it is called new birth rather than healing. It is like the birth of a child, or even more, like the conception of a child. It is totally gracious. The one to be conceived does nothing to bring it about. We are born again through "water and the Holy Spirit," as Jesus says to Nicodemus in our text.[17] We are passive just as a child is passive at his or her birth.[18] It is God who gives us the new birth; as we have it in Ezekiel 36:26-27, "I will give you a new heart; a new spirit I will put within you." The point Ezekiel makes is that something completely new is brought about and one becomes what one was not before.

In our natural birth we are conceived and born by our parents, and therefore we belong to them. And so from creation we are children of God, as we find it in Malachi 2:10. Have we not all one Father; has not one God created us? Yet there is a more profound sense in which those who have been born again are children of God.[19]

Another passage Spener uses to throw light on the text is James 1:17-18, which tells us that the Father of Light has begotten us, according to his will, through the Word of truth. Just as our text tells us that the new birth is through water and spirit, James tells us that it is the work of the Father through his Word. Spener develops this thought at some length, speaking of the new birth in terms of the Father, in terms of the Son, and

14. Spener, *von der Wiedergeburt*, p. 4.
15. Spener, *von der Wiedergeburt*, p. 5.
16. The German translation of the Greek could read "von neuen geboren werden" or "von oben her geboren werden." Spener, *von der Wiedergeburt*, p. 6.
17. Spener, *von der Wiedergeburt*, p. 6.
18. Spener, *von der Wiedergeburt*, p. 7.
19. Spener, *von der Wiedergeburt*, p. 8.

in terms of the Holy Spirit. Each person of the Trinity is active, working through both Word and sacrament.

On the one hand, it is true that it is easy to become a Christian, because it is God who gives us new birth. He makes us new creatures, and when we become new creatures, then everything else flows from that new nature. It all comes from the Holy Spirit and faith. It is the same way with the obedience we owe to God: it flows from this new creation. It is not a forced obedience or an obedience imposed upon us against our wills, but an obedience freely given which springs from a childlike nature.[20]

On the other hand, to be a true Christian demands diligence. Spener is constantly admonishing us to strive to enter by the narrow gate. Jesus himself had taught that we must strive to follow the straight way and enter by the narrow gate if we would achieve eternal life.[21] There are always struggles within and strivings against enemies without. To be sure, we must work out our own salvation with fear and trembling, as the apostle Paul teaches us in Philippians 2:12. Even more, as Jesus taught us, we must take care that our righteousness exceeds that of the scribes and Pharisees. In short, we must be born again and become totally other. And this we must do through faith; otherwise, any hope of salvation is a deception.

With this our preacher begins his conclusion, suggesting several applications. First he urges us to examine ourselves as to whether we have received the new birth. He insists that he is not concerned whether we have at one time received the new birth. It is not enough to have received it at one time. The question Spener would have us ask ourselves is whether we remain newborn.

If we have been born again, Spener assures us, being a true Christian all comes very easily and very naturally. When we are truly repentant and have denied ourselves, and have come to a living faith, from then on the new life which has come from God works from itself, just as a healthy root from itself produces good fruit. God works all in all. Whenever, through the power of the new birth, we enter into a true Christian life, we then live not to ourselves, but to God. It is then that we live in Christ. It is then that we will find that such a life is far more satisfying than the worldly life. Those who are born again live lives that are pleasing to God. That is why they are at peace with God.[22]

---

20. Spener, *von der Wiedergeburt*, p. 11.
21. Spener, *von der Wiedergeburt*, p. 12.
22. Spener, *von der Wiedergeburt*, p. 13.

Until we are born again we remain weak human beings, but once we are born again we are given the power to live lives that please God. We will find that the words of Jesus are true, the yoke of Christ is gentle and his burden is light (Matt. 11:30). Through the new birth this worldly nature becomes ever weaker, and yet, still it persists. Sin has a way of fastening on to us, as we find in Romans 7:24, "O wretched man that I am, who can deliver me from this body of death?" So then it comes to another new birth in which we will be born again to a blessed eternal life. Then the old nature will be completely set aside and all things will become new and all the promises of God will be fulfilled.[23]

The second sermon in the series takes up the same passage of Scripture, John 3:1-15, focusing in on John 3:6, "That which is born of the flesh is flesh." Spener gives his sermon the title "From the Condition of Those Who Have Not Been Born Again." In his introduction he tells us that having heard from the mouth of Christ how necessary it is to be born again, we now need to hear why it is so necessary. The reason is simply that because of our sinful corruption, we are flesh, born of flesh.[24]

Our preacher begins to examine the text. There is a long discussion of the various ways the word "flesh" is used in the Bible. Sometimes it simply means humanity in general.[25] More significantly is it used to speak of that which comes only from human strength, understanding, or desire. In such passages flesh means that which resists God. A good number of Bible verses are quoted to demonstrate this meaning.[26]

After devoting considerable time to this subject, Spener considers how flesh spreads, or is propagated. It is planted in us from our birth. We are flesh because we are born of flesh. That is what is meant by the text, that which is born of the flesh is flesh.[27]

Coming to Spener's *Lehr-Puncten,* or doctrine, we find several points. For one thing, it is the nature of our human flesh that we no longer have that God-given maturity, righteousness, or sanctity which Adam and Eve had before the fall. All that is lost. Our first parents were created in the image of God; they reflected that image, but all that is gone. We now live according to the flesh. This is particularly true for our under-

---

23. Spener, *von der Wiedergeburt,* p. 14.
24. Spener, *von der Wiedergeburt,* p. 15.
25. Spener, *von der Wiedergeburt,* p. 16.
26. Spener, *von der Wiedergeburt,* p. 17.
27. Spener, *von der Wiedergeburt,* pp. 18-19.

standing, our memory, and our will.[28] The members of our body, as well, are corrupt, and we have lost the ability to function according to the will of God. In fact, the natural man lives in enmity with God. He hates God.[29] Ever since the fall this has been the nature of human flesh, the human flesh we all inherit. And even if we have devout parents, we still inherit this flesh. We are still born in sin. The seed of sin is spread through the whole world. We are flesh through and through, and no simple cleaning or polishing us up will be enough to save us. Or, to put it another way, we do not simply need to be spiritually fattened up. We need to be completely remade, transformed, and converted. This, according to Spener, is exactly what Johann Arndt had taught in his famous work on true Christianity.[30]

The conclusion of the sermon is much more positive. As Christians we should take comfort. Although the flesh is at enmity with God and has provoked the divine anger, still God himself is so kindly that he has taken pity on us. He knows that we are flesh and cannot change ourselves. As we find it in Psalm 103, as a father has mercy on his children, so the Lord has mercy on those who fear him. He knows how we are made; he remembers that we are dust.

Then, even beyond this, those who have been born again can have comfort, for we are also spirit, born of the Spirit. This is the beginning of a new creation in which we are re-created after the image of God. When we are in Christ Jesus and are united with him by faith and follow after him in our lives, there is then no condemnation upon us. Although the flesh still clings to us, we are alive because of the Spirit. We are born of the Spirit and yet we still bear the cross. This frustration, however, lasts only in this life. In the life to come we will fully and completely reflect the image of God.[31]

Spener's pietism is very similar to the late medieval pietism Luther had found so oppressive. It was so depressingly introspective. Even those who had been born again were consistently encouraged to reexamine themselves to be sure they really had been born again. That was just what Luther was trying to get away from.

---

28. Spener, *von der Wiedergeburt*, p. 21.
29. Spener, *von der Wiedergeburt*, p. 24.
30. Spener, *von der Wiedergeburt*, p. 27.
31. Spener, *von der Wiedergeburt*, p. 29.

B. Pietism as Protestant Mysticism

The third sermon in the series returns to John 3:1-15, to the words of Jesus, "That which is born of the Spirit is spirit."[32] In the introduction our preacher summarizes his first two sermons, telling us that in this discourse with Nicodemus our blessed Savior wanted to teach about the new birth. Spener explains that in opening up this discourse we first spoke of the necessity of the new birth. What Jesus taught was that the new birth is necessary for entrance into the kingdom of God. The new birth is the only way to escape the corruption of the flesh. Second, Spener tells us, we spoke of the source of this corruption. We are corrupt because our flesh is born of the flesh. It inevitably harbors enmity toward God. Now, however, our preacher continues, we want to speak of the origin of the new man.

As he always does, Spener spends considerable time opening up his text. Here he tells us that there is an analogy between natural birth and spiritual birth. Just as the flesh is born of the flesh, so the spirit is born of the Spirit. What is true of the spirit is no less true than what is true of the flesh. What is true of the spirit is not just imagination. It is every bit as true as what is said concerning the flesh.[33] What our preacher seems to want to get across is that when the Scriptures speak about being born again, it is not simply a metaphor for our salvation. He seems to be saying that to be a Christian one has to go through a conversion experience. One gathers that this is a sort of mystical experience. What is a bit disturbing, however, is that as much as Spener may intend to be a good Lutheran, this conversion experience seems to have taken the place of justification by faith. In good nominalist fashion, Spener seems to be saying that the crucial matter in our salvation is our experience of conversion rather than God's mighty acts of salvation in the death and resurrection of Christ.

Titus 3:5 is an important text for Spener's understanding of the born-again experience. God saves us through the bath of regeneration, that is, the experience of being born again together with the renewal of the Holy Spirit which God has poured out upon us richly through Jesus Christ, our Savior.[34] The King James Version translates "bath of regenera-

32. Spener, *von der Wiedergeburt*, p. 30.
33. Spener, *von der Wiedergeburt*, p. 31.
34. The German text as quoted by Spener is as follows: "Gott machet uns selig durch das bad der wiedergeburt und erneuerung des Heiligen Geistes / welchen er ausgegossen hat über uns reichlich durch Jesum Christum unsern Heyland." Spener, *von*

tion." The German text, however, suggests much more readily that being "born anew" as spoken of in John 3 is an experience of being born again. It is also very clear here that for Spener the text is not really talking about baptism, but the mystical experience of being born again. Spener says the water of baptism would have no power to give us new birth, or to transform our hearts, if it were not that the Spirit works through it. It is the inner working of the Holy Spirit which brings about the new birth. One can understand why the orthodox Lutheran theologians of the day might have had their reservations.

Another important parallel passage for Spener is Ezekiel 36:27, which tells us that God will give us his Spirit and will make the sort of men and women out of us that walk in God's commandments. Ezekiel 36:25-28 was important to Spener. This passage makes the washing of water a sign of spiritual renewal, and even more, promises the gift of the Holy Spirit to God's people.

Even more significant here is the use Spener makes of the nativity narratives in both Matthew and Luke.[35] He tells us that our beloved Savior was conceived by the Holy Spirit. It was just as the angel spoke to the Blessed Virgin Mary: the Holy Spirit will come upon you, and the power of the Most High will overshadow you (Luke 1:35). It was much the same when the angel spoke to Joseph in a dream and told him that the child to be born was from the Holy Spirit (Matt. 1:20). There it is, Spener insists; all Christians must be born from this same Holy Spirit and become lively members of the Body of Christ.

What is interesting here is how similar this interpretation of Christ's conception is to that of John Tauler, the fourteenth-century Strasbourg preacher. Strasbourg was, we remember, the hometown of Spener, but what is interesting for us is that Tauler was a particularly able interpreter of medieval mysticism.[36] For Tauler, as for many another medieval mystic, what was interesting about the nativity narratives was what they said not so much about the birth of Christ, but much more about the spiritual rebirth of the Christian. Spener has clearly picked up much of medieval German mysticism.

---

der Wiedergeburt, p. 32. It is only in this text, Titus 3:5, that the word *wiedergeburt* appears in the New Testament.

35. Spener, *von der Wiedergeburt,* p. 32.

36. See Hughes Oliphant Old, *The Reading and Preaching of the Scriptures in the Worship of the Christian Church,* vol. 3, *The Medieval Church* (Grand Rapids: Wm. B. Eerdmans Publishing Co., 1999), pp. 452-58.

Another fundamental text for Spener is I Peter 1:23, which tells us that we are born again not of perishable seed, but of imperishable seed. We are born again from the living Word of God that abides forever.[37]

Turning now to the doctrines Spener wants to bring out of his text, we find two points right at the beginning. The nobility of those born again comes first from the fact that they are born of God through the working of his Spirit, and secondly, that they actually reflect God's nature. As we find it in James 1:18, out of his own will he brought us forth by the Word of truth that we should be a sort of firstfruits of his creatures.[38] Those born again actually are noble. They have an inner compulsion to do the good.[39] Not only are they begotten of God, but they share his nature. The compulsion of the flesh does not move them, but the compulsion of their God-given born-again nature. When the apostle says since you have been raised with Christ seek the things that are above (Col. 3:1), we should understand that we are to follow his transcendent way of life.[40]

But there is another point to be made. The nobility of one born again is also to be found in the fact that he or she pleases God. God takes pleasure in those who are like him. We have fellowship with him because we are like him. This is a surprising nobility; it pleases God and makes it possible to be united to him and to obtain the full rights of the kingdom.

Here we see the mystical dimension of pietism with special clarity. Holiness is essential to those who would have communion with God.

Coming to the conclusion of his sermon, Spener exhorts us to guard against the permissiveness of those who are always excusing human weakness. There is nothing more perverse than claiming to be Christian but ending up going along with the world and living a worldly life. There is nothing more dangerous to a devout life than giving the excuse that we are no more than human beings, mere flesh and blood. Indeed we are flesh and blood, but we should have an inclination, even a preference, for the things that are not of this world but rather of the world to come. Be well assured, Spener tells us, that as mere worldly human beings we cannot be saved. If we would be saved, we must become something more than a mere human being of flesh and blood. We must become some-

37. Spener, *von der Wiedergeburt*, p. 33.
38. Spener, *von der Wiedergeburt*, p. 38.
39. Spener, *von der Wiedergeburt*, p. 39.
40. Spener, *von der Wiedergeburt*, p. 40.

thing altogether different.[41] To this end, therefore, we must stir ourselves up to seek after the things of God and leave behind the things of this world. And yet we should not imagine that it comes from our striving, but rather from the Spirit of God within us.[42]

The classical Protestantism of the sixteenth century had turned away from the mysticism of the late Middle Ages, preferring a more objective religious experience. Pietism as revived by Spener was a return to a more subjective piety. Protestants began to look within to find God. The question is whether in doing this they lost a basic insight of the Reformation.

C. Pietist Morality

These introductory sermons are of special interest to us because they show the thinking behind the pietist approach to the Christian life, but the great majority of the sermons in the series treat one moral issue after another. In Spener's pulpit, pietist preaching is heavily moralistic. A simple list of the sermon titles for these sixty-six sermons makes the point.

Sermons 4 through 14 continue to develop the theological themes introduced in the first three sermons, but starting with sermon 15 we find sermon after sermon devoted to the characteristics of those who have been born again. The sermon titles are as follows:

> Sermon 15, "Dependence on the Righteousness of Christ" (Phil. 3:8-9)
> Sermon 16, "Love of God" (I John 5:2)
> Sermon 17, "A Childlike Fear of God" (Mal. 1:6)
> Sermon 18, "Obedience to God" (Ezek. 36:27)
> Sermon 19, "The Difference between Legalistic and Evangelical Obedience" (I John 5:3)
> Sermon 20, "Constant Prayer" (Gal. 4:6)
> Sermon 21, "Cherishing Spiritual Things and Despising Worldly Things" (Col. 3:1-2)
> Sermon 22, "Desire for the Means of God's Grace" (I Pet. 2:2)
> Sermon 23, "Patience in Suffering" (Heb. 12:7-10)

41. Spener, *von der Wiedergeburt,* p. 41.
42. Spener, *von der Wiedergeburt,* p. 42.

Sermon 24, "Patience in Suffering" (continued) (Heb. 12:7-10)

Sermon 25, "Looking Forward to a Blessed Departure from This Life" (Phil. 1:22-24)

Sermon 26, "Looking Forward to a Blessed Departure from This Life" (continued) (Phil. 1:22-24)

Sermon 27, "Diligence for Constant Cleansing from Sin" (II Cor. 7:1)

Sermon 28, "Diligence for Constant Cleansing from Sin" (continued) (II Cor. 7:1)

Sermon 29, "Diligence for Growth in Righteousness" (II Cor. 7:1)

Sermon 30, "Self-Denial" (Matt. 16:24)

Sermon 31, "Self-Denial" (continued) (Matt. 16:24)

Sermon 32, "Love for the Neighbor" (I John 4:7-8)

Sermon 33, "Love for the Neighbor" (continued) (I John 4:7-8)

Sermon 36,[43] "Diligence in Edification of One's Neighbor" (I Thess. 5:11)

Sermon 35, "Love for the Neighbor in Bearing His Burdens" (I John 3:16)

Sermon 36, "Helping the Needy" (I John 3:17)

Sermon 37, "Helping the Needy" (continued) (I John 3:17)

Sermon 38, "Gentleness, Patience, and Willingness for Reconciliation" (Col. 3:12-13)

Sermon 39, "Gentleness, Patience, and Willingness for Reconciliation" (continued) (Col. 3:12-13)

Sermon 40, "Humility" (Phil. 2:3-8)

Sermon 41, "Humility" (continued) (Phil. 2:3-8)

Sermon 42, "Brotherly Love" (Rom. 12:10)

Sermon 43, "Brotherly Love" (continued) (Rom. 12:10)

As much as evangelical pietism may have emphasized the inward experience of faith, in actual practice it had an astounding effect on practical piety and charitable works. As much as it may have stressed the religion of the heart rather than the religion of the head, it was strong on the religion of the hands and feet as well. The pietists were ever involved in foreign missions, from Greenland to the Caribbean and from India to the American frontier. Pietism's orphanages, hospitals, schools, and universi-

---

43. The edition on which this study is based has numbered the sermons incorrectly. This should obviously be sermon 34.

ties gave the eighteenth century a heart that the Enlightenment could not match.

II. August Hermann Francke (1663-1727)

In the middle of the seventeenth century the Hanseatic city of Lübeck was an important center of a vast commercial empire. Redbrick Gothic churches crowned the city with a dignified and learned Lutheran culture. Dietrich Buxtehude, the genius of the north German baroque, built the superb organ of Lübeck's Marienkirche and composed splendid sacred cantatas, choral preludes, and fugues for the services of worship. It was in this capital city of the Baltic world that August Hermann Francke was born.[44] His father was a lawyer and a man of considerable piety. He, as so many of his contemporaries, was an avid reader of Arndt's *True Christianity*. While Francke was still a very young child, his father was engaged by Ernst, duke of Saxe-Gotha, to help in the restoration of his territory. The duke was the most devout sort of Lutheran prince, the sort to whom Spener's criticism obviously did not apply. The serious and benevolent piety of this prince was effective in educational reforms and philanthropic foundations which were very similar to the kinds of reforms Francke would institute in later years.

In Lübeck Francke started his studies at the gymnasium and began to show considerable ability in the study of languages. He went to Hamburg to study with a famous Hebrew teacher, and is supposed to have read through the Hebrew Bible six times while there. All the while his devotional life was deepening. At home Francke and his sister read the Scriptures together as well as the standard devotional works of the day. After beginning his university studies at Erfurt, he transferred to Kiel, and there roomed in the home of Pastor Christian Kortholt, a leader of the reform party among the orthodox Lutherans of the period.

Eventually his proficiency in Hebrew earned him a position at the University of Leipzig. While there he translated *The Spiritual Guide,* the

---

44. For biographical information on Francke, see Gary R. Sattler, *God's Glory, Neighbor's Good: A Brief Introduction to the Life and Writings of August Hermann Francke* (Chicago: Covenant Press, 1982). See also Martin Brecht, "August Hermann Francke und der Hallische Pietismus," in Brecht, *Der Pietismus vom siebzehnten bis zum frühen achtzehnten Jahrhundert,* 2 vols. (Göttingen: Vandenhoeck & Ruprecht, 1993), 1:440-540.

controversial work of a contemporary, Italian quietist Miguel de Molinos, from the Italian. The intensity of Francke's religious quest finally came to a climax when he was invited to preach at Lüneburg. It was then that he had the conversion experience so important to pietism.

As he prepared his sermon he began to realize that he himself did not have a steadfast assurance of the faith he wanted to preach, even though he had studied theology for many years. He began to weep over his lack of faith. For several days he became increasingly aware of the weakness of his faith. He really could not be sure that even the Scriptures could be counted on. Then one evening while he poured out his heart to God, suddenly he had faith. It came in an instant, as in the turning of a hand. Immediately he was filled with joy. Recalling the words of Luther in his famous introduction to the commentary on Romans, he realized that now he had the sort of saving faith the Reformer had spoken of. This was the saving faith that overcame reason and brought one into a holy life. Francke understood this new faith as that divine work which changes life. This was for him the new birth. Now he could preach the faith he could not preach before. Now he could renounce ungodly ways and the desires of the world. He could turn away from the idol of education and devote himself to a more serious Christianity.

After this conversion experience he remained in Lüneburg for some months and then returned to Leipzig. But before taking up his work there, he received an invitation from Philipp Spener to visit him in Dresden. Francke accepted, and ended up staying there two months before returning to his work at the university. Arriving in Leipzig early in 1689, he began to lecture on the Scriptures and to organize the typical small fellowships so important to the pietist program. His work was so enthusiastically followed by the students that they began to neglect their regular lectures. Understandably the theology professors became resentful. Finally Francke had to leave Leipzig. He was invited to Erfurt to assist the Lutheran pastor there, and soon gathered around himself a devoted following. In the meantime Spener had received his call to Berlin and was busy with the founding of the University of Halle. Before long Spener had him appointed professor of Greek and the Oriental languages. Francke arrived in Halle in 1692, and there began his many-faceted program of reform which was destined to have such far-reaching effects on the history of Protestant Christianity.

One could go on at considerable length about Francke's educational reforms at Halle. The University of Halle under his guidance became what some have called the first modern university. It led the way in the study of modern languages and the natural sciences, and instruction in the vernacular. His Latin school and school for the children of poor families introduced many new concepts of education and teacher training. His concern for the poor was profound. The orphanage, publishing house, and dispensary he established encouraged Christian benevolence to develop in a great variety of directions. Pietistic reform throughout Europe and America consistently followed the lead of the *Francke'sche Stiftungen,* that is, Francke's foundations. For our concerns, however, Francke is of particular interest because he developed the pietistic approach to preaching. While Spener had advocated significant homiletical reforms, he himself continued to preach in much the same manner as the typical German pastors of his day.

One of the best introductions to Francke's approach to preaching originally was written by Francke as a letter in reply to a friend's question on how one should preach. This letter is of particular interest because it was translated into English and published in London in 1736 with a preface by Isaac Watts. This was only two years before Whitefield and Wesley began to preach the Evangelical Revival in England. Five years later it was published in Boston at the height of the Great Awakening, just after Whitefield had preached his way through New England with the kinds of sermons the great professor of Halle had advocated. This letter quite obviously had a profound effect on both English and American preaching.

The work begins with a clear statement of the purpose of preaching.[45] It is to edify the souls of those who listen, to win souls for Christ, and to inflame their hearts with a growing love for their Savior.[46] The word "edify" was very important for the German pietists. In the German language the word *Erbauung,* which we translate "edification," is a very rich word. It is used to translate Paul's comments in I Corinthians that in the service of worship everything should be done for edification. Basically the word means to build, but it also means to instruct. By connotation it suggests the kind of instruction that builds character and develops piety.

---

45. The edition of this work I used was in the personal library of Samuel Miller, professor at Princeton Seminary. August Hermann Francke, "Of the Most Useful Way of Preaching," in *The Christian Preacher; or, Discourses on Preaching by Several Eminent Divines, English and Foreign,* edited, revised, and abridged by Edward Williams (Philadelphia: William Woolward, 1810), hereafter Francke, *Preaching.*

46. Francke, *Preaching,* p. 78.

Preaching, as Francke understood it, should aim at changing lives.[47] It should aim at winning souls for Christ, that is, bringing sinners into a conversion experience and then building on that conversion experience, leading the convert through the process of transforming his or her behavior. Essential to this transformation is the inflaming of the heart. Preaching should ignite those who hear. That, of course, is just what the preaching of John Wesley, Gilbert Tennent, and above all, George Whitefield did.

Francke develops his theme by mentioning a number of subjects that preaching should treat. A minister should frequently lay down in his sermons the distinguishing marks and characteristics of both the converted and the unconverted so that each hearer can judge to which class he or she belongs.[48] A minister who has experienced the work of grace in his own heart will have no difficulty describing it to others in such a way that they will know whether they have experienced it or not. A minister should instruct his hearers in the duty of self-examination so that each one may discover his or her right relation to God.[49] One should inquire whether one has been awakened from the natural sleep of sin and whether one can identify the marks of a true conversion. It is important to make clear that conventional morality is not the same thing as true religion (and that people understand which is which), nor is a legal approach to faith the same as an evangelical, and it is important that people know which approach they take.[50] Are they really Christians or not?

Obviously, as Francke understands it, the preacher is to spend quite a bit of time in his sermon probing the consciences of his hearers. Another major concern of Francke's is that the minister preach the necessity of conversion, and explain very frequently the nature and process of conversion.[51] Quite contrary to the claims of certain contemporary scholars, the pietists could become quite insistent on the necessity of a conversion experience. Here we see that Francke is quite explicit that conversion is necessary. It was not an optional experience to which more devout Christians attain. In this description of what preaching should be, at least, Francke sees conversion as a very definite process which can be described and needs to be described so that the minister by his sermon can lead his

47. Francke, *Preaching,* p. 81.
48. Francke, *Preaching,* p. 78.
49. Francke, *Preaching,* p. 79.
50. Francke, *Preaching,* p. 80.
51. Francke, *Preaching,* p. 81.

hearers into that experience. People need to be shown how they must repent of their sins, what they must do to be saved from their misery, and how they may obtain full salvation. In short, Francke tells us, a faithful minister must make sure everyone who hears him can give an answer to that most essential of all questions, what must I do to be saved?[52]

The next point Francke makes may come as a bit of a surprise, but it is very revealing for the pietist approach to preaching. As opposed to classical Protestantism, Francke says the minister should not devote too much time to explaining the text of Scripture.[53] He should make his exposition as brief as possible and then hasten to the application. It is to the concerns of the practical Christian life here and now that the minister is to address himself with all seriousness and earnestness. The application should be made to both saints and sinners.[54] Pietist preachers could go on at some length applying their message to all kinds of people among their hearers. In fact, one finds that they paid very little attention to the analysis of the text in their sermons. While strong on evangelistic sermons, they were weak on expository sermons. On the other hand, a minister should frequently display in the most lively colors the excellency and glory of Christ's person, the kindness of his heart, and the exceeding riches of his grace.[55] Christ should be portrayed in both his heavenly glory and his earthly humility. Francke tells us that the preacher should insist on the love of Christ because this attracts us to Christ. In order to win people to Christ, it is important to portray Christ. Through portraying the love of Christ and winning an ardent love for Christ in the hearts of Christian people, they will perform their religious duties with much greater enthusiasm.

From this point Francke goes on to a subject characteristic of the pietists, namely, the conversion of the ministry.[56] They were ever vigilant of the danger of an unconverted ministry. The most important point Francke wants to make in this description of effective preaching is that every minister must look to his own heart to discover if he himself really loves Christ fervently, otherwise he is nothing more than sounding brass and tinkling cymbal. For without a sincere love of Christ in his own soul, there is little probability of his awakening love for Christ in others. If his

52. Francke, *Preaching,* p. 82.
53. Francke, *Preaching,* p. 84.
54. Francke, *Preaching,* p. 85.
55. Francke, *Preaching,* p. 86.
56. Francke, *Preaching,* p. 87.

own heart is not warmed with this sacred love, his sermons will be cold and lifeless and will bear little fruit. If a preacher preaches well, he must love Christ much. Surely one of the most effective dimensions of pietist preaching was personal witness. It was important for a sermon to be fervent and impassioned in its delivery in order to make clear the complete sincerity of the preacher.[57] This sincerity and ardor was regarded as the seal of the witness. This ring of absolute sincerity and conviction was evidently the most important characteristic of the preaching of both Spener and Francke. Neither has ever been classed among the giants of the pulpit, although their preaching was surely very effective in its day. It is true that Francke's sermons are not particularly moving when read as homiletical literature. When preached, however, they were very moving.[58] This has often been the case with great preachers, particularly the greatest preachers. With preachers such as Francke the transparent sincerity, the spiritual intensity, catches the attention of the congregation.

Francke takes up another subject he feels needs to be treated frequently in sermons. The duties of self-denial are an essential feature of day-to-day Christian life.[59] The minister must wean his congregation away from the world and its pleasures, from all things of sense and time. Pietism, whether in the fifteenth century or in the eighteenth century, is inescapably ascetic. As we shall see, the pietist preacher was forever devoting whole sermons to such subjects as the evils of drink, the perils of dancing, and the immodesty of women's fashions.

Preaching was obviously extremely important for Francke. He himself gave a great deal of time to it, but for him it was most effective when done in the context of a warm fellowship of serious, lively and growing Christians. Particularly important to that context is the gift of prayer.[60] Francke tells us that as live coals kindle one another, the fervent prayers of warm and lively Christians are a means of kindling the fire of divine life. To be sure, he does not have in mind reading the prayers of the Lutheran liturgy, nor the sort of premeditated, or "conceived," prayer the Puritans advocated. He meant extemporary or ecstatic prayer which by enthusiasm and simplicity proved that it came from the heart. Prayer, particularly the prayer of the intimate fellowship group, helps enkindle the heart to re-

57. Francke, *Preaching*, p. 88.
58. Few of Francke's sermons are available in English. A small collection is, however, available in Sattler's introduction to the life and works of Francke mentioned above.
59. Francke, *Preaching*, p. 88.
60. Francke, *Preaching*, p. 83.

ceive the gospel message. It is the same way, Francke makes clear, with the rich treasure of sacred hymns, both ancient and modern. As one sees more and more in studying the worship of the pietists, hymnody was understood to have an essential place in worship. Ecstatic prayer and fervent hymnody helped make conversion a community experience.

Francke paid careful attention to catechetical preaching, and normally devoted the afternoon sermon to preaching through Luther's catechism. We have two collections of his catechetical sermons. First are the sermons he preached as he began his ministry at the church in Glauche, many of which have come down in manuscript form.[61] More than twenty years later a second collection of Francke's catechetical sermons was published in Halle.[62]

Francke's preaching needs to be seen alongside the study of Scripture in his small-group fellowships. As Spener before him, he was concerned that the regular preaching of Scripture in public worship be supplemented by a more informal type of Bible study in which the people were free to ask questions and share their own understanding of the text. The priesthood of all believers, as Spener and Francke understood it, implied that every sincere Christian should be involved in searching out the meaning of the Bible. The ministry of the Word was not limited to preaching. It needed to be supported by the common study of Scripture by the whole church or at least by the *ecclesiola in ecclesia*. When these conventicles or midweek Bible studies met, very often in private homes or other places than the church, the minister was not expected to prepare a sermon or give a discourse. It was supposed to be an informal discussion of the Bible and what it meant for everyday life.

As for formal preaching in a service of worship, Francke emphasized two types: preaching that focused on the conversion experience and preaching that edified the Christian, that is, showed one how to live the Christian life. To put it in the terminology we have been using, Francke

---

61. Erhard Peschke, *Die frühen Katechismus Predigten August Hermann Franckes, 1693-1695* (Göttingen: Vandenhoeck & Ruprecht, 1992).

62. Sad to say, we have not been able to locate a modern edition of the regular Sunday sermons of Francke. The following editions are known to have been published in the early eighteenth century, although they have not been available for this study: *Buss-Predigten*, 2 pts. (Halle, 1706); *Predigten über die Sonn- und Fest-Tags Episteln* (Halle, 1729); *Sonn- Fest- und Apostel-Tags Predigten*, 3 pts. (Halle, 1704); *Sonn- und Fest-Tags Predigten, Welche Teils in Halle, Teils an verschiedenen auswärtigen Oertern . . . gehalten worden* (Halle, 1740).

was concerned about evangelistic preaching and moral catechism. He was perfectly happy to do this within the framework of the lectionary, but he seemed to have no qualms about departing from it.

Francke did not feel that the preacher needed to spend much time discussing the text.

III. Johann Albrecht Bengel (1687-1752)

Swabian Protestantism has always had a very distinct character. A large part of Swabia is within the borders of the old principality of Württemberg, a rather large territory in southwest Germany. Today the main city is Stuttgart, but Tübingen is home to the Swabian university, and this prestigious university has set the spiritual tone of the area for centuries.

Johann Brenz was the Swabian Reformer. We spoke of his exemplary expository preaching in the previous volume. Solidly backed by his prince, Eberhard the Bearded, he led Swabian Protestantism in a solidly Lutheran direction, and yet the Christian humanism of the high Rhenish Reformers such as Oecolampadius, Ambrosius Blaurer, and Martin Bucer had considerable influence. Spener had spent some time in Tübingen, and while there he strongly influenced several of the younger faculty members through establishing small groups for prayer and Bible study. These small groups were destined to play a major role in the spread of pietism. The *ecclesiola in ecclesia* has been a major force in Swabian Protestantism down to the present.

One usually thinks of the University of Halle when one speaks of pietism. This is quite appropriate, of course, because Halle was founded by pietists, in Saxony in northeast Germany. The tremendous educational innovations of pietism were built into the academic program there, and Francke, Spener's disciple, had tremendous influence. Tübingen was a much older university, going back before the Reformation, and yet it was one of the fountainheads of pietism as well.

A. Pietist Biblical Studies

The foremost biblical scholar of German pietism was Johann Albrecht Bengel. Bengel was the child of Swabian pietism, and at the same time one of the fathers of pietism.[63] He was born in Winnenden, about ten miles north and east of Stuttgart. His father died when he was six years old. A family friend took over the responsibility of educating the boy. Soon young Bengel's guardian became master of the gymnasium in Stuttgart. This availed the future theologian with the best possible philological training, especially in Latin, Greek, and Hebrew. In 1703 Bengel entered the Stift in Tübingen, one of the great theological institutions of the world, sort of a theological fraternity house for the University of Tübingen. Before the Reformation it had been a convent for one of the monastic orders. Afterward it was turned into a dormitory for young men who wanted to enter the ministry. Those accepted in the Stift not only received room and board free while attending the university, but the Stift provided tutors to help them with their studies. Definite spiritual disciplines were maintained as well.

There was considerable competition to win a place in the Tübingen Stift. In many ways it was something of an exclusive club, but whatever else may be said about it, it did foster among its students a high degree of scholarly competence. Many years ago while a student in Tübingen, I had a friend in the Stift and I was often there. Some of the greatest theological discussions I have ever experienced took place in that prestigious institution. Those discussions convinced me there was no place in the world where Bible study was carried on with such intellectual vigor.

In 1707 Bengel entered the ministry and was sent to Metzingen, a small town in the Swabian Alb, near Urach. Before too long, however, he was recalled to the Tübingen Stift to serve as a tutor. For a number of years he continued in this position while preaching on weekends in the surrounding towns and villages. In 1713 he was sent to Denkendorf as director of what might be called a theological prep school, one of four in Württemberg. Like the Tübingen Stift, these schools had been established at the time of the Reformation in four different former monasteries in the principality. Again like the Tübingen Stift, they were a unique feature of Swabian Protestantism. They were designed to provide the church of Württemberg with well-prepared theology students. Those who mastered their Latin, Greek, and Hebrew most thoroughly were then sent on

63. For a recent work on Bengel and Swabian pietism, see Martin Brecht, "Der Württembergische Pietismus," in Brecht et al., *Geschichte des Pietismus,* 2:225-95. On Bengel especially, see pp. 251-59. See as well Kurt Aland, "Bibel und Bibeltexte bei August Hermann Francke und Johann Albrecht Bengel," in *Pietismus und Bible,* ed. Kurt Aland (Wittenberg: Luther Verlag, 1970), pp. 89-147.

to the Tübingen Stift for their university work. This system of theological education provided a ministry especially proficient in the arts of biblical interpretation. Thanks to these schools, the typical Swabian pastor did know his Bible.

For twenty-eight years Bengel continued as director of the theological preparatory school at Denkendorf. During this time he pursued a rigorous discipline of study. In 1734 he published an edition of the Greek New Testament which gave special attention to problems of textual criticism. His work was of far-reaching importance. In fact, it marks the beginning of modern textual criticism. Then in 1742 he published his commentary on the New Testament, *Gnomon Novi Testamenti*. This commentary was greatly admired by eighteenth-century pietists. John Wesley, for example, relied very heavily on it. Even today it is much used and greatly beloved.

In older years Bengel received a number of prestigious appointments commensurate with the reputation of his scholarly publications. Appointed to the Württemberg consistory, he became a prominent supporter of pietist causes. His person gave prestige to the movement and helped prevent a breach between pietism and the established church of Württemberg.

B. The Pietist Hermeneutic

What is really of the greatest interest in the sermons of Bengel is the pietist hermeneutic. His impressive philological study of the text always tended to the preaching of the Christian life. Matters of doctrine, or more precisely, doctrinal polemic, simply did not interest him. What he heard from Scripture was how one was to live the Christian life, how one was to pray, how one was to bear tribulation and suffering, and how one was to gain the assurance of salvation. For Bengel the Christian life demanded a great deal of inner reflection and meditation.

A sermon which demonstrates this pietist hermeneutic is one Bengel preached on the story of the healing of the paralytic in Matthew 9:1-8, the Gospel for the nineteenth Sunday after Trinity.[64] The sermon

---

64. Johann Albrecht Bengel, *Du Wort des Vaters, rede Du!: Ausgewählte Schriften, Predigten und Lieder* (Metzingen, Württemberg: Verlag Ernst Franz, 1962), pp. 83-93, hereafter Bengel, *Ausgewählte Predigten*.

begins with a formal introduction suggesting several passages of Scripture that teach the same truth that our preacher intends to show is found in the Gospel lesson. We learn from Exodus 15:26 that the Lord is a physician. After bringing the children of Israel through the Red Sea, he gave them as a precept these words: "I am the Lord, your physician." Bengel goes on to say that from the very beginning God created us in such perfection that we would not need a physician. Our souls were in a most beautiful maturity and our bodies in a marvelous harmony, but with the fall all that changed. Instead of the soul being the perfect image of God, it took a shameful and sinful form.[65]

As we find it in Isaiah 1:5-6, the whole head is sick and the heart is faint. From the sole of the foot even to the head, there is no soundness in the body, but bruises and sores and bleeding wounds. To these words of Isaiah our preacher remarks, the body must bear this suffering to remind us that we are still here on earth, and thus illnesses, hardships, and tribulations come upon us as intimations of that death which is the inevitable end of every human life. Thanks be to God, however, for he has provided us with sufficient means to uphold us in these difficulties. For the devout these tribulations are but the fatherly discipline of our faithful God. Today's Gospel, Bengel assures us, is another passage of Scripture which teaches us that God is our physician. In spite of all the contradictions of Satan, God is a physician in our suffering both of body and soul.

Dividing up his text, our preacher tells us he intends to make the following points: First, we see how this healing miracle begins with the healing of the soul. Second, the unjustified thoughts of the scribes are exposed as too harsh and misguided. Third, we will see how the body of the sick man was marvelously healed. With this Bengel offers up a prayer for illumination, asking that the congregation so concentrate on the teaching found in the text that the Holy Spirit would write it deep in their hearts.

In good classic expository style, Bengel takes up the first line of his passage, "And behold, they brought him a paralytic, lying on his bed" (Matt. 9:2a RSV). Our learned New Testament scholar comments that from the circumstances recorded in the text we recognize that these people who brought the pitiful man to Jesus were hoping Jesus would heal him. Jesus had already gotten a reputation for healing people of their physical injuries. The kind of healing they were looking for, however, was

---

65. Bengel, *Ausgewählte Predigten,* p. 83.

not what Jesus was really concerned with. Bengel quotes the next line of his text, "'Take heart, my son; your sins are forgiven'" (9:2b RSV). From this Bengel draws attention to the theological fact that sin is the basic cause of all our sicknesses and frustrations. Is it surprising, then, that Christ began by first assuring the man that his sins were forgiven? Jesus confirmed his faith. God is the source of all comfort and all healing, and when this man knew himself to be at peace with God, then healing came quite naturally. In fact, Jesus is assuring the man of his salvation simply by addressing him as "my son."[66] Bengel reminds us of that great text from the apostle Paul: "Therefore, since we are justified by faith, we have peace with God through our Lord Jesus Christ" (Rom. 5:1 RSV).

This interpretation of one of the healing stories of the Gospels is typical of pietism. It stands behind the numerous pietist social concerns all the way through the eighteenth and nineteenth centuries. The Protestantism of an earlier day would have been more interested in the way the story illustrates the doctrine of justification by faith, but in this sermon we find only a trace of doctrinal polemic. Much more we find a concern for spiritual health. With pietism we have a new hermeneutic.

Returning to the text, Bengel points out that the people who brought this sick man to Jesus were believers. We read that Jesus saw their faith. He saw into their hearts just as he saw into the hearts of the scribes and recognized their evil thoughts. Seeing the faith of the friends of the paralytic, Jesus healed the man. So it often is that God heals sick people because of the prayers of believing friends and relatives.

But we should see something else here, our New Testament scholar tells us. From this story it is very clear that those who have a sense of their need of a spiritual physician have immediate access to the Savior, who is indeed the good physician. When we know we have displeased our Creator, our Provider, our Savior, let us quickly seek him out that we might be healed. Bengel assures us that this is what the gospel is all about. Meticulous scholar though he may be, Bengel sounds more and more pastoral as he encourages his people. Bring to Christ your hearts and your souls, so broken, so filled with suffering, so disgraced though they may be. Discover the true healer of your soul. Bewail your need before your faithful Savior. Cry out to him for help. Approach him with faith. He will heal your sickness; he will bind up your wounds.[67]

66. Bengel, *Ausgewählte Predigten*, p. 84.
67. Bengel, *Ausgewählte Predigten*, pp. 85-86.

The point of this sermon is made very clear. Our greatest concern should be to make sure our sins are forgiven through the blood of Christ, that spiritually we are in good health, that we be assured we are children of God, that we be in fellowship with Christ. We need to be confident that Christ has spoken personally with us. Here again we see the typical pietist hermeneutic. As Christ spoke personally to the paralytic, he will speak personally to us. That is what a Gospel story like this should say to us. This sort of spiritual intimacy with God is of the essence of pietism. This sort of pietism, as we have seen, was very popular in the late Middle Ages, especially in nominalist circles. Now, in the eighteenth century, we find it again.

We have every reason to see to the healing of our souls, our Swabian pastor exhorts us. With a series of rhetorical questions he continues. Think, my dearly beloved, why has God called us into this life? Has he done it that we might heap up piles of gold? Has he created us that we might pursue the pleasures of this world? Has he not called us into existence that we might feel after him and sense his presence? Has he not put us here on earth that we might prepare ourselves for eternity? Are we not supposed to be a temple in which the divine glory might dwell, that we might have fellowship with him?

Having raised these questions, Bengel exhorts us to think of the exalted source and divine heritage of our souls, which can never be satisfied with transient things. Bengel becomes more and more eloquent. Soon we must leave this temporal world, he reminds us. None of these worldly goods can we take with us. The body must return to the earth, but what about the immortal soul? When we stand before the judgment throne, will we be a beloved son or an offending criminal?[68]

Bengel continues at some length to exhort us. This is typical of the pietist sermon, which normally puts a strong emphasis on exhortation. Our preacher reminds us of the transience of life. For most of us life is more than half done. Have we not already spent the better part of our days and years? Let us consider, have we spent more time cultivating the pleasures and comforts of this life rather than searching out the depths of the love of our heavenly Father? Have we heeded the admonition of the apostle John that we love not the world nor the things of the world? Alas, those who love this world do not have the love of the Father in them. Oh, let us wisely consider that what one sows one also reaps. Let us think of the crown of life

---

68. Bengel, *Ausgewählte Predigten,* p. 87.

that awaits the children of God. Let us devote ourselves to obtaining these heavenly joys. Let us diligently attend to our spiritual health.

Bengel returns to his text to consider how Jesus not only healed the paralytic but also confronted the scribes who stood there quite silently, but inwardly were very critical. No doubt, our Swabian New Testament scholar speculates, the scribes regarded Jesus as nothing more than an ordinary human being, a man, plain and simple. They must indeed have thought it strange that Jesus should tell the paralytic that his sins were forgiven.[69] What they saw, however, was not all there was. Jesus was also true God, and as such he had authority to forgive sins.

As a sort of excursus Bengel suggests there is something here we should stop and consider. Completely ignoring the Aristotelian unities, our pietist preacher follows instead the logic of the text. Much more in the tradition of the biblical expository sermon than the homiletical tradition of Scholasticism, Bengel brings in a thought which is not complementary to the central theme of the sermon. Here he is following Luther and the sixteenth-century Reformers rather than the Schoolmen. What Bengel draws from his text at this point is that it is not always wise to say everything one thinks.[70] One cannot always look into the heart and make true judgments. God can do that, to be sure, but we cannot. We therefore ought to avoid harsh thoughts and severe judgments of our neighbors. Think of the unfair judgment of Eli when Hannah was praying at the sanctuary of Shiloh, or the thoughts of the Pharisees about the woman who anointed the feet of Jesus.

Again Bengel goes back to his text, this time to focus on the actual healing of the paralytic. What he finds there is that Christ spoke to the sick man and told him to stand up and go home. As Bengel interprets it, the purpose of this was that all might openly see that the healing word of Christ was not an empty word but an almighty word, a powerful word.[71] It is a word which can heal, a word the wind and seas obey, a word that opens the eyes of the blind, opens the mouth of the dumb, opens the ears of the deaf, and opens the grave of the dead. Bengel was famous for deft turns of rhetoric like this. His commentary on the New Testament is filled with them. In fact, for centuries New Testament commentators have mined his works for gems like this.

69. Bengel, *Ausgewählte Predigten,* p. 88.
70. Bengel, *Ausgewählte Predigten,* p. 89.
71. Bengel, *Ausgewählte Predigten,* p. 91.

But something else here deserves our attention, and that is the implications of this passage for how one understands the place of the Word in worship. The Word has authority and power. It is the Word of God. Swabian pietism may be brushed off as *biblicistisch* by some, but it was on to something very real. God is present through his Word. We noticed this already in the *Didache*. This concept of the kerygmatic presence keeps appearing all the way through the history of Christian worship. It is through his Word that we come to know God, but also it is through his Word that we come to experience his healing presence.

Bengel's understanding of the Word is such that it is quite natural that the Word could heal the paralytic. So it was that Jesus simply said to the paralytic, stand up and go! We should learn from this, our preacher continues, how we should order our lives. It is appropriate that we should thankfully acknowledge God's grace, that we should live accordingly and offer to God praise, laud, honor, and glory. The ultimate thanksgiving, however, is to live our lives to the praise of God. If God has brought us to new birth through his Word, if he has enlightened us through his Word, then we ought to be his people. If he has called us from darkness to his wonderful light, then we are obligated to proclaim his excellent virtues.[72]

Here, too, we find a very clear theology of worship. Worship is thanksgiving, the thanksgiving we owe to God for our healing, for our redemption. It is a covenant obligation. Because we have come to God to be healed, because God has heard our cry, answered our prayers, and given us healing, we are obligated to offer to him our praise and thanksgiving, our obedience, and our lifelong service.

One more word needs to be said about the pietist hermeneutic. The stress on personal intimacy with the Savior tends to leave aside a more corporate understanding of worship. All too often for pietism, it's "me and Jesus all the way," as a member of my congregation one time put it. This personal confrontation between Jesus and the paralytic is certainly to be found in the passage Bengel's sermon wants to interpret. The friends and family of the paralytic bring in a more corporate dimension, but that is not what Bengel develops. For Bengel, as for eighteenth-century pietism in general, the reading and preaching of the Bible was a means of grace in that it promoted a personal intimacy with Christ. Call it *Biblicismus* if you will; for many it was a source of spiritual health and vitality. That's a pretty good step forward!

---

72. Bengel, *Ausgewählte Predigten,* p. 92.

IV. Theodorus Jacobus Frelinghuysen (1692-1747)

Along with Jonathan Edwards, Thomas Shepard, the Mathers and the Tennents, Theodorus Jacobus Frelinghuysen deserves to be recognized as one of the fathers of American Christianity. In 1720 he arrived in New York to organize the Dutch Reformed churches in New Jersey's Raritan Valley. He began in New Brunswick, at the mouth of the Raritan, and organized a dozen or so congregations up the Raritan and the North Branch. He organized strong churches. His Dutch Calvinism was disciplined by a vigorous study of the Scriptures in the original Greek and Hebrew, and yet it was a profoundly personal piety with a strong sense of the presence of God. This very practical worldly piety he engendered in Dutch farmers who were busy making New Jersey a prosperous "Garden State." The importance of Frelinghuysen lay not so much in his theological position as in his spiritual intensity. He was a very pious man, and demanded of his congregation an intensity of devotion few pastors would ever dream of, and even more surprisingly, he got it.[73]

Frelinghuysen, strangely enough, was not a Dutchman at all. He was born in Hagen in Westphalia, and did not learn Dutch until he was a university student. His father was pastor of the Reformed church in Hagen. In those days the German Reformed churches of the Rhineland were much more closely related to the Dutch-speaking Reformed churches of the Netherlands than to the German-speaking Reformed churches of Switzerland. In 1711 Frelinghuysen began his studies at the University of Lingen, which had recently passed from the Netherlands into the domains of the elector of Brandenburg. In spite of the political shift, the university was devoted to that strain of Dutch Calvinism which had been strongly influenced by Gisbertus Voetius. This strain was particularly pietistic, although not in the manner of Spener, Francke, and Zinzendorf. In fact, the Dutch Calvinists were very suspicious of this tradition and made quite clear their distinction from it. Frelinghuysen was a distinguished student, and upon completing his studies, was called to a church in East Friesland near Emden.

He was not exactly inexperienced when he arrived in the Raritan Valley, but he was not yet thirty years old and proceeded to make the mis-

---

73. For information on Frelinghuysen, see James Tanis, *Dutch Calvinistic Pietism in the Middle Colonies: A Study in the Life and Times of Theodorus Jacobus Frelinghuysen* (The Hague: Martinus Nijhoff, 1967).

takes typical of youthful, enthusiastic pastors. He tended to look at his older colleagues as spiritually dead and tried to evangelize those who thought of themselves as pillars of the church. He offended people to whom he was never reconciled, but even at that, it is a tribute to his congregation that they stayed with him. The more mature recognized his very genuine piety, his obvious learning, and his courageous determination to tame the wilderness.

When he arrived in New Brunswick in 1720, the town was on the frontier. He was the first resident pastor. The town had a good number of English-speaking residents, but only the occasional services of Joseph Morgan, the Presbyterian minister at Freehold, New Jersey. In 1726 Gilbert Tennent arrived in New Brunswick to organize an English-speaking Presbyterian church in the rapidly growing town. Providentially the ministers became fast friends. Frelinghuysen, unfortunately, spoke no English, and the two had to converse in Latin. Tennent recognized the gifts of his colleague and respected the obvious success he had in bringing his congregation to conversion. From Frelinghuysen Tennent learned a new approach to preaching, the purpose of which was to bring the congregation to conversion. To Frelinghuysen's delight, Tennent learned his method well, and with even greater ability than his teacher was able to evangelize the English-speaking townspeople. The Raritan Valley began to experience revival under Frelinghuysen and Tennent much as the Connecticut Valley had under Stoddard and Edwards. This was the situation when George Whitefield arrived in New Brunswick in 1739 and again in 1740. The revival for which the two pastors had worked so long finally blossomed. At the high point of the Great Awakening, Whitefield's preaching drew between seven thousand and eight thousand people per assembly in New Brunswick. Those assemblies, presided over by Frelinghuysen, Tennent, and Whitefield, were the prototypes of the American revival.

Let us look at this method of evangelistic preaching which Frelinghuysen bequeathed to the American church. Ultimately his homiletics is based on the *ordo salutis* of pietism, which, although capable of a number of variations, basically offers three steps of salvation: conviction, conversion, and holiness. Conviction is the discovery that one is a sinner and that God's wrath is against all sinners. Conversion is the experience of new birth, an inward experience of God's grace to sinners, the realization that I myself am the object of God's grace. Holiness is the living of the Christian life. It is walking in the narrow way. Most pietists would admit that one could not really obtain perfection in this life, but they felt one who was really converted could experience holiness; one could come very close to perfection. This is certainly not the Calvinist *ordo salutis*. It is, in fact, much closer to the Anabaptist *ordo salutis*. Except for not requiring baptism as a step of salvation, the pietists clearly adopted the Anabaptist approach of salvation through conversion experience. Although Frelinghuysen worked the typical Calvinist doctrines of justification by faith and election into his system, the three-point *ordo salutis* was operative for his homiletics. Preaching had the responsibility, first, of convicting sinners of their sin and the dreadful judgment of God this entailed; second, of proclaiming the promises of the gospel so that they be believed; and third, of instructing the converted in the life of holiness.

Frelinghuysen developed certain methods for doing this in his ministry in New Brunswick. As he understood it, the most important part of his ministry in the Raritan Valley was to bring the great mass of unconverted church attenders into conviction. He had three methods of doing this. To use the terminology of Martin Lodge, the first was the "preaching of terrors"; the second, "holding the mirror to the hearer's soul"; and the third, the "searching method." The preaching of terrors was nothing more than the hellfire and damnation approach of frightening people into conversion. The holding of the mirror to the hearer's soul aimed to depict the failures of the unregenerate soul in such a way that the hearer recognized himself as being still unconverted. The searching method entailed analyzing the excuses of sinners and showing how they are of no avail.[74] Through these three approaches the preacher tried to bring his hearers into a spiritual despair which would prompt them to reach out to the promises of the gospel. Reaching out to accept the promises of the gospel was the conversion experience Frelinghuysen and the Great Awakening generally were concerned to promote.

One is not surprised that the older Dutch pastors in America were less than enthusiastic about his ministry. It was strange to their Calvinist tradition. It was an approach to the Christian life influenced by Calvinist theology, to be sure, but it was basically pietist. As we shall see, the reaction against this kind of pietism will be an important chapter in the history of American Christianity.

74. Cf. Martin E. Lodge, "The Crisis of the Church in the Middle Colonies, 1720-1750," in *Interpreting Colonial America: Selected Readings,* ed. James Kirby Martin (New York: Dodd and Mead, 1973); Herman Harmelink, "Another Look at Frelinghuysen and His Awakening," *Church History* 37 (December 1968): 423-38.

V. Gilbert Tennent (1703-64)

The members of the Tennent family were among the major promoters of the Great Awakening in colonial America. William Tennent, Sr., came to America from Ulster in 1718, and several years later became pastor of the Neshaminy Presbyterian Church in Bucks County, up the Delaware River from Philadelphia. Well known for his piety and learning, the elder Tennent attracted to himself a group of young men eager to prepare for the ministry. This group, prominent among whom were Tennent's own sons, formed what today we call the Log College, the forerunner of Princeton Theological Seminary. As informal as Tennent's Log College may have been, it had a tremendous effect on the religious life of the middle colonies in the eighteenth century.

Gilbert's first church was in New Brunswick, at the mouth of the Raritan River. He began his charge in 1726. According to Milton J. Coalter, he learned from his father a strong distrust of any kind of arid rationalism and a high admiration for inward piety, but at New Brunswick he came under the influence of Frelinghuysen, who infused his Scotch-Irish piety with a strong dose of Friesian pietism and the typical pietistic approach to worship and preaching. While pastor there Tennent came to understand conversion as the chief purpose of preaching, to be brought about by preaching the terrors which awaited those who were unconverted and then by applying the balm of the gospel.

An example of his evangelistic message is found in his sermon "The Espousals Or a Passionate Perswasive. To a Marriage with the Lamb of God, Wherein the Sinners Misery and the Redeemers Glory is Unvailed in A Sermon upon Gen. 24 49. Preach'd at N. Brunswyck, June the 22d 1735."[75] One notices that the conversion experience is thought out in the imagery which had been so common to medieval mysticism. True to the heritage of Scotch-Irish Presbyterianism, Tennent's piety gave cardinal importance to the sacrament of the Lord's Supper. A number of his early communion sermons were published in a volume *Sermons on Sacramental Occasions by Divers Ministers,* published in Boston in 1739. Special series of sacramental sermons had become an important feature of Reformed

---

75. Gilbert Tennent, *The Espousals Or a Passionate Perswasive. To a Marriage with the Lamb of God, Wherein the Sinners Misery and the Redeemers Glory is Unvailed in A Sermon upon Gen. 24 49. Preach'd at N. Brunswyck, June the 22d 1735* (New York: J. Peter Zenger, 1735).

preaching. In fact, in Reformed homiletics, communion meditations has become a significant genre of preaching. We have already spoken of the sacramental sermons of Jean Daillé, John Flavel, and several of the New England Puritans.

Tennent had thoroughly mastered the pietist approach to evangelism by the time George Whitefield arrived in Philadelphia in 1739 and adopted him as his chief American lieutenant. The two men traveled together through New Jersey and New York, attracting large crowds. From New York Whitefield went on to New England while Tennent returned to New Brunswick. Whitefield, who had already won a great reputation for his revivals in England, had equal if not greater success in America than ever before. All the emotional fervor, all the personal magnetism, all the oratorical genius with which he won his crowds in Great Britain he now used to win crowds in America, and Tennent watched the great pulpit orator with admiration. Leading pietists, including Whitefield, had made it a point of honor that their sermons and prayers were impassioned and spontaneous, that they preached without notes, and that this proved that it all came from the heart. One of the most attractive features of Whitefield's ministry for many was his disregard of ecclesiastical structures. Formally he was a minister of the Church of England, but he had a total disregard for the niceties of Anglican ritual and polity. He, as Wesley, had the highest regard for German pietists such as Zinzendorf and his followers. When in New England he acted as a Congregationalist, when in New Jersey as a Presbyterian. If the pietists tended to ignore ecclesiastical structure, they showed even less concern for theological consistency. Any concern for theological precision was regarded as head religion instead of heart religion. Whitefield's disregard for theological issues was very attractive to many. All this Tennent emulated even though Whitefield was his junior by ten years. Tennent found in Whitefield's ministry a model for the revival of piety.

The following year Whitefield sent Tennent on a follow-up tour of New England. Although he inherited opposition from the same quarters that had objected to Whitefield, he was received at least as well as his British colleague even though he had nothing like his natural gifts of oratory. The winter of 1740-41 was a very hard winter, and Tennent braved the snowbound roads of the northern colonies all the way to Maine and back. He was received with the same enthusiasm and the same opposition as his more famous colleague.

As time went on Tennent began to take the opposition of other ministers more seriously. Originally he was one of the Awakeners who spoke most openly of the danger of an "unconverted ministry." As the converts of the Great Awakening, and even some of its leaders, began to show a carelessness for matters of doctrine, formal worship, and church structure, Tennent began to realize that these matters were more important than Frelinghuysen and Whitefield had led him to believe. The Great Awakening had precipitated a schism in the Presbyterian church. Tennent and his friends had managed to alienate their more conservative colleagues, and this evidently did not settle too well in Tennent's conscience. He was still as convinced of the importance of an inward religious experience as ever, but more and more he began to emphasize that love rather than a conversion experience was the proof of saving faith.

In 1744 Whitefield's followers in Philadelphia called Tennent to be pastor of the church they had organized. This congregation met in a building built for Whitefield called the New Building. It had not been intended as a church but rather as a meetinghouse for revival preachers regardless of denomination. This, of course, was all quite in the spirit of Whitefield's mission. He was quite content to be ecclesiastically unaligned. More and more Tennent became uncomfortable with the ecclesiastical haziness of the situation. Benjamin Franklin was asked to be a trustee of the New Building, and under his influence it became the first home of the University of Pennsylvania. Although a Deist, Franklin was known to have had a high regard for Whitefield. If Franklin was to secularize the Whitefield legacy, Tennent was to bring it firmly into a reunited Presbyterian Church. Tennent took his congregation, left the New Building, and built for it the stately Second Presbyterian Church. At the same time, he began to work for the reunion of the Presbyterian church, which he and other supporters of the Great Awakening had done so much to disrupt.

This new concern to balance an enthusiastic piety with theological integrity and ecclesiastical order affected Tennent's preaching program. In 1744 he published a series of sermons called *Westminster Shorter Catechism, Twenty-Three Sermons upon the Chief End of Man, the Divine Authority of the Sacred Scriptures, the Being and Attributes of God and the Doctrine of the Trinity.* This was followed the next year by *Discourses on Several Important Subjects,* which was a second series of sermons on the catechism, this one devoted to the questions of the *ordo salutis:* election, justification, sanctification, saving faith, and good works. One can well imagine that behind these publications was a systematic preaching through of the catechism to which the better part of several years may have been given. These sermons may have been confined to the Sunday evening service or even the midweek service. Preaching through the catechism was a well-established practice among the Calvinists of the seventeenth and eighteenth centuries, as we have often seen.

As Tennent sought more and more to balance his ministry, he began to leave aside some of the emblems of pietism. He began to wear the black preaching gown of the traditional Protestant pastor. He worked out his sermons in carefully prepared notes before preaching, and had no qualms about referring to them in the course of the sermon. In the same way he began to give more careful attention to the disciplines of prayer. In 1749 he published several sermons on prayer and fasting in which the traditional Puritan concerns reappear. With all his concern to reclaim the heritage of classical Protestantism, he never gave up those basic concerns for inward religious experience which he had inherited from his family's Scotch-Irish Presbyterianism. The practice of personal piety, the cultivation of classical Christian theology, a respect for ecclesiastical order — he finally brought these into significant balance. This was not, however, a merely private pilgrimage. In his pilgrimage he, as well as anyone else, knew what the role of the Presbyterian Church would be in American Christianity.

VI. John Wesley (1703-91)

Rarely has a Christian preacher spoken to the need of his day quite so profoundly as John Wesley.[76] Wesley was a preacher of holiness in an age

76. The literature on Wesley and his place in the Evangelical Revival of the eighteenth century is extensive. The following works have proved especially helpful: Robert E. Cushman, *John Wesley's Experimental Divinity* (Nashville: Abingdon, 1989); Horton Davies, "The Methodist Revolution in Popular Preaching," in Davies, *Worship and Theology in England,* vol. 3, *From Watts and Wesley to Maurice, 1690-1850* (Grand Rapids: Wm. B. Eerdmans Publishing Co., 1996), pp. 143-83; Maldwyn Lloyd Edwards, *John Wesley and the Eighteenth Century* (London: G. Allen & Unwin, 1933); Richard P. Heitzenrater, *Wesley and the People Called Methodists* (Nashville: Abingdon, 1995); David Hempton, *The Religion of the People: Methodism and Popular Religion, c. 1750-1900* (London and New York: Routledge, 1996); Harald Lindström, *Wesley and Sanctification: A Study in the Doctrine of Salvation* (Stockholm: Nya Bokförlage aktiebolaget, Almgvist & Wiksells Boktryckeri A.B., 1946); Thomas C. Oden, *Wesley's Scriptural Christianity: A Plain Exposition of His Teaching on Christian Doctrine* (Grand Rapids: Zondervan, 1994);

of frivolity. Courageously he preached the righteousness of Christ when libertinism and lawlessness had become fashionable. In the face of the brutalisms of eighteenth-century rationalism, the slave trade, the Industrial Revolution, the gin mill, Deism, and laissez-faire morality, Wesley made clear the Christian way of life. The rift which had developed in Western society between the rich and the poor, the educated and the ignorant, the religious and the irreligious had by the middle of the eighteenth century become a chasm. By the end of the century it brought a revolution in France. In England other forces were at work, and the Evangelical Revival was one of the most important of them.[77]

Wesley was an effective preacher of this revival. He was not its greatest preacher — Whitefield was — but his organizational genius made his preaching far more effective than Whitefield's. The greatness of Wesley was not his oratory but the inclusiveness of his ministry. He preached holiness to coal miners, mill workers, and scrub maids. Even more, he preached it in such a way that they heard it and lived it. Wesley was not one of the creative theologians of Christian history, but he was one of the great popularizers.[78] He pressed beyond the usual confines of the Church, the chapels of Oxford, the quaint village churches, and the fashionable parish churches of London, addressing himself to the common people. With such people the polite preaching of the genteel English parson had lost touch. Wesley could preach to prisoners, to soldiers, and to mobs about the essentials of the Christian gospel, about justification by faith, the sanctification of life, the new birth, and the assurance of salvation. He was one of the greatest evangelists the Christian Church has ever produced. He was the Protestant Francis of Assisi, and yet he was unique.

Albert C. Outler, *The Wesleyan Theological Tradition: Essays of Albert Outler,* ed. Thomas C. Oden and Leicester R. Longden (Grand Rapids: Zondervan, 1991); Maximin Piette, *John Wesley in the Evolution of Protestantism* (New York: Sheed and Ward, 1937); John Ernest Rattenbury, *The Conversion of the Wesleys: A Critical Study* (London: Epworth Press, 1938); Norman Sykes, *Church and State in England in the Eighteenth Century* (Cambridge: University Press, 1934); Norman Sykes, *From Sheldon to Secker: Aspects of English Church History, 1660-1768* (Cambridge: University Press, 1959); Charles Yrigoyen, *John Wesley: Holiness of Heart and Life* (New York: Mission Education and Cultivation Program Department for the Women's Division, General Board of Global Ministries, United Methodist Church, 1996).

77. Several recent studies have been published on Wesley and his significance in the context of the social claims of his day. See especially Hempton, *The Religion of the People.*

78. The work of Albert Outler has done much to show us the theological personality of Wesley. See Outler, *The Wesleyan Theological Tradition.*

Seen in the English context, the Evangelical Revival was a reaffirmation of classical Protestantism. It was a recovery of the doctrine of justification by faith and a revival of the popular piety of historic Protestantism. It developed in a very different context and addressed a very different set of circumstances than did German pietism, even though in many ways the two movements were very similar. With the restoration of the Stuart monarchy in 1661, the Anglicans expelled the Puritans from the Church of England and monopolized the official religion of the nation. Essential Protestant doctrine was compromised by High Church Anglicans such as Bishop George Bull. Any kind of religious intensity was suspected as nonconformity. Popular devotion had plummeted as more and more the established church catered to the taste of fashionable society.

The Church of England in which Wesley was born and educated was a terribly run-down church. While both of his parents had come from devout Puritan families, they had themselves accepted the Anglican compromise. Neither his mother nor his father had any sympathy with the Puritanism of their ancestors. They struggled to maintain some kind of piety, but it was an embattled kind of devotion which feared the onslaught of the world. When young Wesley went to Oxford to study theology, the religious life he entered was equally besieged. The assaults of Deism on Protestant orthodoxy had produced ponderous tomes of the driest theology ever written. Wesley steeped himself in the old Anglican standby, Jeremy Taylor. He read the medieval mystic Thomas à Kempis and carefully studied William Law's *Serious Call to a Devout and Holy Life* soon after it was published. It all made him into a rigorist, a Holy Joe who in the end was terribly afraid that he might not make it through the pearly gates. And yet, like his Puritan ancestors, he had a passionate thirst for holiness. One can hardly resist the suggestion that in Wesley there is a rebirth of the Puritanism of his ancestors. And yet there were other things at work, too.

Under Wesley the Evangelical Revival was an infusion of pietism in the mainstream of English Christianity. Wesley's adaptation of pietism was a distinctive combination of several strands of Christian piety. He was one of a number of eighteenth-century Christian leaders who were devoted to recovering a more experiential type of Christianity. Pietism appeared in all forms of Western Christianity during this period, whether Catholic, Lutheran, Anglican, or Reformed, but the pietism of Wesley was a particularly well balanced form. We already spoke of the importance for Wesley's spiritual development of Thomas à Kempis, one of the major expressions of nominalist pietism in the late Middle Ages. Taylor was an important forerunner of Anglican pietism, as were most of the Arminian Anglicans of the seventeenth century. During that century Anglicanism had gone far in the direction of Arminianism, and Wesley persevered in this throughout his life.

Wesley was well on the road to pietism when he sailed for Georgia in 1735 and came into contact with a group of Moravians. On his return to London he came under the influence of Peter Böhler, a Moravian missionary in London, who guided him through his conversion experience at Aldersgate on 24 May 1738. This conversion experience made Wesley one of the leaders of the Evangelical Revival. While the introduction to Martin Luther's commentary on Romans was being read, Wesley's heart was strangely warmed and he knew that the salvation about which both the apostle and the Reformer had spoken had graciously been bestowed upon him as well. He knew he was justified by faith in Christ, and this justification had become a personal experience. It was a matter of the warming of the heart rather than the enlightening of the mind. This experience brought Wesley to classical Protestantism through pietism. The experience was typically pietistic, but what was experienced was justification by faith as taught by classical Protestantism. One might call it a rebirth of Protestantism in terms of eighteenth-century England.

Within a few months Wesley was on his way to Germany to visit one of the centers of European pietism, Herrnhut, on the estate of Count Nikolaus von Zinzendorf. Returning to England in September of 1738, Wesley began his astounding evangelistic career. For the next fifty years he traveled the whole of England, Ireland, Scotland, and Wales, preaching in every conceivable place. He preached at the venerable Saint Mary's Church in Oxford, at the coal mines of Wales, in the parks and squares of London, and in the chapel of the countess of Huntingdon. In England particularly the pulpits of the established Church were closed to him, and so he often preached in the open air. Sometimes he preached in the open air simply because the crowds were too large for any available building; crowds of four thousand or five thousand were quite normal. Wesley developed a very definite approach to preaching in these circumstances. His favorite time for preaching was five o'clock in the morning. When one considers that he was trying to reach the common people, this made considerable sense. He wanted to reach them before they went to work. He preached short sermons accompanied by short extemporaneous prayers and the singing of the famous Methodist hymns. All this Wesley insisted must be done within an hour. What he sacrificed in the shortness of his sermons he made up for in their frequency. Normally he preached three times on the Lord's Day and twice each day during the week.

We know considerably more about how Wesley carried out his preaching ministry than most of the preachers we have studied up to this point. There is, of course, an obvious reason for this: Wesley was still alive a bit more than two hundred years ago, and such times are not so remote. Even more significantly, the great evangelist kept a journal in which he recorded his itinerations: the cities or villages in which he preached, the buildings he used, the size and temper of the congregations, the title or text of the sermon, and many other particulars which enable us to get a clearer picture of his preaching ministry. One of the things which becomes very clear is that he used a sermon barrel. We spoke of sermon barrels when discussing the medieval preaching orders, especially the evangelistic preaching of Bernardino da Siena. Wesley used a certain number of sermons over and over again. He carefully wrote them out early in his ministry and adapted them to particular situations as occasion demanded. As time went along these "standard sermons" were published with the intention that they would define the teaching of the Methodist movement. They became the doctrinal standards of the Methodist church, an approach to doctrinal definition which has much to recommend it and was quite natural to eighteenth-century pietism. As we will see throughout the eighteenth century, the major religious leaders of the day tended to publish their ideas in series of sermons rather than in volumes of systematic theology. Because of the importance these standard sermons began to have, Wesley issued a number of sermons as a means of clarifying his position, but the core of the standard sermons is indeed what he normally preached.

In 1746 Wesley published the first volume of these standard sermons.[79] In the preface he claimed they were representative of what he had preached for the preceding eight or nine years. By 1760 he had published three more volumes of these standard sermons, making a collection of forty-four sermons. The edition of Wesley's complete works published eleven years later, in 1771, contains nine more sermons, giving us the sermons in the collection called today the *Standard Sermons.* Something like a hundred other sermons of his have come down to us, but they do not belong to this basic collection.

---

79. The edition on which this study is based is *Wesley's Standard Sermons,* ed. Edward H. Sugden, 2 vols. (London: Epworth Press, 1921).

The preface to the first volume of sermons gives us an important statement of his approach to preaching. The first thing one notices is that with all his Anglican nurture and education, Wesley has very clearly chosen the Puritan "plain style" of preaching. "Nothing here appears in an elaborate, elegant, or oratorical dress."[80] Wesley assures us he has no wish to display his learning by quoting authors ancient or modern. He does not wish to engage in philosophical speculations or intricate reasoning. "For I now write, as I generally speak, *ad populum* — to the bulk of mankind, to those who neither relish nor understand the art of speaking."

As much as Wesley's approach to preaching may constitute a revival of many of the best insights of Puritanism, it includes certain elements of eighteenth-century pietism which are quite different from Puritanism. Puritanism never had the disdain for learning pietism had. While Wesley is more moderate in this respect than a great number of pietists, one does find traces of this pietistic disdain of learning when he says, "Nay, my design is, in some sense, to forget all that ever I have read in my life."[81]

> Let me be *homo unius libri*. Here then I am, far from the busy ways of men. I sit down alone: only God is here. In His presence I open, I read His book; for this end, to find the way to heaven. Is there a doubt concerning the meaning of what I read? Does anything appear dark or intricate? I lift up my heart to the Father of Lights: "Lord, is it not Thy word, 'If any man lack wisdom, let him ask of God'? Thou 'givest liberally, and upbraidest not.' Thou hast said, 'If any be willing to do Thy will, he shall know.' I am willing to do, let me know, Thy will."[82]

Wesley was a very well educated man. He was, after all, an Oxford don, something not many of those who dismissed him as an ignorant enthusiast had themselves attained. He had, in fact, read widely in both sacred and secular literature. He had read a good number of the Church Fathers, the classics of medieval Christianity, and the standard theological works of the Continental Reformation. He knew the works of the Reformed Church of England, both the Anglicans and the Puritans of the seventeenth century, and the contemporary theological and philosophical works of his own day. He was proficient in the use of the ordinary tools of biblical interpretation and thoroughly schooled in formal exegesis. One

---

80. *Wesley's Standard Sermons*, 1:29.
81. *Wesley's Standard Sermons*, 1:30.
82. *Wesley's Standard Sermons*, 1:32.

did not, after all, become a fellow of Lincoln College even in the beginning of the eighteenth century without a considerable competence in the science of theology. In spite of all this, the pietist tendency toward illuminism often comes through with considerable vigor.

Something else comes out very clearly in this preface, something not found in the Puritans: populism. Wesley uses the classic phrase *"ad populum"* to describe his sermons, but he gives it a different ring. It is characteristic of the eighteenth century that the division between the cultured and educated of society and the common ordinary workers began to widen. As never before, the fabric of human culture was being ripped apart by the animosities of rich and poor. Ever wider grew the chasm between the scholars of Oxford and Cambridge and the mill workers of Bristol and Liverpool. The Puritans were quite confident they could teach the farmers and artisans of their day the theological vocabulary. They set out to make every Christian a theologian. The Presbyterians of Scotland had the same vision. To a large extent they succeeded. But with the Industrial Revolution, the gulf between the learned and the ignorant became too wide for even a man of Wesley's vision to imagine that it could be bridged. How could a Welsh coal miner become a theologian? Wesley could at least envision that Welsh coal miners could understand the gospel, and that was a very brave vision for the eighteenth century.

Wesley's sermons were basically of two kinds. There were those intended to bring his hearers to the experience of conversion and those intended to direct the converted in the life of holiness, or, to use the terms we have developed through our study, evangelistic sermons and sermons of moral catechesis. Let us look at some typical examples of each type.

A. Salvation by Faith

The sermon Wesley chose to put first in the collection of standard sermons has the title "Salvation by Faith." Not only does this sermon sum up his basic message, but it was, in the unfolding of his ministry, the first formal announcement of the gospel he would preach for the next fifty years. While this sermon, in the form it was published, was first preached at the celebrated Saint Mary's Church on the High Street in Oxford, it was in substance delivered all over the United Kingdom. Its preaching in Saint Mary's on 11 June 1738, less than three weeks after his conversion experience at Aldersgate, was, however, a momentous occasion. It has often been called the first trumpet blast of the Methodist revival.

As Wesley's sermons frequently are, this one is a masterpiece of chaste brevity. In its arrangement it is simple, clear, and to the point. It is the old ship of three masts with a matter-of-fact introduction and an obvious conclusion. First the text is announced: "By grace are ye saved through faith" (Eph. 2:8).[83] The sermon itself begins with the introduction. Wesley is a master of the sober sermon introduction. Introductions are not designed to grab the ears of his hearers so much as to introduce the subject. They never aim at being clever or colorful. Wesley introduces this sermon with a short essay on grace quite naturally suggested by his text. He tells us that our creation is by grace, that God's providential care of us is a work of divine grace, and that all the good works we do are done by the grace of God.[84] Man has nothing of his own to present to God, and therefore if a sinful humanity is saved at all, it is a matter of grace upon grace. "'By grace' then 'are ye saved through faith.' Grace is the source, faith the condition, of salvation."[85] A good Reformation scholar might preface a statement recognizing grace as the cause and faith the means of our salvation, but be that as it may, this is the subject on which Wesley intends to preach.

The first point Wesley makes is to define the faith by which we are saved. He begins by making it clear that what passes for faith at Oxford is not the kind of faith which saves. Wesley is openly attacking the religion of Oxford. The heathen have a sort of faith, he tells us. They believe God exists, and that he rewards those who diligently seek him. They seek God by glorifying him as God, by giving thanks to him for all things, and by carefully cultivating moral virtues. In short, Wesley draws a picture of the faith of Deism and unmasks it as nothing less than the faith of the virtuous heathen of ancient Greece and Rome. Deism had won a great following in England by the middle of the eighteenth century, and Wesley knew he was challenging the religious beliefs of a substantial number of his hearers.

Then he attacks another segment of the population of Oxford. He tells us that if the faith of the heathen does not save us, then neither does the faith of the devils. They, too, believe, but they believe and tremble. At

---

83. It is the practice in this study to quote the Bible as the preacher quotes it. Wesley habitually quotes the King James Version.

84. *Wesley's Standard Sermons,* 1:37.

85. *Wesley's Standard Sermons,* 1:38.

this point our preacher shows that the devils had all the orthodox beliefs of the Church. They believed Jesus was the Messiah, the Son of the Most High.[86] Unlike the heathen, they believed in the deity of Christ, but they did not know him as Lord of their lives, nor did they serve him as Master. This is clearly an attack on the orthodoxy of Oxford. When Wesley comes down to defining the faith that saves, he puts it in thoroughly pietistic terms. "It is not barely a speculative, rational thing, a cold, lifeless assent, a train of ideas in the head; but also a disposition of the heart."[87] The pietistic dichotomy between head religion and heart religion comes to clear expression. In contrast to the Deists, the faith Wesley preaches is thoroughly christocentric; it acknowledges the necessity and merit of Christ's death and the power of his resurrection.[88] There is no question but that for Wesley faith must be at least orthodox. But it must be more than simply the holding of orthodox beliefs.

Here we see Wesley presenting pietism as the alternative to Deism on one hand and cold orthodoxy on the other.

> Christian faith is, then, not only an assent to the whole gospel of Christ, but also a full reliance on the blood of Christ; a trust in the merits of His life, death, and resurrection; a recumbency upon Him as our atonement and our life, *as given for us,* and *living in us.* [It is a sure confidence which a man hath in God, that through the merits of Christ, *his* sins are forgiven . . .] and, in consequence hereof, a closing with Him, and cleaving to Him, as our "wisdom, righteousness, sanctification, and redemption," or, in one word, our salvation.[89]

For his second point Wesley addresses what the salvation is that comes by faith. He insists this salvation is a present salvation. Whatever else it may imply about the future, it is attainable here on earth. It is a reality for the here and now. Wesley reminds his congregation that the text is in the present tense rather than the future. "Ye are saved by faith," not "Ye shall be saved by faith." This is developed in three subpoints. We are saved from the guilt of sin, we are saved from the fear of punishment for sin, and we are saved from the power of sin.

---

86. *Wesley's Standard Sermons,* 1:39.
87. *Wesley's Standard Sermons,* 1:40.
88. *Wesley's Standard Sermons,* 1:42.
89. *Wesley's Standard Sermons,* 1:40-41, emphasis Wesley's. The sentence in brackets was added by Wesley in a subsequent edition.

In explaining that we are saved from the power of sin, Wesley makes one of the affirmations which were characteristic of the Wesleyan movement. Quoting from I John 3:7ff., "Little children, let no man deceive you. He that committeth sin is of the devil. Whosoever believeth is born of God. And whosoever is born of God doth not commit sin; for His seed remaineth in him: and he cannot sin, because he is born of God," Wesley insists,

He that is, by faith, born of God sinneth not (1) by any habitual sin; for all habitual sin is sin reigning: but sin cannot reign in any that believeth. Nor (2) by any wilful sin; for his will, while he abideth in the faith, is utterly set against all sin, and abhorreth it as deadly poison. Nor (3) by any sinful desire; for he continually desireth the holy and perfect will of God; and any tendency to an unholy desire, he by the grace of God, stifleth in the birth. Nor (4) doth he sin by infirmities, whether in act, word, or thought; for his infirmities have no concurrence of his will; and without this they are not properly sins. Thus, "he that is born of God doth not commit sin": and though he cannot say he hath not sinned, yet now "he sinneth not."[90]

For his third point Wesley addresses some possible objections to what he has already said. The first is that preaching salvation by faith will undermine holiness and good works. This objection, our preacher points out, was raised against the apostle Paul when he preached the same doctrine. Wesley's answer is, "It would be so, if we spake, as some do, of a faith that was separate from these; but we speak of a faith which is not so, but [necessarily] productive of all good works, and all holiness."[91] Wesley is making an important point here which in fact his ministry for the next fifty years held with considerable integrity. His whole concept of salvation puts the matter of faith and works in such close relation that it is hard to charge him with antinomianism.

The second objection Wesley anticipates is that preaching salvation by faith may lead to pride. He shows that Paul anticipated this objection, too, as is clear from the context of Ephesians. It is exactly the point the apostle wants to make in this epistle: salvation by faith removes the grounds of pride, for the faith which brings salvation is the gift of God, "lest any man should boast."[92] A third objection is that the doctrine en-

90. *Wesley's Standard Sermons,* 1:44-45.
91. *Wesley's Standard Sermons,* 1:46.
92. *Wesley's Standard Sermons,* 1:47.

courages people to sin. Paul spoke to this objection in Romans 6. Indeed it may, Wesley admits.[93] Many will continue in sin that grace may abound, but when they do, they do it to their own judgment.

Wesley concludes his sermon by insisting that a return to the doctrine of justification by faith is just what is needed for the situation that the United Kingdom faced in that day. "Nothing but this can effectually prevent the increase of the Romish delusion among us."[94] One remembers, of course, that when Wesley preached this sermon a considerable part of the population supported the restoration of Charles Edward Stuart, the Catholic heir of the Stuart dynasty. In 1745 Bonnie Prince Charlie landed in Scotland and made a serious attempt to recover his throne from the House of Hanover. But while Wesley rejected the Anglican theory that a theological compromise between Protestantism and Catholicism would keep England free from popery, he was not terribly concerned with the preservation of a merely political Protestantism.

He was much more concerned with the libertinism and moral decay which had become fashionable in eighteenth-century England. Deism had brought with it a general decline of morality in spite of its interest in law, that is, the laws of nature. Wesley attacks Deism with consummate eloquence. "Nothing but this can give a check to that immorality which hath 'overspread the land as a flood.' Can you empty the great deep, drop by drop? Then you may reform us by dissuasives from particular vices. But let the 'righteousness which is of God by faith' be brought in, and so shall its proud waves be stayed."[95] There were many in England for whom Protestantism was only political. It was quite another matter for Wesley.

For Wesley, what was needed was a profound religious revival.

Nothing but this can stop the mouths of those who "glory in their shame, and openly deny the Lord that bought them." They can talk as sublimely of the law, as he that hath it written by God in his heart. To hear them speak on this head might incline one to think they were not far from the kingdom of God: but take them out of the law into the gospel; begin with the righteousness of faith; with Christ, "the end of the law to every one that believeth"; and those who but now appeared almost, if not altogether, Christians, stand confessed the sons of perdi-

93. *Wesley's Standard Sermons,* 1:48.
94. *Wesley's Standard Sermons,* 1:50.
95. *Wesley's Standard Sermons,* 1:50-51.

tion; as far from life and salvation (God be merciful unto them!) as the depth of hell from the height of heaven.[96]

For Wesley the doctrine of justification by faith as found in the New Testament, both in the Johannine and Pauline writings, and which less than three weeks before he had personally experienced at Aldersgate while hearing the reading of Martin Luther's commentary to Romans, was the basis of a great revival of Christian faith. Wesley clearly saw himself in the tradition of Luther and the Reformed Church of England. The conclusion of this sermon with its extended quotation from Luther makes it very clear that Wesley intends a revival of classical Protestantism. He had a great gift for discerning the times, and for adapting his message to the needs of a very particular age. He did his best to make the classical Protestantism of the sixteenth century speak to England in the eighteenth century.

B. *The Almost Christian*

The second sermon in the collection is equally emblematic of Wesley's preaching, although it too was preached at Saint Mary's Church in Oxford. It was preached some three years after the sermon we have just considered, and in the meantime Wesley and the Methodist movement had become well known throughout England. A tremendous crowd awaited Wesley's appearance, many there out of curiosity. Hostile reports had stirred up a blaze of criticism. People wanted to know just what he really had to say. This sermon bears the title "The Almost Christian," and takes as its text Acts 26:28, "Almost thou persuadest me to be a Christian." Wesley's sermon is courageously provocative. It is a challenge to the polite religion of his day, which he brands as almost Christian but not altogether Christian. The sermon never gets around to dealing with the text. The text is rather used as a pejorative label for conventional Christianity, which, as Wesley makes very clear, is no Christianity at all.

The sermon is divided into two points. First, our preacher speaks of what an almost Christian is. Agrippa, the puppet king before whom the apostle Paul was brought for trial, may have been almost persuaded to become a Christian on hearing Paul's defense, but he remained a pagan.[97]

---

96. *Wesley's Standard Sermons,* 1:51.
97. *Wesley's Standard Sermons,* 1:54.

Evidently Wesley assumes, and probably quite correctly, that his hearers knew the story very well, and so he wastes no time explaining the text and its implications. Once again he begins to make his charge that both the Deism and the dry orthodoxy of England's theological fountainhead were no more than paganism. Deism is nothing more than a reinterpretation of pagan philosophy, and Anglican orthodoxy is but a mere outward form of godliness.[98] The almost Christian practices with sincerity all the ordinances of the established Church.[99] But in the end Wesley gives both the orthodox Anglicans and the unorthodox Deists the same label. They are almost Christian, but not really Christian.

Having made such a sweeping condemnation of the religion of his listeners, he uses a masterpiece of rhetoric to enforce his point. He asks if it is possible to practice Christianity so carefully and still not really be a Christian. Yes, indeed, Wesley assures his congregation. He himself had been the most meticulous sort of Anglican minister and still was no more than an almost Christian.[100] What could be more infuriating than a man of such impeccable ecclesiastical background making such a confession in Saint Mary's, Oxford, one of the great citadels of respectable English churchmanship?

Having devoted the first part of the sermon to discussing the almost Christian, Wesley turns to the altogether Christian. To be an altogether Christian is, first of all, to love God, and second, to love the neighbor. This Wesley develops with thoughts from I Corinthians 13, Paul's great chapter on love. The kind of love demanded of the altogether Christian is the kind that engrosses the whole heart and offers up the whole life to God. This kind of love is a totally absorbing experience.[101] It is obviously the kind of experience that goes far beyond the lukewarm love of the conventional Christianity of the eighteenth century.

Having spoken of love, Wesley turns to faith. Faith is the foundation of all the rest. It is by faith that we are saved. But be not deceived, Wesley insists; faith which does not produce repentance, love, and good works saves no one. With this Wesley quotes at length the sixteenth sermon from the official book of homilies of the Church of England: "'The right and true Christian faith is' (to go on in the words of our own

---

98. *Wesley's Standard Sermons*, 1:56.
99. *Wesley's Standard Sermons*, 1:57.
100. *Wesley's Standard Sermons*, 1:61.
101. *Wesley's Standard Sermons*, 1:62.

Church), 'not only to believe that Holy Scripture and the Articles of our Faith are true, but also to have a sure trust and confidence to be saved from everlasting damnation by Christ. It is a sure trust and confidence which a man hath in God, that, by the merits of Christ, his sins are forgiven, and he reconciled to the favour of God; whereof doth follow a loving heart, to obey His commandments.'"[102] The point Wesley wants to make is that the classic Protestantism of the Reformed Church of England taught that faith was an experience of personal trust in Christ.

For Wesley, as for the Reformers of the sixteenth century, saving faith is a passion.

> Now, whosoever has this faith, which "purifies the heart" (by the power of God, who dwelleth therein) from pride, anger, desire, "from all unrighteousness," from "all filthiness of flesh and spirit"; which fills it with love stronger than death, both to God and to all mankind; love that doeth the works of God, glorying to spend and to be spent for all men, and that endureth with joy, not only the reproach of Christ, the being mocked, despised, and hated of all men, but whatsoever the wisdom of God permits the malice of men or devils to inflict, — whosoever has this faith, thus working by love, is not almost only, but altogether, a Christian.

Wesley concludes the sermon with a challenge: "Are not many of you conscious that you never came thus far; that you have not been even *almost a Christian;* that you have not come up to the standard of heathen honesty; at least, not to the form of Christian godliness?"[103] Having thus made clear his accusation of conventional religion, Wesley exhorts his congregation to awaken from their sleep and seek the living God.[104]

C. Justification by Faith

Another sermon Wesley preached frequently is entitled simply "Justification by Faith," which appears as number 5 in the *Standard Sermons*. To what occasion we owe the published form of the sermon we do not know. The editors of the edition of the *Standard Sermons* we are using suggest it

102. *Wesley's Standard Sermons,* 1:63.
103. *Wesley's Standard Sermons,* 1:64.
104. *Wesley's Standard Sermons,* 1:65-67.

was first preached in Gloucester on 6 October 1739. Wesley is known to have preached it from his father's tombstone at Epworth on 8 June 1742 and on other occasions throughout his ministry. It is intended as a clear statement of historic Protestant doctrine, as propounded by Luther and adhered to by the Reformed Church of England.

The strength of the sermon is that the doctrine of justification by faith is presented in biblical language. The traditional biblical terminology and imagery are used throughout the sermon. There is no suggestion that the biblical language is beyond the grasp of coal miners and mill workers.

The sermon begins with an account of our creation in the image of God, our state of uprightness and perfection in the Garden of Eden, and our fall through the sin of Adam. Wesley comments, "Thus 'by one man sin entered into the world, and death by sin. And so death passed upon all men,' as being contained in him who was the common father and representative of us all. Thus, 'through the offence of one,' all are dead, dead to God, dead in sin, dwelling in a corruptible, mortal body, shortly to be dissolved, and under the sentence of death eternal. For as 'by one man's disobedience' all 'were made sinners'; so, by that offence of one 'judgement came upon all men to condemnation' (Rom. v.12, &c.)."[105] This is, to be sure, but a restatement of what we find in Romans. If for Luther the doctrine of justification was above all the Pauline doctrine of justification, for Wesley it was just as Johannine as it was Pauline. "In this state we were, even all mankind, when 'God so loved the world, that He gave His only begotten Son, to the end we might not perish, but have everlasting life.' In the fullness of time He was made man, another common Head of mankind, a second general Parent and Representative of the whole human race." Then taking up the imagery of Isaiah 53, Wesley gives an exposition of the doctrine of Christ's vicarious atonement.[106]

For his second point Wesley answers the question, what is justification? Justification is not that the sinner is actually made just and righteous. That is what is meant by sanctification. Sanctification is, to be sure, the fruit of justification, but nevertheless the two are distinct and different. "The one implies, what God does for us through His Son; the other, what He works in us by His Spirit."[107] At this point at least Wesley

105. *Wesley's Standard Sermons*, 1:117-18.
106. *Wesley's Standard Sermons*, 1:118-19.
107. *Wesley's Standard Sermons*, 1:119.

is assuming not the pietistic *ordo salutis* but the Reformed. He continues, "The plain scriptural notion of justification is pardon, the forgiveness of sins."[108] It is the act of God the Father by which, for the sake of the propitiation made by the blood of his Son, he shows forth his mercy, the remission of past sins. Justification means that God does not count our sin. He does not reckon it to our condemnation. He will not condemn us because of our sin either in this world or the next. "He loves, and blesses, and watches over us for good, even as if we had never sinned."[109]

Next Wesley directs himself to the question of who is justified. It is the ungodly, he insists, "the ungodly of every kind and degree; and none but the ungodly."[110] The point he wants to make is that holiness is not a prerequisite for justification. "Does then the Good Shepherd seek and save only those that are found already? No. He seeks and saves that which is lost."[111] Wesley is very clearly denying the position of seventeenth-century Anglican theologians who wanted to insist that certain works of repentance and charity were required for someone to be justified. The controversy is not explicitly opened up in this sermon, but Wesley knows English Protestants had been subjected to this kind of teaching for several generations, and that he must be very clear on this subject.

Finally Wesley takes up his fourth point — on what grounds the ungodly are justified. They are justified on the grounds of faith and faith alone.[112] To establish this point Wesley quotes a number of New Testament texts. Then he attempts to make clear what is meant by faith, and to that purpose gives a brief exposition of Hebrews 11:1, "Now faith is the substance of things hoped for, the evidence of things not seen." Briefly he speaks of the meaning of the Greek text. He concludes, "Justifying faith implies, not only a divine evidence or conviction that 'God was in Christ, reconciling the world unto Himself,' but a sure trust and confidence that Christ died for *my* sins, that He loved *me,* and gave Himself for *me.*"[113] By way of illustration he quotes two passages from *The Book of Homilies.* Once again Wesley is making clear that what he is preaching is the faith of the Reformed Church of England, not the faith of eighteenth-century Anglicanism.

108. *Wesley's Standard Sermons,* 1:120.
109. *Wesley's Standard Sermons,* 1:121.
110. *Wesley's Standard Sermons,* 1:122.
111. *Wesley's Standard Sermons,* 1:123.
112. *Wesley's Standard Sermons,* 1:124.
113. *Wesley's Standard Sermons,* 1:125.

The conclusion of the sermon is a challenge to accept God's justification in Christ for one's own salvation.

> Thou ungodly one, who hearest or readest these words! thou vile, helpless, miserable sinner! I charge thee before God the Judge of all, go straight unto Him, with all thy ungodliness. Take heed thou destroy not thy own soul by pleading thy righteousness, more or less. Go as altogether ungodly, guilty, lost, destroyed, deserving and dropping into hell; and thou shalt then find favour in His sight, and know that He justifieth the ungodly. . . . I challenge *thee* for a child of God by faith! The Lord hath need of thee. Thou who feelest thou art just fit for hell, art just fit to advance His glory; the glory of His free grace, justifying the ungodly and him that worketh not. O come quickly! Believe in the Lord Jesus, and thou, even thou, art reconciled to God.[114]

D. Christian Perfection

The next sermon we want to take up bears the title "Christian Perfection." It is commonly regarded as the classic statement of one of Wesley's characteristic positions. Here we see the great evangelist in one of his more pietistic aspects. The sermon is number 35 of the *Standard Sermons,* first published in 1741 and coming several years after his conversion. Historians of the Wesleyan movement think it presents a considerable development in Wesley's position from his earlier sermons. He had originally, it is claimed, advocated a much more thoroughly perfectionist position. Wesley himself, however, always thought he had maintained the same position on this subject throughout his ministry.

The sermon opens with one of Wesley's clear and precise introductions. He tells us what he is going to preach about and why it is important. He announces his text, Philippians 3:12, "Not as though I had already attained, either were already perfect," and then a few verses later in 3:15, "Let us, as many as be perfect, be thus minded." Concerning this text, Wesley says, "There is scarce any expression in holy writ, which has given more offence than this. The word *perfect* is what many cannot bear. The very sound of it is an abomination to them; and whosoever *preaches perfection* . . . runs great hazard of being accounted by them worse than a

---

114. *Wesley's Standard Sermons,* 1:130.

heathen man or a publican."[115] Wesley, as we have noted before, gives special importance to maintaining the biblical terminology.

> We may not, therefore, lay these expressions aside, seeing they are the words of God and not of man. But we may and ought to explain the meaning of them; that those who are sincere of heart may not err to the right hand or left, from the mark of the prize of their high calling. And this is the more needful to be done, because, in the verse already repeated, the Apostle speaks of himself as not perfect: "Not," saith he, "as though I were already perfect." And yet immediately after, in the fifteenth verse, he speaks of himself, yea, and many others, as perfect: "Let us," saith he, "as many as be perfect, be thus minded."[116]

In order to remove any difficulty from this apparent contradiction, Wesley is to speak about two subjects: in what sense Christians are not perfect, and in what sense they are.

Christians are not perfect, Wesley tells us, in that they do not have a perfect knowledge of all things. They can and do make mistakes. Furthermore, they suffer from various infirmities, such as illness and the like. Finally, they experience temptations even if they do not give in to them.[117]

As for Christians being perfect, Wesley says we must first consider that there are different stages in the Christian life. As we find it in I John, some are spiritually little children, some are spiritually young men, and some are spiritually fathers. It is about the fathers, the mature Christians, that Wesley is chiefly concerned. He supports his point first from Romans 6:1-12, where we find that those who are born again cannot continue in sin. Having been born again to a new life, they cannot live in the old life of sin any longer. This passage, Wesley notes, is speaking about even the most ordinary, the most elementary sort of Christian. It is not talking about the most mature sort of Christian.[118]

From this crucial passage in Romans Wesley turns, as he so often does, to the Johannine literature. In I John 3:9 he finds, "Whosoever is born of God does not commit sin; for His seed remaineth in him: and he cannot sin, because he is born of God." Then again in I John 5:18, "We

115. *Wesley's Standard Sermons,* 2:150.
116. *Wesley's Standard Sermons,* 2:151.
117. *Wesley's Standard Sermons,* 2:152-56.
118. *Wesley's Standard Sermons,* 2:157.

know that whosoever is born of God sinneth not."[119] Wesley discusses a number of interpretations which have been proposed to explain these passages, but in the end one must take very seriously the Johannine demand for holiness.

Wesley then treats a number of passages of Scripture which are urged against his position, first from the Old Testament, then from the New. They are all tightly argued and take quite a number of printed pages.[120] Then he returns to making his point in a more positive way, showing that a Christian is perfect in regard to evil thoughts and tempers.[121] "This is the glorious privilege of every Christian."[122] Again Wesley makes his point by a clear and precise argument from one Scripture after another. One wonders if a couple thousand coal miners standing out in the cold weather could possibly have been interested in all this. Evidently plenty of people in those crowds were. And after all, should we really be surprised? When a man, who himself glows with holiness, opens up the way for others to follow, should we really be surprised when suddenly all other considerations fall away? The cold, the coal dust, the Oxford accent, the Cornish brogue, the lateness of the hour, even time itself kneel before the glory of eternity. The promise of holiness Wesley made, in the language and imagery of Scripture, was of surpassing interest: "We fix this conclusion, — *a Christian is so far perfect, as not to commit sin.*"[123]

The conclusion of the sermon is an exhortation to press on to Christian perfection. Then all those glorious experiences promised by the prophets will be fulfilled. Wesley appeals to Psalm 51:10, "Create in me a clean heart, O God; and renew a right Spirit within me," and then to Ezekiel 36:26, "A new heart also will I give you, and a new spirit will I put within you." Having painted these promises in glowing colors, the glowing colors of biblical language, Wesley concludes with a paraphrase of the apostle Paul: "'This one thing let us do, forgetting those things which are behind, and reaching forth unto those things which are before, let us press toward the mark for the prize of the high calling of God in Christ Jesus'; crying unto Him day and night, till we also are 'delivered from the bondage of corruption, into the glorious liberty of the sons of God'!"[124]

119. *Wesley's Standard Sermons*, 2:158-59.
120. *Wesley's Standard Sermons*, 2:160-68.
121. *Wesley's Standard Sermons*, 2:169-73.
122. *Wesley's Standard Sermons*, 2:169.
123. *Wesley's Standard Sermons*, 2:169.
124. *Wesley's Standard Sermons*, 2:174.

An interesting feature of this sermon is that when it was first published, it appeared as a separate tract. In this tract the sermon is followed by one of Charles Wesley's greatest hymns, "God of all power, and truth, and grace." The hymn, which is twenty-eight stanzas long, is based on Ezekiel 36, which had figured so prominently in John Wesley's sermon. The hymn is a marvelous interiorizing of the sermon. This fact gives us an important insight into the relation of Wesley's preaching to the worship of the earliest Methodist congregations. Preaching always led to hymnody. This is not only characteristic of Wesleyan worship; it is true of pietist worship generally. Preaching was followed by a hymn that gave the congregation the opportunity of experiencing and responding to the message that was preached. This made a great deal of sense in the whole pietist understanding of worship.

E. The New Birth

Wesley's sermon "The New Birth," sermon 39 in the *Standard Sermons,* is another important example of his evangelistic preaching. It is developed from the text "Ye must be born again" (John 3:7). Wesley introduces his sermon by telling us that if there be any two doctrines which can be called fundamental, they are the doctrine of justification and the doctrine of the new birth. Justification is the work God does for us in forgiving our sins; the new birth, or regeneration, is the work God does in us, to renew our fallen nature.[125]

First our preacher addresses why we must be born again. It is because in the fall we died spiritually. As God said to our first parents in the Garden of Eden, "In the day that thou eatest thereof thou shalt surely die" (Gen. 2:17). Adam and Eve did eat of the forbidden fruit, and they died spiritually. "Hence it is, that, being born in sin, we must be 'born again.'"[126]

Next he addresses the nature of the new birth. One cannot give a systematic analysis of it because, as Jesus tells Nicodemus, it is like the wind which no one can see. No one can say where it comes from or where it goes; one can only see its effects as the trees bend before it. This is an interesting point. Here we notice that Wesley disclaims a systematic theo-

---

125. *Wesley's Standard Sermons,* 2:226-27.
126. *Wesley's Standard Sermons,* 2:231.

logical analysis, but insists that one can say enough about it so that one can experience it. Obviously his interest is not theological but pastoral. "However, it suffices for every rational and Christian purpose, that, without descending into curious, critical inquiries, we can give a plain scriptural account of the nature of the new birth. This will satisfy every reasonable man, who desires only the salvation of his soul."[127] This statement is indicative of Wesley's religious quest. The experiential search is quite separate from the intellectual search.

Wesley's description of the new birth as something nontheological and experiential, pietist as it may be, is certainly eloquent.

> But as soon as he is born of God, there is a total change in all these particulars. The "eyes of his understanding are opened" (such is the language of the great Apostle); and, He who of old "commanded light to shine out of darkness shining on his heart, he sees the light of the glory of God," His glorious love, "in the face of Jesus Christ." His ears being opened, he is now capable of hearing the inward voice of God, saying, "Be of good cheer; thy sins are forgiven thee"; "Go and sin no more." This is the purport of what God speaks to his heart; although perhaps not in these very words. He is now ready to hear whatsoever "He that teacheth man knowledge" is pleased, from time to time, to reveal to him.[128]

One cannot help but notice here the typical eighteenth-century emphasis on the empirical, the religious experience of the senses, the hearing, the seeing.

This religious experience is more, of course, than outward feelings. The newborn Christian "feels, is inwardly sensible of, the graces which the Spirit of God works in his heart. He feels, he is conscious of, a 'peace which passeth all understanding.' He many times feels such a joy in God as is 'unspeakable, and full of glory.' He feels 'the love of God shed abroad in his heart by the Holy Ghost which is given unto him'; and all his spiritual senses are then exercised to discern spiritual good and evil. By the use of these, he is daily increasing in the knowledge of God, of Jesus Christ whom He hath sent, and of all the things pertaining to His inward kingdom." Wesley obviously gives great importance to inner feeling; he, as the late medieval mystics, knows its value for Christian maturity.

127. *Wesley's Standard Sermons*, 2:231-32.
128. *Wesley's Standard Sermons*, 2:233.

Without this experiential dimension the Christian cannot be complete, but with it the Christian begins to mature. Wesley continues,

> And now he may be properly said to live: God having quickened him by His Spirit, he is alive to God through Jesus Christ. He lives a life which the world knoweth not of, a "life which is hid with Christ in God." God is continually breathing, as it were, upon the soul; and his soul is breathing unto God. Grace is descending into his heart; and prayer and praise ascending to heaven: and by this intercourse between God and man, this fellowship with the Father and the Son, as by a kind of spiritual respiration, the life of God in the soul is sustained; and the child of God grows up, till he comes to the "full measure of the stature of Christ."

Surely a large part of the eloquence of this passage is the way Wesley quotes Scripture. He is a master of the biblical allusion. He sets up his biblical quotations as a jeweler mounts precious gems. This ability obviously comes from a profound familiarity with Scripture. What he obviously wants to say is what Scripture indeed says, and so the expressions of Scripture naturally fall into place as he unfolds his message.

We find something else here, something we have often found with great preachers: that Wesley has a way of unfolding the biblical imagery. It is not that he finds new and more literary images to clothe a biblical idea. It is rather that he presents the biblical imagery in a fresh, vivid, and arresting manner. This is what he has done here with the biblical image of the new birth. In fact, one might say that this is part of the secret of his effectiveness as an evangelist. He makes clear the imagery of the Bible. He makes clear what salvation is and how one receives it.

After this magnificent imagery, Wesley defines the new birth. This paragraph deserves to be considered among the classics of theological literature:

> From hence it manifestly appears, what is the nature of the new birth. It is that great change which God works in the soul when He brings it into life; when He raises it from the death of sin to the life of righteousness. It is the change wrought in the whole soul by the almighty Spirit of God when it is "created anew in Christ Jesus"; when it is "renewed after the image of God in righteousness and true holiness"; when the love of the world is changed into the love of God; pride into humility; passion into meekness; hatred, envy, malice, into a sincere, tender, dis-

interested love for all mankind. In a word, it is that change whereby the earthly, sensual, devilish mind is turned into the "mind which was in Christ Jesus." This is the nature of the new birth: "so is every one that is born of the Spirit."[129]

Wesley continues to his third point, the necessity of the new birth. First, its necessity is "in order to holiness";[130] second, it is necessary to salvation; and third, it is necessary for us to experience happiness in this world. Again and again Wesley makes it clear that the salvation about which he speaks is no "pie in the sky by and by." Wesley's thoroughly Protestant approach to holiness makes it clear that its beauty is to be enjoyed in this life and from here to eternity.

Having made these three major points, our preacher takes up the relation of the new birth to baptism.[131] This we find of particular interest because we have tried to make the point in this study that evangelistic preaching has a particularly strong relation to baptism. For Wesley, if I understand him correctly, this was not an important consideration. He wants to make it very clear that baptism and the new birth are not the same thing. While the distinction he makes here is certainly valid, in effect he makes baptism of very little significance in our salvation. In Wesley's remarks, as far as I can see, there is no trace of a covenant theology of baptism. For him, as for the pietists in general, baptism does not really figure in the *ordo salutis*. Baptism is not the same as new birth, nor do the two necessarily accompany each other.

Having looked now at five of Wesley's evangelistic sermons, what can we say about his evangelistic preaching?

Certainly we can say he preached about the central experiences of the *ordo salutis* in such a way that others could experience them as well. He spoke about salvation by faith, about justification, the new birth, adoption, sanctification, and Christian perfection, and he opened up these experiences in such a way that others could follow him into them. He spoke about them in a way that was primarily personal and therefore experiential. It was clear to those who heard that he was speaking about things he had experienced. One is never too sure just exactly how Wesley understood the *ordo salutis*. Although he often speaks of the elements of the Reformed *ordo salutis*, particularly justification and sanctification, he

129. *Wesley's Standard Sermons*, 2:234.
130. *Wesley's Standard Sermons*, 2:235.
131. *Wesley's Standard Sermons*, 2:237ff.

was not willing to speak of any kind of election or predestination. Wesley was not a Calvinist. He was not really an Arminian either, for that matter. Typical of his age, he saw things in terms of inner experience rather than eternal reality. Then, too, his doctrine of Christian perfection was really quite different from the Reformed doctrine of glorification. Again, typical of his age, Wesley wants to make holiness a present inward experience rather than an eternal hope. One cannot really say he followed the pietist *ordo salutis* of conviction, conversion, and holiness either. Wesley's pietism is most evident in that he seems little interested in such things as predestination and glorification which are outside of man's immediate experience. His whole approach to evangelism was experiential.

Surely one reason for the effectiveness of Wesley's approach to evangelism is that he used the biblical vocabulary about salvation. This vocabulary and this imagery is tremendously accessible, and Wesley proved its value in speaking to the workers of the rising Industrial Revolution.

Finally, Wesley's evangelism was effective because he himself radiated holiness. It was not just that he appeared to be a man of God. He was what he appeared to be.

F. The Sermon on the Mount

As Wesley traveled around the British Isles ministering to the congregations that had been born from his evangelistic preaching, he developed several series of expository sermons. Included in the *Standard Sermons* is a series of expositions of the Sermon on the Mount that actually fits into his program of evangelistic preaching. He used it to portray the life of holiness. He often preached the series in the open air before great crowds, feeling that he was preaching the sermon as Jesus preached it. Wesley understood the Sermon on the Mount as a summary of the Christian life, presented in all its beauty and all its attractiveness. It never occurred to him that it might be an impossible ideal. This was the Christian life as it was meant to be lived. The Sermon on the Mount was an invitation to holiness, an invitation Jesus issued to the multitudes and which Wesley himself issued to the multitudes.

These expositions are a marvelous example of expository preaching. Wesley devotes thirteen sermons to three chapters, taking up each saying in turn. While his more usual evangelistic sermons often use texts to define the subject to be discussed in the sermon, these expositions are much more classically expository. No attempt is made to limit a sermon to a single theme or subject. The preacher follows the text from one subject to another as long as time permits. Another classic feature of expository preaching which we find in these sermons is that Wesley explains Scripture by Scripture. In explaining "Blessed are the merciful," he tells us that Jesus is really teaching about love and therefore explains this beatitude by going over the apostle Paul's chapter on love, I Corinthians 13. He goes through this chapter very thoroughly, explaining the different qualities of love. For many of us today Wesley's approach tends toward moralism, the kind of pietistic moralism which we find not too attractive, and yet in his own day it must have been very attractive. The presentation of the Sermon on the Mount as the Christian Law surely appealed to an age so devoted to the concept of natural law. One can see how this *lectio continua* of the Sermon on the Mount must have excited crowds of people in the eighteenth century. Wesley tells us that when he preached this series at Cardiff, his heart was so enlarged that he continued for three hours.

While Wesley on occasion put expository preaching to the service of evangelism, he was much more apt to use it in the more intimate meetings of his gathered disciples, the Methodist class meetings. At such meetings he would often go through such central books as I John or Romans.[132] Wesley recognized the need of thoroughly grounding his converts in basic biblical teaching, and his faithfulness in this is surely one of the major reasons his ministry had such long-lasting effects.

Pietism generally gave great attention to moral catechism. If it often neglected doctrinal catechism and had no interest whatsoever in liturgical catechism, it more than made up for it with a very meticulous moral catechism. Wesley was no exception to this general pietistic tendency. He was a very neat, orderly, and precise man. He was devoted to rising early in the morning and had no hesitations about preaching this virtue to others. He despised slovenliness on one hand and sartorial luxury on the other. He was quite free with advice on how Christians should dress. While one might find this a bit oppressive today, one should remember that the eighteenth century had rather excessive styles in clothing. The wealthy often indulged themselves in all kinds of luxurious clothing. One only has to look at the portraits of Gainsborough and Reynolds to get an idea of the money that must have been poured out on silks and satins. On the other hand, such ornate clothing could easily become sloppy, as the etch-

132. See the notes in *Wesley's Standard Sermons,* 1:162 and 314.

ings of Hogarth show with such amusing satire. Wesley's preaching against fashion was no more out of place in his day than Bernardino da Siena's was in fifteenth-century Florence.

It was the same way with Wesley's preaching on temperance. The gin shop was a curse on the Industrial Revolution. The miners and mill workers of England turned to alcohol for escape from the hard realities of their life, and even the more comfortable elements of the population turned to wines and spirits as a source of pleasure and relaxation. That Wesley and the Evangelical Revival generally should have preached so often against the evils of drinking was for that time prophetic.

Nowhere is Wesley's essential Protestantism clearer than in his sermons on stewardship. While he is often compared to Francis of Assisi because the two shared such concern for evangelism and such passion for holiness, they had very different approaches to the use of wealth. While Francis idealized poverty, Wesley saw poverty as an infirmity and cultivated the Protestant concept of stewardship. He preached frequently on such subjects as the use of money, the danger of riches, and good stewardship. Sociologists and historians have for some time pointed out the great benefits of Wesley's concern for practical moral catechism.

VII. George Whitefield (1714-70)

George Whitefield was a powerful orator.[133] Even Benjamin Franklin, Philadelphia's leading Deist, was captivated by his prowess as a public speaker. With consummate ease he could address a crowd of thirty thousand in the open air, and even with the usual noises of the city street he could be heard from Arch Street all the way down to Walnut, at least five blocks away. In England he charmed the fops and dandies of Bristol and yet moved the coal miners of the West Country to tears. Whitefield was

133. For biographical material on George Whitefield, see Albert D. Belden, *George Whitefield, the Awakener: A Modern Study of the Evangelical Revival* (London: S. Law, Marston and Co., 1930); Horton Davies, *Worship and Theology,* 3:143-209; John Gillies, *Memoirs of the Life of the Reverend George Whitefield, M.A.* (London: Printed for Edward and Charles Dilly, 1772); James Paterson Gledstone, *George Whitefield, Field Preacher* (New York: American Tract Society, [1901]); Douglas M. Strong, "Whitefield, George," in *Historical Dictionary of Methodism,* ed. Charles Yrigoyen, Jr., and Susan E. Warrick (Lanham, Md., and London: Scarecrow Press, 1996), pp. 225-27; Henry Stuart, *George Whitefield, Wayfaring Witness* (New York and Nashville: Abingdon, 1957).

born and brought up in the Church of England, and yet he ministered to the whole of Anglo-Saxon Protestantism in a way none of the other leaders of the Evangelical Revival were able to do. His attempt at ecumenism was perhaps more successful than that of other pietists simply because he aspired to be nothing more than a preacher. In spite of the ecumenical thrust of his pietism, Whitefield appealed to the Calvinism of the Thirty-nine Articles and the homilies of the Reformed Church of England. He had obviously been nourished on the Puritans of the seventeenth century. He set the aggressive style of the Evangelical Revival by preaching from tabletops in the open air, in marketplaces, churchyards, and street corners. He was an itinerant evangelist, and his evangelistic tours of the American colonies first began to tie those colonies together into a religious unity. The Great Awakening, of which he was the popular symbol, gave American Christians a consciousness of identity which has never been lost. Whitefield made a strong imprint on the character of the American church.

He began life in Gloucester as the son of an innkeeper. This cathedral city had an excellent school, and having done well in this school, the future evangelist was sent up to Pembroke College in Oxford. He soon became one of the members of John Wesley's Holy Club, the group that was first called "Methodists," which was only a fellowship of intensely devout young men at the time, as Wesley had not yet had his conversion experience. It was hardly the first Methodist church. Whitefield was ten years younger than Wesley, and Wesley's influence must have been great on the young student. In 1736, two years before Wesley's Aldersgate experience, Whitefield got his degree from Oxford, was ordained by Bishop Benson at Gloucester, and began preaching in London. His preaching caused an immediate sensation. Governor Oglethorpe enlisted him for the cause of founding Georgia, and he spent a year in Savannah working for the establishment of his famous orphanage. Returning to England in 1738, he found that pulpits were closed to him. He had been branded an enthusiast. In 1739 he found himself in Bristol, where he began preaching to coal miners at Kingswood, a suburb. The positive response of these coal miners changed the course of Whitefield's ministry. Two months later he began to do the same thing at London. Having been invited to preach at Islington by the minister, he was at the last minute refused entrance to the pulpit by the church wardens, so he decided to preach in the churchyard. Two days later he preached at Moorfields and then at Kennington Common, where no less than thirty thousand people are supposed to have been present.

During the summer months Whitefield itinerated through Great Britain, but during the winter he maintained a ministry at the Tabernacle on Tottenham Court Road in London. This ministry included daily preaching and weekly Communion.

The literary legacy of Whitefield's sermons is not of the highest quality.[134] He preached extemporaneously, and only under the pressure of his friends, compounded by the demands of the printing industry, did he try to put sermons down on paper. His sermons were very popular with publishers because they sold well. Some of his printed sermons are indeed moving, and in them we find his magnificent figures of speech. Even at that, the printed sermons, as we have so often found, give us only a hint of his superb oratory. Some have claimed he was the greatest orator the English-speaking world has ever heard. It is hard, of course, to substantiate such a claim. And in the end one does not really need to make such decisions. The literary remains, as imperfect as they are, show that he was indeed a great artist — great enough, surely, for any of us to sit at his feet.

A particularly fine sermon is "Christ the Believer's Wisdom, Righteousness, Sanctification, and Redemption."[135] The text is I Corinthians 1:30, "But of him are ye in Christ Jesus, who of God is made unto us wisdom, and righteousness, and sanctification, and redemption."[136] In the briefest sort of introduction Whitefield tells us that this text gives us a comprehensive statement of Christ's saving work and that he intends to speak, first, of how our salvation flows from Christ, and second, of our salvation in terms of the four words in our text: "wisdom," "righteousness," "sanctification," and "redemption." Having thus divided up his text, Whitefield proceeds to speak of "the fountain, from which all those blessings flow, that the elect of God partake of in Jesus." It is from the love of the Father for the Son that all our salvation flows. Jesus Christ the Son is the mediator of the divine blessing to us, but "God the Father is the fountain of the Deity." The Son is divine just as is the Father, and between the Father and the Son there

---

134. This study is based on a collection of Whitefield's sermons by the famous Anglican bishop, J. C. Ryle: *Select Sermons of George Whitefield,* ed. J. C. Ryle (London: Banner of Truth Trust, 1959), hereafter Whitefield, *Sermons.* For a more complete edition of Whitefield's sermons, see George Whitefield, *Works,* 6 vols. (London: Printed by Edward and Charles Dilly, 1771), and Whitefield, *Sermons on Important Subjects* (London: Henry Fischer, Son and P. Jackson, 1831).

135. This sermon is found in Whitefield, *Sermons,* pp. 61-71.

136. Whitefield, *Sermons,* p. 61. He habitually cites the King James Version.

is a covenant, as we find it in the Psalms, "I have made a covenant with my chosen."[137] It is on the basis of that covenant that the Son prays to the Father in the intercessory prayer of John 17. Because of that covenant Jesus approaches the Father with confidence when he intercedes for us. And we need to understand the mystery of election on the basis of that covenant. This is what our text is referring to when it says, "But of him," that is, of the Father, "are you in Christ Jesus." It is by the love of the Father that we are in Christ Jesus, and therefore receive the saving blessings of wisdom, righteousness, sanctification, and redemption. However much a pietist Whitefield may have been, his strong doctrine of election could not let him present salvation as a merely personal experience here and now. Salvation is an eternal reality rooted in the relationship of the persons of the Trinity. The love of the Father for the Son is and has been from all eternity electing, covenanting love.

Having spoken of election, our preacher now turns to the blessings which through Christ are made once to the elect. He begins with wisdom.

> But wherein does true wisdom consist? Were I to ask some of you, perhaps you would say, in indulging the lust of the flesh, and saying to your souls, eat, drink, and be merry: but this is only the wisdom of brutes; they have as good a gust and relish for sensual pleasures, as the greatest epicure on earth. Others would tell me, true wisdom consisted in adding house to house, and field to field, and calling lands after their own names: but this cannot be true wisdom; for riches often take to themselves wings, and fly away, like an eagle towards heaven. Even wisdom itself assures us, "that a man's life doth not consist in the abundance of the things which he possesses"; vanity, vanity, all these things are vanity; for, if riches leave not the owner, the owners must soon leave them; "for rich men must also die, and leave their riches for others"; their riches cannot procure them redemption from the grave, whither we are all hastening apace.[138]

The rhetoric of this passage is interesting. What Whitefield is saying is rather commonplace. It is the sort of thing preachers had said century after century. The scriptural allusions are so well known as to be almost tedious. How many times we have all heard the line, "Eat, drink, and be merry," but then our preacher follows it with a line like "But this is only

137. Whitefield, *Sermons*, p. 61.
138. Whitefield, *Sermons*, p. 62.

the wisdom of brutes; they have as good a gust and relish for sensual plea-sures." All of a sudden it picks up sparkle. Again our preacher takes up an all too familiar line, "Vanity, vanity, all these things are vanity." He, as a million pedantic preachers, is warning his congregation against the vanity of riches, but then he follows it with "If riches leave not the owner, the owners must soon leave them," and suddenly the pedantic becomes mem-orable. Whitefield turns to the subject of book knowledge and sets beside it the impossibility of knowing the number of the stars. He takes up the subject of self-knowledge and says the usual things, but then stops us short with "Before, they were darkness; now, they are light in the Lord; and in that light they see their own darkness."[139] Flashes of wisdom like this fill Whitefield's sermons. He says a few more things about wisdom, but that is not the real purpose of this sermon.

Our preacher now takes up the subject of righteousness. Here he makes a full statement of the doctrine of justification by faith. In Christ God the Father has given us the divine righteousness. It is a vicarious righteousness, but it atones for human sin. Then, taking up the imagery of the final verses of Romans 8, Whitefield ascends into a hymn of praise for the redemptive work of Christ that concludes with a thunderous para-phrase of that mighty chapter. He sets up the words of Scripture as an or-ganist introduces a hymn. When the hymn tune finally begins, one knows it is the most beautiful melody in the world.

> And what a privilege is here! Well might the angels at the birth of Christ say to the humble shepherds, "Behold, I bring you glad tidings of great joy"; unto you that believe in Christ, "a Saviour is born." And well may angels rejoice at the conversion of poor sinners; for the Lord is their righteousness; they have peace with God through faith in Christ's blood, and shall never enter into condemnation. O believers! (for this discourse is intended in a special manner for you) lift up your heads; "rejoice in the Lord always; again I say, rejoice." Christ is made to you, of God, righteousness, what then should you fear? You are made the righteous-ness of God in him; you may be called, "The Lord our righteousness." Of what then should you be afraid? What shall separate you hence for-ward from the love of Christ? "Shall tribulation, or distress, or persecu-tion, or famine, or nakedness, or peril, or sword? No, I am persuaded, neither death, not life, nor angels, nor principalities, nor powers, nor things present, nor things to come, nor height, nor depth, nor any other

139. Whitefield, *Sermons*, p. 63.

creature, shall be able to separate you from the love of God, which is in Christ Jesus our Lord," who of God is made unto you righteousness.[140]

What a fugue of homiletical doxology!

Having spoken of election and justification, Whitefield presses on to sanctification. He assures his congregation that the gift of justification is surely a marvelous privilege, but it is only the beginning of the happiness of believers. The Father has even greater gifts to bestow upon us in Christ, and with this Whitefield gives us a full exposition of the doctrine of sanctification. Our preacher's rhetoric is magnificent as he tells us several things he does not mean by sanctification. Having put it negatively, he then puts it positively.

> Their understandings, which were dark before, now become light in the Lord; and their wills, before contrary to, now become one with the will of God; their affections are now set on things above; their memory is now filled with divine things; their natural consciences are now enlightened; their members, which were before instruments of uncleanness, and of iniquity unto iniquity, are now instruments of righteousness and true holiness; in short, they are new creatures; "old things are passed away, all things are become new," in their hearts: sin has now no longer dominion over them; they are freed from the power, though not the indwelling and being, of it; they are holy both in heart and life, in all manner of conversation; they are made partakers of a divine nature, and from Jesus Christ, they receive grace for grace; and every grace that is in Christ, is copied and transcribed into their souls; they are transformed into his likeness; he is formed within them; they dwell in him, and he in them; they are led by the Spirit, and bring forth the fruits thereof; they know that Christ is their Emmanuel, God with and in them; they are living temples of the Holy Ghost. And therefore, being a holy habitation unto the Lord, the whole Trinity dwells and walks in them; even here, they sit together with Christ in heavenly places, and are vitally united to him, their Head, by a living faith; their Redeemer, their Maker, is their husband; they are flesh of his flesh, bone of his bone; they talk, they walk with him, as a man talketh and walketh with his friend; in short, they are one with Christ, even as Jesus Christ and the Father are one.[141]

140. Whitefield, *Sermons*, pp. 63-64.

141. Whitefield, *Sermons*, p. 64. We have quoted Whitefield at much greater length than ordinarily would be considered proper simply to give a sense of the flow of his oratory.

Here again we see Whitefield's marvelous ability to paraphrase Scripture and set together this magnificent picture of sanctification by a whole series of biblical allusions.

Even from a purely literary standpoint, Whitefield's presentation of sanctification is as beautiful as anything in all of Christian literature. Again we quote at length:

> O what an unspeakable blessing is this! I almost stand amazed at the contemplation thereof. Well might the apostle exhort believers to rejoice in the Lord; indeed they have reason always to rejoice, yea, to rejoice on a dying bed; for the kingdom of God is in them; they are changed from glory to glory, even by the Spirit of the Lord: well may this be a mystery to the natural, for it is a mystery even to the spiritual man himself, a mystery which he cannot fathom. Does it not often dazzle your eyes, O ye children of God, to look at your own brightness, when the candle of the Lord shines out, and your Redeemer lifts up the light of his blessed countenance upon your souls? Are not you astonished, when you feel the love of God shed abroad in your hearts by the Holy Ghost, and God holds out the golden sceptre of his mercy, and bids you ask what you will, and it shall be given you? Does not that peace of God, which keeps and rules your hearts, surpass the utmost limits of your understandings? And is not the joy you feel unspeakable? Is it not full of glory? I am persuaded it is; and in your secret communion, when the Lord's love flows in upon your souls, you are as it were swallowed up in, or, to use the apostle's phrase, "filled with all the fulness of God." Are not you ready to cry out with Solomon, "And will the Lord, indeed, dwell thus with men!" How is it that we should be thus thy sons and daughters, O Lord God Almighty!

The rhetorical questions, the marvelous biblical metaphor of the golden scepter of King Ahasuerus, and the quotation from Solomon all make this a superb paragraph. Noble language, as any one trained in classical rhetoric knows, must stem from a noble subject, and what subject could be more noble than holiness? Even as written literature, such language is high art. One can only imagine how a preacher with a sense of rhythm, timing, and pace might have turned this into great oratory. According to all reports, Whitefield had this sense of flow, and with it his prose became poetry.

But Whitefield has an even more sublime subject to treat than sanctification, and he announces this with another biblical metaphor. "O believer! what thou hast already received are only the first-fruits, like the cluster of grapes brought out of the land of Canaan; only an earnest and pledge of yet infinitely better things to come: the harvest is to follow; thy grace is hereafter to be swallowed up in glory."[142] From sanctification Whitefield intends to ascend the *ordo salutis* to the subject of glorification. But before he does, he has a few theological criticisms to make. It is part of his oratorical skill to move back and forth between inspiration and argument, between the preaching of terrors and the preaching of glory, between theological depth and emotional intensity. As every artist knows, a broad palette fascinates the eye. In rapid succession Whitefield takes on first the Arminians and then the antinomians.

Finally he comes back to glorification, which he finds in his text under the term "redemption." The Father has made Christ our "wisdom, righteousness, and sanctification, but also redemption." Whitefield starts out in the terminology made so famous by William Perkins: "This is a golden chain indeed! and, what is best of all, not one link can ever be broken asunder from another. Was there no other text in the book of God, this single one sufficiently proves the final perseverance of true believers: for never did God yet justify a man, whom he did not sanctify; nor sanctify one, whom he did not completely redeem and glorify."[143] The allusions to a number of passages of the New Testament are clear. As an orator, Whitefield knows how to build to a climax, and of course, the whole theological system of the golden chain is a climax. Those God called he also justified, and those he justified he also sanctified, and those he sanctified he also glorified. The literary form follows the theological argument.

> As for God, his way, his work, is perfect; he always carried on and finished the work he begun; thus it was in the first, so it is in the new creation; when God says, "Let there be light," there was light, that shines more and more unto the perfect day, when believers enter into their eternal rest, as God entered into his. Those whom God has justified, he has in effect glorified: for as a man's worthiness was not the cause of God's giving him Christ's righteousness; so neither shall his unworthiness be a cause of his taking it away; God's gifts and callings are without repentance; and I cannot think they are clear in the notion of Christ's righteousness, who deny the final perseverance of the saints; I fear they understand justification in that low sense, which I understood it in a

142. Whitefield, *Sermons,* p. 65.
143. Whitefield, *Sermons,* pp. 66-67.

few years ago, as implying no more than remission of sins: but it not only signifies remission of sins past, but also a *federal right* to all good things to come. If God has given us his only Son, how shall he not with him freely give us all things? Therefore, the apostle, after he says, "Who of God is made unto us righteousness," does not say, perhaps he may be made to us sanctification and redemption: but, "he is made": for there is an eternal, indissoluble connexion between these blessed privileges. As the obedience of Christ is imputed to believers, so his perseverance in that obedience is to be imputed to them also; and it argues great ignorance of the covenant of grace and redemption, to object against it.[144]

Not only is this great oratory, it is carefully argued theology. When one reads this sermon, one can hardly dismiss Whitefield as merely an orator with a facile tongue.

Now that the sermon is in full progress, it is clear that it intends to present a vision of holiness that is beyond any kind of pietistic perfectionism. Whitefield, as other pietists, is concerned for holiness, but he insists that holiness is ultimately beyond the here and now. To be sure, there is a holiness that we can experience here and now, but it is only a foretaste of that which is to come. Again we quote at length:

But be not weary, be not faint in your minds: the time of your complete redemption draweth nigh. In heaven the wicked one shall cease from troubling you, and your weary souls shall enjoy an everlasting rest; his fiery darts cannot reach those blissful regions: Satan will never come any more to appear with, disturb, or accuse the sons of God, when once the Lord Jesus Christ shuts the door. Your righteous souls are now grieved, day by day, at the ungodly conversation of the wicked; tares now grow up among the wheat; wolves come in sheep's clothing: but the redemption spoken of in the text, will free your souls from all anxiety on these accounts; hereafter you shall enjoy a perfect communion of saints; nothing that is unholy or unsanctified shall enter into the holy of holies, which is prepared for you above: this, and all manner of evil whatsoever, you shall be delivered from, when your redemption is hereafter made complete in heaven; not only so, but you shall enter into the full enjoyment of all good. It is true, all saints will not have the same degree of happiness, but all will be as happy as their hearts can de-

144. Whitefield, *Sermons*, p. 67.

sire. Believers, you shall judge the evil, and familiarly converse with good, angels: you shall sit down with Abraham, Isaac, Jacob, and all the spirits of just men made perfect; and, to sum up all your happiness in one word, you shall see God the Father, Son, and Holy Ghost; and, by seeing God, be more and more like unto him, and pass from glory to glory, even to all eternity.[145]

Once again we notice the superb sense of climax.

But we also notice an important theological point. The pietism of Whitefield escapes the pietism of the medieval nominalists. It knows there is infinitely more to the Christian life than the inner experiences of here and now. Christian perfection is in the end the glory of the there and then, the glory of eternity. This is made clear by two more of Whitefield's biblical allusions. "Were I to entertain you whole ages with an account of it, when you come to heaven, you must say, with the queen of Sheba, 'Not half, no, not one thousandth part was told us.' All we can do here, is to go upon mount Pisgah, and, by the eye of faith, take a distant view of the promised land."[146]

Whitefield concludes the sermon by urging the congregation to accept Christ as wisdom, righteousness, sanctification, and redemption. For each point he poses a rhetorical question. What will your wisdom avail you if it does not make you wise unto salvation? Why will you not submit to the righteousness of Christ? Do you think your own righteousness will save you? "Why then will you not come to Christ for sanctification? Do you not desire to die the death of the righteous, and that your future state may be like theirs; I am persuaded you cannot bear the thoughts of being annihilated, much less of being miserable for ever. Whatever you may pretend, if you speak truth, you must confess, that conscience breaks in upon you in your more sober intervals whether you will or not, and even constrains you to believe that hell is no painted fire. And why then will you not come to Christ?"[147] This is without question an aggressive presentation of the gospel. The rhetoric is forceful! The sermon no doubt offended many who listened to it. Whitefield never gave a second thought or the shadow of a scruple about offending his listeners. Still, it is a great sermon and a great piece of oratory.

It raises a number of questions about the sorts of things usually said

145. Whitefield, *Sermons*, p. 69.
146. Whitefield, *Sermons*, p. 69.
147. Whitefield, *Sermons*, p. 70.

about George Whitefield. He always claimed to preach extemporaneously, and yet his use of rhetoric is so skilled one wonders how it was possible. The literary prowess of these sermons is every bit as impressive and memorable as Donne or Bossuet, yet no one seems to speak of Whitefield in the same breath as these widely recognized princes of the pulpit. Theologically Whitefield is frequently quite eloquent. His greatest fault seems to be that he was so aggressive. But, then, Jesus and his apostles would no doubt have to be hauled into court on the same charge.

Let us look at another sermon which conforms a bit more to the stereotype which has come down to us of the preachers of the Great Awakening. "The Method of Grace" takes as its text "They have healed also the hurt of the daughter of my people slightly, saying, Peace, peace, when there is no peace" (Jer. 6:14).

In the introduction Whitefield comments at some length on the ministry of Jeremiah. He lived in a day when there were many prophets who had a smooth and comforting message which people liked to hear. They preached peace, peace, when God had not sent them to preach peace. "As God can send a nation or people no greater blessing than to give them faithful, sincere, and upright ministers, so the greatest curse that God can possibly send upon a people in this world, is to give them over to blind, unregenerate, carnal, lukewarm, and unskilful guides." Whitefield was, of course, greatly criticized for his attacks on an unconverted ministry, of which this is an example. Secular writers and satirists of the eighteenth century attacked the clergy even more bitterly, but for a member of the clergy to say the same thing was not considered good form. Whitefield obviously sees great similarities between the ministry Jeremiah had been called to perform and the one he had been given. "The prophet gives a thundering message, that they might be terrified and have some convictions and inclinations to repent; but it seems that the false prophets, the false priests, went about stifling people's convictions, and when they were hurt or a little terrified, they were for daubing over the wound, telling them that Jeremiah was but an enthusiastic preacher."[148] Whitefield would not want to follow the example of the false prophets of Jeremiah's day. The members of his congregation are indeed right in suspecting things are not right between them and God, and Whitefield would want to show them how to set things right. Here we find a skillful example of a text being used as a springboard for diving into the subject.

148. Whitefield, *Sermons,* p. 49.

While the text serves as an introduction to the sermon, the rest of the sermon is hardly an exposition of it.

Before our preacher begins to explain the method of grace, he makes two cautions. "I take it for granted you believe religion to be an inward thing; you believe it to be a work in the heart, a work wrought in the soul by the power of the Spirit of God." But it also needs to be said that while God does not always work the same way in every heart, there is a pattern of God's work in our hearts, and this pattern is what Whitefield wants to speak about. In other words, this is to be a sermon on the *ordo salutis,* the steps to salvation. This is a standard method of the eighteenth-century evangelists to bring one to salvation: they describe the process. The empirical scientists of the period were doing this, and the pietists were too. What is interesting, however, is that this sermon preaches a different *ordo salutis* than the one we spoke of in the previous sermon.

The first step to salvation is conviction. "First, then, before you can speak peace to your hearts, you must be made to see, made to feel, made to weep over, made to bewail, your actual transgressions against the law of God."[149] This emphasis on feeling is, to be sure, of the very essence of pietism. Whitefield labors this point, expanding it into the various aspects of how one feels this conviction of sin. One must feel God's wrath against those who transgress his laws, that is, God's displeasure with particular sins, but one must also experience God's wrath against original sin.[150] One must feel and experience the justice of God's rejection of sin.[151] One must recognize the sin of self-righteousness. It is not enough to talk about it. One must feel it.[152] One can hardly be surprised that as Whitefield and Wesley and others preached this kind of experiential penance, those who listened wept and wailed as they felt God's anger against sin.

The second step in the process of salvation Whitefield describes in this sermon is laying hold of Christ. He makes a strong point that a historical faith is not the same thing as saving faith. Many people know about Christ and believe in his divinity, go to church every Sunday, maintain family prayers, and still have not felt Christ in their hearts. The sermon was preached in Scotland, we gather from the text, because

---

149. Whitefield, *Sermons,* p. 50.
150. Whitefield, *Sermons,* p. 51.
151. Whitefield, *Sermons,* p. 52.
152. Whitefield, *Sermons,* p. 53.

Whitefield compliments the people of Scotland for having good religious traditions. He warns his hearers that if they think they have always all their lives believed in Christ, they are deluded. He introduces the example of a certain Mr. Marshall, who thought he had been a Christian all his life but afterwards discovered he was mistaken. "Before you can speak peace to your heart, . . . you must be enabled to lay hold upon the perfect righteousness, the all-sufficient righteousness, of the Lord Jesus Christ; you must lay hold by faith on the righteousness of Jesus Christ, and then you shall have peace."[153]

Here we need to point out a sermon illustration which, more than anything we have heard before, draws on a personal experience. We have no idea who Mr. Marshall might have been. This is not a biblical figure nor a well-known historical figure. In all probability he was an ordinary person who had been reached by Whitefield's ministry. This kind of sermon illustration is very popular in our day, but before the days of evangelical pietism it was almost unheard of. It was, however, a development completely consistent with the aim and purposes of Whitefield and his colleagues.

Once again our preacher emphasizes that he is talking about a personal inward experience. "Did Jesus Christ ever give himself to you? Did you ever close with Christ by a lively faith, so as to feel Christ in your hearts, so as to hear him speaking peace to your souls? Did peace ever flow in upon your hearts like a river? Did you ever feel that peace that Christ spoke to his disciples? I pray God he may come and speak peace to you. These things you must experience."[154]

The third step in this *ordo salutis* is the Christian walk.

> But then, my dear friends, beware of resting on your first conversion. You that are young believers in Christ, you should be looking out for fresh discoveries of the Lord Jesus Christ every moment; you must not build upon your past experiences, you must not build upon a work within you, but always come out of yourselves to the righteousness of Jesus Christ without you; you must be always coming as poor sinners to draw water out of the wells of salvation; you must be forgetting the things that are behind, and be continually pressing forward to the things that are before. My dear friends, you must keep up a tender, close walk with the Lord Jesus Christ.

153. Whitefield, *Sermons*, pp. 53-54.
154. Whitefield, *Sermons*, p. 55.

Whitefield is constrained to affirm the doctrine of the perseverance of the saints, but he also is aware of the problem of backsliding. "If you cannot fall finally, you may fall foully, and may go with broken bones all your days."[155] Presumably he wants to say that those who have been saved once will in the end be saved even if through backsliding they suffer many miseries yet in this life. This sermon is not primarily occupied with this subject. Whitefield often got distracted in the course of his preaching. But now he returns to his subject. Here he is obviously addressing those who do not and never have had peace with God.

He begins the conclusion of his sermon:

> But what shall I say to you that have got no peace with God? — and these are, perhaps, the most of this congregation: it makes me weep to think of it. Most of you, if you examine your hearts, must confess that God never yet spoke peace to you; you are children of the devil, if Christ is not in you, if God has not spoken peace to your heart. Poor soul! what a cursed condition are you in. I would not be in your case for ten thousand, thousand worlds. Why? You are just hanging over hell. What peace can you have when God is your enemy, when the wrath of God is abiding upon your poor soul? Awake, then, you that are sleeping in a false peace; awake, ye carnal professors, ye hypocrites that go to church, receive the sacrament, read your Bibles, and never felt the power of God upon your hearts; you that are formal professors, you that are baptized heathens; awake, awake, and do not rest on a false bottom.[156]

Here the offense of the Evangelical Revival is made quite explicit. Whitefield assumes that most Christians who live in the fellowship of the church and make use of the means of grace are no Christians at all, but rather hypocrites. But even if one objects to what he is saying, one cannot help but be carried along by his rhetoric. "Blame me not for addressing myself to you; indeed, it is out of love to your souls. I see you are lingering in your Sodom, and wanting to stay there; but I come to you as the angel did to Lot, to take you by the hand. Come away, my dear brethren — fly, fly, fly for your lives to Jesus Christ, fly to a bleeding God, fly to a throne of grace; and beg of God to break your hearts, beg of God to convince you of your actual sins, beg of God to convince you of your original sin,

155. Whitefield, *Sermons,* p. 56.
156. Whitefield, *Sermons,* p. 57.

beg of God to convince you of your self-righteousness — beg of God to give you faith, and to enable you to close with Jesus Christ."[157] And now, as the most potent argument possible for the pietist, our preacher speaks of his own personal experience. Very rarely have we seen up to this point in the history of Christian preaching a preacher share his personal religious experience, but here we have it, just as we find it in the apostle Paul's sermon before Agrippa. "I know by sad experience what it is to be lulled asleep with a false peace; long was I lulled asleep, long did I think myself a Christian, when I knew nothing of the Lord Jesus Christ. I went perhaps farther than many of you do; I used to fast twice a-week, I used to pray sometimes nine times a-day, I used to receive the sacrament constantly every Lord's-day; and yet I knew nothing of Jesus Christ in my heart, I knew not that I must be a new creature — I knew nothing of inward religion in my soul."[158]

Whitefield never found anything inconsistent with his supposed Calvinism in arguing people into a conversion experience. In this sermon he invokes the wrath of God as an inducement to awaken from spiritual sleep.

> But there is no peace to the wicked. I know what it is to live a life of sin; I was obliged to sin in order to stifle conviction. And I am sure this is the way many of you take; If you get into company, you drive off conviction. But you had better go to the bottom at once; it must be done — your wound must be searched, or you must be damned. If it were a matter of indifference, I would not speak one word about it. But you will be damned without Christ. He is the way, he is the truth, and the life. I cannot think you should go to hell without Christ. How can you dwell with everlasting burnings? How can you abide the thought of living with the devil for ever? Is it not better to have some soul-trouble here, than to be sent to hell by Jesus Christ hereafter? What is hell, but to be absent from Christ? If there were no other hell, that would be hell enough. It will be hell to be tormented with the devil for ever.[159]

No one today is very sympathetic with this kind of preaching, and yet it seems to have been most effective in awakening the Church from a period of very dry formalism, sexual immorality, and deep-reaching heresy. One

157. Whitefield, *Sermons,* pp. 57-58.
158. Whitefield, *Sermons,* p. 58.
159. Whitefield, *Sermons,* pp. 59-60.

may very well conclude that Whitefield and Wesley were sent by God with this threat of damnation every bit as much as Jeremiah had been before them.

Another typical sermon, which in substance Whitefield preached again and again, is "The Lord Our Righteousness." Apparently this was an early sermon, perhaps taken down stenographically. Again a text from Jeremiah has been chosen, but this time the sermon is even less closely related to the text. The text does express the theme of the sermon, but not much more. With the first sentence Whitefield attacks his subject: "Whoever is acquainted with the nature of mankind in general, or the propensity of his own heart in particular, must acknowledge, that *self-righteousness* is the last idol that is rooted out of the heart: being once born under a covenant of works, it is natural for us all to have recourse to a covenant of works for our everlasting salvation." As Whitefield sees it, this is reason for the great popularity of the Pelagianism of so many Roman Catholics and the Arminianism of so many Anglicans. "I am sure, we are all Arminians by nature; and, therefore, no wonder so many natural men embrace that scheme."

After developing this theme a bit more, our preacher puts his thought in a rather far-out biblical metaphor.

> The righteousness of Jesus Christ is one of those great mysteries which the angels desire to look into, and seems to be one of the first lessons that God taught men after the fall. For, what were the coats that God made to put on our first parents, but types of the application of the merits or righteousness of Jesus Christ to believers' hearts? We are told, that those coats were made of skins of beasts; and, as beasts were not then food for men, we may fairly infer, that those beasts were slain in sacrifice, in commemoration of the great sacrifice, Jesus Christ, thereafter to be offered. And the skins of the beasts thus slain, being put on Adam and Eve, they were hereby taught how their nakedness was to be covered with the righteousness of the Lamb of God.[160]

As clever as this allegory is, some of us will find it a bit irreverent. It does show us, however, that Whitefield at least had an active imagination.

Our preacher, in good homiletical form, divides up his text, "The Lord our Righteousness." First, he intends to speak on whom we are to understand as Lord. Second, he intends to speak on how the Lord is our

160. Whitefield, *Sermons*, p. 72.

righteousness. Third, he will treat some objections to this doctrine. Fourth, he will point out some ill consequences which follow from denying it, and finally, he intends to conclude with an exhortation to come to Christ by faith, that we may say with the prophet, "The Lord our Righteousness." This is to be a five-point sermon.

If Whitefield began his sermon with an aggressive attack on Arminianism, he now continues it with an equally aggressive attack on Deism. The Deists he labels Arians, and Socinians. As Whitefield sees it, Jeremiah 23 speaks about the coming Messiah, and regards this Messiah as being God himself. Whitefield has, of course, in great brevity, given the historic Christian interpretation of the text. He believed the Deists were sufficiently answered by showing that their ideas are contrary to Scripture as the Church has always understood it. Deism is no more to be followed in the eighteenth century than Arianism was in the fourth century or Socinianism in the sixteenth century.[161]

Coming to how the Lord is to be our righteousness, Whitefield puts it in one word. It is by imputation. With this he goes briefly through the story of our fall in Adam and our redemption in Christ. There is nothing new or remarkable about this presentation. It is a standard recounting of the vicarious atonement of Christ. He sees this as "the amazing scene of *divine philanthropy.*"[162] One can hardly resist the temptation to suggest that somewhere Whitefield has gotten hold of the Greek Fathers, because this whole passage suggests acquaintance with the theology of Eastern Orthodoxy. This sermon treats Christ as "very God of very God." It sees God's redemptive work as "the divine condescension," and here takes up the subject of God's "philanthropia."

Whitefield is, to be sure, far too often painted in primitive colors, a sort of ministerial frontiersman, but he was in fact the spokesman of historic, orthodox Christianity when it had lost sight of its heritage in a terribly artificial age. The eighteenth century was supposed to have been the age of reason, yet its artificiality was unbounded. Its fashions in clothing were immediately evident, but perhaps more profound was its gardening. Eighteenth-century gardeners trimmed their lawns and hedges with mathematical precision, forcing nature into the contours of rococo geometry. Their philosophers tried to do the same thing with Christian theology, with equally deformed results. As one reads Whitefield's sermons two

---

161. Whitefield, *Sermons,* p. 73.
162. Whitefield, *Sermons,* p. 74, emphasis Whitefield's.

and a half centuries later, they look far more classical than they were perceived to be in the middle of the eighteenth century.

The greater part of this sermon is argumentation in support of the doctrine of justification by faith as Whitefield has advanced it. Basically his argument is that this is the doctrine Scripture teaches. He begins with the Sermon on the Mount, which his opponents advance as proof that one must live a moral life in order to be saved.[163] Whitefield counters by saying the Beatitudes show us that it is the inclination of the heart, meekness, poverty of spirit, and purity of heart which God requires, and these qualities of heart are different aspects of faith. His point is well taken, to be sure, but it hardly needs to be said that he is not at his best as an expounder of Scripture. Even if we agree with his theological point, it is not because we are convinced by his interpretation of the Scriptures. Whitefield brings up the story of the rich young ruler and the parable of the sheep and the goats and tries to answer his opponents' interpretation. Both these passages have frequently been used to counter justification by faith. With the parable Whitefield is fairly convincing. He points to the fact that the righteous are surprised to hear their good works are commended. Even though he does not have the great ability at exposition that preachers such as Luther, or Calvin, or Manton have shown, one finds it interesting that Whitefield, as great an orator as he was, did find it of value to argue a point of theology in a sermon. As anti-intellectual as many of the pietists were, they still were perfectly happy to carry on doctrinal controversy from the pulpit. In fact, they found it quite edifying.

The conclusion of this frankly aggressive sermon is an exhortation to accept the righteousness of Christ. First, Whitefield addresses sinners in general, then he addresses all kinds of different categories of people and calls them to saving faith. Often we notice that he makes several different applications of his sermons, adapting his message to the different spiritual states he perceives his congregation to represent. What is amazing is that this aggressive argumentation over a point of doctrine is the driving power behind an evangelistic appeal.

All in all, Whitefield's message was much the same as that of Wesley, Spener, and the other leading pietists we have spoken of in this chapter. What sets him apart is the way he developed a style of pulpit oratory that fit his message. If pietism sought to develop a religion of the heart, it had really been very slow to shape rhetorical forms suitable to these aims. In

163. Whitefield, *Sermons*, p. 76.

the pulpit Spener sounded much like the traditional German Lutheran preacher. In fact, he was not really at his best in the pulpit; apparently he shone most brightly in his small groups. Francke advocated more attention to admonition and less attention to the exposition of the Scriptures, but his own preaching never set the stellar example of what he advocated. Wesley was so straight that he seemed almost the antithesis of the religion of the heart. Whitefield, on the other hand, was an orator of pathos, a public speaker who moved the hearts of those to whom he spoke.

It was Whitefield who convinced Wesley of the legitimacy of preaching in the open air. Little of that had been done in England since the heyday of the friars. The Franciscans and the Dominicans had been masters of it, but it seems to have all but disappeared by the end of the seventeenth century. "Field preaching," as it was called at the time, was a mark of enthusiasts, and as we have seen, enthusiasm was always a most shameful sin in the eyes of the Anglican establishment. Better stodgy than hearty! But with the field preaching came extemporaneous preaching. Once Whitefield disposed of the carefully written manuscript and began preaching to his congregation face to face and eye to eye, somehow a religion of the heart took fire.

Cicero had always said orators learn their art quickly or not at all. The Greeks and Romans well understood that oratory is a passion which wells up from the heart. Yes, there is something inescapably pietistic about real oratory. Whitefield had that passion, the naive spiritual passion of youth, and driven on by it he brought all the drama, the gestures, and the anecdotes of a natural-born storyteller into his sermons. Stories of his travels, personal reminiscences, and human interest stories filled his sermons. He used the most shameless puns, the most far-fetched allegories. Satire, invective, and even ridicule spice his sermons. Protestant plain style was over the hill once Whitefield took to the fields.

Even his most sympathetic admirers admitted that whatever organization his published sermons may have had, the sermons he preached were often poorly organized. They lacked structure and meandered from topic to topic. True, the sort of extemporaneous preaching he advocated has its negative side, but there is something very admirable about it as well. Whitefield brought vitality to the pulpit, a vitality which for several generations had been sadly lacking.

VIII. Samuel Davies (1723-61)

The apostle of the Great Awakening in Virginia, Samuel Davies was the most well balanced, the most literate, the most popular in his appeal, and at the same time the most theologically cogent American preacher of the eighteenth century.[164] Writing about the time of the Civil War, William Sprague, the learned historian of the American pulpit, quite simply called him the greatest all-round preacher America had produced. For more than a century after his death, Davies' three-volume collection of sermons was widely read throughout America, because he was such an excellent spokesman for the Evangelical Revival. He may not have been the original theologian of surpassing genius that Jonathan Edwards was, but he was a capable theologian who had a gift for putting theological truths simply and clearly.[165] His sermons are theologically sound, but even more importantly, they are theologically perceptive. Davies drew large crowds and was a popular preacher, as were George Whitefield and Gilbert Tennent, and yet we never hear of emotional outbursts attending his preaching. He was a consummate orator, yet never a rabble-rouser. He was prophetic and preached about sensitive problems of the day without any trace of the contentiousness we find in some of the New Lights of lesser magnitude. He seemed to be equally at home preaching to black slaves and to Virginia planters. His preaching was both fervent and gentlemanly.

Davies was born of a pious Welsh family which had come to Pennsylvania very early and had settled in Merion Township across the Schuylkill from Philadelphia. A good number of other Welsh families had gathered in the same area, as one gathers even today from all the Welsh

164. On the life of Samuel Davies, see Wesley M. Gewehr, *The Great Awakening in Virginia, 1740-1790* (Durham, N.C.: Duke University Press, 1930); George William Pilcher, *Samuel Davies: Apostle of Dissent in Colonial Virginia* (Knoxville: University of Tennessee Press, [1971]); and William Buell Sprague, *Annals of the American Pulpit, or Commemorative Notices of Distinguished American Clergymen of Various Denominations* (New York: Robert Carter & Brothers, 1857-[1869]). Further information is available in the introductory essay by William Buell Sprague in *Sermons of the Rev. Samuel Davies, A.M.,* 3 vols. (Philadelphia: Presbyterian Board of Publication, 1854; reprint, Morgan, Pa.: Soli Deo Gloria Publications, 1993-95), hereafter Samuel Davies, *Sermons.*

165. On how Davies fits into the Great Awakening generally, see Gewehr, *The Great Awakening in Virginia, 1740-1790;* Alan Heimert and Perry Miller, eds., *The Great Awakening* (Indianapolis and New York: Bobbs-Merrill, 1967); and Charles Hartshorn Maxson, *The Great Awakening in the Middle Colonies* (Chicago: University of Chicago Press, 1920).

place-names in the area, from Bala Cynwyd to Bryn Mawr. Most of the settlers were engaged in farming. The actual homesite of the Davies family is on the campus of Haverford College. After a generation in Pennsylvania, the family moved to Delaware to another Welsh community not far from New Castle. It was in Delaware that Samuel was born. Apparently neither of his parents could read or write, but young Samuel was put in the local school until he was fifteen or sixteen years old, when he was sent off to the academy of the Reverend Samuel Blair in Faggs Manor.

The academy was an excellent school. Blair had studied with the Tennents at the Log College in Neshaminy and was particularly proficient at the classical languages. Presbyterians of either Old Light or New Light persuasion strongly emphasized the study of the classical languages, as one could easily gather because they chose the name "academy" for their schools. They may have started these schools on the frontier, but the tradition of Christian humanism they inherited from the Reformation was still strong. Blair was respected as a minister of considerable learning, but even more he was beloved as one of the most ardent preachers of the Great Awakening. Davies studied at Faggs Manor for something more than six years. He must have been there in 1740 when George Whitefield preached to twelve thousand people.

In 1746, when Davies presented himself to New Castle Presbytery for licensure, he had thoroughly imbibed the spirit of the Great Awakening. Davies' services were needed all over Pennsylvania, Delaware, and Maryland. Many new churches were springing into existence, and the demand for young ministers who could preach the Awakening was heavy. Less than a year later the Presbytery of New Castle ordained him as an evangelist to Virginia, at a time when no settled preacher of the Awakening was in the colony. Several preachers who represented the movement had itinerated through the colony, but the Anglican clergy was uniformly closed to the movement. Not even Whitefield, himself an Anglican, was welcomed by the clergy of the established Church. There was, however, a significant group of adherents to the movement, particularly in Hanover County, just north of Richmond. Two years later Davies finally became the official pastor of the Presbyterian Church in Hanover. Having paid a visit to the royal governor in Williamsburg, he had managed to charm him so thoroughly that he won a license from him to preach. Governor William Gooch was impressed by the sincerity and orderliness of Davies' approach. He also recognized that as a Presbyterian he had a certain claim on the support of the Crown. If Presbyterianism was the established

Church of Scotland, why could it not at least be tolerated in Virginia? The Church of England was not eager to lose her position of privilege in Virginia, and Davies had a major work of diplomacy ahead of him in order to win a place for the Presbyterian congregations he spawned in the colony. Davies was a man of irenic spirit, as was the governor, and it was to the credit of both that the spiritual power of the Great Awakening manifested itself so peacefully in Virginia.

One often asks how the Great Awakening came to have such a following in Virginia when Anglicanism was so completely established, and so completely closed to it. Some Presbyterian churches in the middle colonies and some Congregational churches in New England were closed to the Great Awakening, but others were not. If one wanted to be part of the revival in Virginia, one had to leave the Anglican Church and join the Presbyterian Church. The reason usually given for the attraction of the Great Awakening is that it was dealing with the profound spiritual realities of life whereas the Anglicanism of Virginia tended to preach an abstract sort of moralism, cooked up in the theological leisure of Oxford and Cambridge and served lukewarm by clergymen who for one reason or another were unable to get "a good church" back in England. The preachers of the Great Awakening, on the other hand, these New Light preachers, had had a profound experience of the presence of God. They had entered into the holy of holies and heard the seraphic song. They knew they were men of unclean lips dwelling in the midst of a people of unclean lips, and yet their guilt had been taken away. Their lips had been touched with glowing coals from the altar, and therefore they preached. They knew they had been called by none other than God himself to do their preaching. The preachers of the Great Awakening may have studied at some log college on the frontier and may well have lacked the patina of the leading academic institutions, but they had studied the Scriptures, and they had even studied them in the classical languages. They had read the great theologians of the past as well. They had studied and studied hard, but somehow one detected more than the patina of learning. One sensed the glow of holiness. The preachers of the Great Awakening clearly knew God.

Davies' sermons are remarkable in that they treat the great religious issues, the issues of sin and holiness, of heaven and hell, of eternal blessedness and eternal damnation. It has often been suggested that these issues were particularly urgent on the frontier because death was so imminent. It is imagined that human mortality was much more an issue out in the colonies than back in London or even in Boston or Williamsburg. Perhaps that does explain something of the success of the Great Awakening, but it really does not do justice to the question. Whitefield got almost as many hearers in London as he did in Philadelphia. England had its awakening just as America did, and the two occurred almost simultaneously. It was not really a matter of the threat of death being particularly acute at that time and place so much as that the great questions of life had a way of surfacing again and again. They may be forgotten for a while. People may be diverted from thinking about them, but in the end the ultimate questions of life and death, faith and reason, or time and eternity keep reasserting themselves simply because they are the ultimate questions. It was about these questions that Davies preached, and that is why people flocked to hear him. He was completely devoted to preaching about the most important concerns of life.

His sermon "The Method of Salvation through Jesus Christ" offers a good example of his ability to treat the ultimate subjects of religion.[166] In fact, the sermon's introduction makes the point that he wants to speak about the most central of all subjects, that which will lead most directly to saving the souls of his hearers.[167] This is why he chose as his text the words of Jesus to Nicodemus, "For God so loved the world, that he gave his only begotten Son, that whosoever believeth in him should not perish, but have everlasting life" (John 3:16 KJV). Davies' concern is that of an itinerant evangelist who cannot count on the same congregation gathered around his pulpit year after year. In theory he was a settled pastor of a church in Hanover, Virginia, but in fact he was Sunday by Sunday preaching to different people. He saw himself as an evangelist preaching to people who had never heard the gospel. He did a great deal of itinerating, and this was the way the preaching of the Great Awakening was approached. The preachers were all at heart itinerant preachers like Whitefield and Wesley or like Francis and Dominic even if, like Davies, they at least had to appear to be settled pastors of local congregations. Being ever aware that he was constantly preaching to people who did not know the cardinal points of the gospel, he preached again and again on this text which he regarded as the epitome of the gospel. Even a brief look at the list of sermon titles makes it clear how often he preached on the subject of salvation and how it was to be received:

166. Samuel Davies, *Sermons,* 1:109-36.
167. Samuel Davies, *Sermons,* 1:109.

"Sinner Entreated to Be Reconciled to God"
"The Nature and Process of Spiritual Life"
"The Compassion of Christ to Weak Believers"
"The Divine Mercy to Mourning Penitents"

Davies had been ordained as an evangelist by the Presbytery of New Castle, and consequently his preaching dealt with the central concerns of the gospel.

What is particularly interesting in this sermon is its balance and clarity. The first point Davies wants to make is that we are in a perishing condition. It was, of course, the ability and willingness of the evangelical preachers to deal with the question of human fallibility which commended them to their age. It was this by which so many of their contemporaries came to realize that they were the realists of the day. So much in the eighteenth century was frivolous and artificial, and yet the artificiality fooled no one. It was an age of satire as well, yet few people were willing to speak of death and judgment, at least not as honestly as such evangelical preachers as Wesley, Edwards, and Davies. But Davies was also willing to speak of God's redemptive work in Christ. This is the second point of the sermon. The text, John 3:16, makes particularly clear that a way of salvation has been opened. God has given his Son for our salvation. This is particularly characteristic of Davies' message. He emphasized the objectivity of God's redemptive work in Christ. Pietists had a tendency to focus on the subjective religious experience of the individual and pass by the objective historical act by which Christ made atonement for our sins. Davies does indeed preach that Christ made atonement for sin. He tries to show the appropriateness and reasonableness of the doctrine of the vicarious atonement. For Davies it is important that this be known and understood.

Having laid this groundwork, our evangelist tells us how this redemptive work of Christ brings us to salvation. It is by faith that we are enabled to appropriate Christ's redemptive work for our own salvation, and Davies proceeds to tell us just what faith is. First, faith presupposes a deep sense of our helplessness.[168] One needs to be aware of the need of a savior before Christ can be embraced as Savior.

I wish and pray you may this day see yourselves in this true, though mortifying light. It is the want of this sense of things that keeps such

168. Samuel Davies, *Sermons,* 1:124.

crowds of persons unbelievers among us. It is the want of this that causes the Lord Jesus to be so little esteemed, so little sought for, so little desired among us. In short, it is the want of this that is the great occasion of so many perishing from under the gospel, and, as it were, from between the hands of a Savior. It is this, alas! that causes them to perish, like the impenitent thief on the cross, with a Savior by their side. O that you once rightly knew yourselves, you would then soon know Jesus Christ, and receive salvation from his hand.[169]

Second, faith implies the enlightening of our understanding. This is a particularly important point for Davies. God enlightens our understanding in order that we might have faith. "While the sinner lies undone and helpless in himself, and looking about in vain for some relief, it pleases a gracious God to shine into his heart, and enable him to see his glory in the face of Jesus Christ. Now this once neglected Saviour appears not only absolutely necessary, but also all-glorious and lovely, and the sinner's heart is wrapt away, and for ever captivated with his beauty: now the neglected gospel appears in a new light, as different from all his former apprehensions as if it were quite another thing." Now that the understanding has been enlightened,

> The sinner is enabled to embrace this Saviour with all his heart, and to give a voluntary, cheerful consent to this glorious scheme of salvation. Now all his former unwillingness and reluctance are subdued, and his heart no more draws back from the terms of the gospel, but he complies with them, and that not merely out of constraint and necessity, but out of free choice, and with the greatest pleasure and delight. How does his heart now cling to the blessed Jesus with the most affectionate endearment! How is he lost in wonder, joy, and gratitude, at the survey of the divine perfections, as displayed in this method of redemption![170]

Finally Davies makes the point that faith in Christ implies a humble trust or dependence upon Christ for the forgiveness of sin, communion with God, and every blessing.[171]

As we have already indicated, the preaching of judgment, or as they put it, "the terrors of the Lord," was an essential characteristic of this school of preaching. Protestants of the nineteenth and early twentieth

169. Samuel Davies, *Sermons,* 1:124-25.
170. Samuel Davies, *Sermons,* 1:125-26.
171. Samuel Davies, *Sermons,* 1:126.

centuries found this very embarrassing. And we immediately dismiss it as "hellfire and damnation" preaching. As we shall say in our section on Jonathan Edwards and his famous sermon, "Sinners in the Hands of an Angry God," there was more to it than its more recent critics have realized.

Davies' sermon "The Doom of the Incorrigible Sinner" is an example of how he preached hellfire and damnation. The sermon takes as its text Proverbs 29:1 (KJV), "He that being often reproved, hardeneth his neck, shall suddenly be destroyed, and that without remedy." The sermon begins with a fine presentation of the character of the book of Proverbs and the nature of proverbs in general.[172] One finds again and again in Davies' sermons a very serious attempt to give us a clear exposition of the text of Scripture. Here again we find in Davies something not typical of the pietist movement. The sermon is divided under the three phrases of the text. First he addresses the phrase "He that being often reproved." He speaks of how we have often been warned against wickedness by the wisdom of other men, by the providence of God, by the Word of God itself, and even by our own consciences.[173] At one place our preacher reminds his hearers of the chastening hand of providence in the French and Indian War which had struck such fear into the colonists. "The providence of God has also reproved us, in common with our countrymen, by the public calamities that have hovered over or fallen upon our land and nation; and particularly by the ravages and desolations of war. Providence has commissioned Indian savages and French papists to be our reprovers, and loudly admonished us with the horrid roar of cannons, the clangor of martial trumpets, and all the dread artillery of ruin and death. What ear among us has not heard, what heart has not trembled, at this terrible warning!" Here we find our preacher interpreting the fears, the defeats, and the tragedies of life as it was being experienced by the people of his own day. Davies continues:

> But has he [that is, God] not often laid aside all instruments, and reproved you more immediately by his Spirit? Has not his Spirit been long and frequently striving with you; reproving you of sin; alarming you with apprehensions of your danger; exciting in you good resolutions, and serious thoughts of reformation? Has not the blessed Spirit at times borne home the word upon your hearts with unusual power,

172. Samuel Davies, *Sermons,* 2:316-18.
173. Samuel Davies, *Sermons,* 2:318.

and roused your conscience to fall upon you with terrible though friendly violence? Which leads me to add,

You have been your own monitors; I mean your consciences have often admonished and warned you; have whispered in your breasts, that "this course of vice and irreligion will not do: this carelessness and indifferency in the concerns of your souls, this stupid neglect of God and eternal things will not end well." Conscience has often honestly pronounced your doom: "Thou art a guilty, wicked creature, under the displeasure of God. Thou art destitute of true vital religion, and hast no title to the divine favour. If thou die in this condition, thou wilt be undone for ever." Thus has conscience warned you; and you have, no doubt, sometimes sweated and agonized under its chastisements. Though you have preposterously labored to bribe it, or suppress it by violence; yet it has still borne at least a faint testimony for its Master, and against you. Thus you always carry a reprover in your own bosoms wherever you go; and though every mouth around you should be silent, this will speak, if you do but attend, and give it fair play.[174]

Our preacher now turns to the phrase "hardeneth his neck." This, he explains, is a metaphor often used in Scripture "to signify an unyielding, incorrigible spirit, resolute in disobedience in spite of all restraints; in spite of advice, dissuasives, and reproofs."[175] He tells his congregation that he does not like to presume that any of them have hardened their necks against the warnings of God, but it is a common problem, and so he must ask them to examine their own consciences to see if they have resisted the leading of God's Spirit. He asks them in a series of questions if they have refused the promptings of God to lead a more devout life and to treat their neighbor with greater consideration. Finally he presses on to the third phrase of the text, "shall suddenly be destroyed, and that without remedy." There can be no medicine to the self-willed, headstrong creature, Davies warns. He will not apply it himself and pushes off every friendly hand that would apply it.

Reproofs and admonitions from God and men, and our own consciences, are the great means to recover sinners: and while these are ineffectual, no other can possibly have any effect. How can he be reclaimed from sin, who will sin in opposition to all restraints! In

---

174. Samuel Davies, *Sermons,* 2:323-24.
175. Samuel Davies, *Sermons,* 2:326.

opposition to the checks of conscience, and the strivings of the holy Spirit within, and the united dissuasives and rebukes of Providence, of the word of God, and of all his friends from without! Neither God nor all his creatures can reform and save such a wretch, while he continues proof against all the means of reformation and salvation. It is unavoidable, that he should suddenly be destroyed; and there is no help for it; he must be given up as an incurable. The whole universe may look on, and pity him; but, alas! they cannot help him; he has the instrument of self-murder in his own hand: and he will not part with it, but uses it against his own life, without control.[176]

Read in its entirety, this is an exceptionally fine sermon. It is a good exposition of the text. It has a fine grasp of the ways of the human heart, and it is a superb piece of oratory. One could admire it for its literary beauty alone, but the question our age most naturally asks is whether sermons on the judgment of God really have a place in the Christian pulpit. Should not such preaching be left to the Old Testament prophets and John the Baptist? In actual fact, Christian preachers have usually felt that the faithful preacher must treat these subjects. Even Jesus could preach hellfire and damnation sermons, as demonstrated by his sermon on the Last Judgment in Mark 13 and Matthew 24. Warning humanity of the dangers of sin and the ruin caused by sin has a legitimate place in the ministry of the Word. In fact, one could go so far as to say that any preaching ministry which neglects the subject of God's judgment against sin, the fact of human fallibility, and the fact of man's rebellion against God's law and resistance to God's grace has not really dealt with the whole picture of human existence.

The eighteenth century was remarkable in its exaltation of frivolity. It tried so hard to paint life in the prettiest colors possible. Watteau, Fragonard, and Bouchet insisted that life was all satin and roses. Today we recognize the utter unreality of their paintings. The court of Versailles tried to believe in a life without care or tears, without the demands of justice or righteousness, and by the end of the century its final judgment descended in the fury of the French Revolution. The preachers of the Great Awakening, on the other hand, were among the realists of their century. Their sermons interpreted the failures of life and penetrated its tragedies. They dealt with the shortness and the insecurities of life. They named the naivetés of life and exposed them for what they really are. They taught

176. Samuel Davies, *Sermons*, 2:331.

their hearers to respect the laws of God as guides for living. They insisted that the ways of God are indeed the best ways. They taught the kindly intentions of even the most difficult ways of providence. If great crowds listened to these sermons, it was because the message dealt with the life the listeners were experiencing. Its realism was recognized.

Another essential religious issue Davies addressed was holiness, as in the sermon "The Connection between Present Holiness and Future Felicity."[177] The text is Hebrews 12:14 (KJV), "Follow . . . holiness, without which no man shall see the Lord." The most interesting part of the sermon is its description of holiness. Davies begins by defining holiness as "conformity in heart and practice to the revealed will of God." A bit further on he says, "We are holy when his image is stamped upon our hearts and reflected in our lives."[178] For human beings holiness is a joyful reflection of the holiness of God. That is the principle behind this text. Without holiness we cannot see God because without this disposition toward him we could never be happy in the enjoyment of him. Those who are not happily disposed toward God's will would hardly be content where God's will is perfectly obeyed. In elaborating this Davies first makes the point that true holiness delights in God's holiness. His exposition of this is remarkable.

> Self-love may prompt us to love him for his goodness to us; and so, many unregenerate men may have a selfish love to God on this account. But to love God because he is infinitely holy, because he bears an infinite detestation to all sin, and will not indulge his creatures in the neglect of the least instance of holiness, but commands them to be holy as he is holy, this is a disposition connatural to a renewed soul only, and argues a conformity to his image. Every nature is most agreeable to itself, and a holy nature is most agreeable to a holy nature.[179]

Next he makes the point that holiness delights in the law of God because of its purity.[180] Then he speaks of holiness as delight in the gospel of salvation. The passage is so rich we have to cite it in full:

> Now, it is evident, that without either of these the moral perfections of the Deity, particularly his holiness, could not be illustrated, or even se-

177. Samuel Davies, *Sermons,* 1:268-84.
178. Samuel Davies, *Sermons,* 1:271.
179. Samuel Davies, *Sermons,* 1:272.
180. Samuel Davies, *Sermons,* 1:274.

cured in the salvation of a sinner. Had he received an apostate race into favour, who had conspired in the most unnatural rebellion against him, without any satisfaction, his holiness would have been eclipsed; it would not have appeared that he had so invincible an abhorrence of sin, so zealous a regard for the vindication of his own holy law; or to his veracity, which had threatened condign punishment to offenders. But by the satisfaction of Christ, his holiness is illustrated in the most conspicuous manner: now it appears, that God would upon no terms save a sinner but that of adequate satisfaction, and that no other was sufficient but the suffering of his co-equal Son, otherwise he would not have appointed him to sustain the character of a Mediator; and now it appears that his hatred of sin is such that he would not let it pass unpunished even in his own Son, when only imputed to him. In like manner, if sinners, while unholy, were admitted into communion with God in heaven, it would obscure the glory of his holiness, and it would not then appear that such was the purity of his nature that he could have no fellowship with sin. But now it is evident, that even the blood of Immanuel cannot purchase heaven to be enjoyed by a sinner while unholy, but that every one that arrives at heaven must first be sanctified. An unholy sinner can no more be saved, while such, by the gospel than by the law; but here lies the difference, that the gospel makes provision for his sanctification, which is gradually carried on here, and perfected at death, before his admission into the heavenly glory.[181]

One who is holy delights in both law and gospel because they are the revelation of the God who is holy. He is not forced into a servile compliance with God's will for fear of punishment, but in his innermost being he delights in holiness and the ways of holiness. It is from this that true religion springs. Here is no place for antinomian licentiousness or a merely formal religion. Holiness delights in the duties of holiness toward both God and man and earnestly desires communion with God through the performing of these duties. The service of God is the pleasure of a holy soul. One thing will holiness have: to dwell in the house of the Lord and behold his beauty. The sermon must have been tremendously moving when it was preached by a minister who was greatly beloved for his holiness. Even when read today, it is a sermon of astounding beauty. No wonder there was a great awakening! When eternal priorities like this are proclaimed with integrity, there is no mystery as to why there is a revival.

181. Samuel Davies, *Sermons,* 1:276.

Samuel Davies is one of those preachers who is distinguished both by the purity of his message and by the excellence of his oratorical gifts. People listened to him because of the gospel he preached, but he preached it magnificently. He also wrote it down with great literary ability. One finds oneself moved almost as much by reading his sermons as one would have been hearing them preached. Unlike many of the preachers of the Great Awakening, Davies wrote his sermons out in full and then memorized them. He often extemporized on his written manuscript and appeared in the pulpit to be free of his manuscript. Pietism encouraged its preachers to preach extemporaneously. Whitefield was among the most extemporaneous of preachers, and those most influenced by him tended to think that real preaching had to be extemporaneous. Spontaneity was thought of as the proof that the sermon came from the heart. Again we find in Davies an exception to the usual patterns of pietism. In his sermons was a recognition that oratory is quite different from written prose. Even in reading the sermons we are aware that it is oratory we are reading. He seems to have fused the two traditions. His sermons contain both the careful organization of thought characteristic of the written sermon and the vitality of extemporaneous speech.

One interesting bit of history which testifies to Davies' great oratorical ability is that when Patrick Henry, one of America's greatest political orators, was a boy, he frequently sat under Davies' pulpit in Hanover, Virginia. He, as his father, was a member of the Church of England. His uncle, also named Patrick Henry, was minister of the Episcopal church in Hanover, but his mother was a Presbyterian, and she regularly took her to church and, Sunday by Sunday, heard Davies preach. Davies' influence on the future orator of the American Revolution seems to have been considerable.[182]

One way Davies was typical of eighteenth-century pietism was his interest in hymnody. He has a claim to being the first American hymn writer.[183] He frequently wrote a hymn for the conclusion of his sermons, much as the Wesleys were doing at the same time in England. In fact, the Wesleys even included one of Davies' hymns in the Methodist hymnal. For the pietists the singing of an appropriate hymn at the conclusion of the sermon was an opportunity for the congregation to affirm or seal the

182. Cf. Pilcher, *Samuel Davies*, pp. 83-85.
183. Cf. Louis F. Benson, "President Davies as a Hymnwriter," *Journal of the Presbyterian Historical Society* 2 (1903): 277-86.

165

gospel that had been proclaimed. Their hymnody had covenantal significance. It was a doxological profession of faith, an acclamation of the saving presence of God with his people. As time went on, congregations
strongly influenced by pietism would normally sing a hymn immediately
after the sermon. If for Calvin the sermon led to prayer, for the pietists
preaching led to hymnody. It was surely their hymnody that was their
greatest contribution to the worship of Protestantism.

Davies was above all an evangelist, as we have had several occasions
to remark. What is of particular interest was that he saw a strong connection between evangelism and the celebration of Communion. Evangelism
was a call to join with God's people in the celebration of the Sacrament.
This is particularly clear in his sermon "The Sufferings of Christ, and
Their Consequent Joys and Blessings."[184] The text for the sermon, obviously preached at the celebration of the Lord's Supper, is Isaiah 53:10-11.
The sermon clearly shows that the way Davies expected his converts to
express their conversion was at the celebration of Communion. It was
there that those who received the gospel affirmed the covenant. The theology of the Sacrament which the sermon expresses is clearly covenantal.
It is in Christ's blood that the covenant is sealed, and it is by sharing in
the bread and receiving the cup of the new covenant that the believer receives Christ and the blessing of his redemption. To think of evangelistic
preaching in terms of the celebration of the Lord's Supper was characteristic of Scottish Presbyterianism from the time of the Reformation. We see
here that the idea lived on in the earliest Presbyterian churches in America, even after the advent of pietism.

Samuel Davies' success in establishing the Great Awakening in Virginia rapidly became known throughout the colonies. He was recognized
as one of the best spokesmen of the movement, and thus was asked by the
trustees of the College of New Jersey to accompany Gilbert Tennent to
Great Britain to raise funds for the fledgling institution. Davies arrived in
London on Christmas Day of 1753. He was received as a preacher with
even more enthusiasm than Tennent, and a year later was able to return to
America with sufficient funds to build Nassau Hall. Returning to Virginia, he continued to strengthen the congregations which had been organized by the disciples of the Great Awakening. More and more the movement was recognized as a cohesive force in binding together the colonists
as they faced the challenges of the French and Indian War and began to

---

184. Samuel Davies, *Sermons,* 2:9-32.

166

expand toward the west. Five years later, when the College of New Jersey was looking for a new president to succeed Jonathan Edwards, Davies was invited to be the new president, and in 1759 left Virginia to take up those responsibilities in Princeton. The young president, not yet forty years old, entered into his work with considerable enthusiasm. In the course of his second year he fell ill and died. It was with great sorrow that the College of New Jersey buried yet another young president. Edwards had likewise died in the presidency of Princeton in 1758. Now Davies, another very promising young leader of the Great Awakening, had died as well. Even at that, in his short life Samuel Davies, like Edwards, had brought America a long way toward achieving spiritual maturity. With the Great Awakening the American church became independent in a way that the American state would not become until a generation later.

CHAPTER III

New England

There are good reasons for treating the Puritans of New England in the chapter we devoted to the Puritans of old England. There is much that bound together the Puritans of the Old World and the New World. They shared many of the same insights into the nature of the ministry of the Word and its place in the worship of the Church. Their passion for preaching was much the same. The plain style was a common feature — and much else. There is one overriding reason, however, for treating New England separately: their preachers were confronted with a very different situation. In England Puritans were a minority, except for a brief period, but in New England they had the responsibility of guiding a whole society. The ministry of the Word in New England had a unique preeminence in a society that looked to it for guidance in all aspects of life. New England expected more of the ministry of the Word than any other society. Professor Stout claims that never before or since has a society listened so intently to so many sermons, supported so many learned and conscientious preachers, or taken the reading and preaching of the Scriptures with such seriousness.[1] For this reason we will look at the ministry of the Word in New England separately.[2]

1. Harry S. Stout, *The New England Soul: Preaching and Religious Culture in Colonial New England* (New York and Oxford: Oxford University Press, 1986).
2. For general works on New England Puritanism and its preaching, see the following: Sacvan Bercovitch, *The American Jeremiad* (Madison: University of Wisconsin Press, 1978); Sargent Bush, Jr., *The Writings of Thomas Hooker: Spiritual Adventure in Two Worlds* (Madison: University of Wisconsin Press, 1980); Emory Elliott, *Power and the Pul-*

This unique situation is undoubtedly why the Church of New England gave such great attention to developing two genres of the ministry of the Word: the evangelistic ministry and the prophetic ministry. It is interesting that this double emphasis has, ever since the first generation of New England preachers, continued through the whole history of the American church. To be sure, the preachers of colonial New England had a very particular way of understanding evangelistic preaching, which will become evident as we go along. Harry Stout has pointed out this double emphasis. Having read through all available sermons, published sermons as well as ministers' manuscript sermons, and even the notes of those who heard these sermons, Professor Stout tells us that while the prophetic sermons preached on fast days and other occasions were the sermons most frequently published, the regular weekly sermons for the Lord's Day tended to be devoted more to what we have called evangelistic sermons. The typical Lord's Day sermon was primarily concerned with showing the way of salvation — and not only with starting out on that way, but even more with continuing in it.[3] The famous jeremiads were preached on fast days, not on the Lord's Day. As time went by they took on greater and greater prominence. The regular Sunday-by-Sunday preaching, however, tended to be devoted to preaching through individual books or even more often chapters of Scripture.[4] There were great numbers of series of sermons on shorter passages of Scripture such as the parable of the ten virgins or the Beatitudes. There were whole series on single verses. Both evangelistic and prophetic sermons were always expository. That was a basic principle of Puritan preaching. A sermon was basically expository, whatever else it was supposed to be.

---

pit in Puritan New England (Princeton: Princeton University Press, 1975); Everett H. Emerson, John Cotton (New Haven: College and University Press with Twayne Publishers, 1965); David D. Hall, The Faithful Shepherd: A History of the New England Ministry in the Seventeenth Century (Chapel Hill: University of North Carolina Press, 1972); E. Brooks Holifield, The Covenant Sealed: The Development of Puritan Sacramental Theology in Old and New England, 1570-1720 (New Haven: Yale University Press, 1974); Babette May Levy, Preaching in the First Half Century of New England (Hartford: American Society of Church History, 1945); Robert Middlekauff, The Mathers: Three Generations of Puritan Intellectuals, 1596-1728 (New York: Oxford University Press, 1971); Perry Miller, Errand into the Wilderness (Cambridge: Harvard University Press, Belknap Press, 1956); Norman Pettit, The Heart Prepared: Grace and Conversion in Puritan Spiritual Life (New Haven: Yale University Press, 1966); and Frank Shuffleton, Thomas Hooker, 1586-1647 (Princeton: Princeton University Press, 1977).

3. Stout, The New England Soul, pp. 38f.
4. Stout, The New England Soul, p. 34.

I. The Liturgical Setting of the Puritan Sermon

Nothing helps us understand the New England sermon quite so much as its liturgical context. In England the Puritans were frequently forced to preach at some other time than the regular service of worship. This was not their preference, but the compromise forced upon them by the established Church. In New England they were free to preach at worship, and this they valued greatly. They understood preaching to be worship, as we will show. The reading and preaching of the Word of God was the sacred service of the whole congregation. It was properly approached with prayer and praise, and it appropriately led to the celebration of the sacraments and the giving of alms.

The Puritan churches of New England never produced either a prayer book or a directory for worship.[5] When they began to worship in Plymouth Plantation or in Massachusetts Bay Colony, the *Westminster Directory for Worship* had not yet been written. No doubt they were guided to some extent by the *Genevan Psalter* of 1542, but there must have been other influences. There was no uniformity. We know that both John Davenport and Thomas Hooker in Connecticut had some original ideas. One of the best documents, although brief, comes from John Cotton. In two places he briefly describes the worship of First Church in Boston: in *The True Constitution of a Particular Visible Church,* published in 1642,[6] and in *The Way of the Churches of Christ in New England,* published in 1645.[7] As time went on, however, the influence of the *Westminster Directory* seems to have increased.

The impression one gets from John Cotton is that the service began rather abruptly with the pastoral prayer:

---

5. There is much work to be done on this subject. See Charles E. Hambrick-Stowe, *The Practice of Piety: Puritan Devotional Disciplines in Seventeenth-Century New England* (Chapel Hill: Published for the Institute of Early American History and Culture, Williamsburg, Virginia, by the University of North Carolina Press, 1982), and Horton Davies, *The Worship of the American Puritans, 1629-1730* (New York: P. Lang, 1990).

6. John Cotton, *The True Constitution of a particular visible Church, proved by Scripture* (London: Printed for Samuel Satterthwaite, 1642), reprinted in John Cotton, *The New England Way,* Library of American Puritan Writings, vol. 12, ed. Sacvan Bercovitch (New York: AMS Press, 1984).

7. John Cotton, *The Way of the Churches of Christ in New-England, Measured and examined by the Golden Reed of the Sanctuary* (London: Printed by Matthew Simmons, 1645), reprinted in Cotton, *The New England Way.*

> First then when we come together in the Church, according to the Apostles direction, *I Tim.* 3.1. [correct to I Tim. 2.1.] we make prayers and intercessions and thanksgivings for our selves and for all men, not in any *prescribed* forme of prayer, or *studied Liturgie,* but in such a manner; as the Spirit of Grace and of prayer (who teacheth all people of God, what and how to praye, *Rom.* 8.26, 27) helpeth our infirmities, we having respect therein to the necessities of the people; the estate of the times, and the worke of Christ in our hands.[8]

From other documents we learn it was a common practice to sing psalms as the people were gathering. As any pastor knows, it takes a bit of time to settle the congregation, and one has to allow for latecomers. The singing of a psalm would have accomplished this. Besides that, Psalm 100 was often inscribed on the walls of Reformed churches: "Enter into his gates with thanksgiving and into his courts with praise." That worship should begin with a hymn of praise could be deduced from many a passage of Scripture.

The *Westminster Directory* made the point that when the congregation had reverently assembled, the minister was to offer an invocation.[9] Fairly generally the Puritan service of worship began with a psalm, followed by an invocation, for which the congregation stood. This opening prayer constituted the worshiping assembly in the name of Jesus, hallowed the divine name, and dwelt at length on God's glory. Its purpose, to use their expression, was to "own" God, that is, to claim God as their own God, the God to whom they belonged. In terms of covenant theology, the prayer was a "votum" in which the congregation vowed to be God's own people. It confessed human sin and recognized the unworthiness of the congregation to enter God's presence and worship him worthily. It acclaimed the worthiness of Christ and invoked the empowering of the Holy Spirit that their worship be in spirit and in truth. The invocation was an epiclesis, that is, an invocation of the Holy Spirit, asking that the Holy Spirit guide the preacher and open the hearts of the people in attendance. It was essential for the Puritans that the ministry of the Word be a means of grace. Generally the prayer concluded with a trinitarian doxology. Far from being simply an opening prayer, it had a definite liturgical shape which the congregation recognized and the minister scrupulously followed using his own words. These prayers were not left to the inspira-

8. Cotton, *Way of the Churches,* pp. 66-67.
9. "Of the Assembling of the Congregation," in *Westminster Directory for Worship.*

tion of the moment but were carefully prepared in the devotional life of the minister, who constantly sought to cultivate the gift of leading prayer.

Reading the Scriptures was a major component of the service of worship. It was common to look to the story of Ezra's public reading of the book of the law of Moses in Nehemiah 8:1-11 as the biblical exemplar of the rite. John Cotton tells us that in the churches of New England, "either the *Pastor* or *Teacher,* readeth a Chapter in the Bible, and *expoundeth* it, giving the *sense, to cause the people to understand the reading,* according to *Neh.* 8.8. And in sundry Churches the other (whether *Pastor* or *Teacher*) who *expoundeth* not, he *preacheth* the Word, and in the afternoone the other who *preached* in the morning doth usually (if there be time) *read* and *preach* and he that *expounded* in the morning *preacheth* after him."[10] In fact, Cotton goes so far in his *True Constitution* to say that when the minister is dispensing this service, he customarily "stands above the people in a Pulpit of wood and the Elders on both sides while the people harken unto them with Reverence and Attention."[11] Here there is a reference to Nehemiah 8:4-5 in the margin.

Several things are not clear here, but the *Westminster Directory* clears them up.[12] Many Reformed churches tried to establish a fourfold ministry, namely, deacons, elders, pastors, and teachers. Consequently a church such as First Church in Boston had both a pastor and a teacher. Cotton was "teacher" there while John Wilson was "pastor." One would read a chapter of the New Testament in the morning and the other would read a chapter of the Old Testament in the evening. The Scriptures were read on the principle of the *lectio continua,* with the reading beginning at one service where it had left off the service before. And not only would a chapter be read but there would also be an exposition of that chapter. The Puritans had a great dislike for "dumb reading," that is, reading without comment. Then later on in both the morning and the evening service a full sermon would be preached on some other passage of Scripture. If the teacher read and expounded in the morning, then the pastor preached later on in the service. If the pastor read and expounded in the morning, then he preached in the evening. Each service thus had a long Scripture lesson followed by an exposition of that lesson and a sermon that was

10. Cotton, *Way of the Churches,* p. 67.
11. Cotton, *True Constitution,* p. 6.
12. "Of Publick Reading of the Holy Scriptures," in *Westminster Directory for Worship.*

more than likely based on a much shorter text. This made for a service of worship which did full justice to both the reading and the preaching of Scripture. But it also meant that the Scripture lesson and the sermon drifted away from each other, and that each service had two "addresses," one the exposition of the lesson, the other the sermon proper.

This rather unusual practice seemed to develop because preachers using the *lectio continua* method had a tendency to slow it down to the point that in one sermon they covered only a single verse. Sometimes it got so slow that it took three or four sermons to cover a single verse. This made for rather short Scripture lessons. To preserve the solemnity of the public reading of Scripture as we find it in Nehemiah 8:1-11, many of the Puritan divines insisted on reading at least a chapter of the Old Testament and a chapter of the New Testament. This had been a major feature of English Protestant worship from the beginning of the Reformation.[13]

In actual fact, there was real diversity in practice. Cotton is quite clear that there was but one lesson at each service at First Church in Boston. According to the *Westminster Directory,* a chapter of the Old Testament and a chapter of the New Testament were read at each service.[14] Cotton tells us that Nehemiah 8 was the pattern followed in the reading of Scripture.[15] Apparently in John Davenport's church in New Haven the congregation stood for the reading, quite literally following Nehemiah 8. Increase Mather at Second Church in Boston, on the other hand, was supposed to have read only the passage on which he intended to preach.

According to the *Westminster Directory,* reading of the Scriptures was followed by the Pastoral Prayer, which, like the invocation, had a definite liturgical shape. It was the major prayer of the morning, and half an hour or more might be devoted to it. While it began with praise and humble confessions before the divine majesty, it was devoted to supplications and intercessions.[16] In many ways it resembled the major prayer of the synagogue, the Prayer of the Eighteen Benedictions. It was a pastoral prayer in that it prayed for the needs of the flock, both material and spiritual. It regularly went through the classical intercessions for the Church universal, the ministry of the Church, the Christian nation and her leaders, the peace of the world, and the relief of the suffering. The whole

13. See vol. IV above.

14. "Of Publick Reading of the Holy Scriptures."

15. Cotton, *True Constitution,* p. 6.

16. For a full description of the Pastoral Prayer, cf. "Of Publick Prayer before the Sermon," in *Westminster Directory for Worship.*

prayer was laced with expressions of praise and adoration, and drew heavily on the vocabulary and imagery of Scripture. There was a very definite typology of prayer which the minister had learned by his study of the prayers found in the Bible, and particularly in the Psalms.

One of the things scholars have yet to figure out is why the Puritans all seem to have moved the Pastoral Prayer from its ancient position after the sermon and before the Lord's Supper to a position after the Scripture lesson and before the sermon. The most likely explanation is that this was how it was done in the Anglican prayer book. With the Reformation, morning prayer rather than the Eucharist became the more popular service for regular Sunday morning worship. If there was to be a sermon, it would most advantageously have come after the order of morning prayer. Those not interested in the sermon could then leave at the end of morning prayer. The *Westminster Directory* was a compromise document, and while many would have preferred the order of the *Genevan Psalter,* they yielded to what seemed a practical solution.

The Pastoral Prayer was followed by the singing of a psalm. One or more psalms may have been sung as the congregation gathered, but there would always be a psalm after the Pastoral Prayer and before the sermon. Another psalm would be sung at the conclusion of the service.[17] Among the first tasks to which the founding fathers set themselves was the production of a psalter. The "old version," that is, the psalter of Sternhold and Hopkins, had served English Protestants for almost a century, but many felt it was not sufficiently faithful to the original Hebrew. Richard Mather, Nathaniel Ward, and Thomas Shepard devoted themselves to producing a psalter which, when published in 1640, became the first book printed in the English-speaking colonies. *The Whole Booke of Psalmes Faithfully Translated into English Meter* was very popular, going through some seventy editions until it was replaced by the psalms of Isaac Watts. The famous *Bay Psalm Book,* as it is popularly called, has never been particularly admired for its poetry, but then that was not what the churches of New England were looking for. From a liturgical standpoint it was fairly successful. Those who sang the psalm versions in it had a sense that they were indeed singing the utterances of the Holy Spirit, and that was what they wanted to do. From diaries and other sources we frequently hear that the singing of the psalms by the congregation was a moving part of the service.

17. Just where the psalms were sung in the service does not seem to have been an issue. See "On the Singing of Psalms," in *Westminster Directory for Worship.*

The service had up to this point taken something like an hour, with considerable time having been devoted to prayer, praise, and the reading and exposition of the lesson. It was now time for the sermon.[18] One could usually depend on the sermon having four basic parts. First the text was opened, which led to the second part, the stating of the doctrine, that is, the teaching to be found in the text. This doctrine was sometimes elaborated at length before the preacher went on to the third part, the reasons that explained or defended the doctrine. It was not uncommon for three, four, or more reasons to be advanced. Finally the ideas which had been developed would be applied to the experience of the congregation, in a number of "uses." The first use might be for rebuke, the second for edification, and a third might exhort the congregation to thanksgiving. Very rarely do we find anything approaching the elaborate introductions or conclusions which the famous French orators of the same period so carefully cultivated.

The sermon would take at least an hour. Anything less the congregation would have considered inadequate. If the hourglass was turned a second time, the congregation more than likely admired the faithfulness of their pastor in providing for them such an abundant feast of the Word. It is perhaps difficult for the mainline American Protestant to realize the intensity with which our ancestors listened to sermons. They delighted in ministers who had thoroughly explored the Scriptures, and they gladly listened to the fruit of their minister's labors. They regularly took notes during the sermon and then returned home to study those notes, discuss them with family and friends, and rehearse them with their children. The very fact that ministers knew their sermons would be heard with such attention spurred them to prepare with the utmost care. They knew their congregations longed to hear the Word, and this was a constant inspiration to them.

Quite logically the celebration of Communion followed the preaching of the Word.[19] Cotton tells us, "After the Word (which is the Covenant of God) the Seales of the Covenant are next to bee administered; Baptisme and the Lords Supper."[20] One notices here that there is a strong relation between Word and sacrament. The preaching of the Word is understood as the proclaiming of the covenant promises, while the sacraments are understood as the sealing of those promises.

---

18. "Of the Preaching of the Word," in *Westminster Directory for Worship.*

19. "On the Administration of the Sacraments," in *Westminster Directory of Worship.*

20. Cotton, *True Constitution,* p. 6.

Once a month the Lord's Supper was celebrated at the Sunday morning service. If it was not, then there might be a baptism. Baptisms could be celebrated after the sermon in the afternoon service as well. The celebration of the sacraments was often the occasion for special sermons or exhortations. We have a number of collections of sacramental sermons. They become for the Puritans a special genre of sermon, and could either precede or follow the celebrations. They might also take the form of preparatory sermons preached on a weekday before the celebration. The celebration of the sacraments was a high point in the piety of the Puritans, and it demanded long and careful preparation in both public and private worship. As for their sacramental piety, the Puritans did not confuse frequency with intensity.

The giving of alms was an important part of the service as Cotton reports it. "The Collection for the Saints was by the Apostles Ordinance to be made: for the time every Lords day, for the measure as God had prospered every man, for the manner, not of constraint but freely, brought by the givers as an offering to the Lord & laid down as a first [fruits] before the Apostles, so afterwards by their appointment, before the Deacons of the Church, as into a common Treasurie by them to be distributed to the supply of the Ministry and of the poore Saints according to their need and of all the outward Service of the Church."[21]

The service was concluded with the giving of the benediction. The benediction most frequently used was the Aaronic benediction, although other scriptural benedictions might be used.[22]

This order of service would be used both morning and evening on the Lord's Day as well as on fast days, days of thanksgiving, and the midweek lecture. The Puritans had a highly developed understanding of the Lord's Day as the Christian Sabbath.[23] It is significant that Thomas Shepard, one of the liturgical scholars of American Puritanism, wrote a major work on the subject. The Sabbath was above all the day of worship. It was a little Easter celebrated weekly. The typology of the Sabbath was the source of a very rich devotion. Of the essence of this was the whole understanding of the Sabbath of the Old Testament as fulfilled in Christ and his resurrection. The day of resurrection had succeeded the day of

21. Cotton, *True Constitution*, pp. 7-8.
22. Cotton, *True Constitution*, p. 8; "Of Prayer after Sermon," in *Westminster Directory for Worship*.
23. "Of the Sanctification of the Lord's Day," in *Westminster Directory for Worship*.

rest. It was the eighth day, the first day of the new creation. All this magnificent typology was intimated when one used the word "Sabbath" for the first day of the week. Typology, as we have often pointed out, was the key to the Puritan theology of worship. It was on the Sabbath that the congregation gathered for public worship, but the public worship was balanced by family worship held by every household at the beginning and close of each day. These daily offices were devoted primarily to praise, prayer, and the reading of a chapter from the family Bible.

The weekday lecture, in spite of the name, was a regular service of worship. In liturgical form it differed in no way from the Sabbath services except that the sacraments were not celebrated. (There was probably no collection, either.) Originally, the sermon preached was supposed to be of a more theological nature. When Samuel Willard gave his monumental series of catechetical sermons, he gave them at the midweek lecture. When Increase Mather preached his highly speculative sermons on Revelation, he did the same, not only because he could count on the attendance of other ministers, but also because he recognized that his project was a bit eccentric and the sermons of the Lord's Day should deal with central matters of the faith. However nicely such distinctions might occasionally appear, the lectures were considered services of worship and the sermons given at them were acts of worship. One could not say that just because a sermon was delivered at the Tuesday lecture in Cambridge or the Thursday lecture at Old North Church in Boston, it was not really a sermon.

Very important to the liturgical life of New England were the special days of fasting and special days of thanksgiving that were called by the civil magistrate.[24] A day of fasting might be called because of the threat of military attack or natural disaster. People were to humble themselves before God and search the Scriptures and examine their consciences to discover why God in his providence might be bringing disaster on them. The minister very particularly had a great responsibility. It was expected that through the ministry of the Word God would make his will clear, and it was the minister's job to search the Scriptures for a word of guidance, a word of rebuke or a word of comfort. A day of thanksgiving was regularly called for a good harvest.[25] Our American Thanksgiving Day is one surviving vestige

24. "Of Publick Solemn Fasting," in *Westminster Directory for Worship*.
25. "Of the Observation of Days of Publick Thanksgiving," in *Westminster Directory for Worship*.

of this practice. Fast-day sermons became a particularly significant genre of Puritan sermons, as did the thanksgiving day sermon.

Occasional sermons were also extremely important to the Puritans. Sermons were preached on all possible occasions. Funerals called for sermons; the mustering of the militia, marriages, ordinations — all required sermons that one might be guided by the Word of God through these events. The most important occasional sermon was the annual election sermon. To be asked to give the election sermon for the year was considered the greatest honor that could be bestowed on a minister in colonial New England. It therefore summoned his best effort, and would more than likely be published. But aside from these considerations, the election sermon had the highest significance to the whole community. It was preached at the request of the civil magistrate in order that the Christian society might know God's will for it. New England understood itself as a covenant community. It was a community which existed to serve God, and therefore it must regularly hear from God how it was to serve him. The minister selected to preach to the assembled magistrates on election day had the responsibility then of inquiring of the Lord, of searching the Scriptures for a word from God which would speak to the Christian community of its meaning in history and its future in the world. The election sermon was the time, above all other times, when the minister was expected to fulfill the role of a Christian prophet.

II. John Cotton (1584-1652)

The reputation of John Cotton had already been established in old England before he came to New England.[26] As lecturer at Immanuel College in Cambridge, he had attained a recognized place among the preachers of the university when he himself underwent a conversion experience. He credited this to the preaching of Richard Sibbes. Already recognized as a significant scholar, Cotton realized that his conversion entailed a radical

---

26. For biographical material on John Cotton, see John Norton, *Abel being Dead yet Speaketh; or, The Life and Death of that deservedly Famous Man of God Mr. John Cotton, Late Teacher of the Church of Christ, at Boston in New-England* (London: Tho. Newcomb for Lodowick Lloyd, 1658), in Cotton, *The New England Way;* Everett Emerson, *John Cotton,* rev. ed. (Boston: Twayne Publishers, 1990); and Larzer Ziff, *The Career of John Cotton: Puritanism and the American Experience* (Princeton: Princeton University Press, 1962).

shift in his preaching style. Putting aside the scholarly showmanship that was ordinarily employed in university pulpits, he strove to develop a simpler style. Sibbes had begun moving in the same direction a few years before him. The story, as Perry Miller remarks, is often told of how John Preston went to hear Cotton, expecting the usual sort of learned sermon. He was at first shocked by the plain style, but then realized he was hearing the gospel proclaimed with a purity he had never before experienced. Preston underwent a similar conversion experience as a result of Cotton's ministry. In time Preston became the most influential Puritan preacher in England, and using the same plain style, did much to establish this simple approach to preaching as the trademark of Puritan preaching. While still in England, Cotton made a memorable contribution to the development of Puritan preaching.

In 1612 Cotton became vicar of Saint Botolph's Church in Boston, one of the larger towns in the county of Lincolnshire, England. For the next twenty years he developed the Puritan tendencies to which he had become devoted in Cambridge. He began to reorganize his parish along congregational lines. Cotton was one of the originators of Congregationalism as a form of church polity. As one would expect, he soon won the ire of Archbishop Laud. He went into hiding and stayed there for almost a year. Finally in 1633 he, too, set out for New England. Large numbers of his old congregation had preceded him and had named their settlement Boston. On arrival he was chosen teacher of the Church of Boston in New England and preached there until his death in 1652.

Cotton was regarded along with Thomas Shepard of Cambridge and Thomas Hooker of Hartford as one of the most able of the first generation of New England preachers. In almost twenty years of preaching in his new Boston, Cotton preached through almost all the books of the Bible. Preaching three or four times a week, he covered the Old Testament up through the middle of Isaiah. He is supposed to have preached through all the books of the New Testament at least once, and most books twice. Several of these series were published as commentaries. Particularly noteworthy were his sermons on Ecclesiastes and his series on the Song of Solomon. Many Puritans gave great attention to the Song of Solomon because it spoke of Christ's love for the Church and the love of the Church for Christ. The reason his series on the Song of Solomon and Ecclesiastes were published is no doubt that they were thought of as particularly difficult books, and since Cotton was widely respected as an interpreter, his interpretation was of special interest. In addition to these *lectio continua* sermons, several series on covenant theology have been published. Many were published posthumously from the notes of those who heard them.

While the sermons on Ecclesiastes and the Song of Solomon were edited and published as commentaries, fourteen of Cotton's sermons on I John were published as actual sermons.[27] It is not too clear whether they were preached in England or in New England. One thing would seem clear — they give us a vivid impression of how Cotton normally preached, whether in the old country or at First Church in Boston.

Several things are of particular interest in these sermons. First, they give us a good example of how effective the plain style of preaching could be in the hands of one who apparently did much to develop it. There is something very beautiful about these sermons. One gets the feeling while reading them of approaching the inner sanctuary of the Word of God. One is moved to fall down and remove one's shoes from one's feet and listen in silence. They have a holy beauty about them. This is not the beauty of the baroque. It is a beauty far away from the high style of the seventeenth century. It is a beauty with neither pomp nor circumstance. It is a simple, solemn beauty.

The first sermon claims our attention because Cotton has some thoughts on worship. This being at the center of our inquiry, we do well to note what our Pilgrim Father has to say.

In his *lectio continua* of I John our preacher has come to 5:12, "He that hath the Son hath Life, and he that hath not the Son hath not life."[28] He sets down the doctrine he has drawn from the text in the opening paragraph. According to that text, having or not having life depends on having or not having Christ. Cotton claims this carries special weight in our Christian experience, and therefore we must take special care in opening it. We have this doctrine in several other passages of Scripture as well. Proverbs 8:35 tells us that "He that findeth me hath life."[29] A similar thought is expressed in Ephesians 2:12. Paul tells the Ephesians that in times past they were without Christ; they were strangers to the commonwealth of Israel; they had no part in the covenant, no hope, and they were

27. John Cotton, *Christ the Fountaine of Life; or, Sundry Choyse Sermons on Part of the Fifth Chapter of the First Epistle of St. John* (Boston: Robert Ibbitson, 1651), hereafter Cotton, *Sermons on I John*.

28. Cotton, *Sermons on I John*, p. 1.

29. The Geneva Bible and the King James Version read a bit differently. We assume Cotton was translating the Hebrew text for himself. He was particularly admired for his facility with the original languages.

without God in the world. Only when they came to have Christ did they come to have life.

The sermon offers several reasons why real life, that is, eternal life, is given only to those who have Christ.[30] First, it is the very nature of creaturely existence that we do not have life in ourselves.[31] Secondly, it has pleased the Father that in Christ all the fullness of life should dwell, as we find it in Colossians 1:19.[32]

With this our preacher moves on to how we can know whether we have Christ. The first way is that we truly worship him. It takes several sermons to treat the different ways we know that we have Christ, but for the remainder of the first sermon in this collection Cotton discusses true worship. One should notice at this point that worship is first on the list.

The very worshiping of Christ is having him. This is implied in the first commandment, "Thou shalt have no other gods before me" (Exod. 20:3). Earlier in Exodus, in the song of victory the children of Israel sang when they crossed the Red Sea, they claimed God as their God and that he had become the God of their salvation; he is their God and was the God of their fathers, therefore they exalted in him. Cotton comments that we worship God when we set him up as preeminent in our hearts and our lives. That is what it is to have Christ. To worship Christ is to have him in mind, in heart, in life, both in our obedience to his commands and in the patient suffering we yield to him when things become difficult. By all this we worship Christ, and so have him.[33]

First, let us think what it is to worship Christ in our minds. It is to hold Christ in high estimation. The worship and honor that we owe Christ is to prize him.[34] Once again Cotton calls on the Song of Solomon. To worship Christ is to adore him above all the delights of life. To have such love for another is to prefer another to oneself, to give the other preference. This is what we have in the story of John the Baptist. John recognized in Jesus the one who was worthy of all praise but whose sandal strap he was not even worthy to loosen.

To worship Christ is to praise him above all other blessings. The apostle Paul gave us an example of this when he said he wanted to know

---

30. Cotton, *Sermons on I John*, p. 2.
31. Cotton, *Sermons on I John*, p. 3.
32. Cotton, *Sermons on I John*, p. 5.
33. Cotton, *Sermons on I John*, p. 6.
34. Cotton, *Sermons on I John*, p. 7.

nothing except Jesus Christ and him crucified (Phil. 3:7-10). For Paul worship of Christ was to know him as preeminent in all things.[35]

But along with worshiping Christ in our minds, we must worship him in our wills and our affections. It is not enough to worship him in our wills alone.[36] In Psalm 42 a saint is alienated from the public worship of God's people as it was celebrated in the Temple. He yearns to return to that festive worship. He laments his spiritual loneliness, and that sorrow is the deepest and most profound of true worship.[37] Cotton understood so well that our tears are the most precious of offerings. To cry before God is to worship him from the depths of our souls.

A third part of true worship is obedience to the will of Christ. Worship is a respect for the commands of Christ because they are his commandments, and that is why we suffer them as our duty. We deny ourselves and our will, our desires, and our purposes that we might do his will.[38] We prefer his will, and we wait upon his will. In the story of Job there is a glorious worship in patience. As did Job, we quietly wait upon the Lord, for the Lord gives and the Lord takes away; blessed be the name of the Lord.[39] In quietness and silence of heart we bear the yoke of Christ. God is the God of our salvation when we keep silence before him. When we recognize that we are but clay in the hand of the potter, this is solemn worship. Even more, as in I Peter 4:14-17, if we suffer for Christ and bear it not only patiently but joyfully, then the glory of Christ rests upon us.[40] There is, of course, much else that one could say about worship, but there is something basic and fundamental about these words of our Pilgrim Father. One would hope that the worship of the American church might never be distracted from the wisdom here expressed.

Another passage in these sermons speaks to the central concerns of our study. In sermon XIII Cotton quotes I John 5:13, where John tells his readers that he has written this epistle "That you may beleeve on the Name of the Son of God." The doctrine Cotton derives from this is that "It is an holy end of the holy Scriptures that beleevers may beleeve." Here we find the reason John wrote not only this epistle but his Gospel as well. This sermon has much to say about the purpose of the whole ministry of

35. Cotton, *Sermons on I John*, p. 8.
36. Cotton, *Sermons on I John*, p. 9.
37. Cotton, *Sermons on I John*, p. 10.
38. Cotton, *Sermons on I John*, p. 12.
39. Cotton, *Sermons on I John*, p. 13.
40. Cotton, *Sermons on I John*, p. 14.

the Word. The Scriptures are given to us that we might believe, that faith be born in us and we might grow in it. Although we have saving faith, we need to advance in faith throughout the whole of life. As Paul writes at the beginning of Romans, we need to go from faith to faith (1:17).[41] The ministry of the Word nurtures faith.

The preacher of the First Church in Boston goes through the New Testament to show that even those who have saving faith need to grow in that faith. Preaching faith was a cardinal component of the ministry of the Word from the very beginning of our history, and is basic to Protestant preaching. Luther himself made that very clear. Evangelistic preaching even among profoundly Christian people is a continuing need. As recounted in the Gospel of John, Thomas, as devoted as he was to Christ, needed to grow in his faith. He needed to learn that the Christ who died on the cross had risen.[42] Sometimes our faith weakens and needs to grow stronger, like the faith of Peter when he set out to meet Christ on the stormy sea. His faith began well, but in the tempest it began to sink.[43]

We all need to grow in our faith, to deepen it, correct it, and confirm it. It is the Word of God which supplies this need. "The Word of God is mighty, and mighty to this end." The Scriptures have the power to supply our faith. "*The Scriptures are mighty through God,* whether *preached* or *read,* or *heard,* or *conferred* upon, or *meditated* upon."[44] The Scriptures are sanctified of God to no other use than this. Cotton then elaborates these five ways the Scriptures supply our faith. Our faith is supplied by the preaching of the Scriptures, by conferences on the Scriptures with others, by reading them, by examining them in private, and by meditating on them in our hearts. Let us look at each of these.

Preaching supplies and supports our faith, Cotton tells us, "For . . . there is a mighty power in the Scriptures preached, for he writes these things that they may be preached."[45] Paul writes that the gospel is the power of God to salvation, for therein the righteousness of God is revealed from faith to faith to lead on even the believer to believe, not to rest in believing but to grow in believing. Paul also tells the Thessalonians

---

41. Cotton, *Sermons on I John,* p. 193.
42. Cotton, *Sermons on I John,* p. 194.
43. Cotton, *Sermons on I John,* p. 196.
44. Cotton, *Sermons on I John,* p. 198.
45. Cotton, *Sermons on I John,* p. 199.

he wants to come to them so that his personal presence in preaching and conferences can be added to the reading of the Word alone.

Secondly, the Word supplies faith through conferring, that is, through discussing the Word. A good example of conferences as a means of strengthening faith is the two disciples who spoke with the risen Christ on the road to Emmaus (Luke 24). They were doubtful whether Jesus was the Christ or not. So Jesus, as yet unrecognized by them, beginning with Moses and the prophets, opened to them the Scriptures so that their hearts burned within them. The Word was opened by means of a conference. It was the same way when Philip met with the Ethiopian eunuch (Acts 8:27). The eunuch had been reading the book of Isaiah, but he had not understood it. A discussion or conference nourished the first beginnings of faith which the eunuch already had in his heart.

Thirdly, reading the Scriptures supplies our faith. We find this in John 20:30-31. Says Cotton, "There is a mighty power of God that accompanies the reading of the word . . . to strengthen men in the faith, that such as beleeve already, may beleeve more, and bee established in their perswasion of the truth of God."[46] Here Cotton is obviously developing that basic affirmation of Reformed theology that the Holy Spirit works through the reading and preaching of the Scriptures, giving an inner testimony to our hearts which in the end makes the Word effective to our salvation.

Fourthly, our faith is strengthened by examining the Scriptures. When we have heard a sermon, we should go home and examine what was taught and compare it to what we find in our Bible and see if the preacher was right. The Bible is the measure. We find a good example of this in Acts 17:11-12, where the Bereans received the Word gladly but then examined the Scriptures to see whether what was said to them was so.[47] The sermon is comment on and interpretation of the Bible. There is something very beautiful here in Cotton's teaching. He seems to have a feel for the dynamic between the reading of the Scriptures, the preaching of them, discussion of them among the faithful, and meditating on them in private. This is something we have all experienced, but it is not often spelled out like this in theological discussion.

Finally, our Pilgrim Father speaks of meditation. When a Christian has heard the Word, he needs to think about it while doing his work, rid-

---

46. Cotton, *Sermons on I John,* p. 200.
47. Cotton, *Sermons on I John,* p. 201.

ing about, or lying in bed at night. This is the way it is received into our hearts. This is the way it is planted deep within us. The Word has a power within it to take root and grow. In the First Psalm the blessed are those who delight in the Law of the Lord and meditate upon it day and night. When we delight in the Word, it grows and prospers and at last bears fruit. When this fruit is produced, then God's glory is magnified.[48]

This dynamic between the reading and preaching of Scripture in public, the discussing of it among friends, and the examining and meditating on it in private is surely one of the things that makes the ministry of the Word a vital part of Christian worship. As one reads through these sermons in all their simplicity and directness, one senses that Cotton had discovered far more than a new land: he had found a depth of Christian truth that the age of the baroque with all its pretensions never perceived.

III. Thomas Hooker (1586-1647)

Among the first generation of preachers in New England, Thomas Hooker was particularly popular.[49] Back in England he had received an excellent education. In 1604 he entered Cambridge, receiving in 1608 his bachelor of arts degree and in 1611 his master of arts. At Cambridge he came under the influence of both Richard Sibbes and William Ames. Ames seems to have had a particularly strong influence on him. Hooker served as both lecturer and catechist there from 1611 to 1618.

Sometime after 1620 he was appointed to a lectureship at Chelmsford in Essex. These lectureships were being established all over England at the time as a way for the Puritans to get serious, scholarly, high-quality preaching, in spite of the officially appointed priests who either could not or would not preach, and they proved very effective in doing that. Hooker soon won a reputation for his "fervent evangelical ad-

48. Cotton, *Sermons on I John,* p. 202.

49. Regrettably there does not seem to be a comprehensive modern collection of Hooker's sermons. This study relies largely on the following collections of sermons: Thomas Hooker, *The Poor Doubting Christian Drawn to Christ,* photolithographic edition of a collection of five sermons published in 1845 (Keyser, W.Va.: Odom Publications, 1991); Hooker, *Redemption, Three Sermons,* introduction by Everett H. Emerson (Gainesville, Fla.: Scholars Facsimiles and Reprints, 1956); and Thomas Hooker et al., *Salvation in New England: Selections from the Sermons of the First Preachers,* ed. Phyllis M. Jones and Nicholas R. Jones (Austin and London: University of Texas Press, 1977).

dresses." His forthright preaching on the essential matters of the gospel was especially well received, and consequently Archbishop Laud, the determined enemy of Puritanism, had his lectureship revoked.

In 1630 Hooker was cited to appear before the Court of High Commission. Fleeing to Holland, he took up pastoral responsibilities in the English-speaking congregation at Delft. In the meantime a group of people who had followed his preaching in Chelmsford had organized themselves as a company and emigrated to New England. They invited Hooker to follow them and become their pastor, which he did in 1633. With Hooker sailed John Cotton, another of the most popular preachers of the first generation in New England, who was destined to become pastor of First Church in Boston. Hooker's company settled up the Charles River from Boston, but by 1636 had decided to move on to Connecticut, where they founded Hartford. The reason always given for the move was that the land on the Charles was less than ideal, and therefore they sought a better building site. The chances are, however, that Hooker and Cotton simply did not get along. Whatever the reasons, Hartford became an important community in the Christian commonwealth of New England, and both Hooker and Cotton were recognized as leading preachers.

As a preacher, Hooker had some very specific concerns. Enough of his sermons survive to give us at least some idea of what he preached. Regrettably, however, it has to be said that his preaching does not come into as sharp focus as that of either Cotton or Shepard. Several years after his death a number of his sermons were put together and published under the title *The Application of Redemption by the Effectual Work of the Word and Spirit of Christ.*[50] Apparently these sermons were fragments of a larger projected work. Hooker preached through the outline of this work three times during his ministry, and if he had not been struck down by an epidemic in 1647, he probably would have completed it for publication. A number of the sermons were published separately. We have, for instance, the following:

"The Soul's Preparation for Christ"
"The Soul's Redemption"
"The Soul's Humiliation"
"The Soul's Ingrafting into Christ"
"The Soul's Vocation"

50. Thomas Hooker, *The Application of Redemption by the Effectual Work of the Word and Spirit of Christ* (London: Printed by Peter Cole, 1657).

"The Soul's Implantation"
"The Soul's Possession of Christ"
"The Soul's Exaltation"

We recognize here the themes of the *ordo salutis,* the steps of salvation. Hooker was concerned in his preaching to show his people how one moves from a life enslaved to sin to the experience of conversion, being united to Christ through faith and final exaltation to eternal glory.

IV. John Eliot (1604-90) — the Gospel in Algonquian

Known today as the Apostle to the Indians, John Eliot was born in old England, the son of a prosperous farmer.[51] In 1622 he received a bachelor of arts degree from Cambridge University, having studied at Jesus College. While at Cambridge he gave special attention to the study of languages; Hebrew and Greek were of particular interest to him. On graduating he became the assistant of Thomas Hooker. For a number of years Hooker exercised a very popular ministry, and young Eliot must have learned much from him. Eventually Laud moved to have Hooker silenced. Soon after Hooker was suspended from his parish, Eliot emigrated to Massachusetts and, on arrival, was employed to help in the ministry at First Church in Boston. Soon, however, he was given a more permanent position as teacher in the church at Roxbury. Over the years he served under several different pastors, but even after he began his ministry to the Algonquians he maintained his connection with the church at Roxbury. Soon after arriving in Roxbury he married Hannah Mulford, to whom he had been betrothed while still in England. She was his constant helper in his work.

Eliot's work with the Algonquians was inspired by a strong sense of

51. On the life and work of John Eliot, see *John Eliot and the Indians, being letters addressed to the Rev. Jonathan Hanmer of Barnstable* (New York: [Adams and Grace Press], 1915); *John Eliot's Indian Dialogues* (Westport, Conn.: Greenwood Press, 1980); and Richard Baxter, *Some Unpublished Correspondence of the Reverend Richard Baxter and the Reverend John Eliot, the Apostle of the American Indians* (Manchester: Manchester University Press, 1931). See also Henry W. Bowden and James P. Ronda, *John Eliot's Indian Dialogues, a Study in Cultural Interaction* (Westport, Conn., and London: Greenwood Press, 1980); Alden T. Vaughan, *The New England Frontier: Puritans and Indians, 1620-1675* (Boston: Little, Brown, 1965); Williston Walker, *Ten New England Leaders* (New York and Boston: Silver, Burdett and Co., 1901); and Ola Elizabeth Winslow, *John Eliot, Apostle to the Indians* (Boston: Houghton Mifflin, 1968).

call. It was God himself who laid the call upon him. The New Testament makes a strong point of the missionary challenge, and as Eliot studied his Bible it became more and more clear to him that God had appointed him to this ministry.

The first thing he had to do was learn the Indian language. The Algonquian language, although widely spoken by the Native American population of New England, was spoken in a number of dialects. To learn it Eliot took a young man into his home as a language teacher. Rather early he began translating a number of passages of Scripture such as the Ten Commandments and the Lord's Prayer. By 1646 he was able to preach to an assembly of Algonquians at Nonantum. The first attempt to preach was not too successful. The Indians responded to his sermon with questions about all kinds of things which puzzled them. They wanted an explanation of thunder, and the phases of the moon, and the changing of the tides. Eliot was not expecting such questions, and his linguistic ability failed him. He sharpened his language skills some more and tried again. After his third attempt to preach, several Algonquians declared themselves converted. A good number followed suit in succeeding weeks, to the great delight of the Christian population. Rapturous letters were sent back to England reporting the dawning of the gospel in the wilderness.

The success of the work was so great that in 1649 Parliament, which by this time was thoroughly committed to Puritanism, established the Society for the Propagation of the Gospel in New England. Their first appeal for funds brought in £11,000, an amazing amount of money, raised mostly from private individuals in both England and New England. Nothing, of course, could have demonstrated more clearly the popular support of this missionary work.

The success of this work led to the establishing of a Christian Indian town at Natick in 1651, with both a meetinghouse and a schoolhouse. A second Indian town was established in Punkapaog in 1654. In time similar towns of "praying Indians" were established at Hassanamasilt, Magunkaquog, Martha's Vineyard, and Nantucket.[52] Eliot was careful to train Native Americans as catechists and lay preachers. Each Christian village had its own exhorters and a number of its own preachers.[53] By 1674 the Christian Indian population had reached four thousand people.

52. Bowden and Ronda, *Study,* p. 37.
53. Bowden and Ronda, *Study,* p. 42.

From the beginning, Eliot translated portions of Scripture into the Algonquian language. By 1661 he was able to publish a New Testament, and two years later an Old Testament. Several other ministers followed his example and learned the different Indian dialects.[54]

Rarely do missionaries leave us manuscripts of their sermons, as we have observed all the way down through the history of preaching.[55] Eliot has, however, left us a work which tells us much about his preaching. This document, known as the *Indian Dialogues,* was a manual for the training of Native American preachers and catechists.[56] It is cast in the form of four dialogues. The first is between two Massachuset tribesmen, Piumbukhou, a Christian who lives in a Christian village, and his kinsman who lives in the village of Nashaurreg, farther into the backcountry, where the gospel has not been preached. The second dialogue is between Waban, one of the first converts from the Massachuset tribe, and Peneovot, who has not yet become a Christian.

The third dialogue supposedly takes place when William Abaliton, a particularly talented Christian preacher from the "praying town" of Punkapaog, is sent by his church to present the gospel to King Philip, the sachem of the Wampanoag tribe, a tribe quite different from the Massachuset, although sharing the Algonquian language. Only five years after these dialogues were published, King Philip became the leader of the Indian revolt called King Philip's War. Finally, the fourth dialogue brings us back to Natick where John Speen, one of the preachers of that Christian town, ministers the assurance of salvation to an Indian who has believed the preaching of the Church.

Although the material is presented as dialogues between Christian Indian preachers and Indians who had not yet received the gospel, it is no

---

54. Other works of Eliot help put his work in perspective: John Eliot, *A Brief Narrative of the Progress of the Gospel Among the Indians of New England* (Cambridge, Mass., 1670); Eliot, *The Indian Primer* (Cambridge, Mass., 1669); and John Eliot and Thomas Mayhew, Jr., *Tears of Repentance; or, A Further Narrative of the Progress of the Gospel Amongst the Indians in New England* (London, 1663). These books have not been available for this study.

55. We will notice the same problem later in this volume, in the chapter devoted to the missionary preaching of the Spanish Franciscans among the Native American population in California. What we will not find in California is the translation of the Scriptures into the Native American languages.

56. John Eliot, *Indian Dialogues, for their instruction in that great service of Christ, in calling home their Countrymen to the Knowledge of God, and of themselves, and of Iesus Christ* (Cambridge: Marmaduke Johnson, 1671).

doubt a crystallization of the evangelistic preaching of Eliot himself. Several most interesting features stand out. In the first place, much importance is given to portraying the way of perdition on one hand and the way of salvation on the other. We noticed in our first volume that this approach played an important role in the *Didache,* which was, after all, the first missionary manual that has come down to us. Joined with this is a certain amount of polemic directed against the way of perdition.

In the second place, it is obvious that the *Westminster Shorter Catechism* was an important missionary tool. Eliot had translated it into Algonquian rather early in his ministry, and as is quite apparent from these discourses, the Native American catechists used it extensively.

In the third place we notice that these dialogues give much attention to going through the *ordo salutis.* This was, to be sure, part of the catechism, but especially in the second and fourth dialogues the material is elaborated at length. Here, too, we find several interesting parallels with the ancient Church. We find the same thing in Augustine's work on introducing the faith, *De catechizandis rudibus,* as well as in several of the missionary manuals of those who evangelized the barbarians of northern Europe in the early Middle Ages. The New Englanders placed the same, strong emphasis on conversion in their missionary work that they did in their ministry to the Anglo population. Further on in this volume, in our chapter on the missionary preaching of the Spanish Franciscans among the Native American population in California, we will find much less emphasis on conversion.

Certainly an important dimension of the New Englanders' missionary work among the Native American population was the translation of the Bible into the Algonquian language. The Spanish missionaries were slow to do this in Mexico, as we noticed in the previous volume. Later we will see that this was not a priority in their work in California either. The Spanish Franciscans established their mission islands, as it were, of Christian civilization. By a sort of cultural assimilation the Native American population was made Christian. For Eliot, however, conversion was obviously a top priority. To become Christian meant to turn away from the ways of perdition and follow the ways of God. The New Englanders preached conversion to the Native American population just as they preached conversion to their white, Anglo-Saxon population.

V. Thomas Shepard (1605-49)

While Thomas Shepard was recognized as one of the better preachers among the founding fathers, he is today recognized as the best theologian of the Massachusetts Bay Colony. And yet as a theologian he was not so much a systematic theologian as what Catholics call a spiritual theologian. In more Protestant terminology, we might say the field of his theological inquiry was the Christian life. There was nothing dry or abstract about his theology. It was highly introspective and capable of the most poetic expression. In those days Richard Mather was perhaps the most highly regarded of the first generation of Puritan ministers for his piety, but as more recent scholars have read Shepard's spiritual journal, they have discovered it to be an amazing record of interiority. All this is, of course, reflected in his sermons, above all his sermons on the parable of the wise and foolish virgins.

Shepard was born the youngest son of a large, not particularly religious family.[57] His father was a grocer in the town of Towcester in Northamptonshire,[58] having been apprenticed to the grocer and in time marrying his daughter and succeeding to the business. Young Thomas was brought up with eight brothers and sisters, but when he was about four years old his mother died and his life under the rule of his stepmother was not happy. When he was ten, his father died and he was shipped from one relative to another. Finally his older brother John took charge of him and eventually saw to it that he was sent off to college. As it happened, he was sent to Emmanuel College in Cambridge, where John Preston was principal.

Not trained by a strong religious family, he fell into rather unruly ways at college. Nevertheless, he did get interested in Christian teaching. He read Richard Rogers's *Practice of Christianity.*[59] Rogers was a strong

---

57. For biographical material on Shepard, see John A. Albro, *The Life of Thomas Shepard,* found as the memoir prefacing *The Works of Thomas Shepard, First Pastor of the First Church, Cambridge,* 3 vols. (Boston: Boston Tract and Book Society, 1853; reprint, New York: AMS Press, 1967); *God's Plot, the Paradoxes of Puritan Piety, Being the Autobiography and Journal of Thomas Shepard,* edited with an introduction by Michael McGiffert (Amherst: University of Massachusetts Press, 1972), hereafter Shepard, *Autobiography;* Thomas Werge, *Thomas Shepard* (Boston: Twayne Publishers, 1987); and Alexander Whyte, *Thomas Shepard: Pilgrim Father and Founder of Harvard: His Spiritual Experience and Experimental Preaching* (Edinburgh: Oliphant and Ferrier, 1909).

58. Shepard, *Autobiography,* p. 39.

59. Shepard, *Autobiography,* p. 45.

leader for the Puritan cause. Typically Puritan, he put a major emphasis on the Christian way of life. Preston's preaching was a strong influence on young Shepard as well. It was from him that he came to understand the importance of receiving Christ as Lord and Savior,[60] and in time he had a profound conversion experience. Shepard was in Cambridge for seven or eight years. Constantly under the influence of Thomas Goodwin and Preston, he became a strong supporter of the Puritan cause. On receiving his master's degree, he was ordained and received a call as lecturer in Essex. There he was welcomed into the company of a number of neighboring pastors who in time would become leaders of the church in New England, notably Hooker, who was pastor at Chelmsford, and Thomas Weld at Terling.[61]

For three years he continued as lecturer at Earles-Colne. During this time Weld took him into his home, and his ministry prospered. His preaching was well received, and more and more his work was valued by the leading Puritans of the area. Sad to say, William Laud, the archbishop of Canterbury so intent on driving the Puritans from the Church of England, heard of how well Shepard's preaching was being received. In fact, when Shepard was called before him, the autocratic prelate had a fit.[62] Laud forbade him to preach further.

As Shepard himself understood it, providence had other plans for him.[63] He was given a position as family chaplain in the home of Sir Richard Darley in Yorkshire. There he was able to preach privately. But also there he met a relative of Sir Richard, Margaret Touteville, whom he married in July of 1632. He spent something like two years preaching in the north of England. At one point he was invited to preach at Heddon in Northumberland, but Laud, ever the oppressor of Puritanism, heard of it and notified the authorities. Again he was forced into hiding. Not being allowed to preach publicly, he began to believe that God was calling him to emigrate to New England.[64] Traveling in secrecy, he returned to the south. Friends sheltered him and his wife, and in these clandestine conditions their first child was born. They attempted to sail from Harwich at the beginning of the winter, but stormy weather drove their ship back. It had been a frightening experience in which they almost lost their lives.

60. Shepard, *Autobiography,* p. 45.
61. Shepard, *Autobiography,* pp. 48-49.
62. Shepard, *Autobiography,* p. 51.
63. Shepard, *Autobiography,* p. 52.
64. Shepard, *Autobiography,* pp. 55-56.

The experience did weaken the health of their child so that he soon died. All this discouragement the couple bore in secrecy while waiting for another attempt to sail for New England.[65] Another son was born to them, and at the end of the summer God opened another way for them to escape. They arrived in Boston on 3 October 1635.

Once in New England, Shepard was chosen as pastor of the church of Cambridge. The spiritual journey of our preacher was still filled with tribulations, though, as his wife Margaret fell ill and died even before they were able to establish a home. But our young preacher was determined to find a good mother for his surviving son and soon married Joanna, the daughter of Thomas Hooker. Hooker had been his friend and patron during his ministry in Essex, and he had emigrated only a short time before Shepard. It turned out to be a good match, and for the next nine years Joanna was a constant support to Shepard and a devoted mother to his son. The Shepard family grew, and we learn so much about the spirituality of being both a pastor and a family man from the journals Shepard kept.[66]

Soon after Shepard arrived in Cambridge, he helped establish Harvard College. From the beginning of his ministry in Cambridge he was looked to as a leader of the church in New England. Not only was his leadership expressed in being the de facto chaplain of the college, but also he was one of those who framed the congregational polity of New England. He was a well-rounded theologian, and even more important, a strong supporter of the mission to the Indians. He often lent his support to the work of John Eliot, who busily learned the language of the Native Americans and began preaching to them in their own language. Finally, Shepard was among those who produced the *Bay Psalter*, the first American liturgical publication.

Not yet fifty years old, Shepard died in 1649. He left behind the notes of his sermons on the parable of the wise and foolish virgins, a remarkable series of sermons which is a fitting proclamation of the ministry of the Word at the founding of America.

---

65. Shepard, *Autobiography*, p. 62.

66. In addition to the *Autobiography*, there are portions of Shepard's journal included in Thomas Shepard, *God's Plot: Puritan Spirituality in Thomas Shepard's Cambridge*, ed. Michael McGiffert, rev. and expanded ed. (Amherst: University of Massachusetts Press, 1994).

A. Sermons on the Parable of the Ten Virgins

One might say the spiritual foundation of America was set with this re-markable series of sermons. Even a century later it was regarded by Jona-than Edwards, David Brainerd, and their contemporaries as the classic work of American theology. It is on sanctification, but not simply per-sonal sanctification: it is on the sanctification of the Christian nation. Yes, the seeds of the American Social Gospel are already to be found in this prophetic series of sermons. These seeds have been sown in the ground of personal piety, that is, the brilliant exegetical insight which carries this whole series. Shepard starts with Jesus' parable of the ten virgins and on the one hand draws into it the Christian interpretation of the Song of Sol-omon, and then, on the other hand, he uses the prophetic revelation of the seven churches of Asia to challenge the churches of New England to await the coming of the Lord in holiness. This is magnificent biblical in-terpretation!

The Puritans were fascinated with the Song of Solomon. This will no doubt come as a surprise to those whose only knowledge about them comes from the standard high school course on the history of American literature. The Puritans produced many commentaries and devotional works based on the Song. We spoke above of series of sermons on the book done by both Richard Sibbes and John Cotton, whose Christian in-terpretation followed the broad lines of interpretation the Church had followed for centuries. We also spoke of Bernard of Clairvaux's series. All the way through the Middle Ages series of sermons were devoted to this book in order to develop the doctrine of Christian love. The standard in-terpretation on which all these are based is that the Song speaks of the love of Christ for the Church and the love of the Church for Christ. While Origen and the Alexandrian School emphasized that the book was an allegory of the soul's ascent to the divine love, a more conservative use of the Antiochene School found many passages of the New Testament which assumed that the Song was a type of the love between the Church and her Bridegroom. Even Calvin had defended this interpretation in his famous controversy with Sebastian Castellion. What is interesting about Shepard's series is that he approaches these themes of divine love from one of the parables of Jesus, the parable of the wise and foolish virgins. The parable obviously assumes the Wisdom theology. Five of the virgins are wise and five foolish. Christ is presented in the figure of the Bridegroom, and the coming of the kingdom as the wedding feast.

194

As Shepard and his contemporaries understood it, this series of sermons treated the Christian doctrine of sanctification. The Puritans generally understood four steps to salvation: election, justification, sanctification, and glorification. If the first generation of the Protestant Reformers had been chiefly concerned with the doctrine of justification by faith, the second generation was concerned with sanctification. Just as the Protestant doctrine of justification insisted that justification was by faith, so on sanctification did Protestantism insist it was by faith as well. The first Protestant century saw the reform of many churches. Protestantism became institutionalized in many parts of Europe, but the spirit of reform pressed on for more than institutional reform. This was inevitable. The devout wanted a reform of life. They wanted a deepening of Christian experience. What happened in Protestantism in the seventeenth century was very similar to what happened to the Church after Constantine established Christianity as the official religion of the Empire. By the end of the fourth century Christians were fleeing the established imperial church for monasteries in the wilderness and devoting themselves to the cultivation of the inner life. The churches of New England were churches in the wilderness, and we find it in no way surprising that in their preaching they turned to the Scriptures to learn what the Word of God had to teach them about the deepening of the Christian life. This, to be sure, is the responsibility of the ministry of the Word in every age. The Puritans of New England preached very differently from the Reformers of the continent of Europe in the century before them. This is as it should be. If they had preached as Luther and Calvin or even as Chrysostom and Augustine, their churches would have starved. Each age needs its own sermons.

The Parable of the Ten Virgins was published in 1659 by Thomas Shepard's son, who was minister at Charlestown, and Jonathan Mitchell, his successor at Cambridge.[67] It was a transcription, Mitchell tells us in his preface, of the preacher's notes, which are in many places much briefer than the sermons themselves. Many of the most moving passages of the sermons were never written out, and yet the notes contain the heart of what was preached, according to Mitchell. Unfortunately, the transcription has divided the material into forty-one chapters which may or may not have been separate sermons. The chapters sometimes appear to be

67. Thomas Shepard, *The Parable of the Ten Virgins Opened and Applied,* in *The Works of Thomas Shepard,* vol. 2 (Doctrinal Tract and Book Society, 1853; reprint, New York: AMS Press, 1967).

complete sermons, but frequently one gets the impression that a sermon has been divided into several chapters or that a chapter is only the fragment of a sermon. The sermons were preached from June 1636 to May 1640. The series was interrupted by Shepard's illness, but we do not know how long his illness lasted. Besides this, they were preached at the midweek service. This meant that many of the ministers, as well as others from nearby churches, would have been present in addition to the usual congregation. Midweek lectures, as they were called, were at this period in the colony rotated among the churches to allow people to hear other ministers, but this also meant that any individual minister might not preach at a midweek service more than once a month.

Even though the edition of these sermons on which we must base our study does not allow us to discover everything we would like to know, we nevertheless get a powerful impression of how Shepard exercised the ministry of the Word. In the preaching of the Word, God revealed his will to his people at a particular time and in a particular place. As we have already said, again and again Shepard weaves the themes of the book of Revelation into his sermons. He seems to have understood the ministry of the Word much as John understood his messages to the seven churches of Asia: "He who has an ear, let him hear what the Spirit says to the churches" (Rev. 2:7, 11, 17, 29; 3:6, 13, 22). John received his revelation when he was in the Spirit on the Lord's Day. This was what happened in worship in the New Testament Church, whether the worship was on the Lord's Day or any other day. The Word of the Lord was revealed to his glory. Even if this Word was a Word of correction and warning, the revelation of this Word glorified God, and was therefore worship. It was Shepard's strong sense that the Word he had been sent to preach was the Word of God that made preaching for him worship.

One takes this parallel between these sermons and the messages to the seven churches of Asia even further. A different Word was preached to each of the seven churches. Each church was in a different situation, and each church had different strengths and weaknesses.[68] There was, of course, one light although seven candlesticks; nevertheless, Shepard's sermons have a particularly strong sense of the importance of preaching a particular message to the churches of New England. His message was for those days after they had made their heroic act of faith and gone out into the wilderness to practice a more complete obedience, and it had become

68. Shepard, *Ten Virgins,* p. 21.

clear that they had succeeded in establishing their Christian community. The new danger they faced was that they were beginning to rest from their labors and fall asleep while waiting for the Bridegroom. The churches of New England were in the same danger as the church of Ephesus. They were beginning to lose their first love (Rev. 2:4).

Let us look now at the text of these sermons, making allowances for the fact that one cannot always be sure where a sermon begins or ends. The first three chapters are very brief introductory remarks. They may indeed represent three separate sermons, and we will assume for our discussion that they do, but often Shepard takes three or four sermons to get through the plain-style sermon outline of text, doctrine, reasons, and uses. Whatever strengths these sermons may have, organization is not one of them.

The introductory sermons of the series are filled with the richest insights of congregational polity. The ten virgins are ten churches.[69] They have all made their Christian profession, although some are wise and some are foolish. Jesus told the parable, Shepard tells us, about the situation of the Church between the ascension and the second coming of Christ,[70] of the visible Church on earth as she awaits the coming of the Bridegroom.[71] While the ten virgins can also be understood as individual members of the churches, the underlying assumption recurs again and again through the series that they are different local churches in the same way as the seven churches of Asia were local churches.[72] This underlying assumption gives the whole series its strong ecclesial orientation. This is the genius of congregational polity. It recognizes the full ecclesiality of each worshiping congregation. A worshiping assembly of Christians is a church in the fullest sense of the word. It is as a member of a church, a visible local church, that the promises of the parable are true for the individual Christian. Shepard tells us that Christ reigns as king over both heaven and earth. Here on earth the saints are commanded to rejoice because of the presence of their king among them. It is in the Church that Christ rules in this world. To be sure, he is present with every one of his people severally, but much more jointly when two or three of them meet together in his name.[73] Here we see one of the great differences between

69. Shepard, *Ten Virgins*, pp. 24 and 25.
70. Shepard, *Ten Virgins*, p. 24.
71. Shepard, *Ten Virgins*, p. 16.
72. Shepard, *Ten Virgins*, p. 26.
73. Shepard, *Ten Virgins*, p. 17.

Catholic mysticism and classical Protestant piety. For Protestants, particularly Congregationalists, piety is always rooted in the worshiping assembly of the congregation.

Sermon 6 makes the point that a true church, as well as a true Christian, is one which, being disengaged from the world, loves Christ and Christ alone, and with single-hearted devotion. This sermon begins by exhorting the congregation to devote her love to Christ. "Here is a match for you! Choose him! If your hearts are entangled with another, get unattached, and bestow your love on him alone!" Make the commitment of faith, not the commitment of a dead, lifeless faith, but of a faith which is animated by love. The apostle Paul tells us of a "faith which works through love" (Gal. 5:6). Let Christ have this love! Love Christ for himself and set your dearest affections on him.[74] This is a rather startling way for a Puritan sermon to begin, but Shepard seems to have departed from the usual homiletical forms of the day quite often.[75]

Having begun with this exhortation, Shepard explains that to press the suit of the Bridegroom is the office of the minister of the Word. He tells us that in doing this the minister is following the office of John the Baptist (John 3:29), who was the friend of the Bridegroom. "And truely it is the main work of the ministry to woo for Christ, and so to present chaste virgins to Christ. This shall be my work now."[76] Here Shepard gives us an important biblical image for the place of the ministry of the Word in worship. Worship is the communion between the Bridegroom and the Bride, between Christ and the Church, and preaching is the Word of love which wins the heart of the Bride.

Shepard tells his congregation to consider the glory of the Christ whose suit his sermon presses.[77] When Christ's glory is revealed and our eyes are opened to see him, our hearts are won for him. Obviously for Shepard the purpose of the sermon is to reveal the glory of Christ, the

---

74. Shepard, *Ten Virgins,* p. 41.

75. Chapter VI begins with the notation "use 3." This suggests that either we are dealing with a sermon which began several chapters earlier, that is, with chapter 3, or that Shepard has taken the traditional sermon outline of the day — doctrine, reasons, uses — and spread it out over a number of sermons. Apparently the whole of chapter VI is devoted to the third use. Chapter VII begins with the notation "use 4" (p. 50). That chapter VI is one complete sermon may be gathered from the final sentence, "Let this day be the beginning of eternal glory to thy soul, and the God of peace be with thee" (p. 50).

76. Shepard, *Ten Virgins,* p. 41.

77. Shepard, *Ten Virgins,* p. 42.

glory that changes the human heart, and his sermon is a whole series of considerations which would bring his listeners to glimpse that glory. One of the most moving of these is that we should love Christ because he is the wonderment of saints in heaven. Shepard uses a marvelous biblical simile to make his point. The queen of Sheba heard of Solomon and therefore wanted to see him. At first she only imagined what she would see, but when she came into his presence she was rapt out of herself. Here in this life the saints hear of the Lord Jesus, of his beauty and glory, and this draws them to enter his presence, and when they do they see what they never had seen before. They fall down in everlasting admiration at this mystery, for their blessedness is to see Christ in his glory. "Now this lies in an infinite good; this cannot be seen in a finite time. Hence saints shall be piercing their eyes deeper and deeper into this mystery, and shall ever see more and more, but never see all; and this is their joy and glory in heaven. Is it so? what think you, is Christ worthy of your love, or not?"[78] This may be Puritan plain style, and these may be only the preacher's preparatory notes, but they are as fervent and eloquent an appeal to love Christ as any preacher ever preached. We can well understand why, almost twenty years after these sermons were preached, Shepard's friends and colleagues pressed for the publication of these notes, however fragmentary they might have been.

The tenth sermon considers the words about the virgins, that they "went to meet the bridegroom" (Matt. 25:1). Our preacher asks what it is to go forth to meet the Bridegroom.[79] It is the soul going forth in faith. To go forth to meet Christ is to see Christ with the mind, to feel after him with the affections, and to fasten upon him with the will. These ten virgins are espoused to Christ already. They have been justified by faith, and now they would go to be glorified with him. Again we see that Shepard thought out this sermon in terms of the Puritan *ordo salutis,* the four steps of salvation: election, justification, sanctification, and glorification. This going forth to meet the Bridegroom is first of all a departing from this world and its joys that one might enter into a far greater joy. Shepard broadens out these thoughts by two vivid biblical images. The Bride of Christ goes out of this world by trampling the moon under her feet as the woman clothed with the sun in Revelation 12. Then the Bride of Christ enters into the king's palace for the wedding feast of the Lamb as the bride

---

78. Shepard, *Ten Virgins,* p. 44.
79. Shepard, *Ten Virgins,* p. 111.

of Solomon entered the ivory palaces of Jerusalem, forgetting her father's house, as in the Forty-fifth Psalm. Here again we see how Shepard joins together the Wisdom imagery of the Solomonic tradition and the apocalyptic imagery of the Johannine tradition. Going forth from this world to meet the Bridegroom, Shepard goes on to tell us, is an act of faith wrought by two affections of the soul, the one hope and the other faith. Here again we are given a marvelous image. Hope and desire are like a blind man and a lame man traveling together.[80] Separately they cannot make the journey, but together they can. Hope, like the eye, goes out and looks; desire, like the feet, runs out and longs. Going forth to meet Christ entails, first, a real expectation of him, and second, a longing desire to be with him. "Hope goes on the top of the world, and cries, O, I see him; desire stands by, and longs for him; O, come, Lord."[81] "A careless, blind world looks not for him, the bride doth." She cries out as the faithful in Revelation, "O, come, Lord Jesus, come quickly" (cf. 22:17 and 20).[82]

The chief point of this sermon is that it is to the person of Jesus Christ himself that faith looks. It is Jesus that the faithful desire, not his gifts of merciful providence or even eternal salvation. The Bride longs for the Bridegroom, not the wedding presents or the new station in life. "It is the bridegroom himself that virgins have to do withal; they are espoused to him as in marriage; there is a giving of themselves one unto another; they make themselves ready for him, they go out to meet him. It is him they love, it is him they want, it is him they look for, it is him they chose withal."[83] As simple and straightforward as this is, it is marvelous rhetoric! The imagery is perfectly suited to make the point the preacher wants to make, and yet it is the biblical imagery. The rhythm of the sentences is superb and yet quite straightforward and quite simple. It is so simple that no one would think to call it great rhetoric. What one recognizes from beginning to end is that to be a Christian is to have a personal relation with Jesus Christ. Shepard makes the point that the best American evangelists have tried to make ever since. He might be called a mystic by those who like that terminology, but the point that becomes so obvious here is that for him the Christian faith is a personal experience. No matter how one

80. Shepard, *Ten Virgins,* p. 112.
81. Shepard, *Ten Virgins,* p. 113.
82. This is obviously not a direct quotation of the King James text, but rather a free paraphrase. As elsewhere in these volumes, we quote Scripture as the preacher we are studying quotes it. Shepard, *Ten Virgins,* p. 113.
83. Shepard, *Ten Virgins,* p. 113.

becomes engaged to Christ, or how one begins the Christian life, in the end it will become a personal experience.

Shepard goes on to explain that it is because the Father wants to give us Christ as our greatest treasure that he withholds many other blessings from us. One must learn to turn away from the secondary blessings that one may learn the primary blessing. Jacob had to experience famine in the land of Canaan that he might discover his son Joseph in a far country. So there is a famine of spirit for the Christian, which often lasts long, in order that the soul might come to see, to embrace, and to rejoice in the Lord Jesus. The most flourishing trees in God's house shall have their winter season, and cast their coat, that they might preserve themselves in their root. This is the great wound of many believing souls for a time. Many a Christian loses the happiness that is in his own hand that he might have it from another hand. But let us not be discouraged, "for faith is an unconquerable grace."[84] Even though the Christian often experiences great joy in the Christian life, in prayer, in hearing the Word, and in divine thoughts, presently the joy leaves us and we wonder why. Commenting on Colossians 3:3, "For you have died, and your life is hid with Christ in God," Shepard assures us that Christ is alive even when we are dead. We are in him and his life is ours.[85] Shepard has a strong doctrine of the perseverance of the saints. Here is a preacher who had gone through many trials; for him tribulation in this life is but an evidence that we are of the elect, and by divine providence we are being prepared for the life to come.

Another point Shepard wants to make is that we are sanctified by faith. What brings us into this communion with the person of Christ is seeing and knowing him.[86] There is a vision of Christ, according to Shepard, which produces a sanctifying faith, as the Christian goes through the trying experiences of mortal life. These visions, or intimations, come through the ordinances, that is, the ordinary means of grace: Word, prayer, and sacraments. When Christ reveals himself to us in Word, prayer, and sacraments, this revelation is irresistible. The Lord reveals himself in such a way that he causes the soul to believe.[87] The very power of it awakens sanctifying faith. Shepard asks, what then is this

84. Shepard, *Ten Virgins,* p. 116.
85. Shepard, *Ten Virgins,* p. 117.
86. Shepard, *Ten Virgins,* p. 120.
87. Shepard, *Ten Virgins,* p. 125.

knowing or seeing of Christ? There is a seeing of Christ after a man believes which is Christ in his love, but our preacher wants to speak of the
light that causes sanctification. This light is an intuitive sight, a very real
sight, to be sure, but it is a sight of Christ in his glory. It is one thing to
see Christ in his merciful love toward us, to know that he seeks us in love.
This intimation of Christ's love wins our love and engages us to Christ,
but to catch sight of Christ in his glory goes beyond even that. It assures
us of his victory over sin. Now, this vision or knowledge which the saints
have of Christ is not by bare word only, but also by Spirit. The word relates to Christ, but the Spirit is the interpreter of the word. It is not that
the Spirit reveals things other than the word, beyond the word, or better
than the word. It is by the word that the Spirit enlightens.[88] Our bare
knowledge is illumined by the Holy Spirit.[89]

As the Christian grows in grace and his sanctification progresses, the
desire for glorification increases. The Puritan *ordo salutis* puts glorification as the fourth and final step of salvation. In the proper sense of the
word, glorification is experienced only in eternity, but glorification was
what the ten virgins were waiting for. Their waiting for the Bridegroom
was the time of their sanctification, but that waiting would come to an
end when the Bridegroom would come and lead them into the ivory palace, and the wedding feast of the Lamb. Commenting on the words of
Paul, "Now we see in a mirror dimly, but then face to face" (I Cor. 13:12),
Shepard tells us that the estate of the saints is translated into a state of
glory. Those who have been justified will be glorified. Sanctification is the
beginning of the life of glory. The light God puts into our minds in order
to sanctify us is the beginning of the light of glory. "Hence, as in heaven,
the soul sees Christ by the full light of glory perfectly, face to face, so in
this life the soul sees Christ really as he is, yet, as in a glass, imperfectly.
Hence, we are said to 'see in part.'"

Now our preacher relates his text to covenant theology. True saving
knowledge and sight of Christ consists in the sight of the glory of his person, especially now "caught up to heaven, and sitting at the right hand of
God, in all the glory of the Father."[90] It is true, Christ will in the end be
seen even by the wicked, but that seeing will not be by faith but by the

88. Shepard, *Ten Virgins*, p. 123.
89. One can hardly imagine that Shepard ever read Saint Gregory of Palamas or
even heard of the discussion of the Byzantine monks over the vision of God, but there are
some striking parallels.
90. Shepard, *Ten Virgins*, p. 124.

senses only. It will be understood by their minds, but it will not shine into their hearts so that it kindles an infinite esteem of him. In our beholding the Lord as he appears in the glory of his covenant, the Lord reveals himself so as to cause us to believe, and to make us his people by entering into covenant with us.[91] When the Lord made Israel his people at Mount Sinai, Moses came down from God with the tablets of the covenant. So when Christ comes to make us his people, he comes as mediator of a better testament.

Christ appears and we behold his glory, full of grace and truth (John 1:14). He appears as one who saves us from our sins and enriches us with his holiness. It is a rule that saving knowledge of Christ is dependent upon a sensible knowledge of ourselves. "Let a Christian in Christ lie in his sins, and comfort himself in remission of them without repentance, he may talk of Christ, but no beauty will appear in Christ. So it is at first; the soul feels sin, and that God is holy, and will hate him; then the Lord shows Christ came to call such. Yea; but I have no good, and can not help myself. Christ appears fit to seek out such. O, but I can not see, nor believe, nor be affected; Christ appears one fit to do all, full of wisdom to perform the second covenant." One cannot help but notice the skillful rhetoric here. Shepard was an accomplished orator: "O, but I want all things; Christ appears all-sufficient. O, but I shall fall; Christ appears constant in his love. O, but he is far to seek; Christ appears present. O, but I shall sin; Christ appears merciful to bear with and heal infirmities. O, but I shall believe too soon; he is fit to prepare and dispose. O, but all the world will be against me; Christ, therefore, appears fit to rule all for me. O, but death and grave may hurt me; Christ appears fit, who has conquered all, and this is ever in the saints."

Shepard is what some call "a master of spirituality," that is, in more Protestant parlance, a teacher of the Christian life. But he is also a master of devotional rhetoric. Notice this series of similes. The poverties of this world, like the comforts of this world, are like fireflies. They are noticed only in the night. When the day comes they are not to be seen. Our weaknesses compared to Christ's strength are like stars that fade before the rising sun. Like Stephen when he was being stoned, the Christian is transported from every pain when he catches sight of Christ in his heavenly glory.[92] As Shepard understands it, to behold Christ in his glory brings us irresistibly to make our covenant with him.

91. Shepard, *Ten Virgins*, p. 125.
92. Shepard, *Ten Virgins*, p. 127.

Shepard now devotes several sermons to the difference between the wise virgins and the foolish virgins. The essential difference is that some are wise and some are foolish. The illuminating wisdom comes from the Word of God which the Holy Spirit applies to the souls of the elect. The foolish virgins are hypocrites whose understanding has not been illuminated and whose use of the means of grace has been ineffectual. They hear the Word preached, but like those Jews who heard Christ preach and did not believe, they do not believe the Word that is preached to them.

Sermon 18 discusses the vessels the wise virgins carried. Shepard tells us the souls of the faithful are vessels made only to receive and preserve the Spirit and grace of Christ. The notes for this sermon are particularly brief, but they do indicate the rich biblical imagery our preacher used to expound his text. And this is particularly interesting because the expanding and elaborating of the biblical imagery is Shepard's consummate charm. By oil is meant the Holy Spirit and his graces with which Christ anoints the elect. Shepard calls on I John 2:27 to make the point that the Holy Spirit is the anointing we have received from Christ. This anointing abides in us and teaches us all things. The graces of Christ are the fragrant oils of the Bridegroom mentioned in the Song of Solomon. These spiritual graces are the anointing on the head of Aaron which runs down into his priestly robes (Ps. 133:2). The anointing produces the graces. Now as Christ himself had not the Spirit without the graces nor the graces without the Spirit, so both are poured out upon us from him who is the fountain of all grace. They are in him as in a fountain and in us as in vessels.[93] Christ being the fountain of all grace and having the Spirit without measure are the source of the golden oil, but we, alluding to II Corinthians 4:7, have these treasures in earthen vessels. With this our preacher turns from the oil to the vessels in which the oil is contained.

As Paul tells us, there are vessels made for menial use and vessels made for noble use (Rom. 9:23). God has made the elect vessels of glory, prepared for glory.[94]

Shepard finds the same imagery in another passage of Scripture, II Timothy 2:20-21 (RSV): "In a great house there are not only vessels of gold and silver but also of wood and earthenware, and some for noble use, some for ignoble. If any one purifies himself from what is ignoble, then he will be a vessel for noble use, consecrated and useful to the master of

93. Shepard, *Ten Virgins*, p. 261.
94. Shepard, *Ten Virgins*, p. 262.

the house, ready for any good work." Our preacher comments: "The Church is God's house." The best vessels are in the house for the master's use only. Sometimes they are filled with puddle water when the master wants to use them, but when the puddle water is thrown out and the vessels purified, then they are ready for the master's use. (Shepard's notes are very sketchy here, but the point is clear enough.) The gold and silver vessels are meant only for the master's table, and then only for the feast days. Although the Spirit may withdraw for some time, and the noble vessels are not used at all and are unable to do any good works, yet they have been made for the Spirit and for the works of the Spirit, and the time will come when they will perform the works for which they have been made.[95]

There is something very moving about the way Shepard puts together the biblical imagery. It makes his sermons pictorial, and even more it gives us the imagery to understand the most profound mysteries of life. It is of the very nature of Scripture that the revelation is at least as pictorial as it is conceptual. If God forbade the making of images "by the art and imagination of men" (cf. Acts 17:29), he nevertheless revealed himself in a most pictorial literature. Preachers who have somehow understood that God has graciously given them the biblical imagery and have cultivated this imagery in their preaching have found it to have in itself a tremendous power.

Sermon 19 develops at length the doctrine of the Holy Spirit. It begins rather abruptly with a statement of the second doctrine Shepard develops from the text on the supply of oil that the wise virgins had with them. Within these vessels is an inward principle of life and grace.[96] The burning, shining profession of the faithful proceeds from an inward principle of the Spirit of grace. It is from the inward work of the Holy Spirit that their lamp burns and their profession shines. The oil in the vessel is the Spirit of Jesus. The Holy Spirit does not originate from ourselves but rather is received in us. It does not merely come upon us or the "Balaamitish ravishments" which may from time to time fall upon the foolish virgins. This biblical image is important to Shepard. Balaam was the priest of Midian who was bribed by the Amalekites to curse the children of Israel. He rode his ass out to perform this infamous task, and his ass saw the angel of the Lord standing in his path preventing his journey,

95. Shepard, *Ten Virgins*, p. 263.
96. Shepard, *Ten Virgins*, p. 268.

but still Balaam was determined to curse Israel. When he opened his mouth to curse, the Spirit of the Lord made him utter an oracle of blessing rather than a curse. Such Balaamitish ravishments are to be distinguished from the work of the indwelling Holy Spirit. The Lord Jesus dwells within us through his Holy Spirit, even the Spirit of life, from whence all our actions spring. This is the oil from which our lamps burn. The profession of the faithful does not spring from outward motives or principles as do the actions of hypocrites. Hypocrites are moved by outward principles, "sometimes sudden praise, sometimes gain, sometimes fears, sometimes fleshly hopes, sometimes sudden conceit and fancy, sometimes irruptions and rushings of the Spirit upon them." Sometimes they are moved by the great power of the Spirit in the ordinances of public worship.[97] The wise virgins have a spring within them, a spring of living water welling up unto eternal life (John 4:14).

In making his application Shepard several times brings up the spiritual problems of the churches of New England.[98] Again and again in this series of sermons he returns to the biblical imagery of the seven churches of Asia in Revelation. At one point he alludes to the church of Laodicea, which had a reputation for being rich but was in fact poor.[99] Here in New England our churches have rich hangings, glorious professions, burning lamps, and astonishing reformations. We have left popery, but we still have our new moons.[100] There is a double meaning here. Even Protestant churches, yes, even the Puritan churches of New England, can be foolish virgins. Their worship, as reformed as it may have been in outward ceremonies, can easily be motivated not by the inward work of the Holy Spirit but by outward concerns. Like the church of Sardis, which had a reputation for good works and then fell asleep, the churches of New England, having begun well, can ignore the moving of the Spirit and be overly concerned for preserving the reputation for being a model of reformation.[101]

The twenty-third sermon takes as its text Matthew 25:5, "While the bridegroom tarried they all slumbered and slept." With this text Shepard begins to concentrate on the meaning of the parable to the churches of New England. As he understands it, the characteristic of churches in the

97. Shepard, *Ten Virgins*, p. 269.
98. Shepard, *Ten Virgins*, pp. 282-89.
99. Shepard, *Ten Virgins*, p. 282.
100. Shepard, *Ten Virgins*, pp. 288-89.
101. Shepard, *Ten Virgins*, pp. 274-75.

last day is that having established themselves securely, they fall asleep.[102] When they are purged from the gross pollutions of the world, then there is a general security and they forget the work they have to do. God warned his people of this danger when they entered the Promised Land. When you come into such a land, beware lest you forget the Lord your God (Deut. 6:12). Like the disciples of Jesus in the Garden of Gethsemane, they fall asleep even though the Lord asked them to pray that they fall not into temptation.[103] When we achieve carnal security, the spirit of prayer becomes silent in spite of knocks of conscience, cries of the ministry, and even woundings from the Lord.[104] Shepard finds this doctrine again and again in both the Old and the New Testaments.

At this point Shepard begins to develop his application. "Let us therefore examine whether this sin be not our sin in this country." Are our churches here beginning to fall asleep?

> We have all our beds and lodgings provided. . . . We never looked for such days in New England. . . . We have ordinances to the full, sermons too long, and lectures too many, and private meetings too frequent; a large profession many have made; but are you not weary? if weary, not sleepy, not slumbering? it may be on you before you are aware, and you not know it; and when so it is, it may be so sweet that you may be loth to see it, that so you may forsake it. Let me knock again: is it not so? Let me come to every man's bedside, and ask your consciences.[105]

Our preacher reinforces his point with a pointed remark about a recent attack on the colonists by the Pequot Indians. "I believe we should not have had those Pequot furies upon us, but God saw we began to sleep."[106] Although everyone is housed and our fields are planted, we still have work to do; we cannot fall asleep now. Shepard urges the establishment of schools, that a new generation of magistrates and ministers might be raised up.

Having made these very specific applications, he returns to the basic passages of Scripture which have guided his whole interpretation of the parable: the seven churches of Asia and the Song of Solomon. Many of

102. Shepard, *Ten Virgins,* p. 371.
103. Shepard, *Ten Virgins,* p. 372.
104. Shepard, *Ten Virgins,* p. 373.
105. Shepard, *Ten Virgins,* p. 375.
106. Shepard, *Ten Virgins,* p. 376.

the same problems which faced the churches of Asia now do indeed face the church of New England. It is not as we read in Song of Solomon 5:2, "I sleep, but my heart waketh." It should be thus, but alas, it is not.[107] Again, we can hardly avoid noticing the beautiful rhetoric.

Before completing our study of Shepard's sermons on the ten virgins, let us look at a sermon he devoted to the subject of the ministry of the Word. As Shepard interprets the parable, the foolish virgins must go to the ministers of the Word if they are to find oil for their lamps.[108] The point our preacher wants to make in this sermon is, "That the Spirit of grace is principally and most abundantly dispensed in the ministry of the gospel by the ministers thereof; . . . this is their business, and trade, and work, like the olive tree to the candlestick (Zech. v.5, 6 [4:11-12]) which taking rooting in the courts of God to this end, to drop in their golden oil; but still observe it is as servants under the Lord Jesus, who gives what and when he will by them."[109] Referring to II Corinthians 3:7, Shepard says the gospel is the ministration of the Spirit in the mouths of the apostles and their successors. The ministrations of the gospel are more glorious than the ministrations of the Law delivered on tablets of stone. Then referring to Galatians 3:2, he asks us, Did you receive the Spirit by works of the Law or by hearing with faith? It is through hearing the preaching of the gospel that the Holy Spirit is revealed and dispensed. For Shepard the reading and preaching of the Word of God in the worship of the Church is the means God has given for the pouring out of his Spirit upon his people.

The reason the public reading and preaching of the Scriptures does this is that God has set aside the ministry of the Word for this purpose. When God sets something apart to any particular end, then it has a strange power to accomplish that end. This is so even if what is set apart seems unlikely or inappropriate for that purpose.[110] A brazen serpent, for example, seems like a strange thing to bring about healing. But it was effective because God set it apart and sanctified it to that end. When God sets something apart as an ordinance, he is present with that ordinance. It is the same way with the setting apart of Aaron and his sons for the service of the Tabernacle.

As we have pointed out before, Shepard's typology is essential to his

107. Shepard, *Ten Virgins*, p. 377.
108. Shepard, *Ten Virgins*, p. 494.
109. Shepard, *Ten Virgins*, p. 495.
110. Shepard, *Ten Virgins*, p. 496.

message, and one finds in this sermon two types of the gospel ministry: the priestly ministry of Aaron and the prophetic ministry of Amos. Puritans commonly thought of the gospel ministry in these terms. They saw the ministers of the gospel as the ministers of the New Covenant, to use the phrase of the apostle Paul (cf. II Cor. 3:6). That is why they called their preachers ministers: they were ministers of the New Covenant. And as such, they were the successors of the ministers of the Old Covenant, that is, Aaron and his sons. There was a distinction between the two ministries, and that was in their function. The ministry of the Old Covenant was instituted to perform the ceremonies and sacrifices of the Law, while the ministry of the New Covenant was to proclaim the gospel.

The type of gospel ministry that receives the most attention in the sermon is the prophetic ministry of Amos.[111] William Perkins, at the very beginning of the Puritan movement, had spoken of the minister of the gospel as the successor of the prophets as well as the apostles. As Shepard speaks about the ministry of Amos and the way the priest of Bethel, Amaziah, forbade him to preach in the king's sanctuary, one inescapably thinks of Archbishop Laud, who for so many years drove the Puritans out of the Church of England. Our preacher never explicitly identifies Laud with Amaziah, but when the reason for driving the prophets out of the Temple is given as "This is the king's sanctuary," no Puritan would have failed to get the point.

To be sure, other perfectly competent sermons were preached when our ancestors first came to these shores. Some were preached in New England and some in Virginia. Some were even preached in California, and even before that in New Mexico, but somehow these sermons stake out the foundations of a new and very special Christian civilization. They are foundation stones most profoundly laid.

B. Sermons on Calvin's Catechism

Shepard's preaching ministry is of particular interest to us because its length and breadth are so well documented. That records of this sort were kept at all in the early days is a tribute to the spiritual intensity of the colony. Aside from the series on the ten virgins, several other series are found in the three volumes of his published works. We know, for example, of a

---

111. Shepard, *Ten Virgins,* pp. 501ff.

long series he did on the Ten Commandments. And even beyond that, there was a particularly important series on Calvin's catechism. The Bibles most of the founding fathers brought with them were Geneva Bibles, and they often had them bound with Calvin's catechism. Shepard is supposed to have preached through this catechism. In fact, he is supposed to have preached through it frequently. This would, of course, have been especially appropriate after Harvard College was established just across the square from Shepard's church.

C. A Wholesome Caveat

Conversion has been a central concern of American preaching ever since the founding of New England. Shepard was regarded as a man who had a conversion experience, and as a preacher he manifested it in a most effective pulpit ministry. It was to this experience of conversion, so important to the newly established churches of New England, that he was able to give voice in his preaching. We find this particularly in a series of sermons preached in 1641, to which the title has been given, *A Wholesome Caveat in a Time of Liberty.*[112]

This series of sermons has two prefaces in the 1853 edition of *The Works of Thomas Shepard.* The first preface is dated 1652 and was possibly written by Shepard's son Thomas, who had prepared a number of his father's manuscripts for publication. Young Shepard followed his father into the ministry, becoming pastor in Charlestown, Massachusetts. Or possibly it was written by Jonathan Mitchell, the successor of the elder Thomas in the church in Cambridge. This preface tells us that these sermons were taken down as notes by a listener. "They are now transcribed by a godly brother, partly from the author's own notes, partly from what he took from his mouth."[113]

A second preface was written for what must have been a second edition. It is signed by William Greenhill and Samuel Mather. Here we are told that notes on the sermons are printed rather than the full text. "These notes may well be thought to be less accurate than if the author himself had published them, and to want some polishments and trim-

---

112. Thomas Shepard, *A Wholesome Caveat in a Time of Liberty,* in *The Works of Thomas Shepard,* 3:285-360.

113. Shepard, *A Wholesome Caveat,* 3:283.

mings, which it were not fit for any other to add; however, thou wilt find them full of useful truths, and mayest easily discern his spirit, and a spirit above his own breathing in them."[114] It has to be admitted that what has come down to us lacks the literary polish which Shepard might easily have achieved in less primitive conditions. Still, these notes taken down by some unknown hand convey the spiritual passion of what might be called the apostolic age of American Christianity.

An interesting thing about this second preface, for our purposes at least, is that it remarks how preaching was considered worship by these spiritual ancestors of ours. It begins: "One of the sweetest refreshing mercies of God, to his New England people, amidst all their wilderness trials, and straits and sorrows, wherewith they at first conflicted in those ends of the earth, hath been their sanctuary enjoyments, in the beauties of holiness, where they have seen and met with Him whom their souls love, and had familiar and full converse with him, above what they could then enjoy in the land from whence they came. This is that that hath sweetened many a bitter cup to the remnant of Israel."[115] How beautifully put — "their sanctuary enjoyments, in the beauties of holiness!" With these words in mind, it should be quite clear that when a New England congregation came together to hear the reading and preaching of Scripture, it had a genuine sense of communion with God. For there they experienced full and familiar converse with God. This is a high doctrine of the pulpit ministry.

Another remark in this preface gives us a valuable insight into the preaching experienced in the first Congregational church in Cambridge:

His manner of preaching was close and searching, and with abundance of affection and compassion to his hearers. He took great pains in his preparations for his public labors, accounting it a cursed thing to do the work of the Lord negligently; and therefore spending usually two or three whole days in preparing for the work of the Sabbath, had his sermons finished usually on Saturday by two of the clock. He hath sometimes expressed himself thus in public: "God will curse that man's labors that lumbers up and down in the world all the week, and then upon Saturday in the afternoon goes to his study, whenas God knows that time were little enough to pray and weep in, and to get his heart in frame, etc." He affected plainness together with power in preaching, not seeking abstrusities, nor liking to hover and soar aloft in dark ex-

114. Shepard, *A Wholesome Caveat,* 3:275.
115. Shepard, *A Wholesome Caveat,* 3:275.

pressions, and so shoot his arrows (as many preachers do) over the head of his hearers.[116]

Shepard was obviously respected as a preacher who fulfilled the expectations of the first generation of New Englanders. One notices immediately that he spoke to his hearers with an "abundance of affection and compassion." He was obviously a studious preacher. That was expected of the Puritan preacher, just as it was in Lutheran Germany. The scholar pastor was the ideal. The pastor was generally expected to spend all week in his study. Calling and other forms of pastoral work might interrupt his studies earlier in the week, but toward the end of the week his whole time would be taken up by sermon preparation.

But we need to point out one more thing. We are told that Shepard "affected plainness." This may not be the way we would say it today, but what is meant here is very clear. In the age of the baroque, that most ornate of ages, one more regularly "affected" anything but "plainness." One affected grandeur, drama, and opulence. Among many the ecclesiastical came very close to the theatrical. What Shepard obviously projected was a saintly and simple dignity, a plainness that was honest and serious.

But let us look at these sermons to learn what their message is. The notes we have no longer make it possible to recover these sermons in their homiletical form. Where one sermon ended and another began is difficult to decipher. Even at that, we find some meaningful passages, especially on conversion, or what it means to receive Christ.

Shepard starts out by pressing the distinction between the outward forms of religion and the inward realities.[117] As Christians we have been called into God's service, and that service has two aspects, the internal and the external. We understand that the internal service has to do with the kingdom of God. Christ teaches us that the kingdom comes not by observances and outward pomp, "For, behold, the kingdom of God is within you" (Luke 17:21).[118] "This is nothing else . . . but when the Lord doth by his Spirit in the word of his grace cause the whole soul willingly to submit and subject itself to the whole will of God as far as it is made

---

116. Shepard, *A Wholesome Caveat*, 3:277-78.

117. Shepard, *A Wholesome Caveat*, 3:288-89.

118. While this quotation follows the King James translation, a number of the Scripture citations are a bit free. The preface made clear that the sermons were taken down as notes and that the editor would make no attempt to revise them. Here we follow the editor.

known to it. 'This is the inward kingdom of God and government of Christ in the soul.'"[119] We read about this in Romans: "So many as are led by the Spirit of God are sons of God" (cf. Rom. 8:14). Here Shepard brings out a whole battery of parallel texts. It was, of course, this sort of thing that delighted the Puritan congregation. This sort of pastoral erudition never ceased to amaze them.

As for the external or outward service, we find that this aspect of the service of God is "to set up and help forward the inward service." The Puritans were not spiritualists. We must recognize the difference between much of the pietism of the eighteenth century and the Puritanism of the seventeenth century. Far from being spiritualists who see the physical as irrelevant to the spiritual, the Puritans insisted that the physical serve the spiritual. While it is true that "external ordinances are nothing in themselves, . . . but as they are appointed and sanctified for this end, they are most glorious."[120] Again Shepard goes on at some length, giving biblical examples of the blessings we receive from serving God in outward and external things. And yet, far more is required than outward service. The inward service of the heart is what God would have from us.

Where the problem comes in is that all too often our hearts become cold before God and we yield him grudging service.[121] From this come the miseries of life. These miseries are recounted at some length. Alas! We too quickly tire of our service to God. Although we have tasted the liberty of the gospel, we too easily slip away into compromises with the world.[122] This is the reason the Lord so often deprives his churches of their liberty and subjects them to iron yokes and pressures. They have cast off the government of the Lord. They have tired of his discipline.[123]

It is here that the question of conversion comes in. How is the heart changed so that one willingly gives to God the service he has called us to perform? How is it that one comes to serve God for his purposes and his glory?[124] Our preacher responds with several points. First, conversion comes about when the soul gives entertainment unto the Lord himself to come into it. To put it simply, it is a matter of receiving Christ. "I say, then, the soul is under the inward kingdom or government of Christ,

119. Shepard, *A Wholesome Caveat*, 3:288.
120. Shepard, *A Wholesome Caveat*, 3:289.
121. Shepard, *A Wholesome Caveat*, 3:292.
122. Shepard, *A Wholesome Caveat*, 3:293.
123. Shepard, *A Wholesome Caveat*, 3:294.
124. Shepard, *A Wholesome Caveat*, 3:300.

when the whole soul gives entertainment to the Lord of lords, the Lord himself, with all his train, . . . for when Christ himself is thus received, the kingdom of God is come to that soul, and entered into that heart; and hence (Mark i.14, 15) the gospel is called the gospel of the kingdom, and when John and Christ preached, 'Believe and repent, for the kingdom of God is at hand.'" Receiving Jesus Christ as Lord is at the center of preaching the gospel. Whether it is Billy Graham in our own day; Charles Finney in the heyday of the New School revival; the Methodist circuit riders on the frontier; Jonathan Edwards in the Great Awakening; George Truett at First Baptist in Dallas; or Henry Boardman, the Old School pastor at Tenth Presbyterian in Philadelphia, this is what the mainstream of American Christianity has understood by conversion. It is a matter of receiving Christ to be the Lord of one's life. This message, so clearly preached at the First Congregational Church in Cambridge, Massachusetts, has been the continuing message of American Protestant preaching. What we find interesting about Shepard's sermons is that this gospel goes back to the first generation of American preachers.

The language of Shepard's gospel may be archaic, the notes taken down by some listener may be a bit clumsy, but the message is clear: "[T]he gospel firstly and primarily offers Christ himself, and faith doth pitch on Christ himself, and doth 'open those everlasting doors that the King of glory may come in.' John i.12, It is said, 'So many as received him, he gave power to be the sons of God.'"[125] Then a bit further on: "Then Christ comes into the soul when the whole soul takes the Lord for himself, Christ, and all that Christ hath, Christ in a pardon, and Christ in a promise: at that very day the Lord gave the heart to receive him, then is the kingdom of God come in that heart, and with him all, life, peace, joy, and glory, God, Spirit, and all."[126] To be sure, there has always been plenty of discussion as to its details, but at the center of it the message is clear: conversion is to receive Christ as Savior.

Unfolding this basic principle, Shepard warns his congregation that to receive Christ as Savior is to receive him as Lord, that is, the one who is to direct our lives.[127] "When the whole soul closeth with the whole will of Christ, having thus received him; for if a prince be come, and people will not be ruled by him nor any laws that he makes, though never so

125. Shepard, *A Wholesome Caveat*, 3:301.
126. Shepard, *A Wholesome Caveat*, 3:302.
127. Shepard, *A Wholesome Caveat*, 3:304ff.

good, but what they list, the kingdom is cast off; for, beloved, there is a marvelous common deceit in men's hearts, they would not for all the world but have Christ; ay, but the will of Christ is neglected, that is a clog, and the burden of the Lord of hosts. Christ is sweet and his will is bitter, Christ is precious and his will is vile."[128] Here is the caveat referred to in the title. Shepard would warn us against the inconsistency of many who claim Christ as Lord but who resist his leading.

As Shepard understood it, conversion is a lifelong process. Only a few years later the *Westminster Catechism* would put it the same way; it was a matter of more and more dying unto sin and living unto righteousness. It was a matter of sanctification. Conversion was not like the mystery religions of pagan antiquity, a once-and-for-all experience that one never had to repeat. The caveat Shepard would issue was for those who had entered into the kingdom. He was preaching to Christians that they not fall away through indolence, the cooling of their hearts, or contentment and self-confidence.

When Shepard preached these sermons, the *Westminster Shorter Catechism* had not yet been written. That was another four or five years down the road. Even at that, Shepard's theological understanding of conversion was very close to that of the Westminster standards. As is very clear from these sermons, conversion is a work of God's grace. "When the soul doth thus submit to the will of Christ, by virtue of the power and spirit of Christ, i.e., when the soul doth not submit by virtue of its own power, strength, or ability, for this is foreign power. But as it doth seek to submit to the will of Christ, so it would have Christ himself act it and rule it, and so enable it to submit thereto. Now is the kingdom of God come near to that heart."[129] It is by the power of Christ that our lives are changed. It is by his grace that we do his will from our hearts. The grace of Christ has great power to transform us into his own image. "When the soul doth lie under the power of the Lord Jesus Christ, when the soul doth lie like wax before the Lord Jesus, when the soul saith, Lord, there was never any change of my nature; the good Lord change it, and if there be any change, the good Lord increase and stir up the graces of thy Spirit in my soul, and do thou lead me and guide me, — brethren, the kingdom of Christ is come to this soul."[130] When a Christian is grappling with his

---

128. Shepard, *A Wholesome Caveat,* 3:304.
129. Shepard, *A Wholesome Caveat,* 3:306.
130. Shepard, *A Wholesome Caveat,* 3:307.

own heart, he will never be able to overcome the resistance of his natural human nature. What the Christian must do is bring his heart to the Lord Jesus Christ. When any man, woman, or child does this, then the yoke of Christ becomes easy and the burden light. Then is Christ's name glorified. "Nothing glorifies Christ so much as this, when Jesus doth work in a Christian; now the kingdom of Christ is come to that soul, and that in power."[131]

One more point. As Shepard sees it, we must be careful to yield to Christ for Christ's ends. Our first-generation American preacher has yet more to his caveat. Our wretched hearts, so clever and so subtle, would have us glorify the Christ that he might glorify us in turn. "Now, if a man shall submit, go to Christ for gifts and parts, that is to set up another king, to advance a man's self; . . . and Christ must be made a servant for this end."[132] We must beware of trying to turn the tables on our Lord. True conversion glorifies Christ for Christ's sake. It is to make his ends our ends. "Man's chief end is to glorify God and to enjoy him forever." The *Westminster Shorter Catechism* may not yet have been written, but its central affirmation was already well understood. In the end our highest joy is his infinite glory.

D. Shepard as Evangelist

Shepard saw preaching primarily as evangelism, and yet a very comprehensive evangelism. It was a matter of continually calling God's people to an ever newer and ever more complete obedience. Shepard also had a comprehensive understanding of worship. He saw it as rendering to Christ the high and holy service of sincere obedience. It is a matter of serving Christ for Christ's glory, not our own, of listening to his word and receiving it and living it. Evangelism is worship because it claims our service, our homage, and our acceptance of his lordship.

Evangelism is the service of the wise virgins keeping watch for the Bridegroom. They listen for his voice and are supported in their waiting by the ministry of the Word. And when he comes, they rejoice in his Word and listen to it attentively. They listen to the preaching of the Word, that they might learn of his coming. They listen for the good news

---

131. Shepard, *A Wholesome Caveat*, 3:308.
132. Shepard, *A Wholesome Caveat*, 3:309.

that he comes. Through the long wait they need to be assured again and again. When evangelism is understood this way, then we understand why even the most mature Christians are constantly in need of it.

But there is another way the ministry of the Word is worship. As we have noticed, Shepard understands the ministry of the Word as the ministry of the friends of the Bridegroom. Like John the Baptist, ministers of the gospel today are the friends of the Bridegroom. The main work of the ministry is to woo for Christ. Preaching prepares the Bride to be presented to Christ without spot or wrinkle. The word of love wins the heart of the Bride.

Yet there is more. The ministry of the Word is sacred worship because when the Bride has been united to the Bridegroom, the conversation of Bride and Bridegroom is a most holy communion. When Christ finally comes, the wise virgins rejoice and listen to his Word attentively. But even more, the Word of Christ is the constant delight of every true Christian. It calls us to awaken us, it teaches us to prepare us, it assures us support. In the end it simply delights.

VI. Increase Mather (1639-1723)

Increase Mather is the most well known of the second generation of New England ministers.[133] He was born in Dorchester where his father, Richard Mather, was recognized as one of the leading ministers of the first generation, one of the founding fathers of New England. Increase grew up in New England and at twelve years old was sent off to Harvard, where he received his basic education and preparation for the ministry. In 1657 he was sent to Ireland, where his older brother Samuel Mather was a minister. After receiving the master of arts degree from Trinity College, he preached in various parts of England for several years until the restoration of Charles II. He returned to Boston in 1661. A few years later he was called to Second Church in Boston, Old North Church, where he remained for more than fifty years.

During that long pastorate Increase Mather became one of the most

133. On the life of Increase Mather, see Michael G. Hall, *The Last American Puritan: The Life of Increase Mather, 1639-1723* (Middletown, Conn.: Wesleyan University Press, 1988); Mason I. Lowance, Jr., *Increase Mather* (New York: Twayne Publishers, [1974]); and Middlekauff, *The Mathers*.

vocal, and most frequently published voices, of established Puritanism in New England. He is usually regarded as the spokesman of Congregational orthodoxy, defending what he regarded as the original purposes of the founding fathers with a rigorous filial piety. The orthodoxy he defended was a particular strain of Puritan thought. He believed in a theocracy controlled by the visible saints for the spiritual good of the whole commonwealth. A strict Congregationalist, he passionately resisted any drift toward Presbyterianism. He regarded it as the duty of the magistracy to maintain order in the commonwealth by laws based on Scripture. New England was a covenant community, as he saw it, with a holy mission in the world to set an example of Christian society. The maintaining of the discipline of godliness was his main concern as a preacher, and to this end he devoted his pulpit ministry.

In spite of his reputation as the voice of Puritan orthodoxy, one notices in his sermons a decided shift. The emphasis on expository preaching so characteristic of the earlier Puritan preachers both in England and America is replaced by what we might call disciplinary preaching. One would like to call these sermons prophetic, but the impression one gets of Mather's preaching ministry falls short of this. He seems more concerned with preserving the order established by the founding fathers than with keeping fresh their vision. While it is true that the apostle Paul had spoken of "reproof, for correction, and for training in righteousness" as one of the functions of preaching (II Tim. 3:16), Mather's approach to this all too often degenerates into attacks on one vice after another. He is often regarded as the great practitioner of the jeremiad, but unlike Jeremiah, he provides no word of consolation. If one reads too much of him, one gets the impression that New England was a failure, something quite opposite to what his son, Cotton Mather, so eloquently claimed in his *Magnalia opera Christi*.

Several published series of sermons show him at his most disciplinary. In 1673 a series of sermons was published against drunkenness, *Wo to Drunkards*. In 1685 a sermon was published, *An Arrow Against Prophane and Promiscuous Dancing*. In 1682 he published a series of sermons delivered to his own congregation, *Practical Truths to Promote Godliness*, outlining the disciplines of piety.[134] There are several sermons on the duties of prayer, the obligation incumbent on Christians by virtue of their bap-

---

134. For a complete listing of the published sermons of Increase Mather, see Thomas James Holmes, *Increase Mather: A Bibliography of His Works* (Cleveland: [Printed at the Harvard University Press], 1931).

tism, the obligation to receive the Lord's Supper, the necessity of avoiding vain persons, and the evils of sleeping during the sermon. One is amazed at the way Mather concentrates on all the externalities of the means of grace while neglecting their inner realities.

In 1687 Mather published *A Testimony Against Several Prophane and Superstitious Customs*.[135] In this series of sermons he attacked health drinking (toasting), playing cards, dice and other games of chance, profane Christmas celebrations, keeping Shrove Tuesday, and cockfighting. The series coincided with the introduction of the Anglican liturgy by the court of the royal governor at the Towne House, and was no doubt precipitated by the introduction of worldly manners and Anglican observances by members of the governor's court. One must say that the level at which Mather treated these subjects is not very profound.[136] To be sure, he was not the first preacher to attack dicing, the theater, and holiday carousing. No one could have gone after the theater more ferociously than John Chrysostom. Gregory of Nazianzus attacked holiday carousing only a generation after the feast of Christmas was introduced. And Mather's sermon against dicing pales before that of Bernardino of Siena. The chances are that John Preston, Thomas Shepard, and Thomas Manton felt much the same way as Mather about these subjects, but one does not find sermon after sermon devoted to them. If Bernardino of Siena devotes a sermon to condemning games of chance, or luxurious clothing or some other vice, it is in the context of a long series of Lenten sermons which culminates in the celebration of Good Friday and Easter. Mather apparently had no scruples about devoting a whole Sunday morning sermon to the evils of drink. One might well ask if this did not compromise the Puritan concept of the Lord's Day even more seriously than the observance of Shrove Tuesday.

The recounting of Mather's preaching ministry thus far suggests that he was one who put the emphasis on the externalities of the Christian faith. His sermons on the Beatitudes, however, show that he had some much more profound thoughts, although, even at that, he lacks the theological consistency of a really profound preacher. Let us look at several characteristics of these sermons.

There is no question but that they are an exposition of the Scrip-

---

135. Increase Mather, *Testimony against Prophane Customs,* introduction and notes by William Peden (1687; reprint, Charlottesville: Published by the University of Virginia Press for the Tracy W. McGregor Library, 1953).

136. Cf. Lowance, *Increase Mather,* pp. 119-26.

tures. Mather's intention is to explain this classic passage of the Bible which so many have preached on before.[137] The sermons follow the homiletical forms of Protestant scholasticism as the English Puritans had developed them. Text, doctrine, reasons, and use divide up each sermon. There is a very conservative Protestant plain style with no high rhetoric. On the other hand, occasionally one finds references to authoritative theologians such as Martin Luther, James Ussher, Richard Baxter, or John Bradford.[138] The chief beauty of these sermons is the sparkling array of parallel texts which we find again and again.

One does have to admit that these sermons occasionally offer some very perceptive thoughts on the nature of public worship. Apparently Mather had a very rich understanding of our participation in the worship assembly. His father, Richard, was a man of prayer and was regarded by the first generation of colonists as setting an especially worthy example of the life of prayer. It may well be that some of these deeper insights are to be traced to Richard rather than Increase. In the sermon on "Blessed are they that mourn" is a beautiful passage on the prayers of lamentation which the Christian offers for those who suffer. Our preacher reminds us that in worship we are united together into the body of Christ. We worship together as one body. One may not be suffering oneself, but one joins oneself to those who do suffer by supporting them in prayer, mourning with them for their suffering.[139]

In his sermon on the pure in heart seeing God, Mather has a beautiful passage on spiritual sight. He tells us that in the meetinghouse, in the course of worship, angels are present. We do not see them, but they are there to assist us in our worship.[140] They could be seen if we had spiritual sight. It is like the servant of Elisha who could not see the hosts of the Lord, drawn up to protect God's people, until suddenly as a miracle he was given spiritual sight (II Kings 6:17).

---

137. In the preface of this volume Mather notes that he realizes that he cannot surpass the sermons Jeremiah Burroughs had preached on the Beatitudes. For a modern edition of these sermons, see Jeremiah Burroughs, *The Saints' Happiness,* photolithographic reproduction (Beaver Falls, Pa.: Soli Deo Gloria Publications, [1989?]).

138. Increase Mather, *Sermons Wherein Those Eight Characters of the Blessed Commonly Called the Beatitudes, are Opened and Applyed in Fifteen Discourses. To which is added, a Sermon concerning the Assurance of the Love of Christ* (Boston: Printed by B. Green for Daniel Henchman, 1718), p. 44, hereafter Mather, *Beatitudes.*

139. Mather, *Beatitudes,* p. 38.

140. Mather, *Beatitudes,* p. 165.

A bit further on in the same sermon we find a passage on public worship as communion with God. The service of worship is the coming together of the covenant community. In this we experience a covenantal communion. "Believers while in this World enjoy God in respect of that blessed Communion which they have with Him. They have Communion with Him in His holy Ordinances. All our Communion with God while in this world, is in and by some Ordinance or other."[141] By ordinances is meant such things as the sacraments, the reading and preaching of Scripture, psalmody, prayer, and the observance of the Lord's Day. The Holy Spirit quickens these ordinances and makes them alive, and thus the means of our having communion with God. The Holy Spirit makes the outward physical forms of worship serve an inward and spiritual communion with God.[142]

As much as these sermons shed light on this weighty passage of Scripture, there are, at least in my opinion, places where he has missed the meaning of the text. The biggest problem is that when Mather gets finished with the Beatitudes, they sound more like a list of qualifications for enjoying the favor of God, and what's more, very demanding qualifications that would tend to discourage the average churchgoer from even trying. In fact, Mather sounds rather like the Pharisees who laid burdens on the common people that were more than they could bear. At the very beginning of the first sermon he tells us that the whole point of the Sermon on the Mount is to show us the spiritual dimension of the moral law, showing not only what external obedience is required but what internal obedience as well. "It condemns not only sinful works and words, but all sinful thoughts also."[143]

In the sermon on the blessedness of those who mourn, Mather ends up making the Christian life sound terribly dismal. He begins by saying that there is a difference between spiritual mourning and sinful mourning.[144] Spiritual mourning is that which is under the afflicting hand of God. It is blessed because it ultimately serves our spiritual growth.[145] Mather gets caught up in legalism in his explanation of this beatitude. He seems to forget that beatitudes should be gospel. He tells us that while the Christian faith forbids neither rejoicing nor mourning, it does regulate

141. Mather, *Beatitudes*, p. 169.
142. Mather, *Beatitudes*, p. 170.
143. Mather, *Beatitudes*, p. 32.
144. Mather, *Beatitudes*, p. 36.
145. Mather, *Beatitudes*, p. 37.

them. This does not sound like a particularly comforting thought; however, it does launch him into a long series of biblical examples of mourning which is spiritually profitable. An example would be the mourning of the exiled Jews by the waters of Babylon in Psalm 137.[146] Then there is the mourning of the bride in the Song of Solomon (5:6), and the mourning of Mary Magdalene at the tomb of Jesus (John 20:11).[147] It is in the piling up of these biblical examples that Mather is at his best.

The ninth sermon, which takes as its text "Blessed are the pure in heart," starts out by telling us the eight beatitudes are "Eight several Characters describing the truly blessed Man."[148] Something very similar has been said in the introduction to a number of these sermons. In several cases the impression is quite strong that these characters are understood as qualifications for God's blessing. In this case it is particularly clear. Without purity one cannot expect to be blessed.[149] The sermon as a whole confirms this moralistic interpretation of the text. At one point Mather tells us that one can tell one's justification by one's sanctification.[150] This seems like a rather tough test to pass. Referring to Psalm 84:11, he tells us that God will give grace and glory to those who walk uprightly.[151] However Mather may have reconciled his interpretation of this text with classical Protestant teaching, we find that he has ended up a long way from Protestant orthodoxy, in spite of his reputation for being a stalwart defender of the New England tradition. At another point he even says that those who are not pure in their lives and conversations cannot expect to be blessed.[152] One gets the impression that those who curse and swear in the open street are not the pure in heart, but rather foul and undisciplined.[153] This sermon in particular I find myself reading to my discouragement. It is condemnation and judgment rather than gospel.

Another characteristic of Mather's sermons on the Beatitudes is their strong emphasis on inherent righteousness rather than imputed righteousness.[154] To put it another way, Mather seems more interested in

146. Mather, *Beatitudes*, p. 38.
147. Mather, *Beatitudes*, p. 39.
148. Mather, *Beatitudes*, p. 146.
149. Mather, *Beatitudes*, p. 147.
150. Mather, *Beatitudes*, p. 157.
151. Mather, *Beatitudes*, p. 158.
152. Mather, *Beatitudes*, p. 161.
153. Mather, *Beatitudes*, p. 162.
154. Mather, *Beatitudes*, pp. 113-14.

sanctification than in justification. One might expect this as a sort of second-generation development. The first generation of Protestants were attracted by the doctrine of justification by faith, but the second generation became more interested in sanctification, or the attaining of inherent righteousness. The problem is that Mather has taken this to a regrettable extreme. In the first sermon of the series he distinguishes between the two. He states very clearly that by nature we are poor and have nothing in the way of spiritual riches. Only by grace do we become rich. We are the poor in spirit until we are blessed with God's grace. By grace we have faith and through faith we have imputed righteousness, but also by grace we have sanctification, or inherent righteousness.[155] Sanctifying grace, particularly the grace of love, is even more desirable than justifying grace.[156] This is how Mather understands I Corinthians 13: faith, hope, and love, and the greatest of these is love. All the way through this series one gets the impression that the Beatitudes teach the Christian the highest levels of holiness. One might say that it is a manifesto for spiritual athletes rather than a gospel for the crowds of humanity.

This often happens in the history of the Church. The enthusiasm of the gospel cools into a spiritual elitism. Or, perhaps, the first generation of spiritual genius is succeeded by a generation that is well trained in going through the motions, but somehow misses the heart of the matter. In my opinion, at least, Increase Mather is an embarrassing example.

VII. Samuel Willard (1640-1707)

Samuel Willard was born and raised in New England. He was educated at Harvard, and after a first pastorate on the frontier, became pastor of Third Church in Boston and finally president of Harvard. He was New England through and through, a worthy example of its best traditions.[157]

Willard was born in Concord, a town on the frontier his father Simon had helped found only a few years before. Simon Willard was a devout man, one of the pillars of the Massachusetts Bay Colony. His leader-

---

155. Mather, *Beatitudes,* p. 113.

156. Mather, *Beatitudes,* p. 114.

157. For a good introduction to the life and thought of Samuel Willard, see Seymour Van Dyken, *Samuel Willard: Preacher of Orthodoxy in an Era of Change* (Grand Rapids: Wm. B. Eerdmans Publishing Co., 1971). Van Dyken gives us an invaluable look into the pastoral ministry as exercised in colonial New England.

ship of the Concord militia eventually made him sergeant major of Middlesex County. He was justice of the peace in Concord and representative at the General Court for fifteen years. For twenty-two years he served on the supreme judiciary of Massachusetts Bay. In addition to all this, he was superintendent of the colonial fur trade. He had particularly good relations with the Indians and was a particularly good friend with John Eliot, so well known for his ministry to Native Americans. Eliot's ministry had been quite successful, and one of the villages of Christian Indians had made Simon its recorder.

As Seymour Van Dyken speculates, young Samuel more than likely received his earliest education at home and learned his Latin at the parsonage. The minister at Concord was none other than Peter Bulkeley, a gentleman theologian quite competent to prepare the more promising young men in his parish for entrance into Harvard. In 1608 Bulkeley completed his master's degree at Saint John's College in Cambridge. He was the son of a clergyman who had independent means, and his mother was of the nobility. As a young man he had inherited a handsome estate and had succeeded to his father's ministry. He was very well situated in England, but Archbishop Laud in his attempt to harrow the Puritans out of the land had him suspended. That prompted him to emigrate, with his family, his servants, and a number of members of his congregation. Peter Bulkeley, having more prosperous means than most ministers, had a substantial library, which in later years he contributed to Harvard. In all probability young Samuel became more than passingly familiar with it.

The Harvard young Willard attended provided much the sort of education as given at one of the colleges at Oxford or Cambridge at the time. The bachelor of arts aimed at giving students a broad, general education with a strong emphasis on the Greek and Latin classics. Lectures were given in Latin. Chapel was held morning and evening and sermons preached frequently, as they were in both Oxford and Cambridge. It was not until one began the master's degree, however, that the academic study of theology began. Here the typical student would have studied the standard commentaries on Scripture and works of systematic theology which were valued by Reformed theologians of the period. The works of John Calvin were quite popular. Such English Reformed theologians as William Perkins, William Ames, John Preston, and Richard Sibbes would have been highly regarded as well. A number of Continental Reformed theologians such as Cornelius à Lapide (1567-1637), Johannes Wollebius (1586-1629), Petrus Ramus (1515-72), and the theologians of the Synod of Dort would have been studied as well. Our young candidate for the ministry is supposed to have finished his formal theological education in about 1662, receiving the master of arts degree.

In 1663 Willard was offered his first call, to the town of Groton, thirty-five miles northwest of Boston. Groton was on the frontier and had been founded only two years before. The first minister fell ill and died a year after being installed. It might seem a hard job for a young man not yet twenty-five years old to be pastor of a village on the frontier, but he had been brought up in a frontier village himself. The hardships of frontier life he had known in his own family. He had lost his mother at an early age and helped bury two sisters. For a young man with that kind of background, theology was not apt to be some sort of idle speculation.

Willard was pastor of Groton for more than a decade. He saw his congregation through one tribulation after another. One troubling pastoral problem was the mental illness of a woman in the congregation. In those days such things were usually understood as demonic possession. As pastor, Willard led his congregation through the prayers and fastings that such problems occasioned. There were days of fasting and humiliation and Willard preached repentance, but the situation remained unresolved until the outbreak of a far more serious tribulation.

In 1675, after a long period of peaceful coexistence with the Indians, there was a full-scale revolt, commonly called King Philip's War. It first broke out in the Plymouth Colony but rapidly spread. All summer long and into the fall one frontier town after another was attacked. The obvious intention was the extermination of the English population. Things quieted down during the winter. Major Simon Willard, our preacher's father, was trying to organize garrisons of soldiers in the frontier towns, but then, on 10 March 1676, Groton was attacked. A Christian Indian had warned that hostilities were about to break out again, but the warning came too late for the town to organize an effective defense. Suddenly about four hundred Indians fell on Groton and put the whole village to the torch. Several people were killed and their bodies desecrated. When the Indians retired, the surviving townspeople decided to abandon Groton and scattered to any community where they could find shelter. For Willard it was above all a spiritual disaster. He must have prayed through the Lamentations of Jeremiah again and again.

In 1678, some two years after he left the smoldering ruins of Groton, he became pastor of South Church in Boston. South Church was the "third gathered church" of the metropolis. From such a pulpit he was able to address the whole of New England. In a very short time he won a high reputation as a preacher.

A. Sermons on Psalm 32

The best sustained look we can get into the regular Sunday-by-Sunday preaching of Samuel Willard is afforded by a series of expository sermons entitled *The Truly Blessed Man, or, the way to be happy here, and for ever: being the substance of divers sermons preached on, Psalm XXXII.*[158] In the preface he tells us this work is a summary of a course of sermons in which he endeavored to lay open this psalm to the congregation to which he had been sent as pastor. In other words, these are expository sermons preached to his own congregation, South Church in Boston, where by 1700 he had been pastor for over twenty years.

The reason Willard chose to preach on Psalm 32, he tells us, is that it speaks very clearly to those central doctrines of justification and sanctification which were so important to the theological concerns of Protestant piety.

These are sermon briefs rather than fully written-out sermons he read from the pulpit. They probably never were written out in full. The briefs had been recast after their preaching as a treatise so that now one cannot tell where one sermon stops and another begins, and yet they are clearly sermons. Logically the Puritan sermon should start with observations on the text, continue with the discussion of the doctrines found in the text, and conclude with a number of uses. With some preachers, however, the discussion of the doctrine, that is, the second part of the sermon, might continue into a second or even a third preaching session. At other times the uses might go into more than one preaching session. The result was that a single sermon, from a formal standpoint, actually ended up being two or three sermons.

The parallel passages in this collection are merely cited by book, chapter, and verse rather than quoted or explained. For the Puritan sermon the parallel passages were of more than passing interest. One wonders if other kinds of exempla or illustrative matter might have been in-

---

158. Samuel Willard, *The Truly Blessed Man, or, the way to be happy here, and for ever: being the substance of divers sermons preached on, Psalm XXXII* (Boston: Printed by B. Green and J. Allen for Michael Perry, 1700), hereafter Willard, *Psalm 32.*

cluded in the preached sermon of which there is little trace in the published sermon. In reading these sermons we easily imagine that we do not have everything that passed over the pulpit.

A good indication of what Willard said in these sermons is given by the list of sermon titles at the end of the volume. Admittedly we use the term "sermon title" a bit loosely, but that is the way our Yankee preacher seems to have organized his publication. Over six hundred octavo pages are found in this work, and thirty-eight sermon titles. Allowing that frequently one sermon stretched out over both morning and evening services, or even more than one Lord's Day, we probably have five or six months of sermons in this volume. The titles are as follows:

1. "A Pardoned Man Is a Blessed Man"
2. "God's Forgiveness Extends to All Sin"
3. "Pardon Removes the Load of Sin from the Sinner"
4. "Forgiveness Covereth Sin"
5. "Pardon Consists in the Non-imputation of Sin"
6. "A Pardoned Man, Is One without Guile"
7. "The Distress of a Conscience Burdened with Sin"
8. "Guilt Apprehended, Distressing to God's Children"
9. "The Danger and Mischief of Sinful Silence and Evasions"
10. "The Distress of Conscience from God's Heavy Hand"
11. "Right Confession, Its Nature and Usefulness"
12. "God's Readiness to Forgive on Penitent Confession"
13. "Examples of Pardoned Sinners, Our Encouragement"
14. "Forgiveness Obtained in a Way of Prayer"
15. "God to Be Sought in a Finding Time"
16. "The Safety of Pardoned Ones in Worst Times"
17. "God Is the Pardoned Man's Hiding Place"
18. "God Will Keep Them from Trouble, Whose Hiding Place He Is"
19. "Faith Engageth the Heart in Making Returns to God for Deliverance"
20. "Experienced Christians Fittest to Teach Others"
21. "Particular Application, the Best Way of Teaching"
22. "Divine Teachings Are to Guide Us in Our Way"
23. "Contumacy to Be Avoided, If We Would Have True Peace"
24. "Untractableness under Teachings, a Vote of Brutishness"
25. "To Go No Farther in God's Service Than Forced, an Ill Sign"
26. "Untractableness under Means, a Character of a Wicked Man"

27. "Wicked Men's Sorrows Great and Innumerable"
28. "Faith the Foundation of True Obedience"
29. "The Rewards of Obedience, Fruits of Meer Mercy"
30. "Every True Believer Is Compassed with Mercy"
31. "There Are Some Righteous in God's Account"
32. "Uprightness of Heart Is Inseparable from a Righteous One"
33. "The Duty and Priviledge of the Righteous and Upright to Rejoyce"
34. "None but the Righteous Can Claim This Priviledge"
35. "The Righteous Should Always Rejoyce"
36. "The Righteous Should Rejoyce Abundantly"
37. "They Should Give Highest Expressions of Their Joy"
38. "Our Rejoycing Should Be in the Lord"

1. The Blessings of God

Let us look more closely at several of these sermons, and first, the introductory sermon, "A Pardoned Man Is a Blessed Man." This first sermon, along with several which follow it, is taken from the first two verses of Psalm 32:

> Blessed is he whose Transgression is forgiven,
>   whose Sin is covered.
> Blessed is the man unto whom the Lord imputeth not iniquity,
>   and in whose spirit there is no guile.[159]

The opening of the text is fairly extensive. Willard considers the occasion for the composing of this psalm. While the text does not reveal this, our preacher speculates that it must have been written when the psalmist was "under sore distress of mind, by reason of the deep sense of his Sin."[160] God had relieved him of his guilt, and he wrote the psalm as a thanksgiving for God's mercy. Willard, who had no doubt searched out the commentaries, reports that it is generally thought that it was occasioned by David's sin against Uriah. Willard notices it has a title; it is "a Maschil of David." Some scholars figure this refers to the musical instruments to be used to accompany the psalm. More than likely, however, this title means it is a psalm of teaching. While some psalms are hymns of praise and others are penitential prayers, this is a doctrinal psalm. The

159. Ps. 32:1-2, as quoted in Willard, *Psalm 32*, p. 7.
160. Willard, *Psalm 32*, p. 7.

doctrine it intends to teach is "to point to us the way how we may come to be truly happy."[161]

Our preacher, still carefully reporting what he has read in the commentaries, discusses at length the meaning of the word "blessed" as found in the original Hebrew text of the Old Testament. Among the most important commentaries would have been those of Immanuel Tremellius (1510-80), an Italian Jew who had been baptized and had in time embraced the Reformation and eventually became professor of Hebrew at Cambridge, and Johann Buxtorf (1564-1629), a distinguished Christian rabbinical scholar who had taught at the University of Basel.[162] Several more words are examined, and the grammar of the text is discussed. Our preacher calls attention to the fact that much of the language here is metaphysical. All this, of course, was thought of as necessary preliminaries to the presentation of the doctrine, or teaching, to be drawn from the text.[163]

The first doctrine he presents to his congregation is "A Pardoned Man, is a Blessed Man."[164] This our native-born Yankee wants to develop in two directions. He wants to discuss first the evils and miseries this pardon frees us from, and second, the privileges it confers upon us. The pardon of God frees us from the condemnation of the Law. As we have it in Romans 8:1, there is now no condemnation for those who are in Christ. No longer is the Law a threat to us, for we have been pardoned from our sin, and therefore the Law has no power over us. Its punishments cannot be executed. God's pardon pacifies his anger.[165] Until that time when we hear the gospel of God's free pardon, we are all conscious of God's anger. As Psalm 7:11 tells us, "God is angry with the wicked every day," and the mature sinner is aware of this. God's anger against sin is the natural reaction of his holiness, which is offended by our sin. Sinners who are under the guilt of sin are therefore the objects of God's displeasure. It is a dreadful misery to be under the anger of God. As we have it in Psalm 76:7, "Who may stand in thy sight when once thou art angry?"[166] But when a pardon comes, then all that anger is set aside.

161. Willard, *Psalm 32*, p. 8.
162. Willard, *Psalm 32*, p. 9.
163. Willard, *Psalm 32*, p. 10.
164. Willard, *Psalm 32*, p. 11.
165. Willard, *Psalm 32*, pp. 12-13.
166. Willard, *Psalm 32*, p. 13. The quotations of Pss. 7:11 and 76:7 are as quoted by Willard.

When God grants us his pardon, then we are discharged from the curse. There is a curse upon all who have sinned under the Law, as we find it in Galatians 3:10, aside from any consideration of the Last Judgment and the world to come. To live this life under the curse of the Law is a very miserable thing. For those who are pardoned, however, the curse has been taken away. We find this taught explicitly in Revelation 22:3, "There shall be no more curse."[167]

The pardon of God stops the mouths of all accusers. "Who shall lay any thing to the charge of God's Elect?" Romans 8:33 asks.[168] An unpardoned sinner is liable to the clamor of every accuser and the turmoil of his own conscience, but God's pardon overcomes all that. When in his own heart a sinner hears the accusations of Satan and Satan seeks to terrify him with the most dreadful representations of sin and the Law, the forgiven sinner has a defense. He needs only hold up his pardon, he "hath his pardon to shew, Signed and Sealed by the Spirit of God; so that he can think of his sins with deepest abasement, and soul humbling thoughts, and yet not be terrified with them."[169] Finally, the pardon of God takes away the terrors of the grave and quenches the fires of hell.[170]

Having discussed the evils and miseries God's pardon frees us from, Willard considers the privileges God's pardon gives us. First, God's pardon grants to us the substance of happiness, not merely its shadow. "Pardon of Sin brings with it all the benefits of Christ." It is in Christ that we are blessed, and from being in him that all that blessedness flows. It is from the imputation of his righteousness that all the privileges flow. It is by faith, therefore, that we receive all the benefits of being in Christ.

Those that are pardoned are justified. "There are two things that belong to the justification of a Sinner, and this is one of them: their sins are forgiven, and they are adjudged righteous, and these are never parted; for, where God pardoneth sin, there he imputeth Righteousness, and thence the man comes to be Justified, so the Apostle argueth, Rom. 4.6, 7. and certainly, he that is Justified is blessed." Here Willard is advancing classical Protestantism as clearly as Luther and Calvin did at the Reformation. Willard sews up his case with a classic proof text, "[F]or indeed, as all misery is rooted in Condemnation, so all felicity flows from Justification: the

---

167. Rev. 22:3, as quoted in Willard, *Psalm 32,* p. 14.
168. Rom. 8:33, as quoted in Willard, *Psalm 32,* p. 15.
169. Willard, *Psalm 32,* p. 15.
170. Willard, *Psalm 32,* p. 16.

Apostle therefore puts them together, Rom. 8.30. 'Whom he hath Justified, them he hath Glorified.'"[171]

Secondly, those that are pardoned have the basis of all peace in the soul. The conscience of the wicked is like a raging sea, always tumbling and tossing, but there is a calm and quiet in the conscience of those to whom God has granted pardon. Conscience is now their friend and accuses them no longer. It gives them confidence. In fact, conscience now testifies for them, as we learn in II Corinthians 1:12.

Thirdly, they that are pardoned are adopted. Paul names adoption one of the great delights of our redemption in Christ.[172] We find in Galatians 4:5 that God sent his Son into the world that we might receive the adoption of sons. Ephesians 1:4 and 5 tell us that the Father destined us in love to be his children through Jesus Christ. Our adoption into his family is one of the high purposes of God. Fourthly, following from this, those pardoned by God and brought into the household of faith become heirs and joint heirs with Christ, as Romans 8:17 says.[173] As a fifth point Willard assures his congregation that those who receive the pardon of God are welcomed into intimate communion with God. Here our preacher uses the imagery of John: "Truly our fellowship is with God the Father, and with his Son Jesus Christ."[174]

Finally, after insisting on the temporal safety of those God has pardoned, Willard opens up their heavenly security. "The pardoned sinner, shall without doubt be made a glorious Saint in Heaven." Christ came to bring about the salvation of sinners, as we learn from I Timothy 1:15. Matthew 1:21 says the Son of God "was made a Jesus" to save us from our sins.[175] Here we have a biblical pun which Willard's congregation would have understood. The name Jesus meant "He will save his people," as explained in Matthew 1:21. Jesus was sent into the world to bring about our salvation, and this is evident from his very name.

Willard, with his strong pastoral concern, was particularly perceptive. Recognizing that not all in his congregation were in the same spiritual condition, he always directed the teachings he drew from the Scripture toward a variety of applications. Ever since Gregory the Great first formulated this principle in his book *On the Pastoral Office,* this insight

171. Willard, *Psalm 32,* p. 17.
172. Willard, *Psalm 32,* p. 18.
173. Willard, *Psalm 32,* p. 19.
174. I John 1:3, as quoted in Willard, *Psalm 32,* p. 19.
175. Willard, *Psalm 32,* p. 20.

has figured as a major feature of homiletical theory. In the sermon before us three different uses are suggested.

The first use is for the spiritually apathetic. The teachings presented in this sermon should awaken those who have ignored spiritual matters to the great joy and blessedness that is available to those who find God's pardon. This is a constant problem which faces the preacher. One always finds among one's listeners those who are in a spiritual torpor. It is not simply that some in our congregations are not yet Christians. The problem runs through all of us. Willard makes this very clear: "Let this then serve to awaken all of us to seek after this pardon."[176] Willard, as many another New England preacher, was quite aware that he was preaching to Christians who were intensely committed, and yet in even the most committed congregations spiritual drowsiness easily puts many asleep. The genius of Puritanism is that while many Christian communities had settled for a religion of low intensity, Puritanism constantly strove for high intensity. It simply could not be content with a Christianity of minimal commitment.

Willard's second use concerns the same problem. He suggests that we should constantly test out or put on trial our spiritual condition. We should always be asking ourselves if we are spiritually awake. This was of the essence of Puritan piety, as it is of any truly Christian spirituality. The Puritans were always afraid that they be "dead asleep in a Lethargy of carnal security."[177] With a good pastor, as Willard was, there is always a balance between the worries of those who are spiritually sensitive and the assurances a Christian receives in the gospel. This is where the third use comes in. This teaching should serve to give us assurance. Certainly those who have heard and understood the teaching of this sermon should be comforted by it. These sermons preach gospel more than all else. One can hardly refrain from pointing out that the message of this sermon is almost the antithesis of the message we found in the sermons of Increase Mather on the Beatitudes.

2. God Our Hiding Place in Affliction

We turn now to three sermons in the middle of the series which show us Willard's preaching at its most pastoral. They are all based on Psalm 32:7,

176. Willard, *Psalm 32*, p. 21.
177. Willard, *Psalm 32*, p. 25.

"Thou art mine hiding place, thou shalt preserve me from trouble: thou shalt compass me with songs of deliverance."[178] The first doctrine Willard would draw from this text is, "A Pardoned Believer hath this security against floods of Affliction, that God is his hiding place."[179] Our preacher then proposes to elaborate his doctrine through three questions: (1) In what respect is God a hiding place? (2) What safety does this afford to God's people? and (3) What consolation can we draw from this?

The pastoral nature of Willard's preaching is evident. This is typical of Puritanism both in England and here in America. While the sixteenth-century Reformers had great devotion to systematic theology, or even more, to biblical theology, the Puritans, following the Reformers by a century or more, were much more interested in questions of piety, or as some would put it, in moral theology or spiritual theology. This we have said elsewhere and often. If one wants to understand Protestant "spirituality," one does not study Luther and Calvin so much as Richard Sibbes, Matthew Henry, and Thomas Shepard. Willard, obviously, is yet another example.

Taking up the first of his three questions, namely, in what respect God is a hiding place, Willard suggests that we recognize that the expression is metaphorical. If we take it as a metaphor, this text tells us that God is everything his people expect from a hiding place. That is, he gives them safe protection from all that threatens to harm them. He is therefore their defense, as we find it in several other psalms. Other words are used, but the meaning is the same. The opening verses of Psalm 18, for example, give a particularly ample list of divine titles: the Lord is our rock, our fortress, our deliverer; he is our rock of refuge, our shield, and the horn of our salvation.[180] All these titles speak of God's protective nature.

In answer to the second question, what safety the Christian has against afflictions, Willard brings out a marvelous collage of Scripture passages.[181] The Song of Moses assures us that the eternal God is our dwelling place and underneath are his everlasting arms (Deut. 33:27). From Proverbs we learn that the name of the Lord is a strong tower; the righteous run into it and are safe (Prov. 18:10). Paul's epistle to the Romans reminds us that if God is for us, no mere human being can be

---

178. Ps. 32:7, as quoted in Willard, *Psalm 32,* p. 382.
179. Willard, *Psalm 32,* p. 383.
180. Willard, *Psalm 32,* p. 384.
181. Willard, *Psalm 32,* p. 386.

against us (Rom. 8:31). These are, to be sure, classic verses of assurance that most of his congregation had known by heart since childhood. Here we have classic expository preaching in the service of a very traditional pastoral function.

The pastoral concern of Willard's preaching is even more explicit for his third question, about what confidence we can take from this doctrine. "Whatever fears a Child of God may be exercised with, whiles under sense of Guilt, by reason of some provoking sin, yet upon his receiving a sealed pardon, he hath all grounds of fear removed, and may be humbly bold." What a beautiful oxymoron, "humbly bold"! Plain style indeed! He was a skillful wordsmith. Willard opens this up in four points. First, a child of God being justified by faith is in a state of grace in spite of whatever sins may have discouraged him. Obviously Willard has a strong doctrine of eternal security. Second, the terrors of sin are now removed. Third, even though we might temporarily fall away, God will not let us be finally lost. "God usually gives more than ordinary Testimonies of his endeared love at such a time. After broken bones and bitter sorrows for sin, God is wont to make great discoveries of his reconciled favor."[182] Fourth, the child of God may with assured confidence apply all the promises of the New Covenant to himself. In all this one has the sense that Willard is speaking not only from Scripture but from his own Christian experience. It could all be a bit tedious with all his proof texts coming one after another, except that one senses he has gone through it all himself. It is of the very nature of true preaching that personal experience witnesses to divine authority.

Having expounded the doctrine he finds in his text, he now takes up the use of the doctrine. For this sermon Willard enumerates two uses; the first is for those who ignore God and pay little attention to spiritual matters. Let those who have little claim to being children of God beware of building their house on the sand, as we have it in the parable of Jesus. The whole sermon presupposes the imagery of the parable. Afflictions are like floods of rain which carry away the house not built on the rock. Any who see a storm coming should beware and think about where they will turn for refuge.[183] Is God your hiding place? Willard presses his congregation to take the question seriously. We often notice in these sermons that Willard is very good at rhetorical questions. Having prompted his

---

182. Willard, *Psalm 32*, p. 387.
183. Willard, *Psalm 32*, p. 388.

flock to think these things over, he assures them, "God, and he alone, can be a safe shelter to you. If he undertake for you, there is no fear: as his power is infinite, so his truth is unchangeable: if he promise, he will perform, if he say he will be your Salvation, he will give being to his word; if he be under a promise, all is settled."[184] What chaste rhetoric!

The second use is directed to the children of God. If you would have God as your hiding place, see that all stands well between you and God. Willard exhorts his congregation to purity of heart and singleness of purpose. While it is true that the title "children of God" belongs to all believers, God is not equally accessible to all his children. Our preacher assumes that his congregation will return home after the service of worship and ponder the preaching they have heard. The Puritan sermon was supposed to stimulate devotional meditation. This is one of the matters our preacher suggests for their meditation. Is there some sin in your life which stands between you and God? As long as there is, God will hide himself from you.

The trouble is that this sin discourages us. It weakens us spiritually. As long as such sin stands unconfessed and unforgiven, "You will certainly be at a woful loss, till you have, by a soaking repentance, made up the breach."[185] And yet, when we see trouble and we fly to God, we honor God. It is true worship when we come to God in our need. When we return to obedience and apply ourselves to the means of grace, God is pleased, and yet that is not what saves us. What saves us is that we put our trust in God and no other to save us. Here Willard becomes eloquent. "Be sure when floods come to make him alone your hiding place. . . . There is safety no where else. If you leave your rock, you will find nothing else to be that to you, which that will certainly be, if you rely on it. . . . With him you shall be in safety. If he be your fortress, all the floods and storms that can beat upon you, will not be able to harm you; you can bid defiance on all that earth and hell can do to you, Psalm 125:1. 'They that trust in the Lord, shall be as Mount Zion, which cannot be removed.'"[186] There is a simple, straightforward beauty to the words of Willard. It might be considered crude in the court chapel at Versailles, but in the context of eternity it is the very soul of eloquence.

---

184. Willard, *Psalm 32*, p. 389.
185. Willard, *Psalm 32*, p. 390.
186. Willard, *Psalm 32*, pp. 390-91.

3. God Our Protection in Tribulation

Sermon 18 again takes up Psalm 32:7, "Thou art mine hiding place, thou shalt preserve me from trouble," but this time elaborating it in a different direction. It focuses on God's protecting care when we are in trouble. The sermon begins with a simple statement of the doctrine the preacher wishes to convey: "They that have made God their hiding place, may and ought believingly to depend upon him."[187]

Coming from long Christian tradition, going back to most-ancient biblical times, Willard understands that the troubles Christians suffer are in reality tribulations and trials. They may be painful, but they have spiritual value. Willard had spoken of this at length earlier in this series of sermons, but the text before him brings him back to the subject again. He speaks about how God saves us from our troubles in such a way that we still receive the benefits of these troubles. Sometimes God simply delivers us from trouble itself. Sometimes he saves us in our troubles. The troubles are not solved, but in the midst of them we are supported so we can bear them. Sometimes God preserves us by turning our troubles into blessings.[188] All this our preacher works out at length. He knows that many in his congregation are undergoing a variety of troubles and need to understand that there is meaning in their suffering.

When Willard finally comes to the third part of his sermon, the uses, he is far more pastoral than theological. When we have to face troubles, we need to recognize that our faith is being tried.[189] Many there are who come to faith and at first experience spiritual prosperity. As in the parable Jesus told of the soils, they receive the Word with joy, but when adversity comes their faith withers away. This is not necessarily the end of the story. Even the truest of Christians can experience a failure of faith, as Peter did when he tried to walk on the water. Yet there are those whose faith survives. They are like Noah and his family. "They have secured their preservation in the day of trouble: they have an Ark in which they are sheltered, and may sleep quietly, though the Floods rise so as to cover the loftiest mountains (Psalm 91:9-10)."[190]

Our preacher proposes four rules for those who would have God's protection in time of tribulation. The first is, you must foresee the prospect

187. Willard, *Psalm 32*, p. 392.
188. Willard, *Psalm 32*, p. 393.
189. Willard, *Psalm 32*, p. 397.
190. Willard, *Psalm 32*, p. 398.

of evil. As we find it in the Epistle to the Hebrews, Noah, being warned of God, was moved with fear and prepared an ark. If God warns us, we must heed that warning. Second, you must see the vanity of other hiding places and renounce them. Third, you must be "Lifted up by a mighty arm into the rock that is higher than you. You did not go into this hiding place by your own strength, but were brought into it by Almighty power; and have accordingly apprehended your own strengthlessness, and felt the efficacy of his grace in causing you to believe; if he had not drawn you, you had not run after him." One easily recognizes the sense of humility as our native-born Yankee witnesses to the graciousness of God's protective care. Willard knew all about this from his living out the Christian life in very difficult days. The final rule he gives is that you must "have taken Christ for your all."[191] If you have made him your hiding place, you have also received him for your Lord and King. Truly to trust him is to be saved by him. It is to have submitted to his government from one's heart.

4. Worship as Thanksgiving

Sermon 19 attracts our attention because of its covenantal understanding of prayer. The title our preacher gives to this sermon is "Faith engageth the heart in making returns to God for Deliverance."[192] Again we are being given an interpretation of Psalm 32:7, but this time of the last phrase, "Thou shalt compass me with songs of deliverance." Our pastor-theologian says the verse refers to the votive prayers of thanksgiving which were offered in the Temple when God had answered prayers for deliverance. Votive thanksgiving prayers were an important part of the worship of the Temple. Psalm 32 was no doubt such a prayer, and the psalm as a whole does indeed teach us much about a covenantal theology of prayer. It is because of the covenant relation between God and his people that prayer in time of need is a logical expression of our worship. The fact that we go to our God and to no other when we are in need honors God. It patently confesses him as our Savior. Prayer in time of need makes clear in whom we have faith. This is particularly clear when our supplications are made in steadfast faith. When we turn to God in constant expectation of his deliverance, this is a clear witness to God's faithfulness. This belongs to a covenantal understanding of prayer.

191. Willard, *Psalm 32,* p. 400.
192. Willard, *Psalm 32,* p. 403.

A covenantal understanding of prayer underlines that prayer is a privilege the Father has given to his children. We pray because God is our God and we are his people. He has a claim on us and therefore we have a claim on him. On the basis of the covenantal relationship we are entitled to pray, and even beyond this, God has promised to hear our prayers because we are his people. Willard quotes a number of passages of Scripture to show that God directs us to pray to him in time of need and promises to hear such prayers. "Hence . . . [faith] directs us to go to God in prayer for this deliverance. If we would have it, not only must we go no where else, but we must repair to him, he hath appointed prayer to be a medium of obtaining, Ezek 37.27. Hence . . . James 5.13. Is any afflicted: let him pray. Thus are we to acknowledge our dependance on him."[193]

Willard brings out another aspect of a covenantal theology of prayer very clearly. When God delivers us from our troubles, we are obligated to witness to his deliverance, and this we do in songs of thanksgiving and praise, that is, "songs of deliverance."[194] Not only that, the true prayer of faith has an eye on the ultimate end of God's glory.[195] We must consider what we should render unto God for all his benefits toward us. We should offer our constant service to him and our heartfelt praise and thanksgiving. We must "pay our Testimonies of gratitude to our benefactor."[196] Here our Yankee theologian has put his fingers on a cardinal dimension of the theology of worship.

From the sermons he has left behind, we cannot help but conclude that Samuel Willard exercised the ministry of the Word with an amazing breadth. He was both theologian and pastor, biblical scholar and spiritual physician. Furthermore, it was not just that on one hand he was professor of theology and on the other hand he was a pastor. It was rather that his theology was at its very roots pastoral, and that is why his preaching was worship. His preaching bore witness to the comforting, the healing, the supporting, yes, to the saving glory of God.

---

193. Willard, *Psalm 32,* pp. 403-4.
194. Willard, *Psalm 32,* p. 405.
195. Willard, *Psalm 32,* p. 406.
196. Willard, *Psalm 32,* p. 408.

B. Sermons on the Catechism

Willard was regarded by his peers as above all a systematic theologian. He produced the first American systematic theology.[197] While not published until after his death, it was the substance of his Tuesday lectures, held once a month, starting in 1688. These lectures, in which he exposited the *Westminster Shorter Catechism*, were enthusiastically heard by the intellectually elite of Boston, and are supposed to be the first attempt at catechetical preaching in New England, although Thomas Shepard had preached through Calvin's catechism many years earlier, as we noted above. In England it was fairly common to preach through this catechism, the most notable example being Thomas Watson's *A Body of Practical Divinity*, first published in 1692.[198] Willard preceded Watson by several years.

By the end of the seventeenth century Protestant theology had produced quite a library of significant theological works. Willard, as we can tell from the margins of his catechetical lectures, was well versed in them. He had obviously read widely in the classical Reformers — Luther, Calvin, Bucer, and even Martin Chemnitz, a notable Lutheran theologian closely associated with Philipp Melanchthon. He had also read the works of Zacharias Ursinus (1534-83), who produced and commented on the *Heidelberg Catechism*. He knew his successor David Pareus and his *Explicatio catecheseos*. Johannes Wollebius (1586-1629), the Reformed preacher at the cathedral of Basel and professor of theology at the University of Basel, was another of his favorites; his compendium of Christian theology was a standard theological textbook. Johannes Piscator (1546-1625), the famous theologian of the Academy of Herborn in the German Rhineland, was another frequently consulted guide.

Willard's study was in no way limited to the theologians of Continental Protestantism. The English Puritans began to produce an impressive collection of theological works toward the end of the reign of Elizabeth I and into the seventeenth century. The thought of William Gouge, William Ames, Richard Sibbes, William Perkins, Thomas Goodwin, and John Preston all shaped this substantial folio volume. That such an im-

197. Samuel Willard, *A Compleat Body of Divinity in Two Hundred and Fifty Expository Lectures on the Assembly's Shorter Catechism* (Boston: Printed by B. Green and S. Kneeland for B. Eliot and D. Henchman, 1726).
198. For a discussion of this work, see Hughes Oliphant Old, *The Reading and Preaching of the Scriptures in the Worship of the Christian Church*, vol. 4, *The Age of the Reformation* (Grand Rapids: Wm. B. Eerdmans Publishing Co., 2002), p. 317.

pressive work could be produced in the colonies before the end of its first century was truly amazing.

C. A Classic Jeremiad

Many occasions demanded that Willard preach a jeremiad.[199] We have already spoken of these Puritan fast-day sermons in our chapter on the Puritans of England in volume IV.[200] As the Puritans saw it, penitential sermons were part of the ministry of the Word as understood from earliest times. Amos, Jeremiah, and John the Baptist had set the example long ago.

A jeremiad Willard preached in 1694 can be considered a classic of the genre. It comes in the later years of his ministry at Old South Church in Boston and was published under the title *Reformation, the Great Duty of an Afflicted People.*[201] In many ways it sums up the fast-day sermons our Yankee theologian preached ever since his first congregation at Groton was disbanded by the terrors of King Philip's War. In fact, the occasion for calling this fast on 23 August 1694 was not unlike the disaster of twenty years before. This time it was the Jesuit missionaries from Canada who stirred up the Indians to attack several outlying New England settlements, which by this time had been rebuilt. On 16 July Oyster River had been attacked and many of its inhabitants massacred. Then a few days later Portsmouth, Exeter, Dover, and once again Groton were attacked.[202] For Willard, we can easily understand, the animosities of the Canadians on the one hand and the savagery of the Native American tribes on the other were a continuing problem, a problem with a deeper

199. On the jeremiad as a particular genre of the New England sermon, see Bercovitch, *The American Jeremiad,* and Stout, *The New England Soul,* pp. 62-63. Apparently the term was coined by Perry Miller. See also Samuel Willard, *The Fiery Tryal No Strange Thing* (Boston, 1682), and Stout's commentary on this sermon in *The New England Soul,* pp. 110f.

200. See also the sections on the preaching of Thomas Goodwin and Jodocus van Lodenstein above.

201. Samuel Willard, *Reformation, the Great Duty of an Afflicted People: Setting Forth the Sin and Danger There Is of Neglecting of It, Under the Continued and Repented Judgments of God: Being the Substance of What Was Preached on a Solemn Day of Humiliation Kept by the 3rd Gathered Church in Boston, on Aug. 23, 1694* (Boston: Printed by Barth, 1694).

202. Van Dyken, *Samuel Willard,* p. 80.

spiritual root. If only the Christians of New England had offered a purer witness of Christian faith before the Native American population, they would never have had the disastrous hostility.

But there was more. The English government had ignored New England for years. The colony had governed itself, but then in 1684 the English government annulled the original charter. A royal governor was sent over who was obliged to be an Anglican. King's Chapel was established in Boston and the Anglican liturgy instituted to the embarrassment of the Congregational Church. During the administration of Governor Andros the affliction was sore and grievous. With the accession of William and Mary the arrogance of the Anglicans was definitely ameliorated, but when Governor Phips arrived as the new governor things deteriorated, and once more the church of New England sensed itself afflicted. In reading through Willard's *Reformation,* it is never clear just what the affliction was. The preacher had to be diplomatic, but there is no doubt both the preacher and the congregation understood several things as afflictions.

The text Willard chose to expound on this occasion is Leviticus 26:23-24: "'And if by this discipline you are not turned to me, but walk contrary to me, then I also will walk contrary to you, and I myself will smite you sevenfold for your sins.'"[203] In good Puritan tradition Willard begins with a few observations on the text. He makes clear that there is a difference between the way God treats his New Covenant people and the way he treats the children of Israel. Children need to be treated with more strictness.[204] God was stricter with the children of Israel than he is with us. We are not under the covenant of Law but under the covenant of grace. Nevertheless, we should take God's judgment on Israel as a warning, as we find in I Corinthians 10:11.[205] The threatenings of the law that we read about in Deuteronomy 28:14-15 stand as a hedge of thorns to keep God's people in a straight way. If they transgress they will scratch themselves. Continued sin, however, breaks down the hedge, and soon God's people will become lost and wild beasts will devour them.[206] Plain style as Willard may be, he often develops the biblical imagery like this.

Willard also says the wording of the text is very emphatic and there

203. This text is taken from the Revised Standard Version. Willard is apparently translating from the Hebrew text, but the full text is not written out in the printed edition.

204. Willard, *Reformation,* p. 6.

205. Willard, *Reformation,* p. 8.

206. Willard, *Reformation,* p. 9.

is an unexpressed assumption that the divine judgments on Israel do not produce reform. It is presumed that they have sinned against the covenant before, and still remain impenitent. Consequently God declares that he will walk contrary to them. He will punish them for their sin.[207]

Having made several similar observations on the text, Willard draws from it his first doctrine, "The Great design of all Gods Judgments on a Professing People is to Reform them."[208] Public calamities may be the lot of a people that claim to be Christian in any case, for the true emblem of the Church militant is a burning bush. Usually, however, they draw on themselves these afflictions because of some apostasy.[209] God may indeed use affliction to strengthen their faith and train them in obedience. I Peter 3:13 teaches that those who innocently suffer will in the end suffer no harm, but will be blessed through the experience. On the other hand, some judgments are tokens of God's displeasure. "They are of the Discipline which God, by Covenant, engageth to Exercise toward his People." In Hebrews 12:6 the Lord disciplines the son he loves.[210] Such corrections are called rods because they evidence God's anger, but at the same time suppose a love which stands behind it. The rod is always used for reformation of those who receive it.[211]

In the usual manner of Puritan homiletics, this doctrine is followed by several uses. First, from this we should learn that if a professing people perish at last, they must blame themselves. To make his point Willard calls on several biblical examples.[212] As a second use our preacher suggests that this should serve to point us to our present duty. Willard admonishes his congregation with real passion. God "hath wasted us by smiting us many ways, and we are reduced to great distresses. . . . What, then, remains but that we set upon a real and a thorough Reformation?" No doubt the passion is fueled by the memory of the disaster at Groton so many years before. Again our Yankee prophet issues a rhetorical question, "Is there not a fearful decay of love, and zeal, and holiness among us?"[213] Again several prophetic texts are brought forward to encourage a reform.

Our New England prophet draws a second doctrine from his text:

207. Willard, *Reformation*, p. 10.
208. Willard, *Reformation*, p. 11.
209. Willard, *Reformation*, p. 12.
210. Willard, *Reformation*, p. 13.
211. Willard, *Reformation*, p. 14.
212. Willard, *Reformation*, p. 16.
213. Willard, *Reformation*, pp. 17-18.

"A declined Professing People, may meet with sore Judgments and yet remain unreformed."[214] There are many examples of this, especially in the Old Testament, and Willard makes his sermon especially vivid by going through them. Jeremiah, not surprisingly, is frequently cited in this sermon. As Willard sees it, "natural man" has a recurrent dislike for the ways of God.[215] We should recognize, however, that afflictions and judgments do not have in themselves the virtue of reforming. They are nevertheless often used by God to change our hearts. It is just part of our human nature that the guilty are slow to accept responsibility for God's disfavor. Indeed, until God pours out his Holy Spirit, human beings have a way of being stupid and senseless.[216]

Willard proposes two uses to this doctrine. We should realize that just because God has sent afflictions, we can count on everything working out well. It only means that God hopes that his people will finally reform.[217] But this teaching should be put to another use as well. It is not enough simply to call solemn assemblies, make lamentation, offer up prayers of confession, and formally renew the covenant. Typically Puritan, Willard insists there must be sincere reformation. This point has been emphasized since the prophet Amos, and made again and again: repentance must go beyond simply participating in a penitential liturgy.

Willard's sermon draws a third doctrine from his text: "If Gods Judgments do not reform a backslidden People, the blame lies in their willfulness."[218] If people refuse to repent, there is no other reason than their obstinacy. It must be granted that they cannot reform themselves, but it is a mistake to give this as a reason for their refusal to reform. The real problem is their willfulness. This Jesus himself made clear in Matthew 23:37, when he spoke of how often he would have gathered his people to himself as a mother hen does her chicks, but they would not.[219] Several other passages are used to make the same point. Then Willard advances some reasons. A considerable part of our refusal to repent lies in the depravity of our wills. Besides that, we are only too willing to shut our eyes and stop our ears against the convictions which are leveled against us and would logically lead to reform. Too many people simply refuse to ac-

214. Willard, *Reformation,* p. 19.
215. Willard, *Reformation,* p. 22.
216. Willard, *Reformation,* p. 23.
217. Willard, *Reformation,* p. 26.
218. Willard, *Reformation,* p. 27.
219. Willard, *Reformation,* p. 28.

cept the help that would bring them out of the difficulties they find themselves in.[220] They really do not want to forsake their sins.

This means two things for our Yankee prophet. First, it should make clear how inexcusable we are, and second, it should humble us.[221] We have been as oxen unaccustomed to the yoke. Even in his straightforward language, Willard is vehement. Surely here there is a genuine revival of both the prophetic message and the prophetic imagery. The Holy Spirit who spoke through the prophets, to use the phrase of the Nicene Creed, that same Holy Spirit who spoke through Jean Gerson and Girolamo Savonarola, obviously was speaking through Samuel Willard.

The fourth and final doctrine Willard drew from his text is that an unreformed professing people do all the while walk contrary to God.[222] All apostasy is a revolt against God. A people that are in covenant with God have accepted God's sovereignty over them. They have owned him to be their Lord and king, and they have bound themselves to be obedient to his commandments. When they are disobedient they depart from their allegiance. Jeremiah 5:23 says they revolt against God. When they continue in their apostasy they provoke God to jealousy.[223] They thereby withstand his glory, but when they repent they do glorify him. This was the sense of Jeremiah's famous temple sermon in Jeremiah 7:1-15. Again Willard finds himself following the message of Jeremiah, making it alive once more in seventeenth-century America. The jeremiad of colonial New England was a notable attempt to continue the prophetic dimension of preaching. Willard exercised this genre magnificently.

Few preachers have offered such a well-balanced pulpit ministry. Willard was a magnificent expositor, a capable systematic theologian, a teacher and catechist, a counselor and pastor, and a prophet as well. The diversity of his ministerial gifts was truly admirable.

VIII. Benjamin Colman (1673-1747)

Benjamin Colman, one of the most urbane and cosmopolitan ministers of New England, presided over Boston's Brattle Street Church for the first

---

220. Willard, *Reformation,* pp. 29-30.
221. Willard, *Reformation,* p. 32.
222. Willard, *Reformation,* p. 36.
223. Willard, *Reformation,* pp. 37-38.

half of the eighteenth century. He made the church the voice of a progressive, irenic, and open-minded Puritanism.[224] Colman was by nature a man of light and warmth, who encouraged his colleagues, supported philanthropic causes, and corresponded with the most advanced spirits of his age. He must have been one of colonial America's most profuse letter writers, keeping in constant touch with Christian leaders from Great Britain to the French and Indian frontier. It was as a letter to him that Jonathan Edwards's *Surprising Narrative* began to evolve. His letters encouraged the leaders of the Great Awakening such as George Whitefield and Gilbert Tennent. He always insisted on the basic validity of the religious experience of the movement and defended it in Boston's most prestigious circles. He also corresponded with the Society for the Promotion of Christian Knowledge in Edinburgh, and through their efforts was granted a doctor of divinity degree by the University of Glasgow in 1731. He was a tireless supporter of missionary work with the Indians. Energetically he worked for Harvard College, and at one point was chosen president, although he finally preferred to remain minister of Brattle Street Church.

Colman brought a fresh spirit to the Boston pulpit. He was almost the antithesis of Increase Mather. Colman represented a broad sort of evangelicalism much like that of Matthew Henry. While he was born and educated in Boston, and spent seven years at Harvard studying liberal arts and divinity, he finished his education with several years in England. There he came under the influence of men such as John Howe, London's ecumenically inclined Presbyterian preacher. As a preacher Howe was literate and intellectually stimulating. Howe was a Puritan of moderation and tact who, although at one time Oliver Cromwell's domestic chaplain, managed to stay on the most friendly terms with more tolerant Anglicans such as Archbishop Tillotson. Howe was one of the chief promoters of the union between Congregationalists and Presbyterians. Very wisely, as Christopher Reaske puts it, Colman took Howe as his role model. He emulated his moderation as well as his eloquence.

Colman was a man of refinement, thoroughly at home in Boston, but who had enjoyed the polite society of London as well. His sermons

224. For biographical information on Benjamin Colman, see Ebenezer Turell, *The Life and Character of the Reverend Benjamin Colman, D.D. (1749)*, facsimile reproduction with introduction by Christopher R. Reaske (Delmar, N.Y.: Scholars' Facsimiles & Reprints, 1972).

were well composed, and were written out with an eye to good literary taste. Colman's son-in-law and biographer, Ebenezer Turell, tells us how his father-in-law prepared them. After prayer asking God's assistance, he chose his text and consulted the best commentaries. Not surprisingly, Matthew Henry, whose commentary on the whole Bible was completed early in Colman's ministry, was his favorite. At that point he would begin to make notes and observations on separate sheets of paper. After some time he would draw up an outline. Then he collected quotations from authors and sought out passages of Scripture to support his theme. Colman would finally write out the sermon in full. This he did rapidly, often in the course of a single morning. This text was written in a beautiful hand on folded sheets of paper stitched together into a small booklet. Preachers of the period were accustomed to taking such booklets into the pulpit with them and then keeping them to be used later as occasion suggested. Colman kept great numbers of his sermons, and they are preserved to this day.[225] Well over a hundred of these were published, particularly funeral sermons, as was the custom in those days. These funeral sermons had a distinct liturgical or, perhaps better, devotional function. They were an opportunity to affirm the Christian faith in eternal life and to meditate on the Christian witness of an outstanding Christian. There are a number of occasional sermons prompted by the fast days and feast days of the community. Such sermons were usually expanded and published as tracts for devotional purposes. Only one extended series of Colman's sermons seems to have been published, a collection of twenty communion sermons, *On the Glories of Christ,* which appeared in 1728.

Brattle Street Church had been founded with very distinct liturgical reforms in mind. Those who organized it were not happy about the

---

225. While we have been unable to find a larger collection of the sermons of Benjamin Colman published as a single volume, many single sermons of his were published during his lifetime. Among the sermons preserved are Benjamin Colman, *The Blessing of Zebulun and Issachar* (Boston: Printed by B. Green, Printer to His Excellency the Governour and Council for Samuel Gerrish, at his shop, 1719); Colman, *Case of Satan's Fiery Darts in Blasphemous Suggestions and Hellish Annoyances* (Boston: Printed by Rogers and Fowle, 1744); Colman, *Credibility of the Christian Doctrine of the Resurrection* (Boston: Printed for Thos. Hancock, 1729); Colman, *A Humble Discourse of the Incomprehensibleness of God* (Boston: Printed by J. Draper, for D. Henchman, 1740); and Colman, *The Judgments of Providence in the Hand of Christ* (Boston: Printed for J. Phillips . . . and T. Hancock, 1727).

disappearance of the public reading of the Scriptures in the service of worship. Under the leadership of the Mathers, only the passage to be preached on was read by the minister. The *Westminster Directory for Worship* had provided for the reading of a chapter of the Old Testament and a chapter of the New Testament at each service, and the organizers of Brattle Street Church wanted to revive this practice. They also wanted to restore the use of the Lord's Prayer in worship. This had been vigorously debated among the Puritans and was perceived as one of the distinctions between Presbyterians and Congregationalists, Presbyterians being in favor of its use and Congregationalists against. A third concern in the founding of the new church was a less stringent policy in admission to the Lord's Supper. This, too, was a favorite topic of discussion among the Puritans of New England. Solomon Stoddard understood Communion as a converting ordinance and therefore advocated open communion. Increase Mather, on the other hand, advocated the strictest fencing of the table. As Mather saw it, only those should be admitted to the table who could relate to the church a distinct conversion experience. The organizers of Brattle Street Church advocated a mediating position between the two extremes. When the young Colman was invited to become the first pastor of the new church, it was already committed to a program of liturgical reform, which Increase Mather denominated as a sort of creeping Presbyterianism. In fact, with an obvious play on the name of the church, he called them a bunch of Presbyterian brats. Nevertheless, by the time the church actually got under way, Mather agreed to preach at the dedication.

Presbyterian brats or not, Brattle Street Church took its place among the Congregational churches of New England, and Colman, who had been ordained by the presbytery in London in 1699, became the leader of this unique congregation. He encouraged the liturgical reforms the founders had envisioned. The Scriptures were read in course, chapter by chapter; the Lord's Prayer was recited after the invocation at the beginning of each service; and believers were admitted to the Lord's Supper in a rather free and open spirit. As the hymns and psalm paraphrases of Isaac Watts began to appear, Colman welcomed them and warmly recommended them to his congregation. It is significant that he began preaching in the Brattle Street pulpit on 24 December 1699, the next to the last Lord's Day of the old century. With that service American Protestantism began to turn from the Puritanism of the old century to the evangelicalism of the new.

IX. Jonathan Edwards (1703-58)

A star of first magnitude in the firmament of American intellectual life, Jonathan Edwards has helped to set the course of the religious life of our nation for over 250 years.[226] His influence in philosophy, theology, and piety is clearly discernible even in our own day.[227] Edwards, theologian, mystic, evangelist, missionary, pastoral counselor, and above all preacher, was a man of balance. He was a man of both breadth and depth. And what makes all this so impressive is that he was nurtured on the frontier. His education was the work of his father, who had studied theology at Harvard, his mother, who was the daughter of Solomon Stoddard, and his older sisters. He went off to Yale at an early age, but Yale at the time was not much older than he was. He never crossed the Atlantic, remaining all his life in the American colonies, and even here he did little traveling. He was a product of colonial America. Even more he was the natural heir of New England Puritanism. One might even say he was the flowering of colonial American Christianity.

One often points to the similarity between Edwards and the pietists of the eighteenth century such as Spener, Francke, and Zinzendorf in Germany and Wesley and Whitefield in England. As similar as they undoubtedly were, Edwards seems to have come to his piety from other sources. The Puritans had always promoted a personal and inward religion. Already the great Elizabethan Puritans had put a strong emphasis on personal piety. Thomas Shepard had preached an almost mystical communion with Christ, and he was hardly unique among the first generation of American preachers. For men like John Cotton, Richard Mather, and Thomas Hooker, religion was intensely personal.

226. For biographical information on Edwards, see David C. Brand, *Profile of the Last Puritan: Jonathan Edwards, Self-Love, and the Dawn of the Beatific* (Atlanta: Scholars, 1991); Conrad Cherry, *The Theology of Jonathan Edwards: A Reappraisal* (Bloomington: Indiana University Press, 1990); John H. Gerstner, *The Rational Biblical Theology of Jonathan Edwards* (Powhatan, Va.: Berea Publications; Orlando: Ligonier Ministries, 1991-92); Nathan O. Hatch and Harry S. Stout, eds., *Jonathan Edwards and the American Experience* (New York: Oxford University Press, 1988); Robert W. Jenson, *America's Theologian: A Recommendation of Jonathan Edwards* (New York: Oxford University Press, 1988); Perry Miller, *Jonathan Edwards* (Cleveland: World Publishing, 1964); and Iain Hamish Murray, *Jonathan Edwards: A New Biography* (Edinburgh and Carlisle, Pa.: Banner of Truth Trust, 1987).

227. Appreciation should be expressed to Daniel Ledwith, one of my students, who has for many years had a special interest in Jonathan Edwards and who has been of great assistance in my research for this chapter.

In New England, where Congregationalism held sway, the Church was understood as a community of visible saints who could testify to a conversion experience and to a daily communion with God. This, at least, was a tendency in New England Congregationalism. Those who had Presbyterian leanings put less stress on conversion, but even at that they were interested in a religion that was personally experienced. That was of the essence of Puritanism. Jonathan Edwards's grandfather, Solomon Stoddard, had somewhat liberalized some of the traditional Puritan attitudes, developing a more inclusive understanding of church membership, but even at that Stoddard could speak of a congregation which had experienced several awakenings during his long pastorate.

Benjamin Colman, pastor of the famous Brattle Street Church in Boston, also had a more inclusive approach to church membership. One did not have to relate a conversion experience to become a member of Brattle Street Church; nevertheless, Colman preached an experiential religion and was one of the strongest supporters of the Great Awakening among the ministers of Boston. Puritanism had traditionally emphasized strong personal commitment, an intense discipline of personal prayer, and serious study of the Bible, aspects of the Christian faith the pietists were recovering. It was only natural that Whitefield, Wesley, Edwards, and Colman should become allies in the spiritual struggles of the eighteenth century. In the same way, it was quite appropriate for Theodorus Jacobus Frelinghuysen and Gilbert Tennent to work so well together in New Jersey, but neither Edwards, nor Colman, nor Tennent was really a pietist.

What makes Edwards such a brilliant star on the horizon of American Christianity is his conjunction of learning and piety. In this he reminds us of no one quite so much as Jean Gerson, the chancellor of the University of Paris who tried to evangelize the fathers of the Council of Constance and then spent his last days catechizing children in an impoverished suburb of Lyon. Edwards was a man of learning even if he did not boast impressive diplomas on his wall. Back in those days Yale was not as impressive as it is today. His reading, however, was intense. He studied the Scriptures with the best tools available. He knew his ancient languages and had read the classics of Reformed theology. While at Yale he read John Locke's *Essay concerning Human Understanding*, which provided a philosophical matrix for him to understand his religious experience, and yet even his wide and intense reading was not the key to his learning. That was his study of religious experience, both his own and that of others. He had a keen eye for observing matters of the soul. He approached it as an empirical scientist. He wrote down his observations constantly. In this he reminds one of Pascal. Edwards thought deeply about his religious experiences and those of his congregation.

Edwards was above all a man who delighted in God. From earliest childhood he was surrounded by devout people. He was the only son in a family of eleven children. His mother, like Susannah Wesley, was a woman of profound spirit, and one gathers that Edwards's childhood home must have been a very happy place. His own marriage was very happy, and he and his wife had ten children of their own. The two were particularly well suited to each other. She was the great-granddaughter of Thomas Hooker, and so quite obviously shared the New England spiritual heritage with her husband. Even as a girl she knew transports of religious experience at which her future husband marveled. At the height of the controversy over the Great Awakening, Edwards published a full spiritual biography of his wife in order to present the awakenings experienced in his congregation in their best possible light. He did not at the time reveal that it was about his wife that he was writing. The interesting thing is that no one so perfectly exemplified his idea of holiness as his own wife. What a delight she obviously was to him! His piety was thoroughly Protestant. It was anchored in home and family as much as in church and congregation. In the common blessings of life, Edwards discovered the glory of God and delighted in that glory.

Edwards was fascinated by nature, and could well have been a naturalist, a botanist, or a zoologist. While still quite young, he wrote a treatise on the habits of the spider. This was the sort of thing an eighteenth-century naturalist did. It was a careful observation, a delight in the constantly unfolding variety of God's creation. The piety of Edwards was as far removed from the piety of Neoplatonic asceticism as the epistemology of John Locke was removed from that of Plato.

Yet his delight in God was preeminently expressed in worship. The Christian Sabbath was a source of great joy to Edwards. He tells us very specifically that he noticed that those who had been converted came to have a great love for the Lord's Day: "There was no time so prized as the Lord's Day, and no place in this world so desired as God's house."[228] In his *Faithful Narrative* Edwards tells of a young woman, Abigail Hutchin-

---

228. Jonathan Edwards, *A Faithful Narrative,* in Edwards, *The Great Awakening,* ed. C. C. Goen, in *The Works of Jonathan Edwards,* vol. 4 (New Haven and London: Yale University Press, 1972), p. 184. Subsequent references to Edwards's works will be cited as Edwards, *Works,* followed by volume and page numbers.

son, who was spiritually awakened, and how she began to discover the delight of psalmody, prayer, and Bible reading.[229] The study of the Bible was a tremendous pleasure to Edwards, as it was to his congregation. They found nothing more interesting than three solid sermons per week. The more spiritual treasures the preacher could produce for any given sermon, the better. Time was not nearly as important as thoroughness and soundness. It was true for Edwards and the Puritans of New England, as it was for the psalmist: "But his delight is in the law of the Lord; and in his law doth he meditate day and night" (Ps. 1:2 KJV).

In his *Faithful Narrative* Edwards speaks of the tokens of God's presence in Northampton during the Awakening:

> God's day was a delight, and his tabernacles were amiable [Ps. 84:1]. Our public assemblies were then beautiful; the congregation was alive in God's service, everyone earnestly intent on the public worship, every hearer eager to drink in the words of the minister as they came from his mouth; the assembly in general were, from time to time, in tears while the Word was preached; some weeping with sorrow and distress, others with joy and love, others with pity and concern for the souls of their neighbors.
>
> Our public praises were then greatly enlivened; God was then served in our psalmody, in some measure, in the beauty of holiness [Ps. 96:9]. It has been observable that there has been scarce any part of divine worship, wherein good men amongst us have had grace so drawn forth and their hearts so lifted up in the ways of God, as in singing his praises. Our congregation excelled all that ever I knew in the external part of the duty before, generally carrying regularly and well three parts of music, and the women a part by themselves. But now they were evidently wont to sing with unusual elevation of heart and voice, which made the duty pleasant indeed.[230]

As one reads the works of Edwards, it becomes very clear that the celebration of the Lord's Supper was a sort of spiritual harvest time. The height of the revival came when, at the celebration of the Lord's Supper, a hundred new converts made their profession of faith and were received into church membership.[231]

229. Edwards, *Works,* 4:191-99.
230. Edwards, *Works,* 4:151.
231. Edwards, *Works,* 4:157.

This delighting in God's presence and delighting in holiness and all its ways was nothing new in Puritanism. Particularly in America it was fairly common to find man's chief end understood as to glorify God and to enjoy him forever. In all this Edwards was but following such founding fathers as John Cotton and above all Thomas Shepard. The Puritans were particularly fond of developing love toward Christ in terms of the nuptial imagery of both Old and New Testaments. This is found with particular clarity in both Cotton's and Sibbes's sermons on the Song of Solomon, as well as in Shepard's long series of sermons on the ten virgins. Edwards was particularly fond of the Song of Solomon, and that magnificent book was often the theme of his meditations on the love of Christ. It was only natural that someone so interested in the religious affections, as Edwards undoubtedly was, should develop a theology of love toward God with such care. He developed this not only in his study of Scripture but also in his study of the religious experience of others.

Edwards, we remember, brought the experiences of David Brainerd to the world. Brainerd, the young missionary to the Indians, was overwhelmed with the love of God and had the most intense experiences of it, and it was for that love that he spent his life in the service of the Indians. Edwards's description of the religious experiences of Abigail Hutchinson and Phebe Bartlett makes clear the same thing. Edwards tells us these women had many extraordinary discoveries of the glory of God. One time while reciting the *Westminster Shorter Catechism* on the divine attributes, Hutchinson had an overwhelming sense of the wisdom, justice, goodness, and truth of God, particularly of the last. "Her mind was so swallowed up with a sense of the glory of God's truth . . . that she said it seemed as though her life was going, and that she saw it was easy with God to take away her life by discoveries of himself."[232] A bit further on Edwards tells us of another one of her experiences "of the excellency and loveliness of Christ in his meekness." She often had overpowering senses of the worthiness of the Lamb that was slain, of the dying love of Christ, and again of his ascended glory. Edwards concluded, "It seemed to me she dwelt for days together in a kind of beatific vision of God."[233] As with Brainerd, this intense experience of the love of God led Hutchinson to a longing for the salvation of all peoples. This coupling of intense awareness of God's presence and the missionary concern has remained a feature

232. Edwards, *Works*, 4:194.
233. Edwards, *Works*, 4:195.

of American piety ever since. Hutchinson delighted in God, in her family, in her household tasks, in her neighbors, and even, Edwards tells us, in her minister.

Edwards was a preacher of revival. And yet he was a revival preacher to a people that was already intensely religious. By 1730 things may have gotten a bit dry, or a bit tedious, in the churches of Puritan New England. After all, New England had been founded more than a century earlier, and it is a bit much to expect enthusiasm for any kind of movement to remain at a high pitch for more than a hundred years. Even at that, the Puritan commonwealth of New England was doing rather well in the years Edwards was pastor at Northampton. The apostasy which troubled a man like Edwards, most pastors today would hardly worry about. The problem was not that the pews were empty in the Congregational churches of New England, but that those who sat there, all quite steadfastly enough, were falling asleep. But Edwards had a vision of Christian society that surpassed by far what had already been accomplished by New England even in the days when its vision was most fresh and its devotion most ardent. Edwards was eager to press on to an even more godly society. He wanted to see people awaken to the most profound realities of the spiritual life. The hopes of the founding fathers had not yet been realized; the millennium had not yet come, but the hope was still very much alive, and Edwards's yearning for spiritual awakening was evidence that the New England vision was indeed still very much alive. His preaching was not a reaction against the old Puritanism of New England; it was its flowering.

Edwards's preaching was clearly the old Protestant plain style. One finds the same time-honored types of sermon outlines. Without any sort of elaborate introduction the sermon begins with a few observations about the text, which lead to a formulation of what is taught by the text, what they called the doctrine. This doctrine is then elaborated, explained, or defended. Reasons are suggested to support it or objections are refuted, and finally applications are made. The applications usually took up the last third of the sermon, and were often made to particular segments of the congregation, to those who had found assurance of salvation and to those who had not; to parents, to children, and to servants; to those who were careful in their religious obligations and to those who were careless. This tradition, which went as far back as Gregory the Great's *Regula pastoralis,* experienced a revival among the Puritans. We noticed it was often used by George Whitefield as well.

The applications might also follow the schema of II Timothy 3:16, that all Scripture is profitable for teaching, for reproof, for correction, and for training in righteousness. This text suggests four types of application: teaching, reproof, correction, and training. Not all four were appropriate to every sermon, but Edwards was rather good at adjusting his theories to the realities he preached. Edwards would quite simply say that in the application we first find that this teaches us the following things. Then, after making that clear, he would go on to say, second, the text reproves us in the following ways, and so forth, until he had covered the types of applications suggested by the apostle. After this had been done, the sermon was ended.

One might have expected that with all his interest in the religious affections, he might have developed a homiletical style more calculated to stir the emotions. The great French pulpit orators were still in vogue in his day. Massillon was still alive when the Great Awakening began. Yet one finds little of grand oratory in Edwards's preaching. There are no arresting introductions, no dramatic apostrophes, no entertaining exempla or stirring conclusions. The reason is that while Edwards believed the religious affections motivated human behavior, he was confident it was at God's initiative that they arose. He was a true Calvinist from first to last. It was by the Word, prayer, and sacrament that the Holy Spirit could be expected to work. To have infused his preaching with emotional appeal would have been much too Arminian, much too Pelagian, much too manipulative for Edwards.

For generations Edwards has been held up to the ridicule of every American high school student as the original preacher of hell, fire, and damnation. The typical high school English teacher in the required American literature course all too often perceives Edwards to be the source of all that made up the worst of American revivalism down to Billy Sunday and Jim Bakker. In the popular imagination Edwards has a bad reputation, and the protestations of serious scholars have been heard only by intellectuals. In his own lifetime there were plenty who grabbed his ideas and ran. Unfortunately they had neither the intellectual nor the spiritual maturity fully to understand what they were doing. What makes Edwards such a significant theologian was his balance, a balance many he influenced lacked. Plenty of other thinkers in the eighteenth century would have been horrified if they had even an inkling of what their ideas would produce. How many of the French philosophes would have been pleased with the horrors of the French Revolution which their ideas fomented? The situation of Edwards is somewhat analogous. His recognition that the religious affections play a major role in our religious experience and his empirical studies of religious experience were a significant advance in the science of theology. That there were those such as Charles Chauncy who saw him only as an outbreak of emotionalism is unfortunate. On the other side were those such as James Davenport whose wild preaching was only a caricature of the Great Awakening. Edwards very carefully avoided the emotionalism feared by Chauncy and exemplified by Davenport.

In his important address at the Yale commencement in 1741, *The Distinguishing Marks of a Work of the Spirit of God,* Edwards made clear the distinction between the work of the Holy Spirit warming our hearts, moving our wills, and enlightening our minds, and whipping up a crowd by an emotional appeal.[234] In this work the leading point is that a revival is essentially a work of the Spirit of God. The last thing Edwards was interested in was how people could be manipulated into a conversion experience by an appeal to the emotions. Not surprisingly the only people who seemed to understand him were those who had experienced the transcendent joys of which he spoke, and they were many.

A. Sermons on I Corinthians 13

Looking at Edwards as preacher, we can find no better place to begin than his expository sermons on the thirteenth chapter of I Corinthians. Here we see him dealing with the religious affections in terms of biblical theology.

To begin his series Edwards takes the first three verses of the chapter: "Though I speak with the tongues of men and of angels, and have not charity, I am become as sounding brass, or a tinkling cymbal. And though I have the gift of prophecy, and understand all mysteries, and all knowledge; and though I have all faith, so that I could remove mountains, and have not charity, I am nothing. And though I bestow all my goods to feed the poor, and though I give my body to be burned, and have not charity, it profiteth me nothing."[235] In his typically unassuming way, Edwards

---

234. Jonathan Edwards, *Distinguishing Marks of a Work of the Spirit of God* (Boston: S. Kneeland, 1741). A modern version is found in Edwards, *Works,* 4:213-88.

235. I Cor. 13:1-3, as quoted in Jonathan Edwards, *Charity and Its Fruits,* in Edwards, *Ethical Writings,* ed. Paul Ramsey, in *The Works of Jonathan Edwards,* vol. 8 (New Haven and London: Yale University Press, 1989), p. 129. In this study, unless otherwise noted, the Scriptures are quoted as the preacher quotes them.

begins his sermon by observing that the subject of this chapter of Scripture is charity, and surely charity is "peculiarly essential in Christians." Jesus and his apostles frequently speak of it; in fact, there is no virtue so much insisted upon by them. To be sure, Edwards reminds us, the English word "charity" does not really give us the full sense of the original Greek word *agape*. The original word used by the apostle had a much broader significance, and might have been better rendered by the English word "love."[236] Most modern translations use the word "love," but as those of us who were brought up on the King James Version will remember, the older translation spoke of charity rather than love. Edwards's text here might be a bit obscure to the modern reader who does not remember the old King James Version.

Edwards usually begins his sermons with a few observations on the text. This observation about a better translation is rather commonplace, but he follows it with a more sophisticated bit of biblical philology. He points out that in this same epistle, at the beginning of the eighth chapter, the word is used to speak both of kindly deeds toward the neighbor and of love for God. The point Edwards wants to make is that what his text calls "charity" is Christian love in its broadest and most profound sense, both to other human beings and to God himself.

His next observation about his text is that those spiritual gifts or pious works mentioned in it such as wisdom, prophecy, the performing of faith healings and mighty works, ascetic rigors and almsgiving are among the greatest gifts one can receive. They are, however, vain if not motivated by love.[237] The sort of thing the apostle opposes is the arrogant wisdom and the hypocritical devotion of the Pharisees. Christ condemned their blindness in John 9:40-41. They pretended to great wisdom, but Christ called them blind. They could prophesy, cast out demons, and do mighty works, as we find in Matthew 7:22. They gave much money to feed the poor, and yet their hearts were cold to those they fed. These observations, though brief, give us a masterful collection of parallel passages. Edwards does know how to do his exegesis.

Having made his observations on the text, our preacher continues with the second part of the traditional Puritan sermon, the drawing out of the doctrine found in the text. That doctrine is simply that all saving virtue is summed up in love. "Let a man have what he will, and let him do

---

236. Edwards, *Works,* 8:129.
237. Edwards, *Works,* 8:130.

what he will, it signifies nothing without charity."[238] Charity is the life and soul of all religion. Without it all other things that bear the name of religion are empty and vain. Even faith, as our text explicitly says, is nothing without it. "That faith which has not love in it, though it be to such degree that men could remove mountains, yet is nothing, like an empty, vain thing, and like the body without the spirit."[239] Here is the essential "doctrine," or teaching, of the text.

Edwards intends to open up this doctrine by showing, first, something of the nature of Christian love and then the truth of the doctrine. By its very nature Christian love is "one and the same in its principle. It may be various in its exercises and objects, it may be exercised towards God or towards men; but it is the same principle in the heart which is the foundation of the exercises of a truly Christian love, whether to God or men." Christian love, quite different from natural love, comes from the Spirit. It is from the Holy Spirit, influencing the heart. "The Spirit of God is a spirit of love. And therefore when the Spirit of God enters into the soul, love enters. God is love, and he who has God dwelling in him by his Spirit will have love dwelling in him. The nature of the Holy Spirit is love; and it is by communicating himself, or his own nature, that the hearts of the saints are filled with love or charity." This emphasis on the work of the Holy Spirit is characteristic of Christian pietism, as we have seen in a number of pietistic preachers down through the centuries.

What is interesting here is that after this strong statement that Christian virtues are the work of the Holy Spirit in the human heart, he tells us that this is why "the saints are said to be 'partakers of the divine nature'" (II Pet. 1:4).[240]

Conversion, for Edwards, is the work of the Holy Spirit. "The Spirit of God in the work of conversion renews the heart by giving it a divine temper. Eph. 4:23, 'and be renewed in the spirit of your mind.' And it is the same divine temper which is wrought in the heart that flows out in love to both God and men."

The nature of Christian love is defined by its motive. "When God is loved aright he is loved for his excellency, the beauty of his nature, especially the holiness of his nature."[241] We love other Christians from the

---

238. Edwards, *Works,* 8:131.
239. Edwards, *Works,* 8:131-32.
240. Edwards, *Works,* 8:132.
241. Edwards, *Works,* 8:133.

same motive: for holiness' sake. "Love to God is the foundation of a gracious love to men. Men are loved either because they are in some respect like God, either they have the same nature or spiritual image of God; or because of their relation to God as his children."[242] Essentially Edwards understands Christian love as a religious affection for God, either as encountered in God himself or in other human beings.

The religious affections are what really motivate our spiritual lives. This was the great insight of Jonathan Edwards. His book *The Religious Affections* is his major contribution to the philosophy of religion. In these sermons love is clearly identified as one of the religious affections, in fact the principal religious affection.

In the usual way of a scholastic mind, Edwards wants to show that this doctrine is true. He wants to defend it or prove it both by reason and by revelation. Typically scholastic, as so many Protestant theologians were at the beginning of the eighteenth century, Edwards firmly believed Christianity was reasonable, and an important part of a sermon like this was demonstrating the reasonableness of Christian teaching. At length our preacher tries to show that "love will dispose to all proper acts of respect to both God and men."[243] The servant who loves his master, just as the subject who loves his prince, will be disposed to proper subjection and obedience. Love will dispose us to all proper duties toward our neighbor. "If men have a hearty love to their neighbors, it will dispose them to all acts of justice toward them. Men are not disposed to wrong those whom they truly love."[244]

Going even further, our preacher insists that reason teaches that whatever virtues or good works we seem to have are hypocritical if not motivated by love. If there be no love in what we do, then our actions are insincere. From this, surely, reason must conclude that there is no sincerity in obedience performed without love.

We learn this from revelation as well, our preacher says; it is what Scripture teaches. Edwards takes up Romans 13:10, where the apostle Paul says love is the fulfillment of the Law. "Now unless love was the sum of what the law requires, the law could not be wholly fulfilled in love. A law is not fulfilled but by obedience to the sum, or whole of what it contains."[245]

---

242. Edwards, *Works,* 8:133-34.
243. Edwards, *Works,* 8:134.
244. Edwards, *Works,* 8:135.
245. Edwards, *Works,* 8:137.

Next our preacher takes up the saying of Jesus on the summary of the Law in Matthew 22:37-39. There we are commanded to love God with everything that we are and to love our neighbor as ourselves, because this is the fulfillment of the Law.[246] We find the same thing in Galatians 5:14, where Paul teaches that the Law is fulfilled in one word, and that word is to love our neighbor as ourselves. The apostle James seems to have the same thing in mind, Edwards suggests, when he tells us that if we love our neighbor as ourselves we fulfill the "royal law."[247]

Finally Edwards gets to the third part of the Puritan sermon, the use, or application. For this sermon he has three uses, one for self-examination, one for instruction, and one for exhortation. Pietism typically gives much attention to self-examination, and here Edwards indeed looks very pietistic. He would have us ask ourselves if we have this spirit of love within us.[248] Do we delight in God, and rejoice in his worship and in magnifying his holy name? Delighting in God is a very important concept in Edwards. In fact, it is a major dimension of his thought on worship. One could almost say that for Edwards worship is delighting in God.

The second application Edwards suggests is instruction. We should learn from this teaching that love is essential to faith. "When persons experience a right belief of the truth of the gospel, such a belief is accompanied with love."[249] Edwards's third use, exhortation, follows closely on this. He urges us to seek this love and grow in it as much as we are able. "If your heart is full of love, it will find vent; you will find or make ways enough to express your love in deeds. When a fountain abounds in water, it will send forth streams. Consider that as a principle of love is the main principle in the heart of a real Christian, so the labor of love is the main business of the Christian life."[250]

The second sermon in this series on I Corinthians 13 takes up once more the first two verses. "Though I speak with the tongues of men and of angels, and have not charity, I am become as sounding brass, or a tinkling cymbal. And though I have the gift of prophecy and understand all mysteries, and all knowledge; and though I have all faith, so that I could remove mountains, and have not charity, I am nothing."[251] Again, in his

246. Edwards, *Works,* 8:138.
247. Edwards, *Works,* 8:139.
248. Edwards, *Works,* 8:142.
249. Edwards, *Works,* 8:146.
250. Edwards, *Works,* 8:148.
251. Edwards, *Works,* 8:149.

usual way, Edwards makes a few observations on the text. Compared to many preachers of his day, Edwards is very conscientious about his observations on the text, but still, for the most part these observations give the impression of being rather preliminary, serving merely to set up the doctrine of the sermon. Here Edwards's exegetical remarks are in considerable detail. First, he wants to speak of the extraordinary spiritual gifts, distinguishing them from the ordinary spiritual gifts. Second, he wants to show that as much as the extraordinary gifts are a great privilege, there is a definite preference given to the ordinary gifts.

As to the extraordinary gifts, the text specifically mentions four.[252] First, there is the gift of tongues, a gift poured out on the Day of Pentecost, frequently mentioned throughout Acts and specifically discussed in I Corinthians 14. Second, there is the gift of prophecy, which Paul also discusses in chapter 14, specifically indicating that it is the most desirable of the extraordinary gifts. The third is knowledge. As Edwards sees it, this refers to "all speculative knowledge of things of religion."[253] The fourth is the sort of faith that produces mighty works and miracles.

On the other hand, the ordinary gifts are fundamental and essential to our existence as Christians. These are faith, hope, and love, and the greatest of these is love. The doctrine this sermon expounds, then, is that the ordinary influence of God's Spirit, working saving grace in the heart, is a more excellent blessing than any of the extraordinary gifts of the Spirit.[254] Today, this sermon Edwards preached two and a half centuries ago is of particular interest because it takes up a question which is at the heart of the debate over the charismatic movement.

The doctrine, or second, part of the traditional Puritan sermon is devoted to nine reasons why the ordinary gifts are to be preferred. Again we see Edwards's concern to show the reasonableness of the Christian faith, and yet the quality of exegesis here is very high. He goes through the whole of the Bible to show that the extraordinary gifts are subservient to the ordinary gifts. We do not need to go through all nine reasons for it to become clear that our preacher has indeed searched the Scriptures very carefully in his attempt to expound to his congregation the passage of the Bible before them.

The third part of the Puritan sermon, the use, or application, pre-

252. Edwards, *Works,* 8:150.
253. Edwards, *Works,* 8:151.
254. Edwards, *Works,* 8:152.

sents four "instructions" for our consideration. First, the ordinary gift of saving grace is the greatest gift God has ever given to any of his creatures. Edwards gives us an especially appropriate biblical illustration at this point.

> Great was the privilege which God bestowed on the blessed virgin Mary, in granting that of her should be born the Son of God; that a person who was infinitely more honorable than the angels, who was the Creator and King of heaven and earth and the great Savior of the world, should be conceived in her womb, born of her, and nursed at her breast, was a far greater privilege than to be the mother of the child of the greatest earthly prince that ever existed. But yet, surely that was not so great a privilege as it was to have the grace of God in the heart, to have Christ, as it were, born in the soul, as Christ himself does expressly teach us. Luke 11:27-28.[255]

The text from Luke gave Edwards everything he needs for his argument. "'Blessed is the womb that bare thee, and the paps which thou hast sucked. But he said, Yea, rather blessed are they that hear the word of God, and keep it.'"[256]

Second, it is clear that extraordinary gifts are not signs the person is saved.[257] The best evidence of saving grace is the fruits of the Spirit. Third, the extraordinary gifts have ceased and will not come back. As Edwards saw it, these gifts are no longer needed by the Church, because it has matured beyond them. Not everyone today would agree with him, but this clearly was the way he regarded such things as the gift of tongues and miracles of healing.[258] Fourth, the fact that God has given us such great and incredible grace is cause for praising God and giving him glory and honor. The blessing we have received in the gift of God's love is far greater than any number of extraordinary gifts.[259]

Even though the Puritans made no special effort to conclude their sermons with an eloquent peroration, the final paragraph of this sermon is magnificent. It is a great statement on the doxological function of preaching. Having received such wondrous grace from God, let us praise

---

255. Edwards, *Works*, 8:166.
256. Edwards, *Works*, 8:167.
257. Edwards, *Works*, 8:168.
258. Edwards, *Works*, 8:171.
259. Edwards, *Works*, 8:172.

and adore him, our preacher exhorts his congregation. Here is first-class rhetoric! In a series of rhetorical questions he urges us to live to God's glory, to exalt his name. In honor of Christ let us consider how we ought to live. We who are so privileged, how can we do anything else than consider how we can live in humble submission to such a generous God? As the psalmist puts it, "What shall I render unto the Lord for all his benefits towards me?" (Ps. 116:12).[260]

Sermon 3 takes up the third verse of I Corinthians 13: "And though I bestow all my goods to feed the poor, and though I give my body to be burned, and have not charity, it profiteth me nothing."[261] On the previous Sabbath our preacher made the point that the extraordinary gifts of grace are nothing without love; now he says moral action is nothing without love. No matter how good an act may look on the outside, without love it is nothing. Neither performances of duties, benevolent contributions, nor heroic suffering really matter apart from it. He develops the text by giving five reasons why this is so. Following this he applies it by urging those who find insincerity in themselves to strive for this spiritual virtue. The sermon as a whole illustrates the highly introspective nature of Edwards's faith.

The fourth sermon brings us to the next verse, "Charity suffereth long and is kind." Originally this sermon was preached over three Sunday mornings. This means that the traditional organization of the sermon into text, doctrine, and use gets a bit lost, but this often happens in Puritan sermons. Even at that, the sermon is filled with fascinating material.

The sermon begins with a few words summarizing what had been said in the three earlier sermons, but we find no remarks on the text, which traditionally was the first part of the Puritan sermon. In all fairness, however, much of the sermon could justifiably be called exegetical comments or observations. The whole sermon might be called an expository essay on the biblical meaning of long-suffering or meekness.

The doctrine or teaching this sermon intends to impart is that "A Christian spirit disposes persons meekly to bear ill that is received from others, and cheerfully and freely to do good to others."[262] Jesus himself made a great point of the value of meekness when he invited us to himself: Come unto me all ye that labor and are heavy leaden (Matt. 11:28).

260. Edwards, *Works,* 8:173.
261. Edwards, *Works,* 8:174.
262. Edwards, *Works,* 8:185.

Learn of me, for I am meek and lowly of heart (11:29). This meekness and lowliness is what is meant by long-suffering in Scripture. It is mentioned as one of the fruits of the Spirit in Galatians 5:22.[263] Edwards is very good at defining biblical terms by showing how they are used in parallel passages of the Bible.

In a particularly fine passage, Edwards gives us four signs of true long-suffering or meekness. First, Christian meekness bears injuries without looking for revenge.[264] Second, it bears injuries while maintaining love to those who caused them. Third, it is born with quietness of mind. Fourth, it is willing to "suffer considerably in our own interest for the sake of peace rather than to do what we have the opportunity to do to defend ourselves."[265] Love to God produces this kind of meekness because we imitate what we love. God treats us with this kind of long-suffering and meekness, as we frequently find in Scripture. With this Edwards brings out a host of examples, which are treated at length.[266] Here we find Edwards's gifts of exposition at their best, and we could very profitably study this sermon in much detail, but we must move on.

The next sermons in the series, following the text of I Corinthians 13, develop the meaning of Christian love. Sermon 5 takes as its text, "Charity envieth not."[267] Here the Christian virtue of charity is considered over against the opposite vice, namely, envy. Our preacher defines envy as "a spirit of opposition to others' comparative happiness, or to the happiness of others considered as compared with their own."[268] Sermon 6 defines Christian love in terms of humility, while sermon 7 shows what Christian love is over against selfishness.

Sermon 7 is of particular note. Its text is the apostle's word concerning love, that it "seeketh not her own." This gives Edwards an opportunity to consider what it means to love oneself.[269] In this sermon he wants to show how the apostle indicates "the nature of charity with respect to our own good, in that it is contrary to pride and selfishness. First, it is contrary to pride. Charity disposes persons not to be proud of what good

263. Edwards, *Works,* 8:186.
264. Edwards, *Works,* 8:190.
265. Edwards, *Works,* 8:191.
266. Edwards, *Works,* 8:193.
267. Edwards, *Works,* 8:218.
268. Edwards, *Works,* 8:219.
269. On this subject see Paul Ramsey in the introduction to the Yale edition, Edwards, *Works,* 8:12-27.

they possess. It is expressed in these words, 'charity vaunteth not itself, doth not behave itself unseemly.' Second, it is contrary to selfishness; it seeks not her own."[270] As Edwards sees it, not all self-love is opposed to a Christian spirit. Quite the contrary, there is a certain sense in which the right kind of self-love is an important Christian trait.

> It is not a thing contrary to Christianity that a man should love himself; or what is the same thing, that he should love his own happiness. Christianity does not tend to destroy a man's love to his own happiness; it would therein tend to destroy the humanity. Christianity is not destructive of humanity. That a man should love his own happiness is necessary to his nature, as a faculty of will is; and it is impossible that it should be destroyed in any other way than by destroying his being. The saints love their own happiness; yea, those that are perfect in holiness. The saints and angels in heaven love their own happiness. Otherwise their happiness, which God has given them, would be no happiness to them; for that which anyone does not love he can enjoy no happiness in.[271]

Other theologians have of course made the same point. Among them is, to be sure, Augustine. Whether or not Edwards is aware of this we cannot say. It ought to be fairly obvious, however, to someone who knew his Bible as well as Edwards. Our frontier theologian continues:

> That to love ourselves is not unlawful is evident from that, that the law of God makes it a rule and measure by which our love to others should be regulated. Thus God commands, "Thou shalt love thy neighbor as thyself" [Matt. 19:19]; which command certainly supposes that we may and must love ourselves. And it also appears from this, that the Scripture from one end of the Bible to the other is full of things which are there held forth to work upon a principle of self-love. Such are all the promises and threatenings of the Word of God, and all its calls and invitations; its counsels to seek our own good, and its warnings to beware of misery.[272]

Being a Christian, as Edwards sees it, does not entail putting aside one's own happiness or neglecting to seek one's own good, but rather regulating

270. Edwards, *Works,* 8:252.
271. Edwards, *Works,* 8:254.
272. Edwards, *Works,* 8:254-55.

it so that it stands in proper relation to one's love of God and love of others. "The alteration which is made in man when he is converted and sanctified is not by diminishing his love to happiness, but only by regulating it with respect to its exercises and influence, and the objects to which it leads."

Edwards's thought at this point contains a realism which makes him much more attractive than many a moral philosopher:

> A man may love his own happiness as much as anybody, and may be in an high exercise of love to his own happiness, earnestly longing after happiness, and yet he may place that happiness so that he may in the same act be in an high exercise of love to God. As for instance, when the happiness for which he longs is to enjoy God, and to behold the glory of God, or to enjoy communion with God. Or a man may place his happiness in glorifying God; it may seem the greatest happiness to him that he can conceive of to give God glory as he ought to do, and he may long for this happiness. Now in longing for this happiness he loves that which he looks on as his happiness. If he did not love what he esteemed his happiness he would not long for it. And to love his happiness is to love himself. But yet in the same act he loves God, because he places his happiness in God. What can more properly be called love to any being, or any thing, than to place one's happiness in that thing?[273]

The logic of this can hardly be improved upon. Edwards continues: "So persons may place their happiness considerably in the good of others, the good of their neighbor, and desiring that happiness, which consists in seeking their good. They love themselves; they love their own happiness. But yet this is not selfishness, because it is not a confined self-love, because his self-love flows out in such a channel as to take in others with himself. The self which he loves is, as it were, enlarged and multiplied, so that in those same acts wherein he loves himself he loves others."[274] The eighteenth century produced quite a number of prominent moral philosophers. It was a favorite subject of the day, and many of the classics of moral philosophy were produced by contemporaries of Edwards. One thinks of Bentham, the earl of Shaftesbury, Hume, Kant, and Voltaire. Edwards was by no means the least of them.

Another point Edwards makes in this sermon is that a Christian

273. Edwards, *Works*, 8:255.
274. Edwards, *Works*, 8:258.

spirit is contrary to a selfish spirit because "a Christian spirit seeks to please and glorify God."[275] From this flows a natural concern for the good of others. This seeking good for others manifests itself in being merciful to others, in being liberal in mercy and in kindness, and in being concerned for the public good. Edwards seems to make a connection between having a true Christian spirit and being a patriot. "A Christian spirited man will be also concerned for the good of his country, and it disposes him to lay himself out for it." He also connects this concern for others with being active in politics: "Especially will a Christian spirit dispose those who stand in public capacity, such as ministers and magistrates and all public officers, to seek the public good."[276]

Another excellent point made in this sermon is that the reason the Christian spirit is like this is that God is like this. God's love begins with himself and then overflows to others, much like the love of Christ, which begins with love of the Father and then extends out to the neighbor.[277]

Sermons 8 and 9 present love again in terms of its opposites. Love is the opposite of both an angry spirit and a contrary spirit.

Sermon 10 takes up practical love. It is based on I Corinthians 13:6, "Rejoiceth not in iniquity but rejoiceth in the truth." It insists that grace tends to holy practice.[278] Saving grace is not static; it leads to action. It is alive and expansive. Edwards puts it quite explicitly: "If any have a notion of grace that it is something put into the heart there to be confined and lie dormant, and that its influence does not govern the man as an active being, or that the alteration of the heart which is made when grace is infused, though it indeed mends the heart, yet has no tendency to a proportionable emendation of life, they have a quite wrong notion of it."[279] For Edwards good theology is practical theology. Good grace is practical grace. Good love is practical love. The Christian life is about practicing one's theology. Surely this is one of the major themes of American Christianity, clearly expressed in the eighteenth century, firmly believed down to the present.

In the usual manner of the Puritan sermon, this doctrine is supported by a number of reasons, in this case five. The first is that "practice is the aim of that eternal election which is the ground of the bestowment

275. Edwards, *Works,* 8:259.
276. Edwards, *Works,* 8:261.
277. Edwards, *Works,* 8:263.
278. Edwards, *Works,* 8:293.
279. Edwards, *Works,* 8:294.

of all true grace."[280] The second is, "That redemption by which grace is purchased, is to that end."[281] Third, "Effectual calling, or that saving conversion in which grace is infused, is to this end." Fourth, "A true knowledge of God and divine things is a practical knowledge."[282] Fifth, this same thing "appears by the more immediate consideration of the principle of grace itself. This also will show that the tendency of all Christian grace is to practice."[283]

Long, enumerated lists of arguments like this are typical of the sermons of scholasticism in both its Catholic and Protestant forms. In Edwards's day, when church people delighted in long, detailed sermons, this kind of exhaustive enumeration reached its height. The fifth argument here opens up into another series of five arguments. When Edwards moves on to show that not only is general grace pointed toward practice, but that particular graces are as well, he enumerates this in twelve points. Only with this is the doctrine of this particular sermon exhausted. Taking up the application, Edwards then gives us seven points. Even if we are amazed by the enumerations of a sermon such as this, we cannot help but be even more delighted with the rich material that is conveyed.

Sermon 11 takes up I Corinthians 13:7, "Beareth all things." Edwards summarizes the doctrine of this sermon by saying, "They who are truly gracious have a spirit for Christ's sake to undergo all sufferings to which they may be exposed in the way of their duty."[284] The point the sermon makes is that love is willing to suffer for the good of those one loves. Willingness to suffer comes from love for Christ, because in love for Christ we participate in his willingness to suffer. In loving Christ we become like him, even in his suffering love. The theme of sermon 12 follows, making the point that all graces are connected together. They all go together. Where there is love there are faith and hope. All the graces depend on each other because they all come from the work of the same Holy Spirit in our hearts.

In the application of this sermon Edwards takes up conversion, the subject which so fascinates him. Pietism has always put a strong emphasis on conversion, and here again we see Edwards coming very close to pietism, as so many in his day did. He tells us that in the vital connec-

280. Edwards, *Works,* 8:294-95.
281. Edwards, *Works,* 8:295-96.
282. Edwards, *Works,* 8:296.
283. Edwards, *Works,* 8:297.
284. Edwards, *Works,* 8:314.

tion of all these graces we come "to understand in what sense old things are said to be done away and all things become new in conversion. This is what the Apostle teaches in II Cor. 5:17, 'If any man be in Christ, he is a new creature; old things are passed away; behold, all things are become new.'" A bit further on Edwards says: "It is in the new birth, as it is with the first birth. The infant in the womb has all the parts of a man. Though they are in a very imperfect state, yet unless it be a monster, there is not one part wanting. Such an infant has as many members as a man in full stature and strength. And therefore what is wrought in regeneration is called the new man; not only new eyes, new ears, or a new head or new hands, but a new man in all the members."[285] For Edwards the practice of love is possible only through conversion. To live a life of true love demands the transformation of our complete being. It is this transformation which is conversion.

In sermon 13 our preacher addresses the text which tells us that charity "endureth all things."[286] This is followed by sermon 14, which begins with a summary of the whole series:

> This chapter is an encomium on charity, and the drift of the Apostle through the whole is to show the preference of charity to all other gifts of the Spirit. He sets forth the excellence of charity in this chapter by three things. (1) By showing that it is the most essential thing, and that all other gifts are nothing without it, in the three first verses. And (2) by showing how charity is that from which all good dispositions and behavior do arise, the stock on which all good fruit grows, and the fountain in which all that is good is contained and from whence it flows, in the four next verses to the end of the seventh. And (3) he shows its preference above other gifts in its being more durable, and in its remaining when the church of God shall be in its most perfect state after other gifts of the Spirit are vanished away, beginning with this eighth verse, the verse of the text, to the end of the twelfth verse. And then the Apostle sums up his conclusion in the thirteenth verse, and so ends the chapter.[287]

The point, of course, is that here in this chapter we have a very full definition of Christian love as understood in Scripture. The message Edwards

---

285. Edwards, *Works,* 8:334-35.
286. Edwards, *Works,* 8:339.
287. Edwards, *Works,* 8:351.

wants to get across in these sermons is that love is the mainspring of the Christian life.

The final sermon in the series, number 15, "Heaven Is a World of Love," is one of the classics of the American pulpit. The text encompasses three verses, "Charity never faileth but whether there be prophecies, they shall fail; whether there be tongues, they shall cease; whether there be knowledge, it shall vanish away. For we know in part, and we prophesy in part. But when that which is perfect is come, then that which is in part shall be done away."[288] Strangely enough the last verses of the chapter are omitted.

In his observations on the text Edwards tells us that the Church exists in two stages. One stage started in the days of the apostles and continues as long as the Church is here on earth. This is the Church militant, the childhood of the Church. But there is another stage, and that is the Church triumphant. That is the mature stage of the Church; it is its heavenly existence, for only in heaven does the Church come to the measure of the stature of the fullness of Christ. It is about this mature, adult state of the Church that the apostle speaks in the concluding verses of this chapter. Here we read, "'When that which is perfect is come, that which is in part shall be done away.' 'Now we see through a glass darkly; but then face to face; now I know in part; but then shall I know, even as also I am known.'"[289]

Coming to the "doctrine" of the sermon, Edwards tells us, "The Apostle in the text speaks of a state of the church which is perfect, and therefore a state in which the Holy Spirit shall more perfectly and abundantly be given to the church than it now is. But the way in which it shall be given, when it is so abundantly poured forth, will be in that great fruit of the Spirit, holy and divine love in the hearts of all the blessed inhabitants of that world."[290]

To make clear how heaven is a world of love, our preacher gives us six points of doctrine he has taken from his text. First, he would consider the great cause and fountain of love which is there. Heaven is the dwelling place of God. "Heaven is the palace, or presence-chamber, of the Supreme Being who is both the cause and source of all holy love." Indeed, God is everywhere, for he fills heaven and earth and yet is said to dwell in Israel

288. Edwards, *Works,* 8:366.
289. Edwards, *Works,* 8:367.
290. Edwards, *Works,* 8:368.

above all lands, and in Jerusalem above all cities, and in the Temple above all other houses in the city, and in the Holy of Holies above all other apartments in that Temple, and on the mercy seat over the ark above all other places in the Holy of Holies. So it is said that God's dwelling place is in heaven above all other places in the universe. What superb rhetoric!

Essential to understanding how Edwards communicates is his remark at this point: "Those places in which he was said to dwell of old were all but types of this." Our preacher well understands the function of types in the Scriptures, and he richly uses the classical Christian typology. "Heaven is a part of the creation which God has built for this end, to be the place of his glorious presence. And it is his abode forever. Here he will dwell and gloriously manifest himself to eternity. And this renders heaven a world of love; for God is the fountain of love, as the sun is the fountain of light."[291] God himself is the fountain of love, and God himself makes heaven a world of love.

Second, Edwards would have us consider heaven in regard to the objects of love it contains.[292] Here he develops the typology of the book of Revelation. He quotes Revelation 21:27 to the effect that nothing defiled, no abomination, no lie or untruth shall enter into the heavenly city. From chapter 22 he takes the imagery of the crystal fountain. "There the Holy Spirit shall be poured forth with perfect sweetness, as a pure river of water of life, clear as crystal, . . . a river whose waters are without any manner of pollution. And every member of that glorious society shall be without blemish of sin or imprudence or any kind of failure." Then he develops the type of the Bride of Christ to show that the objects of Christian love in heaven will be altogether lovely and pure, without spot or wrinkle.[293]

Third, our preacher invites us to consider the love which is there in regard to the subjects of the heavenly city. The heart of God is the original seat or subject of the divine love. "Divine love is in him not as a subject which receives from another, but as its original seat, where it is of itself." With this Edwards introduces once more his highly developed typology. "Love is in God as light is in the sun, which does not shine by a reflected light as the moon and the planets do; but by his own light, and as the fountain of light." But because God is the fountain of love, this love flows

291. Edwards, *Works,* 8:369.
292. Edwards, *Works,* 8:370.
293. Edwards, *Works,* 8:371.

out to others. First it flows out to the Son, and then to the elect. It flows out to all the inhabitants of heaven.

> And the Son of God is not only the infinite object of love, but he is also an infinite subject of it. He is not only the infinite object of the Father's love, but he also infinitely loves the Father. The infinite essential love of God is, as it were, an infinite and eternal mutual holy energy between the Father and the Son, a pure, holy act whereby the Deity becomes nothing but an infinite and unchangeable act of love, which proceeds from both the Father and the Son. Thus divine love has its seat in the Deity as it is exercised within the Deity, or in God towards himself.

Here is high theological preaching as brilliant as has ever been preached.

Edwards has much more to say under this point. He speaks of the love of God to the saints and angels. The love of God "flows out in innumerable streams towards all the created inhabitants of heaven; he loves all the saints and angels there."[294]

Fourth, our preacher wants to "say something of the principle . . . which fills the heavenly world." The principle is of course love itself, and we need to speak of both its nature and its degree. In nature it is altogether holy and divine. The love that is experienced in heaven is never compromised by mixed motives, by self-centeredness, or by impure desires. "There love is a pure flame. The saints there love God for his own sake, and each other for God's sake, for the sake of that relation which they bear to God, and that image of God which is upon them." As to its degree, it is perfect, with an absolute, infinite, and divine perfection. Here Edwards provides a good biblical simile: "That which was in the heart as but a grain of mustard seed in this world shall there be as a great tree."[295]

Fifth, our preacher wants to consider "some of the excellent circumstances in which love shall be expressed and enjoyed in heaven."[296] Ten subpoints are opened up under this subject. Heavenly love always meets with a return. The joy of heaven shall never be interrupted by jealousy. It will be expressed in perfect decency and wisdom. In heaven there will be nothing to hinder the perfect enjoyment of this mutual love. Again calling on the imagery of the Song of Solomon, Edwards insists that in heav-

---

294. Edwards, *Works*, 8:373.
295. Edwards, *Works*, 8:374.
296. Edwards, *Works*, 8:376.

enly love there will be a mutual propriety. "'My beloved is mine and I am his,' as Cant. 2:16. And in heaven all shall not only be related one to another, but they shall be each other's. The saints shall be God's. He brings them hence to him in glory, as that part of the creation which he has chosen for his peculiar treasure. And on the other hand God shall be theirs."[297] In heaven the creatures of God will enjoy each other's love in perfect prosperity.[298]

And sixth, Edwards wants to speak of "the blessed fruits of this love, exercised and enjoyed in these circumstances."[299] In heaven the saints will be perfect in their behavior, in their worship, and in their mutual serving of one another. They will serve God in praise and one another in good works. Heavenly love will be exercised in perfect tranquillity and joy. "In that soul where divine love reigns, and is in lively exercise, nothing can raise a storm."[300]

Edwards is strong on the doctrinal element of the traditional Puritan sermon, which was divided into text, doctrine, and use. Unlike the typical eighteenth-century pietist, who most often emphasized the use, or application, Edwards is always very conscientious in making clear the doctrine. On the other hand, classical Protestantism would have emphasized the text. Edwards and other Puritans, it must be admitted, gave it far less attention than did Luther, Zwingli, and Calvin.

This concluding sermon of the series does give us several detailed uses. Ever since Gregory the Great said the conscientious pastor should recognize the variety of spiritual needs in the congregation and apply the Scripture differently to different needs, preachers have taken to heart this responsibility. This was especially true with the eighteenth-century pietists. We noticed this in George Whitefield, Edwards's colleague in the preaching of the Great Awakening. Edwards here makes applications to several kinds of hearers in his congregation, but what interests us most is the application he makes to those who have not yet experienced conversion.

He suggests to them that what he said earlier of heaven should stir them to seek after it. "If heaven be such a blessed world, then let this be our chosen country, and the inheritance we seek. Let us turn our course this way." However Calvinist he may be, Edwards clearly believes in free

---

297. Edwards, *Works,* 8:380.
298. Edwards, *Works,* 8:381.
299. Edwards, *Works,* 8:383.
300. Edwards, *Works,* 8:384.

will. The offer of the gospel is made to all. A truly orthodox Calvinist believes both in predestination and free will, and here Edwards makes it evident that he quite understands the function of free will. "It is not impossible that this glorious world may be obtained by us. It is offered to us. Though it be so excellent and blessed a country, yet God stands ready to give us an inheritance there, if this be the country we choose, and upon which we set our hearts, and spend our time chiefly in seeking it. God gives men their choice."[301] Edwards does not treat free will as a theological illusion. He believes in both free will and divine election.

With this Edwards urges those in his congregation who have not experienced conversion to make the choice. He takes some time making clear the way to salvation. Finally he exhorts his people, "If you would be in the way to the world of love, you must live a life of love."[302] Here he is preaching to everyone in the congregation. His concluding word is: "By living a life of love, you will be in the way to heaven. As heaven is a world of love, so the way to heaven is the way of love. This will best prepare you for heaven, and make you meet for an inheritance with the saints in that land of light and love. And if ever you arrive at heaven, faith and love must be the wings which must carry you there."[303] What a superb metaphor to end this superb sermon!

It was many years ago that I first attempted to read Edwards's series of sermons on charity and its fruits. I found it tough going and, to be truthful, tedious. But I was in my freshman year of college. The next time I read it was during my first year of research at the Center for Theological Inquiry. At the time Paul Ramsey was a member of the Center as well, and he was in the middle of producing the Yale edition of this famous work. I often heard him discussing it. His admiration for these sermons was unbounded. It seemed foolish for me to base my study on one of the older editions of the work. I set it aside until his edition should appear. So now, fifteen years later, I return to it, having read through the whole history of Christian preaching. Now I realize that it is one of the classics of Christian preaching. It ranks with Bernard of Clairvaux's sermons on the Gospels of the liturgical calendar, Augustine's sermons on the First Epistle of John, and Basil's *Hexaemeron.* Even more, with Shepard's sermons on the ten virgins, it is one of the foundation stones of American Christianity.

301. Edwards, *Works,* 8:392.
302. Edwards, *Works,* 8:395-96.
303. Edwards, *Works,* 8:396-97.

In this series we see Edwards as the biblical expositor rather than the evangelist. There are certainly elements of evangelism in these sermons, but that is not their primary aim. It is an attempt to help Edwards's congregation understand what Christian love is. It is not so much an exhortation to love one another, or to love God, although that element is certainly there. It is much more an analysis of what Scripture has to say about it. Edwards is very clear about what the apostle Paul says about it, but in the end the ultimate word on the subject for Edwards, as for the apostle, is the example of the obedient, self-sacrificing love of Christ. The words of Paul are for Edwards a witness to the Savior.

His exposition is clearly christocentric. As an expositor he is perceptive and precise. He is often, in fact very often, quite original in his interpretation of the text. Philological discussions of the text are found only occasionally, and when they are they are simple. Edwards makes no attempt to display erudition. Even at that, he gives more attention to the analysis of the text than was common in the eighteenth century. In most sermons there is a good balance between explanation and application.

It was fairly common in the eighteenth century to rush through the exposition of the text and then devote most of the hour to the application. As we have seen, Spener himself, the father of eighteenth-century pietism, recommended this approach. Right from the beginning, these sermons of Jonathan Edwards claim one's attention because of the careful analysis of the text. Because of their strong expository nature, and because they are so clearly christocentric, they easily escape the sort of moralism so often characteristic of the great mass of ethical instruction which has so often overwhelmed Christian preaching. Each sermon is thoughtful and has a good balance between profundity, clarity, and practical application.

B. Preaching the Terrors of the Lord

There is no question about it, Edwards did preach the terrors of the Lord just as the Old Testament prophets did, just as John the Baptist did, and, one has to be honest about it, just as Jesus did. Most of those who inspired the great revivals of the eighteenth century did as well, whether it was Edwards or Whitefield or Tennent or Frelinghuysen or Wesley. This has always been an element in great preaching. God himself made it very clear to Amos, Isaiah, and Micah that they were to preach his approaching judgment to a people who had become careless in their service of

God. Jeremiah had recognized that it was the false prophets who preached peace, peace, when there was no peace. It was a degenerate priesthood that spoke of the inviolability of the Church: "This is the Temple of the Lord. This is the Temple of the Lord." The true prophets preached judgment to God's people, and judgment came. God could not tolerate a corrupt Temple to stand. It was an offense to him because it confused the revelation. It belied the nature of holiness. The prophets preached hellfire to God's people because that people had betrayed a sacred trust. It was in this sense that Edwards preached the terrors of the Lord to New England. New England was a covenant people, a very religious people, and yet a people beginning to assume faith and presume upon God. This has a way of happening to religious communities. Faith is like the manna; it has to be gathered new each day. It is like French bread; it is stale by the second day.

As Edwards understood his generation, he saw that it needed to overcome its complacency. No matter how strong or pure the religion of New England was, salvation can never be assumed. It will be lost if it becomes the talent buried in the ground, preserved and held on to but never used. Edwards figured the best way to bring his congregation out of their religious presumption was to emphasize the pure graciousness of salvation. It cannot be assumed because it is so gracious. Natural humanity can only assume damnation. We cannot assume salvation as our natural right, as so many in Edwards's congregation apparently did. They figured they were good Protestants. They had a right to be saved. But, as Edwards understood it, when they did this they completely corrupted the essence of the Protestant faith. They lost sight of the gracious nature of salvation. Humanity has no natural right to salvation. Humanity in the course of nature will be damned. Edwards's message was, by grace are you saved through faith, not by right, lest any man assume salvation. It was against the presumptions of natural humanity that Edwards preached the terrors of the Lord.

His most famous sermon, "Sinners in the Hands of an Angry God," is the perfect example of how he preached the terrors of the Lord.[304] Sad to say, the sermon is usually read out of context. To be read in context it

---

304. The sermon is reproduced in many anthologies. The Yale edition, as of this writing, has not yet appeared. The edition used for this study is *The Sermons of Jonathan Edwards: A Reader,* ed. Wilson H. Kimnach, Kenneth P. Minkema, and Douglas A. Sweeney (New Haven and London: Yale University Press, 1999), pp. 49-65, hereafter Edwards, *Sermons.*

must be read along with a sermon on the delights of the Lord, which we shall do further on. But it is a great sermon, and we need to understand why.

One could call it great because it was appropriate in its historical and geographical context. It is often pointed out that the little town of Enfield where it was preached was a particularly stodgy place where the population was especially smug in its self-righteousness and blatantly careless in its religious observance. This may be quite true. Surely the sermon was quite effective in turning the congregation around. Its hearers did repent and turn to God. Edwards understood his New Englanders well, and he knew how to get his message across to them. That is certainly one of the things which goes into a great sermon.

But there is more than that. A great sermon, as any literary classic, must speak to more than just one isolated place, in this case a town in the Connecticut River Valley. This sermon was appropriate to the eighteenth century — that most frivolous of centuries with its lace collars, its powdered wigs, and its pink satin waistcoats. Was there ever an age when man tried so hard to hide himself from his fallibility? Was there ever an age more sure of its reason, more demanding of its rights, than the age of Voltaire? This particular sermon spoke to the problem of an age. If only there had been someone to preach this sermon at the court of Versailles, if only there had been a preacher to break through the decorum of the court chapel, how might history have gone?

But there is still more than that. The sermon speaks to something universal: to the precariousness of human existence, the transience of our happiness, the fallibility of our very nature. This is a great sermon because it speaks about something that is true, even if we do not like to hear it. It is the nature of heaven and earth to pass away. It is the nature of man to die, just as it is the nature of grass to wither and the flower to fall. That we should be lifted up to eternity is miraculous and can only be a surprising, gracious act. The greatness of the sermon is its honesty. It tells us what we should like to forget, but what we know is true just the same.

The power of this sermon is easy to understand from a literary standpoint. It evokes the images the human psyche naturally uses to deal with the precariousness of our human existence. It evokes the imagery of mortality and fallibility. Our perceptive New Englander begins with a text which is extremely pictorial: "Their foot shall slide in due time" (Deut. 32:35). He develops the imagery by speaking of Psalm 73:18-19, "Surely thou didst set them in slippery places; thou castedst them down into destruction. How are they brought into desolation as in a moment?" These words easily bring before us the human propensity for falling. The wicked are liable to fall of themselves, Edwards tells us, "without being thrown down by the hand of another. As he that stands or walks on slippery ground, needs nothing but his own weight to throw him down."[305] Another image Edwards uses repeatedly in this sermon is the spider's web.[306] He uses it to evoke the slender thread on which human life hangs. To the same effect he uses the images of the whirlwind, the devouring flame, and the storming waves of the sea.[307] These, of course, are only the simplest images. The image of the underworld which seems to occur in so many cultures is vastly more complex.[308] Being devoured by lions or demonic beasts is another universal image of terror before the unknown.[309] Edwards uses all these together with some of the more specifically biblical images for our fears of the future.[310]

These feelings of fallibility are in every human breast, no matter how much we may cover them up with elaborate lace and expensive satin. The greatest artists, the greatest poets and preachers, have all spoken of it in their turn: Sophocles in his tragedies, Dante in his *Inferno*, Michelangelo in his frescoes in the Sistine Chapel or his Pietà in the Duomo at Florence. And then Mozart, born during Edwards's lifetime, one of the most sensitive spirits of the eighteenth century, wrote it clearly in *Don Giovanni* and even more clearly in the *Dies irae* of his *Requiem*. For an artist to neglect the subject of human fallibility or fail to admit our anxiety about the Last Judgment is to court a final verdict of unreality. The question, of course, is whether the poet or the prophet is able to see beyond the Last Judgment, whether his apocalypse catches the vision of the kingdom of God as well. Some of the greatest poets have been far more eloquent in their paradise lost than in their paradise regained. This is where the true greatness of Edwards is discovered; he was as eloquent when he spoke of the delights of the Lord as when he spoke of the terrors of the Lord.

305. Edwards, *Sermons*, p. 49.
306. Edwards, *Sermons*, p. 56.
307. Edwards, *Sermons*, p. 57.
308. Edwards, *Sermons*, p. 55.
309. Edwards, *Sermons*, p. 52.
310. Edwards, *Sermons*, p. 61.

C. Preaching the Delights of the Lord

No one has ever spoken better of the joy of finding salvation than Jonathan Edwards, whether speaking of Abigail Hutchinson in his *Faithful Narrative* or publishing the journal of David Brainerd. Neither of these, of course, is written in sermonic form. Surely one sermon which speaks at length of the delights of the Lord is the last sermon from the series we just studied. A good example of this is his sermon, "The Excellency of Christ." In this sermon we find the religious affections at their most appealing.[311]

The sermon takes its text from Revelation 5:5-6, "And one of the elders saith unto me, Weep not: behold the Lion of the tribe of Judah, the root of David, hath prevailed to open the book, and to loose the seven seals thereof. And I beheld, and lo in the midst of the throne, and of the four beasts, and in the midst of the elders, stood a Lamb, as it had been slain."[312] In his observation on the text our preacher points to the strange paradox of this passage of Scripture that it speaks of the exalted Christ both as the Lion of the tribe of Judah and as the Lamb that was slain.[313] Paradox was a favorite rhetorical device of classical antiquity, and in this sermon Edwards plays this paradox to its fullest. Dividing up his text, he tells us that first he intends to show how in the person of Christ there is "an admirable conjunction of diverse excellencies."[314]

The first of these paradoxes is that while in Christ we meet the infinite highness of his divinity, we also meet the infinite condescension of his humanity. Condescension was a favorite theme in the Christology of John Chrysostom as well as in that of many another Church Father. We have spoken of this at some length. It was also a favorite theological term of Luther and Calvin. Here is one of those many places where we see how classical Edwards's theology really was. "Christ, as he is God, is infinitely great and high above all. He is higher than the kings of the earth; for he is King of kings, and Lord of lords." Edwards quotes a wonderful line from Proverbs 30:4, "What is his name, and what is his Son's name, if thou canst tell?" Edwards comments, "Our understandings, if we stretch them ever so far, can't reach up to his divine glory."

---

311. "The Excellency of Christ" has not yet appeared in the Yale edition. For the text we rely on Edwards, *Sermons*, pp. 161-96.

312. Edwards, *Sermons*, p. 161.

313. Edwards, *Sermons*, p. 162.

314. Edwards, *Sermons*, p. 163.

Then our preacher cites a line from Job 11:8, "It is high as heaven, what canst thou do?" and comments, "Christ is the Creator, and great possessor of heaven and earth: he is sovereign Lord of all: he rules over the whole universe, and doth whatsoever pleaseth him: his knowledge is without bound: his wisdom is perfect, and what none can circumvent: his power is infinite, and none can resist him: his riches are immense and inexhaustible: his majesty is infinitely awful."[315] One cannot help but be inspired by the Wisdom Christology which Edwards has so obviously mastered.

If Edwards presents the exaltation of Christ with great art, he presents Christ's condescension fully as well. "Yea, so great is his condescension, that it is not only sufficient to take some gracious notice of such as these, but sufficient for every thing that is an act of condescension. His condescension is great enough to become their friend: 'tis great enough to become their companion, to unite their souls to him in spiritual marriage: 'tis great enough to take their nature upon him, to become one of them, that he may be one with them."[316]

Again Edwards's sermon wonders at the admirable conjunction of innocence and worthiness on one hand and patient suffering on the other. Christ was completely innocent and righteous, and yet he was unjustly prosecuted and persecuted, and rather than railing and angrily denouncing his enemies he patiently bore his sufferings. Again, in the person of Christ are joined a perfect spirit of obedience and the supreme dominion over heaven and earth. As Edwards presents it, Christ is Lord of all in two respects. "He is so as he is God-man, and Mediator; and so his dominion is appointed, and given of the Father, and is by delegation from God, and he is, as it were, the Father's viceregent. But he is the Lord of all things in another respect, viz., as he is (by his original nature) God. And so he is by natural right, the Lord of all, and supreme over all, as much as the Father. Thus he has dominion over the world, not by delegation, but in his own right: he is not an under-God, as the Arians suppose, but to all intents and purposes, supreme God."[317]

The paradox continues when we notice that in Christ we have conjoined absolute sovereignty and perfect resignation. Christ, as he is God, is the sovereign disposer of all events. "'Tis he that worketh all things ac-

315. Edwards, *Sermons,* p. 164.
316. Edwards, *Sermons,* p. 165.
317. Edwards, *Sermons,* p. 169.

cording to the council of his own will." With this he quotes Colossians 1:16-17, "By him, and through him, and to him, are all things." Then he quotes John 5:17, "The Father worketh hitherto, and I work." He follows this with Matthew 8:3, "I will, be thou clean."[318] These words of healing are an obvious expression of Christ's divine sovereignty. Edwards, too, is a master in the use of parallel texts.

Jesus also had complete resignation, as we find in the story of his prayer in the Garden of Gethsemane. His intense prayer put all things into the hands of the Father as he realized he was approaching a painful and ignominious death. He prayed that he not have to drink the bitter cup of suffering, and yet he resigned himself to what was coming when he prayed that it not be his will which would prevail but the will of the Father. As Edwards presents it in this sermon, the perfect resignation of Christ in his sacrificial death was in fact his highest glory. "Never was he subject to such ignominy as then; never did he suffer so much pain in his body, or so much sorrow in his soul; never was he in so great an exercise of his condescension, humility, meekness, and patience, as he was in these last sufferings; never was his divine glory and majesty covered with so thick and dark a veil; never did he so empty himself, and make himself of no reputation, as at this same time: and yet never was his divine glory so manifested, by an act of his, as in that act, of yielding himself up to these sufferings."[319] Here the delicacy of Edwards's expression is remarkable.

One wonders how Edwards's congregation received this sermon. As one reads it today, one finds it most beautiful. One hesitates to leave out a single word, although in the edition before us it goes on for thirty pages. One simply has to read it for oneself. It is about as lyrical a treatise on Christology as the Church has ever produced. Here is doctrinal preaching at its most doxological!

When Edwards turns to application, he makes a most interesting statement about the purpose of preaching delights. "Let the consideration of this wonderful meeting of diverse excellencies in Christ induce you to accept of him, and close with him as your Savior. As all manner of excellencies meet in him, so there are concurring in him all manner of arguments and motives, to move you to choose him for your Savior, and everything that tends to encourage poor sinners to come and put their trust in him: his fullness and all-sufficiency as a Savior, gloriously appear in

318. Edwards, *Sermons,* p. 170.
319. Edwards, *Sermons,* p. 176.

that variety of excellencies that has been spoken of."[320] All that has been said about the excellency of Christ should encourage the sinner to claim Christ as Savior. The doxological and evangelistic functions of preaching go hand in hand. Here we have it at the heart of the American tradition of preaching. Preaching stirs up and encourages the religious affections and therefore brings us to the most profound worship. This would be a great sermon if it stopped here. It certainly speaks to the first concern of our study, namely, how preaching is worship.

Edwards goes on. In this sermon, at least, the application is brilliantly worked out. In choosing Christ for our Savior and our friend, we discover that Christ gives himself to us. All those excellencies we find in Christ he gives us for our enjoyment. "He will ever after treat you as his dear friend; and you shall ere long be where he is, and shall behold his glory, and shall dwell with him, in most free and intimate communion and enjoyment."[321] This is all beautifully elaborated with, interestingly enough, frequent references to John 17, Christ's High Priestly Prayer. The final paragraph we have to quote in full. It is a theological grand finale:

> This is the design of Christ, to bring it to pass, that he, and his Father, and his people, might all be united in one. John 17:21-23, "That they all may be one; as thou Father art in me, and I in thee; that they also may be one in us; that the world may believe that thou hast sent me. And the glory which thou hast given me, I have given them, that they may be one, even as we are one; I in them, and thou in me; that they may be made perfect in one." Christ has brought it to pass, that those that the Father has given him, should be brought into the household of God; that he, and his Father, and his people, should be as it were one society, one family; that the church should be as it were admitted into the society of the blessed Trinity.[322]

Knowing how the Puritans worked things out, this may well have been preached in as many as three or four sessions. It reminds one of the great theological orations which Gregory of Nazianzus preached in Constantinople at the time Arianism was finally put to flight and orthodox Christology was reestablished by the Council of Constantinople.

---

320. Edwards, *Sermons*, p. 184.
321. Edwards, *Sermons*, p. 192.
322. Edwards, *Sermons*, p. 196.

D. Preaching to the Mohicans and the Mohawks

Edwards had become one of the most influential ministers in New England when a controversy over admission to Communion led to his alienation from his own congregation. In June of 1750 he was dismissed and began to look for another position. It was more than a year before he found one, a position which in many ways seemed quite inappropriate. He received a call to the Indian mission at Stockbridge.

More than fifteen years before, a mission to the Indians had been established at Stockbridge in the far west of Massachusetts, close to the New York border.[323] Stockbridge was about halfway between Northampton and Albany. John Sergeant began the mission with the support of the Society for the Propagation of the Gospel, a missionary organization with headquarters in Scotland. The work of the Society in New England was under the direction of a board of commissioners in Boston.

Sergeant had begun the mission very well. He could preach to the Indians in their own language. He seems to have been sufficiently fluent in the Housatonic dialect to gather a congregation between two Indian settlements and maintain a school there during the week, at least during the winter months.[324] He apparently could also communicate with the Iroquois. He is supposed to have known the Indians, their ways, and their languages sufficiently to have been a moving preacher. Unhappily Sergeant died in 1749 after beginning his work so well. When Edwards arrived, things were disheartening. This was largely due to the beginnings of the French and Indian War and the attempts of the French not only to evangelize the Indians but to turn them against the English. This was especially an issue with the Iroquois.

323. On the Stockbridge mission, see Jonathan Edwards, *The Life of David Brainerd,* ed. Norman Pettit, in *The Works of Jonathan Edwards,* vol. 7 (New Haven and London: Yale University Press, 1985), pp. 16-18. See also the chapter "Missionary to the Indians" in Murray, *Jonathan Edwards,* pp. 385-98.

324. The literature is not clear as to which tribes the mission at Stockbridge ministered. The Mohawk, Mohican or Mahican, Housatonic, and Iroquois are mentioned. The mission originally was established to reach the Housatonic branch of the Mohican tribe. The Mohicans (sometimes Mahicans) were a branch of the Algonquians and spoke a dialect of the Algonquian language which John Eliot had learned early in the history of the colony. The Mohawks, speaking a very different language, began to move into the area just before Edwards arrived. The mission was optimistically trying to reach the Mohawks as well. The Iroquois were too far north and west to have had much contact with the mission at Stockbridge.

Edwards, brilliant as he was, could not master any of the Indian dialects. His son, Jonathan Edwards, Jr., on the other hand, learned the street language of the village as he grew up, and even maintained his fluency in older years. When Edwards arrived, John Wauwaumppequunnaunt, a devout Christian Indian, was able to translate for him. He had been an assistant to Timothy Woodbridge, who had sometime earlier developed a ministry to the Indians. In 1752 Gideon Hawley arrived, having studied at Yale and having been greatly inspired by Edwards's publication of the journal of David Brainerd. Hawley knew several Indian dialects, and he was able to translate Edwards's sermons. For a good part of Edwards's ministry at Stockbridge services were held for the Mohawks as well as separate services for the Mohicans. Edwards preached the same sermon, but the translations were given in the different Indian languages. In time the mission began once again to bear some modest fruit.

Edwards may not have been too well suited to be a missionary. He was a pastor, to be sure, and he did manifest a real pastoral concern for the Indians to whom he had been sent, but he was above all a theologian who spoke to theologians. He was amazingly successful at preaching to the theologians in his congregation, even to the point of raising up a whole church of amateur theologians. Theology was obviously his first vocation, and yet he was an enthusiastic supporter of the mission to the Indians. From the very beginning of the Puritan colonization there had been a conscientious attempt to share the gospel with the Native American population.[325] A considerable amount of effort was given to their evangelization and to the translation of the Bible into various Native American languages and dialects. There were a good number of Christian Indian congregations in spite of the inevitable tensions which began to arise as the Anglo-Americans populated more and more of the land.

Edwards's interest in the mission to the Indians became increasingly evident as he edited and published the journal of David Brainerd. For Brainerd the mission to the Indians was a mystical vocation, and Edwards recognized the sanctity of the missionary call. The publication of Brainerd's work did much to give American spirituality a profound dedication to the missionary challenge.

A good number of the sermons Edwards preached to his Indian

325. Cf. the section above on the ministry of John Eliot.

congregation have been preserved, at least in manuscript form.[326] Two of his sermons to the Mohawk Indians have been published, "To the Mohawks at the Treaty, August 16, 1751" and "He That Believeth Shall Be Saved."[327] The sermons are very simple and straightforward. Apparently most of them are revisions of sermons he had preached to his congregation at Northampton. We find that, typical of the missionary preaching we have looked at, a strong emphasis is put on recounting the history of salvation. But then we find the typical schema of preaching terrors on one hand and delights on the other. A salient feature of these sermons is that they are written in very short paragraphs. This was to facilitate the work of the translator, as those of us who have preached with a translator will recognize. The translation goes much more easily if the sermon is preached one sentence at a time and the translation of that single sentence given before going on to a second sentence.

One hesitates to say too much about these sermons, when the bulk of them has yet to be published. What is important is that Edwards recognized the missionary task as essential to true Christianity. It is of the nature of Christian worship that it is a witness to the saving power of God before all peoples and tribes, all clans and nations. Edwards's concern for missionary preaching has helped make this an indelible characteristic of American Christianity.

E. Doctrinal Preaching

Although there were plenty of other dimensions to Edwards's preaching, he was primarily a doctrinal preacher. He was fascinated by doctrine and was constantly concerned to justify classical Christian doctrine. While he followed the traditional arrangement of the Puritan sermon — text, doctrine, and use — it was ever and again doctrine to which he gave the greatest attention.

Abstract doctrine did not fascinate him. He always focused in on pastoral doctrine, that is, doctrine about how one was to follow the way to salvation. The doctrine which fascinated him was soteriology, to use

326. On these sermons see the introductory study on Edwards's preaching by Wilson H. Kimnach in Jonathan Edwards, *Sermons and Discourses, 1720-1723,* ed. Wilson H. Kimnach, in *The Works of Jonathan Edwards,* vol. 10 (New Haven and London: Yale University Press, 1992), pp. 125-29.

327. Edwards, *Sermons,* pp. 105-10 and 111-20 respectively.

the technical term. Or put another way, the *ordo salutis,* or the steps to salvation, was at the heart of his theological pursuits.

In some ways his preaching seems rather introspective. He preached neither the lectionary nor the *lectio continua* but about what fascinated him, for the most part. Sunday by Sunday throughout his ministry he took up the theological subjects which interested him, and yet he was a committed pastor. He was interested in what he as a pastor needed to preach to lead his congregation to an ever more Christian experience. His interests were thoroughly pastoral. As is often said in pious circles, he had a genuine passion for souls.

Let us look at two of his most treasured sermons which show him as a doctrinal preacher with a pastor's heart.

1. "God Glorified in the Work of Redemption"[328]

Edwards preached this sermon in 1731, when he was invited to Boston to preach to the ministers of the New England metropolis. He was beginning to achieve a reputation as a preacher, and the Boston preachers wanted to hear what this young preacher had to say. Edwards on his part was worried about the ministers of Boston beginning to drift toward Arminianism, and he therefore decided to preach a sermon reaffirming the basic principles of classical Protestantism. The point of the sermon is that the doctrine of justification by faith leads us to true worship. The importance of the occasion led, therefore, to the publication of the sermon.

For a text Edwards chose I Corinthians 1:29-31, "That no flesh should glory in his presence. But of him are ye in Christ Jesus, who of God is made unto us wisdom, and righteousness, and sanctification, and redemption. That, according as it is written, He that glorieth, let him glory in the Lord."[329] In the usual way Edwards begins with a few observations on the text. He explains that the apostle Paul addressed his epistle to Christians who lived in a part of the ancient world where philosophy was greatly respected. The city of Corinth was very close to Athens, which was the center of the philosophical tradition. Paul tells the Corinthians, however, that God has "brought to naught, their human wisdom." With all their great wisdom they had not come to know God. "But after they had done their utmost to no effect, it pleased God at length, to reveal

328. The text of this sermon is in Edwards, *Sermons,* pp. 66-82.
329. I Cor. 1:29-31, as quoted in Edwards, *Sermons,* p. 66.

himself by the gospel which they accounted foolishness: he 'chose the foolish things of the world to confound the wise. . . .'"[330] The reason God did this, according to our text, is "'That no flesh should glory in his presence. . . . That according as it is written, He that glorieth, let him glory in the Lord.'"

When it comes to our redemption, we are totally dependent on God. It is in Christ that we have the true wisdom that the Greeks so long sought. But God has given us even more than that wisdom, for in Christ we have righteousness and our sanctification and our redemption, as our text so clearly teaches us. Edwards goes on to point out that this dependence is unfolded in a trinitarian manner. We are dependent on the Father, who has given us his Son; we are dependent on the Son because it is in him that we have all these blessings; we are dependent on the Holy Spirit, because it is by his sanctifying work that we have faith and are thereby united to Christ.[331]

Edwards then proceeds to the second part of the traditional Puritan sermon, the doctrine. As we see again and again, this is the part that interests our preacher the most. Here he proposes to show "That there is an absolute and universal dependence of the redeemed on God for all their good. And, that God hereby is exalted and glorified in the work of redemption."

This dependence is evident in several ways. Christians have all their good *of* him, they have all their good *through* him, and they have all their good *in* him. (Edwards uses italics.) He elaborates each point at length. First, he would have us understand, "The redeemed have all their good *of* God. God is the great Author of it; he is the first cause of it, and not only so but he is the proper cause."

At this point Edwards uses a very effective piece of rhetoric. It is a very simple plain-style sort of rhetoric, but nevertheless it shows us that Edwards was a natural orator. We will need to quote at length here to show how a single repeated phrase, *"'tis of God,"* can drive in a point.

> *'Tis of God* that we have our Redeemer. *'Tis God* that has provided a Savior for us. Jesus Christ is not only of God in his person, as he is the only begotten Son of God; but he is from God as we are concerned in him, and in his office of mediator; he is the gift of God to us: God

---

330. Edwards, *Sermons*, p. 66.
331. Edwards, *Sermons*, p. 67.

chose and anointed him, appointed him his work, and sent him into the world.

And as it is God that gives, so 'tis God that accepts the Savior. As it is God that provides and gives the Redeemer to buy salvation for us, so it is of God that the salvation is bought: he gives the purchaser, and he affords the thing purchased.

'Tis of God that Christ becomes ours, that we are brought to him, and are united to him: 'tis of God that we receive faith to close with him, that we may have an interest in him. Eph. 2:8, "For by grace ye are saved, through faith; and that not of yourselves, it is the gift of God." 'Tis of God that we actually do receive all the benefits that Christ has purchased. 'Tis of God that pardons and justifies, and delivers from going down to hell, and 'tis his favor that the redeemed are received into, and are made the objects of, when they are justified. So it is God that delivers from the dominion of sin, and cleanses us from our filthiness, and changes us from our deformity. 'Tis of God that the redeemed do receive all their true excellency, wisdom and holiness; and that two ways, viz. as the Holy Ghost by whom these things are immediately wrought is from God, proceeds from him, and is sent by him; and also as the Holy Ghost himself is God, by whose operation and indwelling, the knowledge of God and divine things, and a holy disposition, and all grace are conferred and upheld.

And though means are made use of in conferring grace on men's souls, yet 'tis of God that we have these means of grace, and 'tis of God that makes them effectual. 'Tis of God that we have the holy Scriptures; they are the Word of God. 'Tis of God that we have ordinances, and their efficacy depends on the immediate influence of the Spirit of God. The ministers of the gospel are sent of God, and all their sufficiency is of him. II Cor. 4:7, "We have this treasure in earthen vessels, that the excellency of the power may be of God, and not of us." Their success depends entirely and absolutely on the immediate blessing and influence of God.[332]

This rhetorical device gives a sense of passion to Edwards's sermon, and this sense of passion was characteristic of pietistic preaching even if sometimes the sermon was fully written out and faithfully read from the manuscript.

Edwards goes on to insist that not only are God's blessings of God, they are through God as well. The redeemed are also dependent on God

---

332. Edwards, Sermons, pp. 68-69, emphasis added.

for all, because they have all *through* him. "'Tis God that is the medium of it, as well as the author and fountain of it. All we have, wisdom, and the pardon of sin, deliverance from hell, acceptance into God's favor, grace and holiness, true comfort and happiness, eternal life and glory, we have from God by a mediator; and this mediator is God."[333] Again we have an effective piece of rhetoric which helps convey Edwards's passion for his subject. The long list of blessings we have through God in his Son impresses us with its fullness. All this is tacked down by a beautiful proof text, I Corinthians 8:6, "But to us there is but one God, the Father, of whom are all things, and we in him; and one Lord Jesus Christ, by whom are all things, and we by him."

This text, of course, leads into his next point. "The redeemed have all their good *in* God. We not only have it *of* him and *through* him, but it consists *in* him; he *is* all our good."[334] Again we have a beautiful piece of simple, basic rhetoric as Edwards brings out the treasures of the biblical vocabulary. "God himself is the great good which they are brought to the possession and enjoyment of by redemption. He is the highest good, and the sum of all that good which Christ purchased. God is the inheritance of the saints; he is the portion of their souls. God is their wealth and treasure, their food, their life, their dwelling place, their ornament and diadem, and their everlasting honor and glory. They have none in heaven but God; he is the great good which the redeemed are received to at death, and which they are to rise to at the end of the world."[335] When Edwards begins to contemplate the blessings of heaven, his sermon becomes rapturous. Our blessings are in God, for "[H]e is the light of the heavenly Jerusalem; and is the 'river of the water of life' that runs, and the tree of life that grows, 'in the midst of the paradise of God' [Rev. 2:7]."

In discussing the blessings we have in God, Edwards speaks of the doctrine of the Holy Spirit. He tells us that we have a spiritual excellency and joy by a kind of participation in God. "They are made excellent by a communication of God's excellency: God puts his own beauty, i.e. his beautiful likeness upon their souls: they are made 'partakers of the divine nature,' or moral image of God (II Peter 1:4). They are holy by being made partakers of God's holiness (Heb. 12:10)."[336] This is all by the gift

333. Edwards, *Sermons*, p. 73.
334. Edwards, *Sermons*, p. 74, emphasis Edwards's.
335. Edwards, *Sermons*, pp. 74-75.
336. Edwards, *Sermons*, p. 75.

of the Holy Spirit and his dwelling in our hearts. "'Tis by partaking of the Holy Spirit, that they have communion with Christ in his fullness."[337]

So it is that our redemption is from beginning to end a glorious act of God. Paul devotes the first eleven chapters of Romans to a full account of our redemption in Christ. Then in conclusion he sums it up in a great doxology. As Edwards reads the Greek, it says, "for *of* him, and *through* him, and *in* him are all things" (Rom. 11:36).[338]

The second point of doctrine Edwards makes is that God is glorified in the work of redemption. This universal dependence of the redeemed on God for all the blessings of their existence glorifies God. In other words, when we recognize that God is sufficient for all our needs, that he is abundant in all his blessings, that is, when we experience his grace, then we participate in the right relationship with him. The right relationship consists of worship, praise, prayer and adoration, and even more, communion.[339]

Our preacher now turns to the use to which the doctrine should be applied. The complete sufficiency of God to supply our insufficiency is in the end what serves God's glory. Our redemption is in the end the ultimate worship. "Though God be pleased to lift man out of that dismal abyss of sin and woe into which he has fallen, and exceedingly to exalt him in excellency and honor, and to an high pitch of glory and blessedness, yet the creature hath nothing in any respect to glory of; all the glory evidently belongs to God, all is in a mere, and most absolute and divine dependence on the Father, Son, and Holy Ghost."[340] We notice the trinitarian dimension of Edwards's concept of worship. "And each person of the Trinity is equally glorified in this work: there is an absolute dependence of the creature on every one for all: all is *of* the Father, all *through* the Son, and all *in* the Holy Ghost. Thus God appears in the work of redemption as 'all in all.' 'Tis fit that he that 'is, and there is nothing else,' should be the Alpha and Omega, the first and the last, the all and the only, in this work."[341] Edwards very clearly understands that worship is the work of the Holy Spirit, in the body of Christ, to the glory of the Father. This was Calvin's understanding of worship as well.

It is in the doctrine of justification by faith that the nature of true

337. Edwards, *Sermons,* p. 76.
338. Edwards, *Sermons,* p. 77.
339. Edwards, *Sermons,* p. 78.
340. Edwards, *Sermons,* p. 79.
341. Edwards, *Sermons,* pp. 79-80, emphasis Edwards's.

worship becomes clear. True worship recognizes the sufficiency of God. It realizes the mercy, the covenant faithfulness, and ultimately the love of God toward his people. True worship is a communion with God in which we are nourished, and that unto eternal life. "Faith is a sensibleness of what is real in the work of redemption; and as we do really wholly depend on God, so the soul that believes doth entirely depend on God for all salvation, in its own sense, and act. Faith abases men, and exalts God; it gives all the glory of redemption to God alone." Justification by faith teaches us to approach God in humility. It teaches us to worship God in simplicity because we stand before his majesty. In the end justification by faith "should teach us to exalt God alone as by trust and reliance, so by praise. 'Let him that glories, glory in the Lord.'"[342]

2. "A Divine and Supernatural Light"

Another beautiful example of Edwards's doctrinal preaching is his "A Divine and Supernatural Light, Immediately Imparted to the Soul by the Spirit of God, Shown to Be Both a Scriptural, and Rational Doctrine."[343] For this sermon our New Englander chose as his text Matthew 16:17, "And Jesus answered and said unto him, Blessed art thou, Simon Barjona: for flesh and blood hath not revealed it unto thee, but my Father which is in heaven."[344]

The observations on the text put it in the context of Peter's confession of faith that Jesus is the Christ, the Son of the living God. Here, as Edwards understands it, Jesus himself says the essence of saving faith comes not from the usual sources of human knowledge, but directly from God himself.

Our preacher goes on to give us an interpretive paraphrase of the words of Jesus: "'This is such knowledge as my Father which [is] in heaven only can give: it is too high and excellent to be communicated by such means as other knowledge is. Thou art blessed, that thou knowest that which God alone can teach thee.'"[345] An interpretive paraphrase like this is a rhetorical device often used by expository preachers. It was, for example, a favorite rhetorical device of Calvin.

---

342. Edwards, *Sermons,* p. 81.
343. The text of this sermon is in Edwards, *Sermons,* pp. 121-40.
344. Edwards, *Sermons,* p. 121.
345. Edwards, *Sermons,* p. 122.

Edwards really bores in on his point in the second part of the Puritan sermon, the doctrine. He wants to make three points. The first is to show what this divine light is. The second is to explain how it is given immediately by God, and not obtained by natural means. The third is to show the truth of this doctrine. Then, as a conclusion, he intends to give us a brief suggestion as to its application.[346]

Our preacher first proposes to show what this divine light is by showing what it is not. It is not our conviction of our sin and misery. This comes to us quite naturally from our natural knowledge, nor is it to be confused with the conscience. The conscience gives us a sense of right and wrong and makes us aware of our need of a Savior. "But in the renewing and sanctifying work of the Holy Ghost, those things are wrought in the soul that are above nature."[347] This is what Edwards wants us to consider.

Edwards has a highly developed doctrine of the Holy Spirit, and in this sermon we have a particularly fine opening of it. He points out that "the Spirit of God, in acting in the soul of a godly man, exerts and communicates himself there in his own proper nature. Holiness is the proper nature of the Spirit of God. The Holy Spirit operates in the minds of the godly, by uniting himself to them, and living in them, and exerting his own nature in the exercise of their faculties." The work of the Holy Spirit is to anoint our spirits with his holiness, but this is not his only work. "The Spirit of God may act upon a creature, and yet not in acting communicate himself. The Spirit of God may act upon inanimate creatures; as, 'The Spirit moved upon the face of the waters' [Gen. 1:2] in the beginning of the creation. . . . For instance, he may excite thoughts in them, may assist their natural reason and understanding, or may assist other natural principles, and this without any union with the soul, but may act, as it were, as upon an external object." The really proper work of the Holy Spirit is sanctification. "But as he acts in his holy influences, and spiritual operations, he acts in a way of peculiar communication of himself, so that the subject is thence denominated *spiritual*."[348]

Another negative point Edwards wants to make is that this spiritual light does not suggest any new truths or doctrines not contained in the Word of God. It is not to be confused with the inspiration under which the prophets and apostles wrote the canonical Scriptures. Even today, Ed-

346. Edwards, *Sermons,* p. 123.
347. Edwards, *Sermons,* p. 124.
348. Edwards, *Sermons,* p. 125, emphasis Edwards's.

wards points out, there are enthusiasts who claim to have this kind of illumination. No doubt Edwards had in mind the Quakers, who were actively proselytizing in New England at the time. Illuminism is the furthest thing from Edwards's mind. "But this spiritual light that I am speaking of, is quite a different thing from inspiration: it reveals no new doctrine, it suggests no new propositions to the mind, it teaches no new thing of God, or Christ, or another world, not taught in the Bible; but only gives a due apprehension of those things that are taught in the Word of God."

From these negative observations we move to a more positive statement of Edwards's doctrine. This divine light is "a true sense of the divine excellency of the things revealed in the Word of God, and a conviction of the truth and reality of them."[349] This is the Holy Spirit's anointing of our understanding, as some have called it, or the inner testimony of the Holy Spirit to the authority of Scripture, which was important in the thinking of the Reformers. This divine light, as Edwards sees it, is a "true sense of the divine and superlative excellency of the things of religion; a real sense of the excellency of God, and Jesus Christ, and of the work of redemption, and the ways and works of God revealed in the gospel."

There is a difference, Edwards tells us, between having "an opinion that God is holy and gracious, and having a sense of the loveliness and beauty of holiness and grace. There is a difference between having a rational judgment that honey is sweet, and having a sense of its sweetness."[350] What Edwards seems to be saying here is that beyond any rational understanding of God such as the philosophers seek there is a religious sensitivity within the heart that opens our eyes to the truth of the things of God. Even more, "There is a wide difference between mere speculative, rational judging anything to be excellent, and having a sense of its sweetness, and beauty. The former rests only in the head, speculation only is concerned in it; but the heart is concerned in the latter."[351]

This is a remarkable sermon, especially as a doctrinal sermon, and yet Edwards preached many sermons of intense doctrinal content. It witnesses not only to the theological maturity of the preacher, but also to the theological perception of the New England churchgoer in the eighteenth century. New England had a high preaching culture. With such high

349. Edwards, *Sermons*, p. 126.
350. Edwards, *Sermons*, p. 127.
351. Edwards, *Sermons*, p. 128.

quality of preaching, one is hardly surprised that New England maintained a spiritual leadership in America that continued for many generations.

Something else needs to be said. To understand the preaching of Edwards, in fact, to understand American Christianity generally, one needs to realize what was at work in his *Religious Affections,* and at the same time what was really going on with the Great Awakening. It was not so much that Edwards gave us a new theology or a new piety, or a new program of evangelism. Thomas Shepard was already working on these ideas when he preached to the first students at Harvard a hundred years beforehand. One finds it in the poetry of Anne Bradstreet, the missionary journal of David Brainerd, and the fast-day sermons of Samuel Willard. What was distinct about the religious life of New England? It was a passion for God. Call it a delight in God; call it conversion; call it charity; call it religious affection; it all amounted to the same thing, a passionate love for God. When all is said about the sermons of Edwards, they have a sacred passion about them. His sermons are intellectually brilliant, morally perceptive, theologically challenging — all of this, to be sure — but above all they have a passionate holiness about them which brings us to delight in God. For Edwards, it was this delighting in God which was worship.

CHAPTER IV

Preaching in the Austro-Hungarian Empire

Between the Hapsburgs and the Jesuits a unique culture was established in eastern Europe from the beginning of the seventeenth century through most of the eighteenth century.[1] This Austro-Hungarian baroque culture was quite distinct from what was going on in western Europe, and this is especially noticeable in preaching. There is a world of difference between the great French preachers such as Bossuet, Bourdaloue, and Massillon and their Austrian contemporaries Abraham a Sancta Clara and Franz Peikhart. True, the Frenchmen were baroque as well, but they went about it so differently. The absolutism of the Bourbons was splendid, almost to the point of being convincing. The Hapsburgs, on the other hand, were never quite as believable.

What sets Austro-Hungarian baroque apart is a certain lightheartedness. The Austrian preachers never became the classic orators of the German language that Bossuet, Bourdaloue, and Massillon became of French. Austro-Hungarian baroque at its best entertains us more than it enlightens us. The French baroque preachers had something monumental about them. The Austro-Hungarian baroque never attained anything like that. They were often charming but rarely grand.

1. The libraries to which I have access are not particularly well stocked with the source materials I would like to have read for this chapter. If this chapter is necessarily incomplete, it is nevertheless able to report the existence of a fascinating field of inquiry yet to be explored.

We treated the Counter-Reformation in Italy, Spain, and France at length in volume IV. Much of the material which follows could have been taken up in that volume, but as the research developed it just happened that the Austro-Hungarian baroque came into view more slowly.

Austro-Hungarian baroque culture had a dark side to it, just as French baroque culture did. It was just as absolutist, in fact even more. From the very outset of the Reformation the Hapsburg dynasty was determined to crush Protestantism. The Hapsburgs sensed, and quite rightly, that Protestantism and absolutism were essentially incompatible. This was as true in Austria as in Spain. In Spain Protestantism never got a foothold, but in Bohemia and Hungary it was a very different matter. One of the sources of Protestantism first sprang forth in Bohemia, and Hungary received Protestantism enthusiastically from the early sixteenth century to well after the middle of the seventeenth century. Much of the preaching of the Austro-Hungarian Empire, therefore, was determinedly Counter-Reformation.

There was also Protestant preaching in the Austro-Hungarian Empire. One thinks of Jan Amos Comenius (1592-1670). Refusing to convert to the Catholicism of the Hapsburgs, he lived in exile for many years. For a time, however, he was able to teach in the famous Reformed Academy of Sárospatale in Transylvania, where he was out of the reach of the Hapsburgs. A strong Lutheran church in Slovakia was able to maintain itself down to the present day. In Hungary Protestantism refused to die, heroically maintaining its witness to this day, even under twentieth-century communism.[2] The witnesses of István Kis preaching in chains in the marketplace and of the Hungarian Reformed ministers whom the archbishop of Esztergom condemned to the Spanish galley ships are among the most heroic confessions of faith ever made. When those who found their way back to Hungary were able to preach to their fellow countrymen, their sermons hardly needed baroque flourishes to keep the people listening. Hungarian Protestant preaching was the antithesis of Austrian baroque, but it is still part of the picture.

Péter Pázmány (1570-1637) was surely one of the great preachers of the Counter-Reformation. From a literary standpoint alone, his preach-

---

2. Unless one reads Hungarian, it is hard to do much research about Hungarian preaching. With help from some of my Hungarian friends, of which I have a number, I have been able to piece together something of the story of Hungarian preaching. What a treasure! While my knowledge of the subject is modest, I persevere in my efforts with the hope that it might inspire others to open up this subject more fully.

ing deserves attention. Unlike the Counter-Reformation preaching of Adam Kravařský in Bohemia, Pázmány's preaching was directed toward the Hungarian aristocracy. Intellectually refined as he was, Pázmány had a completely feudal understanding of evangelism: convince the upper classes and force the rest. Even today, in spite of his failings, Pázmány is regarded by Hungarians with great respect. I have never heard even the most Protestant of Hungarians speak of him without somewhere along the line expressing admiration.

Having recognized the dark side of Austro-Hungarian preaching, we will at last look at some of its masterpieces. The Lenten sermon of Pázmány is certainly among those masterpieces. By common consent, however, the most typical of Austro-Hungarian baroque preachers is Abraham a Sancta Clara (1644-1709), court preacher to the Holy Roman Emperor Leopold I. While one is slow to recognize another Austrian preacher who so fully represents the ethos of the Austrian baroque, the funeral sermon of Franz Peikhart (1684-1752) for Prince Eugen of Savoy is perhaps the single sermon which sums up Austrian baroque Catholicism.

I. The Hapsburg Conquest of Bohemia, 1526-1620

As we have already seen, the Czech Reform began a good century before Luther.[3] During the fifteenth century support for this reform had largely won the population of Bohemia. Very quickly had it spread to Moravia as well.[4] The Hussite movement had developed in several directions. Some were closer to what we call evangelical Protestantism than others, but all

3. See above, Hughes Oliphant Old, *The Reading and Preaching of the Scriptures in the Worship of the Christian Church,* vol. 3, *The Medieval Church* (Grand Rapids: Wm. B. Eerdmans Publishing Co., 1999), pp. 459-89. For further information on Czech Protestantism, see Thomas A. Fudge, "Myth, Heresy and Propaganda in the Radical Hussite Movement" (Diss., University of Cambridge, 1992); Anton Grindly, *Geschichte der Gegenreformation in Böhmen* (Leipzig: Verlag von Duncker und Humbolt, 1894); Harold Kaminsky, *A History of the Hussite Revolution* (Berkeley and Los Angeles: University of California Press, 1967); Rudolf Říčan, *Das Reich Gottes in den Böhmischen Ländern* (Stuttgart: Evangelisches Verlagswerk, 1957); Matthew Spinka, *John Hus, a Biography* (Princeton: Princeton University Press, 1968); Paul de Vooght, *L'hérésie de Jean Hus* (Louvain: Publications Universitaires du Louvain, 1960).

4. See George Huntston Williams, *The Radical Reformation,* 3d ed. (Kirksville, Mo.: Sixteenth Century Journal Publishers, 1992), especially the chapter "Radical Christianity in the Kingdom of Bohemia and the Markgraviate of Moravia," pp. 204-33.

agreed on two things: Communion in both kinds and preaching in the Czech language.[5] They wanted plenty of preaching, not just occasional sermons on feast days. During the reign of King Vladislav the Czech religious reforms were respected, and so it continued under his son Louis. But then Czech independence began to come apart. Louis was killed at the Battle of Mohács in 1526, leaving no male heir. Ferdinand, the archduke of Austria, claimed the Bohemian throne because his wife Anna was the daughter of Vladislav and the sister of Louis. There were a number of other claimants to the throne of Bohemia, but the estates, or parliament, of Bohemia chose Ferdinand because in 1526, at least, he seemed to be open to church reform. The Protestant Reformation in Germany had only recently begun in 1526. Of much more concern to the Protestant nobles in Bohemia was that Ferdinand would help defend them from the Turks. So it was that the Hapsburg archduke of Austria was chosen by the Bohemian estates as king of Bohemia.

For some time the Hapsburgs had wanted to add both Bohemia and Hungary to their hereditary lands. In both places the king had to be elected, which was also true of the Holy Roman Empire, whose emperor German nobles had by long tradition elected. The driving ambition of the Hapsburgs was to become the hereditary emperor of the Holy Roman Empire and the hereditary king of both Bohemia and Hungary. To be simply archduke of Austria was never enough.

Their imperial ambitions had a religious dimension. There was nothing new about this. Charlemagne had much the same vision seven hundred years before. It was going to be with religious sanctions that the Hapsburgs would open up a vast empire to the east. The Turks would finally be pushed back across the Bosporus, and a Christian emperor would rule from Vienna down the Danube to Constantinople. That, the Hapsburgs understood, was the destiny of Austria, to be the Eastern Christian Empire.[6]

The trouble was, the Hapsburgs had a hard time subduing both the Bohemians and the Hungarians. As the sixteenth century progressed, the Czech Reform began to make common cause with the Protestant Reformation. A good part of the German-speaking population went in the di-

---

5. On the growth of the Czech Reform, see particularly Říčan, *Das Reich Gottes in den Böhmischen Ländern*, pp. 55-106.

6. The German name for Austria, Österreich, makes this clear. It means, quite simply, the Eastern Empire.

rection of Luther while the tendency among the Czech-speaking population was to go in the direction of the Swiss Reformation. The Hapsburgs became more and more impatient with the Protestant inclinations of their Czech subjects as their Protestantism was becoming more explicit and beginning to spread into Moravia to the east of Bohemia.

In 1541 a fire in Prague destroyed a number of state documents. Ferdinand insisted that when the documents were redrawn, it be made clear that he was king of Bohemia by his wife's inheritance, not by his election by the estates. Very foolishly the estates agreed to this. Only a few years later they began to realize their mistake. Ferdinand wanted his Bohemian nobles to provide soldiers for his brother's wars against the Protestants. The estates, firmly Protestant as they were, refused to aid him. By the end of 1550 Ferdinand's brother Charles V was having notable military success in his attempt to quell the Protestant princes as well as those free cities which had chosen Protestantism. Ferdinand fought by his brother's side through the 1550s, leading an army strengthened by a considerable number of Spanish mercenaries. By 1560 the imperial forces were largely in control of Europe and Ferdinand returned to Bohemia with his own mercenary army and a good supply of Jesuits.

By 1560 Ferdinand was much more in control of Bohemia than he had been twenty years earlier. He figured he was strong enough to move against what he considered the arrogance of the Protestants. Appealing to the principle of *cuius regio, eius religio,* he figured the Bohemians were obligated to adopt his Roman Catholicism. For over a century Prague had refused the presence of a Catholic archbishop, and therefore in 1561 Ferdinand brought in his own. This was followed by the establishment of a Jesuit college.

Three years later, having secured the election of his son Maximilian to the Bohemian throne, Ferdinand died. With Maximilian on their throne from 1564 to 1576, the Bohemian estates pressed for a formal recognition of religious liberty on the basis of the Bohemian Confession of 1575. Sad to say, the Bohemians did not receive anything more than an oral assurance during the reign of Maximilian.

Rudolf von Hapsburg came to the throne in 1576 as Rudolf II. He did not push Catholicism as energetically as other members of his family. In fact, he was more interested in being a patron of the arts than in the religious politics of the day. He reigned from 1576 to 1612 in spite of the attempts of other members of the Hapsburg family to replace him. Finally in 1609 he granted with a written and signed document, commonly called the "Letter of Majesty," the religious liberty demanded by the Czech nobility.

Rudolf had no male heir, however, and in 1612 he was succeeded by his brother Matthias. By this time the Jesuits were very active in the Czech lands, that is, in both Bohemia and Moravia. In 1600 they were joined by the Capuchin brothers, a branch of the Franciscan Order. Matthias was a much more typical Counter-Reformation monarch than Rudolf had been. The Bohemian estates, especially those of strong Protestant inclination, saw him as much too autocratic. Far too often he violated the religious liberty to which they had been accustomed for almost two centuries. Finally, this religious liberty, as we have said, had been formally granted to them in Rudolf's "Letter of Majesty." The Czech nobility expected their king to recognize religious liberty.

Matthias was on the throne but a short time. He, too, died without a male heir, whereupon a Hapsburg cousin, Ferdinand of Styria, claimed the throne. Ferdinand had been educated by the Jesuits in their college at Ingolstadt, and had already gained a reputation of severity toward the Protestants of Styria. In 1617 he managed to be crowned as Ferdinand II, king of Bohemia, but the Czech nobility, still largely Protestant, resented him thoroughly. On 26 August 1618 the Bohemian estates met and deposed him in favor of the Protestant Elector Palatine, Frederick, who came to be known as the "Winter King." The election of Frederick infuriated the Hapsburgs and their allies, especially the Bavarians. Gathering an army under the famous general Johann Tserclaes Graf von Tilly, the German Catholic forces entered Bohemia in September of 1620. Quickly this became a major focus of the Thirty Years' War. Rapidly Tilly's army crushed the resistance of the Czechs. The crucial battle occurred on 6 November 1620, at White Mountain outside Prague. The German Catholic forces thoroughly won the battle in a spectacular show of military superiority. On entering Prague they demanded unconditional conversion to Catholicism. Those who refused were to be exiled and their property confiscated. Many of the Protestant nobility, refusing to convert, were executed. Those who escaped execution fled, many going into exile throughout Europe.

Protestant ministers were ordered to leave Prague in three days and the country within six, on pain of death. Protestant books were burned and their churches turned over to the Catholics. Even the renowned Charles University was closed and the Jesuits were put in charge of education throughout the land. Officially, at least, Bohemia had converted to Catholicism.

299

One cannot but regret that after two hundred years Czech Protestantism was brought to an end. And yet the ways of God are past finding out. Call it chance; call it providence. For many of us it seems a clear act of divine providence. On 6 November 1620 the Protestants were defeated at the Battle of White Mountain, but that very day the *Mayflower* was on its way to America. Less than a week later it would arrive in Massachusetts Bay. There the Pilgrim Fathers would found a Christian commonwealth that would surpass anything the Holy Roman Empire could ever have imagined. In time a company of Czech exiles, now called the Moravian Brethren, would find a haven both in Bethlehem, Pennsylvania, and in Winston-Salem, North Carolina. These Moravians would raise the spiritual level of Protestantism for another two hundred years, be it here in North America, in Herrnhut, Saxony, or in the Caribbean Islands or even South India. They would be a blessing to Protestant leaders such as Count Nikolaus von Zinzendorf, John Wesley, Friedrich Schleiermacher, and Dietrich Bonhoeffer, and to less well known believers such as my own grandmother, a graduate of Moravian Female Seminary in Bethlehem, Pennsylvania, who, being a good Presbyterian all her life, was educated by the heirs of Jan Hus and the Czech Reformation.

II. Counter-Reformation Preaching in Bohemia, 1620-1750

Having deprived the Czech Protestants of their pastors and teachers and having either put their nobility to the sword or hounded them into exile, the Austrians besieged the Czechs with Jesuits prepared to instruct them in the true faith. The Jesuits were given charge of the educational system both in Bohemia and Moravia, but they also recognized the need to send out preachers. At first not many could preach in the Czech language, but the Jesuits gave much attention to developing such preachers.

The most prominent of these preachers was Adam Kravařský.[7] He was not a Czech by birth, having been born in Silesia in 1585. He attended the Jesuit college first at Olmütz in Moravia, then at Kommotau, where he

---

7. The information about Kravařský is quoted from a Jesuit historian named Pelzel in Christian Adolf Pescheck, *The Reformation and Anti-Reformation in Bohemia,* 2 vols. (London: Houlston and Stoneman, 1845), 2:99-109. Just how objective this source might or might not be we hesitate to say. For further information on Kravařský, see John Krajcar and Michael Lacko, "Czechoslovakia," in *New Catholic Encyclopedia,* 17 vols. (Washington, D.C.: Catholic University of America Press, 1968), 4:592.

was admitted to the Jesuit Order in 1607. Following the Battle of White Mountain, when the land had been rid of Protestant leadership, Kravařský was sent to preach at Prachatitz, then Wodnian, and finally Pisek, towns thoroughly committed to the Protestant cause. Apparently his mission was not too successful.[8] Before long he was recalled to Prague. It was thought that things were still a bit too heated to preach a gospel of reconciliation.

Father Kravařský's first successful preaching mission in Bohemia was in Kossumberg, an area in the domains of the Slawata family, a family that had apparently profited substantially from the confiscation of the lands of the Protestant nobility and was eager to rid their newly acquired lands of any trace of Protestantism. There Kravařský labored with great zeal, and within a few months five hundred people abjured their faith and converted to Catholicism. The official record was very clear that they did this without compulsion. They received Communion as good Catholics should, taking the bread but not the wine.

Following this success Kravařský was sent to Rakonitz, a district, according to Catholic author Pelzel, more infected with heresy than any place in the empire. He arrived with letters from the emperor, the archbishop, and the estates commissioning him to instruct the inhabitants in the official faith of the Holy Roman Empire. He was met by very angry peasants who often armed themselves as best they could. Our Jesuit evangelist apparently felt it advisable to confine himself to the fortified castle of Bürglitz. Finally, we are told, his affability in conversation began to win people over, and increasingly people came willingly to be instructed by him. First were the leading citizens of the area, who set a good example, and then the simple country people. Within a year ten thousand Bohemians had converted to the Holy Roman faith. When this was reported to the emperor, he was overjoyed![9] That the Spanish soldiers of General von Lichtenstein rounded up these people to hear Kravařský's preaching is not mentioned. This was, however, the usual practice.[10]

Another mission assigned to Kravařský was the conversion of Trebnitz.[11] In this area the Bohemian Brethren were especially strong, having developed in a more Calvinist direction. As the Jesuit historian tells us, Kravařský preached daily to the people in their own language,

---

8. Pescheck, *Bohemia,* 2:100.
9. Pescheck, *Bohemia,* 2:101.
10. Pescheck, *Bohemia,* 2:94.
11. Pescheck, *Bohemia,* 2:101.

and before long five thousand people were converted to the Catholic Church. Again, this was reported to the emperor Ferdinand, who forwarded his personal thanks to Kravařský. What is interesting in this report of the preaching of Father Kravařský, biased as it may be, is what can be read between the lines. These Jesuits were learning to preach to an angry mob, compelled to listen by mercenary soldiers. The traditional liturgical setting and the usual manuals of homiletics just did not work. New approaches had to be developed.

Kravařský's next mission was to Karlstein, at the special request of Baron John Kawka of Rziczan. As the Jesuit historian Pelzel relates the story, the people of the region were as wild as the countryside itself. They were generally confused, having had very little Catholic teaching. If one became passionate in one's preaching, they would often take offense. The women would flee from the church; the men would become hostile and would often walk out on the preacher. Sometimes they came to his sermons armed and would threaten him with their muskets. Kravařský preached every day, explaining the catechism to the ignorant. One day two strong men with axes appeared. They obviously had evil intentions. They started to argue with the preacher, and the people, fearing the intervention of the soldiers, disappeared. Kravařský, however, stood his ground and very calmly and patiently answered their questions. His labors eventually bore fruit, we are assured, and five hundred people abjured the heresies they had imbibed from the Czech Reform.

Finally Kravařský was called back to Prague to preach in the new town which, as the Jesuits saw it, was the center of Protestant obstinacy. They absolutely refused to be taught the true faith of the Holy Roman Empire, but the Jesuits persevered. They were masters of intimidation. General von Lichtenstein's soldiers were everywhere insisting that the Protestants listen to the sermons of the Jesuits. Gradually Kravařský gained respect by his preaching, our Jesuit historian insists. After a while he began to visit the leading citizens in their homes. He "divested them of their useless scruples, shewed them the antiquity and glory of our own religion, and abolished from their souls all remembrance of their former errors. Whoever still hesitated he moved by the prospect of commendation."[12] Just what this "prospect of commendation" was is not clear. Pelzel goes on: "As soon as he thus by degrees restored to the faith the principal families, the common people quickly yielded, induced by the example of

12. Pescheck, *Bohemia,* 2:102.

the rich; so that in the course of that year, above 4000 came to the light of divine faith in that city."[13]

As he grew older and more experienced in the methods of converting the unwilling, Kravařský remained more and more often in Prague teaching the younger Jesuits the most effective methods of convincing Protestants of their errors. As the seventeenth century advanced, these Jesuits produced a new school of preaching. Responding to the demands of their mission, this baroque school of preaching concentrated on how to make one's case, how to convince, and how to impress one's listeners with the glory of the faith of the Holy Roman Empire. This was what the age of the baroque was all about. Here, certainly, was one of the sources of the Austrian baroque school of preaching.

A new aristocracy arose in Prague. The old Czech nobility had been chased out and their confiscated property awarded to the soldiers of fortune who had secured Bohemia for the Hapsburgs and their brand of Catholicism. New palaces were built for this new German-speaking aristocracy. They were masterpieces of baroque art, and even today they still stand in Prague, giving the city a distinct architectural flavor. The style of preaching the Jesuits developed fit in very well with the baroque palaces and churches which began to dominate the city.[14]

By the end of the seventeenth century this new school of preaching began to develop considerable refinement. The names of Ondřej de Waldt and Antonin Dvořàk of Bor are particularly remembered. There had always been a tradition of Catholic preaching in the Czech language. One preacher, Tomáš Bavoroský, the Catholic pastor of Plzeň, published a book of Czech sermons, *Česká postila,* in 1557. More and more, however, Catholic preaching was in German. Somehow the feeling developed that to preach in Czech was not truly Catholic. The Czech language supposedly had been compromised by the Czech Reform. Jan Hus and his followers had been as insistent on Czech preaching as they were on Communion in both kinds. After the Battle of White Mountain Protestant books were burned, especially Protestant Bibles in the Czech language. The effect of this was catastrophic for the Czech language. For the next two centuries Czech literature would decline seriously. The Hapsburgs

13. Pescheck, *Bohemia,* 2:102-3.

14. For an introduction to Czech art and culture, see Mojmír Svatopluk Frinta, "Czechoslovakian Art," in *New Catholic Encyclopedia,* 4:598-605; Krajcar and Lacko, "Czechoslovakia," 4:589-92; Bohdan Chudoba, "Czech Literature," in *New Catholic Encyclopedia,* 4:585-88. These articles have extensive bibliographical references.

were determined to make both their Hungarian subjects and their Bohemian subjects not only Catholics, but German-speaking Catholics.

The problem with all this was that it cultivated a certain insincerity in matters of religion. One's religion became a matter of one's politics. Outward conformity became the standard. Baroque religion became oppressively artificial, just as baroque art. The same thing happened in France. Louis XIV set the stage in France for Madame Guyon, just as the Hapsburg emperor Ferdinand II set the stage for Herrnhut and the pietism of the Moravian Brethren. It was the devotional fire of those exiled disciples of the Czech Reform which Zinzendorf molded into the community of Herrnhut, one of the powerhouses of Protestant pietism. Pietism turned its back on everything the Jesuits understood religion to be. The glories of baroque spirituality tempted the pietist not in the least. Pietism moved in the opposite direction. It insisted on a religion of the heart. The years of persecution only deepened pietists' devotion.

III. Preaching the Reformation in Hungary

Now we must say something of the Hungarian Reformation.[15] It had not been ten years after Luther had posted his Ninety-five Theses on the door of the church of Wittenberg that the kingdom of Hungary suffered a catastrophic military defeat at the hands of the Turks. In 1526, at the Battle of Mohács, the defeat of the Hungarians was so complete that the kingdom of Hungary never recovered as an independent kingdom. As mentioned above, Louis II, who wore the crown of Saint Stephen as well as the crown of Bohemia, was killed in battle, leaving no son as his heir. As a result of this military tragedy Ferdinand von Hapsburg, archduke of Austria, was able to claim the Hungarian throne, as he claimed the Bohemian throne, by virtue of his wife, sister of King Louis II of Hungary.

The Hungarians, like the Bohemians, figured that by offering their

---

15. On the history of Protestantism in Hungary, see Dominic G. Kosáry, *A History of Hungary* (Cleveland and New York: Benjamin Franklin Bibliophile Society, 1941); Imre Lukinich, *A History of Hungary in Biographical Sketches,* trans. Catherine Dallas (Freeport, N.Y.: Books for Libraries Press, 1968); István Nemeskürty, Lázsló Orosz, Béla G. Németh, and Attila Tomás, *A History of Hungarian Literature,* ed. Tibor Klaniczay (Budapest: Corvina, 1982); and Denis Sinor, *History of Hungary* (Westport, Conn.: Greenwood Press, 1976). My appreciation is expressed to Rev. Dr. Lazslo Kovacs, a friend of many years, for pointing me to these works.

throne to Ferdinand von Hapsburg, the brother of Charles V, emperor of the Holy Roman Empire, they had the best hope of making a comeback and reclaiming the territory they had lost to the Turks. That the Hapsburgs might subjugate them as mercilessly as had the Turks had not occurred to them.

The Reformation was already beginning to be preached in Hungary, particularly in those cities with a strong German-speaking representation. While the nobles and the people of the land were normally Hungarians or, as they called themselves, Magyars, the commercial classes in the cities were more apt to be German or, as they liked to refer to themselves, Saxons. Preaching in a Protestant direction, especially among the Saxons, was beginning to be well received even before the devastating Battle of Mohács.

A. The Earliest Protestant Preachers

In the Magyar population we hear more clearly of Protestant preaching after 1526. One of the first Protestant preachers we have records of is Michael Sztári, who served as a chaplain at the Battle of Mohács.[16] He got his early schooling in Hungary but then studied in Italy. He earned a doctorate at Padua and wore the habit of Saint Francis. Whether he had received the Reformation before the dreadful battle we are not sure, but he did manage to escape with his life, and for the next twenty years ministered to his conquered countrymen. Through his vigorous preaching he is supposed to have organized the reform in over 120 churches. He was a powerful orator, well known for his bold, rich, and colorful use of the Hungarian language.

Another early preacher of the Reformation was Matthias Biró Dévai. We first hear of him being in prison for his Protestant preaching. This was in 1531. Apparently he was the first Hungarian student to find his way to the University of Wittenberg to study under Luther and Melanchthon. He returned to Hungary, where he was called the Hungarian Luther. He proclaimed the gospel in a number of towns. Finally he was imprisoned in the castle of Buda and died there about 1545.[17]

---

16. Imre Revesz, *History of the Hungarian Reformed Church,* trans. George A. F. Knight (Washington, D.C.: Hungarian Reformed Federation of America, 1956), pp. 12-14.
   17. Revesz, *History,* pp. 11-12.

Another early Protestant preacher was Gal Huszár.[18] He preached in the northwest of Hungary, in the Hapsburg-controlled area. Very rapidly he moved from place to place, being rather bold, preaching right under the noses of the Roman bishops. He was in and out of prison several times. Wherever he went he set up printing presses. In Hungary, as in many other areas, it was the printing press as much as the pulpit which did the work of evangelism. Huszár printed not only his sermons but the metrical psalms which became so popular in Protestant worship. He was one of those leaders of the Reformation who corresponded with Henry Bullinger, Zwingli's successor in Zürich. Bullinger's letters did much to win the Protestants of eastern Europe to the thinking of the Swiss Reformation.

B. István Kis of Szeged (1505-72), Doctor of Theology

An early Hungarian Protestant preacher about whom we know considerably more is István Kis of Szeged.[19] He began his studies in Hungary but went to Vienna to continue them. Before the actual beginning of the Reformation, the University of Vienna was a center of Christian humanist studies. Zwingli, for example, studied there before taking up his pastoral responsibilities in the Swiss canton of Glarus. That was where Celsius taught the Latin classics. From there young Kis went on to the University of Cracow, another important center of Christian humanism in the early years of the Reformation. At Cracow he began the study of Greek and probably Hebrew. In time he was given teaching responsibilities for Latin literature. Kis was developing into a Christian humanist scholar. From Cracow he went to Wittenberg, where he studied under Luther and Melanchthon for several years and eventually won his doctorate.

Returning to Hungary in 1544, Dr. Kis became the object of the jealousy of a local official responsible for church affairs. As a result, his library of several hundred books was confiscated. For those days this was a large and valuable library, having been acquired in Vienna, Cracow, and

18. Revesz, *History,* p. 18.
19. Alexander Sándor Unghváry, *The Hungarian Protestant Reformation in the Sixteenth Century under the Ottoman Impact,* Texts and Studies in Religion, vol. 48 (Lewiston, Lampeter, and Queenston: Edwin Mellen Press, 1989), pp. 143-61; Revesz, *History,* pp. 15-17. Further, see William Toth, "Stephen Kis of Szeged, Hungarian Reformer," *Archiv für Reformationsgeschichte* (1953): 86-102.

Wittenberg. For the next twenty years Kis won a reputation for his learned preaching and his devout interpretation of the Holy Scriptures. He became the leading voice of Protestantism in the area around Szeged, a major city in the southern part of Hungary, which had been under Turkish rule since the Battle of Mohács in 1526.

Preaching the gospel under Turkish domination was difficult. The learned Dr. Kis preached at great personal cost. So it was that in 1561 a woman who had taken offense at one of his sermons denounced him to the Turkish authorities.[20] According to her, Kis was a spy for the Austrians. The Turks arrested the preacher, put him in prison, and posted a sum for which he could be ransomed. This was a frequent way the Turks raised money in eastern Europe, as it had been for the Moors in Spain. In order to shame the Protestants into raising the ransom price, they would have this Protestant pastor preach in the marketplace in one town after another, wearing his chains on both hands and feet. When the faithful had almost raised the money, the Turks would raise the price. The Protestants eventually paid twelve hundred pieces of gold to hear their preacher proclaim the treasures of the gospel.

The word of Kis was highly valued, not only in Turkish-occupied Hungary but in western Europe as well. In 1592 a volume of his biblical expositions in sermonic form was published in Switzerland. Then in 1608 Theodore Beza published his defense of the doctrine of the Trinity. This work was occasioned by the antitrinitarian preaching of George Blandrata, an Italian humanist who appeared in Transylvania as early as 1563. Toward the end of the sixteenth century Unitarianism enjoyed a certain popularity, for a short time, but the Hungarian Reformed Church resisted it vigorously.[21] Hungarian Protestantism remained staunchly trinitarian.

Kis is usually presented as a mediating theologian who tried to keep a balance between Luther and Calvin. He is supposed to have been especially fond of Melanchthon on the one hand and Bullinger on the other. The general tendency in Hungarian Protestantism has been that while the German-speaking population stuck with Lutheranism, especially the

20. For more detail of this fascinating story, see the chapter "Stephen Kis of Szeged, a Hungarian Reformer during the Ottoman Occupation, 1505-1572," in Unghváry, *Reformation,* p. 145. See as well in this same work still further details, p. 55.

21. On the antitrinitarian movement in Hungary, see George Huntston Williams, *The Radical Reformation* (Philadelphia: Westminster, 1962), pp. 709-32, chapter entitled "The Rise of Unitarianism in Transylvania."

Transylvania Saxons, the Magyars were inclined toward the Swiss Reformers. Bullinger was especially influential in the Hungarian Reformed Church, and his Second Helvetic Confession was by far the favorite confessional statement.[22]

The picture of István Kis, noted biblical scholar and doctor of theology, preaching in the marketplace in chains has always been a symbol of the preaching ministry of the Hungarian Reformed Church. It speaks of the humility of the true preacher of the gospel. It reminds us of the example of the apostle Paul, who preached before the officials of the Roman government although in chains. A true minister of the gospel is a servant of his Lord, who came not to be served but to serve. This was the whole tenor of the preaching of this mediating, conciliatory preacher. Both in his sermons and in his theological literature he was a man of humility.[23]

C. Gáspár Károlyi (ca. 1520-91) and the Hungarian Bible

Just as the German Bible, translated from the original sources into the language of the people by Martin Luther, was the decisive act of the Reformation, and just as the work of Tyndale, Coverdale, and Lancelot Andrewes in producing the King James Bible in 1611 was a major accomplishment for the English Reformation, so the final publication of the Vizsoly Bible of 1590 was a decisive step forward in the reformation of Hungary. This accomplishment was largely the work of Gáspár Károlyi.[24]

Several attempts had already been made at producing a Hungarian Bible, or at least sizable portions of the Bible. Benedek Kamjáthy published a Hungarian New Testament in 1533.[25] It was largely based on the Latin New Testament of Erasmus. The Old Testament scholar János Szilveszter, professor of Hebrew at the University of Vienna, made considerable progress in translating a portion of the Hebrew Bible. A Unitarian attempt at translating certain portions of the Bible was also made by Gáspár Heltai. The Reformed pastor of Debrecen, Péter Juhász (Melius), made an attempt, but it was far from complete. The history of the En-

22. Unghváry, *Reformation,* pp. 156f.
23. A volume of English translations of his sermons would be a welcomed contribution to our knowledge of the Reformation in eastern Europe.
24. Unghváry, *Reformation,* p. 148; Revesz, *History,* p. 16.
25. On the various attempts to produce a Hungarian Bible, see Nemeskürty et al., *History of Hungarian Literature,* pp. 50-52.

glish Bible, as we have seen, was really a cooperative effort.[26] The same must be said about the Hungarian Bible, and yet it must be said that it was the continuous work of Károlyi that finally brought out the complete work.

Károlyi was the son of a noble family who had been able to study abroad. As so many Hungarian students, he spent several years at the University of Cracow. From there he went to Wittenberg and then, with the curiosity typical of students in every age, to Zürich, then Basel, then Strasbourg. When he was about forty years old, he returned to his native land. Finding the Turks to be much more of a menace than he expected, he had to take refuge in the fortress at Szatmár. When he was called to be pastor at Göncz in 1562, he moved there although it was in territory controlled by the Ottoman Empire. He was constantly exposed to the danger of being sold into slavery and offered his freedom at a high ransom. The Turks apparently were more interested in collecting ransom from Christians than converting them to Islam.

The publication of the Vizsoly Bible was hampered by the necessity of hiding the printing presses. The Counter-Reformation opposed vernacular translations of the Bible, which made it dangerous to do this work in the part of Hungary under the control of the Hapsburgs. It had to be done in Transylvania, where the Hapsburgs had no authority.

Károlyi was an accomplished scholar and able to use the work of biblical philologists in a variety of lands. Among those he consulted were the Dominican scholar Santes Paganinus (d. 1541); the Parisian Hebraist François Vatable (d. 1552); Sebastian Münster (d. 1552), who had been professor of Hebrew in Basel; and Immanuel Tremellias, a baptized Jew who was professor of Hebrew at Heidelberg. The Latin translation of Theodore Beza as well as his commentaries had a particularly strong influence on Károlyi. The intensive work "the godly old man" expended on his translation apparently wore him out. The work was finished in 1590, and he died in 1591, crowned with the respect of his countrymen.

---

26. See above, Hughes Oliphant Old, *The Reading and Preaching of the Scriptures in the Worship of the Christian Church,* vol. 4, *The Age of the Reformation* (Grand Rapids: Wm. B. Eerdmans Publishing Co., 2002), pp. 136f.

D. Péter Bornemissza (ca. 1535-84), Lutheran Bishop

Young Péter Bornemissza was scarcely six years old when his father was beheaded by the Turks because of his opposition to their policies.[27] The Bornemissza family was a highly respected noble family. Relatives took the young man under their protection, raising him on the family estate in Upper Hungary, a territory today included in Slovakia. Before long the scholarly life began to attract the future Lutheran bishop. Accordingly, he was sent off to the University of Cracow. There an English scholar, Leonard Cox, introduced young Bornemissza to Protestant ideas. At eighteen years old he was already inclined toward the Reformation.

Part of an education in those days was traveling from one university to another and sampling different philosophies of life. From Cracow in the south of Poland our young scholar traveled to Italy, where he learned how the Italian humanists understood the world. Bornemissza was not too impressed, so he turned to Wittenberg, where he grew much more favorably inclined toward the Christian humanism of Melanchthon. From Wittenberg he went to Vienna, at the time a center of Erasmian Christian humanism. There he came to know a Hungarian biblical scholar named János Szilveszter. Szilveszter was a typical Erasmian Christian humanist. He believed in reform, but not necessarily the sort of reform Luther had in mind. Bornemissza was as much interested in literature as in theology. In Vienna at this time the influence of the Reformation was definitely being felt, even if the court would hear nothing of it. While Bornemissza was there a young Jesuit, Peter Canisius, who was destined to become the leader of the Counter-Reformation in German-speaking Europe, was preaching in the pulpit of the cathedral of Saint Stephen.[28] His message was not well received, and Ferdinand von Hapsburg had to call out his troops to protect him. During this time young Bornemissza began to preach the Reformation to other students in his apartment. He had strong connections at the Hapsburg court, where he was a notary, but he still kept brooding over the ideas of Melanchthon.

Returning home to Upper Hungary, he set up a printing press for publishing Protestant literature. Apparently he continued to preach, but

27. Katalin Péter, "Bornemisza, Péter," in *The Oxford Encyclopedia of the Reformation*, 4 vols. (New York and Oxford: Oxford University Press, 1996), 1:201-2; Unghváry, *Reformation*, pp. 225-51. See also Nemeskürty et al., *History of Hungarian Literature*, pp. 54-56.

28. On Peter Canisius, see Old, *Reading and Preaching*, 4:190f.

not in a ministerial capacity. Around 1564 he was ordained as a Lutheran pastor, and for the next twenty years organized Lutheran churches in northwest Hungary.[29]

Bornemissza's outstanding literary accomplishment was his five volumes of sermons that he published at his printing press in Šintava, Slovakia. These *Postilla* were published for much the same purpose as Luther had published his *postils*.[30] He wanted to provide homiletical material for preachers to use in their preaching. The material followed the traditional Gospels and Epistles of the medieval liturgical calendar. These pattern sermons included a variety of materials. They range from very introspective confessions and meditations to stories, anecdotes, and fables, according to Katalin Péter. They contain a considerable amount of social criticism, as well as edifying personal admonitions.[31] Another large collection of his sermons called *Foliopostilla* appeared in 1584, the year before his death. Bornemissza wrote in a very classic Hungarian style which did much to increase the facility of the language.

E. Péter Juhász (Melius) (1536-72)

Péter Somogyi Juhász was the leading pastor of the church of Debrecen. As many scholars of his day, he went by a Latinized form of his name, Petrus Melius. Because he was born in northeast Hungary, which was at the time under Turkish control, he grew up knowing both Turkish and Arabic. It was because of this that the sultan supposedly tried to get him to translate the Koran into Hungarian.[32]

In those tumultuous times records were not kept too well, and the records that were made were often destroyed. Melius is supposed to have been of noble birth.[33] He is supposed to have been educated in a Turkish school, which would explain his knowledge of Arabic. Like so many lead-

---

29. On the specifically Lutheran Reformation in Hungary, see the extensive work of David P. Daniel, especially his article "Hungary," in *The Oxford Encyclopedia of the Reformation*, 2:272-76, with its extensive bibliography.

30. See Old, *Reading and Preaching,* 4:12.

31. The sermons of Bornemissza have not been available for this study. It is hoped that the work of Katalin Péter will eventually be published. Péter, "Bornemisza, Péter," p. 202.

32. Unghváry, *Reformation,* p. 276.

33. Unghváry, *Reformation,* p. 277.

ers of the Hungarian Reformation, Melius was sent off to study in Wittenberg. Arriving there in 1556, the future Reformer drank deeply from the Christian humanism of Melanchthon, taking special care to learn Greek and Hebrew. He stayed there long enough to earn his master's degree.

In 1558 he was called back to Debrecen to employ his classical theological training in the defense of the trinitarian teaching of classical Protestantism. Transylvania had become a center of Unitarian preaching, and the Reformed churches reacted quickly to check its spread. For many Hungarians it seemed like an attempt to find a theological compromise with Islam, and was therefore rather quickly rejected.

In the sixteenth century Debrecen was a large frontier town. It was caught between the Hapsburgs on the west, the Ottoman Empire on the south, and the Tartars to the northeast. It was a large town, larger than Wittenberg, Zürich, or Basel, and a wild town, one of the crossroads of eastern Europe, a town much like Geneva before the time of Calvin. During the pastorate of Melius the city was burned to the ground three times and plundered twice between the Turks, the Hapsburgs, and the Tartars. And yet, like Geneva, the town was eventually transformed, often called even to this day the Calvinist Rome.

Melius's contribution was largely theological. He led efforts to publish the Debrecen Confession of 1562, and to a great extent actually formulated it. In time the Hungarian Reformed Church adopted both the *Heidelberg Catechism* and the Second Helvetic Confession. Melius was also active in compiling a Hungarian hymnbook. For our purposes, however, his sermons are of greater interest. Some two hundred of them have come down to us.

The first collection of his sermons to have been published is his *Sermons on Christ's Intercession,* which appeared in 1561. This series of sermons came out of the controversy over the divinity of Christ. The preacher makes the point that because Christ is indeed the Son of God, truly man and truly God, he is in a unique position to intercede for Christians.[34] The sermons were, to be sure, very polemical. Apparently they were preached to answer the charges of the Unitarians.

Melius had a clear understanding of what a sermon should be. As he

---

34. There had been a debate in Debrecen between Melius and the Italian Jew Francisco Stancaro, at one time professor of Hebrew at the University of Padua. Unghváry, *Reformation,* pp. 328-31.

wrote in the Debrecen Confession, God's Word is the essential element. The sermon should be above all gospel, and Scripture alone brings us to understand what is meant by the gospel. Melius was obviously following the old principle Augustine had formulated so long ago. Scripture is to be interpreted by Scripture. The sermon should be nothing more than an exposition and an application of the passage of Scripture read as the lesson.[35] This apparently was understood in much the same way the Reformers of Zürich, Strasbourg, and Basel had understood it. Among his two hundred sermons is a series of seventy-six *lectio continua* sermons on Romans.[36] Another series of *lectio continua* sermons which has been preserved is his fifty-eight sermons on Revelation. Melius seems to have been inspired by the sermons of Henry Bullinger, Zwingli's successor in Zürich. Bullinger, one of the most prolific letter writers of the sixteenth century, corresponded often with Melius. His sermons on Revelation, being a model of exegetical good sense, were greatly admired at the time. In fact, Queen Elizabeth had them translated into English and placed in every parish church in England. Millenarian speculation was rampant in eastern Europe at the time, and Melius's series on Revelation was more than timely. What it suggests to us, however, is that the Reformer of Debrecen was an important supporter of the homiletical practice of the Reformed churches of western Europe.[37]

F. Albert Szenci Molnár (1574-1637)

Let us look at one more Hungarian Reformer to round out our picture. The story of Albert Szenci Molnár brings us well into the seventeenth century.[38] Here is a man who was a theologian and preacher, to be sure, but also a publisher — a rather ingenious publisher in fact, who knew how to provide the Hungarian Protestants of his day with the literature they needed.

Molnár was the son of a prosperous miller and vintner born in Szenc, in western Hungary. His parents were devoted Protestants.

35. Unghváry, *Reformation,* pp. 287-89.
36. Unghváry, *Reformation,* p. 288.
37. Here again we suggest that an English translation of a volume of Melius's sermons would be of great value in demonstrating the breadth and depth of Protestant preaching.
38. Unghváry, *Reformation,* pp. 201-24.

Growing up he was given the opportunity to study in various schools in Hungary. Especially important for his education was the Reformed theological college of Debrecen. From an early age he found himself fascinated by the art of printing. At sixteen he visited Gáspár Károlyi, who was at the time finishing his edition of the Bible. In the next forty years he visited most of the great publishing houses of Europe, writing and publishing some twenty volumes of his own. Molnár was the typical wandering scholar. He was a true pilgrim, always open to the new and the unfamiliar. His journal has come down to us, showing how he learned about the world through his ceaseless traveling about, meeting great people and people of no distinction at all, talking with them, and collecting impressions, hearing new and different ideas. Molnár's journal is to this day a witness to the importance of travel to a genuine education.

In 1591 he arrived in Wittenberg, always an important post for the Hungarian itinerant education. After a while there he went on to Heidelberg, which at the end of the sixteenth century was one of the most exciting theological centers of Europe. The Hungarians were especially fond of Heidelberg! From Heidelberg he went to Strasbourg, where he earned a baccalaureate degree. Then he went to Geneva, where he came to know Theodore Beza, Calvin's successor. He found the old man charming, and as Beza recounted his stories about Calvin, Molnár began to realize that Calvin was indeed a real saint, a theological hero he would do well to emulate. These personal impressions of the great Reformer that Beza communicated were important, because in time Molnár would translate Calvin's *Institutes* into Hungarian and disseminate the published volumes of that theological classic to his fellow countrymen.

From Geneva Molnár went to Rome. Somehow he had gotten to know an emissary of the Spanish king. The two men enjoyed talking with each other as they traveled, and before long they were in the Eternal City, but since the weather was hot, Pope Clement VIII was in his summer palace, Mount Caballi. Molnár found his way to Mount Caballi, and was even invited to dine at the papal table. Bright young students are able to get away with that sort of thing.

Back in Heidelberg, Molnár began to work on a Latin-Hungarian dictionary. Nothing like this had ever been done with the Hungarian language. Hungarian is a unique language, having no similarity to any other European language. It was a major step forward for Hungarian literature, and therefore of the greatest possible importance for the reading and preaching of the Scriptures. Molnár, quite understandably, dedicated his epoch-making dictionary to the Hungarian king, Rudolf II, who, as we said above, was more interested in being a patron of literature and the arts than in pushing through the usual Hapsburg religious politics. Molnár went to Prague, found his way into the royal presence, and personally presented his dictionary to Rudolf. As king of Hungary he was delighted, and presented Molnár with fifty pieces of gold.[39] What an operator young Molnár must have been!

Molnár undertook several other major publishing projects as well. He produced a Hungarian hymnal inspired by the *Genevan Psalter* of Clément Marot and his old friend Theodore Beza. He also used the German psalms of Ambrosius Lobwasser as a model.[40] He printed the psalters at Herborn in 1607 with the hope of smuggling them past the watchful eyes of the Hapsburg authorities.

Molnár at this point in his career was always back and forth between Hungary and Germany, where he did his printing of Hungarian Protestant literature. While in Hungary he still apparently did quite a bit of preaching in his native language. He later published two volumes of these sermons in the Rhineland city of Oppenheim.[41]

One of Molnár's most important publications was his translation of Calvin's *Institutes*. He dedicated the work to the prince of Transylvania, Gábor Bethlen,[42] who financially underwrote the work and rewarded Molnár substantially. The work's great value is the high quality of the translation.[43] Molnár stabilized the Hungarian theological vocabulary, linking Hungarian theological terms with the classic Latin theological vocabulary. This translation gave the Hungarians a classic of Protestant theology which has made it possible for them to maintain a significant witness in eastern Europe even to this day.

For more than 150 years the Hungarian Reformed church offered a vigorous preaching ministry in spite of the Hapsburg dynasty in Vienna and the Ottoman Empire in Constantinople. As the seventeenth century progressed, however, this pressure to convert to Catholicism increased as the Austrians tightened their grip on Hungary.

39. Unghváry, *Reformation,* pp. 209-10.
40. On the poetic excellence of Molnár's psalms, see Nemeskürty et al., *History of Hungarian Literature,* pp. 73f.
41. Unghváry, *Reformation,* p. 219.
42. Gábor Bethlen, prince of Transylvania from 1609 to 1629, was a devout Calvinist who brought Transylvania to its zenith.
43. Unghváry, *Reformation,* pp. 217-18.

IV. Péter Pázmány (1570-1637)

By the beginning of the seventeenth century, Protestantism had won the devotion of the great majority of Hungarians. The success of the Hungarian Reformation, however, was a major impediment to the imperial ambitions of the Austrians. For Cardinal Klesl (1552-1630), who for almost twenty years virtually ran the Austro-Hungarian Empire, the Hungarians were rebels by nature, just as the Bohemians were.[44] They must therefore be forced into conformity with the broader purposes of the Holy Roman Empire. Cardinal Klesl was one of the chief architects of Austrian absolutism, but it was Péter Pázmány who was to activate the Austrian program in Hungary.[45]

Although born to a Protestant nobleman, Pázmány was converted to Catholicism at the age of twelve by his stepmother. At seventeen he joined the Jesuit Order and studied in Cracow, Vienna, and then Rome. His first assignment was to teach philosophy and theology at the Jesuit college in Graz from 1597 to 1607. Thoroughly indoctrinated by Austrian ideology, he returned to Hungary in 1607 to be the councillor of the Catholic primate of Hungary, Cardinal Forgách. Under Forgách Pázmány's first reform was to bring order and discipline to the Catholic clergy. One must give considerable credit to the Jesuits for insisting on the moral discipline of their members and the Catholic clergy in general. This was always a major plank in the reforms of the Counter-Reformation. It was, however, the political dimension of Pázmány's program which was to have the most long-reaching effects.

Pázmány was by this time a staunch supporter of the Hapsburg monarchy. The Hapsburgs, as we have said, saw themselves as the champions of a Holy Roman Empire, which by divine appointment was to establish and maintain Catholic civilization in eastern Europe. As Pázmány saw it, submission to the Hapsburg monarchy offered the best hope of driving the Turks from Hungarian soil. The point of absolutism is that it is all of one piece — Catholic faith, Catholic empire, and Catholic civili-

44. Melchior Klesl (sometimes Khlesl or Klesel) (1552-1630) studied philosophy at Vienna, receiving his doctorate in 1579. See Joseph Felicijan, "Klesl, Melchior," in *New Catholic Encyclopedia*, 8:212.

45. For biographical material on Pázmány, see Odo Joseph Egres, "Pázmány, Péter," in *New Catholic Encyclopedia*, 11:35; J. Kornis, *Le Cardinal Pázmány, 1570-1637* (Paris, 1937), which was not available for this study; Lukinich, *History of Hungary*, pp. 153-60; and Nemeskürty et al., *History of Hungarian Literature*, pp. 85f.

zation. Complete obedience to each in its proper sphere is required. Conversion to Catholicism, then, quite logically, was the first step to establishing this goal. In eastern Europe absolutism became, in fact, the Jesuit gospel.

Pázmány was very convincing. He was a magnetic orator, and he preached his Jesuit gospel throughout Hungary. He won many converts. In fact, he has often been called the Hungarian Cicero. His rhetoric was sparkling, witty, and vivacious. His intensity was captivating. As a writer he used the Hungarian language with distinction. He set up Jesuit schools for the children of the nobility. His program was to convince the upper classes that Catholicism offered the best hope of reestablishing a united Hungary, and when that was accomplished, the lower classes could be forced into the Catholic fold. He believed quite thoroughly in *cuius regio eius religio*. By the time he died in 1637, he had converted some fifty families from the Hungarian nobility. The rest would be easy.

Let us look at one of his most famous sermons, a sermon delivered in Lent of 1636.[46] Its title might be freely translated as "Knowing Ourselves as the First Step to Salvation."[47] The Gospel reading for the day was apparently the story of how the Pharisees came to Jesus and asked him, "Who are you?" (John 8:25). Not paying very much attention to the context of this question in the Scriptures, Pázmány takes this question as his text, but strangely enough, he looks at it in the context of Greek philosophy. This maxim goes back to Apollo, according to our preacher. It is very important for us as Christians to know ourselves, but it is typical of us human beings that we can see what others are doing but not what we are doing ourselves. The human eye sees everything but itself. We see the dirt on someone else's face, but we cannot see the dirt on our own face.

This is why Mother Church puts ashes on our foreheads at the be-

---

46. In 1636 Pázmány completed publishing his sermons. It is not clear from the sources available to me whether the text we have was first preached in Lent of 1636 or whether it was published in 1636. At any rate, Pázmány is supposed to have worked very hard in his last years finishing up and publishing his sermons. He died shortly after publication.

47. For the sermons of Pázmány, see Péter Pázmány, *Predikácziók* (Budapest: Nyomatott a M. Kir. Tud.-Egyetemi Nyomdában, 1905). Appreciation is expressed to the Reverend Professor Botond Gaál for a copy of the text of this sermon and to the Reverend Professor John Bütösi for a summary of it in English. Given the importance of these sermons to the history of preaching, it is hoped that the sermons of Pázmány might be translated into English.

ginning of Lent and tells us to remember that we are dust and ashes. Mother Church does this to remind us who we are, that we might know ourselves. This is important when we realize that at the beginning God told Adam, You are dust, and to dust you must return. Let us never forget this: we are no more than dust and ashes. The prophets spoke of how we are clay in the hands of the potter. We dare not, therefore, be proud.

Looking at the Gospels, Pázmány continues, we find that when various sick people asked Jesus to heal them, our Savior would ask them what they wanted of him. He asked this question so that they would come to know themselves. He wanted them to know their sickness. Should we wonder, then, that in so many ways God desires that we know ourselves? There is no knowledge more useful for bringing us to salvation than knowing ourselves. To know ourselves is a spiritual science. It is unique among the sciences in that it teaches us humility. Most sciences puff us up and make us proud. To know ourselves is a science of humility.

No one, Pázmány assures us, can be saved unless he knows himself. Our preacher puts it in a striking metaphor. God says to the pious fiancée, If you do not know yourself, you cannot live with the bridegroom. You cannot become enticing or attractive to him without humility. You must be chased away from his house. While this metaphor may seem exaggerated at best, it is, I am assured, Hungarian humor, part of the literary charm of Pázmány's sermons.

Our preacher continues. It is better and more praiseworthy for a person to know himself than to know the orbits of the sky, the strength of the stars, and the paths of the beasts of the earth. This is because the knowledge of ourselves kills pride and implants the wisdom of fearing God.

The perfection of humility is to realize that God has established the foundations of the earth on nothing. God created the world out of nothing. In the same way Christian humility digs into the unfathomable depths of existence and finally discovers that we are nothing. The knowledge of where we came from and where we are going ultimately brings humility. Pázmány turns to us and asks, Come now, Christian, who have you been and what are you now and what are you to become? Self-knowledge comes if you are able to answer these questions. Here, then, is Pázmány's division of his text. To know ourselves is to know who we have been, what we are, and what we are to be. We have before us a traditional three-point sermon.

If we are to know who we really are, we must open our spiritual lives

318

to the knowledge of ourselves in order to enlighten our minds. Sober and diligent thinking requires that we know who we are and what kind of being we are. Not only is our nature lowly, but our moral behavior is full of failures. We can know ourselves in two ways: by comparing ourselves to others and by comparing ourselves to God. David tells us in the Psalms that when we compare ourselves to God we are nothing. The same thing is told us by Saint Paul, who insists that not only is he nothing, but the whole human race is emptiness and vanity. Think about the logic of it, our archbishop urges. Whatever is outside God is nothing because God's name is "I am who I am." Everything outside of God is like a drop of dew, a morning mist, emptiness and vanity. God himself, however, is limitless. His strength is almighty and his power is without end. Before God, how impure is our purity, how angry is our meekness, how proud is our humility, how cruel is our mercy. How weak is our strength if we look at it through the mirror of Christ.

Saint Augustine tells us that in the sight of God we are nothing. All comparison shows our sinfulness, our smallness, our nothingness. With this prestigious authority supporting him, our preacher asks us, What are we made of? First we must say that from all eternity we were nothing. God's free grace brought us to life, but God did not intend our bodies to be created without means. First God created the earth, and from the earth he created mud, and from mud he created the first human body. To make this very clear he called the first man Adam, which means earth. In Latin it is *Homo,* which also means earth. We are from the earth, and our bodies, at least, will return to the earth.

At first we imagine that the mud and the nothingness are only in the bodies of our ancestors and forebears. But as we take a closer look, we recognize that it is passed on to us through our mother's womb. Just as the milk is sucked from the mother's breast, in the same way, the Scriptures tell us, our bodies were made of blood and semen. For ten months we are in a dark, smelly enclosure, a shitty and ugly prison.[48] We are enclosed in that which no light could enter. There is no voice of comfort, no kind of food, drink, or enjoyment but what we took in through the umbilical cord from our mother's blood. From there we began our suffering

---

48. In an American pulpit even in this day and age, such language would not be tolerated, but in that day it would not have been nearly as shocking. Still, I am assured, it would have some shock value. Pázmány as an orator was apparently somewhat sensationalist. Sensationalism, of course, was typical of baroque art.

and growing. From this prison we move out when we are born, accompanied with our mother's pain, even sometimes her deadly pain.

You may understand, the archbishop continues, what you have been. First nothing, then earth and clay and mud. Finally you were conceived among shit, subject to immeasurable miseries, worthy of eternal damnation, because of your original sin. Don't you have reason to be humble? But let us go further!

Do you want to know who you are, and what you are? Whether in body or soul, danger, ugliness, and insufficiency characterize everything you do. One of the saints has said that our bodies are nothing more than sacks of shit. When we eat much, we simply fill more sacks of shit. Just look at how much smelly shit, snot, spit, and piss pass out of our bodies in the course of a day. Yes! Human beings are like a bunch of smelly latrines. Pázmány says the Scriptures speak with great disdain about our bodies so we will learn to hate them. Pázmány says they call the body the dungeon of the soul, the chains that drag down our spirits. While we have this body, we are like a prisoner in chains. On this subject Pázmány was neither the first nor the last to be confused. It certainly leaves us asking questions about the extent of his theological erudition and, even more, about his mastery of Scripture. However, he is a master orator!

But you may say, Pázmány continues, that there are many good things in our bodies such as strength and beauty, but how closely they are linked with fallibility and failure. At this point Pázmány gives us a number of illustrations. He was famous for his vivid, colorful illustrations! Let us consider, our preacher reminds us: Even if worldly goods were really good, think how uncertain and short-lived they are. Even our very life passes away like smoke, bursts like a bubble, fades like a flower, and ends like a dream. Here is a preacher who knew all the tricks of rhetoric for holding on to our ears! He may be theologically confused, but he is rhetorically astute. He has obviously mixed Manichaeism and Neoplatonism with biblical Christianity, but he does get our attention!

The body is a constant threat, Pázmány continues. It conspires with the devil against our souls. It is a mortal weapon of lewdness. It drives us to drunkenness and gluttony. Our tongues consistently entangle us in lies and slanders and foul talk. This is why God has commanded through Saint Paul that we not pamper our bodies and satisfy our desires. We are not created to serve our bodies, but to treat them as donkeys. We should scourge our bodies and keep them under control.

We need to go further, according to Pázmány. What sorts of good works can we do which will lead to salvation? We are so weak, so fumbling, so incapable. We cannot even think about doing good without God's aid. It is God who works in us the will to do good works and the strength actually to perform them. As the eye cannot see without light, the body cannot live without food, so we cannot do good works without God's aid. Here our preacher works in the standard sorts of illustrations. Good works have to come like the fruit of the vine. The strength comes from the root, but that strength brings the fruit through the branches. The same is true with oil from the olive trees, and with seed sown on the ground — it produces only if heaven grants the rain.

If we do any good, the glory belongs to God and not to us. If someone knows himself and views the ugliness of his deeds, he realizes that his deeds do not deserve any praise, payment, or reward, but only shame and dishonor. He looks at himself as a smelly carcass, the sins of which are still working corruption. It is just as we find it in the Bible, where David compares himself to a dead dog.

But there is another consideration. If we would truly know ourselves, we must consider what we will be at the end of our miseries when we finally are freed from this life and the miseries of this world. How will we stand in relation to God, before whom we will appear at last on the day of judgment? What is the future of our souls? Shall we escape the fire of hell?

If we would truly understand ourselves, we must think of the coming of old age with all its pain and misery. Our eyes will grow dim, our hearing will fail, we will not be able to enjoy the taste of our food, nor sleep at night. Even our mental abilities will fail us and we will have no pleasure in them. But this is nothing compared to death and what follows it. As the Scriptures tell us, first comes death and then comes judgment. Unpleasant experiences may precede death, but when we die the body becomes awful and smellier than any animal. In the grave the body becomes the food of snakes and worms until it finally disintegrates into dirt and once again we are dust. Even more terrifying, the soul is taken in total solitude to the throne of God's judgment, where all secrets will be revealed and no prayer will help. Here eternal damnation or happiness will be determined.

Several things should be noticed in this sermon. Pázmány was a Jesuit, and part of the Jesuit spirituality was the discipline of meditating on the eternal verities. One meditated in the most vivid way possible on both the glories of heaven and the horrors of hell. That was one of the things baroque art was all about. As we find in the *Spiritual Exercises* of Ignatius Loyola, a Jesuit spirituality fostered a vivid meditation on the pains of death. To meditate on the cross one went into all the blood, all the stink, and all the cries of pain. The Jesuits encouraged people to visualize it, to make mental pictures. This indeed was the mainspring of baroque art. If we find this sermon a bit extreme in its meditation on human depravity, we can be sure Pázmány preached in the same overdrawn way about the rewards awaiting those who deny the pleasures of this world. We can well imagine that he could be just as visual and as detailed about the mercies of the Virgin and the glories of heaven. That was part of the Jesuit spirituality as well! The baroque altars of eastern European churches are covered with it.

What interests us much more is the way Pázmány interprets the Gospel lesson he tells us he is preaching on.[49] As he has it, the Pharisees asked Jesus, "Who are you?" This is not at all the same question implied by the maxim so popular among the Greeks, "Know thyself." Much more is at stake when Jesus is asked "Who are you?" than when we ask ourselves who we are. In John 8 the implication is that the Pharisees are asking Jesus whether he is seriously claiming to be the Messiah, just as the Jews asked John the Baptist whether he was indeed the Christ. The exegesis of our preacher, at least in this case, shows a very naive understanding of Scripture. Even worse, it shows a rather insensitive mixing of Christian Scripture and pagan philosophy.

As a matter of fact, Pázmány had a reputation for rather inept interpretations of Scripture. Lázsló Ravasz, the most famous Hungarian preacher of the twentieth century, tells us that in spite of Pázmány's genius as an orator, he had a rather weak understanding of Scripture.[50] He used the Bible as a sourcebook for illustrations of how beneficial the moral teachings of Catholicism are and how dangerous it is to try to wander outside the bounds of the Catholic Church. The Bible and the preaching of the Bible are of value, according to Pázmány, only when used to bring us to obedience to the laws of the Catholic Church. Pázmány had little sense that the Bible is the Word of God, nor did he con-

---

49. Apparently Pázmány has taken as his text John 8:25, in which the opponents of Jesus ask him, "Who are you?" Possibly he has conflated this with John 1:19, in which we are told that the priests and Levites were sent from Jerusalem to ask John the Baptist, "Who are you?"

50. Appreciation is expressed to Dr. Bütösi for a summary of Lázsló Ravasz, *A Gyülekezeti Igehirdetés Elmélete (Homiletika)* (Pápa, Hungary: Református Fôiskola, 1915).

sider it essential to the Christian life to sit at the feet of the Master and learn of him as Luther did. One finds no suggestion from Pázmány that to proclaim the Word of God is central to Christian worship, or that the purpose of preaching is to glorify God. As Pázmány understood it, the Bible could be a very dangerous book; to be too concerned about what it taught he regarded as superstitious. He believed those who used it unlawfully or touched it with unclean hands, as the Protestants did, ran the danger of blindness or insanity. Pázmány's interest in the Bible was primarily polemical.

Finally, we notice that this sermon is concerned to emphasize a position at odds with Protestantism. Protestants, and especially Calvinists, have always opposed the asceticism of both Lent and Advent. Asceticism drives a sharp division between the physical and the spiritual. Much pagan philosophy, especially Manichaeism and Neoplatonism, sees our physical existence as the source of sin and corruption. It is pagan philosophy, not biblical Christianity, which teaches that the physical body is a prison that enslaves the human spirit. This has always been a major point of controversy between Catholicism and Protestantism. We notice in this sermon what we have often noticed in Jesuit preaching, that it is much more polemical than kerygmatic.

Pázmány is supposed to represent the best of the preaching of the Counter-Reformation in eastern Europe. We have to take the word of others for this, but as the seventeenth century advanced, Catholic preaching deteriorated considerably. In both Bohemia and Hungary it tended to pound in the Catholic doctrines which Protestants had challenged. The preaching of the Marian devotions, pilgrimages, Lenten observances, and saints' days became increasingly important. This will be evident further on when we come to Abraham a Sancta Clara.

V. Pál Medgyesi (fl. 1650-60)

By the middle of the seventeenth century the Counter-Reformation was having notable success in converting Protestants to Catholicism in the western part of Hungary where the Austrians were sufficiently in control to insist on their understanding of Christian civilization. It was another matter in the eastern portions of Hungary. There Stephen Bocskay, Gábor Bethlen, and György Rákóczi I organized the principality of Transylvania, where Protestantism established itself and flourished for several generations.[51] Under Bethlen and György I, both staunch Calvinists, civil order was established, economic prosperity advanced, and religious toleration was guaranteed. For almost a century the armies of Transylvania were able to keep the Turkish forces at a respectful distance. Transylvania became an island of tranquillity in the tempestuous sea of eastern Europe.

Three important colleges were founded by the Hungarian Protestants during this time. Bethlen established a college in his capital at Gyulafehérvár. Leading Protestant scholars from western Europe were brought in and scholarships were endowed, making it possible for students of poorer means to obtain an education. The Rákóczi family endowed a college at Sárospatak, which for a time was under the leadership of Johann Amos Comenius, famous for his progressive theories of education. Then there was the college in Debrecen, founded by the city council early in the Reformation. Debrecen was for several generations a center of Hungarian Protestant scholarship. It was especially well known for supporting students of modest financial means. The Protestant Theological Academy of Debrecen is to this day a major center of theological studies.

There were two problems, however: the principality of Transylvania had not been able to throw off its fealty to the Turks, and even more disastrous, several of its princes had conflicting political ambitions. Some were, alas, like too many of the magistrates of Christendom, ambiguous in their religious loyalties. This was particularly the case with György Rákóczi II. Unlike other members of his family, György II was vain, ambitious, and disinterested in the larger concerns of his fellow countrymen. By the mid-1650s conditions in Poland were confused. Although John Casimir had the title of king of Poland, he was far from being in control of the country. Therefore György decided to claim Poland for himself, and in January 1657 he invaded. The venture was a disaster. The army of Transylvania, which for the past fifty years had won relative peace and independence for the principality, was discredited, and once again the Turks reasserted their authority in eastern Hungary. A few years later, in 1660, very unrealistically, György rallied the Hungarian forces again and attacked the Turks, but he fell mortally wounded on the battlefield. His widow, Zsofie Bathon, and their infant son, Ferenc, converted to Catholicism. Transylvania never recovered.

51. On the history of Transylvania and its courageous attempt at religious freedom, see Sinor, *History of Hungary,* pp. 188-97.

It was in those sorrowful days of the decline of Transylvania that the preaching of Pál Medgyesi began to play an important role.[52] Although often called the first Hungarian pietist, his preaching seems more Puritan than pietist.[53] He is known to have studied the works of William Ames, the English Puritan who taught at the theological academy at Franeker in the Netherlands. A number of English Puritans, such as William Perkins, seem to have been well known to him.

In 1650 Medgyesi published a manual on how to preach and conduct public prayer, entitled *Doce nos orare quin et praedicare.* He emphasized strongly the devotional preparation for preaching as well as the prayerful study of the biblical text. He tells us at one point that only a God-fearing and God-glorifying preacher can be a true preacher. Medgyesi urges preachers to deal not only with doctrinal questions but also with personal religious experiences. Here, indeed, early as it is, is a pietist theme.

Let us look at a sermon he preached at Sárospatak in the discouraging days after György II returned from his disastrous attack on Poland.[54] The text for this double-barreled sermon is Lamentations 5:15-16 (RSV): "The joy of our hearts has ceased; our dancing has been turned to mourning. The crown has fallen from our head; woe to us, for we have sinned!"[55] The preacher sets the text in its context. The book of Lamentations, according to the traditional view, is a series of five songs of complaint written by the prophet Jeremiah. Medgyesi explains that while some scholars think this fifth lamentation concerns the death of King Josiah, probably more correctly, like the rest of the book, it concerns the fall of Jerusalem.

---

52. Appreciation is expressed to Prof. Gaál for providing the Hungarian text of two sermons of Pál Medgyesi, and likewise to Dr. Bütösi for providing me with a free English summary of these sermons as well as material on the significance of Medgyesi to the history of Hungarian preaching.

53. Hungarians often speak of the "first homiletical controversy." It was a controversy between the pietist approach to preaching and the approach of Protestant orthodoxy. Medgyesi advocated the pietist approach, while the approach of orthodoxy was advocated by István Geleji, who produced two volumes of sermons under the title *Praeconium Evangelicum,* containing 212 sermons, and three volumes, *Valtsag Titka (The Mystery of Salvation),* containing 228 sermons.

54. The sermon appears to have been preached in two parts, the first part in the morning and the second part in the evening of the same day, 2 September 1657.

55. The sermon text was taken from Pál Medgyesi, *Erdély romlásának okairól* (Budapest: Magvetö Kiadó, n.d.).

Our preacher goes over the specific complaints of the fifth song. The land had been turned over to aliens and the people's homes to foreigners. The situation of Judah in the days of Jeremiah was similar to that in Hungary under the domination of the Turks. Our preacher points out the parallels. The people of Judah under the Babylonian occupation had to pay the conquerors for water from their own wells and firewood from their own forests. The Hungarians knew all about this. The Babylonians had marched off the young men of Judah to be enslaved in a foreign land and had ravished their young women. The Hungarians knew all about this as well. The Lamentations of Jeremiah could well be the lamentations of the Hungarians under the Turks.

Our text, Pastor Medgyesi tells us, says two things about the joy of our hearts and the crown of our heads. We should realize what is the basis of a truly joyful people. The crown is a symbol of glory. When a people enjoys their national sovereignty, it is because the nation lives in righteousness, honesty, and justice. The joy of a nation depends on its moral character. But when a nation refuses to abide by the laws of justice and honesty, when it refuses to live by the truth, then its people lose both the joy in their hearts and the crown from their heads.

The sermon presses in on what causes a nation to flourish. Here three points are made. A nation prospers if it has good civil government, not only godly princes but all those in civil service. At this point Medgyesi brings Deuteronomy into the discussion. There we learn that those who lead a nation should commit to heart the Law of God. They should take care not to turn from it either to the right or to the left. A godly prince should maintain a godly court. As we find it in Proverbs 16:12 (RSV),

> It is an abomination to kings to do evil,
>   for the throne is established by righteousness.

But the people must also abide by the Word of God. It is important for the people carefully to listen to the teachings of the Scriptures and to maintain a high standard of morality. The whole people must maintain an honest life and a sincere devotion. The pure worship of God must be maintained. This is supported with a number of parallel passages and biblical illustrations.

When the people become careless about the things of God, they are liable to disaster. This is especially clear from Psalm 73:18 (RSV):

326

Truly thou dost set them in slippery places;
thou dost make them fall to ruin.

Our preacher draws the first installment of this sermon to a close by recounting how the sins of the sons of Eli brought about the conquest of Israel by the Philistines. The ark was captured, Eli fell dead, and the heir to that priestly line was born and named by his dying mother Ichabod, which means "The glory of the Lord has departed from Israel." After that tragically appropriate illustration, Medgyesi pronounces an apostolic ascription of praise which gave his congregation a hint of hope: "Now to him who by the power at work within us is able to do far more abundantly than all that we ask or think, to him be glory in the church and in Christ Jesus to all generations, for ever and ever. Amen" (Eph. 3:20-21 RSV).

Medgyesi begins the second session of this sermon by quoting the words of the apostle Paul that we should rejoice with those who rejoice and weep with those who weep. A time of weeping has come upon us. The greater part of the Hungarian nation lives in misery and ruin. Many have been killed. Many live in the cruel prisons of the pagan Turks. Will they ever be free? Is it not appropriate that we hold a day of prayer and fasting in honor of their suffering?

But something else needs to be said. True, we should lament because our brethren are suffering, but even more we should cry out to God because we have sinned. Once more Medgyesi turns to the biblical stories of the decline of ancient Israel. Certainly one important element in that decline was Israel's repeated apostasy. Again and again Israel took part in the sacrifices of the Canaanites and the idolatry of the Philistines. Our preacher goes into detail about several of these. Those well versed in the history of the times will no doubt recognize the parallels easily enough.

There is one thing we Hungarians can do, Medgyesi says, as we see the decline of our nation: repent. Medgyesi elaborates the sort of repentance that would be appropriate. First, he says, we who up to this time have given ourselves to sin should commit ourselves as those who have risen from the dead to the Lord, our true God. We should build on the good foundations our ancestors set rather than deserting them and giving ourselves once more to sin and idolatry. We should turn to God in prayer like the prodigal son. From here on, we should endeavor to find new ways to do good. We should give our whole lives to the glory of God. We should remember the words of our Lord Jesus not to be afraid of those who kill the body but cannot kill the soul, but rather be afraid of the one who can destroy both body and soul in hell. We must refrain from the violence that has become so characteristic of our day. Finally, if we will just repent, and that wholeheartedly, we can be sure God will fulfill his gracious promises to us. Our darkness will turn to light and our sadness to joy.

One easily recognizes here the typical fast-day sermon so popular among the Dutch Calvinists and the Puritans of both England and America.[56]

It is easy to conclude from these two sermons of Pál Medgyesi that the preaching of Hungarian Protestantism, like that of Reformed Protestantism at its best, gave high importance to a sound and practical exposition of Scripture. Nothing indicates that the Hungarian Protestants had only a backwoods version of classical Protestantism. Quite to the contrary, it is like the Protestant preaching of seventeenth-century New England, or seventeenth-century France — worship at its most profound offered under the most difficult conditions.

As the situation of Hungarian Protestantism became more and more difficult, the devotional life became more and more intense. Pietism was in many respects a reaction against absolutism. It was in their sufferings that the Word of God spoke most clearly to the Protestants of Hungary.

VI. The Witness of the Hungarian Galley Slaves

Cardinal Pázmány died in 1637. His preaching ministry no one seems to have taken up, but his religious politics were followed with a vengeance. He had convinced many of the nobility that to recover the large section of Hungary lost to the Turks, they needed to submit to the Hapsburgs and convert to Catholicism. Sad to say, those whom Pázmány's successors could not convince they now began to force. The first step was to rid the Protestants of their pastors.

The years 1671-81 are known as the "Dark Decade" among Hungarian Protestants, for during these years the Counter-Reformation did its worst to force the conversion of the Hungarians to Catholicism.

---

56. For Puritan fast-day sermons and for Dutch fast-day sermons, see Old, *Reading and Preaching*, 4:296f. and 464f. For New England, see above in this volume, pp. 177-78 and 240-44.

Leopold I had become emperor in 1658, when he was only eighteen years old. He was supposed to succeed his uncle as prince archbishop of Passau, and had therefore received his education in the Jesuit college at Ingolstadt, the foremost theological school of the German-speaking Counter-Reformation, where Abraham a Sancta Clara was also trained about the same time, that is, about 1655. Leopold was determined to put down Hungarian Protestantism the same way his predecessors had put down Czech Protestantism.

In the early 1670s Hungarian Protestant ministers were summoned to a special court at Pozsny.[57] The primate of Hungary, archbishop of Esztergom, presided.[58] Three hundred Hungarian Protestant ministers in the course of two years were assembled from the territories ruled by the Hapsburgs. They were sentenced to death and confiscation of their property unless they would convert. For almost a year they were starved and tortured. During this torture some died and some renounced their faith and signed a document pleading their conversion. Some feigned conversion and then escaped to territories under Turkish rule. Some stood firm, called by God to give the ultimate witness. The strongest of these were chained together, marched off to Trieste, and then shipped to Naples. Along the way some escaped and some died. On 7 May 1675 forty-one survivors of the march were sold to the Spanish navy as galley slaves. In time a physician, Nicholas Zaffius, discovered this deplorable cruelty. Scandalized, he wrote letters to leading statesmen and scholars throughout Europe.

The strongest protest arose in the Netherlands, where many Hungarian ministers had studied. They had colleagues, former professors, and friends in the Netherlands. Synods of the Dutch Reformed Church made impassioned pleas to the Estates General, the Dutch parliament. There was a strong Dutch fleet in the Mediterranean at the time. A message was sent to one of the admirals to investigate, and on 12 December 1675 Vice Admiral Jan de Staen sailed into the Bay of Naples to discover if the stories were true. The chaplain of the ship interviewed each of the ministers chained to his bench in the galley. The full Dutch fleet was off the coast

---

57. The German name for this city was Pressburg. Today it is part of the modern nation of Slovakia and is called Bratislava.

58. For an account of this story in English, see Revesz, *History,* pp. 60-67. An account was written by a survivor of the ordeal, Bálint Kocsi Csergö, *Narratio brevis de oppressione libertatis Ecclesiarum Hungaricum.* See M. Eugene Osterhaven, "Reformed Galley Slaves," *Reformatusok Lapja,* pp. 3-4; and Nemeskürty et al., *History of Hungarian Literature,* p. 79.

of Sicily at the time, and the vice admiral reported the findings to Admiral Michael de Ruyter, the "Old Sea Dog," the greatest admiral ever to sail under the flag of the Netherlands.

Admiral de Ruyter prepared his strategy, took the necessary diplomatic steps, and in a few weeks, when all was ready, raised full sail and entered the Bay of Naples, surrounding the Spanish fleet and aiming his cannons at the city. The admiral demanded the ministers be released from their chains.[59] On 11 February 1676 the chaplain of the Dutch fleet, accompanied by an honor guard of naval officers, boarded the Spanish ships and freed the forty-one ministers who had survived. Once on board the Dutch man-of-war, the ministers knelt on the deck for prayer and all joined in singing Psalm 116, "I love the Lord, because he has heard the voice of my supplication."

The next morning the ministers, now fed, bathed, their wounds cared for, and wearing more suitable clothing, were brought to the flagship, *De Zeven Provicien,* to be presented to the "Old Sea Dog." He, however, would accept no thanks. We are only God's instruments, he insisted. *Soli Deo gloria,* to God alone give glory! As Admiral de Ruyter regarded it, "Of all my victories, not one has caused me so much joy as the deliverance of Christ's innocent ministers from this intolerable yoke."[60]

For some time these ministers lived in the Netherlands. Leopold's clerical advisers had made it very clear that they were not to seek any kind of revenge or compensation. Particularly they were not to try to return to Hungary. Neither the elector of Saxony nor the Dutch Estates General, however, would let the matter drop, insisting that the ministers be allowed to return. The emperor, feeling embarrassed about the affair, finally allowed them to return to Hungary.

VII. Abraham a Sancta Clara (1644-1709)

Only now, having looked at Protestant preaching in the Austro-Hungarian Empire and the frantic determination of the Hapsburgs to stamp out Protestantism, can we understand Austrian baroque preaching. This preaching had its source in the Counter-Reformation polemic first of Father

---

59. Some accounts suggest that two Swiss merchants by the name of Welz were at the same time arranging to ransom the ministers.

60. Osterhaven, "Reformed Galley Slaves."

Kravařský in Bohemia, who learned how to charm the hostile, and second in the rhetoric of Cardinal Pázmány, who learned the art of impressing the prestigious with his wit, his intensity, and his aristocratic bearing. It came to full vigor in the triumphal age which followed the deliverance of Vienna from the siege of the Turks in 1683, and continued through the age of Maria Theresa toward the end of the eighteenth century.

Johann Baptist Schneyer, a leading Catholic authority on the history of preaching, has singled out Abraham a Sancta Clara as the most significant German-speaking preacher of the baroque period.[61] He was born Johann Ulrich Mergerlin, the son of a tavern keeper in Kreenhein-stetten, near Vienna.[62] We remember that George Whitefield, the great pulpit orator of the following generation, was also the son of a tavern keeper. It is often suggested that hearing the folk language of the tavern would have given these young men a solid handle on the popular speech of the day. Abraham, as Whitefield, knew how to capture people's ears. He knew how to tell a story, paint a word picture, and tell a joke. He no doubt learned it from earliest childhood.

Abraham may have learned the gift of gab in his father's tavern, but before long his father sent him to the Jesuit college at Ingolstadt. There he was thoroughly immersed in the typical Jesuit education. Christian humanism, as the Jesuits had developed it, had a distinct approach to learning. At the heart of it was the catechism of Peter Canisius (1521-97). Students memorized this catechism and repeated it again and again, as memorization was understood as the secret of education. The teaching of the catechism was generously supported by Scholastic philosophy, the logic of Aristotle, and proof texts from Scripture. Essential to this education were the literary studies of Christian humanism. One read the classics of Greek and Roman antiquity. Jesuit learning took place in Latin, the language of both philosophy and theology, both learning and prayer. It was the universal language of the intellect, transcendent wisdom, and ancient tradition. All this, of course, was quite appropriate for a preacher to the Holy Roman Empire.

---

61. Johann Baptist Schneyer, *Geschichte des katholischen Predigt* (Freiburg im Breisgau: Seelsorge Verlag, 1969), p. 287.

62. For biographical material on Abraham, see L. Bianchi, *Studien zur Beurteilung des Abraham a Santa Clara* (Heidelberg, 1924); A. J. Clark, "Abraham of Sancta Clara," in *New Catholic Encyclopedia*, 1:35; T. G. von Karajan, *Abraham a Sancta Clara* (Vienna, 1867); and F. Lodi, *Menschen im Barock: Abraham a Santa Clara über des religiosesittliche im Österreich 1670-1710* (Vienna, 1938).

Three years later the future preacher's father died, and an uncle, Abraham Mergerlin, took charge of his education. The uncle was a priest of some standing, being a canon of Altöting. He transferred Abraham to the Benedictine College in Salzburg in 1659, no doubt because it was much closer to Altöting. In 1662 our future preacher entered the Augustinian Order, taking as his religious name Abraham in honor of his uncle. He did his novitiate at Mariabrunn, near Vienna. In 1668 he was ordained in Vienna, and as his first assignment was sent to the pilgrimage church of Taxa near Augsburg. Almost immediately he became popular as a preacher, drawing large crowds.

Soon young Abraham was called back to Vienna and assigned to the Augustinian church in the center of the city, close to the imperial court. A few years later, in 1677, he was named preacher to the court and is supposed to have had considerable influence with the emperor. Abraham was a model court chaplain, having neither political ambition nor a craving for the honors of the court. Apparently he had a genuine love for preaching. In fact, it is said that he loved preaching so much that he became a priest so that he could be a preacher. In 1679 Vienna was devastated by an outbreak of the pest. This occasioned many sermons and warnings of human mortality. Abraham's preaching had a sobering effect on the city. Eventually he cooked down his sermons to a devotional writing, *Merk's Wien!* In this work he gives graphic descriptions of the plague, making the point that death comes to all of us. Another important theme of his preaching was the awakening of Vienna to the danger of the Turkish invasion. These sermons also were reduced to a book, *Auf, auf, ihr Christen,* which appeared in Vienna in 1683.[63] That, of course, was the year the Austrians did rise up, lift the Turkish siege of Vienna, and chase the forces of the Ottoman Empire back down the Danube, putting all of Hungary firmly in Austrian hands.

Some were very critical of Abraham, calling him a buffoon in the pulpit. (As one wag put it, he was Franz Lehár in clerical garb.) His personal conduct, however, was beyond reproach, and some of the most meticulous of German literary critics have admired his preaching for its originality, its wit, and its colorful humor. We hesitate to make judgments

---

63. For a collection of Abraham's works, see Abraham a Sancta Clara, *Sämmtliche Werke,* 21 vols. (Lindau: Verlag von Johann Thomas Stettner, 1846). A selection of his works was published in Vienna by H. Strigil between 1904 and 1907. The first edition of his complete works is supposed to have been published in Passau from 1835 to 1847.

about the artistic value of German oratory. We prefer instead to repeat the opinion of Schneyer, who credits Abraham's phenomenal popularity to his gift of careful observation of the human scene and his incisive and appropriate evaluation of the situation. He had an amazing memory for stories he had heard from childhood and material he had read years before. His recall for what he had learned back in his school days was quick and ready. Even more, here was a preacher with the ability to savor his speech with humor, to give it sparkle with his clever satire. His sermons fairly bubble over with enthusiasm and fun. Abraham was vivacious; he was the soul of Austrian baroque culture. In his sermons we find picture after picture; anecdote after anecdote; a profusion of fables, legends, and fairy tales; jokes, poetry, and rhymes. He was a master of the short story, a gifted painter of the comedy of manners, in short, a poet of God's grace, as Schneyer has put it.[64]

Apparently, Abraham a Sancta Clara was one of those who prepared the way for the comic operas of Mozart, the amusement park of the prince-archbishop of Salzburg, and the Viennese operettas of the nineteenth century. Indeed, he was one of the creators of the Austrian baroque. What a unique world it was, so different from the Protestantism of England and America! As we have said, it is more lighthearted, but as we shall see, it does have its serious moments. The Austrian baroque may start with its *Così Fan Tutte* and its *Magic Flute,* but it ends with its *Don Giovanni* and finally with the Mozart *Requiem.*

A. Sermon for Christmas Eve[65]

Sometime in the 1670s Abraham was invited to a neighboring church in Vienna to bring to a conclusion a novena, a nine-day series of devotions. Apparently it was the custom in Vienna to hold such a novena in preparation for the feast of Christmas. The sponsoring church was Saint Michael's, a particularly prestigious congregation, for it was the *Hofpfarrkirche,* the parish church of the court.[66]

---

64. Schneyer, *Geschichte des katholischen Predigt,* p. 289.

65. The following study is based on Abraham a Sancta Clara, *Neun neue Predigten von Abraham a Sancta Clara, Aus der Wiener Handschrift cod. 11571,* ed. Karl Bertsche (Halle: Max Niemeyer Verlag, 1930), hereafter Abraham, *Predigten.*

66. Cf. Bertsche's introduction to the text of this sermon, Abraham, *Predigten,* pp. xivff.

The sermon is organized around four newspaper reports. The first is from the newspaper of the kingdom of heaven, the second from the newspaper of Bethlehem, the third from the newspaper of Rome, and the fourth from the newspaper of Vienna. The preacher to the court of the Hapsburgs was in no way lacking in imagination, it would seem.

Our preacher takes up the heavenly newspaper first. It reports that in a field scarcely a mile outside the City of David an angelic courier had arrived with the report, *"Invenietis infantem positum in praesepio"* (Luke 2:12).[67] Catholic preachers from the time of the Counter-Reformation usually quoted Scripture in the Latin Vulgate. The Latin text is then followed by a translation, "You will find the child lying in a manger." Our preacher asks his listeners a rhetorical question: Is this not a blessed newspaper report for us to read? The great God has appeared on earth as a little child. O Great God, our preacher expatiates, whose greatness has no measure, no end, no counting, whose greatness fills heaven and earth, whose greatness no human eye can see, next to whom Pompey, Alexander, and even Julius Caesar are all but a shadow, how is it that you have made yourself so small?[68] God's love for his creation is the final cause. It is, in the end, God's love that brings his almighty majesty to come to rest in this simple manger.

Our preacher once more turns to the Gospel of Luke, which tells us why Mary and Joseph journeyed to Bethlehem. It was in obedience to the imperial decree that all had to be taxed. Mary made the journey even though she was expecting her first child. The preacher discusses the details of the journey at some length. It was surely a difficult journey for a woman in such a condition. One wonders if she really made the journey by foot. Could not a carriage have been provided? The opinions of several learned theologians are reviewed. Maldonatus, a sixteenth-century Jesuit biblical scholar, and even Saint Bernard of Clairvaux had tried to explain the difficulty. But the point seems to be that the incarnate God was born among us in the most difficult of circumstances. It is, in the end, the love of God which brought all this about.

To make this point the preacher tells the old fable, used so often in all kinds of edifying literature, of the sun and the wind. It seems that Lady Sun and Lord Wind got into an argument about who had more power. The wind blew ferociously and brought about all kinds of destruction.

67. Abraham, *Predigten,* p. 62.
68. Abraham, *Predigten,* p. 63.

Everyone was impressed at the power of Lord Wind, but then Lady Sun had her turn. She began to send out her rays and warm things up, and all of a sudden everyone began to throw off their coats, come out of doors, and enjoy the warm weather. The sun may not have had the power of destruction, but it did have the power of enlightenment and warmth and pleasure. Our Viennese court preacher says a somewhat similar argument arose in the kingdom of heaven, this one about the relative power of justice on the one hand and love on the other. The righteousness of God tried to show its power for four thousand years. All this we learn about in the stories of the Old Testament. God's judgments on Pharaoh, Jezebel, and Sennacherib are given as examples. Then with the incarnation the love of God had its turn to demonstrate its power. When God became incarnate in the pure, virginal womb of blessed Mary and was born as a little child and then laid in a manger, then the power of God's love, as the mellifluous Saint Bernard put it, began to triumph.[69]

Having made his first point, our preacher takes out his second newspaper. This newspaper is from Bethlehem and is dated 24 December. According to this report, the second person of the Trinity was born "incognito" in a stall between an ox and an ass. Saint Jerome, some four hundred years after the birth of Christ, tells us Christ was born in a cave. In Latin our preacher asks his congregation, *"Quid quaerit hic Jesus apud bovem? Ovem."* That is, What does Jesus seek here among the cattle?[70]

Saint Ambrose tells us that the Christ child was born among the cattle in order to make it clear from the very beginning that he came to save sinners, even the dumbest oxen and the silliest asses of the human race.

At some length our preacher makes the point that we human beings are a bunch of dumbheads, oxen and asses all together. Adam so foolishly took the word of Eve rather than the word of God, and so the two of them, Adam and Eve, both together, were exiled from paradise. *"Quid quaeris apud bovem? Ovem."* Then our preacher speaks for Jesus, answering the question. I came into the world as a physician, Jesus tells us, to heal the wounds of men, the wounds inflicted by the serpent. I came into the world as a fountain of water to quench the thirst of human beings. *"Quid quaeris?"* I came into the world to seek out the lost sheep and, with

---

69. Abraham, *Predigten,* p. 65.

70. Abraham, *Predigten,* p. 66. Apparently our preacher makes a pun here. He follows the word *bovem* with *ovem,* the Latin word for sheep. It can also mean simpleton. The pun, of course, can be understood only by those who know Latin.

a shepherd's staff, to bring them into the fold again. *"Venio peccatores salvos facere."* I came to save sinners.[71]

Again Abraham addresses the Savior: Your Spiritual Majesty, we have but one question: Why did you come into this world "incognito," clothed in human flesh? Our preacher, again demonstrating his erudition, tells us that the blessed Drogo wrote that the humanity of God must have been in some sense a mirror.[72] To illustrate his point, Abraham tells a story about Augustus Caesar, who had a raven that would on a signal cry out, "Ave Caesar." Now, as Abraham has it, the way to train a raven to speak is to put a mirror in front of the bird. Then, hidden behind the mirror, the trainer cries out a phrase repeatedly and the raven thinks it is hearing the bird in the mirror crying out the phrase and decides to copy it. And so the bird learns to speak. Our preacher makes the point that God took on human flesh to teach us how we should behave. God teaches us to be good by giving us a good example. It is the incarnate Son of God who is this good example. The moral influence theory of the atonement comes through loud and clear.

Our preacher moves to his third newspaper, dated 25 December from Rome. A courier reports a wonderful discovery of a prophecy that the anointed Messiah is to be born the prince of peace. He is not to be wild and rough but soft and gentle. In the Old Testament God is often called a roaring lion, *ein brilender leb,* because of his uncompromising righteousness. The God of the Old Testament is a grim God, a hard, fierce God. He is called *catulus leonis Juda,* the young lion of Judah, and yet as soon as he was born of Mary, he was called the Lamb of God who takes away the sin of the world.[73]

Abraham tells another story from Pliny's natural history about some creature in a faraway land. It is clear that the point of it all is that the God of the Old Testament is an angry, vengeful God, but that once God is born of the chaste virgin Mary, God is soft and gentle. Once God has been clothed with mortal flesh, then he is quite calm and friendly.[74] He is no longer a lion but a lamb. No longer is he a god of vengeance, but now he is a prince of peace, *Princeps pacis.* Indeed, God has become a little child.

71. Abraham, *Predigten,* p. 67.
72. The *New Catholic Encyclopedia* mentions three people by the name of Drogo. None of them, however, is recognized as a theologian.
73. Abraham, *Predigten,* p. 70.
74. Abraham, *Predigten,* p. 71.

To prove how gentle God is, Abraham tells the story of Alphonsus Viliega, who had lived a century before in Spain. It seems the man was a heretic and wanted to prove that the consecrated eucharistic bread was nothing more than common table bread. So he went to mass and took the host into his mouth, but did not swallow it. Instead he went home and took the host out of his mouth and threw it into the fire. The host was not burned in the fire, but rather proved itself to be the incarnate body of Christ by producing little drops of blood. The experiment was repeated with the same result, and Alphonsus was converted to true Catholic faith.[75] This miracle surely shows us how, after God took on human flesh in the womb of the Virgin, he became more gentle. Well, at least, it was sufficient proof for the court chapel of the Austro-Hungarian Empire.

Returning to his subject, Abraham exhorts his listeners: Go to the manger, my children. With trust and confidence kneel down there and seek from the newborn Messiah forgiveness of your sins. Give to him the shiny red apple of your heart, for he is indeed quite kindly disposed.[76]

Again our preacher turns to the ancient Roman naturalist for an example of how occurrences of nature confirm the gospel. As Pliny tells us, all the rivers of the world get their waters from the sea. We find the same truth taught in Scripture, for we read *"ad locum unde exeunt flumina revertuntur,"* which translated says,

> All streams run to the sea,
>   but the sea is not full;
> to the place where the streams flow,
>   there they flow again. (Eccles. 1:7 RSV)

With this our preacher plunges into a long explanation of how the Danube begins in the little streams of the Black Forest. Tributary after tributary flows into it until it is a mighty river when it passes through Vienna and then on through Hungary and Romania into the Black Sea. Saint Basil of Caesarea tells us the same thing in his sermons on the six days of creation, Abraham explains. In the beginning all water is bitter, but when it flows through the earth it becomes sweet. So it is with our humanity. What from the beginning flowed from Adam's rib was sour, but when it flowed through Mary's virgin womb it became sweet.[77] Abraham may

---

75. Abraham, *Predigten,* p. 72.
76. Abraham, *Predigten,* p. 73.
77. Abraham, *Predigten,* pp. 73-74.

have delighted the devout of Vienna, but for some of us his theology is a bit muddled. However, we have all heard plenty of muddled theology in our own pulpits right here in America, especially at Christmas. The parallels are embarrassing.

Before we can finish with this festal sermon, we have one more newspaper to look at. This paper dated 24 December was published in Vienna itself. The report tells us that here in the capital city of the Austro-Hungarian Empire everyone is well prepared for the coming of the great king. This, of course, is appropriate only when one considers his importance. Jacobus Megerus writes that when Philip, the count of Flanders, was to be born, there was a miraculous proclamation, *Vacuate mihi domum.* This can be translated, "Empty the house for me," that is, clean the house, prepare it for my arrival, decorate this place which is to be my home.[78] So we should clean out our hearts of all filthiness, dishonor, and immaturity. With this our preacher launches into a classical peroration urging the congregation of the Church of Saint Michael to intensify their devotion to make ready for the great feast which approaches.

B. Sermon for Easter

This sermon was probably preached in the early 1670s at the Augustinian church in Vienna.[79] A number of Abraham's Easter sermons have come down to us, but this one is written in the hand of the preacher himself. It is not, however, a finished-up sermon. The text contains rough spots which no doubt were "finished up" in the pulpit. Besides that, there are a number of places where for one reason or another a passage has been lost. Sometimes the preacher's thoughts get a bit tangled, a fact which leads us to believe the manuscript before us was a draft of the sermon our preacher intended to preach.

The introduction certainly catches one's attention. Abraham proposes that crickets, moths, and other small insects often act as eyeglasses by which we come to know the Creator. The brilliance of butterflies and the ingenuity of ants are sometimes the means by which we sense the wonder of the divine workmanship. These little tiny creatures can bring us to faith in the Creator.

78. Abraham, *Predigten,* pp. 74-75.
79. Cf. Bertsche's introduction in Abraham, *Predigten,* pp. xvff.

This is followed by a miracle story from Ávila in Spain that makes the point.[80] There a certain church was built to the honor of the blessed mother of God. The church was built because a blacksmith found a sacred image of the Virgin in a cow stall. The church was named, therefore, Maria de Vaccis. This image is made famous by a miraculous sign. Every year on the second Sunday of May a citywide procession is held in honor of this holy image. It is accompanied with wondrous miracles and healings. Every year when the procession is held, a beautiful white moth, larger than one ever sees otherwise, flies about the image and attaches itself to the veil of the Virgin. Nothing scares it away, neither the drums or trumpets of the musicians, nor the singing of the crowds of people. It never leaves the image of the Virgin. When the moth dies, its wonderful snow-white wings are sent to a prominent person, and miraculously they have curative powers so that often the sick recover their good health.

This is followed by a story from the revelation of Saint Birgitta.[81] It, too, is a rather bizarre legend regarding insects which demonstrates the resurrection of Christ.[82] This leads into a recounting of the biblical types of the resurrection. Noah, Isaac, Jacob, Moses, and David are all recognized as types of Easter. The trail our preacher treads is more than circuitous, and even the strongest supporters of typology will find it a bit strange.

Let us pick up the sermon after this long series of types, at the point where our preacher returns to the subject to which all these types point, the resurrection of Christ. Abraham clearly affirms the resurrection. Whatever failings this sermon may have, it does affirm the resurrection of Christ. Our preacher addresses his congregation: Oh, truly converted listener, we all gladly confess, gladly believe: Christ is risen, *surrexit,* he is risen, and therefore we rejoice. Our preacher lapses into Latin, *"scio quod redemptor meus vivit et in carne mea"* (Job 19:25, "I know that my Redeemer lives and in my flesh . . ."). I, too, will rise again. To be sure, this famous line from Job had a prominent place in the liturgical celebration of Easter. Our preacher probably could count on many in his congregation understanding the Latin; even those who did not were impressed by the sonority of the Latin text and the learned impression it made.[83]

---

80. Abraham, *Predigten,* pp. 79-80.

81. Saint Birgitta of Sweden (Saint Bridget) was a fourteenth-century mystic who had many visions, revelations, and miraculous experiences.

82. Abraham, *Predigten,* pp. 80-81.

83. Abraham, *Predigten,* p. 87.

Our preacher seems almost in ecstasy as he assures his congregation that because Christ rose from the dead we can be sure that we, too, will rise from the grave and enter into eternal life. Abraham reminds us of the words of Jesus about God's care for the sparrows. How much more our heavenly Father cares for us and wants to open up to us eternal life. Again he lapses into Latin, *"Nolite timere: multis passeribus"* (Matt. 10:29-31). Jesus wanted to console his disciples with the hope of eternal life. It was the same way when the risen Christ met Mary Magdalene in the garden. Jesus asks Mary why she weeps and why her heart is cast down. Does she not realize Christ is risen, and that he is the seal of our resurrection? Because he rose again, our preacher assures his congregation, we can be sure that we will rise again, be glorified, and enter into eternal life. *"Haec dies quam fecit Dominus, exultemus et laetemur in ea."* "This is the day the Lord has made; let us rejoice and be glad in it" (Ps. 118:24). Here again, the use of Latin seems almost ecstatic, for the preacher at least, but probably for the congregation as well.[84]

Here is classic Easter preaching. There is no question about it. It is just that for many of us at the beginning of the third Christian millennium, the rococo expression of this eternal truth is compromised by the thick overlay of legends, entertaining stories, and miraculous tales. Like so many of the homiletical jokes and human interest stories of our own day, they seem to compromise the true heavenly mysteries of the eternal Gospel.

Abraham is incorrigible. He ends his sermon with a tale of a bird which is said to inhabit America. The story goes that on Good Friday this bird falls lifeless to the ground until Easter Sunday morning. What a story! One wonders if it strengthened the faith of the Viennese courtiers who filled his church on Easter, or was one of those things like our American Easter bunnies which only confuse those who seek true faith.

C. Sermon for Saint Leopold's Day

Let us look at one more of Abraham's sermons, the sermon for Saint Leopold's Day. Saint Leopold's Day was the name day for Leopold I, the Holy Roman emperor at the time. Leopold lived from 1640 to 1705, and reigned from 1658. He had a rather long and prosperous reign, and was thoroughly devoted to the Catholic Church. The Jesuits had much influ-

---

84. Abraham, *Predigten*, p. 88.

ence at his court. As we have seen, in both Bohemia and Hungary he was determined to crush Protestantism. Like Louis XIV, his French contemporary, he was committed to absolutism. In short, he was a model Counter-Reformation monarch.[85]

The annual name day celebration was in Catholic countries the equivalent of the American birthday celebration. Saint Leopold's Day was a celebration not only of the saint but also of the Holy Roman emperor Leopold I. Leopold was a member of the House of Hapsburg, which for several generations had ruled Austria; in fact, in his reign it had finally secured the right of hereditary succession to the title of Holy Roman emperor. Saint Leopold, on the other hand, was the margrave of Austria in the twelfth century. He lived from 1075 to 1136. He had been educated by Saint Altman of Passau. Pope Innocent II had given him the title Son of Saint Peter because of his loyalty to the papacy during the investiture controversy.

In time, however, the margrave changed his support to Henry V, who was the Holy Roman emperor, and therefore was rewarded with the hand of the emperor's daughter, Agnes. Leopold was a devout prince, and expressed this in founding several important monasteries. One of these was the Augustinian cloister at Klosterneuburg, another was the Cistercian abbey Heiligenkreutz, and a third the famous Benedictine cloister Kleinmariazell. One of his sons became Conrad II, prince-archbishop of Salzburg. Leopold was canonized in 1485 and chosen as patron saint of Austria in 1663, that is, early in the reign of Leopold I. Obviously the Hapsburg dynasty was looking for the sanction of sacred tradition. The sermon, if nothing else, shows us how in the seventeenth and eighteenth centuries the divine right of kings was looking for the support of holy history.

Let us see how Abraham a Sancta Clara preached the feast of Saint Leopold.[86] The sermon begins with a list of amusing insults about the

---

85. On the importance of the Saint Leopold's Day sermon to Austrian preaching, see Maria Kastl, *Das Schriftwort in Leopolds predigten des 17. und 18. Jahrhunderts* (Vienna: Braumüller, 1988).

86. A number of Abraham's sermons for this feast have come down to us. The sermon edited by Karl Bertsche in Abraham, *Predigten*, pp. 102-9, is the subject of our study. There is also a sermon on this same subject in Werner Welzig, *Predigten der Barockzeit: Texte und Kommentar* (Vienna: Österreichischen Akademie der Wissenschaften, 1995), pp. 147-65. The version published by Welzig must have actually been preached at court because it is filled with all the obsequious flattery of proper court etiquette.

court and the life of the court. Abraham was well known for the ingenuity and variety of his rhetorical figures. Here is an example of his clever oratorical devices. Some have called the court a hospital for sick hopes, he says, a grave for all that is lively, a breeding ground for jealousy, a school for pride, a marketplace for falsehood, a home base for cheating, the native land of cursing, a purgatory for true morality, and a hell for virtue. We can well imagine that each of these charges got its laugh in turn.[87] The Viennese, like Americans, to be sure, love a laugh.

Again the tail of the lion is twisted. Our preacher addresses Saint Peter, holy Saint Peter: I have a question for you. I have heard that you stumbled and in fact that you actually fell. Where did you have this problem? Was it among the fishermen? Was it among the craftsmen, the builders, or carpenters? Or was it in the tavern or among the soldiers? Could it have been among the gypsies, or the merchants? Oh, holy Peter, among what people or in what place did you swear that false oath that you did not even know Jesus of Nazareth? We can well imagine that the audacity of the preacher amused the courtiers. Dramatically our preacher embroiders his theme of the scandal of Peter's denial. Finally the prince of the apostles answers our preacher's question: It was at the court that he had denied Christ.[88] Our preacher paraphrases the story from Matthew 26, and then asks a rhetorical question: But how could it have gone otherwise? To maintain virtue and honesty at court requires nothing less than a miracle.

That is what is so surprising about the saint we celebrate today, our preacher continues. Saint Leopold, in spite of the debauchery of the court, remained pure. As a swan swimming in a pond remains dry or a salamander falling into the fire is not burnt, as a rose along a smelly street still sends forth its pleasing smell, his eyes saw purity of life where others saw ugliness, his tongue spoke wisdom where others spoke shame. So Leopold remained a saint even at court.[89] This is all typical medieval sermon filler. Clever as the preacher undoubtedly is, this is a typical hagiographical sermon. In fact, one gets the impression that the description of Leopold's sanctity is richly imaginative. No doubt Abraham fabricated it in much the way the baroque pulpits and altars of Austrian seventeenth-century churches are decorated, brimming with roses and gilded angel's wings.

87. Abraham, *Predigten,* p. 102.
88. Abraham, *Predigten,* p. 103.
89. Abraham, *Predigten,* p. 104.

At some length our preacher speculates on whether someone could marry and still be a saint. Saint Leopold was married, and he and his wife Agnes had eighteen children. It must be possible. To build his case Abraham repeats an apocryphal story regarding the wedding at Cana, reported in John 2. According to this story, the authority for which was none other than Saint Jerome, the bridegroom at that wedding was the beloved apostle, Saint John. The name of the bride was Anatolia. The story goes that Jesus wanted John to marry but not to have sexual relations with his wife.[90] One wonders how the young courtiers of Vienna took that story.

On the other hand, Abraham was quite capable of making his point with reputable biblical material. He may not have his Bible stories quite straight and may draw some rather strange implications from them, but he does try. The story of the transfiguration is introduced to show that there was no question but that Moses was a saint, and yet he was known to be a married man. Moses, it must be remembered, certainly had his experiences at court. Yet the story of his life at court should surely make us aware that the saintly are not always welcome there. Saint Leopold, however, as he became ruler of his kingdom, did much to maintain the disciplines of the Christian life among his courtiers. It is said that he made life at court like the life of a monastery. Things had obviously changed by the time of *Der Rosenkavalier.*

At this point our preacher inserts the story of Emperor Theodosius, an exemplary Christian monarch, as related in the works of Saint Ambrose of Milan. The story is well known, and apparently Abraham did not feel it necessary to write out the whole story in his manuscript. After one of his more bloody battles, Ambrose confronted the emperor with his sin and demanded that he do penance. The emperor did just that. The story is usually told to show the admirable courage of a Christian bishop and the exemplary humility of a Christian emperor.

Saint Leopold was every bit the saintly monarch as Theodosius, as our preacher tells the story. He wanted no one in his court but the staunchest of Catholics.[91] Not only did he say this once, he repeated it hundreds of times, not only in words but in deeds. Heretics were to be pulled out of the court as weeds from the garden of the Catholic Church. Leopold was a faithful Christian who was willing to pour out his noble blood to the honor of the Catholic faith. Apparently Abraham

90. Abraham, *Predigten,* p. 105.
91. Abraham, *Predigten,* p. 106.

a Sancta Clara sees in the patron saint of Austria ample justification for Leopold I's repression of Protestantism in Hungary. That the sermon was preached in Vienna about the same time as the Hungarian pastors were sweating it out in the Spanish galleys seriously compromises the Hapsburg vision. To be sure, Hungary has its place in the Hapsburg vision. Our preacher is careful to make this clear. Leopold was one of those Christian princes like Saint Stephen, king of Hungary, who are the saintly guardians in heaven of the lands and people they protected here on earth.[92]

Much else could be said about this sermon. The conclusion is typical. It is thoroughly baroque, not unlike the famous conclusions of Bossuet. Abraham calls on Saint Leopold to pray before God for his beloved Austria, for surely Leopold will do for Austria as much as Moses did for Israel. Oh, Leopold, you saint, give your benediction over Austria as Joseph over Egypt and as Jacob over Mesopotamia. Bless Austria in the name of the Father and the Son and the Holy Spirit. Amen.[93]

Abraham a Sancta Clara may have been a dramatic orator, he may have drawn large crowds, he may have been a significant expression of Austrian culture, but he was far from rightly expounding the word of truth (cf. II Tim. 2:15). For many of us he betrays a rather naive approach to the interpretation of Scripture. Worst of all, he mixes Scripture and tradition in such a way that it must have been hard for his hearers to detect where Scripture left off and tradition took over.

VIII. Franz Peikhart (1684-1752)

As cathedral preacher in Vienna from 1720 to 1745, Franz Peikhart was a prince of the Austrian pulpit in a day when the Austro-Hungarian Empire had reached its zenith.[94] It had become the sort of empire the Hapsburgs had envisioned, or at least come as close to that vision as it ever would. The absolutism of the Hapsburgs had been even more fragile than that of the Bourbons. Maria Theresa ascended the throne as a twelve-year-old girl in 1740. Her desire was to be the mother of all her people. That may

---

92. Abraham, *Predigten,* p. 107.
93. Abraham, *Predigten,* p. 109.
94. For biographical material on Peikhart, see "Peikhardt, Franz," in *Biographisches Lexikon des Österreichs,* 60 vols., ed. Constant von Wurzbach (Wien: Druck und Verlag der K. K. Hoff — und Staatsdruckerei, 1870), 21:430-31.

have sounded just fine in court circles at Vienna, but in Transylvania or Bohemia it was not quite as believable. The job of Peikhart and preachers like him was to make it as believable as they could.

Peikhart joined the Jesuit Order in 1698. The Jesuits had, for their own purposes of course, been faithful supporters of the Hapsburg emperors. They, too, believed in absolutism. It was the political philosophy of Tridentine Catholicism. The Jesuits had developed a whole approach to preaching based on this baroque absolutism, but by 1720, when Peikhart was named cathedral preacher in Vienna, baroque preaching had become rococo. What we saw in Abraham a Sancta Clara we see again in Peikhart. If anything, we see this Austrian pulpit ideology brought to its fullest expression.

Peikhart's masterpiece is his eulogy for Prince Eugen of Savoy, preached in 1736.[95] The sermon was officially published in a festive booklet and printed and reprinted several times.[96] Prince Eugen was indeed one of the most celebrated generals in military history. Once again the motto of classical rhetoric is proven to be true. Great oratory must have a great subject. The life of Prince Eugen was just such a subject.[97]

The text is taken from the Old Testament Apocrypha, II Maccabees 6:31 (RSV): "So in this way he died, leaving in his death an example of nobility and a memorial of courage, not only to the young but to the great body of his nation." The preacher, of course, repeats the text in Latin, a convention we have noted before. The text of II Maccabees concerns the heroic example of the martyr Eleazar. Surely it was a most ap-

---

95. The text for this sermon is found in Welzig, *Predigten der Barockzeit,* pp. 281-309.

96. The title page is itself an indication of the importance of this sermon. "Lob- und Trauer-Rede / Uber den Todt / Des / Durchleuchtigen Printzen / EUGENII / FRANCISCI, / Hertzogen von Savoyen / und Piemont, etc. etc. / Jhro Römisch-Kayserlichen Majestät / und des Heil. Röm. Reichs / General-Lieutenant, etc. etc. / Da Seine Hohe Leich-Besingnuß / Mit Drey-Tägigen / Grossen Ehren-Gepräng / Jn der allhiesigen *Metropolitan*-Kirchen bey St. Stephan / gehalten worden; / Verfasset, und vorgetragen / Von *P. FRANCISCO PEIKHART,* / aus der Gesellschaft JEsu / der besagten *Metropolitan*-Kirchen Dom-Prediger. / Mit Genehmhaltung Einer Hohen Obrigkeit. / Wienn, gedruckt und zu haben, bey Johann Jgnatz Heyinger, Universitäts-Buchdruckern, 1736." Welzig, *Predigten der Barockzeit,* p. 281.

97. The eleventh edition of the *Encyclopedia Britannica* has a five-column article on this greatest of eighteenth-century Austrian generals. This article is not signed. "Eugene of Savoy," in *Encyclopedia Britannica,* 11th ed., 29 vols. (New York: Encyclopedia Britannica, 1910-11), 9:882-84.

propriate text. Little is done to open it. Our preacher does not even recount the story of the Maccabean heroes. He does, however, divide this text into two points, namely, Prince Eugen was an example of strength and courage on the battlefield, and he was an example of virtue in time of both war and peace.[98]

This sermon is surprisingly interesting. Certainly one of the reasons is that the preacher recounts the story of this military hero with a tremendous amount of detail. It is a colorful story that our preacher rolls out before us.

Peikhart begins by pointing with his hand to the casket covered with its black pall, embroidered with a golden cross, four candles burning, one at each corner. A free translation of his opening words might go something like this: "Here lies one whom we can truly call great, a prince by birth, a soldier by nature, a conqueror over lands and kingdoms, a power holding sway over all, a victor dominating all his enemies, a hero setting an example for every one of us. To put it briefly, here lies the great Eugen-Franz of the royal house of Savoy, a winner in every battle of life."[99]

This dramatic introduction is followed by a series of similes. Our preacher compares the heroic Austrian field marshal to that most astounding and infrequent of heavenly bodies, the comet. The different planets appear from time to time in one place or another, but there are always planets in the sky. A comet, on the other hand, comes once or perhaps twice in a century.[100] Prince Eugen was just such a rare phenomenon. Again, a military commander of such frequent success is to be wondered at as much as the first shipment of gold the Spanish brought back from America. Or still again, we should admire the greatness of the prince of Savoy and Piedmont now at the hour of his death, as we admire

---

98. "EUGENIUS ware ein *Exempl* und Beyspiel der Stärke und der Tugend: und dieses ist mein Zihl. Er ware ein *Exempl* der Stärke in denen Feld-Schlachten und Belägerungen. Er ware ein *Exempl* der Tugend in denen Kriegs- und Friedens-Zeiten: und dieses ist die Abtheilung meiner Rede." Welzig, *Predigten der Barockzeit*, p. 282.

99. "ALlhier ligt in einer Todten-Sarch beysammen / was man immer unter uns Menschen Grosses nennen kan: Ein Printz von Gebert / ein Soldat von der Natur / ein Eroberer so vieler Plätz und Vestungen / ein Bezwinger so vieler Länder und Königreichen / ein Uberwinder aller Feinden; Ein Held / welcher / da er allen gleichen wolte / aus allen einen jeden übertroffen hat. Kurtz zu sagen: allhier ligt der Grosse EUGENIUS, welcher so offt gesieget/als er gestritten. . . ." Welzig, *Predigten der Barockzeit*, p. 281.

100. Welzig, *Predigten der Barockzeit*, p. 282.

the glory of the setting sun which to our eyes, at least, is greatest in size when it sets. Classical rhetoric loves metaphors and similes like this. The literati of Viennese society must have loved this sermon.

Our sacred orator sets forth again. Surely an orator finds himself in difficulty when he must praise a life of such rich accomplishments. Should he only treat the most outstanding deeds? Like a painter who must include in his work a large number of different people in a small space, I find it impossible to do justice to the multitude of this conqueror's miraculous deeds, Peikhart says. My work must be like that of a geographer who must reduce the whole world to a small piece of paper.

Baroque preachers loved the classical forms of the panegyric. We spoke earlier of the panegyrics of Basil of Caesarea and Gregory of Nazianzus. Bossuet's funeral sermons were filled with the forms of the panegyric. Peikhart uses the same literary forms here, but with the Greek Fathers it was always a matter of a sort of spiritual allegory. With Peikhart all that gets turned around, and somehow priests become generals and generals become saints.

The panegyrics of classical antiquity loved to display the noble lineage of their heroes. According to our preacher, Eugen-Franz was a descendant of the royal House of Sardinia.[101] He was also a descendant of the House of Soissons.[102] We know nothing from his childhood, Peikhart tells us. We know very little from his youth except that his noble parents consecrated him to the altar. As a boy he was called "the little priest." In actual fact, we know considerably more about the early years of this renowned Austrian general than our preacher lets on. He was born in Paris, where his parents had a place at the court of Louis XIV but had fallen into the disfavor of the Sun King. The story goes that his mother was accused of attempting to poison his father and several other members of the court. Being a princess of the House of Mancini, she belonged to the highest level of the Roman aristocracy. That Peikhart mentions none of this is strange. All we know, according to Peikhart, is that his parents had decided to take up residence at Vienna. At that time Leopold I was already on the imperial throne, and he was a cousin of the dukes of Savoy. Leopold received Eugen's parents warmly. Prince Eugen

---

101. Welzig, *Predigten der Barockzeit,* p. 283.

102. On the House of Soissons, see "Soissons, Counts of," in *Encyclopedia Britannica,* 25:352-53. Prince Eugen was the son of Eugène Maurice of Savoy, count of Soissons, and Olympia Mancini, niece of Cardinal Mazarin.

apparently had a grudge against Louis XIV and his line for the rest of his life. Peikhart knows, of course, that such things should be glossed over in a eulogy.

At this point our preacher turns to more devotional material. When God's people need a guide and protector, God has a way of choosing those divinely appointed heroes from earliest childhood. Eugen's parents may have chosen him for the priesthood, but God chose him for military leadership. Just as God prepared Moses to be a princely leader with all the training of one educated at court, and just as God cared for Moses in his basket of reeds, hiding him in the bulrushes, so God prepared Prince Eugen for his unique service.[103]

Prince Eugen began to manifest his genius already as a young man. In 1683 this military star of first magnitude began to ascend over the horizon, and in a short time began to spread his glory over the whole of the Holy Roman Empire. Karl, duke of Lorraine, and Ludwig, marquis of Baden, were heroic spirits who often made both the Rhine and the Danube flow red with the blood of their enemies; these two incomparable spirits were the first teachers of our hero.[104] In those distressing wars against the Turks fought on the Hungarian plain, our young officer learned about fire and gunpowder. When things sank so low that the Turks were besieging the very gates of Vienna, our prince lifted the siege.[105] At that moment the eyes of the world were upon Prince Eugen. In these battles he came to know the roar of the cannons and the flashing of sword blades. The smoke of the artillery rose so thick that the eyes of all Europe smarted. Eugen stood side by side with the noble general Maximilian Emanuel, the prince elector of Bavaria. Together they stormed the walls of castles, routed the enemy cavalry, sparing neither courage nor their own blood. Hell itself seemed determined to wound our valiant prince, and so it happened, the first of many a battle wound.

Here was a warrior who was universally recognized as a hero. Who would be surprised to learn that Pope Clement XI, the vicar of Christ on earth, presented him with a golden helmet appropriate to the captain of Christian forces doing battle with the heathen and a diamond-studded

103. Welzig, *Predigten der Barockzeit,* p. 284.
104. Welzig, *Predigten der Barockzeit,* p. 284.
105. The recent attack on the World Trade Center in New York City is, according to some, supposed to have been an act of revenge for the defeat of the Moslems before the gates of Vienna on 11 September 1683.

sword worthy of a protector of the holy Church? Such an honor is scarcely granted more than once in several centuries.[106]

This sermon must have gone on in the same vein for well over two hours. We don't imagine anyone was bored. Everyone of any importance was there to honor a man who deserved all the worldly honors the Holy Roman Empire could bestow. Here was one place where pomp and circumstance was not out of place.

As a work of the art of oratory, we can hardly deny this sermon its well-deserved place, but is it a Christian sermon? One is bothered as one reads this sermon. What troubles us?

One might well cavil at whether the eulogy is really a sermon because it is only formally an exposition of a passage of Scripture. One might quibble over the text being from the Old Testament Apocrypha, but that is not really the problem. Maybe the fox we want to chase is more the question of the appropriateness of a eulogy in Christian worship. The preachers of the age of Louis XIV had a way of giving their best efforts to eulogies for the members of the royal family. One remembers Bossuet's eulogy for Queen Henrietta Maria. Can an oration aimed at praising a great king or queen, a prince or a general, really serve the glory of God? We remember Massillon's eulogy for Louis XIV which began with the words, "Only God is great." Massillon obviously understood the problem. We also remember how the Cappadocian Father Gregory of Nazianzus, in his panegyric for Athanasius, the bishop of Alexandria, spoke of praising God in his saints. True saints reflect the glory of God, and in reflecting it, magnify it; that is, they make the glory of God even greater. Some eulogies really do lead us in the worship of God. No, this is not the fox we want to chase.

So much of the art of the baroque age was used as propaganda for both court and chancel. One thinks first of all of Bernini and second of Rubens. One remembers when a whole room of the Louvre was given over to Rubens's cycle of paintings of the apotheosis of Catherine de Medici. Happily, the last time I was there things had been changed. But the same things bother me with this sermon of a Jesuit preacher at the Cathedral of Saint Stephen. All the ideology of the Hapsburg dynasty is

---

106. "Und wer will sich anjetzo wundern / wann auch alle Christliche Häupter zusamm getretten / EUGENIUM zu belohnen. Pabst CLEMENS XI. Statthalter CHristi auf Erden / hat ihm den kostbaren Hut eines Schützers / und das reiche Schwerdt eines Verfechters der Heiligen Kirchen umgehangen / welche Ehre in vielen Jahrhunderten kaum einen widerfahren ist." Welzig, *Predigten der Barockzeit*, p. 292.

poured into it. By the power of arms the siege of Vienna was lifted, and the Turks were chased from Hungarian soil. The sermon celebrates the victory of the Hapsburg vision, the success of the Jesuit gospel. It is a scintillating justification of absolutism.

We would do well to contemplate this sermon, so far away from American Protestant interests and concerns. One detail of the story has yet to be related. As it happens, Prince Eugen was a fast friend of John Churchill, the duke of Marlborough and the ancestor of Winston Churchill. The two were comrades in arms at the Battle of Blenheim in the War of the Austrian Succession, a war that manifested the ultimate secularization of the old regime. More and more the Christian princes of Europe were being lured into purely secular concerns, even if they claimed spiritual goals. They were learning how to use religion to bolster their shaky thrones, whether it was Queen Anne of England, the last of the Stuarts, or Leopold von Hapsburg of Austria, emperor of the whole Austro-Hungarian Empire.

This is bad enough, but there is something much worse, and this is the reason we must meditate on this sermon. We find reflected in this sermon a bad case of using worldly means to accomplish godly ends. No one supported the Hapsburg vision of a Holy Roman Empire quite so effectively as Prince Eugen-Franz of Savoy, unless it was Jesuits like Franz Peikhart. The Hapsburgs had a way of doing this, generation after generation. What really bothers me, as I have seen the last half of the twentieth century pass by, is that one gets the feeling that we American Protestants, all with the best intentions, to be sure, are doing just the same thing. We have been trying to bring in the kingdom of God with worldly means, either politics, or art, or sacred entertainment, or some configuration of these. We imagine that surely we will be able to bring about what the Word of God can never do, any way near as effectively. Presbyterians even, having forgotten the doctrine of providence and largely lost the discipline of prayer, have become more and more adept at using managerial techniques to force spiritual growth. We can hardly point fingers at the Jesuits.

CHAPTER V

Franciscan Preaching in Spanish California

As a boy growing up in California, I was fascinated by the story of the Franciscan friars who founded the missions all along the coast from San Diego to San Francisco. In school we all learned about Padre Junípero Serra (1713-84) and the churches he founded at San Gabriel, Santa Barbara, and Carmel, and how he and his fellow missionaries walked along El Camino Real from one mission to the next. That was part of California history.[1] As I have grown older and become more and more interested in the history of Christian worship, I naturally have wondered about those padres and how they initiated the ministry of the Word in my native state.[2]

Slowly it has begun to grow on me that the Franciscans had a passion for preaching, and as a Presbyterian I could hardly be anything other than approving. So many California towns are named for great preachers: San Francisco, San Bernardino, San Juan Capistrano, San Antonio, and

---

1. The Franciscan mission to New Mexico was considerably older than the mission to California, but it had nothing like the quality of leadership the mission to California had. Cf. the recent study of Jim Norris, *After "The Year Eighty": The Demise of Franciscan Power in Spanish New Mexico* (Albuquerque: University of New Mexico Press, 2000).

2. While it has been my usual practice to study preaching on the basis of the sermons that have been preserved, in this case I have not found any sermons preached by the Spanish missionaries in California. The missionaries did, however, leave considerable records of their work from which we can learn at least something about their preaching.

Ventura, which is of course short for San Buenaventura. It began to occur to me that I ought to see what I could find out about Franciscan preaching in California during the Spanish colonial period.[3]

I. The Gathering of the Mission Team

Young Junípero Serra was inspired to be a missionary to the American Indians while still in his novitiate,[4] at only seventeen or eighteen years of age. The Franciscan Order was very strong on the island of Majorca, and the Franciscans had already provided many missionaries for the Americas. It was only natural for our future missionary to begin to feel the stirring of his call so early in life. Serra did well in school, and before long he was doing doctoral studies at the University of Palma, a university made famous by the medieval Scholastic theologian Raymond Lull. Serra was particularly interested in the theology of Duns Scotus, one of the most prominent of the Franciscan theologians. In 1742 he received the doctorate of theology from the Lullian University of Palma, and two years later was awarded the Scotistic chair of theology. The eight-hundred-page manuscript of his commentary on Duns Scotus is still preserved in the university library. In time this made Serra the foremost theologian of the university. That, at least, is what Francisco Palóu (1723-89), Serra's friend, records, and by this time Serra and Palóu were fast friends. It was at the university that Serra also came to know Juan Crespi (1721-82), another friend who would labor at his side throughout his life. A mission team was taking shape.

3. There is an abundance of material on the Franciscan missions to California. The following have been especially helpful: Herbert Eugene Bolton, *The Colonization of North America, 1493-1783* (New York: Macmillan, 1920); Bolton, *The Mission as a Frontier Institution in the Spanish-American Colonies* (El Paso: Printed at Texas Western College Press for Academic Reprints, 1960); Maurice N. L. Couve de Murville, *The Man Who Founded California: The Life of Blessed Junípero Serra* (San Francisco: Ignatius, 2000); Omer Englebert, *The Last of the Conquistadors, Junípero Serra (1713-1784)* (New York: Harcourt, Brace and Co., 1956); Maynard Geiger, *Franciscan Missionaries in Hispanic California, 1769-1848: A Biographical Dictionary* (San Marino, Calif.: Huntington Library, 1969); and Adro Xavier, *Junípero Serra* (Barcelona: Editorial Casals, 1986).

4. We are well informed about Serra's early years because of the biography of Francisco Palóu, Serra's lifelong companion and fellow Mallorcan: Francisco Palóu, *Relación historica de la Vida . . . del V. P. Fray Junípero Serra* (Mexico, 1787). An English translation is available: Maynard J. Geiger, O.F.M., trans. and ed., *Palóu's Life of Fray Junípero Serra* (Washington, D.C.: Academy of American Franciscan History, 1945).

Still, devoted Franciscan that he was, Serra was an enthusiastic preacher. Academic theology had not distracted him from his missionary call. European universities traditionally, even to this day, have long vacations, and the records show that Serra used those vacations to develop his preaching skills, doing preaching missions all over Majorca. Apparently he preached the usual university sermons as well. These latter had been a major component of the academic program since medieval times. One year he was appointed to preach the traditional panegyric for Raymond Lull. It was exceptionally well received. All this suggests that generally Serra was thought of as a first-rate preacher.

One day the news came that a prominent Franciscan missionary training college in Mexico City, the College of San Fernando, had sent an agent to Spain to recruit missionaries. Father Serra and his former pupil Palóu decided this was the call they had been waiting for. They set out for Málaga on the Spanish mainland and finally embarked from Cádiz at the end of August in 1749. Along the way their ship called at San Juan, Puerto Rico, and there Father Serra took the time to preach a mission. Apparently the future apostle of California never lost an opportunity to mount the pulpit. The passage from San Juan to Veracruz was stormy, and the nine-month journey to the city of Mexico was not completed until 1 January 1750.

After a few months Serra and Palóu were joined by Crespi, who, like Palóu, had been one of Serra's students in Palma. The first assignment the Mallorcans were given was to restore the missions which had been planted in the Sierra Gorda, a wild, mountainous region almost two hundred miles northeast of the city of Mexico. The native population there was very primitive, unlike that in the Aztec or Mayan areas. A number of missions had been established there in the seventeenth century, but the native population had resented the Spanish invasion of their territory and eventually rebelled and destroyed the missions. The buildings were ruined, the fields burned, the herds of cattle disbanded, the granaries and cellars emptied.

Even with all this, the friars gathered the Indians who had not run back into the mountains to their nomadic way of life. They rebuilt the buildings; replanted the vineyards, olive groves, and fields; and reestablished the herds and flocks. That was the way the Spanish understood missionary work. It was a matter of establishing Christian civilization. The cycles of agriculture and rhythms of liturgical life all went together. Mass was said on Sundays, morning and evening prayers were offered each day, and the sacraments were celebrated as occasion demanded. Feast days came and processions were held. The friars taught the natives to sing their liturgical music. The Indians loved the fiestas! The newborn were baptized and the dying were given the last rites. The soldiers were there to make sure everything was done in good order.

The Indians of Sierra Gorda were members of the Pames nation, and they spoke a distinct language, Otomí.[5] Apparently Father Serra was able to learn the language, and he seems to have been able to preach in it. Actually we know quite a bit about how the Sierra Gorda missions were run. Serra regularly wrote his reports to San Fernando, the mission college back in Mexico City. From these letters it becomes evident that he was a patriarch like Abraham. He was a farm manager, a rancher who knew how to build up the herds, fill the cellars with casks of wine, and stock the granaries with grain, and at the same time he was a doctor of theology. He is supposed to have preached a hundred times a year at his church in Jalpan, and no doubt he preached to them in their own language.[6]

Morning and evening prayers were a part of the daily schedule. The official policy of the Spanish colonial government was that the Indians were to be taught to pray in the Spanish language. Serra and the other Franciscan brothers observed this requirement, but Serra was able to translate these prayers as well as the catechism, portions of which were recited at prayers every day. This the older generation of missionaries in Sierra Gorda had apparently not done. Slowly the Indians began to understand the faith of the missionaries.

With the patience, untiring work, and faith of the Franciscans, the missions began to prosper. The Indians learned to farm; they learned trades such as brick making and tile making. They learned to use the potter's wheel, to do metalwork, spinning, weaving, tanning, and a host of other trades. The missions became prosperous, but the crowning work of the missionaries was the building of a beautiful church. The church of Jalpan is still in use today. With its bell tower, its imposing nave and grand altar, it is a beautiful example of Spanish colonial architecture. Serra carried the stone it is built of, mixed mortar, and lifted the huge

5. Cf. vol. IV on the work of the first Spanish missionaries in Mexico. Otomí was one of the first languages the missionaries learned. Hughes Oliphant Old, *The Reading and Preaching of the Scriptures in the Worship of the Christian Church*, vol. 4, *The Age of the Reformation* (Grand Rapids: Wm. B. Eerdmans Publishing Co., 2002), p. 179.

6. Englebert, *Last of the Conquistadors*, p. 42, and Geiger, *Franciscan Missionaries*, p. 241.

beams with his Indians, just as one would expect a son of Saint Francis to do. Crespi built a very similar church in the neighboring town of Tilaco. This was the way the Spanish missionaries did things, and it worked. The native American population of the Sierra Gorda accepted the Christian culture. After nine years Serra was sent back to the College of San Fernando in the city of Mexico.

Back again in the mission college, Serra became an itinerant evangelist. Apparently he was very popular in this capacity. He was charged with a number of preaching missions in the city. We do not have the careful records of Crespi and Palóu for this period, as both were still serving in the Sierra Gorda. Palóu tells us very little about this period of Serra's life, and we do not have the letters from Serra himself that we have from other periods of his ministry.

We do learn that Serra took to afflicting the flesh while preaching in this period; that is, he flagellated himself or beat his breast with stones in the pulpit. We spoke of the Italian Benedictine preacher of the eleventh century, Peter Damian, doing this sort of thing.[7] While this seems extreme to us, it was just part of Catholic spirituality in that day. Serra had repeated problems with ulcerated feet, and he often aggravated his condition by insisting on walking on his various itinerations. He understood it as a form of doing penance, which for us Protestants seems a serious misunderstanding of the nature of repentance and the forgiveness of sins. But if nothing else, it does indicate the good padre's zeal. Serra, as all the records show, was possessed of an all-commanding zeal.

We hear a few details of Serra's itinerations. He made several missions to the territory of the Huasticanos, one of the more advanced pre-Colombian nations that lived near the Sierra Gorda. Serra's knowledge of the Otomí language may have allowed him to preach to the natives there. We hear of an itineration along the Gulf Coast from Tampico to Veracruz. Here he may have been preaching to the Spanish-speaking population, but it is also possible that he was preaching through an interpreter to the native population as well. That was also Huasticano territory, and again he may have done some of this preaching in Otomí. On the other hand, our preacher also went to Oaxaca in the south, in the center of the Zapotec nation, where the natives spoke a very different lan-

7. On Peter Damian and his ascetic practices, see Hughes Oliphant Old, *The Reading and Preaching of the Scriptures in the Worship of the Christian Church,* vol. 3, *The Medieval Period* (Grand Rapids: Wm. B. Eerdmans Publishing Co., 1999), pp. 226-29.

guage. Here we imagine the good padre did his preaching in Spanish to the Spanish-speaking community. Oaxaca had been an outpost of Spanish colonial civilization since early in the sixteenth century. In the Spanish colonies conversion to Christianity generally entailed adopting both Spanish culture and Spanish language.

We hear of a mission in Tabasco. The hot jungles of Tabasco, even today, make for difficult traveling. Our missionary was indeed going to the uttermost parts of the earth. We hear of his traveling by canoe through crocodile-infested waters. We hear of his going through arid deserts and climbing mountain trails. He covered a good part of that vast and varied land in his nine years as itinerant evangelist. After those nine years he must have been a true missionary explorer, an experienced frontiersman.

As fascinating as these explorations of the backcountry of Mexico are, what interests us more is what kind of preaching Serra did on these missions. When Palóu's biography of Serra speaks of preaching a mission, something specific was understood. These missions would have been like the Lenten missions of Bernardino da Siena, who set the standard of the Lenten preaching mission for the Franciscans.[8] They aimed at first bringing the people to recognize their sin and need of repentance. Then the series would open the way of repentance and prepare the congregation to do their Lenten penance and receive Communion at Easter. The Franciscan preaching mission had a very definite form. Whether at Lent, Advent, or any other time of the year, the typical preaching mission preached through the steps of salvation and helped the people follow through them to the end of a spiritual renewal or revival. In this they were really quite similar to the preaching missions of John Wesley, Serra's Protestant contemporary. To be sure, there were real differences as to how one understood this revival, but there were similarities as well.

II. The Road to California

The mission to California was at first taken on for rather devious reasons. The padres, no doubt, had the highest motives, although the political

8. For a description of the typical Franciscan mission as exemplified by Bernardino, see Old, *Reading and Preaching*, 3:547-64.

motives which enabled the mission were a bit complicated. But then, good Scholastic theologians that they were, the Franciscans had an ingrained appreciation for the importance of secondary causes.

Our story begins on 2 April 1767, the date the Spanish king, Carlos III, suppressed the Jesuit Order. For two hundred years the Jesuits had manipulated the affairs of every court in Europe in order to gain advantages for the Counter-Reformation. But with the Enlightenment, even the most Catholic of kings began to tire of their tactics. Several European courts banished them about this time. In Mexico it happened rather suddenly. On 22 June José Gálvez, the inspector general in New Spain, arrested the 178 Jesuit priests living in Mexico.

As it happened, one of their major missions was establishing churches in Baja California, the peninsula of Lower California now included within the borders of Mexico. The peninsula is almost a thousand miles long, reaching from San Diego halfway to Mexico City. The Jesuits had been entrusted with this mission in 1697 but had developed it very slowly. Baja California is not much more than a desert island. Sand, cactus, and salt flats dominate the countryside. Even today it is sparsely populated. When the Jesuits first arrived, the native population was rather primitive. They knew nothing of the civilization of the Aztecs or the Mayas. In seventy-five years the Jesuits had succeeded in planting only fifteen missions, and they had gathered less than eight thousand baptized Christians, many of whom, the reports tell us, were still running around naked. The Jesuits had become experienced missionaries since the days of Francis Xavier. They had established missions in India and Japan,[9] and been active in a number of mission fields. They had developed their missionary strategy first in the Far East, then in Quebec, throughout the Great Lakes, and down the Mississippi, but Baja California proved difficult. Still, someone had to replace them, and the Franciscan College of San Fernando was given the responsibility.

Apparently the Franciscans saw this as a great opportunity, and they sent the man who by then must have been their most experienced padre, Junípero Serra. The mission college organized quickly, and on 14 July 1767 Serra and his company set out for Baja California, never realizing they were on their way to what would become one of the great population centers of the New World. To Serra, providence had given the opportunity to open the door for Christian civilization in California. Happily the

---

9. Cf. Old, *Reading and Preaching,* 4:186-89.

mission college also sent with him his trusted former students, Francisco Palóu and Juan Crespi. The old team was back together again.[10]

By the end of August the Franciscans had arrived at Tepic, which was where Spanish colonization ended. Yet Tepic was still some twenty miles from the sea. The fishing village of San Blas, although apparently still rather primitive, busily turned itself into a seaport, building and outfitting ships for the expedition to Baja California. The new governor of Baja California, Gaspar de Portolá, occupied himself with supplying the ships and the soldiers during most of that fall. Portolá was able to set sail for La Paz, arriving there in December. La Paz was no more a town than San Blas had been. There were a few government buildings surrounded by the mud huts of the Indians who had tentatively cast their lot with the Spanish by being baptized. It was a few months later, April of 1768, that our padre arrived in La Paz. The Franciscans were quickly sent out to occupy the missions formerly run by the Jesuits. Very soon it became evident that these missions were not as promising as they had been told back in Mexico City. But Baja California was not, apparently, what Providence had in store for Junípero Serra and his company.

In the meantime the Spanish Court had begun to see a far greater significance in Baja California. In fact, the politicians began to think that perhaps Upper California might be very important. Up to this time Spain had no interest in anything above the thirtieth parallel, which is some hundred miles south of present-day San Diego. Rumors, however, had come to the Spanish Court in Madrid that the Russians, under the ambitious czarina Catherine the Great, were sending explorers down the California coast as far as San Francisco. The Pacific coast of Mexico might be in danger.

Within a few months Gálvez was in La Paz. It was his responsibility to transform Baja California into a fortress which could resist the Russians. To this end he founded a naval academy to train seamen as well as a mining school to make the peninsula economically self-sufficient.

Now, however, the vision began to broaden. The Spanish decided to steal the march on the Russians. They decided to occupy what in those days was called Upper California. The California coast had been explored by Juan Rodríguez Cabrillo as early as 1542. Several other explorers sailed

---

10. The story of the Franciscan mission to California was first written by Francisco Palóu: *Historical Memoirs of New California by Francisco Palóu, O.F.M.,* trans. and ed. Herbert Eugene Bolton (New York: Russel and Russel, 1966).

up the coast after him, the most notable of whom was Sebastián Vizcaíno. In 1602 he had gone ashore at Monterey for a few days, at least. He planted a cross on a hill, claimed it in the name of the king of Spain, and gave it the prestigious name of Monterey, Mountain of the King. Subsequent explorers were confused by the name, expecting a mountain rather than a hill, as we shall see. Back in Spain the outline of the colonization was determined. On the basis of the available maps, Monterey was selected as the capital of the new colony. There would be a settlement at San Diego, because San Diego Bay was recognized as a possible port. The Santa Barbara Channel they figured would be another good place for a settlement. These, then, were to be the first settlements: San Diego, Monterey, and Santa Barbara.

Gálvez and Serra came together at La Paz and worked toward developing a plan for the colonization. Basically the plan was to establish a series of missions stretching from San Diego to Monterey. Every forty miles there would be a mission, thus making a highway starting at La Paz, up the Baja Peninsula to San Diego, then on to Santa Barbara and finally up to Monterey. This was to be El Camino Real, the King's Highway. The forty miles between missions allowed a courier on horseback to go from one mission to another in a single day. Those traveling by foot could find shelter every other night.

The first step was to establish the mission at San Diego. Two ships, the *San Carlos* and the *San Antonio,* leaving at different times, were sent ahead with soldiers and supplies. Then two companies set out on foot with more soldiers, the priests, mule drivers, herdsmen, and Christian Indians armed with bows and arrows for hunting and machetes for clearing the road. Hopefully these Christian Indians would be able to translate the language of the Indians along the route.

III. The Founding of the Missions

On 14 May 1769 the first company, led by Captain Rivera and Father Juan Crespi, set out over land. It arrived in San Diego to find that the two ships were already there.[11] The ships had not fared well. Almost two

---

11. For the record of the company, see the diary of Juan Crespi: *Fray Juan Crespí, Missionary Explorer on the Pacific Coast, 1769-1774,* trans. and ed. Herbert Eugene Bolton (Berkeley, 1927; reprint, New York: AMS Press, 1971).

dozen seamen had died. The *San Carlos,* the first of the ships to set sail, had taken 110 days. Devastated by disease, the crew was too weak to launch its longboats and come ashore. The second company, led by Governor Portolá and Father Serra, with a full complement of soldiers, livestock, herdsmen, and Indian guides, set out just after Easter and arrived in San Diego 30 June 1769. The two overland companies buried several men along the way, and many of the Christian Indians deserted them. Altogether the new colony now numbered 126 persons. Yet on Sunday, 16 July 1769, the disheartened expedition came together for worship, dedicating the mission to San Diego of Alcalá. Father Serra preached to an assembly of soldiers, cattle drivers, seamen, a few Christian Indians, and the curious natives of the neighborhood. This, then, was the first Christian sermon in California. It marked the founding of San Diego.

Portolá was eager to press on to Monterey, and so, leaving Serra behind, he began his march up the coast. Crespi went along as his padre, and also recorded the journey carefully in his diary. They headed up along the shore. Crossing the Santa Ana River, they experienced their first California earthquake. They turned inland as the coast went off to the west toward the Palos Verdes Peninsula. They crossed the Los Angeles River, followed through the San Fernando Valley, and then rejoined the shore along the Santa Barbara Channel. For several days they traveled west to Point Conception. Here the records of the earlier explorers were easy to follow. At Point Conception they picked their way north to Morro Bay, but passing Morro Bay they found the Sierra Santa Lucia a difficult barrier. The high mountains go down sharply to the sea. Here their scout, Sergeant José Francisco de Ortega, wisely cut inland and followed the Salinas River down to Monterey Bay.

Alas, the description of Monterey was so exaggerated by Vizcaíno that Portolá and his company did not recognize it. They were looking for Monterey, the Mountain of the King. What the Portolá expedition saw was only a hill, so they pressed on. Coming to Half Moon Bay, so accurately described by Sir Francis Drake, they realized they had gone too far.

But before retracing their steps, they made a momentous discovery. Their food was running low, and they sent out a hunting party which suddenly caught sight of San Francisco Bay. They were the first Westerners to lay eyes on that great natural harbor. The extent of the bay frustrated them. They tried to go around it, but it was too vast. Finally from the hills behind Berkeley they saw the Golden Gate and the sun setting behind it into the Pacific. But they had been sent to settle Monterey, and they turned back south hoping to find it. With the help of their instruments they found the place Vizcaíno had indicated, but they again decided it was not Monterey. They buried a bottle with a message for any future explorers explaining their frustration, and returned to San Diego.

When they got to San Diego, they found a very discouraged group of men. The *San Giorgio*, which was supposed to supply the infant colony, had apparently been lost at sea. No reinforcements had arrived and food was running short. Portolá decided to lead the whole expedition back to Baja California unless they were relieved by a shipload of supplies. At Serra's insistence the governor agreed to wait a few days longer. The zealous padre prayed for the arrival of a ship. He preached hope, but the disheartened settlers prepared to abandon San Diego. Finally the governor insisted that if no ship arrived by 19 March 1770, the mission would be abandoned and the whole company would return to Mexico. The morning of the nineteenth arrived and there was still no sign of relief. At mass Serra again preached hope, but the day passed and no ship appeared on the horizon. Then, just a little before sunset, the sails of the *San Antonio* appeared on the horizon. Help had arrived.

It took a month to regroup, but by Easter Portolá and Serra set out once more for Monterey, this time by sea. Six weeks later they found the elusive site and set to work building the mission and the presidio, and establishing the settlement. On 3 June 1770, Pentecost Sunday, bells were hung from a great live oak, so characteristic of California; a cannonade was fired from the *San Antonio;* and the soldiers reported with their guns. The *Veni creator spiritus* was intoned. The good padre, assisted by Crespi, celebrated mass attended by Portolá, the sailors, and the Christian Indians. No doubt Serra preached. The cabin boy of the *San Antonio* who so sadly succumbed to the rigors of the expedition was buried, and a great cross was raised over the site of these sacred rites.

On 9 July Portolá set sail for Mexico to report the success of the expedition. It was in this way that a new civilization was to be grounded in that most distant land. Providence lent wings to Portolá's triumphant journey! Arriving at San Blas on 1 August, he lost no time setting out for the city of Mexico. He got there in a week, and by 16 August the official announcement under the signature of the viceroy came off the press. Spain had occupied California. Let the Russians and the English take note. Carlos III was lord of California.

Back in Monterey, the first job that had to be done was to organize the herds of cattle, and to plant olive groves and vineyards, vegetable gardens and grainfields. Shelters had to be built and a church constructed. The mission school had to be organized, boys and girls recruited. The children in the school would learn Spanish faster than the priests would learn the native languages. It was a difficult task, for there were so many different local dialects. Father Serra himself did much of the teaching. He taught the children the catechism. He taught them to pray in Spanish. The brightest he trained as altar boys. All the children were taught to sing the Latin hymns, the *Te Deum,* the *Salve regina,* and the *Veni creator spiritus.* They learned the *Pater noster,* the *Credo,* and the canticles of the Mass.

There was, of course, much left to be done.[12] One after another the other missions were founded. On 14 July 1771 the mission of San Antonio was founded inland about halfway between Monterey and Point Conception. It was named in honor of Saint Anthony of Padua, who did so much to shape the preaching ministry of the Franciscan Order. This mission was one of the most successful economically. The good padres ran a very effective ranch there, signaling the tremendous agricultural possibilities of California in a way neither San Diego nor Monterey had manifested. The story is told that at the founding of the mission, again Father Serra had the bells hung in a big California live oak. Energetically the bells were rung, and the good padre was teased about it at length. No Indians appeared; nevertheless, the mass was begun. Then when Father Serra looked up after reading the Gospel and before beginning his sermon, a few Indians very cautiously were beginning to approach. Evangelism, at least as understood by eighteenth-century Franciscans, was beginning to take place.

The founding of San Gabriel a month later, on 15 August, was a big step forward. It was the first step in the establishment of that populous metropolitan area of Los Angeles. But it was something of an embarrassment to the padres because some of the soldiers molested the Indian women. It was hard to preach the gospel when supposed Christian soldiers were raping the native women. The shameful story does not have to be retold, but it still casts a shadow over the history of California. More and more the secular authority began to hinder the work of the padres. The padres and the politicians often had conflicting interests. Both the secular authorities and the soldiers slowed down the founding of the missions and diverted the supplies intended for the missionaries to their personal enrichment.

---

12. For a more detailed account of the founding of the individual missions, see John A. Berger, *The Franciscan Missions of California* (New York: Putnam, [1941]).

The founding of the mission at San Francisco took place in 1776, the year the original thirteen American colonies declared their independence from England. That the earliest explorers should have missed San Francisco Bay and sailed right past the Golden Gate without taking their ships into that dramatic harbor would seem impossible to one who has never lived in California. But for a native, who morning after morning has awakened to find the world veiled in fog, it is only too easy to understand. The entrance to San Francisco Bay is very small. One morning fog could have easily hidden the whole thing. Neither Cabrillo nor Vizcaíno had spotted it. It was not until 1769, when the Portolá expedition saw it from the hills behind Berkeley, that the Golden Gate was finally discovered. From the sea it had gone undetected.

San Diego, the Santa Barbara Channel, Point Conception, and Monterey had already gotten their names before the Franciscans arrived, but San Francisco was a major site the Franciscans were the first to put on the maps, and it was only natural that they gave it the name of their founder, one who had done so much to revitalize Christian preaching.

Serra found it necessary to go to the city of Mexico, and assigned Palóu to replace him in Monterey. Palóu had always been Serra's first lieutenant. Palóu arrived from Baja California, where he had remained, running the mission of San Xavier, one of the missions founded by the Jesuits. He had also preached a mission in Compostela, a neighboring settlement, and seems to have been a capable preacher, like his mentor. He had served as the essential link between California and Mexico.

Serra returned to Monterey from Mexico with considerable support, having won the confidence of the viceroy, Antonio Bucareli. Supplies were now more generous, and the missionaries began to make plans to found a mission at San Francisco. The first expedition set out in the fall of 1774. Palóu accompanied the explorers and planted a cross on the peninsula, and then returned to Monterey a few days later. The settlement itself was not made until the summer of 1776. The company set out from Monterey under the military command of Lieutenant José Joaquín Moraga. He was accompanied by two padres, Palóu and Pedro Benito Cambón, sixteen soldiers, seven colonists, and the usual supporters of such an operation. This was to be the sixth California mission. The presidio was established on 17 September, and the mission was officially established on 9 October.

The San Francisco mission was rather slow in developing. Even though the site was destined to develop into one of America's greatest cities, it was not the best place for raising crops or maintaining the herds of cattle that were the economic basis of a successful mission. Ten years later only about five hundred Indians had been baptized and the village of Christian Indians next to the mission numbered only half that.

Our story could be continued for another generation or two.[13] The Franciscans went on for some years founding their missions. All together they established twenty-one of them. We leave off the story at this point, however, because our sources give us little additional information on the preaching of the Spanish missionaries. More and more the mission work was compromised by the secular concerns of colonists and colonial officials. The mission system became less and less effective. Finally the missions were secularized. The spread of smallpox and other diseases decimated the Native American population in California, as it had in Mexico. Then the Spanish colonial period ended with the Mexican revolution in 1821. With that California became part of Mexico for a short time, but by 1848 it was ceded to the United States, a year before the Gold Rush. The Gold Rush completely changed the population of California, and the Spanish-speaking segment of the population began to lose its former importance. The story of Spanish California may be brief, but it is certainly heroic. California preaching has much ahead of it. This chapter is only the beginning.

Many have been critical of the mission system, charging that the missionaries enslaved the native population.[14] Yet the mission system did establish civilization in California, whereas the native population up to that time knew nothing more than hunting, fishing, and food gathering. Apparently before the missionaries came, the native population had neither herds, nor fields, nor agricultural cultivation.

Our concern in this study is with but a small facet of the broader question of introducing civilization to a more primitive culture. The padres preached, but as yet they had not learned the native languages. That usually takes a generation or two. Regardless of the mission field, learning the local language is a major problem. The New Englanders had wanted

13. For the continuing story of the Franciscan missions in California, see Berger, *The Franciscan Missions of California,* and the journals of Fermín Francisco de Lasuén: *Writings,* trans. and ed. Finbar Kenneally, 2 vols. (Washington, D.C.: Academy of American Franciscan History, 1965).

14. For an evaluation of Serra from the standpoint of liberation theology, see Daniel Fogel, *Junípero Serra, the Vatican, and Enslavement Theology* (San Francisco: ISM Press, 1988).

to preach to the native Indians in their own language. They tell us more of how they went about it than the padres do, but we can assume they went about it in much the same way. Even at that, learning the native language was only part of the story. The padres, as the Puritans before them, helped the baptized Indians establish Christian villages and introduced them to the ways of Christian civilization. The padres, more than the Puritans, insisted that Indians pray in Spanish, listen to Scripture lessons in Latin, and take part in a Latin mass. While the Puritans tried to develop native preachers, we hear little of this from the padres. There must have been some preaching in the local language, but most of it was probably in Spanish.

A story of Juan Crespi gives an important glimpse into the preaching of the mission churches. We are told that the good padre had trouble memorizing his sermons. But since he, like other Franciscans, wanted to preach at the regular Sunday mass, he would quite openly bring a book of sermons into the pulpit and read one to the congregation. These sermons would no doubt have been in Spanish. The preaching orders, we remember, had whole libraries full of sermons that could be used in this way.[15]

Serra's letters and Crespi's and Palóu's diaries tell us often of the young boys and girls who came to live in the missions. They learned their catechisms and took part in daily prayers. In all probability they were doing it in Spanish. The education they received at the mission was above all a matter of learning the Spanish language and Spanish ways. These boys and girls became the servants of the padres. In time they cooked their meals and built their dormitories and their churches, but in the process they learned the language of civilization as well as the language of faith.

What the critics of missions seem to forget is that the Native American population was attracted to Spanish Christian civilization. Even with all its faults they wanted to be part of it. Even if it was frightening, even if they had to enter it as novices, as children, at the lowest level of the social scale, they wanted to be part of it. This has always been part of the agony of passing from one culture to another.

When the missions were successful, they produced a quantity and variety of food the Indians had never experienced before. Serra was well

---

15. Even Franciscan preaching by the end of the seventeenth century was highly conventionalized. First there was lectionary preaching. Anthony of Padua gave the Franciscans a very good example of this, as has already been shown. Then there was the preaching of the regular Advent and Lenten missions. The great Franciscan example of this genre was Bernardino da Siena. See Old, *Reading and Preaching*, 3:547f.

aware of the importance of feeding the hungry. It was not too hard to encourage them to come and live at the mission and take part in the Christian community. In time, of course, it was hoped that these new Christians would be equipped to become full citizens of the pueblo as artisans, merchants, ranchers, and even property owners, full subjects of the king of Spain with all the duties and rights that went with it. That, at least, was the vision of the missionaries. The more secularized colonists were little interested in the salvation of souls, least of all the souls of the native popularion of California.

The padres had a well-thought-out approach to evangelism. It is interesting to compare it to that of the Wesleys, George Whitefield, Jonathan Edwards, Gilbert Tennent, and the preachers of the Great Awakening. They were, after all, exact contemporaries.[16] Their understanding of evangelism was very different. They may have lived in the same century, but they were worlds apart. It is even more interesting to compare the first Californian preachers to the first New England preachers. If we could imagine Junípero Serra and John Eliot sitting down at a table to discuss their different approaches to the evangelization of the native American population, there would certainly be some differences, but there would certainly be some similarities.[17] Above all, let us note that the padres made a heroic attempt to fulfill the apostolic commission to go into all the world and make disciples of all nations, baptizing them and teaching them all that Christ commanded.

16. Edwards and Wesley were born in 1703, while Serra was born in 1713 and Whitefield in 1714.
17. On John Eliot's mission to the Algonquians, see chap. 3 above.

CHAPTER VI

Romanian Orthodoxy under the Turks

The age which brought the Reformation to the Western Church brought the tribulation of the Turkish conquest to the Eastern Church. During the sixteenth and seventeenth centuries, at least in many areas of western Europe, both among Catholics and Protestants, the ministry of the Word came to a fresh flowering while in the East the Moslem hegemony parched the ground of Christian learning, and Christian preaching inevitably withered. The Eastern Church struggled to maintain Christian preaching and teaching, nevertheless. In Romania the Orthodox were particularly successful in accomplishing this sacred task.[1] Those who stoutly proclaimed the gospel often paid the price of martyrdom, as did Antim of Iveria, whose fascinating story we are about to recount. Yet the

---

1. Much of the information in this chapter was personally transmitted to me by my friend Joan Alexandru, whom I met when we were both students in Germany at Christmas in 1969. For a whole year we studied together, and the following Christmas we spent together in Romania. There I met such leaders of the Romanian Orthodox Church as Father Stanaloa; Justinian, future metropolitan of Cluj; and Calinic, future bishop of Curtea de Argeş, Christian leaders for whom I have the highest respect. In spite of changing political circumstances, we have been able to maintain our friendship over the years. In the summer of 1991 I was able to visit my friends in Romania once again. By that time I was well advanced in the study of Christian preaching. To help me in this they sent a young monk, Maxim Nica, who interpreted for me page by page a variety of material on Romanian preaching, especially the sermons of Antim of Iveria.

ministry of the Word was maintained. The Romanians had for centuries almost secretly nurtured their faith in their monasteries. Hidden away in the Carpathian Mountains, these monasteries preserved the manuscripts of the Scriptures. Their libraries contained volume upon volume of commentaries on the Scriptures produced by the Church Fathers. They treasured their sermons as well as their tomes of theology. In the superb Orthodox liturgy, large portions of the Scriptures were read through in a systematic way. In fact, the Orthodox lectionary was much more systematic in its reading of Scripture than the Catholic lectionary. The monks gave a great deal of attention to reading the Bible, memorizing it, and meditating on it. They were the ones who, in their monasteries, preserved the tradition of biblical wisdom during the Moslem conquest.

In the sixteenth century the Romanian-speaking people were for the most part divided among three different lands. One principality, Walachia, ruled the rich alluvial plain north of the Danube and south of the Carpathians, and another, Moldavia, controlled the valley of the Moldau, east of the Carpathians. Then there was Transylvania, north and west of the Carpathians. Ever since the Magyar invasion in the tenth century, Transylvania had been part of the Kingdom of Hungary. The Romanian heartland was really in the Carpathians, although there were enclaves of people who spoke "Ruman," the medieval form of Romanian, south of the Danube and even in the mountains of Albania. For centuries during the barbarian invasion they had been pushed up into the mountains, but in the thirteenth century they began to reclaim the rich plains and valleys their ancestors had once farmed. Their ancestors had been the Roman colonists of the ancient province of Dacia. From the first to the seventh centuries there were lots of Romans in the Balkans. When the barbarians came, it was in the mountains that they preserved their ancient Roman language. They were the heirs of the eastern Roman Empire and thought of themselves as Romans, hence the name Romania. They were, like the emperor Justinian himself, born in the Balkans of Latin-speaking parents. Byzantium, in its origins, was as much Roman as Greek, and these eastern Romans were Orthodox. Both culturally and religiously, it was the Byzantine heritage they wanted to cultivate.

I. The Seventeenth-Century Homiliaries

Homiliaries had often been used as a means of encouraging and guiding Christian preaching.[2] This was especially the case when the Church was not able to provide its preachers with the sort of literary education which helps produce learned and articulate preaching. The Turks did not forbid Christian schools of higher learning so much as they exacted such heavy taxes that it became a luxury few could afford. About the middle of the seventeenth century a significant number of homiliaries were published by the Romanian Orthodox bishops. It is clear from these homiliaries that the Orthodox Church was making a concentrated effort to encourage a preaching ministry.

Between 1633 and 1654 Prince Matei Basarab, although still a vassal of the Turkish sultan, was able to provide Walachia with a moderate amount of stability and even autonomy. During this time Teofil, metropolitan of Bucharest, published a homiliary, or *cazania,* as it is called in Romanian, which, according to Gheorghe Comşa, numbered almost a thousand folios.[3] This important publication was not provided with a title page, which leaves us without a title or a date of publication. We do know, however, that the metropolitan was assisted in this important project by two other Walachian bishops, Ignatie of Rimnic and Stefan of Buzau. It was a major cooperative effort of the church of Walachia. Such a volume provided a village priest with a considerable amount of teaching material. While most of the sermons were for regular Sundays, there were also sermons for the major feast days. These sermons were probably not read out by the priest so much as used as a source of ideas to construct his own sermon. It was clear that the bishops of Walachia expected the priests in their churches to preach a sermon on both regular Sundays and the major holidays.

In 1641 a homiliary appeared in the Transylvanian city of Alba Julia.[4] Sometimes called the Belgrade Cazania, this homiliary contains Romanian translations of classic patristic sermons. It was a reprint of a volume printed in Braşov in 1581, a volume which had been supported

2. On the importance of the Romanian homiliaries, see Moses Gaster, "Rumania: Literature," in *Encyclopedia Britannica,* 11th ed., 29 vols. (New York: Encyclopedia Britannica, 1910-11), 23:844-45.

3. Gheorghe Comşa, *Istoria Predicei la Români* (Bucharest: Tipografia Cărţilor Bisericeşti, 1921), p. 26.

4. Comşa, *Istoria Predicei la Români,* pp. 27-29.

by the Romanian Orthodox bishops fairly generally and had been very popular with the parish priests. The Orthodox metropolitan of Alba Julia, Ghenadie II, paid for the project because there were not enough copies of the older edition to go around and the priests had asked for more. Ghenadie died before the project was completed, but his successor, Elie Iorest, finished it. In the preface he wrote that the volume should make the priests better aware of their responsibility to preach and teach the Word. The Church Fathers had obviously given much time to preaching. It is true, the metropolitan tells us, worship is our primary concern, but worship without preaching is distorted. By long tradition, going back to the Church Fathers, preaching is a part of the liturgy. Without preaching worship is not properly understood. It is cold and lacks human warmth. By preaching a sermon the priest has a chance to give his own personal witness to the tradition which is passed on in the liturgy. From this it is clear that the metropolitan does not have in mind a mechanical reading of the homiliary from the pulpit. The sermons are published as an example for the priest in developing his own sermon, a sermon which is sufficiently the preacher's own work that it conveys the warmth of his own personal witness.

In the following year, 1642, at the Walachian monastery of Câmpulung in Argeş, the abbot Melhisedec published a homiliary made up of his translation of a number of Greek sermons for use in catechetical instruction.[5] The title of the volume might be translated *Short Teachings from the Holy Books for the Use of All Christians Translated in Romanian.*[6] According to Comşa, the following subjects are covered:

1. To Have Love for One Another
2. To Be Patient
3. Against the Love of Money
4. Almsgiving
5. On Hospitality
6. On Repentance
7. On Confession
8. On the Lord's Prayer

5. Comşa, *Istoria Predicei la Români,* p. 30.

6. "Invăşături preste toate zilele alese pre scurt din multe dumnezeeşti cărţi, de folosinţa tuturor creştinilor, prepuse de pre limba grecească pre limba rumânească." Comşa, *Istoria Predicei la Români,* p. 30.

9. On the Sign of the Cross
10. On the Ten Commandments

One notices that the Homiliary of Câmpulung is carefully following the classics of Byzantine moral theology at this point. As we shall see, this list is very similar to the catechetical preaching outlined by Antim at the beginning of the following century.

The Homiliary of Govora was published in 1642.[7] In 1635 Prince Matei Basarab had brought a printer from the Ukraine to help provide Christian literature for his subjects. A printing press was set up at the monastery at Govora, a monastery which even today is treasured for its beauty. The prince provided the financial backing for a translation of the sermons of Petru Movilă, the son of a prominent Romanian noble family who at the time was metropolitan of Kiev. Petru Movilă, sometimes Peter Mogila, had studied at the University of Paris, had gotten a Western education, but had remained faithful to the Orthodox faith. In fact, he became a prominent Orthodox theologian. As metropolitan of Kiev, he had called the famous pan-Orthodox synod in 1642. This synod, the first such synod to meet since the fall of Constantinople two hundred years before, succeeded in drawing delegates from the whole Orthodox world. It even established a constitution for Orthodoxy. More important, however, it served as a rally for the bruised self-consciousness of a very important segment of the Christian Church.

The publication of the homiliary was supervised by the monk Silvestru. Because the book had the financial backing of the prince, great pains were taken to make it beautiful. It was handsomely printed in black and red ink. In the preface Silvestru says this work was taken up for love of country and because it was very important to have good preaching. If their nation were to survive the Turkish conquest it would be through faithfulness to their historic Christian tradition. Today's Romanians recognize the same thing. It was important, therefore, that good preaching and teaching of the essential articles of the faith be maintained.

II. Petru Movilă (1596-1646)

That the sermons of Petru Movilă should be published in his native land had more behind it than patriotism. He was a manifestation of the spirit

---

7. Comşa, *Istoria Predicei la Români,* pp. 30-35.

of Orthodoxy which persisted in spite of the Turkish conquest. Movilă was a man of great learning. It was he who established the Academy of Kiev and introduced the teaching of both Latin and Greek to the Russians. This academy, outside the Turkish empire, to be sure, was the first attempt to provide Russia with a genuine education in the literary arts. Movilă was well aware that good preaching demanded a very special kind of education.

A particularly interesting feature of his sermons is the way Gospel stories are illustrated by parallels from the whole of Scripture. Movilă was well aware of the classic homiletical principle that Scripture is best explained by Scripture.

A generation later, in 1678, Varlaam, metropolitan of Bucharest, not to be confused with Varlaam of Moldavia, published a collection of eighteen feast-day sermons, obviously intended for the guidance of the preachers of Walachia.[8] The title, *Cheia Înțelesului (Key to Understanding)*, suggests the importance the metropolitan gave to preaching.

In 1691 Teodosie, then metropolitan of Bucharest, also published a homiliary, to which he gave the title *Margarita*, or *The Pearls*.[9] It is a collection of patristic sermons from the leading preachers of the Greek Church. Most prominent in the collection are the sermons of John Chrysostom, but there are also sermons from Ephrem the Syrian, Maximus the Confessor, John of Damascus, Athanatius of Mount Sinai, and Symeon the New Theologian. Teodosie provided his publication with two prefaces, the second being an essay on the preaching ministry of Chrysostom. Clearly Chrysostom was regarded as the classic example of Orthodox preaching. Teodosie, of course, was neither the first nor the last to realize the quality of Chrysostom's example. It may be true that the Orthodox were pushed to develop a preaching ministry in self-defense. If Christian preachers did not make clear the fundamentals of the Christian faith, it would be very easy for Christians, ignorant of their faith, to succumb to the faith of their conquerors. Conversion to Islam could win many favors from those in power. Some may have preached simply because Catholic and Protestant preachers were attracting their flock, but it probably is more true that the Orthodox were reexamining their own tradition and were becoming very much aware that they, too, had a great tradition of preaching. The example of Chrysostom, the greatest of all

---

8. Comșa, *Istoria Predicei la Români*, pp. 48-51.
9. Comșa, *Istoria Predicei la Români*, pp. 54-57.

Christian preachers, was impossible for them to forget. As a true Church Father, century after century his memory has begotten again and again a fresh generation of Christian preachers.

This does not at all exhaust the list of homiliaries published by the Romanian Orthodox Church during the Moslem domination. The very fact that so many homiliaries were published during this time is evidence that there was a considerable preaching activity. One does not publish a lot of homiliaries if no one is using them. Priests throughout the Romanian-speaking lands were using these homiliaries as sourcebooks for their own sermons. The culture of the Romanian-speaking church at that time was primarily oral rather than literary, but unlike many oral cultures, it had a rich literary culture from which to draw, namely, the theological culture of the Byzantine Church. In a situation like this, a homiliary can have a profound effect on preaching. It puts into the hands of a priest who may have had little formal education a gold mine of theological insight which could be dug into for years.

III. Varlaam of Moldavia (fl. 1643)

During the seventeenth century Moldavia was a Romanian principality under the hegemony of the Ottoman Empire. It had to cope with pretty much the same set of problems that plagued Walachia. The princes of Moldavia were required to pay heavy taxes to their Turkish overlords. Yet in spite of the repressive measures of the Phanariot regime, which tried to run Moldavia from Constantinople, the princes were able to secure for their people a certain amount of stability. One prince in particular, Basil the Wolf, or as his name is written in Romanian, Vasilie Lupul, was able to do quite a bit to encourage Romanian literary culture. Coming to the throne in 1634, he ruled for twenty years. He worked on codifying the old legal traditions; he encouraged monastic schools and built a printing press. The metropolitan of Jassy, Varlaam Motoc, proved his constant ally. He was the son of an old Moldavian noble family who received a good education in the monastery schools of Moldavia, the only place any kind of education was available in Romania. The Turks were not interested in education, and in fact were notorious for ignoring the educational needs of their subjects. As metropolitan, with the backing of his prince, Varlaam wanted to strengthen education. His special concern was to produce a Christian literature in the common tongue. At the same time he encour-

aged closer relationships with the ecumenical patriarch in Constantinople, Varlaam worked hard to encourage the use of Romanian in both the
reciting of the liturgical prayers and in preaching. For the most part Old
Slavonic was still the liturgical language of most of the Balkans. Varlaam
was very successful in spreading the use of Romanian in worship. In 1643
he published a homiliary of Romanian sermons, half of which were from
Petru Movilă, the remaining half from Varlaam himself.

This homiliary contained a sermon for each Sunday and for the
more important feast days. The book contains almost five hundred folia.
We find sermons on the following subjects:

"On Humility"
"On Punishment"
"On Confession"
"On Repentance"
"On the Second Coming of Christ"
"On Forgiveness"
"On Communion"
"On the Veneration of the Holy Cross"
"On the Power of Faith"
"On the Patience of God"
"On the Calling of the Apostles"
"On the Works of Evil"
"On the Love of Money"
"On Meekness"
"A Sermon for Easter"
"The Pilgrimage of Life"

For feast-day sermons we find the following:

"A Sermon for the Feast of Simon Stylites"
"The Nativity of the Virgin"
"The Glorification of the Holy Cross"
"The Life of Saint Parasceva"
"The Martyr Demetrius"
"A Sermon for the Feast of Saint Nicholas"
"Christmas"
"Epiphany"
"Circumcision"

"A Sermon on Saint Theodor Tiron"
"Saint George"
"Saint John the Moldavian"
"The Decapitation of John the Baptist"

Resources such as these homiliaries did much to keep the homiletical tradition alive under the difficulties of the Turkish domination.

IV. Antim of Iveria (1650-1716)[10]

By the end of the seventeenth century the Ottoman Empire was beginning to show signs of weakness. The Turks never did win Vienna. The Austrians had driven them from their territory and were now beginning to envision an Austrian empire that would flow from Vienna down the Danube, across the Hungarian plain, past the Carpathian Mountains, to the shores of the Black Sea, even to the Golden Horn. Then it would really be *Österreich,* the Eastern Empire. The Hungarians were beginning to drive the Turks out of Hungary as well, but at the cost of surrendering the crown of Saint Stephen to the Austrians. From now on the Hapsburgs would bear the title of king of Hungary. The Hungarian Protestants fiercely objected and for a while were able to maintain a principality in Transylvania, but eventually the Austrians won that as well. The Romanians were no more interested in Austrian Catholic domination than in Turkish Moslem domination, but another possibility was beginning to appear on the horizon. Peter the Great was consolidating all the Russias into a Russian empire, and was beginning to assume the role of champion of the Orthodox peoples of the East. The Turks, however, still ruled over much Christian territory, and they still exacted heavy taxes. They were not about to give up the Balkans without a fight. So the Turkish wars went on devastating the eighteenth century as they had devastated the seventeenth. Orthodox Christianity was humiliated in its very homeland. No longer did the patriarch of Constantinople preside over an imperial Byzantine Church. He was at best the vassal of an Islamic sultan who delighted in submitting him to the indignities of the Phanariot regime.

---

10. The spelling Iveria has been chosen rather than Iberia to avoid confusion. Iberia is most often recognized as the name of the peninsula shared by Spain and Portugal.

A. From Slavery to Martyrdom

During this difficult time the church of Romania was to receive great help from an unexpected land. It was on the other side of the Black Sea, on the slopes of the Caucasian Mountains, in the ancient Christian kingdom of Georgia, that Antim of Iveria, the patron saint of Romanian preaching, was born.[11] There the Orthodox Church had won the allegiance of the population many centuries before and had brought the nation to a high level of culture and learning. Georgia in those days, as Romania, was constantly plundered by the Ottoman Empire. As a young man Antim was enslaved by the Turks. Somewhere along the line he was trained as an artisan, learning wood sculpture, painting, embroidery, and calligraphy. He also learned Greek, Turkish, and Arabic. Apparently he was ransomed by the patriarch of Constantinople and given a theological education in the patriarchal school at Constantinople. As was true of Joseph the Old Testament patriarch, slavery was, in the providence of God, his door of opportunity.

By the end of the seventeenth century the prince of Walachia, Constantin Brîncoveanu, had been able to win for his principality a modicum of peace and stability. For a few years, at least, the Turkish overlords were occupied with other matters, and the prince was able to devote himself to the cultivation of Christian learning. The prince apparently brought Antim to Walachia in 1689 to assist in this program of cultivating Byzantine Christian learning.[12] In 1695 Antim was appointed abbot of the old monastery at Snagov. There he established a publishing center which served the Orthodox Church of a number of different lands under Turkish domination. In the next five years he printed fifteen books in Greek, Romanian, Arabic, and Old Slavonic. Somehow the Turks did not notice that there was a Christian revival going on in the Romanian monasteries. Spiritually they were prospering. Gifted young men were flocking to them. Avidly they studied the books Antim published. Antim did much, by this means, to make Romanian a literary language. He must have had an amazing gift for languages! Before long his use of Romanian was so masterful that no one could detect that it was not his mother tongue. His talent for calligraphy enabled him to create beautiful books

---

11. In addition to Moses Gaster, "Anthim the Iberian," in *Encyclopedia Britannica*, 11th ed., 2:94, see Comşa, *Istoria Predicei la Români*, pp. 72-83.

12. Mircea Pacurariu, *Istoria Bisericii Ortodoxe Române* (Bucharest: Institutul Biblic si de Misiune al Bisericii Ortodoxe Române, 1978), p. 144.

which encouraged the use of Romanian as a literary language. In Romania, once again, we see how the cultivation of preaching and the cultivation of the literary arts go hand in hand.

In 1705 Antim was appointed bishop of Rimnic, being ordained by Metropolitan Teodosie, a prelate who himself had done much for the spiritual growth of his people. As bishop, Antim set about putting things in good order. Being an administrator, he was able to accomplish much in a short time. He was a builder of churches as much as a printer of books, but his most important project was the encouragement of Christian learning among the priests as a means of raising the quality of Christian preaching and teaching. Surely one of the reasons he was so effective was the high example he himself set as a learned preacher who was sensitive to the needs of his people. Steeped in the homiletical traditions of Byzantium, he demonstrated the blessings that can come from seriously undertaking the ministry of the Word. In 1708 he succeeded Metropolitan Teodosie as primate of Walachia. The sermon Antim preached at his consecration has been preserved.[13] In it he says his first responsibility as metropolitan is to be a teacher of the Word of God. He intends to follow the example of Christ, the great physician who healed the world through his gentle wisdom.[14] Ultimately, of course, the example of Christ is what encourages Christians to maintain the ministry of teaching and preaching at the center of their worship. We preach and teach because Christ sent his disciples to do just that (Matt. 28:18-20; Mark 16:15; Luke 24:47). Fear of heresy might be a motive, the example of the Church Fathers might be a motive, but ultimately Christ himself is the inspiration of Christian preaching. Whether in seventeenth-century Romania or contemporary America, Christ is our reason for preaching.

For almost twenty years Antim made an outstanding contribution to the cause of Christ in his adopted land. Providentially it had been a time of peace under a pious prince. The time, brief as it had been, was coming rapidly to an end. Resistance to Turkish rule was becoming more and more obvious in Romania, and Antim took little trouble to hide his distaste for the Moslem conquerors. The Austrians and the Russians were beginning to push the Turks out of the Balkans. Antim was in favor of supporting the Russians. Peter the Great was czar, and he presented him-

---

13. Antim of Iveria, *Opere,* ed. Gabriel Ştrempel (Bucharest: Editora Minerva, 1972), pp. 3-9.

14. Antim of Iveria, *Opere,* p. 3.

self as protector of the Orthodox. The Austrians, on the other hand, threatened to enforce Catholicism. In a desperate effort to hold Walachia, the Turks conducted Brîncoveanu and his four sons to Constantinople, and by bribery tried to induce him to embrace Islam. The prince could not be bribed. Then he was threatened with the death of his oldest son if he did not embrace Islam, but both father and son valued the eternal crown more than anything the Turks could offer, and so he was executed. In the same way the other sons and finally the father won the martyr's crown. This briefly is the story recounted to me by my friend, Joan Alexandru, who unfolded it to me at great length one summer in the cathedral at Curtea de Argeş.

Back in Walachia, Antim refused to leave his flock, until finally by force the Turkish soldiers took him away. Ostensibly they had been ordered to take him to Constantinople, but having crossed the Danube and left Romania behind, they drowned him in the Marita River, so that his ministry, too, was finally crowned with martyrdom.

B. Catechetical Ministry

In 1710, two years after beginning his tenure as metropolitan, Antim published a short catechism designed to encourage his priests to maintain a ministry of catechetical teaching and preaching. The title might be translated as follows: *The Teachings of the Church, What Is Most Needful and Useful for the Priests in Their Teaching Ministry, Printed in This Manner in the Metropolitan Offices of Tirgoviste in the Year of Our Lord, 1710.*[15] This publication outlines fourteen subjects and gives a few indications on how a priest might develop these lessons. This list is interesting, especially since it shows such similarities to the homiliary of Câmpulung mentioned above. It gives us a good idea of what an Orthodox prelate in a land controlled by the Turks considered essential to a Christian education. Let us look briefly at these subjects.

1. The introductory lesson takes up the sign of the cross. It is a sign by which Christians identify themselves, but it is also a weapon against

---

15. *Învăţătura besericească la céle mai trebuinioase şi mai de folos pentru învăţătura preoţilor, acum într-aceasta chip tipărită in sfînta Mitropolie în Tîrgovişte la anul de la Hristos 1710. Să să dea în dar preoţilor.* This study is found in Antim of Iveria, *Opere,* pp. 365-83.

the enemy. As we read in I Corinthians 1, the cross is the power of God and the wisdom of God. The sign of the cross should be made in a very definite way. One should put the first three fingers of the right hand together and trace the cross from the forehead, in the name of the Father, to the navel, in the name of the Son, to the right shoulder and then the left shoulder, in the name of the Holy Spirit. That is the way the Orthodox do it. Nothing is said about the fact that the Catholics do it differently.

2. The second lesson, which one can well imagine took a number of sessions, is devoted to an explanation of the Lord's Prayer. Eight petitions are elaborated, and a text suggested for each. This might be taken as indicating that the metropolitan had in mind a sermon for each petition.

3. The next subject is the Nicene Creed. It is divided into twelve articles, and a text provided for each. Again we would imagine that a session was given to each article. As one would expect from an Orthodox theologian, quite a bit of profound theological material is handled in the exposition of the creed. The doctrines of the Trinity and the person and work of Christ are all to be taught. An explanation of the Nicene Creed would be much more explicit on these subjects than an explanation of the Apostles' Creed, simply because it is more theological in its intention. Antim is careful to make the Orthodox doctrine of the Holy Spirit quite clear and to show its scriptural basis. The Christology of the Gospel of John as explained by Cyril of Alexandria is at the center of these explanations.

The next seven lessons treat the seven sacraments. Again we notice that the treatment has a distinctly Orthodox flavor. The sacraments are listed as baptism, chrism, the liturgy, ordination, confession, marriage, and the anointing of the sick. Rather than a sacrament of confirmation with laying on of hands, Antim tells us about a sacrament of chrism with the anointing of consecrated oil. The controversy between the Orthodox and the Catholics over the epiclesis is mentioned very specifically when discussing the sacrament of the liturgy. The liturgy itself is the transformation of bread and wine into the body and blood of Christ, a statement which seems oblivious to the sophistications of the Schoolmen as well as the questions raised by the Reformation. One notices that while the seven sacraments are delineated, there is nothing like the liturgical catechism so often found in patristic and Byzantine literature, in which the progress of the liturgy is explained step by step.

With this Antim's instruction turns to moral catechism. There is an explanation of each of the Ten Commandments, but there is also an explanation of the nine ecclesiastical commandments. This remains even today a staple of Orthodox moral teaching. The nine commandments are as follows:

1. We need to pray to God with a broken heart and humility.
2. We need to keep the four fasts: the Christmas fast, the Easter fast, the Apostles' fast, and the Dormition fast.
3. We need to honor our spiritual fathers who are praying to God for us, and we need to consult them on spiritual matters.
4. We need to make confession to a spiritual adviser at least four times a year, that is, at each of the four seasons of fasting.
5. We should avoid listening to heretics as well as to those who are ignorant of the Scriptures.
6. We should pray for the priests, for the leaders of the Church and the leaders of state, for soldiers and for all men.
7. We should keep the special fasts prescribed by the bishop.
8. We should not steal from the Church, enrich ourselves from the goods of the Church or divert Church property to our own use.
9. We should not celebrate marriages during fast days.

This sort of enumeration — eight petitions of the Lord's Prayer, twelve articles of the creed, seven sacraments, ten commandments of the Old Testament, nine commandments of the Church, and several more at which we shall look — is typical of catechetical education. Perhaps one might call them catechetical paradigms. Enumeration of this sort is an aid to the memory. In a society in which books are expensive and teaching cannot depend on a wide distribution of inexpensive books, this kind of enumeration plays an important role in education. Explanations of the creed, the Lord's Prayer, the Ten Commandments, and the sacraments had long been staples of catechetical teaching, but here we find significant additions to this material. The very fact that Antim is able to come up with such an impressive number of these paradigms shows us that the Orthodox had been working on catechetical instruction for centuries.

Next we find the seven gifts of the Holy Spirit. This is taken from Isaiah 11. As Antim enumerates them, they are wisdom, understanding, knowledge, desire for spiritual things, happiness, initiative, and reverence. This is not quite the same way a biblical philologist might get them out of the text of Isaiah today, let alone the way the philologists of the Western Church had numbered them, but that is beside the point. For the experienced catechist these lists were the outline for a discourse on Christian moral philosophy. It was the same way with the next lesson, "The Three Acts of Divine Blessing," based on Paul's famous teaching in I Corinthians 13, "Now abideth these three, faith, hope, and love, and the greatest of these is love." One notices that for Antim these are not so much the three theological virtues as three dimensions of God's grace. Moral theology in the West can very often wander off into Pelagianism, and the Western discussion of the theological virtues is a case in point. The Eastern Church just never seemed to see the issues the way the Western Church has, and here is one place where it seems to have a much stronger doctrine of grace. This lesson is followed by "The Four Blessings of the Soul," which are enumerated as courage, wisdom, righteousness, and purity. Then follows "The Four Blessings of Health." One of course recognizes the old discussion of the classical virtues here, but instead of wisdom, courage, temperance, and mercy, one has sliced the subject of moral virtues a bit differently.

"The Seven Deadly Sins" is the subject of another session, and following that is a more positive discussion of the same problem, "The Seven Good Deeds against Sin." The two match up, as is quite evident when we list them. The seven deadly sins are:

1. pride
2. avarice
3. lust
4. anger
5. gluttony
6. jealousy
7. sloth

The seven good deeds are:

1. humility
2. generosity
3. continence
4. patience
5. fasting
6. love
7. industriousness

The last lesson is on the twelve fruits of almsgiving, taken from Matthew 15. Again we seem to have the outline of one or more catechetical sermons.

In previous chapters we have seen several examples of catechetical preaching for those living in monastic communities. *The Spiritual Catechisms* of Symeon the New Theologian are the great example. The word "catechism" originally meant introductory instruction, but as things developed the tradition of catechetical instruction became more and more devoted to a systematic teaching of those well advanced in the Christian life. It is not surprising that this should be preserved in literary form much more frequently than the sort of instruction directed toward those who really were beginners. Antim's catechism is therefore of particular interest because it gives us a look into the catechetical instruction of a church that had a largely oral culture. Furthermore, it was a persecuted church. To be sure, Antim complained that his priests were not too diligent in conducting the instruction he outlined in this catechism, but some must have followed it, and besides, Antim would never have had this material unless others had been using it for centuries. As we have pointed out, it is traditional material which Antim had collected. There was nothing novel about it; Antim had not invented it. It would seem quite evident that we have here the traditional popular catechism of the Byzantine Church.

A remarkable thing about this catechism is that it is relatively free from polemic against either Moslems or other Christian groups. In a few places Antim is careful to define the Orthodox position when it was clearly different from the Catholic position. But the material seems hardly aware that Protestantism taught a number of positions quite different from the Orthodox. Nothing appears either to attack or defend against Moslem teaching. In light of this, it would seem difficult to claim that catechetical teaching was being encouraged primarily as a defense against the encroachments of those preaching another faith. Antim, in encouraging catechetical instruction, for the same reason encourages preaching in the liturgy. That is what Christ sent his apostles out to do, to make disciples of all nations, baptizing them and teaching them (Matt. 28:19). No other reason is necessary.

C. Feast-Day Sermons

The only real sermons of Antim which have been preserved are his festal sermons.[16] Of these we have fewer than thirty. Even at that, they are re-

16. We have three manuscripts of the sermons of Antim. They were discovered

garded today as monuments in the history of Romanian literature. They exemplify a clean, sober style. They are models of directness and clarity. One finds little of the baroque rhetoric which Antim's French contemporaries Bossuet, Bourdaloue, and Massillon took to such heights. It never occurred to Antim that he should dazzle his congregation with oratorical brilliance. He makes no attempt to impress them with his brilliant oratory. Here is a preacher who has the humility of a ransomed slave. He is preaching to a people humbled by the heavy taxation of an alien power. Grand oratory was the last thing on anybody's mind.

That the sermons which have been preserved were festal sermons rather than regular Sunday sermons is not at all surprising. As we have often said, all the way back to the classical civilization of ancient Greece and Rome, a feast day demanded a festive public address, and it was the responsibility of the leader of the community to provide it. Festal sermons would have been prepared with special care, and were apt to be written out either before or after the occasion. The people expected the festal sermon to be an especially significant utterance.

Following Gheorghe Comşa, we find in the collection the following sermons:

Five sermons for Palm Sunday
Three sermons for the transfiguration
Two sermons for the feast of the dormition of the Virgin Mary
Two sermons for Christmas
Two sermons for the feast of SS Constantine and Helena
Two sermons for Saint Demetrius
Two sermons for Saint Nicholas
Two sermons for the beginning of Lent
One sermon for the feast of the circumcision

---

only gradually. The first was discovered by Bishop Melhisedec of Roman in 1886. This was a copy made in 1781 of an older manuscript. On the basis of this manuscript Bishop Melhisedec produced the first published edition of the sermons which was given the title *Didahii.* The second one was discovered in 1887 by Constantin Erbiceanu, and is apparently older than the copy published by Bishop Melhisedec. The third was discovered in 1958, and this is the oldest manuscript which has come down to us. This is the manuscript published by Gabriel Ştrempel. It was copied by Ephrem the Apprentice in 1722 and 1725, that is, shortly after Antim's death. The copy was made in Antim's monastery in Bucharest at the direction of the dean of the monastery, the priest Stantiul. For further information, see Antim of Iveria, *Opere,* p. xlv.

One sermon for the Epiphany
One sermon for Saint Simeon
One sermon for the feast of the SS Apostles Peter and Paul
One sermon for the feast of the SS Archangels
One sermon for the feast of the presentation of the Virgin
One sermon for the Sunday of the Tax Collector and the Pharisee

This obviously is not a systematic collection, but rather a gathering up of all the sermons of which records had survived. One wonders why there are five sermons for Palm Sunday and not a single sermon for Easter. One would hesitate to speculate as to the reason, other than simply to say that these were the sermons which could be found after the soldiers took our preacher away. Antim had not in his lifetime published his sermons, or even prepared them for publication. Their publication was entirely post-humous.

A study of the sermons we have shows that the martyred metropolitan was above all a teaching preacher.[17] In a large portion of the sermons we have, even in those for high feast days, a goodly part of the sermon is devoted simply to retelling the story of the event being celebrated. This is an obvious thing to do. People love to hear stories; besides that, recounting the event the community is celebrating is the primary function of the festal sermon. It is only natural, therefore, that when Antim preaches on the feast of the Epiphany he retells the story of Christ's baptism;[18] when he preaches on the feast of the transfiguration, he tells the story of Jesus taking Peter, John, and James up Mount Tabor and then being transfigured before them.[19] This is what we expect a popular preacher to do, as we have said, but Antim more than most is keenly aware of the teaching opportunity it gives him.

Not only is Antim concerned with the teaching of Holy Scripture, he is also concerned with the teaching of Christian doctrine. In his sermon for Christmas he wants to show that Christ was born to save us from our sins, and therefore he explains what sin is and why we need to be saved from it.[20] In the same sermon we find a long explanation of why it was appropriate for the Son of God to be incarnate in human form rather

17. This study is based on the text as found in Antim of Iveria, *Opere*, pp. 3-238.
18. Antim of Iveria, *Opere*, pp. 66-67.
19. Antim of Iveria, *Opere*, pp. 9-10.
20. Antim of Iveria, *Opere*, pp. 119-26.

than angelic form. A Christmas sermon is without doubt an appropriate place for unfolding the doctrine of the incarnation. Antim never hesitates to give solid doctrinal sermons on even the highest of feast days. In his sermon for the feast of the Epiphany, he offers a long teaching on the nature of the sacrament of baptism.[21] It is a thoroughly doctrinal sermon. To be straight about baptism was of the greatest possible importance to a Christian community living under a Moslem power, for it was baptism that separated Christians from non-Christians. Baptism could not be taken for granted. Christians had to understand the significance of their baptism. It is the same way here in America. Baptism became more and more an issue in the twentieth century because so much of our society lapsed into paganism. In a sermon for Palm Sunday Antim spoke of God's redemption of sinners and the power of Christ to raise the dead. The sermon is a thorough explanation of the doctrine of the resurrection of the dead.[22] It is most appropriate, therefore, that the collection of Antim's festal sermons be given the title *Didahii*, or in English, *Teachings*. Antim was a teaching preacher.

Antim's sermons are marked by a rather conservative use of homiletical devices. The use of parallel passages — one of the most conservative of all homiletical devices — is frequent. Scripture is best explained by Scripture, and Antim is always explaining a passage from the Gospels by a quotation from the Psalms, a reference to Solomon, or an allusion to the apostle Paul. The same is true of his biblical illustrations. In speaking of why Christ was willing to endure his life of humiliation, Antim talks of how Jacob was willing to endure twenty-one years of servitude for the love of Rachel.[23] Knowing that Antim had once been a slave makes this biblical illustration especially eloquent. Occasionally one finds a striking simile or metaphor showing us that Antim must indeed have studied classical Greek rhetoric in the patriarchal academy in Constantinople, but one never gets the impression that he has given a lot of time or effort to produce them. For Antim, as for many of the best Christian preachers, rhetoric is the servant of the Word, not its master. The most elaborate forms of rhetoric, so popular with the preachers to the court of Louis XIV, simply do not appear.

Antim has a very broad concept of the ministry of the Word. We

---

21. Antim of Iveria, *Opere*, pp. 68-73.
22. Antim of Iveria, *Opere*, pp. 140-49.
23. Antim of Iveria, *Opere*, p. 14.

saw his concern for catechetical teaching and how important he regarded the teaching opportunity even in festal sermons. We need, however, to point to the doxological nature of his preaching as well as the didactic. On several occasions his sermon turns to hymnody. His sermon for the feast of the dormition of the Virgin, which for the Orthodox is one of the cardinal feasts of the calendar, becomes, at its climax, a hymn written in rhythmic prose.[24] Apparently this hymn was the work of Antim himself. We find the same thing in a sermon on Saints Constantine and Helena.[25] Here the sermon is introduced by a hymn of five stanzas, apparently an original composition of the preacher. The close connection between hymnody and preaching is an important feature of the worship of Byzantine Christianity. Romanos the Melode is the outstanding example, but we find this feature recurring again and again.[26] The reason behind this amazing feature is the doxological tendency of Orthodox worship in general. It was only natural that preaching should be as doxological as it was didactic. As the Greek Fathers so often demonstrated, God is glorified when his wisdom is expounded.

A most important feature in the preaching of Antim is the way he maintains a balance between the traditional conventions of the Byzantine sermon and the pastoral needs of his congregation. We have spoken at length of the way Byzantine preachers developed a whole series of conventions for the sermons required by the various feasts of the Church. Christmas required both a sermon on the visit of the shepherds to the stable in Bethlehem to adore the Christ child and a sermon on the logos Christology in the prologue to the Gospel of John. The feast of the Epiphany required a sermon on the baptism of Jesus by John in the Jordan River. The first Sunday in Lent required one on the temptation in the wilderness. The Christian celebration of Passover required a wealth of sermons: on the raising of Lazarus, on the Christian meaning of the Passover, on the descent into hell, and on the Holy Myrrhophores, the women who took myrrh to anoint the body of Jesus. These conventions guided the preacher as he developed homiletical icons for his congregation. The only problem with this was that it too often produced stereotyped sermons which soon lost their ability to hold the attention of the congregation.

24. Antim of Iveria, *Opere,* p. 19.
25. Antim of Iveria, *Opere,* p. 113.
26. On the hymnic sermons of Romanos, see Hughes Oliphant Old, *The Reading and Preaching of the Scriptures in the Worship of the Christian Church,* vol. 3, *The Medieval Period* (Grand Rapids: Wm. B. Eerdmans Publishing Co., 1999).

Antim was obviously aware of the problem, for he frequently devoted a festal sermon to meeting the pastoral needs of his congregation rather than executing the homiletical convention for the feast being celebrated on that day. A striking example is found in the five sermons he has left us for Palm Sunday. On Palm Sunday 1710 he completely ignored the story of Christ's triumphal entry into Jerusalem and decided to preach on the devotional disciplines his congregation needed to follow in preparation for receiving Communion on Maundy Thursday.[27] One might say he prioritized the pastoral over the liturgical dimension of preaching. Orthodoxy had been mellowed by pietism sufficiently in those days that this was not thought too shocking. As we saw in the preaching of Symeon the New Theologian, pietism had a long and influential history in Orthodoxy. In this sermon Antim complains about the laxity of his congregation in their preparation for Communion, and now that they are entering into the last week of Lent, he urges them to redouble their disciplines of devotion, to be stricter in their fasting and more generous in their gifts to the poor.[28] Another Palm Sunday, however, produced the more conventional sermon.[29] Antim, as a man who had a wide experience of the Church ranging from his native Georgia to the patriarchal court at Constantinople and finally to the monasteries of the Carpathians, was also a hierarch with a deep pastoral sensitivity. He knew there was place in the worship of the Church for a variety of approaches to preaching.

Finally we come to another, and yet even more interesting, feature of Antim's preaching. Typical of Orthodox piety is that Antim finds preaching to be an invitation to meditation. This is a cardinal dimension of preaching as well as of worship in general. Ever since the psalmist encouraged the faithful:

> but his delight is in the law of the LORD,
> and on his law he meditates day and night (Ps. 1:2 RSV),

meditation on the Scriptures has been regarded as an important component of the worship of the heart both in public and in private. Antim realizes this quite well when he tells us in one of his sermons that we need to open our eyes, not just our bodily eyes, but our spiritual eyes as well, to the picture that is painted before us, because what is portrayed is not

27. Antim of Iveria, *Opere,* pp. 89-96.
28. Antim of Iveria, *Opere,* pp. 94-96.
29. Antim of Iveria, *Opere,* pp. 105-13.

merely an earthly event but a mystical reality.[30] This is a very interesting statement. It is the sort of thing Orthodox theologians usually said about their icons, but here it is said about the sermon. It implied that those listening to the sermon have to do more than simply record what is said. One has to think about it. Only when the congregation takes the meditations of the preacher as a stimulation to their own meditation has the sermon fulfilled its purpose. When real preaching happens, the congregation is not merely passive, it is completely engaged in penetrating the mysteries of God. This is about as stimulating an insight into what should happen in our preaching as any preacher has come up with, East or West, Orthodox or heterodox. Further study might show that it is an idea deeply imbedded in the Orthodox spirituality of preaching. And yet, is it not something we have all experienced in preaching? Sometimes when the preacher is not very eloquent, nor even very learned or sincere, we are confronted by the Word of God almost in spite of him. On the other hand, sometimes what he is as an individual Christian person gives wings to what he says. One cannot always be sure just what it is. Sometimes preaching is so much more than anything the stenographer could even begin to get down on paper, so much more than anything the preacher really said. Sometimes what we hear goes way beyond what was said, and yet we do hear it, and we know it is the Word of God.

30. Antim of Iveria, *Opere,* p. 68.

CHAPTER VII

The Russian Orthodox Church

There is something unique to the preaching of the Russian church.[1] In the last several centuries, from the sixteenth to the nineteenth, the Russian church has produced a remarkable group of preaching saints. But to understand this holy breed of orthodox charismatics, we must begin with the story of the evangelization of Russia. So very different from the evangelization of western Europe and yet at many points so very similar, the evangelization of Russia is the story of the Slavic peoples opening up the road from the Baltic Sea to the Black Sea, down the great rivers of the north, the Don, the Dnieper, and the Volga. It is the story of monks spending years of contemplation not in the deserts of Egypt but in the snow-filled forests east of Novgorod or upriver from Moscow.

The evangelization of Russia is not only the story of the Slavs, it is the story of the Vikings as well. They built the ships that took them down the rivers and, once onto the Black Sea, to Byzantium. We spoke of when the "Rus" first appeared on the horizon of classical civilization — in the ninth century, when the great Photius was patriarch of Constantinople.

1. On the history of the Russian church and in particular its preaching, see George P. Fedotov, *The Russian Religious Mind (I): Kievan Christianity, the Tenth to Thirteenth Centuries,* in *The Collected Works of George P. Fedotov,* vol. 3 (Belmont, Mass.: Nordland, 1975); John Fennell, *A History of the Russian Church to 1448* (London and New York: Longmans, 1995); N. Kataiev, *Geschichte der Predigt in der russischen Kirche,* translated from Russian into German by Alexis Markow (Stuttgart: Verlag von W. Kohlhammer, 1889); and Dimitry Pospielovsky, *The Orthodox Church in the History of Russia* (Crestwood, N.Y.: St. Vladimir's Seminary Press, 1998).

These foreign people arrived in their boats and pillaged the capital of the East. This raid on the second Rome opened up a whole new civilization — the world of the Slavs. Those "Rus" took home more than they knew. They took home a new way of life. They paved a cultural highway which joined the Viking and the Byzantine.

It was an inevitable unfolding of geography that the Russians should receive their Christianity from Constantinople rather than Rome. That was the way the rivers went. In the providence of God something unique was to come out of Russia. It took centuries to develop, and more than likely it will keep on developing, giving to the Church for centuries to come living saints, preaching the Word of God in profound holiness.

I. The Evangelization of Russia

The official history is that Russia was converted to Christianity in the year of our Lord 988, when by a miracle of divine grace Vladimir, heir of the mighty Ryurik, grand prince of Kiev, decreed that his people were to accept the Christian faith.[2] Modern historians have wrangled with these traditions for years, but basically they seem to hold fast. By the end of the tenth century the descendants of Ryurik had established themselves as the rulers of a vast alliance of Slavic peoples. These descendants were probably Viking warriors who had established their right to rule the Slavs. These Vikings were mercenaries, who for several generations had defended Slavic communities such as Novgorod and Moscow, married into the Slavic peoples they had defended, and adopted their language. The story seems to be that they organized the Slavs of the great river basins of the Dnieper, the Don, and the Volga and created what we today call Russia. We Americans should understand this because the civilizing of our continent was also based on the populating of a vast river basin, that of the Ohio, the Missouri, and the Mississippi.

When Fort Duquesne became Pittsburgh, the history of the continent was decided. It was the same way with Kiev. It was the key to a great river basin, and as such the key to the evangelization of Russia. It was, from a geographical point of view, only logical that the evangelization of Russia should begin with Kiev.

Christianity had begun to enter the land of the Rus at least as early

2. Pospielovsky, *The Orthodox Church,* p. 15.

as the ninth century when those Rus who plundered Constantinople in the days of Photius returned to their homeland. Supposedly these pirates accepted Christianity and took missionaries back with them.[3] What may have happened when they returned is a matter of conjecture, but there were Christian churches in Kiev before Vladimir's conversion. We do know that Olga, princess of Kiev, was a Christian. We get the impression that she was a very capable lady. She was the wife of Igor Ryurikovich and the regent of his son Svyatoslav Igorevich and grandmother of Vladimir, who would lead Russia to the Christian faith. She was more than likely baptized in Constantinople in 946.[4] Olga was very much impressed by the culture of Constantinople. In 946 she led a large company of courtiers, merchants, and bodyguards to the capital of the Byzantine Empire, perhaps to find a highborn Christian princess for her son. She no doubt figured that a royal bride, "born to the purple," would be quite suitable for an heir of the House of Ryurik. But the courtiers of Constantinople had no idea of the vastness of the dominions of the Rus, and Olga returned home without her princess. She did add some Orthodox clergy to her sizable entourage. Whether among them there were any conscious missionaries is unknown.

Forty years later Olga's grandson Vladimir, who began his reign enthusiastically supporting paganism, changed his mind and determined that the dominions of the Rus, that is, all the Russias, were to become Christian. This loose federation of Slavic tribes and clans, ruled over by the descendants of Ryurik and his Viking warriors, apparently followed their prince. They were baptized in the Dnieper River shortly after Vladimir himself had been baptized. Vladimir's baptism probably took place at Cherson in the Crimea and was closely connected with an alliance with the Byzantine emperor, Basil II, and Vladimir's marriage to the emperor's sister, Anna.[5] The Russian chronicles give the impression that the Christianization of the land took place almost immediately, but in actual fact it must have unfolded much more slowly. What interests us, of course, is the place of preaching in this Christianization.

3. Fennell, *History*, pp. 22f.
4. Fennell, *History*, pp. 26f.
5. Fennell, *History*, pp. 36-39.

A. Ilarion (d. 1051), Metropolitan of Kiev

The most important document for our understanding of Vladimir's conversion is a sermon preached by Ilarion, the metropolitan of Kiev, about 1050, some sixty years later. Ilarion was the first native-born Russian to be metropolitan of Kiev. He was apparently born and brought up in the newly converted Christian land. He had been educated by the newly founded Christian schools of Kiev and was able to preach about these momentous changes in the Russian tongue, what today we call Old Church Slavonic. At the time Ilarion spoke it, it could be understood from Novgorod in the far north all the way over to the most eastern reaches of the Volga, down to the Black Sea, and as far west as Moravia and Ochrid in Bulgaria. This sermon is one of the first examples of this language which has come down to us. Again we find the principle that preachers created the language just as much as poets did. This sermon was probably preached at Ilarion's consecration as metropolitan of Kiev. On this solemn occasion all the bishops of the Russian church would have assembled in the presence of the grand prince of all the Russias, who by this time was Jaroslav, son of Vladimir. The sermon is a fitting celebration of the founding of the Russian church; it is in form and spirit a panegyric as we find them so often in the Byzantine Church. It had a lengthy title: *Concerning: the Law given by Moses and the Grace and Truth which come by Jesus Christ. And: how the Law departed, and Grace and Truth filled all the earth, and faith spread forth to all nations, even unto our nation of Rus'. And: an encomium to our kagan Volodimer, by whom we were baptized. And a prayer to God from all our land.*[6] With all the jubilance of one of the panegyrics of Gregory of Nazianzus, Ilarion begins his sermon with an allusion not only to the Benedictus but to the salutations of several New Testament epistles.

> (1) Blessed be the Lord God of Israel, the God of Christians, for He has visited and redeemed His people, for He has not abandoned His creatures to remain until the end in the grip of the darkness of idolatry and to perish in the worship of demons. For first He justified the tribe of Abraham through the tablets and the Law; then through His Son He

6. This sermon is found in *Sermons and Rhetoric of Kievan Rus'*, translated and with an introduction by Simon Franklin (Cambridge, Mass.: Distributed by Harvard University Press for the Ukrainian Research Institute of Harvard University, 1991), p. 3, hereafter Ilarion, *Sermon.*

redeemed all the nations; through the Gospel and through baptism He brought them to regeneration, to rebirth into the life eternal. Let us therefore praise Him and glorify Him unceasingly, as He is praised unceasingly by the angels; and let us worship Him constantly, as He is worshiped constantly by the cherubim and the seraphim; for in His watchfulness He has watched over His people.[7]

Here is high rhetoric, the sort which had for centuries been popular in Constantinople. This was the sort of culture which the newly converted warrior princes and their boyars so greatly emulated. How amazing that in sixty years the Russian church could bring forth a preacher who could master Christian rhetoric and produce in the Slavic tongue a sermon of such eloquence!

Not only is this great rhetoric in the Greek tradition, it is great theology. Seen in the context of the eleventh century, it is amazingly profound. While we do have to consider that this sermon, like the liturgical sermons of Bernard of Clairvaux (1090-1153), has come down to us in concentrated form, yet the theological statements are put precisely.[8] Having delivered this jubilant opening statement, Ilarion summarizes the Christian gospel.

(2) He Himself saved us; neither an envoy nor a messenger. He visited earth not as a vision, but truly in the flesh, He suffered for us even unto the grave, and He resurrected us together with Himself. To the people who lived on earth He came clothed in flesh; and to those who abided in Hades He descended through His crucifixion and the sepulcher where He lay: so that both the living and the dead might know of His visitation and of the coming of the Lord; so that they might understand that He is indeed a strong and mighty God, strong and mighty both for the living and for the dead.[9]

Following the forms of classical rhetoric, our newly consecrated metropolitan proposes to discuss first the Law given by Moses and the gospel revealed by Christ. God gave the Law to prepare the human race for truth and salvation. He wanted to draw human nature away from its tendency toward pagan polytheism and bring humanity to faith in one single God.

---

7. Ilarion, *Sermon,* p. 3.
8. One notices that Bernard was born forty years after this sermon was preached.
9. Ilarion, *Sermon,* pp. 3-4.

All this is made clear in the story of Abraham and Sarah, Hagar and Ishmael, and finally Isaac.

The relation between the Law and salvation is made clear by the biblical typology of Hagar and Sarah found in Galatians (4:21f.). Abraham had as his wife a free woman, Sarah, and not the slave Hagar. In the same way God created the world free, and only afterward did sin enter in and enslave the world. Sarah, it happened, had no children. By divine providence it was determined that only in her older years would she give birth.[10] The good metropolitan has stretched the typology rather far, but it is a brilliant and creative interpretation nevertheless. Ilarion continues: just as the birth of Ishmael was a preparation for the birth of Isaac, so the gift of the Law is a preparation for the gift of the gospel of salvation.[11] And even further, in regard to the whole world, the Law is a preparation for the gospel.

At this point Ilarion brings in another elaborate interpretation of an Old Testament story, namely, the story of Gideon's fleece. Before the revelation of the gospel the whole earth was dry except for the fleece, that is, the Jews, who had the dew of God, but with the coming of Christ and his rejection by the Jews, now the whole earth receives the dew of God while Israel is left dry.[12] The hermeneutic seems a bit opportunist at this point, but the occasion, sad to say, seems to invite it. Still, Russia was destined to play a major role in the history of the Jews.

This brings Ilarion to his third point, the exposition of the doctrine of the incarnation.[13] Jesus is true God and true man, and while on earth he demonstrated the characteristics of both natures. With this the newly consecrated metropolitan gives a long series of examples from the ministry of Jesus, all showing him to be true God and at the same time true man. This, no doubt, was the constant theme of the evangelistic preaching Ilarion and his colleagues had been exercising for the last sixty years, sometimes in very elaborate form as we have it here in this festive panegyric, and sometimes in the simple telling of the gospel stories in village after village up and down the great rivers. Telling the story has always been the heart of evangelism.

But the Savior came to bring the gospel not just to those who lived

---

10. Ilarion, *Sermon,* p. 5.
11. Ilarion, *Sermon,* p. 7.
12. Ilarion, *Sermon,* pp. 8f.
13. Ilarion, *Sermon,* p. 10.

in the Holy Land in ancient times, our metropolitan continues.[14] He came to save the peoples of the whole world. To these lands he sent his apostles. Quoting the Great Commission in both the Gospel of Mark and the Gospel of Matthew, Ilarion emphasizes that Jesus himself had intended the gospel to be preached to all lands.[15] So it is that the grace of faith has spread over all the earth and has even reached us here in Russia.[16] What was prophesied has come true. The shadows and the types of the Law have given way to the present time. The promises of Isaiah, David, and Daniel have been fulfilled as the church of Russia has been born, the promised son of the free woman.[17]

With this the sermon becomes an encomium of Grand Prince Vladimir, who led Russia to embrace the Christian faith. The preacher dwells on Vladimir's enlightened desire to bring the Russian people to the Christian faith and to leave paganism behind. He took the lead in presenting himself for baptism and seeing that the name of the Father and the Son and the Holy Ghost was proclaimed in every city of the Russians. If not all were completely convinced of the truth of the faith, all so completely respected our glorious grand prince that they followed suit and had themselves baptized. Pagan sanctuaries were torn down and Christian churches built. Idols were thrown into the river and sacred icons honored.[18] Vladimir, not surprisingly, is compared to Constantine, another prince who brought a whole nation to Christ.[19] The encomium now branches out to the son and successor of Vladimir, who has wisely continued his support of the faith, as has the whole royal family.[20] The sermon concludes with an eloquent prayer invoking the blessing of God on the Russian people, their rulers, and their church.[21]

This sermon is a masterpiece. From the standpoint of a theologian it may come from the other side of the Christian world — what could be more exotic for an American Presbyterian than a medieval Russian sermon? — but even at that it is fascinating. The ideas may be strange but they are interesting. From the standpoint of classical rhetoric one imme-

14. Ilarion, *Sermon*, p. 12.
15. Ilarion, *Sermon*, p. 13.
16. Ilarion, *Sermon*, p. 14.
17. Ilarion, *Sermon*, p. 16.
18. Ilarion, *Sermon*, p. 19.
19. Ilarion, *Sermon*, pp. 22-23.
20. Ilarion, *Sermon*, pp. 24-25.
21. Ilarion, *Sermon*, pp. 26-29.

diately recognizes its sophistication, but even more from the standpoint of Slavic philology it is beautiful oratory. Those who understand such things tell us that the beauty of this sermon as living language is amazing. It is a piece not primarily of written language but of spoken language. This sermon was preached in an oral culture and is therefore best appreciated as oratory.[22] This sermon is a masterpiece indeed, but especially a masterpiece of oratory.

Now, the point is that masterpieces like this do not appear in isolation. They are dependent on a highly developed preaching culture, and the preacher who produces them is hardly a newcomer to the pulpit. He is an experienced preacher. He has to have been brought up in a church in which there is frequent preaching. This sermon is conceivable only as the summary of a whole generation of evangelistic preaching. When Grand Prince Vladimir led his people to the waters of baptism, he must have opened up a century or more of vigorous evangelistic preaching. Ilarion's homiletical masterpiece is the proof of it.

B. Luke of Novgorod (fl. 1050-70)

About the same time Ilarion was metropolitan of Kiev, Luke was bishop of Novgorod, a city in the far north of Russia over toward the Baltic Sea.[23] He is supposed to have been a native of Novgorod, appointed to his office by Grand Prince Jaroslav in one of his visits to the city. As the story goes, Luke was born to a family well known for its patriotism. Novgorod boasted an important Christian school at the time, which was apparently where Luke prepared for the ministry.[24] This consisted of the study of Scripture, the liturgical books, and the writings of the Fathers. As bishop, he presided over an impressive building campaign for the prince of Novgorod. The most important of these buildings was the Church of the Holy Wisdom, but he built other churches and monasteries as well. He is also remembered for his translation of Greek theological literature. For us, however, his collection of catechetical sermons, *Admonitions to the Congregation,* is of special interest.

22. Jean Leclerq made the same point about the sermons of Bernard of Clairvaux. Bernard's sermons for the feasts of the liturgical calendar were put into written form only after they had been preached.
23. Cf. Fedotov, *The Russian Religious Mind,* pp. 229-30.
24. Kataiev, *Geschichte der Predigt,* pp. 11-16.

Admonitions to the Congregation contains a series of rules for the Christian life: rules concerning our responsibilities to God, rules concerning our duties to our neighbor, rules concerning what we owe ourselves, and several special rules concerning the church of Novgorod. He gives special emphasis in his admonitions on our duties to God to believing in but one God and one God alone. Not only are we to believe in but one God, we are to worship him as a holy Trinity — the Father, the Son, and the Holy Ghost. This is what the holy apostles taught and what the Fathers established. Our preacher goes on to speak of the Nicene Creed, which teaches us to believe in one single God. What we seem to have here is only an outline of the first in a series of catechetical sermons. These *Admonitions* are similar to other series of sermons found in other mission fields at about the same stage of Christianization. One might compare them to those of Martin of Braga, Boniface, and Pirmin.

Let us look at the subjects which are treated. There is an admonition on the Christian belief in eternal life, taking up first the resurrection of Christ, then the resurrection of the Christians, and then the rewards of the righteous and the condemnation of the wicked. This is followed by an admonition to prayer. The bishop of Novgorod would have his flock enter the church and stand without distraction, concentrating on the presence of God. When we come to the church to pray, we should not talk with one another or think about anything worldly, but rather pray to God that our sins be forgiven.

Turning to our duties to our neighbor, our preacher makes clear that the basis of all our relationships with others should be love. This is the fundamental Christian virtue. The fruit of this love is openheartedness and integrity. One should have love toward everyone, but particularly toward those who share with you the same Christian faith. Our saintly bishop warns his flock against hypocrites, who have one thing in their hearts and another on their lips. A Christian should not try to do his brother in, for in the end God might be his avenger. A Christian should devote himself to the truth even to the point of giving his life for it. Be careful not to repay evil with evil. Honor one another that you be approved of God. Judge not your brother; instead worry about your own sins lest God condemn you. Have mercy on wanderers, on the poor, on prisoners, and be gentle to the orphaned. Much similar material follows, sketching out the fundamental principles of Christian morality and how they should be applied to life.

The third subject of these catechetical sermons is the Christian's private life. One should not give oneself over to vanity, to immaturity, or to disgusting words. One should not harbor anger or resentment toward another or make fun of anyone. In hard times one should be patient and trust in God. Don't get into fights, the good bishop warns; be not proud or arrogant. Instead be gentle and humble. Follow the commandments of God. The proud should take care lest they enshrine the devil in their hearts and make it difficult for the Word of God to penetrate their hearts.

The fourth subject goes along much the same line. One should respect elderly people, especially one's parents. One should not use God's name in vain nor curse anyone. One should respect the civil authority and the courts of justice in the city of Novgorod. One should not bear false witness, but make good judgments. One should fear God and honor the king, respecting God first and then honoring the rulers of the community. Included in this, of course, are the members of the clergy and the city officials of Novgorod.

There is nothing particularly exciting or interesting about these catechetical sermons. In fact, they are rather standard. They are much the same sorts of teachings we find in the moral catechism taught from New Testament times all the way down through the history of the Church. They summarize the introductory moral teaching of not only Luke of Novgorod but also of a whole host of Christian missionaries who in that day evangelized one of the largest Christian nations ever evangelized.

C. Theodosius of Pechersk (d. 1074)

Another series of sermons from the early years of the Russian Orthodox Church comes from a monk of Pechersk, the famous monastery of the caves in the suburbs of Kiev.[25] Theodosius eventually became the abbot of this monastery, but he was above all beloved as a preacher. While his exact dates are unknown, he must have been a younger contemporary of Luke of Novgorod and Ilarion of Kiev. One dated event in his sermons

25. On the life of Theodosius, see George P. Fedotov, *A Treasury of Russian Spirituality* (Vaduz: Buchervertriebanstalt, 1988), which contains an English translation of the life of Theodosius by Nestor, a medieval hagiographer. Fedotov claims that in spite of the problems of medieval hagiography, it is still the best source we have for the ministry of Theodosius beyond, of course, the sermons themselves. As for the sermons, I have relied largely on Kataiev, *Geschichte der Predigt*, pp. 20-25. Fedotov has himself given us an important biographical study in his great work, *The Russian Religious Mind*, pp. 110-31.

was an incursion of the Polovetsy, a wild, nomadic tribe living on the steppes east of the lands settled by the Russians. The Polovetsy are remembered today because of Borodin's *Polovetsian Dances.* Following the Russian chronicles, this would indicate that his ministry was at its height in 1067, the year following the Norman invasion of England under William the Conqueror.

Theodosius is the perfect example of the Russian holy man who because of his sanctity had enormous authority in the pulpit. He was the Russian Elijah, an ascetic who persevered in long fasts, who in his cave heard the still small voice and its bidding, and who waged a never ending battle with paganism. As George Fedotov has pointed out, the preaching saints of Russian Orthodoxy were distinctive in that they always maintained a pastoral responsibility. They performed heroic feats of asceticism, but they never cut themselves off from the Christian community.[26] That is why these Russian monks had an important preaching ministry in a way many monks before them did not. This tendency to join preaching and monasticism is supposed to have gone back to Theodosius, who was the real founder of Russian monasticism. He was famous for his frequent preaching.[27]

The emphasis of his preaching, we are told, was the saving of souls. He therefore often preached to his monks on the importance of living a God-fearing life, keeping the regular fasts of the Church, participating regularly in the liturgy, devoutly following the service, and exercising love for the neighbor as well as fraternal love to the brethren. As the tradition has come down to us, Theodosius preached to his monks every day.[28] One notices that these sermons to his monks are very similar to those Theodore the Studite preached to his monks in Constantinople, as well as the sermons of spiritual catechism preached by Symeon the New Theologian. In the early days of Russian Christianity, Byzantine monastic literature was very popular. The Byzantine missionaries to Bulgaria had translated many of these works into the Slavic tongue; besides this, pilgrims frequently went to Mount Athos and the monastic centers of the Holy Land. Saint Sabba, near Jerusalem, and even Saint Catherine on Mount Sinai were often visited by Russian monks.

Even more interesting than the sermons Theodosius preached for

26. Fedotov, *The Russian Religious Mind,* pp. 124f.
27. Kataiev, *Geschichte der Predigt,* p. 26.
28. Kataiev, *Geschichte der Predigt,* p. 30.

his monks were those he preached to the common people. Here we see how an eleventh-century Russian preacher battled against the superstitions of paganism as well as the pervasive debauchery of barbarian life. What is interesting is how similar this preaching was to that preached in the West at about the same stage in its Christianization. One thinks especially of Caesarius of Arles.

A particularly interesting sermon Theodosius preached to the general population was occasioned by the vandalism of the Polovetsy. The sermon today bears the title "The Scourges of God." Our preacher blames these raids of barbarian people on the incomplete conversion of the Russians who kept on living like pagans even though they accepted baptism.[29] Our charismatic monk denounces the disputes and riots these barbarian raids have caused. Disorders of this sort are the work of the devil, he says, who has always been our enemy. It is he who will have the shedding of blood, and yet these tribulations are also to be understood as divine punishment for our sins. Theodosius then illustrates his point about the scourges of God with various passages from the Old Testament prophets. Having seen what God has done in the past to his disobedient people, we must take even greater care that righteousness be maintained among us. One senses in even these fragmentary reports of these sermons the voice of a charismatic prophet. Here was an Elijah once again calling a half-converted people to the righteousness appropriate to the elect people of God.

Elijah was obviously Theodosius's model, just as he has guided Russian preaching all the way through its history. Theodosius calls his newly evangelized Russians to establish fair courts of justice, that the accused be brought to trial and judged honestly. Evil ought not be repaid with evil. Justice must replace the taking of revenge. We need to turn to God with love and with fasting and with tears and thereby seek to purify ourselves from sin. We do not want to become Christians in name only, when in fact we still live like heathen.

Our Christian Elijah is clearly preaching to a half-converted nation which worships the God and Father of our Lord Jesus Christ one day and old pagan deities the next. Theodosius comes down heavily on superstitious practices, games of chance, gambling, card playing, dicing, and sorcery. In doing such things one gives oneself over to the devil, one becomes a slave of sin and distances oneself from God further and further.

It may be of special interest to those of us who come from the heri-

29. Kataiev, *Geschichte der Predigt*, p. 27.

tage of Anglo-Saxon American Protestantism that one sermon that has come down to us is a sermon against drunkenness. He makes the point that one is permitted to drink with a meal, but it becomes wrong when drinking becomes drunkenness.[30] Apparently warning Christians of the evils of alcohol goes a long way back in the history of Christian preaching.

D. Kiril of Turov (ca. 1130-82)

Let us look at one more preacher from the era of the evangelization of Russia. Kiril of Turov has left us a collection of about a dozen sermons of the highest literary quality. From a strictly historical point of view, very little is known of Kiril.[31] However obscure the preacher of these sermons, they intimate something of the homiletical treasures of medieval Russia. One cannot read them without admiring the uniqueness of the Russian pulpit.

The tradition handed down about Kiril indicates that he, too, was a monk who spent most of his life in ascetic practices, in prayer, fasting, and the study of the sacred books. In time he was consecrated bishop of Turov, his native city, where, as the son of a prosperous family, he received a good education. Turov was on one of the tributaries of the Dnieper, almost two hundred miles north of Kiev in what today is Belarus. Nowadays it may be hard to find Turov on the map, but in the twelfth century it was a prestigious provincial capital. Kiril was another spiritual Elijah, an ascetic monk who spent his days by the brook Cherith (cf. I Kings 17:1-7), fed only by ravens, a monk who at God's moving would come into the city to preach. Kiril was the sort of monk who would ascend Mount Carmel (cf. 18:19-40) to proclaim the Word of God before a sin-bent world, and then return to the desert. As the story goes, Kiril retired from his office early and settled back into the wilderness to continue his pursuit of the transcendent life.

Kiril's understanding of the purpose of preaching may well be much more elaborate than we are able to discover from the literary corpus he has left behind, but we do have one statement of some of his ideas in the introduction to his sermon "On the Lame and the Blind."[32]

---

30. Kataiev, *Geschichte der Predigt,* p. 29.

31. Cf. *Sermons and Rhetoric,* pp. lxxv-xciv.

32. This sermon is found in *Sermons and Rhetoric,* pp. 55-70, hereafter Kiril of Turov, "On the Lame."

(1) It is good and most profitable, brethren, that we should compre-hend the teachings of the divine Scriptures. For such an understanding chastens the soul, inclines the mind to humility, stirs the heart to strive for virtue, fills man with gratitude, leads one's thought heavenwards to the promises of our Lord, fortifies the body for labors of the spirit, makes one spurn this life, its fame and its wealth, and relieves all the mundane cares of this world. Therefore, I entreat you, be diligent and assiduous in reading the sacred books, so that, nourished by God's words, you may nurture your desire for the ineffable blessings of the age to come. For the blessings of the age to come, though they are in-visible, yet they are immovable and firm, eternal and endless.[33]

For Kiril the reading and preaching of Scripture is a means of grace. It is God's chosen instrument for freeing us from our attachment to the mate-rial things of life and lifting our thoughts and desires to heavenly things. In worship, in the public reading and preaching of Scripture, God does something. He sends forth his Word that we might be raised up to him.

But Kiril goes on to make clear that those who study the sacred Scriptures receive a blessing not only for themselves but for their neigh-bor as well. For the solitary monk to preach to the crowds of the world is the stewardship the Savior requires of those who have been blessed with insight into the sacred Word.

(2) And let us not merely speak what is written, running over it with the tongue; but rather let us discern and absorb what is written, and endeavor to perform it in deed. Sweet is the honeycomb, and sugar is good; but understanding the books is better than both, for the books are treasure houses of eternal life. If in this life a man were to discover earthly treasure, then even if he were not to venture to take it all, but were to take only a single precious stone, still he is already carefree and sated, for he has wealth to the end of his life. Even thus, a man who has discovered the treasure of the sacred books, a man who has found through his understanding the true meaning of the words of the proph-ets and the psalms and the apostles and of the words of salvation of our Savior Christ Himself — such a man helps to bring about salvation not for himself alone but also for the many others who hearken to him. In such a man is made manifest the Gospel parable which says: "Every bookman who has been instructed concerning the kingdom of heaven

33. Kiril of Turov, "On the Lame," p. 55.

is like unto a man who is a householder, who bringeth forth out of his treasure new things and old." But if in his vainglorious solicitude for the great he neglects the lesser and insolently conceals the lord's coins and does not give them to the traders in this life so as to double the king's silver (that is, human souls), then the Lord will see his proud mind and will take his talent from him. For the Lord spurns the proud man, but He gives grace to the meek.[34]

It is to accomplish this service that monks have been set apart and endowed with spiritual gifts. For the monk to hoard up spiritual treasures of wisdom and knowledge without preaching to the poor, the simple, and the worldly is a form of spiritual pride. For the Christian scholar, preaching to the people is essential. Of the very nature of divine wisdom is that it must shine forth in the preaching of the wise. Preaching is the stewardship required of those who have been enlightened.

The Orthodox theology of preaching is based on the biblical Wisdom theology. Preaching is to set forth the divine wisdom. As with the Johannine Christology, it is of the essence of the divine Wisdom to enlighten. It is the purpose of the Church to enshrine the Hagia Sophia, and so it is the purpose of the true monk to witness to the Word of God.

The celebration of Easter in the Russian Orthodox Church even to this day is unparalleled in its splendor. In the Orthodox Church generally, Easter is the feast above all feasts. Happily Kiril has left us a series of eight Easter sermons, including the following:

Sermon for Palm Sunday
Sermon for Easter Sunday
Sermon for the Sunday after Easter
Sermon for the Third Sunday after Easter
Sermon for the Fourth Sunday after Easter
Sermon for the Sixth Sunday after Easter
Sermon for Ascension
Sermon for the Sunday before Pentecost

Let us look briefly at the first three of these sermons.

The sermon for Palm Sunday is an anticipation of Easter. In homiletical form it is a typical patristic commentary on the Scripture les-

---

34. Kiril of Turov, "On the Lame," pp. 55-56.

son. It is a running commentary, taking up one subject after another as they appear in the text. But following in the Byzantine tradition, it is also a panegyric, that is, a piece of festive oratory appropriate to the ceremonies commemorating a great event. Furthermore, it follows closely the conventions established for the Palm Sunday sermon. In fact, these Easter sermons generally follow the conventions established earlier. We spoke of this particularly in regard to Byzantine preaching in the Age of Justinian; in the fifth and sixth centuries the conventions for the preaching of major feasts were more and more codified. In these Easter sermons we find that these conventions are still very much alive.

This sermon is a good example of the continued use of both the patristic and Byzantine homiletical traditions.[35] The worshiping congregation is called to participate in these songs of rejoicing sung by the daughters of the heavenly city. Next our preacher takes up the garments of the apostles which were spread on the road. Allegorically these are the Christian virtues. "O behold the revelation of a glorious mystery! For the garments of the apostles are the Christian virtues: by their teaching the apostles made men of good faith to be as a throne for God and as a dwelling for the Holy Spirit."[36] The waving of the palm and olive branches is commented upon next. These people were the common ordinary sinners who come to God with contrite hearts and humbled souls. After this Kiril interprets those who went before Jesus crying "Hosanna." They are the prophets and apostles. Those who followed are the holy men and the martyrs.[37] All Jerusalem was stirred up and shaken on this day as the Son of God entered the Holy City. Annas and Caiaphas were vexed and the priests were bewildered.[38] They took counsel and plotted how they might kill him who had come to save them. On this day the elders, the scribes, and the Pharisees watch the children singing out "Hosanna to the Son of David." They watch with envy and reject their Lord. And, as Kiril interprets it, they brought upon themselves God's rejection.[39]

Kiril concludes his sermon by admonishing his congregation to accept the Savior who comes to them on this holy day. Be not like the faithless rulers of the Jews, the scribes and the Pharisees. Be rather like the in-

---

35. For the text of this sermon see *Sermons and Rhetoric*, pp. 96-101, hereafter Kiril of Turov, "Sermon for Palm Sunday."

36. Kiril of Turov, "Sermon for Palm Sunday," p. 97.

37. Kiril of Turov, "Sermon for Palm Sunday," p. 98.

38. Kiril of Turov, "Sermon for Palm Sunday," p. 99.

39. Kiril of Turov, "Sermon for Palm Sunday," p. 100.

nocent children who received the Savior singing the hymns of the Church, offering our praises to God, and extolling Christ our Savior.[40] This is very clearly festal preaching; it is not evangelistic preaching. It is doxological preaching which extols the mighty acts of God for our salvation. It is not trying to teach the people what they do not know. It is going over once more what the congregation already knows very well. The conventional story is told in the conventional phrases that the congregation might jubilate in the *magnalia Dei,* the mighty acts of God. That is what is supposed to happen in a festal sermon. We saw this so very well in the Easter sermon of Melito of Sardis, and again in the hymnic sermons of Romanos the Melode. Those who heard this sermon had already heard the evangelistic preaching of the first missionaries. They had already listened to a series of catechetical sermons like those preached by Luke of Novgorod and Theodosius of Pechersk. They had already heard the basic Bible stories read and preached. Sermons for the feast days, like this sermon for Palm Sunday, were an occasion for praising God for his mighty works of salvation in the person of Christ. It was an occasion for doxological preaching.

The sermon for Easter Sunday is similar. Following the long-held tradition of the Orthodox, the Easter sermon begins with the elaborate jubilation: "Redoubled is the rejoicing among all Christians, and unspeakable is the happiness for all the world, because of the feast that has come on this day. . . ."[41] This jubilation continues, after recounting the mystery of Christ's atoning death, with the jubilation of Psalm 24:7, "Lift up your heads, O ye gates, . . . that the king of glory shall came in." As Kiril interprets this, the gates are the gates of hades which crumbled at Christ's resurrection. Two more jubilant acclamations are quoted from Scripture: "For our passover has been sacrificed, even Christ" (I Cor. 5:7) and "O death, where is thy victory? O Hades, where is thy sting?" (I Cor. 15:55).[42] Our preacher has put them all together very beautifully, but these materials are all quite conventional. The congregation would have understood them very well, and they would have expressed the triumphant adoration of the worshiper for the gospel of Christ's victory over death. Acclamation is at the heart of the Orthodox celebration of Easter.

---

40. Kiril of Turov, "Sermon for Palm Sunday," p. 101.

41. For a text of this sermon, see *Sermons and Rhetoric,* pp. 101-8, hereafter Kiril of Turov, "Sermon for Easter Sunday," p. 101.

42. Kiril of Turov, "Sermon for Easter Sunday," p. 102.

Again and again the congregation shouts the acclamation, "Christ is risen! Christ is risen, indeed!"

We observed in earlier volumes that there are several traditional Easter sermons. There is the sermon on the story from Matthew of the women going to the tomb and finding it empty. Another one speaks of Christ's victory over the powers of death, his breaking open the gates of hell and leading the dead to eternal life; this might be called the *Christus Victor* sermon and is usually preached on I Corinthians 15:55, "O death, where is thy victory? O Hades, where is thy sting?" A third traditional Easter sermon is the typological interpretation of Passover, traditionally preached on I Corinthians 5:7, which speaks of Christ as our Passover. One could speak of others, but these are the principal Easter sermons. Kiril's sermon weaves them all together. In fact, it gives, in addition, much space to interpreting the story of Christ's appearance to the two disciples on the road to Emmaus.[43] This is usually the sermon for Easter vespers.

The point is that this sermon is one long jubilation, one continual acclamation. Into it are woven the traditional Easter stories, although one has to admit that they are alluded to more than actually recounted. All of the themes are drawn together and the sermon is completed with a final acclamation, "This is the day which the Lord created; let us rejoice and delight in it, for Thine is the kingdom and Thine, Christ, is the power and the glory with the Father and the Holy Spirit, now and ever."[44] The doxology of Psalm 118:24 is paraphrased in a thoroughly Christian sense. Again we see doxological preaching at its most obvious. In fact, this seems to be characteristic of Orthodox preaching, today even as in the Middle Ages.

II. The Mongolian Conquest

For two and a half centuries (988-1240) the evangelization of Russia advanced with little interruption. Bishops were established in city after city along the great rivers. Churches were built everywhere, schools founded in the towns, and monasteries planted deep in the forests.[45] Then suddenly the Tatars appeared on the eastern horizon. In 1240 these wandering

43. Kiril of Turov, "Sermon for Easter Sunday," pp. 105-7.
44. Kiril of Turov, "Sermon for Easter Sunday," pp. 107-8.
45. Fennell, *History,* pp. 45-90.

Mongolian warriors that Genghis Khan had led to power attacked and defeated the disorganized and feuding warrior bands of the Russian princes. The khans established their capital at Saray on the lower Volga, a thousand miles downriver from Moscow, close to where the river flows into the Caspian Sea. They maintained their hold on much of Russia until the fifteenth century when the princes of Moscow were able to unite their fellow countrymen in opposition to their foreign overlords. It was then, of course, that the leadership of Russia passed from Kiev to Moscow.

The preaching ministry of the Russian church continued to prosper during this period, according to Kataiev.[46] He tells of several important preachers in his history of Russian preaching. Many of the preachers of the late thirteenth and early fourteenth centuries left us anonymous sermons. There were obviously numerous preachers of quality whose names we do not know; they left manuscripts without identification. This may indicate that the preachers were monks or even hermits who functioned as charismatics. During the years of Mongol rule it would be only natural that preachers became even more intense in identifying themselves with Elijah.

There were several important bishops, however, who had a reputation for preaching. Bishops particularly seem to have been aware of their teaching responsibility during this time. Serapion, bishop of Vladimir, is remembered in the Russian chronicles as one who was strong in his knowledge of the Scriptures and a great teacher.[47] About half a dozen of his sermons have come down to us, and according to Kataiev, they show he had considerable pulpit experience behind him. The bishop himself says he preached frequently.[48] His sermons were strongly didactic, indicating that he considered it an important part of his pastoral office to teach his congregation the Christian way of life. Repeatedly he speaks of the importance of doing penance and disciplining one's life.[49]

His sermons tend to have a number of prophetic concerns. He remonstrates with his congregation over their besetting sins. Like the prophets of the Old Testament, he confronts his people with the holdovers of paganism. He denounces the continued practice of witchcraft and sorcery. It is because of this that Russia now suffers the cruelties of

---

46. Kataiev, *Geschichte der Predigt,* pp. 51-77.
47. Kataiev, *Geschichte der Predigt,* p. 56.
48. Kataiev, *Geschichte der Predigt,* p. 56.
49. Kataiev, *Geschichte der Predigt,* p. 59.

the Mongol invasions, their raids and confiscations. He sets all this forth in vivid and picturesque language. In fact, these sermons sometimes tell more about the superstitious practices than we want to know.

Photius, metropolitan of Kiev, was another bishop who had a reputation as a teacher.[50] He was a Greek by birth, and from his youth spent much time as a hermit. How he came to Russia we do not know, but in 1406 he was appointed metropolitan of Kiev by the patriarch of Constantinople. Fifteen of his sermons have come down to us. Possibly they were written out to be read by the pastors of local churches as encyclical letters. However that may be, the metropolitan understood his responsibility to preach even to those under his pastoral care whom he would never see face-to-face. His ministry stood at the beginning of the fifteenth century, when the difficulties of the Mongolian conquest were making the preaching ministry more and more difficult to exercise. Perhaps sending out sermons as encyclical letters was one of the methods he used to overcome these problems.

Finally we must mention one of the successors of Photius, Gregor Ssamvlak, who was consecrated metropolitan of Kiev in 1416.[51] Gregor was a Serbian by birth, and served in Bulgaria and Moldavia before coming to Russia. He has left us a collection of twenty-one sermons. These are much more classical than those of Photius. They give careful attention to the exposition of the passage of Scripture read during the liturgy. He treats the doctrines which can be drawn from the passage.

As the fifteenth century began to unfold, preaching became less and less frequent in Russia. This was no doubt largely due to the difficulty in training preachers. The Mongolian conquerors were not interested in maintaining Christian schools in the towns and cities, much less monastery schools. Both Photius and Gregor were apparently trained before they arrived in Russia. Through much of the fifteenth and sixteenth centuries preaching essentially disappeared from Russia. Sometimes sermons from among the classics of the past were read from the pulpit. Kiril of Turov was popular, as were Russian translations of Byzantine preachers, but often the liturgy was celebrated without a sermon.

---

50. Kataiev, *Geschichte der Predigt*, p. 67.
51. Kataiev, *Geschichte der Predigt*, p. 71.

III. Latin Influence on the Russian Sermon

By the seventeenth century the princes of Moscow were beginning to establish a considerable amount of independence and, at least in the north and east of Russia, were pushing back the Tatars and gaining control of their country. In the south and west the king of Poland was beginning to turn back the Mongols, but he was determined to bring the Russian Orthodox Church under the control of the Roman pope. The Poles used all possible methods to convert their Orthodox subjects to Catholicism, or as they called it, reunion with Rome.

One of these methods was establishing schools run by the Jesuits. The Orthodox tried to counter this by establishing their own schools, but not having the strong academic traditions which the Catholics had developed in the West during more recent centuries, they all too often simply adopted the Scholastic methods of the Jesuits. This was clearly the case in homiletics. Consequently the old Byzantine homiletical traditions, as well as the particularly Russian traditions which had begun to develop in the twelfth and thirteenth centuries, were simply forgotten and the Scholastic approach put in their place.[52]

Scholasticism had made a point of developing a sermon outline in which the text was logically analyzed. The text was unfolded and distinctions were drawn out. Reasons were given to support the doctrines expressed in the text. Particularly important was the citation of other biblical passages and the Church Fathers. Proof texts were very popular, as well as examples and illustrations which would make the basic doctrinal and moral concepts understandable. The Schoolmen had really made great contributions to the art of preaching, and especially in the south these Scholastic methods were eagerly learned and widely practiced. And yet somehow the sermons of Russian Scholasticism never had the doxological intensity of the Byzantine tradition or charismatic fire of the hermit saints schooled in the snow-filled forests of the north. In southern Russia, at least, Scholasticism produced no sons of Elijah.

Even at that, we should mention two prominent seventeenth-century preachers who were schooled in western Scholasticism and made a definite contribution to Russian preaching.

Cyril Tranquillion-Stravrovezky studied in the Lemberg Brotherhood School, eventually becoming a teacher there. He spent some time in

---

52. Kataiev, *Geschichte der Predigt,* pp. 89f.

Vilna in Belorussia, and was finally made archimandrite of Tschernigov by the metropolitan of Kiev. In 1619 he published a book of sermon helps containing material for each Sunday and feast day of the year. It is clearly intended for the use of the Orthodox. One easily recognizes passages which defend the Orthodox against popular Catholic polemic. It is always very indirect so as not to offend the Polish. Protestant ideas, however, are more directly challenged.[53] The sermons are often very critical of the failures of the clergy and the upper classes of society. Living in luxury, love of money, and love of drink are vigorously attacked.[54] The Polish overlords are indirectly admonished against cruelty, insensitivity to the needs of the poor, overworking the serfs, and charging high rents. Cyril's handbook provides much material from the fathers of the Greek Church, Saint Basil the Great, John Chrysostom, Gregory of Nazianzus, Epiphanius, and John of Damascus. The Catholics in the West had been producing preaching helps like this for some time. Cyril produced something very similar for the Orthodox.

Joanniki Goljatowsky was educated by the Mojiljaner College in Kiev, becoming in time a teacher there. He soon developed a reputation as a preacher. In 1659 he published a collection of sermons with the title *The Key to Understanding.* This went through several editions, to which he constantly added new sermons. In 1671 he was called to preach before the czar in Moscow. Finally he was made archimandrite of Tschernigov. Goljatowsky is the most significant of the Scholastic preachers of Russia, not only for the example he set, not even for his extensive collection of sermons, but rather for his book on homiletical theory. This book, *The Art of Preaching,* is the first attempt in Russia to write a treatise on homiletical theory.[55] It was influential for some time.

Goljatowsky's sermons are composed strictly according to Scholastic principles. To us they seem overly concerned with getting the attention of the congregation. Often clever devices are used to elaborate the subject matter, but many of us will find them a bit too trite. The trouble, more than anything else, was that these Scholastic methods were already a bit tired and worn out when the Jesuits brought them to Russia. It soon became clear that Scholasticism was but an old wineskin.

53. Kataiev, *Geschichte der Predigt,* p. 100.
54. Kataiev, *Geschichte der Predigt,* p. 101.
55. Kataiev, *Geschichte der Predigt,* p. 103.

IV. The Preaching Saints

It was about the time the Western Church became involved in the Protestant Reformation that the Russians began to free themselves from the yoke of the Mongols. As we noted above, the princes of Moscow were able to play a large part in this, primarily because they had developed a strong central monarchy, whereas some of the other centers of Russian civilization lacked the strong leadership Moscow had. Kiev in the south was dominated by the king of Poland, and Novgorod was not so much a principality as a merchant republic, being a member of the Hanseatic League.

The military success of the princes of Moscow encouraged them to develop a strong sense of national identity. At the height of this development they boasted that Moscow was the third Rome. The first Rome had fallen to the barbarians; Constantinople, the second Rome, had fallen to the Turks in 1453; and now Moscow, so successful in turning back the Mongols, had taken the leadership of Christendom as the third Rome. In 1547 Ivan IV was crowned czar. The grand prince of Moscow had become the czar of all the Russias, and the bishop of Moscow had been granted patriarchal status. In 1589 Job was installed as the first Russian patriarch.[56]

In spite of all the attempts to Westernize Russia, neither the king of Poland, who wanted to convert Russia to Catholicism, nor Peter the Great, who wanted to open Russia up to northern Europe, or even his heirs who married into a number of German royal houses, some with Protestant leanings, some with Enlightenment leanings, were able to quench the growing sense of Russian self-identity.

This meant that more and more a distinctly Russian approach to preaching developed. The influence of Scholasticism began to wane, and the uniqueness of the Russian Orthodox homiletical tradition began to reappear in the Russian pulpit.[57] Let us look at several leading Russian preachers who demonstrate the recovery of the Russian traditions.

A. Daniel of Moscow (fl. 1540)

Daniel received a good education in the traditions of Russian Orthodoxy and was appointed metropolitan of Moscow early in the sixteenth cen-

---

56. Pospielovsky, *The Orthodox Church*, pp. 57-79.
57. Kataiev, *Geschichte der Predigt*, pp. 130-53.

tury. The sixteenth century was a confusing time in Russia. In a day when political expediency put strong pressures on the Russian church to compromise both its traditions and doctrines, Daniel insisted on the integrity of the historic Russian faith. With the growing military success of the Moscovite state, the government increasingly tried to impose its authority on the Church. For Daniel preaching was an important means of resisting these pressures.

Thirty-one of his sermons have come down to us. For the most part they set down the historic positions of the Orthodox Church over against the Erastianism, the libertinism, and the secularism of the day. Considering the times, these sermons were truly prophetic. Here was a bishop who saw preaching as an important way of fulfilling his pastoral responsibility. In a day when irreligion was rampant, preaching was a way of instilling piety in the minds of the faithful. When many prided themselves on being free thinkers who lived above the morality of the common people, preaching became a way of appealing to the conscience. Preaching gave the metropolitan an opportunity to remind his people that one could not expect the blessings of God if one ignored his commandments. For Daniel preaching was a pastoral responsibility, one of the fundamental responsibilities of his office. His insistence on maintaining a preaching ministry was a logical component of his program of recovering the teachings and practices of Orthodoxy.

Sad to say, I have not been able to find translations of Daniel's sermons. But I have found a rather full summary of a good number of them in Kataiev's history of Russian preaching. While one would like to have more, what Kataiev gives us helps us fill in the picture, although admittedly in a rather indirect way.

In the first sermon Daniel sets forth the basic assumption of his preaching ministry. We must teach, believe, and live according to the counsels of Holy Scripture rather than according to merely human reason. Whenever differences of opinion arise, we must discuss these matters with love and restraint, not with arguments and complaints. In questions of basic doctrine we should be guided by the Scriptures and the traditions of the Church. When teachers arise who deny this authority and do not recognize the ways and customs of those who have gone before us and who introduce new laws which corrupt society, they should be recognized as false teachers.[58]

58. Kataiev, *Geschichte der Predigt,* p. 82.

The theme of the second sermon is that one should stand up for the truth even if it costs one one's life. There is a long discussion of the responsibilities of the pastoral office. Daniel obviously has a high doctrine of the ministry and understands the bishop to have broad authority even over against the state. The sermon applies this to the problems of the day. He is very critical of ministers who betray their office by being careless of spiritual responsibilities or who court the favor of the world and the approval of the mighty.[59] The third sermon continues in much the same vein, telling how when Christ ascended into heaven he left us the Scriptures of the Old and New Testament, the apostles, and after them the Church Fathers. We have therefore two kinds of tradition, written and unwritten. All such traditions we should continually respect. We would like to know what Daniel knew about Protestantism, but our limited sources do not tell us explicitly. It sounds as if he has heard of *sola Scriptura* and is not in accord, but more than that we hesitate to speculate. The fourth sermon goes over the teaching set down in the third sermon and applies it to several customs regarding prayer. Daniel insists on the Orthodox method of making the sign of the cross as opposed to the Catholic method.

The next three sermons in the collection deal more with strictly theological matters. The doctrine of the incarnation is discussed at length as well as Christ's atoning sacrifice on the cross. Several sects had arisen at the time which had been influenced by Jewish ideas. There were already large Jewish settlements in the southeast of Russia, and several of the nomadic tribes had either adopted Judaism or been largely influenced by it. When Daniel speaks of the heresies of the day, he more than likely has these Judaizing doctrines in mind. The Jewish influence was therefore playing a role even as far north as Moscow. That is why our metropolitan found it necessary to stress particularly these doctrines.[60]

Further on we find five sermons which treat ethical questions. The basic principles of Christian morality are of course laid down, but then the metropolitan bears down on the vanities of the time, the wearing of gold and silver rings, elaborate coiffures, lingerie embroidered with costly thread, silken shoes, and fancy waistcoats. Luxurious clothing and frequent bathing are a waste of time and money, he says. The theater is a danger to good morals. Again we find that drunkenness is given the stron-

59. Kataiev, *Geschichte der Predigt,* p. 83.
60. Kataiev, *Geschichte der Predigt,* p. 84.

gest disapproval. Daniel preached a simple ascetic way of life just as John Chrysostom had before him. Actually, one has to admit that the office of metropolitan in Moscow in the sixteenth century was not unlike the position of Chrysostom at the Byzantine court at the beginning of the fifth century. Both courts, although staunchly Christian, were addicted to the most flagrant vanity and the most hopeless hypocrisy.[61]

Finally we must speak of another cluster of sermons the great metropolitan delivered clearly opposing divorce. At issue was the divorce of Grand Prince Basil and his subsequent remarriage. Daniel comes down just as strongly as John the Baptist had come down on Herod. The truly Orthodox could not waver on the matter.

In many ways Daniel's preaching was still thoroughly Scholastic. One finds the usual sermon outlines of the Latin Schoolmen, the usual concern with proof texts, authorities, and illustrations. But most important, one finds a prophetic insistence on the fundamentals of Orthodox faith and life. Obviously the tradition of Chrysostom is being asserted in Moscow in spite of all else. Even more, behind him we clearly discern the features of John the Baptist and, behind him, Elijah.

B. Dimitri of Rostov (1651-1709)

Born in the village of Makarov not far from Kiev, Dimitri of Rostov was able to study at the Brotherhood School. Having completed his studies, he decided to become a monk and entered a monastery. Being a good preacher, he was often invited to preach in various localities throughout Russia. As tradition has it, he was greatly admired by the czar, Peter the Great, and was frequently called to Moscow to preach in the Kremlin. The czar recognized his gifts and in time appointed him metropolitan of Rostov. In Rostov he established a school for the training of preachers. Dimitri, like Daniel of Moscow, had been strongly influenced by Scholasticism, especially in preaching style, but he, too, was devoted to recovering the traditions of Russian Orthodoxy. While this may not have been evident in the outward form of his sermons, it was very clear in the message he preached.[62]

Today Dimitri is regarded as a saint of the Russian Orthodox

61. Kataiev, *Geschichte der Predigt,* p. 85.
62. Kataiev, *Geschichte der Predigt,* pp. 125f.

Church. The published collection of his works contains almost one hundred sermons, but according to his biographer, these represent only his preaching ministry in Moscow. His sermons in Kiev and Rostov have not been preserved. The most remarkable thing about his sermons is that they are constantly filled with an amazing spirit of Christian love. According to Kataiev, his sermons tended to stress moral and devotional practices but not as rules or regulations the Christian was obligated to follow. Rather, he sought to bring his hearers to a true understanding of the spirit of Christian piety.[63] There is something universal about his sermons which makes them of value to Christians of any age. Especially his Sunday sermons gave careful attention to the exposition of the Scripture lesson for the day. He did a considerable amount of theological writing, and yet he rarely did doctrinal preaching. We regret especially that his sermons have not been available for this study because they are supposed to be a good example of the devotional emphasis in Russian Orthodox preaching. Typical of Russian preaching, the devotional element was much stronger than the doctrinal or the didactic.

C. Tikhon of Zadonsk (1724-83)

The figure of Peter the Great dominates the beginning of eighteenth-century Russian history.[64] His intention was to make Russia a modern nation like the nations of northern Europe. In his heavy-handed methods of trying to do this, he never seems to have sensed the deeper movements which had begun to manifest themselves in Russian Orthodoxy. The young theologians who had resisted attempts to foist on them Catholicism in the theological schools of Kiev or Lutheranism in Novgorod and Saint Petersburg were searching out the sources of Orthodoxy in the monasticism of Mount Athos. Nothing, of course, could be further removed from the ideology of Peter the Great than the spirituality of the Holy Mountain. Tikhon of Zadonsk was one of those who led the way to the recovery of Orthodox spirituality in Russia.

With a certain irony one notices that Tikhon was born the year be-

---

63. Kataiev, *Geschichte der Predigt,* p. 127.
64. On this historical background of the eighteenth-century Russian church, see Pospielovsky, *The Orthodox Church,* pp. 105-31, and James Cracraft, *The Church Reform of Peter the Great* (Palo Alto, Calif.: Stanford University Press, 1971).

fore Peter the Great died. He was a younger contemporary of Jonathan Edwards, John Wesley, and Count Nikolaus von Zinzendorf. He, too, was a pietist, but his pietism was distinctly Orthodox and clearly Russian.

Tikhon was born into the lowest class of Russian Orthodox ecclesiastical society. His father was a village sexton. The youngest of six children, he was brought up in poverty. His father died when he was very young, leaving the family destitute. The older brothers and sisters helped as best they could. Somehow he got a place in the theological academy of Novgorod. There he would have studied Old Church Slavonic, which was the liturgical language, somewhat different from the Russian that was spoken on the street. He would have studied Latin, the language of formal theology, and Greek. At the beginning of the eighteenth century Latin theology still dominated the theological academies, as much as one may have wanted to return to the Greek Fathers. Instruction in Greek was not always provided by the theological academy, yet Tikhon did learn it in seminary and was able to read several of the classics of patristic theology. Finally he was appointed professor of Greek. This, of course, gave him access to the Byzantine spiritual heritage.[65]

Tikhon longed to live a monastic life. He made his monastic profession hoping to spend his life in contemplation, but the hierarchy recognized his talents and quickly put him to work, first in the administration of several different academies, then as suffragan bishop of Novgorod, and finally in 1763 as bishop of Voronezh. Voronezh was at that time on the eastern frontier of Russia, in the country of the Don Cossacks, where Christianity had not penetrated the culture as deeply as elsewhere.

In Voronezh he set an extraordinary example of preaching. Not only did he himself preach with great passion and insight, but he established a program of badly needed catechetical preaching to edify the faith of the common people. On Sunday mornings, an hour before the liturgy began, the people would be called to the church by ringing bells. A seminarian would give the people simple instruction in the fundamentals of the Christian life. The instruction was primarily of a moral and devotional nature, rather than theological. It was intended to draw the people away from superstitious practices and instill in them the habits of the Christian life. It was to instruct them in methods of prayer, to encourage them to trust in God, and to instill in them the love of God. In

---

65. Nadejda Gorodetzky, *Saint Tikhon of Zadonsk: Inspirer of Dostoevsky* (Crestwood, N.Y.: St. Vladimir's Seminary Press, 1976), pp. 25-38.

short, the catechists were "to speak clearly and briefly on things pertaining to salvation."[66]

In addition to this catechetical instruction, our bishop cultivated the preaching of sermons on the appointed lesson of the day. On Saturdays the parish priests were called to the cathedral to hear the lessons for the following Sunday read and explained. Large parts of the diocese were too far away for the priest to attend, so Tikhon planned to send catechists out to the villages. To what extent his plans were realized we do not know. What is important is that he had a high respect for the catechetical ministry of the Church. For Tikhon, as for many eighteenth-century Christians, enlightenment and awakening went hand in hand.

Only over time did the population of this rather wild region of the East begin to realize that their bishop was a saint. The Cossacks too often regarded him as one more bureaucrat from Moscow. They thought he had nothing more in mind than centralizing power in the hand of the czars. They could not have been more mistaken. His preaching had a strong element of social criticism. He exercised a Christian critique on all levels of society. Not only that, but his simple life and generous alms were an implicit judgment on the luxurious lifestyle of the upper classes. He was living what he preached, and that began to get through to the Don Cossacks.

But even though he was beginning to see signs of success in his active ministry, Tikhon kept hearing the call to the wilderness. The monasticism of Mount Athos kept beckoning him. Like Elijah, he was being summoned to the desert. He pleaded with the ecclesiastical authorities to be allowed to retire from his office and live in solitude. His pleas were not acknowledged for a long time. In the meantime his health broke, and finally he was pensioned and allowed to retire to a monastery nearby. He finally settled at Zadonsk, a rather poor, run-down monastery in the same region. There he lived for the last fourteen years of his life, absorbed in prayer, his writing, and his generous charitable works. In the tradition of Orthodox monasticism, a monk like Tikhon was regarded as a holy man and many would seek him out for spiritual guidance. The aim of such a monk was to live in constant prayer — the prayer without ceasing. A true monk knows times of ecstasy, when he is a man among the angels and an angel among men. His simple word would be received with special reverence, and when he preached, it had enormous authority. The secret of the

---

66. Gorodetzky, *Saint Tikhon of Zadonsk,* p. 52.

great Russian preachers was that they, like Elijah, had gone forty days into the wilderness to Mount Sinai and there, weak from fasting, heard the still small voice. In its power alone, they went back into the world to proclaim the Word of God.

V. Philaret of Moscow (1782-1867)

Philaret, metropolitan of Moscow, was a leading light of the Russian church during his time.[67] He was distinguished not only as a preacher but also as a biblical scholar. He was largely responsible for translating the Bible into modern Russian, and produced the translation of the Gospel of John himself. The Russian church used the Old Church Slavonic translation, which by the beginning of the nineteenth century the common people had difficulty understanding. There was considerable opposition to this new translation, but Philaret's support is supposed to have done much to facilitate its acceptance.

This distinguished preacher was born Basil Drozdov in Kolomna, south of Moscow. His father was a parish priest and his mother the daughter of a parish priest. Here was a man who came from the heartland of Russia and was trained in traditional piety, a piety that was solid and profound. At seventeen he was placed in the seminary of the Holy Trinity, located in the famous monastery founded by Saint Sergius, some fifty miles from Moscow.

He graduated four years later and was appointed professor of Greek and Hebrew. Soon he was called upon to preach in addition to his other responsibilities. As a preacher, Philaret schooled himself in rhetoric, particularly that of the Byzantine Fathers. Very quickly through his preaching he won the favor of the metropolitan, Platon, who conferred upon him the title "Preacher to the Monastery of the Holy Trinity." This happened while he was yet a layman. In 1808 he took his monastic vows and

---

67. For biographical material on Philaret of Moscow, see Kallistos Timothy Ware, "Metropolitan Philaret of Moscow (1782-1867)," *Eastern Churches Review* 2 (spring 1968): 24-28, and Paul Kalinovitch, "Metropolitan Philaret of Moscow and His Significance for the Russian and Universal Church," trans. Seraphim Englehardt, *Orthodox Life* 46 (July/August 1996): 43-49; and 46 (September/October 1996): 41-49. See as well the biographical introduction to the edition of Philaret's sermons mentioned in n. 68. In addition, see Martin Jugie, "Philarete Drozdov," in *Dictionnaire de théologie catholique* xii (1933): col. 1378.

was given the name Philaret. Then being ordained a deacon, he was appointed professor at the seminary in Saint Petersburg. His patron, Metropolitan Platon, regretted his removal to Saint Petersburg, but there Philaret met new friends, including several friends at court. His renown as a preacher grew.

Coming to the attention of Prince Alexander Galatzine, minister of public instruction, Philaret found himself in the midst of an educational reform movement that was generously supported by Czar Alexander I. But these years were troubled by the Napoleonic Wars, and Alexander was preoccupied by international affairs. Great cultural changes were taking place, and for Philaret to be named rector of the theological academy of Saint Petersburg put him in the center of the discussion. At the height of the Napoleonic Wars Philaret was appointed a member of the Holy Synod of the Russian Orthodox Church. The Holy Synod was the governing body of the Russian church and presided over the religious affairs of the nation.

In 1821 he was made archbishop of Moscow, and in 1826 he was elevated to metropolitan of Moscow. He remained a member of the Holy Synod, which necessitated that he divide his time between Moscow and Saint Petersburg. In 1841 he was permitted to resign from the Holy Synod, which allowed him to live permanently in Moscow. For over forty years Philaret was the greatly respected metropolitan of Moscow.

The legacy of Philaret was important. He set an example as preacher. His study of Scripture was serious and sustained. His advocacy of the modern Russian translation was pivotal in opening up the Bible to the general population.

Philaret deserves to be recognized as a major preacher. He is not better known in the West because most of his sermons have to be read in Russian. But a collection of his sermons has been translated into English. Let us look at a few of these marvelous sermons.[68] We have selected several of his Easter sermons, because Easter is so central to Orthodox spirituality. One might say that the pietism of Orthodoxy is a resurrection pietism. It is the natural heir of the Byzantine theologians of much earlier centuries. As the Byzantine theologians understood it, the resurrection of Christ is the basis of enlightenment. In the eighteenth century, when the West was preoccupied with the Enlightenment, an enlightenment sup-

---

68. *Select Sermons by Philaret of Moscow* (London: J. Masters, 1873), hereafter Philaret, *Sermons*.

posedly based on reason alone, Philaret preached an enlightenment based on the resurrection of Christ and the inner working of the Holy Spirit.

The first Easter sermon in our collection is preached on the text "Then opened He their understanding" (Luke 24:27), taken from the story of Christ's appearance to two disciples on the road to Emmaus.

The sermon begins by setting the theological stage. With Adam's fall, our preacher reminds us, all men have passed through the gates of death. We are held in a prison, waiting until Christ comes and opens the gates unto life. We live in banishment, driven from the Garden of Eden.[69] The gates are locked against us. They can be opened only by the Key of David, the incarnate Christ. "The revealing action of this key is the Resurrection of Christ. By it the prison doors are opened, and its captives released; paradise is opened and receives the banished."[70] The banished now pass through the gates and enter paradise.

While at first we do not recognize that Philaret is speaking about epistemology just as much as does Immanuel Kant (1724-1804), Philaret's older East Prussian contemporary, we can hardly miss the obvious similarity of this prison to Plato's cave. Ever since Gregory of Nyssa, Orthodox theologians have seen the similarity. Philaret was speaking out of a very rich theological tradition.

Christ, the Key of David, unlocks our understanding. This is the meaning of our text, "Then opened He their understanding." The story of Jesus revealing himself to the two disciples on the road to Emmaus teaches us that it is the risen Christ who opens our hearts and minds. "The resurrection of Christ, and faith in that resurrection, opens the locked up human intellect unto the true understanding of sublime and saving truths."

As our preacher understands it, the apostles received enlightenment only after the resurrection. To be sure, they had listened to the teachings of Christ, but not only had they listened to him teach about the kingdom of God, they themselves had gone out and taught the good news of the kingdom while he was yet with them. "Their understanding was yet locked up. This is scarcely credible; and yet, according to the word of the Lord, it is true."[71] Our preacher tries to show how the understanding of the disciples changed in regard to their commission to preach repentance

69. Philaret, *Sermons*, pp. 68-69.
70. Philaret, *Sermons*, p. 69.
71. Philaret, *Sermons*, p. 70.

and remission of sins in his name among all nations, beginning at Jerusalem. Before the resurrection they understood the necessity and the duty of repentance. After Christ rose from the dead they came to realize its fruit and its reward. Before, the resurrection was merely at hand, but now they experienced it. They experienced its actual manifestation "unto themselves and in themselves."[72] Here we begin to see why Philaret, like Søren Kierkegaard (1813-55), is regarded as one of the forerunners of existentialism.

What we seem to have here is a sermon on the conversion experience. The two disciples on the road to Emmaus had a conversion experience, as Philaret interprets it. The risen Christ came to them and their eyes were opened. Up to that point the true Christ was veiled to them. Christ's divinity was veiled in his humanity.

Jesus' public preaching of the resurrection was often veiled. An exception would be his saying about Jonah in the belly of the fish being a type of the burial and resurrection of the Son of Man (Matt. 12:40). Another exception was his saying about going up to Jerusalem to suffer and to rise again on the third day (Luke 18:31-33). Even in this case Luke makes it clear the disciples understand none of these things (Luke 18:34). It was the same way after the transfiguration. Jesus charged the disciples not to speak of it until he should rise from the dead (Mark 9:9-10). It was only after the resurrection that the disciples could be enlightened.[73]

Our preacher now applies the experience of the apostles to his hearers. He admits that much of this will still be a hidden saying. What Philaret wants to do is open up the understanding of his congregation. And yet, this can be done only "by the light of the risen Christ, and by faith in Him."[74] Philaret is to be numbered as one of the great preachers of grace. To make his point he cites the text "By thy light we see light" (Ps. 36:9). This text makes it especially clear that the doctrine of grace is fundamental for a Christian understanding of epistemology.

One should underline at this point that for Philaret the emphasis is on the victory of the resurrection. It is a very objective victory that Christ won in opening the gates of death and passing through them into eternal life. It is a very objective victory over the devil and the forces of sin and death, over the infernal armies. It is a very objective victory, and yet the

72. Philaret, *Sermons*, p. 71.
73. Philaret, *Sermons*, p. 72.
74. Philaret, *Sermons*, p. 73.

victory of the resurrection enlightens our understanding as well. It is also a subjective experience. "To contemplate divine objects, we need a divine light and a condition of the mind in harmony therewith."[75]

Christ provides the divine light that opens man's understanding of the Word of God. Christ works through his Holy Spirit. It is therefore only after Christ is risen and ascended to the Father and has sent forth his Spirit that the Word of Christ and the work of Christ are to be understood. The Spirit is sent only after the resurrection when Christ's divinity is no longer veiled in his humanity. In this postresurrection condition he begins to part the clouds and darkness which encompassed humanity. In this way Christ raises us to a new, heavenly perception of both the Word of God and the work of God.[76] It is this of which the text speaks, "Then opened He their understanding, that they might understand."

Philaret is concerned to make clear that this spiritual light comes suddenly, and yet it also grows in degrees. This is one of those questions which the pietism of the eighteenth century often discussed. In the West as well the matter was often considered. The apostles grew in their experience. On the one hand Jesus breathed the Holy Spirit on the apostles in the Upper Room (John 20:22). It was as the light of day dawning. But after the resurrection, and particularly at Pentecost, it was a greater fullness of light, akin to the light of noonday.[77]

To develop his point our preacher contrasts what he has been saying with spiritual darkness. He speaks of the spiritual darkness of the Jews who reacted to the resurrection by claiming that the disciples came and stole the body of Jesus from the tomb.[78] With this Philaret launches into an apologetic for the historicity of the resurrection. How preposterous that the disciples should be able to steal the body from a tomb sealed by a large stone with armed guards standing watch. The rhetoric is magnificent. "But who is it that bears witness that the body was stolen? The very same sentinels. Do the very same sentinels who slept, and did not awake, bear witness of that which happened during their sleep, and which they did not hear?"

"Unbelief does not reason," Philaret concludes. "It scatters abroad throughout the world words which please it simply, because they savor of

75. Philaret, *Sermons*, p. 75.
76. Philaret, *Sermons*, p. 76.
77. Philaret, *Sermons*, p. 77.
78. Philaret, *Sermons*, p. 78.

unbelief."[79] One cannot help but be impressed with the rationality of this Russian Orthodox mystic. He makes the Western Enlightenment look a bit tawdry. Surely if officials had really suspected the disciples of such a theft, they would have arrested them. Yet these disciples stayed in Jerusalem for at least eight days longer, when they once again came together in the Upper Room. Philaret nails down his argument. His irony is inescapable. His reason is sharpened by his rhetoric. "Is it possible then that after all this, the fable of the stealing away of the body of Jesus by his Disciples could still be circulated among the Jews as something worthy of attention? Yes, possible indeed, for the mind hardened in unbelief, like a bird of night, sees only in the darkness of unbelief, loves only its own dreams, and flees from the light of truth which scorches its eyes."

The conclusion of the sermon makes clear that there is nothing naive about the preaching of this saintly metropolitan who has retired into the monastery. He is fully aware of the problems and fevers of the world he has left behind. He understands full well the unbelief of the eighteenth century. "Dread unbelief!" he warns his congregation. Imitate not the unbelief of Thomas, but rather "Let faith and love draw down upon you the light of life." Let not "sin and unbelief lock from ourselves that which hath been opened unto us by the Key of David."[80]

A second sermon on Easter emphasizes Easter joy. Philaret introduces this sermon with a rather striking figure of speech. Here is a preacher who does know something of rhetoric. Easter is the king of days, he tells us. Just as kings give security and peace to their subjects, so Easter gives security and peace to believers throughout all their other days, freeing us from the fear and bondage of death (cf. Heb. 2:15). As kings bring dignity to their people, so Easter gives our days dignity which otherwise would be of little interest or import.[81] Finally, as a king brings joy to a people by gaining victory over all that people's enemies, so Easter brings joy to all the year.

Easter has a power to cast its light back through history. We read in the Gospel of John that Abraham rejoiced to see the day of Christ (John 8:56). Philaret reminds us of how it took Abraham three days to get to Mount Moriah, the place of sacrifice. He ascended with his son Isaac and then received his son back alive. Hebrews assures us that this was a figure

---

79. Philaret, *Sermons,* p. 79.
80. Philaret, *Sermons,* p. 80.
81. Philaret, *Sermons,* p. 82.

of the resurrection of Christ (Heb. 11:19). The true meaning of the story is understood only once one knows the story of the resurrection of Christ.[82]

In the same way Easter shines its light into the future. We read in John, "But I will see you again, and your heart shall rejoice, and your joy no man taketh from you" (John 16:22). This is the text of the sermon. It tells us that the joy which cannot be taken away must continue forever. Our preacher wants to challenge us continually to increase our Easter joy year by year.

This may seem unrealistic to many. "To some it will perhaps appear, that I am 'asking a hard thing,' that it is too much on my part to desire, and demand that the light and joy of the resurrection of Christ should always increase in us, while their source is ever one and the same."[83] This may seem contrary to human experience and capacity, but when we look carefully at the sermon's text, we notice that Jesus promised the disciples joy when he would see them again. Philaret points out that it is not a matter of their seeing him but of his seeing them which brings them the joy that will never fade away. The source of our joy is when the Savior looks upon us in grace. To be sure, when God looks upon us in his omnipresence, his omnipotence, and his omniscience we are blessed, but when he looks upon us in his grace, then we know true happiness.

Philaret uses analogies with particular insight. Here he compares this spiritual truth to a natural phenomenon. The sun's light is a blessing to men even though they cannot gaze upon it directly. So Christ transforms our humanity even though we know him but faintly, unable to gaze on his glorified humanity.[84] The apostles' joy was not contingent on their seeing him, but on his seeing them.

One easily recognizes that here Philaret is taking up the doctrine of election so vigorously discussed in Western theology. The Greek Church has never gotten as involved in this subject as the Western Church, but here we find a fairly clear statement of it. It is Christ looking on us and not our seeing him with our physical eyes that is important. It is rather "that He should also look down upon us with the bright and luminous eye of grace, with the ardent and glowing look of love, with which He does not look upon all without distinction, but according to His choice."

82. Philaret, *Sermons,* p. 83.
83. Philaret, *Sermons,* p. 84.
84. Philaret, *Sermons,* p. 85.

Indeed, Philaret is very careful to qualify his statement by insisting, "Yet, such is His mercy that He excludes no one from this election who does not exclude himself."[85]

It may well be that at the beginning our joy is mixed with doubt and even fear. We read that when the women came to the tomb and found it empty, they departed "from the sepulcher with fear and great joy" (Matt. 28:8). The women had not seen the risen Jesus. He had not appeared to them, and yet they believed. While Thomas had not seen Jesus and insisted he could not believe until he could touch the risen Jesus, Jesus encountered him in the Upper Room. Thomas saw him and knelt down before him and confessed him to be his Lord and God. With this Jesus pronounced a blessing on those who while they have not seen him believe nevertheless (John 20:29). Philaret, heaping up his parallel passages, reminds us of the text from I Peter where the apostle commends believers for rejoicing in the one they have never seen (I Pet. 1:8-9). Faith does not depend on sight, and in the same way joy does not depend on sight.

Philaret's clinching argument is from Acts 1. He notices that it was on the day of the ascension, after Jesus had departed into the heavens and the apostles could no longer see him, that they "returned to Jerusalem with great joy."[86]

With this our preacher turns to application. The problem for most Christians is that we have a way of resisting the joy of Easter. "Do not set yourselves against divine joy, do not reject, do not stifle it; it will of itself continue; it will increase and develop of itself, until finally it will change into bliss."[87]

Let us look now at a third sermon for Easter. This sermon is based on the prologue to the Gospel of John, "In the beginning was the Word, and the Word was with God, and the Word was God" (John 1:1). It begins with a rhapsody which takes off from the theological affirmation which begins the Fourth Gospel. It reminds us of the festal sermons of Gregory of Nazianzus.

> The Church of Christ has this day announced unto us, in the most solemn manner, the greatest of all glad tidings: "In the beginning was the Word, and the Word was with God, and the Word was God," and so on. Now since we know it to be her custom to reveal to us in the Gos-

85. Philaret, *Sermons*, p. 86.
86. Philaret, *Sermons*, p. 89.
87. Philaret, *Sermons*, p. 90.

pel for the day the significance of the feast, and to afford unto us a subject for pious meditation and spiritual instruction; then what am I to
do now? Shall I strive to raise your souls from the earth, to carry you
above the sun and stars, to transport you into the heaven of heavens,
past the lower and higher orders of Angels unto the extreme heights of
creation, thither where time is not, for there eternity reigns intransient
and indivisible, where space is lost in infinity, and whence by a retro-
spective glance you may be convinced how little exaggerated, how feeble even, is the saying of the wise Solomon, "that the whole world is before God as a little grain in the balance, as a drop of the morning dew
that falleth down upon the earth" [Wis. 11:22]? Shall I require you "to
stand upon the watch" [Hab. 2:1] of contemplation with the holy
Evangelist John, higher even than the Prophet Habakkuk stood upon
his watch, for the prophet contemplated the Son of God manifested in
His incarnation, whereas the Evangelist contemplates Him in the mystery of His eternal birth? Shall I speak to you of the beginning in the
highest sense of that word, of the beginning of the beginning, in the
words of the Prophet-king, of that beginning which long precedes the
beginning of time, and of everything which is in time, of the beginning
from which all things in eternity itself commence, but which itself is
not limited by any further beginning or end? Shall I seek words in
which to bring as near as possible to your understanding that Word,
which not only the human, but even the angelic mind is inadequate to
comprehend, and the tongue to explain, — that Word which was once
for all uttered, and which is eternally uttered, or rather begotten, by the
One Eternal Father of the Word, and which Itself called forth the
whole creation, not nominally into hearing and understanding, but virtually into being and well-being? Shall I paraphrase in some plainer
words the sublime narrative of the great Divine, that in the beginning
was the Word, that is to say, that it had no beginning of such a nature
that you might imagine a time when it was not, but that it always was,
before all time and from all eternity, that it always is, and shall be, because it is everlasting: that the Word was with God, that is to say, that
"the only begotten Son, which is in the bosom of the Father," was not
disunited or separated from God the Father by His birth, but is
consubstantial with the Father and the Holy Ghost; that the Word was
God, that is, that the Name of God in the same true sense as it belongs
to God the Father, equally belongs to the Son of God, and also to the
Holy Ghost, yet so that in the Three Divine Hypostases there is but
One God in substance; that by this hypostatical Word of God, every-

426

thing, without exception, was created, — the earthly as well as the heavenly, the visible as well as the invisible; that in Him is life, or the source of the life of every living thing and more especially of every being living a spiritual and immortal life; that this fountain of life always was and is the light of men which shone upon them in Paradise, was not quite hidden from them on earth, was not extinguished by paganism, though not perceived nor accepted by it, which revealed itself in foreshadowings in the law of Moses, like a dawn in the Prophets, until at last the Word Incarnate revealed Himself as the sun and noon-day, in the full light of truth, with a quickening and miraculous power, and in His life and in His preaching, in His acts, and even in His free passion and death, and above all in His resurrection, "we beheld His glory, the glory as of the only begotten of the Father, full of grace and truth."[88]

We have not often quoted so long a passage from a sermon, but this passage is so majestic, so wondrous! Surely here is doxological preaching at its most exalted. It is the crowning example of the doxological preaching of the Orthodox tradition. It somehow typifies the worship of Orthodox Christianity.

Philaret specifically tells us here that it is the custom of the Church to announce in the reading and preaching of Scripture the subject for pious meditation and spiritual instruction.[89] Meditation is an important part of worship in the Orthodox Church, and the lessons and the sermon were supposed to inspire, direct, and support that meditation.[90] The prologue to the Gospel of John may more normally be thought of as appropriate to Christmas rather than Easter, and yet here it is read at Easter. Why is that? It is because nowhere in Scripture is the supreme mystery of the Christian faith put in more sublime words. Only John could put with such solemnity the gospel of the heavenly glory.

One might ask why for the Easter Gospel we do not have a solemn reading of the story of the resurrection. It is because ultimately we are called to meditate on the Truth itself. Especially at Easter we should penetrate to the deepest truth of the gospel, that is, the doctrine of the incarnation. For this we must lift up our hearts to a holy joy. We must leave behind vanity; we must leave behind the empty, noisy celebrations of this world. "Our festive joy ought to be spiritual, pure, peaceful and exalted;

88. Philaret, *Sermons,* pp. 92-95.
89. Philaret, *Sermons,* p. 92.
90. Philaret, *Sermons,* p. 96.

for such a joy not only does not hinder serious and deep meditation, but even renders a man more than usually capable of lofty contemplations."[91]

Having made the point that the joy of Easter should be a holy joy, he goes on to bring together a number of biblical examples of holy joy. As so many great preachers, Philaret is a master of the parallel text. He tells us of Elizabeth, John the Baptist still in her womb, along with Mary, the Christ child still in her womb, rejoicing together in ecstatic prophecy. Then there was the joy of Thomas, once he believed, who knelt in joy before the Savior and confessed his faith, "My Lord and my God."[92]

We must be careful, our preacher warns, that the spiritual exaltation of Easter not dissipate into mundane entertainments. Let not our "spiritual gladness soon . . . be swallowed up by sensual pleasures."[93] One senses the pastoral realism of our preacher at this point. He goes into some detail about how Easter joy can degenerate into earthly delights, but this tendency can and must be resisted. The apostle Paul is to be understood spiritually when he exhorts us, "Rejoice in the Lord alway: and again I say, Rejoice" (Phil. 4:4). The sermon as a whole is an example of spiritual joy. It is a hymn of praise to Christ who is the resurrection and the life.

In reading these three sermons one senses that those who can read the original Russian have a definite advantage. The sermons intimate so much more than they say. They call me back to that Easter in the late sixties which I celebrated in a Russian Orthodox church in Paris. I had taken a two-week seminar in Orthodox theology and worship sponsored by the World Council of Churches. The seminar had been planned in such a way that it was brought to a conclusion with the Russian celebration of Easter. Now, more than thirty years later, I read these sermons and it all flashes back to me so vividly. What a transporting joy that service of worship was! Preaching like this can be understood only in the context of the liturgy. While here in the West we might assume that preaching is one thing and worship is another, Philaret would never have dreamed of such a separation. For him, as for Orthodoxy generally, preaching is worship. It is nothing less than the contemplation of God's glory.

91. Philaret, *Sermons,* p. 97.
92. Philaret, *Sermons,* p. 98.
93. Philaret, *Sermons,* p. 99.

CHAPTER VIII

Scotland

In few countries over so long a time has the ministry of the Word been so highly prized and so conscientiously exercised as in Scotland. What is remarkable about Scottish preaching is the long continuity of a very distinct tradition beginning with John Knox and continuing through all the vicissitudes of a rather tumultuous history down to our own day. Scottish preaching has always had great variety, and yet it has consistently emphasized the exposition of Holy Scripture with a remarkable combination of high seriousness, evangelical passion, and solid learning.[1]

I. John Knox and His Lieutenants

There is no question but that John Knox is the prototype of Scottish preaching.[2] He was a faithful disciple of the Continental Reformers in his

1. For general works on the church history of Scotland and the role of preaching in Scotland, see William Garden Blaikie, *The Preachers of Scotland* (Edinburgh: T. & T. Clark, 1888); John H. S. Burleigh, *A Church History of Scotland* (London: Oxford University Press, 1960); Gordon Donaldson, *Faith of the Scots* (London: Batsford, 1990); Donaldson, *Scotland: James V to James VII*, rev. ed., Edinburgh History of Scotland, vol. 3 (Edinburgh: Oliver & Boyd, 1987); Donaldson, "Scotland," in *Oxford Encyclopedia of the Reformation*, 4 vols. (New York and Oxford: Oxford University Press, 1996), 4:28-31; Donaldson, *The Scottish Reformation* (reprint, Cambridge: University Press, 1979); James Kirk, *Patterns of Reform* (Edinburgh: T. & T. Clark, 1989); John Macleod, *Scottish Theology in Relation to Church History Since the Reformation* (Edinburgh and Carlisle, Pa.: Banner of Truth Trust, 1974); and David McRoberts, ed., *Essays on the Scottish Reformation* (Glasgow: Burns, 1962).

2. For general works on the life and ministry of John Knox, see Pierre Janton, *John*

concern for a learned exposition of Scripture in the pulpit. He was a popular preacher, and it was his popular preaching that won Scotland for the Reformation. Even more than Luther and Calvin, Knox relied on the preaching of the Word of God to reform the Church. His writings, unlike those of Luther and Calvin, were only of secondary importance; it was his preaching that was paramount. Still, as it happened, his sermons were not taken down and published, and so, alas, we cannot study them in any detail. The effect of his preaching left an indelible impression on Scotland. The picture of John Knox audaciously preaching the Reformation before Mary Queen of Scots is the primary icon of Scottish Protestantism. It is an icon often reproduced in a variety of colors, sometimes fiery and fanatic, sometimes noble and courageous. We wish we knew exactly what he said and how he said it, but we have to be content with this picture worth a thousand words.

A few things can be said about Knox's sermons and how he actually approached the ministry of the Word.[3] It would be a mistake to imagine that his preaching was nothing more than an extemporaneous, free-flowing demand for reform. One would expect that he would have followed the example of the Continental Reformers, especially Calvin, considering he spent several years in Geneva as Calvin's colleague, pastoring the congregation of English-speaking exiles who had taken refuge there during the reign of the infamous Bloody Mary. Reports which have come down to us would seem to support this.[4] His sermons consisted of a care-

---

Knox (ca. 1513-1572): L'homme and l'oeuvre (Paris: Didier, 1967); John Knox, *John Knox's History of the Reformation in Scotland,* ed. William Croft Dickinson (London: Thomas Nelson & Sons; New York: Philosophical Library, 1949); Thomas M'Crie, *Life of John Knox* (Philadelphia: Presbyterian Board of Publication, 1845); Lord Eustace Percy of Newcastle, *John Knox* (Richmond: John Knox, [1965]); Kevin Reed, "John Knox and the Reformation of Worship in the Scottish Reformation," in *Worship in the Presence of God,* ed. David Lachman and Frank J. Smith (Greenville, S.C.: Greenville Seminary Press, 1992); W. Stanford Reid, *Trumpeter of God* (New York: Scribner, 1974); Jasper Ridley, *John Knox* (New York: Oxford University Press, 1968); and Janny Wormald, "Knox, John," in *Oxford Encyclopedia of the Reformation,* 2:380-81.

3. The ingenious study of Janton, *John Knox (ca. 1513-1572),* has thrown considerable light on his preaching. In addition to the very small number of sermons which have come down to us in the usual form, Janton has been able to recover a number of other sermons from letters and other works of the Scottish Reformer. Especially helpful are Janton's three concluding chapters, pp. 403-505, which treat the style and pulpit eloquence of Knox.

4. Blaikie, *The Preachers of Scotland,* p. 64.

ful exposition of Scripture followed by a practical application. It was the applications that characterized his sermons. They were like trumpets that fired the congregation into action. He was a prophetic preacher in the tradition of Elijah, Amos, and Savonarola.

Pierre Janton has recovered the following sermons from Knox either in full or in part. (1) The sermon on Isaiah 26 he wrote out himself after preaching it. (2) The sermon on the Mass he preached in 1550 and revised and published in 1556. These are the only sermons Knox published in their complete form. We find synopses of two other sermons in Knox's *History of the Reformation:* (3) one preached at Saint Andrews in 1547, and (4) another at Stirling in 1558. (5) The *Exposition of Psalm Six* is written in the form of a sermon, even if it was written to his mother-in-law. Then there was (6) *A Godly Letter,* which gives us the material of several sermons he preached in England. It was the same with his (7) *Admonition,* which gives us the substance of a sermon preached in Westminster, his (8) *Epistle to the Inhabitants of New Castle and Berwick,* and his (9) *Brief Exhortation to England.*[5] These sermons, written up as letters, Janton very persuasively argues, reveal much about Knox's preaching.

As Janton presents it, there was a real distinction between the controversial and polemical sermons Knox preached at the beginning of his ministry and the more pastoral sermons he preached after the formal establishment of the Reformed Church of Scotland. His earlier sermons were clearly prophetic, to use the categories we have been using. After the establishment of Protestantism, however, he regularly preached systematic expository sermons from the pulpit of Saint Giles. Janton puts it this way, "The polemical sermons were succeeded by long biblical commentaries, book after book, chapter after chapter, which Knox must have inaugurated even before he took refuge in Geneva, at least on occasion, if we are to judge by his *Exposition of Psalm Six,* but which became the daily bread of the Scots after 1560."[6]

Knox and his predecessors Wishart and Hamilton had apparently learned their preaching from the Swiss Reformers even before Knox went to Geneva. The years in Geneva no doubt only confirmed the strong emphasis on expository preaching as well as the use of the *lectio continua.*

5. Janton, *John Knox (ca. 1513-1572),* pp. 409f.

6. "Au sermon de controverse succède le long commentaire biblique, livre après livre, chapitre après chapitre, que Knox avait dû inaugurer avant de se réfugier à Genève, à en juger par son *Exposition du Psaume Six,* mais qui devient le pain quotidien des Ecossais après 1560." Janton, *John Knox (ca. 1513-1572),* p. 408.

Knox would never have had the effect he had on Scotland had it not been for his lieutenants, of whom we mention only a few. There was John Craig, a former Dominican friar who although born in Scotland, was sent as a young man down to Italy by his order.[7] In the Dominican priory of Bologna he read Calvin's *Institutes* and was thereby won to the Reformation. Returning to Scotland about 1560, he became an active supporter of Knox. Eventually he became minister of the church at the Canongate and ministered to the young king, James VI, at Holyrood Palace.

James Lawson (1538-84) succeeded Knox as minister at Saint Giles.[8] He had been won to the Reformation by Knox. While no son of thunder, he was the man Knox wanted as his successor, and it was at his installation that Knox last appeared in the pulpit of Saint Giles. Lawson studied at Saint Andrews, in its flower at the time with George Buchanan, the brilliant Scottish humanist, thoroughly committed to the Reformation. There he drank deeply of the new biblical exegesis with its emphasis on the study of Greek and Hebrew. After that he taught at the University of Aberdeen. He was above all a scholar. A very gentle and studious man, he won a considerable reputation as a learned preacher. He is credited with having founded both the High School of Edinburgh and the University of Edinburgh. His opposition to episcopacy made it necessary for him to flee Scotland in 1584. Unfortunately none of his sermons have survived.

Robert Bruce (1559-1631) was minister at Saint Giles from 1587 to 1600.[9] He came from one of Scotland's noble families. His father had planned for him to study law and had envisioned that with his family connections he would have a brilliant career at court. After a profound experience of vocation, the young Bruce finally persuaded his father to let him study for the ministry. He studied at Saint Andrews in the days of George Buchanan and Andrew Melville, learning from them the new Renaissance exegesis with its emphasis on the original languages. It was his preaching on the Psalms that steeled the courage of Edinburgh when under the threat of the Spanish Armada.[10] His catechetical sermons on the

---

7. On John Craig see Blaikie, *The Preachers of Scotland*, pp. 69f.

8. On James Lawson see Blaikie, *The Preachers of Scotland*, pp. 71f.

9. On Robert Bruce see Blaikie, *The Preachers of Scotland*, pp. 77-84, and *Sermons by Robert Bruce*, reprinted from the original edition of MDXC and MDXCI with collections for his life by Robert Wodrow, now first printed from the manuscript in the library of the University of Glasgow, ed. William Cunningham (Edinburgh: Wodrow Society, 1843).

10. These sermons have been reprinted in *Sermons by Robert Bruce*, pp. 279-326.

doctrine of the Lord's Supper are to this day regarded as a classic statement of Reformed eucharistic doctrine.[11] Among other sermons which have been preserved is a series on the Epistle to the Hebrews.[12]

Bruce is crucial to our study, because he probably gives us the clearest picture of Scottish sixteenth-century preaching during the age of the Reformation. His six sermons on the illness and subsequent recovery of Hezekiah show us how the lieutenants of John Knox did their regular expository preaching.[13] The minister read the Scripture lesson from Isaiah 38, then introduced his sermon with a brief summary of what is to be learned from the passage. This passage of Scripture, according to Bruce, tells us about the godly King Hezekiah who fell ill of a most serious illness. "It pleased the Lord to exercise this godly king with this heavie tentation."[14] While it is true, Bruce continues, that many men suffer serious illness, the manner in which they behave when under distress is not always as exemplary as was Hezekiah's. Let us listen to this story, our preacher suggests, so that we ourselves may learn how to behave when we must endure serious trials. This is the same kind of simple, direct sort of introduction we find in the sermons of the Continental Reformers.

The sermon follows the text, phrase by phrase and verse by verse. Referring to Exodus 9:9, Bruce suggests that the nature of the disease is the same as that suffered by the Egyptians when they were plagued with boils.[15] Even at that, the illness that fell upon Hezekiah does not indicate divine reprobation. It is more like a kind of pastoral rebuke which God, on occasion, lays upon his chosen people. Bruce suggests that when we look at the previous chapter, Isaiah 37, we find a clear statement that often God rebukes us because we are his people, and this is not to be confused with God cutting us off from himself.[16] Here again Scripture is being interpreted by Scripture, a principle especially beloved by the preachers of the Continental Reformation. A bit further on Bruce uses

---

11. Robert Bruce, *The Mystery of the Lord's Supper,* ed. Thomas F. Torrance (Richmond: John Knox, 1958).

12. Apparently these sermons have never been published, but the manuscripts are preserved in the library of New College, Edinburgh.

13. These sermons first appeared as *Sermons Preached in the Kirk of Edinburgh, by M. Robert Bruce, Minister of Christs Evangel there: as they were received from his mouth* (Edinburgh: Robert Waldegrave, 1591), pp. 163-279, hereafter Bruce, *Sermons.*

14. Bruce, *Sermons,* p. 165.

15. Bruce, *Sermons,* p. 164.

16. Bruce, *Sermons,* p. 165.

parallel passages from the books of Kings and Chronicles to explain his text.[17] From this we see that Bruce knows how to use the new methods of exegesis developed by the Renaissance.

Our preacher rather early in the sermon draws a lesson from his text. He makes clear to his congregation that the present king is, praise God, in good health. The problem is that the kingdom is not in good spiritual health.[18] This should worry us, lest God's judgment suddenly come upon us to reprove us.[19]

Returning to his text, our preacher focuses on Hezekiah's prayer of repentance. This prayer has often been used as one of the classic prayers of the Bible to demonstrate how we should pray in times of special need. Indicating the privacy of his entreaty, the king turned his face to the wall.[20] He reminds God that he has been sincere in his attempts to obey God's Word and to do his duty as a king should. Now, this is not any kind of boasting, Bruce assures us; rather King Hezekiah is simply able to pray to God in good conscience.[21] Bruce goes through a number of examples of how the prayer warriors of Scripture prayed with a good conscience; David, Nehemiah, Daniel, and the apostle Paul all tell us the same thing.[22] Having a good conscience, he still prays to God with a repentant heart. Hezekiah's whole behavior is one of humility and prayer. He turns to God, the same God who laid these trials upon him, and asks that his life might be saved.

Bruce concludes the sermon with the prayer that the king might pray to God in humility to heal the spiritual sickness of the nation.[23] This certainly is a properly respectful sermon to be preached before the king, but it does remind the court that behind all they do is the judgment of God.

The second sermon begins with a review of the first.[24] Again this is typical of the expository sermons of the Continental Reformers. The passage before Bruce is a message of comfort. The Lord has heard Hezekiah's prayer and seen his tears and will grant him another fifteen years of life.

17. Bruce, *Sermons*, p. 166.
18. Bruce, *Sermons*, p. 171.
19. Bruce, *Sermons*, p. 172.
20. Bruce, *Sermons*, p. 173.
21. Bruce, *Sermons*, p. 174.
22. Bruce, *Sermons*, p. 175.
23. Bruce, *Sermons*, p. 178.
24. Bruce, *Sermons*, pp. 179-81.

Our preacher notes that a more detailed version of the story can be found in II Kings 20,[25] and at some length goes into the differences between the two passages. But one thing is clear — God answered the prayer of the king speedily.[26] Bruce reminds us that God is of his very nature merciful, and then launches into an application of the passage, stressing God's faithfulness to those who seek him in prayer. Returning to the passage before him, Bruce speaks of the extent of the blessings God promises to pour out on Hezekiah. Hezekiah had asked only that his health be restored and that the length of his days be increased, and God grants him this, but beyond this he also grants him blessings he had not asked for, that is, victory over the king of Assyria.[27] The point of all this, according to our preacher, is that when we seek our blessings from God, and God alone, then we are blessed beyond all that we ever imagined.[28] The sermon is completed by a doxology.

The third sermon takes up verses 7-11, having to do with the sign God gave Hezekiah that his prayers for long life would be granted. This marvelous sign was given the king to strengthen his faith. The interesting thing about these sermons is how transparent they are. Ostensibly one is talking about the king of Israel, and yet, what is said has much to do with the king of Scotland. Bruce seems to show considerable sympathy for the king of Scotland as he interprets this story of the life of King Hezekiah. Hezekiah was a good king, and yet he was subjected to one trial after another. Again and again his faith was tried, that he might be purified from the sins of this life and rest firmly on the mercy of God. Bruce constantly exhorts the king, and the court as well, to be true to God and approach him humbly in prayer. What one cannot help but notice is the underlying assumption that just as Isaiah had the prophetic responsibility to nurture the faith of King Hezekiah, so Robert Bruce, minister of the gospel, had the responsibility to nourish the faith of King James VI of Scotland.

The sixth and final sermon in the series takes up verses 16-22, and deals with the hymn of thanksgiving King Hezekiah offers for the blessings God has granted him. Our sixteenth-century Isaiah goes on at some length on the importance of giving thanks to God. Thanksgiving secures the gifts of God so that they are poured out to our blessing.[29]

25. Bruce, *Sermons*, p. 182.
26. Bruce, *Sermons*, p. 183.
27. Bruce, *Sermons*, pp. 190-91.
28. Bruce, *Sermons*, p. 192.
29. Bruce, *Sermons*, p. 256.

The different lines of the hymn are interpreted to make the point that God's favor to us is a matter of free grace.[30] It is not a matter of our virtue or our works. The thanksgiving hymn of Hezekiah rejoices in the mercy of God which has cast all our sins behind his back. Our preacher explains this figure of speech as a metaphor indicating that our sin is both forgiven and forgotten. It is not just venial sin which is forgiven while mortal sin remains. The text says all our sin is forgiven. The earthy language of Bruce at this point is vivid. He speaks of original sin as "this foul puddle, this rotten root, of the quhilk all these rotten fruits do flow."[31] Bruce preached in a strong Scots tongue. Scholar though he may have been, he knew how to speak to the common people as well as to the royal court.

Bruce's sermons are full of application. He comments on the text, going along from verse to verse, but as he goes he makes one application after another. Never does he seem terribly concerned to maintain a unity of theme, as though it were some kind of homiletical law, and yet everything seems to fall together by the time he gets through all six of his sermons on his chapter. The unity of these sermons, of course, comes from the Scriptures themselves; the preacher just recognizes it. This is a prophetic series of sermons. Bruce constantly has in mind the need for Scotland to establish a kingdom of peace and righteousness. No doubt those who first heard these sermons understood the political innuendoes well. And though they may not be too clear to us today, we can recognize a few of them at least. For example, God had saved Scotland from the Spanish Armada.[32] This was an act of God's grace and mercy, and it ought to inspire us to live to God's praise and glory. The turmoil, the political confusion, the rebellion which makes every lord king in his own estate, was an obvious criticism of the Scottish nobility that ignored the king's authority.[33] Bruce, a member of the Scottish nobility, could say such things very diplomatically. In fact, he had a responsibility to warn his people. Such behavior will only anger God so that we must constantly be visited by trials and tribulations. But we do not always have to live in a way that displeases God, Bruce insists; there is another way. Let us have recourse to God in all things. Let us crave the blessings of God

30. Bruce, *Sermons*, p. 264.
31. Bruce, *Sermons*, p. 265.
32. Bruce, *Sermons*, p. 272.
33. Bruce, *Sermons*, p. 273.

and live in justice and good order. When we begin with God, continue with God, and end with God, we can count on his blessing. The sermon concludes with a doxology.[34]

If the sermons of John Knox never seem to have been recorded, a good selection of the sermons of Robert Bruce was. His sermons no doubt reflect Knox's very closely in both prophetic fire and homiletical form. Bruce uses the Protestant plain style. His sermons are clear, popular, and vigorous. They were preached in the Scottish vernacular. They clearly carry through the tradition of Calvin, but perhaps even more, of Zwingli, whereas Hugh Latimer, the English Reformer most renowned as a preacher, continued in the Scholastic homiletical tradition. If indeed Bruce is the best guide to the preaching tradition of Knox, then it should be fairly clear that the Scottish Reformers adopted the homiletical methods of the Continental Reformers. In England the Scholastic homiletical tradition never did give way to the homiletical traditions of Continental Protestantism to anywhere near the same extent. Characteristic of Scottish preaching in the sixteenth century was its thoroughly Protestant approach to preaching.

Refusing to go along with James VI's scheme to impose episcopacy on the Church of Scotland, Bruce was banished from Edinburgh. He retired to the family estate at Kinnaird, and since the local church had no pastor, he supplied the pulpit until his death in 1631. This country church at Larbert became the goal of many pilgrims who went to hear him preach. It was there that Alexander Henderson, destined to become such an important leader of the church, was converted on hearing the preaching of the saintly confessor.

John Welch (also spelled Welsh) (1570-1622) was the son-in-law of John Knox.[35] Born in Dumfriesshire, he spent a rather wild youth as a borderer before finally repenting of his ways and returning home. Only after long entreaties did his father receive him back. He was sent off to study at the University of Edinburgh and in time became one of the most saintly ministers of Scotland. His ministry at Ayr had a tremendous effect. He preached daily, and yet he still gave great amounts of time to prayer and pastoral care. Ayr was considered a rather wild town at the

---

34. Bruce, *Sermons,* p. 276.

35. For biographical material see James Young, "Life of John Welsh," in *Dictionary of Scottish Church History and Theology,* ed. Nigel M. de S. Cameron (Edinburgh: T. & T. Clark, 1993), p. 861.

time, and his ministry brought considerable order and calm to the community. In 1605 Welch, too, was banished by James VI for opposing episcopacy. He found his way to Saumur in France, where he studied at the famous Huguenot academy, and having become sufficiently proficient in French, became pastor in the town of St. Jean d'Angely. A volume of thirty-five of his sermons preached at Ayr has come down to us.[36] They are simple, earnest expositions of Scripture which put a high value on the grace of God for our salvation, justification by faith, and the living of an honest and peaceful Christian life.[37]

David Fergusson (ca. 1523-98) of Dunfermline was another outstanding minister.[38] He served as moderator of the General Assembly several times. He came from a very simple background, and only with greatest effort was he able to attain an education. He was noted for his lively humor. When King James VI visited Dunfermline, he loved to converse with the minister because of his kindly wit and simple wisdom. Fergusson contributed considerably to the history of Scottish literature through his collection of folk proverbs. His greatest contribution, however, was in the moral reformation of the town of Dunfermline. Through his direct, simple, and earnest preaching he brought the whole community to an orderly, godly life which it had never known before.

In 1603 when James VI acceded to the throne of England, a great age in the Church of Scotland came to an end. The church had accepted the Reformation in 1560 over the opposition of Mary Queen of Scots; the church and its preachers brought the Reformation to its triumph. Unlike the Church of England, the Church of Scotland owed little of its reform to the Crown. This made for a very independent church, a church which would not tolerate state control. If James VI, the son of Mary Queen of Scots, could not understand why the Church of Scotland would not let him control it with his bishops, the Church of Scotland never could understand what right the king had to control the church. Neither James nor his successors ever gave up their attempt to control the Church of Scotland, and likewise Scotland never felt easy about any state attempt to keep the church under its control. But when James VI of Scotland became James I of England, the Scottish church found itself in a very

36. Blaikie, *The Preachers of Scotland,* p. 87.

37. John Welch, *Forty-eight Select Sermons* (Glasgow: Robert Chapman and Alexander Duncan, 1786).

38. On David Fergusson see Frank D. Bardgett, "Fergusson, David," in *Dictionary of Scottish Church History and Theology,* p. 318.

different place. The church more and more became the defender of Scottish rites and Scottish ways against the increasingly foreign rites of an absentee landlord. As long as James lived, he made moves to impose the English liturgy, English canon law, and episcopacy on Scotland. For James the compatibility of the doctrine of apostolic succession and the divine right of kings was obvious. In 1625 when Charles I succeeded his father, he increased efforts to subject Scotland to episcopacy and even to introduce the English prayer book. This continual attempt of the English state, even though presided over by a Scottish dynasty, to subvert the Reformed Church of Scotland called forth the age of the Covenanters. This age continued for almost a century.

II. The Covenanters

In 1638 the resistance of the Church of Scotland was formalized in the signing of the National League and Covenant in Greyfriars churchyard. This document vowed to uphold the Reformed Church in Scotland with its Calvinist theology and Presbyterian polity. It became the platform of a vigorous revival of Protestantism.

The age of the Covenanters produced a host of preachers. They are characterized not only by their prophetic courage but also by their concern to make clear the Word of God in the affairs of this world. They held dear the Reformed tradition of a learned ministry with a popular evangelical message. That this approach to preaching was maintained in the face of such strong political opposition through much of the century makes it even more remarkable. Let us look very briefly at only a few of the great preachers of the period.

Alexander Henderson (1583-1646) was one of the leading Scottish preachers of the early seventeenth century.[39] He received his education at the University of Saint Andrews. In 1610 he was appointed professor of rhetoric and philosophy. He was presented with a very lucrative parish by

---

39. Blaikie, *The Preachers of Scotland,* pp. 98-102; Thomas M'Crie, *The Life of Alexander Henderson, minister of Edinburgh, and one of the commissioners from the Church of Scotland to the assembly of divines at Westminster* (London: Thomas Nelson, 1847); James Pringle Thomson, *Alexander Henderson, the Covenanter* (Edinburgh: Oliphant, 1912); and J. D. Douglas, "Henderson, Alexander," in *Dictionary of Scottish Church History and Theology,* p. 397. For the historical background of Henderson's ministry, see W. Makey, *The Church of the Covenant, 1637-1651* (Edinburgh: John Donald, 1979).

one of the king's bishops, but his installation was resisted by his congregation. At first his ministry was unexceptional, but after he heard Robert Bruce in the country church of Larbert, he caught fire. Being called to Edinburgh, he was one of the leaders of the revival which culminated in the signing of the National League and Covenant.[40] In 1638 he was chosen as moderator of the General Assembly which restored Presbyterianism. Even Charles I recognized his excellence as a preacher on hearing him preach at Newcastle. Wherever he preached he drew large crowds and commanded rapt attention. Being one of the four Scottish commissioners to the Westminster Assembly in London, he preached before Parliament, and there, too, he won the admiration of his congregation by his learned, imaginative, and practical preaching.[41]

The collection of Henderson's sermons we have is one of the most important liturgical documents for seventeenth-century Reformed worship. It provides us with not only a collection of sermons, but also the text of the major prayers of the service. In addition, we find a sermon for a communion service along with the communion exhortations used at each table. The collection provides us with sermons and prayers for both the preparatory services and the thanksgiving services. In short, it gives us a good look at the worship of the Church of Scotland as men like Henderson understood it, before the *Directory for Worship* of the Westminster Assembly was adopted by the General Assembly of the Church of Scotland.[42]

As for the sermons, one notices that they are thoroughly expository in nature. Those for the communion season take up several verses from Hebrews 11, one of the most popular passages in the Bible on the nature of faith. It goes through the Old Testament heroes to demonstrate how salvation comes by faith. The editor of the sermons suggests they were part of a longer series on Hebrews 11 that was well advanced when the

40. On Henderson's part in the National League and Covenant, see Burleigh, *Church History of Scotland*, pp. 210-32.

41. See *Sermons, Prayers and Pulpit Addresses by Alexander Henderson,* ed. R. Thomson Martin (Edinburgh: John Maclaren, 1867), hereafter Henderson, *Sermons.*

42. One question needs to be raised about these services. How do they relate to the celebration of Easter? The Communion Sunday is given as 15 April, which could have been Easter. If it was, then these prayers and sermons were those of the first Easter following the signing of the National League and Covenant. The five Articles of Perth were the king's attempt to impose Anglican worship on the Church of Scotland. They demanded a celebration of Easter, yet these sermons pointedly do not celebrate Easter.

communion season approached.[43] The sermon for the Sunday morning before the celebration of the Communion takes up Hebrews 11:28, which has to do with Moses' celebration of the Passover by faith.[44] The sermon for Sunday afternoon takes up verse 29. In this sermon Henderson points to how the children of Israel were saved by faith as they followed God's Word and passed through the sea.[45] On Communion Sunday our Covenanter takes the next verse, 30, which tells of the faith of the children of Israel and how it brought down the walls of Jericho.[46] To be sure, it was a communion sermon. The sermon makes clear that saving faith is believing the promises of God. In the communion sermon the promises of God are proclaimed and then sealed in the sharing of the sacred meal. The covenantal theology of our preacher comes out clearly in these sermons. Here, once again, it is obvious that the sacramental theology of the Reformed church is covenantal theology.

The thanksgiving service on Sunday afternoon takes an entirely different passage of Scripture, Psalm 126.[47] This psalm is especially appropriate for a thanksgiving service. On the following Sunday, being the Lord's Day after Communion, our preacher returns to Hebrews 11 by preaching on verse 31, on the faith of Rahab.[48] Presumably Henderson finished the series on Hebrews 11 that spring, although these sermons have not come down to us. Apparently there was a fast day during May, and we find sermons for the occasion in the volume before us.

In the fall Henderson preached a series on Ephesians 6:10-18, the apostle's famous admonition to put on the whole armor of God. In these four sermons our preacher gives a classic running commentary on the text and at the same time explicit admonitions regarding the affairs of the nation. In 1638 Scotland was going through momentous events. King Charles I was determined to control the religious life of his kingdom, but the Church of Scotland was stoutly resisting him. Ephesians 6 gave our Covenanter every text he needed to steel the opposition toward the king. Our preacher challenged his congregation to stand against the wiles of the devil.[49] He assured them it was not against flesh and blood that they were

43. Henderson, *Sermons,* p. 124.
44. Henderson, *Sermons,* pp. 95-115.
45. Henderson, *Sermons,* pp. 124-34.
46. Henderson, *Sermons,* pp. 144-63.
47. Henderson, *Sermons,* p. 190.
48. Henderson, *Sermons,* p. 216.
49. Henderson, *Sermons,* pp. 447-71.

fighting, but against principalities, powers, and rulers of this present darkness.[50] These sermons were about as political as any that have ever been preached. It is hard not to hear echoes of John Knox in them. Preaching in Scotland has again and again been prophetic toward the state. The great tradition of Scottish preaching is that it constantly claimed the right to speak out on public affairs. But these sermons not only recall the tradition of John Knox, they also foreshadow the prophetic tradition in the preaching of Thomson, Chalmers, and Guthrie. Scotland has known its prophets and its sons of the prophets as well.

David Dickson (1583-1663) is surely to be reckoned among Scotland's prophets.[51] Although he was not the national leader Henderson was, he had an even greater reputation as a preacher. After studying and then teaching at the University of Glasgow, in 1618 Dickson was ordained minister at Irvine, a small city on the coast south of Glasgow. There he served for twenty-three years, although King James VI banished him from 1622 to 1623 because of his opposition to the Articles of Perth. While in Irvine he won a reputation as a solid, learned preacher of the Word. He regularly preached on market days, therefore affecting the whole countryside. People even moved to Irvine so they could hear his sermons on a regular basis. In time a significant revival swept the whole area, during which many conversions were experienced. In 1641 Dickson was called to the chair of divinity at the University of Glasgow, and then in 1650 to the same post in Edinburgh. In later years he produced commentaries on Matthew, Hebrews, and the Psalms.

Robert Blair (1593-1666) was another memorable preacher of the period.[52] Born to a prominent family, he sired a whole dynasty of prominent Scottish preachers. His great-grandson, Hugh Blair, whom we will treat later, was the most eminent of the line. Robert both studied and taught at the University of Glasgow. After a pastorate in Ulster he sailed for New England, but the ship turned back and he eventually became pastor at Ayr, where he won a reputation as an able preacher. The General Assembly of 1638 sent him to Saint Andrews, where his preaching was received with considerable enthusiasm.

Samuel Rutherford (1600-1661) is perhaps the best-known

50. Henderson, *Sermons*, pp. 472-88.
51. For biographical material see Louis Igou Hodges, "Dickson, David," in *Dictionary of Scottish Church History and Theology*, p. 243.
52. For biographical material see David C. Lachman, "Blair, Robert," in *Dictionary of Scottish Church History and Theology*, pp. 81-82.

preacher of seventeenth-century Scotland, not because of his sermons but because of the letters of spiritual counsel he wrote while in banishment.[53] In these letters he spoke of his religious experiences much as the English metaphysical poets of the early seventeenth century spoke of theirs. Born in Roxburyshire, Rutherford studied in Edinburgh, and after receiving his master of arts degree, was ordained to be minister of Anwoth, near Galloway. In 1636 his theological treatise on the doctrine of grace was published in Amsterdam. Because this work attacked Arminianism, which Charles I was trying to spread in both England and Scotland, one of the king's Scottish bishops had Rutherford banished and sentenced to confinement in Aberdeen. It was during this time of confinement that he wrote most of his famous letters. They show him to have had a profound sense of the presence of God; he has consequently often been heralded as Scotland's leading mystic. As a matter of fact, our preacher was very well read in medieval theology and was knowledgeable in the theological discussion of the day.

Rutherford may have been a mystic, but except for his time in confinement, he in no way lived a life of retirement. He was a most vigorously active pastor. He was present at the signing of the National League and Covenant. With the Church of Scotland now free to govern its own affairs without the intrusion of the civil government, he was made professor of divinity at the University of Saint Andrews and preacher at the Cathedral. He was one of the most ardent and learned defenders of the Presbyterian polity, publishing during the course of his life several works defining and defending the principles of Presbyterian church government. Rutherford envisioned a church polity free of the authoritarian political models of his day. He saw the church as a republic rather than a monarchy. In 1643 he was sent to London as one of the Scottish commissioners to the Westminster Assembly. While there his famous treatise on constitutional law appeared, *Lex Rex, a Dispute for the Just Prerogative of King and People*. This work was publicly burned on the restoration of the monarchy in 1660.

---

53. For more detailed information on Rutherford, see Sherman Isbell, "Rutherford, Samuel," in *Dictionary of Scottish Church History and Theology*, pp. 735-36; T. Murray, *Life of Samuel Rutherford* (Edinburgh, 1827); Marcus L. Loane, *Makers of Religious Freedom in the Seventeenth Century* (Grand Rapids: Wm. B. Eerdmans Publishing Co., [1961]); James Walker, *The Theology and Theologians of Scotland, 1560-1750* (reprint, Edinburgh: Knox Press, 1982); and Alexander Whyte, *Samuel Rutherford and some of his Correspondents* (Edinburgh and London: Oliphant Anderson and Ferrier, 1894).

By the time he got back to Saint Andrews he was a theologian of international reputation. He spent the next fourteen years preaching, teaching, and writing. But with the restoration of Charles II he was a marked man. He was deprived of all his offices, charged with high treason, and cited to appear before Parliament. At this point his health broke, and before he could come to trial he died with a supreme sense of having overcome the world.

Among those that have come down to us is his series of eight sermons on the parable of the prodigal son.[54] These were taken down by someone in the congregation, and more than likely come from a *lectio continua* series on the Gospel of Luke. They have a beautiful simplicity to them. The vigorous Scottish diction gives them a special charm. Rutherford uses some vivid similes and metaphors, but of even greater interest are his supporting texts and parallel passages. The biblical illustrations give the preacher's observations special authority. But what interests us most about these sermons is that they have not yet succumbed to the homiletical forms of Protestant scholasticism. One still senses the vigor of the classical Protestant expository sermon with its running commentary on the passage of Scripture which had been read. Two or three subjects may be taken up in the course of a sermon. Occasionally the analytical system of Protestant scholasticism may appear with its *text, doctrine,* and *use,* but the overall feel is one of a running commentary. Neither Aristotelian rhetoric nor Scholastic analysis dominates these sermons. While not dated, they were more than likely preached before the appearance of the *Westminster Directory for Worship,* which tended to take preaching more toward Protestant scholasticism than toward classical Reformed expository preaching. These sermons clearly continue the tradition of John Knox.

When Charles II returned from France in 1660, exactly a century after Knox had returned to Scotland from Geneva, he was as determined to rid Scotland of Presbyterianism as he was to rid England of Puritanism. Charles was a crypto-Catholic who, unbeknownst to his subjects, had promised Louis XIV to deliver both England and Scotland to Roman obedience. He saw Scottish Presbyterianism as Protestantism at its worst, and was even more severe in his opposition to the Presbyterians of Scotland than he was to the Puritans in England. Once more episcopacy was

---

54. *Quaint Sermons of Samuel Rutherford,* ed. Andrew A. Bonar (London: Hodder and Stoughton, 1885; photolithographic reprint, Morgan, Pa.: Soli Deo Gloria, 1999).

forced on the Church of Scotland, and those who refused to subscribe were ejected from their churches. For the next thirty years the spiritual leadership of Scotland was in the hands of field preachers who presided at clandestine conventicles. These were heroic times, to be sure, but even more importantly they were the times of tribulation which gave character to the Scottish soul. The preaching of men like Alexander Peden; John Welch, the great-grandson of John Knox; John Blackader; Donald Cargill; Richard Cameron; and James Renwick sustained the faith of the nation. The field preachers were hunted men. Many died as martyrs or ended their years in prison. The faithful who attended the conventicles were liable to heavy fines, and if they could not pay them, to debtor's prison. New Jersey was populated by penalized Presbyterians who had attended conventicles or supported field preachers. Yet with all this, sometimes the field preachers drew crowds of five or six thousand people.

As Principal Blaikie put it, people who risk so much to hear the preaching of the gospel want to hear the gospel, and that was what they heard at the conventicles. These sermons, understandably, have not come down to us, but the memory of them was burned deep into the Scottish soul. The heroic preaching of the Covenanters was worship at its most holy, and those who attended it knew that just to be there was to bear witness to the royal majesty of God. It was to glorify God and God alone as King of kings and Lord of lords.

With the Glorious Revolution of 1688, the suppression of the Reformed faith in Scotland came to an end. William of Orange, a solid supporter of Protestantism, acceded to the thrones of Scotland and England. Episcopacy was once again disestablished in Scotland, and in 1690 the General Assembly was reestablished. A new age in the religious heritage of Scotland began.

III. Thomas Boston (1676-1732)

It was with a generous warmth and compassion that Thomas Boston presented the gospel to the villagers of Ettrick. For more than twenty-five years Boston was a village preacher. He preached simple, solid sermons to the farming people of the Scottish border country. Typically Scottish, there is something both virile and lyrical about his preaching. To be sure, there was nothing important about the little town of Ettrick, nor was there anything important about Boston, yet somehow the twelve volumes

445

of his sermons which have come down to us have come to be regarded as classics of evangelical Protestantism.[55] Here are sermons which put the gospel in a simple, joyful, and straightforward way. They are both disciplined and profound, morally demanding and devotionally inspiring.

Thomas Boston was born in troubled times.[56] Charles II was trying to force Anglicanism on Scotland. This was part of his strategy to eventually make Scotland Catholic. The Covenanters, sworn to maintaining the principles of the Reformation, resisted the king and suffered vigorous persecution. While Boston was yet a boy, his father was imprisoned for supporting the Covenanter position. In those days the soul of Scotland was constantly nourished by field preachers and clandestine conventicles, and young Boston attended these services with his father. In fact, it was in listening to one of these Covenanter preachers that he himself experienced an awakening.

By the time he was ready to go off to school, King James VII of Scotland, better known as James II of England, had been chased from both his thrones and the Protestant succession was assured. William and Mary were ushering in a new age of toleration. In 1694 Boston received his first degree at Edinburgh, and with that he began the study of divinity. As the custom was at the time, he entered on an itinerant ministry after a few months. Both his studies and his preaching were under the care of the presbytery. This would normally go on for several years until the candidate would receive a call to a church.

In 1697 he was licensed by the presbytery, which indicated he had completed his ministerial training. He was ordained in 1699 to be minister of the church of Simprin, one of the smallest parishes in the border country. In 1707 he was called to Ettrick, a neighboring church. This was a larger church, but still a position which, viewed externally, hardly seemed important. Boston remained pastor of these two churches until the end of his life.

Boston may have been minister of two very insignificant churches,

---

55. *The Complete Works of the Late Rev. Thomas Boston, Ettrick,* ed. Samuel M'Millan, 12 vols. (London, 1853; reprint, Wheaton, Ill.: Richard Owen Roberts, Publishers, 1980), hereafter Boston, *Complete Works.*

56. For biographical material on Boston, see Philip Graham Ryken, *Thomas Boston as Preacher of the Four Fold State,* Rutherford Studies in Historical Theology (Edinburgh: Rutherford House, 1999). See esp. p. 2 n. 4, where Ryken discusses the sources available for information on Boston's life. Boston's *Memoirs,* found in *The Complete Works,* is still the best source, but see as well David C. Lachman, "Boston, Thomas," in *Dictionary of Scottish Church History and Theology,* pp. 88-89.

but he took a significant part in the theological discussions of the day. It was he who introduced *The Marrow of Modern Divinity* into the theological discussion of Scotland.[57] The book is supposed to have been written by an English Puritan of the previous century, but even to this day there seems to be no unanimity as to its author.[58] Boston found a copy in the home of one of his parishioners and, on reading it, decided it expressed his theology very well. He recommended it to some of his friends and finally published an edition of it.

What interested them about this book was that while maintaining a strong Calvinistic orthodoxy it insisted that Christ died for all, that he was the Lamb of God who takes away the sin of the world, that the grace of God was therefore open to all, and moreover that repentance and faith were to be preached to all. Not everyone was as favorably impressed with the book. Principal Hadow of Saint Andrews University was very negative about it, claiming it fostered an antinomian theology and a disregard of the moral requirements of the Christian life. The General Assembly of 1720 condemned the work, but Boston and his friends, without success, tried to reverse the decision in the following General Assembly.

Boston's preaching, at least what we have, is strongly weighted toward doctrine. This is not surprising because of the special interest which people had in his doctrinal teaching. As we have noticed several times in this volume, in the seventeenth century sermon preparation was the workbench of the theologian. A good number of the leading theologians of the day, particularly John Wesley, published their theology in the form of sermons. As Philip Ryken puts it, Boston was above all else a preacher.

Although usually thought of as an evangelistic preacher, Boston occupied himself with expository preaching as well. His midweek lecture was normally devoted to a *lectio continua* preaching of different books of the Bible, but each service, according to the *Westminster Directory for Worship,* was also to include the reading of the Bible. With this reading went an exposition of the chapter read. This frequently amounted to a sermon in itself. With preachers like Matthew Henry, a scrupulous follower of the *Westminster Directory,* it produced a double sermon. By principle the Scripture

---

57. On the Marrow Controversy see David C. Lachman, *The Marrow Controversy, 1718-1723: An Historical and Theological Analysis* (Edinburgh: Rutherford House, 1988). See further Burleigh, *Church History of Scotland,* pp. 288f.

58. David Lachman claims the author was Edward Fisher, a physician who reflected the popular Calvinism of sixteenth-century Cambridge Presbyterians. Cf. Lachman, *The Marrow Controversy,* p. 5.

reading followed the *lectio continua,* so each service had both a doctrinal sermon and an expository sermon.[59] Boston probably did his share of expository sermons, but these were not published. What was published were his highly evangelistic doctrinal sermons, because they were unusual. They presented the gospel in a most pastoral way.

A. The Evangelistic Function of Preaching

Early in his ministry Boston wrote an essay on homiletics, *Soliloquy on the Art of Man-Fishing.*[60] The title alone is intriguing. It immediately recalls that very popular Puritan essay on preaching, William Perkins's *The Art of Prophecying.* But it also ties the work to that whole genre of homiletical essays produced toward the later half of the Middle Ages, the *Ars predicandi.* Boston's title is unique in that it clearly concentrates attention on evangelistic preaching. The text on which he develops his soliloquy is the promise of Jesus that he will make those who follow him fishers of men. The essay's theme can be summed up in the author's prayer that his preaching flow from the love of God and the love of souls.

From the outset Boston makes it clear that it is Christ himself who makes a preacher a fisher of men. "I will make you fishers of men," Jesus promised; vocation is the key to the preaching ministry. Jesus called the disciples long ago to follow him, and so he calls ministers today to follow him. And just as it is the vocation of the Savior that makes them preachers, so it is the promise of the Savior that enables and qualifies them. "He makes them fishers as to success; that is, he makes them catch men to himself by the power of his Spirit accompanying the word they preach."[61] One cannot help but notice here, as elsewhere in Boston's work, the importance of the role of the Holy Spirit in his understanding of preaching.

---

59. Appreciation is expressed to my pastor, Dr. Philip Ryken, for pointing out a number of passages in Boston's autobiographical memoirs which indicate the expository nature of Boston's preaching at the midday lecture and that the regular Scripture lessons both followed the *lectio continua* and were accompanied by a detailed exposition. The references are as follows: Boston, *Complete Works,* 12:154, 158, 161f., 203, 209, 218, and 230.

60. Thomas Boston, *A Soliloquy on the Art of Man-Fishing,* ed. D. D. F. MacDonald (Paisley: Gardner, 1900). The edition used in this study is found in Boston, *Complete Works,* 5:5-43.

61. Boston, *Complete Works,* 5:7.

The great pietists, whether the Byzantine preacher Symeon the New Theologian or Jean Gerson, the French conciliarist, all put a strong emphasis on the work of the Holy Spirit, and here we notice for this Scottish Covenanter the same emphasis. There is a strong trinitarian dimension to his understanding of preaching as worship. The ministers of the Word are called by Christ and empowered by his Spirit. Preaching is at its very foundation a divine work.

Boston continues, "Have an eye to this power, when thou art preaching; and think not thou to convert men by the force of reason." At the beginning of the eighteenth century there were many who firmly believed that reason was sufficient to make good Christians of people. Even John Tillotson, the archbishop of Canterbury, who tried very hard to be completely orthodox, emphasized the converting power of reason. Christian thinkers all over Europe were quite confident in the reasonableness of Christianity. Boston was much more reserved. "Be concerned then, in the first place, O my soul, for the presence of God in ordinances, and for his power that will make a change among people." By "ordinances," as was the common parlance of the day, Boston meant the services of worship, the observance of the sacraments, the offering of public praise and prayer, and of course, the preaching of sermons. It was the presence of God in these ordinances that made them effective. "When thou writest a sermon, or dost ruminate on it, then say to God, Lord, this will be altogether weak without thy power accompanying it. O, power and life from God in ordinances is sweet. Seek it for thyself, and seek it for thy hearers."[62] Again, as we have noticed all through the history of preaching, the preaching of the Word is a means of God's kerygmatic presence.

Fishers of men is the biblical metaphor Boston has chosen as the theme of his essay on homiletics. He elaborates this metaphor with considerable detail. "Fishers catch with a net. So preachers have a net to catch souls with. This is the everlasting gospel, the word of peace and reconciliation." Fishermen spread wide the net so that it catches a wide variety of fish. There is nothing selective about a net. "God excludes none from the benefits of the Gospel that will not exclude themselves; it is free to all."

Another way Boston applies his biblical metaphor is by pointing out that "Fish are taken unexpectedly by the net, so are sinners by the Gospel."[63] He expands his point by telling how Zacchaeus had no thought of

---

62. Boston, *Complete Works,* 5:8.
63. Boston, *Complete Works,* 5:11.

being spiritually awakened when he climbed the sycamore tree or how Paul had no intention of encountering Jesus on the Damascus road when he set off on the devil's mission. The same was true for him, Boston reminds himself. Little did he think when he went to hear Henry Erskine preach that in that sermon God would begin to deal with him.

Again, when fish are at first taken by the net, they struggle against it. Our Covenanter remembers his reading of Augustine's *Confessions* and what it says about the ancient theologian struggling to get free from the net. To be sure, one can resist the power of the preached Word. In fact, that is all the natural man can do. Much more important, however, is the overcoming power of God, the *"gratia victrix,"* which comes and makes "the unwilling heart willing."[64]

Our Covenanter draws out a number of other points from his biblical metaphor and then sums up his introduction with a brief prayer: "Observe, . . . O my soul, that the way for me to be a fisher of men, is to follow Christ. What it is to follow thee, O Lord, show me; and, Lord, help me to do it."[65]

This soliloquy is a sort of sermon which our Covenanter preaches to himself. It is based on the text, "Follow me, and I will make you fishers of men" (Matt. 4:19 KJV). Having gotten through his introduction, he now divides up his text. He intends to draw two points from it: to show what following Christ supposes and implies, and wherein Christ is to be followed. Boston bases his ministry on the presupposition that the gifts of the Holy Spirit have been bestowed on him. He assumes that if he really has been sent to preach the gospel, the gifts will be granted as he needs them to fulfill his commission. He elaborates his reasons for this confidence at some length.[66] In the first place he recognizes within himself "a flame of love to Christ" (cf. Rom. 5:5). "My soul loves him above all; and I have felt my love to Christ. . . . Lord, put fuel to this fire. I have a love for his truths, that I know. . . . I find sometimes his word sweeter to me than honey from the comb. It comforts and supports me. I can not but love it; it stirs me up, and quickens my soul."[67]

Again our Covenanter finds confidence in his ministry because he senses within himself a flame of desire. As Jesus taught in the Beatitudes,

64. Boston, *Complete Works,* 5:12.
65. Boston, *Complete Works,* 5:14.
66. Boston, *Complete Works,* 5:14-16.
67. Boston, *Complete Works,* 5:16.

he hungers and thirsts after righteousness (Matt. 5:6). "I find in my heart some heat of zeal for God."[68] All of this encourages him, and yet there is something else: he is equally aware of his frailty. He has a sense of his own weakness, and his need of God's guidance and leading.[69] He well understands that it is in Christ and in the power of his Spirit that the work of God is accomplished. No minister in his own strength can fulfill what he has been sent to do. Every true minister of Christ is utterly dependent on the power of Christ.

To properly exercise the ministry of the Word "implies the renouncing of our own wisdom."[70] Boston reminds himself that the apostle Paul renounced the wisdom of words. He did not follow the rules of worldly wisdom, and our Covenanter wants to continue in the same path. One notices throughout the writings of Boston a consistent humility that is very attractive. He has both a true evangelical confidence and a true evangelical humility. One of the most beautiful things about this essay is the way he balances assurance with humility. He knows he is nothing without God, and yet he is sure God is with him.

His soliloquy now turns to what constitutes following Christ in the preaching ministry. First of all, we should follow Christ in coming at the bidding of the Father. Jesus did not take upon himself the work of preaching the gospel. He was specifically called to it. Boston recalls how Jesus quoted the words of Isaiah 61:1 (KJV), "The Spirit of the Lord GOD is upon me; because the LORD hath anointed me to preach good tidings unto the meek." Those who would be fishers and catchers of men must follow Christ in this. "He was sent by the Father to preach the Gospel; he went not to the work without the Father's commission."[71] Again we notice how Boston thinks this out in a fully trinitarian way. His ministry must be at the Father's call; it must follow the example of Christ and be anointed by the Spirit.

Having spoken of preaching as vocation, Boston addresses preaching as doxology. At this we perk up our ears. Here is the subject we have been asking about all along. Having been brought up on the *Westminster Shorter Catechism,* here is a preacher who had learned that man's chief end is to glorify God and enjoy him forever. If that is what life is really about,

68. Boston, *Complete Works,* 5:17.
69. Boston, *Complete Works,* 5:19.
70. Boston, *Complete Works,* 5:20.
71. Boston, *Complete Works,* 5:23.

then surely preaching is about that, too. Preaching should aim above all to glorify God. When our preaching takes this as its goal, then truly it is worship. Boston tells us that in his preaching Christ sought the glory of his Father. We, too, should seek nothing less. Then he drives his point home by quoting Paul's admonition: "Whatsoever ye do, do all to the glory of God" (I Cor. 10:31 KJV).

A particularly interesting point is that our Covenanter emphasizes that the motive of our worship is gratitude for God's grace to us. It is not a legal consideration which drives us to serve God's glory. It is not so much that we are commanded to worship God and are obedient to the commandment, as that the grace of God has been poured out upon us so generously that we can do nothing else but glorify him in return. We worship God because he has created us to worship him. It is a matter of stewardship — of using the talents he has given us. When we serve God's glory, we fulfill the purpose for which we were created.[72]

Boston has another point to make. Christ had the good of souls in his eye. He came to seek and to save that which was lost. He came to seek out the lost sheep of the house of Israel. Christ had a passion for the saving of souls; so should the preacher today. What is interesting here is that Boston aims at converting the covenant people. They are already God's covenant people, but they still need to be converted. Here is a dimension of Scottish spirituality which is not found everywhere. This was the point the evangelists on the American frontier in the nineteenth century often missed. Boston had a sense that he was evangelizing those who belonged to the covenant people.[73]

Christ was moved to preach because he was merciful. His motive for preaching was pure love. As he looked about Galilee, as he regarded the people of Jerusalem, he had compassion on the multitude because they were as sheep without a shepherd (cf. Matt. 9:36).[74] He pitied their condition. Christ wept over them because so many did not know the peace of God (cf. Luke 19:41-42).[75] Christ was grieved for the hardness of people's hearts.[76] Just as Christ was moved to preach by his love and compassion for a fallen humanity, so our motive for preaching should be nothing other than mercy.

72. Boston, *Complete Works*, 5:25.
73. Boston, *Complete Works*, 5:27-30.
74. Boston, *Complete Works*, 5:30.
75. Boston, *Complete Works*, 5:31.
76. Boston, *Complete Works*, 5:32.

This was the heart of Boston's evangelistic ministry: compassion for the men and women to whom he preached. This is no doubt why he put his emphasis on evangelistic preaching. Moreover, his compassion was particularly for covenant people. He preached to a Christian village. He knew everyone in the congregation, and it was the same congregation every Sunday. Only exceptionally was there a new face. Typically a Scottish preacher in the early eighteenth century had a very stable congregation. He was preaching to a baptized people. They were not strangers to Christ. What Boston yearned to do was lead his congregation to a deeper faith, to have them experience a spiritual awakening that would make them alive to the full blessings of God. In this our Scottish Covenanter was beginning to go along the same path of awakening and revival that so many sincere Christians of his day were beginning to discover.

There is yet another important theme in Boston's *Soliloquy*. Faithful preaching is both born of prayer and bears fruit in prayer. This theme recurs again and again down through the history of preaching. We noticed how important this was for the early Franciscan preachers. For Boston it was a matter of following the example of Christ. Christ was much in prayer, our preacher reminds us. We should be much in prayer as well. Much prayer should go into the making of a sermon. He urges himself to pray "that thy heart may be inflamed with zeal for the glory of the Master; that out of love to God, and love to souls, thy preaching may flow."[77]

This work contains much more of value that we have to pass over. We have given it more time than we usually give preaching manuals because it gives us an important insight into the attitudes typical of the age of awakening. It is a very subjective approach to the ministry of the Word. For some the eighteenth century was an age of enlightenment; for others it was an age of awakening. The two were very different in some respects and much the same in others. What Boston has shown us is the depth and the wisdom of the age of awakening.

B. The Doxological Purpose of Preaching

Thomas Boston gives us an amazingly straightforward statement of the doxological dimension of preaching. This is characteristic of the Scottish

77. Boston, *Complete Works,* 5:34.

school of preaching. The chief end of preaching, as of everything else in life, is to glorify God. What makes Boston of interest is that his emphasis in preaching is clearly evangelistic. His point is that evangelistic preaching has as its chief end God's glory. When the evangelist witnesses to Christ's eternal glory and everlasting authority, the triune God is truly worshiped. God's saving power is magnified in true evangelistic preaching, and that magnifying of God's saving power is truly worship.

This is brilliantly demonstrated in Boston's series of ten sermons, *The Names and Attributes of Christ*.[78] It is an exposition of Isaiah 9:6 (KJV), "For unto us a child is born, unto us a son is given: and the government shall be upon his shoulder: and his name shall be called Wonderful, Counsellor, The mighty God, The everlasting Father, The Prince of Peace." This is, to be sure, one of the traditional Christmas passages. It was apparently preached the Sunday before Christmas in 1725.[79] The second sermon in the series, the editor notes, was preached on the Sunday following Christmas, and the remainder presumably on the succeeding Sundays. A good Covenanter would not have observed Christmas Day. To do so would be to establish an ordinance which God had not commanded, as Boston makes clear in his sermon.[80] Be that as it may, Boston nevertheless chose a text most appropriate for the Christmas season.[81] Apparently he was not entirely convinced that the feast of Christmas should be ignored so long as it was not celebrated on the twenty-fifth of December, the date the pagans of Rome celebrated *sol invictus,* the victory of the sun god over the darkness of winter. The celebration of Christ's nativity on the Lord's Day before or the Lord's Day following, as was the custom in Geneva at the time of the Reformation, was another matter. Of even greater interest to us is the way this series of sermons, so clearly evangelistic in intention, is so thoroughly doxological.

The note of joyful proclamation is evident from the introduction of

---

78. Boston's most important series of sermons, *Human Nature in Its Fourfold State,* has recently received a very thorough study by Philip Ryken in *Thomas Boston as Preacher of the Four Fold State.* We will therefore study another series of sermons, namely, *The Names and Attributes of Christ.* This series is found in Boston, *Complete Works,* 10:178-266.

79. Boston, *Complete Works,* 10:178.

80. Boston, *Complete Works,* 10:185.

81. The Reformers knew that the feast of Christmas was not invented until the mid–fourth century and had pagan origins. This they learned from John Chrysostom, who said the feast was first celebrated ten years before he began his ministry in Antioch.

the first sermon. The words of our text, our preacher assures his congregation, bear a most joyful message.[82] They proclaim a great light which will bring illumination to the children of Israel, and not only to them but to people of all nations. This joy is compared to the joy of the harvest, when the farming community brings in its produce. It is compared with the victorious joy of the armies which conquered their foes and returned home with their bounty. The joy the prophet Isaiah announces is indeed even more profound. Our Savior, Jesus Christ, has done battle with our oppressor, the devil himself. Christ has won the victory and gives us freedom from sin. This is why the prophet calls us to rejoice.[83]

The body of the sermon unfolds the mystery of the incarnation. Jesus Christ is truly God and truly man. Our preacher makes the point that our Savior is our relative, bone of our bone, flesh of our flesh. "For unto us a child is born, for unto us a Son is given." The divine is one of us.[84] The second sermon in the series continues the same point.[85] The doctrine of the incarnation is a major theme of Christian teaching, and our preacher's treatment of it spills over into the following week's sermon. In fact, it is not really until the second sermon that our preacher gets down to his application. Seeing then that Christ has been born for us and is presented to us, let us, like aged Simeon, take him up in the arms of faith, "Knit with him, open your hearts to him." "Unto us a child is born, unto us a child is given," as the text tells us. Let us then receive him.[86]

The sermon is particularly rich in what it says about public worship. It speaks about how in the preaching of the Word Christ is presented to us.[87] We then worship Christ by taking him up in our arms. Our Covenanter quotes Psalm 24:9 (KJV), "Lift up your heads, O ye gates; even lift them up, ye everlasting doors; and the King of glory shall come in." Again Simeon is mentioned. Old Simeon, when Christ was presented in the temple, "took him up in his arms with full satisfaction of soul. . . . He is now in heaven as to his bodily presence; but he is presented to you in the gospel, embrace him by faith, with the heart believing on him for all his salvation."[88] The point is that preaching presents Christ to the

---

82. Boston, *Complete Works,* 10:178.
83. Boston, *Complete Works,* 10:179.
84. Boston, *Complete Works,* 10:180.
85. Boston, *Complete Works,* 10:184.
86. Boston, *Complete Works,* 10:185.
87. Boston, *Complete Works,* 10:186.
88. Boston, *Complete Works,* 10:188.

worshiping congregation to be received by faith. When Christ is so received, God is worshiped.

The conclusion of the sermon, although we only have it sketched out in the briefest words, appears to have been most eloquent. Our Covenanter exhorts his congregation: Worship him! So did the wise men of the East; he is the everlasting God, therefore he is to be adored. He is thy Lord, worship him therefore, thy Husband, thy King, thy God. Worship him with internal worship, consecrate your whole souls to him; and worship him with external worship. Present unto him gifts. So did the wise men. Make a gift of your hearts to him, of yourselves wholly! Glorify him in your souls, and bodies, your substance, your all.[89]

The fourth sermon continues in much the same vein. Here the emphasis is that Christ has been presented to us to guide us and rule over us. The government shall be upon his shoulder by divine appointment.[90] In this sermon Boston takes up the honor, power, and authority belonging to Jesus Christ.[91] The sermon is worship because it proclaims the authority of Christ. In fact, it not only proclaims Christ's authority, but urges it as well.[92]

The fifth sermon has come down to us in very brief form, but still the point is made that the names indicated in the text point to the unconquerable excellence of our Savior. It is none less than the Father who has given the Son these names. They all, various and unusual as they may be, indicate that the name of Jesus is above every name. As found in Philippians 2:9 (KJV), "God . . . hath highly exalted him, and given him a name which is above every name."[93]

The remaining sermons in the series unfold the meanings of the titles given the Messiah in the prophecy of Isaiah. We will not go through them one by one. The point has been sufficiently made: these sermons, evangelistic as they may be, and doctrinal as they may be, are nevertheless thoroughly doxological. In a day when the Enlightenment was very skeptical about basic Christian doctrine, Scottish preachers like Thomas Boston served God's glory by proclaiming the historic doctrines of the Church regarding Christ's person and work. The classical texts of Scrip-

---

89. The text as it has come down to us seems to have been very close to oral discourse. We have used a free hand in editing it.

90. Boston, *Complete Works,* 10:203.

91. Boston, *Complete Works,* 10:206.

92. Boston, *Complete Works,* 10:209.

93. Boston, *Complete Works,* 10:214.

ture are plain enough. These preachers expounded them and urged them, and this is true worship.

IV. John Willison (1680-1750)

As no one else, John Willison represents the historic tradition of Scottish Presbyterian piety.[94] During the first half of the eighteenth century he produced several manuals of devotion which were widely read in Scotland, England, Ireland, and America. His *Treatise concerning the Sanctification of the Lord's Day* appeared in 1712. This was followed in 1716 by *A Sacramental Directory, or Treatise concerning the Sanctification of a Communion Sabbath*. This was several times enlarged and republished. True to the spirit of the eighteenth century, these works speak of Christian worship in terms of the inclination of the heart. They are works not so much on liturgical rites as on liturgical piety. That, of course, was what interested the eighteenth century. In 1737, at the height of that sad controversy in which moderatism tried to suppress the Covenanter spirit, Willison published *The Afflicted Man's Companion* as well as his very influential *Example of Plain Catechising*. While the two works are very different in purpose, both nourished the religious aspirations of the people in a day when ecclesiastical politics seemed to be quenching the spirit.

A. The Piety of the Old School

In 1742 Willison published a series of twelve sermons, *The Balm of Gilead*, which addressed the spiritual maladies of the nation and prayed for a revival. One thing of particular interest to Americans about these sermons is that Willison had obviously read Jonathan Edwards's *A Faithful Narrative*, telling of the spiritual awakening in the Connecticut Valley. Willison greets this news with enthusiasm. Only a few months after the appearance of Willison's work, the famous Cambuslang revival began. *The Balm of Gilead* is a series of prophetic sermons in the truest sense of the word. They offer a vision of the awakening that was to come, not only in America and the British Isles, but even on the continent of Europe. Inspired by the min-

---

94. For biographical information on Willison, see John R. McIntosh, "Willison, John," in *Dictionary of Scottish Church History and Theology*, pp. 873-74.

istry of the French Huguenot prophets in the mountains of southern France, he spoke with amazing clairvoyance of the French Revolution, which would begin in 1792. As Willison saw it, both revolution and revival were on their way. For those who would not repent, there was judgment, but for those who would, there was joy everlasting.

Willison died a very happy man. His long pastorate in Dundee had produced a large and flourishing congregation. The time of refreshment for which he had prayed was showing signs of arrival. It would be easy to see in him a forerunner of pietism, or even to claim him as a Scottish version of eighteenth-century pietism. Such an evaluation, however, would really miss the mark. The piety he encouraged differed from the pietism of Spener, Francke, and Zinzendorf and Wesley and Whitefield in two important respects. First, he addressed himself to the Church rather than to the faithful few within the Church. He was concerned for the *ecclesia,* not the *ecclesiola in ecclesia.* Second, his piety was closely related to the regular worship of the Church. At the center of the sanctification of the Lord's Day is the coming together of the Church for public worship. The celebration of Communion is the high feast of the Christian life. It is there that the covenant vows are made and renewed; it is in publicly participating in the body and blood of Christ that the profession of faith is made. The subjective devotion and the objective celebration are kept closely together. But if not a pietist nor even a forerunner of pietism, Willison was certainly an ally of pietism. He saw it coming and greeted it with enthusiasm. Like Jonathan Edwards, Benjamin Colman, and perhaps, when all is said and done, Gilbert Tennent, Willison had always known a deep personal piety and was therefore one of the first to recognize the spiritual integrity of the pietists, whatever hesitations he may have had about certain aspects of the movement.

B. Sermon and Sacrament

In 1722 Willison published *Five Communion Sermons,* a series of sermons preached during a typical Scottish communion season.[95] Three preparatory sermons were preached during the week before the Sunday morning

95. The text of the sermons used for this study is found in *The Practical Works of the Rev. John Willison,* ed. W. M. Hetherington (London: Blackie and Son, [ca. 1830]), hereafter Willison, *Works.*

celebration and two thanksgiving sermons after, one on Sunday afternoon and the other on Monday. The preparatory and thanksgiving services were an important part of the Scottish communion celebration. Together they formed what was called a communion season. Frequently neighboring ministers were asked to assist in these seasons, preaching one or more of the sermons. The sermon preached at the actual celebration, called the "action sermon," is not included in this series of five sermons. We cannot for certain say why. Perhaps another minister preached it. Willison might, for instance, have been invited to preach at the preparatory and thanksgiving services in another congregation and the host pastor might have urged the publication of sermons afterward. We have a particularly fine "action sermon" from Willison published elsewhere, and we will study that along with the preparatory and thanksgiving sermons in order to get a full picture of how Scottish eucharistic preaching was handled in the eighteenth century.

The first of the three preparatory sermons is devoted to the subject of Christ's presence with his people. This is, to be sure, one of the classic themes of sacramental meditation. The text is Jeremiah 14:8, "O Hope of Israel, the Saviour thereof in time of trouble; why shouldest thou be as a stranger in the land, and as a way-faring man, that turneth aside to tarry for a night?"[96] Jeremiah 14 is a great passage on spiritual drought. After commenting on the meaning of the text and speaking of why God's presence was withdrawn from Israel in the days Jeremiah was sent to preach, Willison draws the following point: "That as it sometimes pleaseth God to withdraw himself, and behave as a stranger to his church and people; so there is nothing in the world that will be such matter of exercise and trouble to the serious seekers of God, as such a dispensation."[97] With great sensitivity he paints the somber tones of spiritual drought. He does it in such a way that we understand it is not only a problem for the people as a whole, but one we all face personally from time to time. "When the Lord denies access to his people in duty, and breaks off his wonted correspondence with them: they come to God's ordinary meeting-places with his people, ordinances both public and private, but he is not there; they seek him, but still they miss him, so as they are put to cry with that holy man, Job xxiii.3, 'O that I knew where I might find him.' O that I knew the place, the duty, the sermon, the sacrament, where I might find him; there I would go and seek

96. Willison, *Works,* p. 309.
97. Willison, *Works,* p. 310.

him; I try prayer, (saith the poor soul) but that brings not to him." Then Willison begins to explore why God sometimes withdraws his presence. His biblical illustrations are superb. When God's people "turn earthly-minded and prefer the delights of sense to precious Christ, then he withdraws, Isa. lvii. 17. They that have a strong relish for the flesh-pots of Egypt, are not fit to taste the hidden manna. When the Gadarenes come that length as to prefer their swine to Christ's presence, he turned his back, and departed from their coasts, Mat. viii.28."[98] One notices here how important the Song of Solomon and the nuptial imagery of both the Old and New Testaments are in Willison's sacramental sermons. In fact, one notices this again and again in the sacramental sermons of the Puritans in both England and New England during the seventeenth and eighteenth centuries.

In treating how the Christian is to deal with these seasons of spiritual drought, Willison tells us to lay hold of all the appointed means of finding God's presence. Like the spouse in the Song of Solomon who sought her beloved all about the city (Song of Sol. 3:2), "In all duties and ordinances, both private and public, our souls should follow hard after him, and pursue him closely, as it were, from one ordinance to another."[99] Our preacher tells us we are to seek God's presence in prayer by pleading with him as Jeremiah does in this text, and as he did in fact in his whole ministry. Jeremiah pleaded the glory of God's name and the helplessness of his people. He pleaded his former mercies and the sufficiency of his power. But what is particularly interesting here is that Willison tells us Jeremiah "pleads the outward symbols and pledges of his presence . . . his temple, his ark, and oracles." The outward forms of worship are obviously quite real for Willison. We find no radical subjectivism here. There is no suggestion that the objective forms of worship and subjective experience of piety are opposed to each other or are in some sort of dialectical relationship. If the objective and subjective are divided, God's people can never be satisfied. "If God be not in the ordinances, nothing can please them, not the most powerful sermons, though an angel were to preach them; nor the most lively communions, though a glorified apostle should come and dispense them. The absence of God is such a great want to them, that nothing in heaven or earth can fill up, but himself."[100] Yet these outward forms of worship can be and often are the means of experi-

98. Willison, *Works,* p. 311.
99. Willison, *Works,* p. 312.
100. Willison, *Works,* p. 313.

encing God's presence. That is what is expected in worship, and Willison preaches this sermon so that the congregation may indeed experience God's presence in the regular celebration of worship. There is no beauty in worship if Christ is absent, but if he is present then there is beauty. "It is his presence that puts a lustre on ordinances, and makes them shine, so as to confirm the friends of the gospel. . . . It is his presence that puts life in communions, and life in communicants, and causes them to prefer a day in 'God's courts to a thousand elsewhere.'"[101]

The second preparatory sermon takes up "the happiness of being in covenant with God." The text is Psalm 144:15, "Happy is that people whose God is the Lord."[102] Our preacher dwells at length on the meaning of this verse in the context of this psalm, and then draws out the point he wants to make. To be in covenant with God and to have God as our God is the greatest happiness we can have.[103] In developing this theme our preacher distinguishes between an outward and an inward participation in the covenant. "All members of a visible church are federally in covenant with God by their profession of Christ, and being baptized in his name." But just as in ancient Israel many belonged to the covenant people outwardly but not inwardly, so among Christians those who do not seek earnestly to make this an inward reality miss the blessings of the covenant relationship. For us to come into the bond of the covenant of grace is a matter of faith. It is by faith in Christ that we inwardly participate in the covenant. Genuinely to enter into the covenant relationship is to be thoroughly convinced of our sin and our inability to achieve our salvation by our own work; it is to accept Christ as our righteousness, our only mediator, surety, and peacemaker. It is to choose God, Father, Son, and Holy Spirit, as our God; it is to give ourselves to Christ and walk with him in newness of life as becomes his covenant people.[104] It is the inward apprehension of faith which makes the covenant relation our greatest happiness. Willison concludes his sermon by appealing to his congregation to go home and in their secret prayers renew their covenant vows and then return to the communion service and make their vows before men and angels.[105] As Willison envisions it, the objective formal act of public worship, if his congregation heeds his word, will be supported by an inner de-

101. Willison, *Works,* p. 315.
102. Willison, *Works,* p. 316.
103. Willison, *Works,* p. 317.
104. Willison, *Works,* p. 318.
105. Willison, *Works,* p. 323.

votion that will make it a great source of blessing. He obviously expects the outward forms to be filled with inward reality. There is no suggestion that only the inner experience is important.

When Willison preached at the communion service, he must have had a tremendous sense of being carried into the highest of heavenly realities. As it has often been said, the Reformed understand the Lord's Supper not so much in terms of the incarnation of Christ as in terms of his ascension. The text for the one "action sermon" we have from Willison is from the Song of Solomon: "He brought me to the banqueting house, and his banner over me was love."[106] One might be tempted to imagine that choosing a text from the Song of Solomon was some sort of eccentric quirk in the piety of one isolated Scottish minister if we did not have a number of Dutch Reformed, Presbyterian, and Congregational communion sermons from the seventeenth and eighteenth centuries which draw heavily on the nuptial imagery to celebrate the mutual relationship of love between Christ and his Church. Obviously the choice of a text like this makes it very clear that the Lord's Supper is not merely a memorial of Christ's death; it is even more a celebration of the wedding feast of the Lamb. The Protestant communion services of that day were not as funereal as some have claimed.

Introducing the sermon, Willison outlines the Christian interpretation of the Song of Solomon.[107] The whole book celebrates the communion between Christ and his Church. Christ is the Bridegroom. Given the Christian interpretation, our text tells us that Christ brings his bride into the wedding feast. He brings her under a banner: "Love is the banner that Christ lifts up and displays this day to engage you to come to him, and enlist yourselves under his banner. Love is that which leads to the banqueting-house."[108] The first point this dour Scotsman wants to make is the richness of the banquet prepared by Christ. Almost as a fanfare Willison brings to our attention a series of biblical images for spiritual food: the feast of the lady Sophia, the fountain of life and the wells of salvation, the hidden manna, the bread of angels, and the grapes of Canaan. Letting his imagination have its play, he suggests seven dishes which are served at this spiritual feast: pardon of sin sealed to the believer, the rare

106. Song of Sol. 2:4, as quoted by Willison, *Works*, p. 303.
107. Samuel Rutherford was another Scottish preacher who developed the nuptial imagery of the Song of Solomon. There was nothing obscure about this at all to Scottish piety.
108. Willison, *Works*, p. 303.

dish of peace and friendship with God, our adoption as heirs and joint heirs with Christ, peace of conscience, comforting and strengthening graces, Christ's presence and the sight of his countenance, and finally that most delectable of dishes, the pouring out of the Holy Spirit.[109] "Thus I have shown you some of the rich provision and noble entertainment prepared in this banquet before you: yea, you see it is not only rich provision, but there are choice rarities here, . . . plenty and variety, . . . food to nourish, strengthen, delight, and refresh the soul. Here is food suitable to all the faculties, light to the mind, peace to the conscience, satisfaction to the will, and food for all the affections. Here love may satisfy itself in clasping the Desire of all nations. Delight may here bathe itself in the rivers of pleasure."[110] The whole sermon is a lyrical proclamation of the love of Christ, and an expression of holy delight in the presence of God.

The Communion held on Sunday morning was followed by thanksgiving services on Sunday afternoon and on Monday. For the first of these services Willison chose the text, "Wherefore thou art no more a servant, but a son: and if a son, then an heir of God through Christ."[111] The sermon is a meditation on the benefits of our redemption. It stresses the filial nature of the new covenant, in which we are adopted as sons of God. Although only our Lord Jesus Christ is the son of God by eternal generation, all believers are sons by grace and adoption. At considerable length Willison draws out the imagery of the spiritual inheritance the Christian has in Christ.[112] Then, in a particularly apt metaphor, he speaks of the Holy Spirit as the executor of the will. The Holy Spirit invests believers in the bequeathed inheritance, "by renewing their souls, working faith in them, and disposing them to close with the Redeemer; planting all gracious habits in them, and thereby giving them the earnest and first fruits of the inheritance."[113] It is by this work of the Holy Spirit that we become heirs not only by adoption but by redemption as well. By the gracious work of the Holy Spirit dwelling within us we become godly by nature. He gives us power actually to become children of God in that we more and more come to share the divine nature.

Within the idea of thanksgiving is the idea that after receiving God's gracious gift of redemption the Christian must give himself to God in

109. Willison, *Works,* pp. 304-5.
110. Willison, *Works,* p. 305.
111. Gal. 4:7, as quoted by Willison, *Works,* p. 333.
112. Willison, *Works,* pp. 335-36.
113. Willison, *Works,* p. 337.

Christian service, in living according to God's will, and in deeds of love toward the neighbor. This is the subject of the second thanksgiving service. The sermon takes as its text Isaiah 40:29, "He giveth power to the faint; and to them that have no might, he increaseth strength."[114] The overall theme is to encourage the communicants to live the Christian life by assuring them of God's support. Only by God's strength can we do God's work, Willison tells us. Then, as so often in sermons of this period, he gives a set of "directions" for receiving such strength. The point, so essential to Reformed theology, that the Christian life is lived in thanksgiving for our salvation is clearly made.

The eucharistic preaching of John Willison is evangelistic. In Scotland it was at the communion seasons that the minister proclaimed the most central and essential matters of the gospel. This was because of the strong covenantal dimension of Reformed theology. It was in receiving the sacred bread and wine that the Christian accepted Christ and promised to live and die in his service. Scottish evangelistic preaching, following the practice of John Calvin's preparatory services during Holy Week in Geneva, was understood in terms of the celebration of the Lord's Supper. It was preparatory to the Lord's Supper, preparing the members of the covenant community to make the vows of faith at the covenant meal.

V. Robert Walker (1716-84)

Here is the preacher whose sermons were commended to me by the portrait of my great-great-grandfather, Robert Chambers. I mentioned this on the first page of the introduction to these volumes. It is a book of Walker's sermons that my lace-collared ancestor holds in his hand in that portrait. The edition he owned was no doubt the one published here in Trenton, New Jersey, in 1820. I always figured that my ancestor, in identifying this book in his hand, was letting his descendants know what he understood the true preaching of the gospel to be.

Robert Walker was born in Edinburgh, Scotland, in 1716, the son of the minister at the Canongate Church.[115] Today the ancient building is still standing on the Royal Mile down close to Holyrood Palace. Young

114. Willison, *Works,* p. 342.
115. For biographical information on Walker, see Macleod, *Scottish Theology,* pp. 207-8.

Robert would have been given all the cultural and educational advantages of the city of Edinburgh, which in the eighteenth century was the Athens of the North, the Weimar of Great Britain, the city of David Hume, the philosopher; Adam Smith, the economist; and Robert Burns, the poet. The Enlightenment was at high tide in the Scottish capital, and Edinburgh was a center of mathematics, medicine, science, and the literary arts. Walker was privileged to study at the University of Edinburgh, which in the eighteenth century was one of Europe's centers of learning.

After completing his university training, the young theologian was sent out to the southwest of Scotland to preach under the guidance of the local pastors. This was the way things were done in Scotland at the time. Internship was an important part of the theological education, a sort of ministerial apprenticeship. In 1737 Walker was licensed to preach by the Presbytery of Kirkcudbright. A year later he was ordained minister of Straiton by the Presbytery of Ayr. Eight years after that he was called to the second charge at South Leith, a suburb of Edinburgh. Finally he was called to be one of the ministers of Edinburgh itself. There he exercised a collegiate ministry at the High Church, at the other end of the Royal Mile from where his father had served. Here Walker was a colleague of the Reverend Hugh Blair, the famous preacher of moderatism. One gets the impression that the two preachers were thought of as balancing each other. Blair's ministry was to the enlightened literati, Walker's to those of more orthodox temper. For almost thirty years he served in that pulpit made sacred by the memory of John Knox.

A. Providence

If one were to choose a single sermon as an example of the preaching of Scottish Protestantism, Walker's sermon on the text "I will never leave thee, nor forsake thee" (Heb. 13:5 KJV) might very well serve the purpose.[116] It is an exemplary sermon. First, it affirms the doctrine of providence, and this in a day when the doctrine was under heavy attack from the Enlightenment. Second, it is an example of Protestant plain style at its

---

116. Robert Walker, *Sermons on Practical Subjects, Late one of the Ministers of the High Church of Edinburgh; to which is prefixed a character of the Author by Hugh Blair, D.D.*, 5th ed., 3 vols. (Edinburgh: C. Elliot and G. Robinson, 1785). The sermon in question is found in 3:332-56.

clearest and most sober. The sermon outline is simple and straightforward. Third, one notices a solid structure of parallel passages and biblical illustrations. Scripture is used to throw light on Scripture. The practical application of the sermon is evident. Finally and most importantly, the sermon conveys a strong sense of grace; it is gospel through and through. Let us look at the sermon in more detail.

True to Protestant plain style, the introduction to the sermon is brief and simple. There is no attempt to grab the ears of the congregation. The introduction simply tells us what the sermon intends to treat. "This comfortable declaration or promise is introduced by the Apostle, to enforce the duty of contentment, to which he had exhorted the Hebrews in the previous part of the verse. Nothing can be more unbecoming to a child of God, than dissatisfaction with his present condition, or anxiety about his future provision in this world."[117] The vocabulary here seems a bit odd, but more than two hundred years have passed since this sermon was preached. A generation ago Marxists would have been waving red flags at this opening sentence, but in the middle of the eighteenth century these words would have fallen on more devout ears. One thing we notice is that already in the introduction our preacher appeals to a parallel passage. He takes up the words of Jesus from the Sermon on the Mount: "Take no thought, saying, What shall we eat? or what shall we drink? or wherewithall shall we be clothed? For after all these things do the Gentiles seek, and your heavenly Father knoweth that ye have need of all these things" (Matt. 6:31-32).[118] Walker comments: "God will support and maintain his own people, as long as he has any service for them in this world. He knows all their wants; and as his goodness constantly inclines him, so his power doth at all times enable him, to bestow every needful supply in its season." Then with a deft twist of classical rhetoric he asks, "And can our interest be lodged in better hands?"

Following this brief introduction our preacher divides his text into three points.[119] First, he intends to show the importance of this gracious promise. Second, he wants to indicate who may claim this promise. Third, he will try to give solid grounds for assurance that this promise will be fulfilled. Dividing the text up like this at the beginning of the sermon was very popular in eighteenth- and nineteenth-century sermons,

117. Walker, *Sermons,* 3:332.
118. Here, as throughout this study, Scripture is quoted as the preacher quotes it.
119. Walker, *Sermons,* 3:334.

and of course the practice has a long lineage, going back to the High Middle Ages.

In his first point, the gracious import of this promise, Walker tells us that God's faithfulness to his word is of the essence of his nature. His promise never to leave us or forsake us wells up naturally from his divine constancy. God is consistent, never changing, and therefore is dependable.[120] There is nothing else on which we can depend. With any creature, as distinguished from the Creator, it is quite different. "How often do we see riches make unto themselves wings, and flee away."[121] A storm at sea or a fire on land will in a few hours consume the labor of many years. Even princes, when they least dreamed of it, have been forced to exchange their palaces for a prison; they have learned by sad experience "that crowns are but tottering emblems of power." "The fairest character may be sullied with the breath of calumny; our friends may prove false, or abandon us."[122] Here Walker's congregation must have admired their preacher's masterful use of words. We seem to have here a very sophisticated use of classical rhetoric, carefully shaped by Protestant plain style.

Walker has given us an eloquent disquisition on the vanity of life, but it is far more. It is a very theological perception of the nature of divine providence. He tells us that frequently the children of God are exercised by the severest trials here on earth. "This mutability of the creatures is not the effect of *chance,* but of *design.*"[123] He obviously has a strong doctrine of providence. That goes along with Scottish Protestantism. Even at the zenith of the Enlightenment our preacher insists that the lives of Christians are guided not by mere chance but by the loving hand of the Father. Going further into the subject, Walker assures us that the Father's design is to keep his children dependent on him alone, and while we are here on earth, to inspire our desires for communion with him and the joys of his kingdom. It is often the case that his dearest children are enticed by other desires. But "When his own children are in danger of being ensnared by them, he pulls them, as it were, with violence, out of their hands." God is ever watchful, constantly defending and protecting his children from their desires and temptations. "He will not suffer them to continue long in so dangerous an error; and he sends the rod to undeceive them: he fre-

120. Walker, *Sermons,* 3:335.
121. Walker, *Sermons,* 3:336.
122. Walker, *Sermons,* 3:337.
123. Walker, *Sermons,* 3:338, emphasis Walker's.

quently repeats the stroke, to remind them that they are only sojourners in a strange land, and to quicken their desires for their Father's house above . . . where alone they shall have fulness of joy, and pleasures forever more."

Our preacher points out that God's presence with his people is sufficient ground of consolation in every state and condition of life.[124] Again he calls on a rich anthology of parallel passages to illustrate his point. He quotes the Twenty-third Psalm at length to make the point that God's presence is the highest joy: "Though I walk through the valley of the shadow of death, . . . thou art with me" (Ps. 23:4). Then he alludes to a passage from the prophet Habakkuk: "Although the fig-tree shall not blossom, neither shall there be fruit in the vines, the labour of the olive tree shall fail, and the fields shall yield no meat, the flock shall be cut off from the fold, and there shall be no herd in the stalls; yet will I rejoice in the Lord, I will joy in the God of my salvation" (Hab. 3:17-18). Walker turns to the book of Daniel and reminds us of the story of Nebuchadnezzar and the three young men in the fiery furnace, and how when the king looked into the furnace he saw not only Shadrach, Meshach, and Abednego but also a fourth presence, one like the Son of God. Even in the fierce tribulations of the Babylonian captivity God was with his people as they walked through the fire.[125] "All the saints who have God really present with them, although they cannot see him with their bodily eyes, have equal cause to rejoice in the midst of tribulation." This long anthology of parallel passages is concluded with the observation that the presence of God is the highest joy that can be afforded. The loss of smaller comforts and joys may cause us distress, but ultimately God's presence compensates for all else. He sums it up in a superb maxim: "Who would mourn the loss of a taper, who enjoys the light of the sun?"[126]

The second matter in this three-point sermon is the identity of those to whom the promise of God's presence is made. It is addressed to those who believe in Christ Jesus, "for this is the order which God hath established. He first gives us his Son; and when this 'unspeakable gift' is thankfully received, then, together 'with him, he freely gives us all other things.'"[127] But it also needs to be said that we never come into a good relation with God on the basis of certain moral qualifications. Here, of

124. Walker, *Sermons*, 3:339.
125. Walker, *Sermons*, 3:340.
126. Walker, *Sermons*, 3:341.
127. Walker, *Sermons*, 3:345.

course, Walker is following along carefully with the classic teachings of the Protestant Reformation. Its consistent Protestantism has always been the backbone of Scottish religion, and here this comes through loud and clear. The just shall live by faith; that, and that alone, is the basis of every theological virtue and every charitable work.

But Walker opens this theme up even more. All the blessings promised in the gospel have been purchased by Christ with the price of his blood. Again we see Walker following along with the classical Protestant teaching of the atoning power of Christ's sacrifice on the cross. The Enlightenment may have faded out the colors of Protestant doctrine elsewhere, but when Robert Walker preached in the High Kirk of Edinburgh, the colors are still fresh and vibrant. It is Christ, and Christ alone, who is our Savior. "Every good . . . gift . . . must be conveyed . . . through his hands." Ever pounding in his message with a sharp text, our preacher reminds us, "Christ himself says (Matth. xi.27), 'All things are delivered unto me of my Father.'"[128] To this he adds several more texts to make the same point. Finally he sums up his second point by telling us that if we depend on Christ alone as our Savior, we can claim Christ's promise that he will never leave us or forsake us.[129]

For the final point of this sermon our preacher wants to assure us that God is faithful to his promises. The first consideration that should give us confidence in the promise of God's constant presence is to remember who made the promise. Again we have a collage of Scripture verses to make clear that divine authority is the basis of these words. "'He is not a man, that he should lie, nor the son of man, that he should repent.' [Num. 23:19] These are the words of God himself, who is incapable of deceit." "'The mountains shall depart, and the hills be removed; but my kindness shall not depart from thee, neither shall the covenant of my peace be removed, saith the Lord that hath mercy upon thee.' [Isa. 54:10] And is not the word, the promise of such a God, a sufficient ground of trust?"[130] Indeed, Walker continues, he not only has said it, he has sworn it as well. He has confirmed it by an oath, the Scriptures tell us. Can our souls desire a better security? What can establish our faith if this does not?

But there is another consideration: "Believers in Christ Jesus are the children of God, adopted into his family, and beautified with his image:

128. Walker, *Sermons*, 3:346.
129. Walker, *Sermons*, 3:348.
130. Walker, *Sermons*, 3:349.

and this is another pledge of his gracious promise; for surely he will never abandon his own offspring."[131]

Yet another consideration is the heavenly intercession of Christ at the right hand of the Father. This is especially important for the text of this sermon because it is in Hebrews that we find a very full exposition of this teaching. "The constant intercession of our glorious High Priest effectually secures the accomplishment of this promise." Jesus has poured out his Holy Spirit to dwell among his people and accomplish his purposes among them.[132] This is clearly taught in John 16, and then in chapter 17 we find an example of Jesus exercising, while still on earth, his high priestly ministry.

The conclusion of the sermon is typical for its day. It is devoted to making an application of the teaching developed in the sermon. In fact, Walker introduces his conclusion with a comment to this effect: "I shall now conclude this discourse with a short practical improvement." Our preacher uses the word "improvement," a word which sounds a bit quaint to us. In those days it was a synonym for "application." Normally in the eighteenth century a sermon was concluded not so much with a peroration as with an application. With the "experiential" concerns of the age, this is naturally expected. It is a twofold application. First, our preacher addresses himself "to those who are yet in a state of alienation from God." He urges such people in his congregation to put their faith in God. He warns them against the foolishness of pursuing vanity, and yet promises them the blessing of God if they will but turn to him.[133]

Second, our preacher addresses those happy souls who are in a state of friendship with God. Here he goes on at considerably more length. One would imagine he does this because he figured most of his congregation sincerely believed in Christ and were therefore devotedly committed to following in his ways. To such of those before him he hopes this promise of God's presence would "excite and encourage you to steadfastness in the ways of religion. 'For if God be with you, who can be against you?' [Rom. 8:31] . . . Your help is laid in One who is mighty to save, and who is no less willing than able to support you under all your trials."[134]

This is not the sort of sermon that brings men, women, and chil-

---

131. Walker, *Sermons,* 3:350.
132. Walker, *Sermons,* 3:351.
133. Walker, *Sermons,* 3:353-54.
134. Walker, *Sermons,* 3:354-55.

dren streaming down the aisles to the anxious bench, but it is evangelism. It is very profound evangelism filled with plenty of gospel and generously offered to all. It has a special devotional temper to it — a sort of simple dignity that well understands that the conversion of our souls comes about not through the power of our oratory but by the inner working of God's Spirit.

B. The Gospel and the Supper

One of the most attractive features of Scottish Protestantism is the way it joins evangelism to the celebration of the Lord's Supper. Repeatedly we find that the most powerful presentations of the gospel are made in the context of the observance of the sacrament of Communion. In the worship of the Reformed churches that was where one made and renewed the covenant vows of faith which brought one into communion with Christ and his Church. Formally it was through Communion that one joined the Church, but more subjectively, participation in the Sacrament was indeed communion, that is, communion with God. Evangelism, then, at its most profound, was the invitation to come and sit at the Lord's Table and receive Christ by sharing in the sacred feast. This is no doubt the reason so many of the best examples of Scottish evangelistic preaching are to be found in communion sermons. The Church of Scotland may have celebrated the Supper but once or twice a year, but those celebrations were the spiritual focal point of their worship.

Like the collection of sacred orations which has come down to us from Gregory of Nazianzus, the collection of Robert Walker's sermons is a selection of the best examples of his preaching art. With Walker's colleague, Hugh Blair, teaching rhetoric at the University of Edinburgh, the interest in the art of oratory was strong in eighteenth-century Scotland. Cultivated Christians liked to read sermons for their literary excellence as well as their devotional value. Sad to say, both for Walker as for Nazianzus, the historical context of the individual sermons has been lost. There are no recognizable series of *lectio continua* sermons or catechetical sermons. Each sermon in this collection stands pretty much on its own. One exception is a group of five sermons which the editor tells us were preached at the celebration of the Lord's Supper. The editor does not indicate whether they were preached in the course of a single Scottish communion season or at different communion services as part of the celebration. However that may be, they are magnificent examples of evangelistic preaching filled with gospel and grace.

The text of the first one is drawn from the Gospel of Matthew: "Come unto me, all ye that labour, and are heavy laden, and I will give you rest" (Matt. 11:28). The text is particularly appropriate for a communion service. Again, Walker's introduction is brief: "It was prophesied of our Lord long before his manifestation in the flesh, that he should 'proclaim liberty to the captives, and the opening of the prison to them that are bound': And lo! here he doth it in the kindest and most endearing manner, offering *rest,* or spiritual relief, to every *labouring and heavy laden* sinner. — *Come unto me all ye that labour, and are heavy laden, and I will give you rest.*"[135]

This is a remarkably short introduction, but it is significant nevertheless. It interprets one of the classic Old Testament texts on evangelism, namely, Isaiah 61:1-3 (KJV):

> The spirit of the Lord GOD is upon me; because the LORD hath anointed me to preach good tidings unto the meek; he hath sent me to bind up the brokenhearted, to proclaim liberty to the captives, and the opening of the prison to *them that are* bound; To proclaim the acceptable year of the LORD, and the day of vengeance of our God; to comfort all that mourn; To appoint unto them that mourn in Zion, to give unto them beauty for ashes, the oil of joy for mourning, the garment of praise for the spirit of heaviness; that they might be called trees of righteousness, the planting of the LORD, that he might be glorified.

Jesus himself had appealed to this text when he preached in the synagogue in Nazareth. As Luke reports it, Jesus used this to explain his preaching ministry. It has been used this way ever since. It makes clear that, for Jesus, his preaching ministry was evangelistic. The Father had sent him and the Holy Spirit had anointed him to preach the gospel. To preach the gospel was to bring the good news of God's grace to the spiritually poor, the weighed down, the mourning and lamenting children of God who were troubled by the reverses, the hardships, and the inequities of life. That was what preaching was for Jesus, and that was what preaching was for Robert Walker.

The division of the text is simple and clear. First, Walker wants to tell us to whom this promise is given. Second, he wants to explain the in-

---

135. Walker, *Sermons,* 1:186, emphasis Walker's.

vitation itself and show what is involved in coming to Christ. Finally, he wants to illustrate the gracious promise of our Lord to grant us rest.[136] Walker begins his first point. Again we notice his clean, sober prose:

> I begin with the character of those to whom the invitation is addressed. They are such, you see, as *labour and are heavy laden;* that is, who feel the unsupportable load of guilt, and the galling fetters of corrupt affections, and earnestly long to be delivered from both; for these were the persons whom our Saviour always regarded as the peculiar objects of his attention and care. — By our fatal apostasy, we forfeited at one our innocence and our happiness; we become doubly miserable, liable to the justice of God, and slaves to Satan and our own corruptions. But few, comparatively speaking, are sensible of this misery! The bulk of mankind are so hot in the pursuit of perishing trifles, that they can find no leisure seriously to examine their spiritual condition. These indeed have a load upon them, of weight more than sufficient to sink them into perdition; but they are not *heavy laden* in the sense of my text. Our Savior plainly speaks to those who feel their burden, and are groaning under it; otherwise the promise of rest, or deliverance, could be no inducement to bring them to him.[137]

There are two reasons why this call is addressed to them. First, because our Lord knew well that no one else would respond to it. Such is the pride of our hearts that each of us would wish to be a savior to himself and to purchase heaven by his own personal merit. Walker makes his point by quoting Romans 10:3: "Being ignorant of God's righteousness, they went about to establish their own righteousness, and did not submit themselves unto the righteousness of God." The soul that is enlightened by the Spirit of God is humble and looks to God for salvation. "It was therefore with peculiar significancy, that our Lord introduced his sermon upon the mount by adjudging the kingdom of heaven to the 'poor in spirit,' placing humility in the front of all the other graces, as being the entrance into a religious temper, the beginning of the divine life, the first step of the soul in its return to God."[138]

The second reason is that if the laboring and heavy laden were not particularly distinguished, they might despair of any hope of salvation.

---

136. Walker, *Sermons,* 1:187.
137. Walker, *Sermons,* 1:187-88.
138. Walker, *Sermons,* 1:188-89.

They would exclude themselves because they imagined they would be considered unworthy of God's mercy. The teaching of Jesus in this matter is very clear. God is merciful: "he 'who will not break the bruised reed, nor quench the smoking flax,' doth kindly encourage them by this special address." This saying of Jesus, taken from Matthew 12:20, is a classic text on God's patience and mercy toward the slow in heart. The bruised reed that cannot stand straight as well as the dimly burning wick God will patiently set in order, just as the shepherd gently carries the exhausted lamb. This invitation is extended not just to the swift and the strong, but to the slow and the weak as well.

The promise of this text is made to those who are troubled about being alienated from God. The very thing that appeared to be the greatest obstacle in the way of mercy might become the means of assuring them that they are the very persons for whom mercy is prepared. Another beautiful passage follows which needs to be quoted in its entirety:

> Let this then encourage every weary selfcondemning sinner: The greater your guilt appears in your own eye, the greater ground you have to expect relief if you apply for it. Mercy looks for nothing but an affecting sense of the need of mercy. Say not, If my burden were of a lesser weight, I might hope to be delivered from it; for no burden is too heavy for Omnipotence: he who is 'mighty to save,' can easily remove the most oppressive load; 'his blood cleanseth from all sin,' and 'by him all who believe, are justified from all things.' — This great physician did not come to heal some slight distempers, but to cure those inveterate plagues, which none beside himself was able to cure.[139]

Not even the sober elegance of Dr. Johnson could improve on these lines.

Building on the *Westminster Shorter Catechism,* which his congregation would have known quite well, Walker explains the second point of the sermon: what it means to come to Christ. The catechism explains it in terms of the three offices of Christ: Christ as prophet, Christ as priest, and Christ as king. Because Christ has been given to us as a prophet, we need to have our minds enlightened by his teaching. Because Christ is our king, we need to submit our wills to his rule. And because Christ is our priest, we need to accept his sacrifice for our atonement.[140] The priestly office of Christ is especially emphasized. We notice this because it shows

139. Walker, *Sermons,* 1:190-91.
140. Walker, *Sermons,* 1:196.

how stoutly Walker insisted on those elements of the Christian faith that the Enlightenment tended to ignore. While the Enlightenment tended to emphasize the prophetic, or teaching, office of Christ as well as the kingly office, or moral and ethical dimensions of the Christian faith, it tended to ignore the priestly, or cultic aspects of the Christian faith. Not so with Walker. Here, as so often in these sermons, the cultic dimensions of Christian faith are given full treatment. This is especially true here because these sermons were preached at a communion service. While Walker would never have thought of the Communion as a sacrifice, he did understand it as the commemoration of Christ's sacrifice. The adoration of that sacrifice was at the heart of the celebration.

The third point our preacher wants to make is that Christ gives rest to those who come to him. Come unto me and I will give you rest, is the promise we have from Christ.

> There can be no doubt that the *rest* here spoken of, must be, at least, of equal extent with the *burthen,* and include a deliverance from every cause of trouble to the soul. But this subject is an ocean without bottom or shore; we cannot measure the length or breadth of it, neither can its depth be fathomed; for "the riches of Christ are unsearchable;" and surely no tongue can express what the mind itself is unable to comprehend. Nevertheless I shall attempt to say a few things which may be of use to help forward your comfort and joy, till eternity shall unfold the whole to your view.[141]

Our preacher builds his point with a series of rhetorical questions. Do the guilt of sin and the curse of the Law lie heavily upon your soul? "'Behold, the Lamb of God, who takes away the sin of the world!'" (John 1:29 RSV). In the sacrifice of Christ there is an infinite merit that can never be exhausted.[142] Do you feel a law in your members warring against the law of your mind? Are you harassed with temptation and weighed down with the preoccupations of the flesh, that you cry out with the apostle Paul, O wretched man, who shall deliver me (cf. Rom. 7:23-24)?[143]

These rhetorical questions all urge the evangelistic invitation. Do you fear he might forsake you? Christ is the Good Shepherd who carries the lambs in his bosom, and therefore they cannot perish, because none is

141. Walker, *Sermons,* 1:198.
142. Walker, *Sermons,* 1:199.
143. Walker, *Sermons,* 1:200.

strong enough to pluck them out of his hand. "The believer is not left to stand by himself; he who is the author is likewise the finisher of his people's faith. Omnipotence is their guardian; and they are 'kept,' not by their own strength, but 'by the power of God, through faith unto salvation' [cf. I Pet. 1:5]."[144] While this part of the sermon is built on a series of rhetorical questions, it is filled with brilliant scriptural allusions. Not every congregation would be able to follow this. Preaching at this level demands a biblically literate congregation, and Scotland had such congregations in the eighteenth century! This final point is summed up by these words:

> Such, my brethren, is that rest which Christ will finally bestow upon his people. They shall "enter into the joy of their Lord." All their burdens shall drop with their natural bodies; none of them can pass beyond the grave. Then faith and hope shall become sight and enjoyment; then love grown perfect shall cast out fear; and nothing shall remain of all their former trials, but the grateful remembrance of that friendly hand which supported them, and hath at length crowned their "light and momentary afflictions," with a "far more exceeding and eternal weight of glory."[145]

As we have noticed, Walker tends to conclude his sermons with very "practical" applications; that is, for the life of faith, they are spiritually and devotionally practical. That, of course, is why his congregation so eagerly listened to them. The practical application in this case is to invite the congregation to receive the Sacrament. The remainder of the sermon is an invitation to receive Christ in the communion service. Now our preacher figures that all who have heard his sermon up to this point should be ready to receive Christ at the Lord's Table. Our preacher draws out the invitation at some length, emphasizing that it is truly made to all. Jesus himself, when he preached in the Temple of Jerusalem, stood up on the last day of the feast and cried, "'If *any man* thirst, let him come to me, and drink' [John 7:37]." Jesus said the same thing to the degenerate church of the Laodiceans: "'Behold, I stand at the door, and knock: If *any man* will hear my voice, and open the door, I will come in to him, and sup with him, and he with me' [Rev. 3:20]."[146] With this passage of Scripture, particularly, the invitation to the Lord's Supper is clearly made to all.

144. Walker, *Sermons,* 1:201.
145. Walker, *Sermons,* 1:203.
146. Walker, *Sermons,* 1:206.

At this point our preacher becomes very specific in his invitation: "Come now and receive the new testament in Christ's blood: — For confirming your faith, and increasing your joy, he hath instituted this visible pledge of his love, this external seal of his gracious covenant."[147] The covenantal dimension of Reformed eucharistic doctrine comes strongly to the fore. To come to the table is to come and take with one's own hand the promise of rest which Christ himself has given. Our preacher urges his congregation to come to the Lord's Table and find in this sacrament "something of that *rest* . . . which he is always ready to dispense to those who feel their need of it, and who know its worth."[148]

The genius of the Scottish communion service was on the one hand its covenantal theology and on the other its evangelistic proclamation. This we find again and again in Scottish communion sermons.

C. Evangelistic Imagery

Let us look at another sermon preached at the celebration of the Lord's Supper. The communion sermons of Robert Walker are filled with a great abundance of biblical imagery. The eucharistic imagery is, to be sure, edifying. Surely there is no way to understand Reformed eucharistic theology quite so profoundly as to study the biblical imagery used in discussing it. We saw this in the eucharistic sermons of the Dutch preacher Jodocus van Lodenstein as well as those of the American Gilbert Tennent. Many more examples could be cited. We find this eucharistic imagery in Walker, too, but we want to focus on another kind of imagery: his evangelistic imagery.

It is in the imagery of the prophet Zechariah that the second of these eucharistic sermons is cast: "Rejoice greatly, O daughter of Zion; shout, O daughter of Jerusalem: behold, thy King cometh unto thee" (Zech. 9:9 KJV). The gospel is presented as the announcement that the divine promise of a Savior has been fulfilled. The preaching of the gospel is kerygma — the proclamation of the coming king. This is a basic biblical image for evangelism. The long-promised, divinely anointed Savior has come; let us receive him. This is, to be sure, eucharistic imagery, but even more it is evangelistic imagery. It is the imagery of kingship and

147. Walker, *Sermons,* 1:211-12.
148. Walker, *Sermons,* 1:212.

court etiquette. This may put us off, with all our republican ideology. But then, as Walker points out, the prophet tells us that the messianic King comes to us with humility.[149] "He is just, and having salvation; lowly, and riding upon an ass, and upon a colt the foal of an ass" (9:9 KJV). Even more, the prophecy of Zechariah continues to promise that the rule of the Messiah will differ completely from the methods of earthly potentates who subdue the peoples with external force. The Christ will rule not by outward power but by inward persuasion. "And I will cut off the chariot from Ephraim, and the horse from Jerusalem, and the battle bow shall be cut off: and he shall speak peace unto the heathen" (9:10a KJV). The text speaks of the chariot, the horse, and the battle bow. All these shall be cut off, "by the preaching of the gospel, accompanied with the powerful operation of the Spirit, which is emphatically called 'speaking peace unto the Heathen.'" It is by spiritual means that the Messiah will establish his kingdom. The happy outcome of the messianic rule will be that Christ's kingdom will be a peaceful kingdom, spread out over all the earth. "And his dominion shall be from sea even to sea, and from the river even to the ends of the earth" (9:10b KJV). As Walker sees it, "[T]he gracious aim of his government is, to set men at liberty from the vilest slavery, and to release them from the most ignominious confinement, by opening their prison-doors."[150]

Right here we discover the root of both evangelical social concerns and the missionary movement which was beginning to develop and would gain momentum well into the nineteenth century. The abolition of slavery, prison reform, and a whole host of other enlightened social concerns were implicit in the basic biblical evangelistic imagery. It was inevitable that these evangelical social concerns would develop as more and more devout Protestants began to understand the gospel more profoundly. Walker, and those like him, were doing the groundwork for the evangelical social reforms of Thomas Chalmers in the century to follow.

We find another important evangelistic image in this sermon, namely, the spiritual anointing prophesied by Isaiah.[151] "The spirit of the Lord GOD is upon me; because the LORD hath anointed me to preach good tidings unto the meek; he hath sent me to bind up the broken-hearted, to proclaim liberty to the captives, and the opening of the prison

---

149. Walker, *Sermons,* 1:213.
150. Walker, *Sermons,* 1:214.
151. Walker, *Sermons,* 1:215.

to them that are bound" (Isa. 61:1 KJV). We mentioned how Walker considered this a significant Scripture for understanding the preaching ministry as Jesus exercised that ministry. For Walker it was obviously Jesus who set the example of evangelistic preaching. When Jesus quoted these words from Isaiah, he gave the Church an important image of at least one dimension of Christian preaching, that is, the evangelistic dimension. The preaching of the gospel liberates those who receive it from the slavery of sin. Liberation from slavery is a key image for evangelistic preaching.

Walker brings up the imagery of Isaiah 61 further on in this sermon as well, giving us additional insights.[152] He points out that according to the Gospel of Luke Jesus himself quoted this text as being prophetic of his own ministry. At the center of his ministry was an evangelistic ministry, a ministry of proclamation. This proclamation was not only of the messianic King but of a messianic age as well. Walker says that for those who have suffered slavery, a double portion of honor has been reserved. "For 'your shame ye shall receive double'" was the prophecy of Isaiah.[153] This is to be understood spiritually. It speaks of the fullness of life in this world, but even more of life in the world to come.[154]

Passing on to the next sermon, we find yet another important biblical image for the evangelistic ministry of the Church. It is the pastoral image. Walker takes his text from I Peter 2:25, "For ye were as sheep going astray; but are now returned unto the shepherd and bishop of your souls."[155] Evangelistic preaching is the pastoral work of the shepherd searching for the lost sheep, the sheep that have gone astray. In the introduction to the sermon our preacher reminds his congregation of two Old Testament rites, the Passover and the feast of dedication. He quotes from the biblical texts which speak of these rites at some length. Both rites commemorated the liberation of God's people. That is particularly clear in the Passover imagery. Walker gives high prominence to the Christian interpretation of Passover: "The gospel-passover, which we are this day to celebrate, commemorates a deliverance from spiritual thraldom."[156] The Scottish communion service often included the singing of the metrical version of Psalm 23 in which the image of the good shepherd is especially strong. The Passover had always been closely connected with pastoral im-

152. Walker, *Sermons,* 1:231f.
153. Walker, *Sermons,* 1:232.
154. Walker, *Sermons,* 1:233.
155. Walker, *Sermons,* 1:237.
156. Walker, *Sermons,* 1:240.

agery. In evangelistic preaching there is the gathering of the flock. The call of the shepherd gathers the flock and leads it into green pastures and beside still waters. This sermon makes very clear that the pastoral imagery is both eucharistic and evangelistic. The imagery can no more be separated than can evangelism be separated from the celebration of the Lord's Supper. The evangelistic dimension of the Eucharist and the eucharistic dimension of evangelism Walker would have us keep closely together.

Yet another image Walker develops in the communion sermons is Christ as our great high priest ascended into heaven, seated at the right hand of eternal glory. This is the imagery of the feast of the atonement. We find this in the fifth of these sermons,[157] for which Walker chooses the text, "Let us therefore come boldly unto the throne of grace, that we may obtain mercy, and find grace to help in time of need" (Heb. 4:16). Again we are dealing with the cultic imagery of ancient Israel, imagery that was fundamental to classic Protestant piety. The image of the high priest provides encouragement to those who seek the blessings of God.[158] It makes clear how efficacious faith in Christ and his atoning sacrifice is. There is no explaining this fundamental biblical imagery without a profound grasp of the vicarious nature of Christ's sacrifice for us.

Imagery is very important to preaching, and part of the secret of great preaching is the ability of the preacher to present to the congregation the biblical imagery. The preacher is not dealing with words alone. Words produce pictures. The imagination is constantly making mental pictures of the words it hears. If Scottish Presbyterian worship had little ceremonial, it did cultivate an exceedingly rich biblical imagery. These communion sermons are a significant example. The biblical imagery is of course a very literary imagery. It is supposed to be literary. To turn it into paintings or drawings would be to abuse it, or perhaps better, to weaken or compromise it. One cannot always go translating one art into another. One art communicates certain things better than another art. This subject we intend to treat elsewhere, but for the present we simply want to point out that Walker's preaching, plain style oratory that it is, has a strong visual dimension. Like the Bible itself, it is rich in imagery.

157. Walker, *Sermons,* 1:259.
158. Walker, *Sermons,* 1:269.

D. Lord's Day Worship

Only after a prolonged study of the history of Reformed worship does it become obvious that one place we can learn about a specifically Reformed approach to worship is in sermons on the sanctification of the Lord's Day. Several Reformed theologians have written treatises on worship which bear titles suggesting that they are treating how the Christian is to observe the fourth commandment. Thomas Shepard, one of the first pastors of New England, for example, wrote his *Theses Sabbaticae,* and in doing so gave us an essay on Christian worship. The Scottish pastor John Willison left us a similar work with the title *On the Sanctification of the Lord's Day.*

The collection of Walker's sermons we have contains two sermons on the fourth commandment. Actually it is a single sermon, preached in two parts.[159] One would imagine these two sermons were originally in a series on the Ten Commandments, but that is not certain. Walker gives no evidence of following any system in his preaching, at least not as a regular procedure. But that may reflect the literary preoccupations of the publisher. On the other hand, the lack of any system was somewhat typical of the eighteenth century. We noticed this particularly with John Tillotson and Jacques Saurin among the moderatists and with George Whitefield and Samuel Davies among the preachers of the Great Awakening.

This doubleheader sermon almost completely dispenses with an introduction. There is but a single sentence: "The too general and growing abuse of the Christian Sabbath must render a discourse on this subject both seasonable and necessary."[160] With this our preacher divides up his text into three points.

First we notice a thoroughly Scholastic approach to worship. It is our duty. Natural religion alone can bring us to understand that as God's creatures we owe our Creator worship.[161] Yet even more, it is particularly clear from Scripture that the observance of one day in seven as a day of worship is instituted of God.[162] This, for a Reformed theology of worship, is a key point. It is because God has called us to worship him that

159. Walker, *Sermons,* 3:170-212.
160. Walker, *Sermons,* 3:170.
161. Walker, *Sermons,* 3:171-72.
162. Walker, *Sermons,* 3:173-74.

this worship serves his glory. As appropriate as it may seem, this appropriateness is not the reason we worship. It is because God has commanded it and we have obediently done it that it serves God's glory.

What is most interesting in this sermon is that it understands worship not in terms of duty or even divine institution but rather in terms of memorial. In explaining why the Christian Sabbath is celebrated on the first day of the week rather than the seventh day, our preacher says it is "in commemoration of our Saviour's resurrection from the dead, the holy rest is transferred to the first day of the week; which hath ever since been called, by way of eminence, *The Lord's Day.*"[163] That word "commemoration" is of the greatest possible importance. The fourth commandment in Exodus begins with the word "remember." Walker points out that our Sabbath memorial as found in the Law in Exodus is a commemoration of the creation, for in six days the Lord made the heavens and the earth and rested on the seventh.[164] The Christian Sabbath, on the other hand, is a commemoration of the resurrection, the new creation.

The sermon continues, showing the usual passages of the New Testament which indicate that already in the earliest Christian churches the Lord's Day was observed as the Christian Sabbath. But then our preacher brings up an equally important subject: the Lord's Day is to be understood as an intimation of the last day. Here is a frequently overlooked dimension of the Reformed understanding of worship. Christian worship from its earliest times had an eschatological aspect. Quite remarkably this is clearly expressed in eighteenth-century Scotland. The Lord's Day, according to Walker, is "a foretaste of the everlasting Sabbath, an earnest of that rest which remains for the people of God."[165] Essentially what Walker is saying is that the Lord's Day is a sacrament of heaven.

This sermon exhibits a very high theology of the Lord's Day, but as always in Walker, his preaching gives ample attention to what in that day was considered the practical application of his exposition. He very carefully goes over just what should be done to sanctify the Lord's Day. The first responsibility is the assembling of ourselves for the public worship of God. Our preacher puts it in an interesting way: "that as many as can conveniently meet in one place may join in paying homage to their com-

163. Walker, *Sermons,* 3:175.
164. Walker, *Sermons,* 3:179.
165. Walker, *Sermons,* 3:182.

mon Lord; and thus contribute their endeavours to make him glorious in the eyes of the world around them."[166] Just assembling ourselves together is an act of worship in itself. In New Testament terms it is the *synaxis* which by itself glorifies God and is a witness to the world (cf. I Cor. 11:17-20 and Heb. 10:25). To be sure, what the assembly does is important as well; indeed, it is even more important, but the assembling of ourselves together belongs to the essence of worship.

The assembly performs a ministry of prayer and praise, to be sure. There is the reading and preaching of the Scriptures as well as the celebration of the sacraments. This Walker assumes but mentions only in passing.[167] What this sermon targets is the worshiper's preparation for the public service in family prayers and the devotions of the "closet," as the term was. As archaic as it sounds today, it was the standard term at the time. Closet prayers were personal, private devotions. This had been a feature of Scottish piety ever since the General Assembly of the Church of Scotland, in adopting the Westminster Standards, added to the *Westminster Directory for Worship* a chapter on private and family prayers.[168] As the Christian Sabbath was practiced in Scotland, the whole day was to be devoted to "the public and private exercises of God's worship."[169]

Time should be spent in "reading and meditating on the word of God." This reading was to be done in a context of prayer. One was to "implore his presence and his blessing, by humble prayer, in the secret retirements of the closet."[170] Walker speaks of how joyful a public service of worship would be if families would arrive at church on the Lord's Day hav-

166. Walker, *Sermons,* 3:185.

167. Walker, *Sermons,* 3:186.

168. Matthew Henry had great influence on the cultivating of family prayers through his book on the life of his father, Philip Henry. This biography describes in great detail the practice of family prayer as developed by his father, a minister of the Church of England who had been ejected from his pastorate in 1662. Matthew Henry served as pastor of the Presbyterian church in Chester, England, from 1687 to 1711, at which time he accepted a call to a church in London. See my article "Matthew Henry and the Puritan Discipline of Family Prayer," in *Calvin Studies VII,* ed. John H. Leith (Davidson, N.C.: Colloquium on Calvin Studies, 1994).

169. *Westminster Shorter Catechism,* q. 60. "How is the Sabbath to be sanctified? A. The Sabbath is to be sanctified by a holy resting all that day, even from such worldly employments and recreations as are lawful on other days; and spending the whole time in the public and private exercises of God's worship, except so much as is to be taken up in the works of necessity and mercy."

170. Walker, *Sermons,* 3:185.

ing come from their family prayers at home.[171] The public service concluded, one should return home and give one's time to meditation. We should "meditate on the marvellous works of God; on his glorious perfections, as they are displayed to us, in creation, providence, and redemption; above all, on that great 'mystery of godliness, God manifest in the flesh, justified in the Spirit, seen of angels, preached unto the Gentiles, believed on in the world, received up into glory'" (I Tim. 3:16).[172] Here again is remembering, the commemoration which is of the essence of worship. It is in this commemoration, this sacred memorial, that the Lord's Day is sanctified, just as we have it in the fourth commandment, "Remember the Sabbath day to keep it holy." It is exactly in this commemoration of God's mighty acts of creation and redemption that we have the essence of both the reading and preaching of Scripture, on one hand, and the celebration of the sacraments, on the other, but in this sermon at least our preacher is aiming at the devotional exercises of his congregation in the privacy of their homes. Those who study the history of the liturgy rarely focus on this very practical concern of worship, but it is an essential part of the whole picture. The liturgy is the public service of worship. Walker draws attention to the private service of worship.

Focusing even more closely on this very subjective aspect of worship, we find a beautiful passage in this sermon which we would like to quote at length. It tells us worlds about the piety, or if you prefer, the spirituality, of Reformed worship.

> In this sacred retirement, we ought to revolve in our minds the various steps of our Lord's humiliation, from his birth in Bethlehem to his burial on Mount Calvary. Thence we should proceed to view the triumphs of his cross, where he bruised the old serpent's head, "finished transgression, made reconciliation for iniquity, and brought in everlasting righteousness." To confirm our faith, and increase our joy, our meditations ought to follow this mighty Conqueror, and to contemplate him breaking the bands of death, and rising from the grave on this first day of the week, ascending up to heaven in the sight of his disciples, and sitting on the right hand of God the Father; from whence he shall come to power and great glory, to judge the world in righteousness, according to this gospel which is now preached in his name. When, by such meditations as these, our hearts are warmed and enliv-

171. Walker, *Sermons,* 3:188.
172. Walker, *Sermons,* 3:189.

ened, we should then with all humility and reverence approach the throne of grace: imploring those mercies which we need for ourselves, and begging a divine blessing to accompany the outward means of grace, that, with our fellow-worshippers, we may be made to taste of the fatness of his house, and may find his ordinances to be indeed the wisdom and the power of God, "the savour of life unto life," to our souls.[173]

This is of the essence of Christian worship, whether in the devotional meditation on Sunday evening after one has returned from the public services at the church, whether in the celebration of the Lord's Supper, or whether in the reading and preaching of the Scriptures in the public worship on the Lord's Day. It is in remembering, proclaiming, and rejoicing in the mighty acts of God for our salvation that we serve God's glory.

To use modern parlance, preaching is eucharistic. As Robert Walker saw it, the proclamation of the gospel recalls the mighty acts of God for our salvation, rejoices in them, and leads the congregation to gather about the Shepherd and dwell in the house of the Lord forever. When our evangelism does this, it indeed serves God's glory.

VI. Hugh Blair (1718-1800)

By the end of his life, Hugh Blair had won an international reputation as one of the most enlightened preachers of Protestantism.[174] Even in Germany the young Friedrich Schleiermacher had studied his sermons as consummate examples of the art of preaching. In 1758 Blair became minister of the High Church in Edinburgh.[175] It was the first pulpit of Scotland, and he occupied the most prestigious ministerial position in Edinburgh in

173. Walker, *Sermons,* 3:189-90.
174. Blair could very well have been treated in chapter 1 of this volume. He was indeed the leading Scottish example of moderatism.
175. For biographical information on Hugh Blair, see Hugh Blair, *Lectures on Rhetoric and Belles Lettres,* edited with a critical introduction by Harold F. Harding, 2 vols. (Carbondale and Edwardsville: Southern Illinois University Press, 1965); James L. Golden and Edward P. Corbett, *The Rhetoric of Blair, Campbell, and Whately: With Updated Bibliographies* (Carbondale and Edwardsville: Southern Illinois University Press, 1990); George A. Kennedy, *Classical Rhetoric and Its Christian and Secular Tradition from Ancient to Modern Times* (Chapel Hill: University of North Carolina Press, 1980), esp. chap. 11; and Robert Morell Schmitz, *Hugh Blair* (New York: King's Crown Press, 1948).

a day when Edinburgh could boast a distinguished literary culture. It was to men and women of taste and culture that Blair preached Sunday by Sunday, and his preaching was well received by his congregation. Toward the close of his ministry he published a collection of his sermons which well sums up his preaching ministry. The work was widely circulated in the British Isles as well as on the continent of Europe and won him a generous pension from King George III. These sermons were not great theology, perceptive expositions of the Bible, nor powerful proclamations of the gospel. They were, however, magnificent essays on Christian morality. Written in the most lucid and attractive English style, they were treasured by cultivated Christians of the day as a significant guide to practical Christianity. They taught a way of life recommended by generations of established Christianity. They are infused with an appreciation for reverence and the solemn service of God's house. They breathe a confidence that the Christian way of life is both rational and blessed. In them we have the testimony of a studious and literate Christian gentleman who can look back over his life and say, yes, the Christian way of life is the good life.

It is not surprising that Blair had this approach to the Christian faith. He was the son of a prosperous Edinburgh merchant and the great-grandson of Robert Blair, the minister of Saint Andrews mentioned earlier. Hugh was born and raised in Edinburgh. From earliest childhood he had known Christians of honesty and integrity. He received his master of arts degree from the University of Edinburgh, where he became regius professor of rhetoric and belles lettres. He was brought up with a high respect for a learned ministry, for the simple dignity of Calvinist worship and the good order of Presbyterian polity. He was heir to the best traditions of that most Christian and literate city which guarded the heritage of Scotland.

He was a Christian moralist, an apologist for the Christian way of life, and he was very much aware that the Christian way of life was under serious attack. His congregation was constantly exposed to the criticism the Enlightenment made of Christianity. David Hume wrote his works on natural religion and ethics during Blair's ministry in Edinburgh, and Adam Smith made his contributions to moral philosophy and economics. The new attitudes of romanticism were beginning to affect Edinburgh, too. In fact, both Robert Burns and Walter Scott became the heroes of literary Edinburgh while Blair was preaching from the pulpit of the High Kirk of Saint Giles. Blair was preaching on subjects that were of keen interest to the intellectuals of his congregation.

Blair was in the center of the intellectual life of his day, and with the greatest moderation and equanimity he advocated a life of Christian morality and piety. The impression we get from his sermons is one of temperance, thoughtfulness, and reflection. In a period when Deism was very popular, he gently affirmed historic Christian doctrine. Although doctrine was not his main concern, and although he showed little interest in doctrinal apologetic, he clearly held to the doctrine of the Trinity, the divinity of Christ, substitutionary atonement, the doctrine of providence, and the inspiration of Scripture. He presented the Christian life in a way designed to win over his congregation and attract them to the Christian way. Succeeding generations have been very critical of his "moderatism," and yet many in his day must have remained in the Church because of the gentle reasonableness of his witness.

If nothing else, the table of contents of Blair's sermons shows that the focus of his ministry was moral catechism. Among his ninety-one published sermons we find the following titles:

"On the Union of Piety and Morality"
"On Gentleness"
"On Devotion"
"On the Duties of the Young"
"On the Duties and Consolation of the Aged"
"On the Mixture of Joy and Fear in Religion"
"On the Motives to Constancy in Virtue"
"On Candor"
"On the Character of Joseph"
"On the Improvement of Time"
"On Fortitude"
"On Envy"
"On Idleness"
"On the Sense of the Divine Presence"
"On Patience"
"On Moderation"
"On Charity as the End of the Commandment"
"On Integrity as the Guide of Life"
"On the Importance of Public Worship"
"On the Submission to the Divine Will"
"On Drawing Near to God"

And this list is only a sample. More than three-fourths of his sermons treat such questions. Blair's sermons usually have a text which is often carefully explained, and sometimes there is real exposition. But at other times the text seems nothing more than a formality. In literary form his sermons are really moral discourses in the tradition of classical antiquity.

Blair's collection of sermons is a studied collection. In his retirement he carefully gathered together his best efforts and spent long hours polishing each piece to reflect his best insights into sacred rhetoric. The first sermon, therefore, we can take as a proper introduction to his pulpit ministry.

It bears the title "On the Union of Piety and Morality." It takes as its text Acts 10:4, "Thy prayers and thine alms are come up for a memorial before God." The text comes from the story of the Roman centurion to whom God sent Peter to present the gospel. God had granted this privilege to this Gentile because he demonstrated both piety in his prayer and morality in his generous alms. Cornelius was, therefore, an example of the union of piety and morality.[176] An explanation of this serves as the introduction to the sermon. It is a very straightforward introduction.

The sermon has two points. First, our preacher endeavors to show "that alms without prayers, or prayers without alms, morality without devotion, or devotion without morality, are extremely defective."[177] As a devotee of moderatism, Blair finds the logic of balance self-evident. His purpose in this sermon is to show the happy effects of the union of devotion and morality. We notice no real exposition of the text, but rather the text serves as an image or figure for the point Blair wants to make. Cornelius, if you will, is a good figure of the preacher's message, a good illustration, especially for Blair's congregation, because he had come to this virtue as a Gentile without the benefits of revelation. Reason alone should be able to see the preacher's point.

Blair begins to talk about alms without prayers. Examples of this are not uncommon in the world. One often finds those who emulate virtue but despise piety. Surely there were those among the Edinburgh literati who felt this way. "They are men of the world, and they claim to be men of honour. They rest upon their humanity, their public spirit, their probity, and their truth. . . . But devout affections, and religious duties, they treat with contempt, as founded on shadowy speculations, and fit to em-

---

176. Hugh Blair, *Sermons*, 5 vols. (London: Printed for A. Strahan and T. Cadell in the Strand; Edinburgh: W. Creech, 1792-96), 1:2.

177. Blair, *Sermons*, 1:3.

ploy the attention only of weak and superstitious minds." Blair's refined rhetoric hits his target. The sermon is aimed at the Enlightenment. He knows their arguments, and in spite of himself is sympathetic with many of their concerns, but he knows their weaknesses, too. "Now, in opposition to such persons, I contend, That this neglect of piety argues depravity of heart."[178]

As Blair sees it, nature itself has so formed the human heart as to have a sense of religion. Man "finds himself placed, by some superiour power, in a vast world, where the wisdom and goodness of the Creator are conspicuous on every side." This was a common sentiment of Christians who had been influenced by the Enlightenment, and David Hume notwithstanding, many educated Christians in the eighteenth century found it convincing. With the beautiful language in which Blair expresses it, it is indeed attractive. "The magnificence, the beauty and order of nature, excite him to admire and adore. When he looks up to that omnipotent hand which operates throughout the universe, he is impressed with reverence."[179] Even natural religion brings us to worship. That human beings should worship is indeed quite reasonable. Here, at least, Blair sounds much like Archbishop Tillotson.

The other extreme is just as undesirable: prayers without alms and devotion without morality.[180] It has often been the case that those of perverse mind have substituted "certain appearances of piety in the place of the great duties of humanity and mercy."[181] Such persons should be assured that their devotion is altogether spurious. Their religious rites and devotional practices are their own creations, having basis in neither reason or the word of God. Here, we notice in passing, Blair appeals both to revelation and reason, even if most of the time, because of the congregation he addresses, he argues from reason. Most of the time he sounds like the Enlightenment, but from time to time one detects the foundations of orthodoxy beneath it all. Quoting a number of passages all through the Bible, Blair shows that obedience is better than sacrifice. As Isaiah would ask, "To what purpose is the multitude of your sacrifices unto me? saith the Lord. Bring no more vain oblations. Incense is an abomination unto me. The new moons and sabbaths, the calling of as-

178. Blair, *Sermons,* 1:4.
179. Blair, *Sermons,* 1:5.
180. Blair, *Sermons,* 1:10.
181. Blair, *Sermons,* 1:11.

semblies, I cannot away with; it is iniquity, even the solemn meetings" (Isa. 1:11 and 14).[182]

All these cultic activities, our preacher continues, are quite vain apart from morality. "It is for the sake of man, not of God, that worship and prayers are required; not that God may be rendered more glorious, but that man may be made better; that he may be confirmed in a proper sense of his dependant state, and acquire those pious and virtuous dispositions in which his highest improvement consists."[183] One notices that one of the purposes of worship is to confirm us in our dependent state. This is very profound, and it makes us realize there is more to Blair's understanding of worship than the Enlightenment had taught him. Blair's orthodox foundations show through again. In worship we experience the humility of the human condition, we experience, more than any other place, our true relationship to reality. We experience both our frailty and fallibility and at the same time discover that we are blessed by God and dear to him as children of our Father.[184]

The second point Blair wants to make is that the union of devotion to God and charity to our fellows is the true character of the Christian.[185] If our worship is supposed to glorify God, then our neglect of our neighbor, our injustice to others, is a contradiction of his glory. It is an insult to God.[186] Our worship is all in vain. When, on the other hand, our virtue and devotion are joined together, then God is truly glorified.

Again our preacher returns to the story of Cornelius the Roman centurion.[187] Here was a man who did both. Great generals and men of arms have come and gone in the history of the world, and to few others has the Almighty granted such grace or indicated such approval. It should be clear from this that God's delight is in those who honor him with both their prayers to him and their charity to their neighbors. To such as fear God and work righteousness God is indeed favorable. "Divine illumination is ready to instruct him. Angels minister to him. They now mark him out on earth as their future associate; and for him they make ready in paradise the white robes, the palms, and the scepters of the just."[188] This

182. Blair, *Sermons,* 1:14.
183. Blair, *Sermons,* 1:15.
184. Blair, *Sermons,* 1:16.
185. Blair, *Sermons,* 1:17.
186. Blair, *Sermons,* 1:18.
187. Blair, *Sermons,* 1:23.
188. Blair, *Sermons,* 1:24.

passage with all its sparkling rhetoric is beautiful, but it is very curious. Cornelius receives "divine illumination"; nothing is said about his conversion. Apparently conversion, illumination, and enlightenment all amount to the same thing.

For eighteenth-century Edinburgh this sermon may well have been a significant piece of apologetic. Given Blair's congregation, it may have even been prophetic. It certainly gives us a strong statement of the prophetic criticism of the worship of ancient Israel. On the other hand, it is hardly gospel. It sounds more Stoic than Christian. Blair has not said much more than Cicero, Seneca, and Marcus Aurelius said in ancient Rome. Like the ancient Christian writer Lactantius, Blair has spoken to a particular temper of his day, not a Christian Platonism but a Christian Stoicism. Even at that, the Stoicism seems to predominate.

Let us look at another sermon. A good example of Blair's approach to the Christian moral discourse is his sermon "On Gentleness," which appears as the sixth sermon in his collection. Appropriately Blair chose a verse from the Epistle of James as his text, "The wisdom that is from above is . . . gentle" (3:17). The sermon begins with a brief introduction in which our preacher distinguishes between being wise in one's own eyes, being wise in the opinion of the world, and being wise in the sight of God. Our wisdom should be a reflection of God's wisdom, according to Blair. It is this we should seek to emulate. Gentleness is one of the chief characteristics of the wisdom that is from above.[189] Having thus introduced his subject, our preacher attempts to explain the nature of this virtue. Gentleness is distinguished from passive tameness of spirit and unlimited compliance with the manners of others. "It is impossible to support the purity and dignity of Christian morals, without opposing the world on various occasions."[190] Gentleness is not to be confounded with "artificial courtesy, that studied smoothness of manners, which is learned in the school of the world."[191] This is frivolous and empty.

> True gentleness is founded on a sense of what we owe to him who made us, and to the common nature of which we all share. It arises from reflection on our own failings and wants; and from just views of the condition and duty of man. It is native feeling, heightened and improved by principle. It is the heart which easily relents; which feels for every

189. Blair, *Sermons,* 1:146.
190. Blair, *Sermons,* 1:147.
191. Blair, *Sermons,* 1:149.

thing that is human; and is backward and slow to inflict the least wound. It is affable in its address, and mild in its demeanour; ever ready to oblige, and willing to be obliged by others; breathing habitual kindness towards friends, courtesy to strangers, long-suffering to enemies. It exercises authority with moderation; administers reproof with tenderness; confers favours with ease and modesty. It is unassuming in opinion, and temperate in zeal. It contends not eagerly about trifles; is slow to contradict, and still slower to blame; but prompt to allay dissension, and to restore peace. It neither intermeddles unnecessarily with the affairs, nor pries inquisitively into the secrets, of others. It delights above all things to alleviate distress, and if it cannot dry up the falling tear, to soothe at least the grieving heart. Where it has not the power of being useful, it is never burdensome. It seeks to please, rather than to shine and dazzle; and conceals with care that superiority, either of talents or of rank, which is oppressive to those who are beneath it.[192]

One cannot help but notice the thoughtfulness, the exact and interesting vocabulary of these lines. The precision of expression demands that we listen very carefully; the maturity of his reflection demands that we listen very seriously. Blair's high art witnesses to his deep understanding. Having given us this brilliant passage of moral philosophy, our preacher follows it with a collage of Scripture. It is gentleness the Gospel commands when it says we are to "bear one another's burdens; rejoice with those who rejoice, and to weep with those who weep; to please everyone his neighbour for his good; to be kind and tender hearted; to be pitiful and courteous; to support the weak, and to be patient towards all men."[193] Essays on moral philosophy though they be, for Blair it is important that his thoughts be at least supported by divine revelation.

Having described the virtue of gentleness, our preacher recommends it to his congregation. First he tells us that gentleness is a duty we owe to God. God is gentle to us. The Scriptures tell us of the divine condescension to the poor, the weak, and the humble. The apostle Paul spoke of the gentleness of Christ in the text, "I beseech you by the meekness and gentleness of Christ" (II Cor. 10:1). Gentleness is in fact characteristic of all three persons of the Trinity, for we read that the Holy Spirit is the Comforter, the Spirit of grace and peace.[194] This is an impressive trinitar-

192. Blair, *Sermons,* 1:150-52.
193. Blair, *Sermons,* 1:152.
194. Blair, *Sermons,* 1:154.

ian unfolding of the gentleness of God. Blair's point is that since God is gentle, so we, too, should be gentle. But there is another reason for us to be gentle. Gentleness promotes harmony in human society. "It softens animosities; renews endearments; and renders the countenance of man a refreshment to man."[195] What a line! If this is not enough to recommend gentleness to us, then let us consider that it is recommended purely from self-interest. Here we see Blair as the apologist. Some in the intellectual circles of Edinburgh were attracted to those moral philosophers of the day who attempted to establish morality on the basis of enlightened self-interest. If one wants to take that approach, our preacher will be happy to recommend the virtue of gentleness by it. Is it not true, Blair asks, that gentle people are appreciated by others much more than those who are harsh? Even more important than that, gentleness promotes inward tranquillity.[196]

Finally our preacher asks how one develops this Christian virtue of gentleness. Most importantly it is developed by considering the hope of eternal life. "But gentleness will, most of all, be promoted by frequent views of those great objects which our holy religion presents. Let the prospects of immortality fill your minds. Look upon this world as a state of passage. Consider yourselves as engaged in the pursuit of higher interests; as acting now, under the eye of God, an introductory part to a more important scene. Elevated by such sentiments, your minds will become calm and sedate."[197]

The fact that Blair chose a text from James is significant. This book, perhaps more than any other in the New Testament, reflects a very specific temper of devotion. It is the devotion of the Wisdom school. It continues the tradition of the Proverbs, Ecclesiastes, and the Wisdom of Sirach. No other New Testament book reflects the Sermon on the Mount quite so closely as James. To choose a text from the Wisdom tradition was natural for Blair because in all his thought he stands very close to that tradition. This sermon comes from the mature reflection of a wise and gentle man who knew from experience the virtue he preached. He expounds his text with a wealth of Scripture, to be sure, but also with a wealth of experience. Surely much is of value in a sermon like this, yet there is little here that one could call gospel.

195. Blair, *Sermons,* 1:160.
196. Blair, *Sermons,* 1:163.
197. Blair, *Sermons,* 1:170.

In Blair's fourth volume we find a sermon, "On the Importance of Public Worship."[198] The text is from Psalm 26:8, "Lord, I have loved the habitation of thy house." Again the text is appropriate to the subject, but there is no exposition of it. In fact, our preacher begins by quoting another text, one of the words of Jesus: "God is a Spirit and they that worship him, must worship him in spirit and in truth" (John 4:24). Blair comments that religion chiefly consists in an inward principle of goodness and that all external services are of value only to the extent that they promote purifying the heart and reforming the life. "Notwithstanding this, it is certain that external services have their own place, and a considerable one too, in the system of religion."[199] It is evident from the outset that the Enlightenment has made considerable inroads in Blair's theology of worship. The Enlightenment had forgotten what the Reformers had maintained, that worship was the subject of the first tablet of the Law while morality was the subject of the second. This was particularly the view of Calvin, as we discussed at length in the previous volume of our study. Even the *Westminster Shorter Catechism,* a century after the Reformation, taught that man's chief end was to glorify God. Blair may have thought he was defending the Christian faith against the Enlightenment, but in fact he gave the Enlightenment considerable ground.

Blair proposes to treat worship first in regard to God, second in respect to the world, and third in respect to ourselves. Our preacher sets forth with his usual eloquence:

> Let us consider it with respect to God. If there exist a Supreme Being, the Creator of the world, no consequence appears more natural and direct than this, that he ought to be worshipped by his creatures, with every outward expression of submission and honour. We need only appeal to every man's heart, whether this be not a principle which carries along with it its own obligation, that to Him who is the Fountain of our life and the Father of our mercies; to Him who has raised up that beautiful structure of the universe in which we dwell, and where we are surrounded with so many blessings and comforts; solemn acknowledgements of gratitude should be made, praises and prayers should be offered, and all suitable marks of dependence on him be expressed.[200]

198. Blair, *Sermons,* 4:224.
199. Blair, *Sermons,* 4:225.
200. Blair, *Sermons,* 4:227-28.

Here, as we notice frequently in Blair, the case for worship is made on the basis of natural religion alone. Again, Blair sounds very much like Tillotson. Only occasionally does he suggest that our worship be according to Scripture, an approach so central to a Reformed theology of worship.

Likewise, it is on the basis of reason that Blair argues for public worship: "This obligation extends beyond the silent and secret sentiments of our hearts. Besides private devotion, it naturally leads to associations for public worship; to open and declared professions of respect for the Deity. Where blessings are received in common, an obligation lies upon the community, jointly to acknowledge them. Sincere gratitude is always of an open and diffusive nature. It loves to pour itself forth; to give free vent to its emotions; and, before the world, to acknowledge and honour a Benefactor."[201] One cannot resist pointing out the beautiful alliteration in "the silent and secret sentiments of our hearts." The whole language of this paragraph lifts up our hearts. One can well imagine that the congregation was thrilled with its eloquence. Today it may sound a bit overblown, but not in the age of Haydn and Handel. Yet behind the eloquence is an undeniably rationalistic theology.

Let us look at another eloquent passage which summarizes the compromise eighteenth-century Protestants made with the Enlightenment. It is long but worth reading in its entirety:

> Survey the societies of men in their rudest state; explore the African deserts, the wilds of America, or the distant islands of the ocean; and you will find that over all the earth some religious ceremonies have obtained. You will every where trace, in one form or other, the temple, the priest, and the offering. The prevalence of the most absurd superstitions furnishes this testimony to the truth, that in the hearts of all men the principle is engraved, of worship being due to that invisible Power who rules the world. — Herein consists the great excellency of the Christian religion, that it hath instructed us in the simple and spiritual nature of that worship. Disencumbered of idle and unmeaning ceremonies, its ritual is pure, and worthy of a divine Author. Its positive institutions are few in number, most significant of spiritual things, and directly conducive to good life and practice. How inexcusable then are we, if, placed in such happy circumstances, the sense of those obligations to the public worship of God shall be obliterated among us,

201. Blair, *Sermons,* 4:228.

which the light of nature inculcated, in some measure, on the most wild and barbarous nations?[202]

We have all heard this sort of thing, for indeed it has shaped much of traditional American religion. What is less well known is that it is the heritage not of classical Protestantism but of the Enlightenment. As any American Protestant knows, this is the common assumption of most of the people in our pews.

The benefit public worship brings to the world is to human society, particularly "the great mass and body of the people."[203] It is from public worship that they receive religious instruction. How else would their rude passions be restrained? How else would they be endued with a conscience? The sages of the past established public worship for good reason. "By bringing the rude multitudes to worship together, and, at stated times and places, to join in hymns and songs to their deities, they gradually restrained them from violence, and trained them to subordination and civilized life."[204] This argument may not carry much weight today, but in the late seventeen hundreds it was very popular. The pulpit played a great role in popular education, and the teaching pulpit was cherished by a large segment of society who had little in the way of books and other forms of communication. For Blair the teaching of good morals to the common people was apparently the chief purpose of preaching, and this he figured the advocates of the Enlightenment would recognize.[205]

The only trouble was that while the upper classes did admit the validity of Blair's argument, they figured they themselves had no need of public worship. It was good for the masses but they were above that. This is what the third point of this sermon is about. Our preacher insists that it is the duty of everyone regardless of station to attend public worship. Again we notice that the appeal is to duty. Attendance at public worship gives warmth to piety and solemnity to morality.[206] Our rhetorician turns to his cultivated listeners and addresses them personally: the truths taught from the pulpit may be well known to you, but the purpose of hearing them is to recall them to your mind, "and their dormant influences awakened; . . . to have serious meditations suggested; to have good dispositions

202. Blair, *Sermons,* 4:228-30.
203. Blair, *Sermons,* 4:234.
204. Blair, *Sermons,* 4:235.
205. Blair, *Sermons,* 4:236.
206. Blair, *Sermons,* 4:239.

raised; to have the heart adjusted to a composed and tranquil frame."[207] But then instruction is not the only purpose of attending public worship. Everyone owes praise and adoration to God. We all should supplicate the Almighty for protection and favor.[208] This, however, seems to be by way of concession; it is not what truly motivated enlightened worship.

The real burden of Blair's apologetic is that public worship is of value because of the instruction it offers. This is clear simply from the great number of his sermons so consistently teaching one moral virtue after another, but then at the conclusion of his sermon our preacher returns to a much more orthodox affirmation. "The ends for which we assemble in the house of God are two; to worship God, and to listen to religious instructions."[209] Again and again Blair argues from natural religion, but then at the close we find a much more traditional assurance. When the great truths of natural and revealed religion are discussed in the sermon, when the important doctrines of the gospel concerning the life and sufferings and death of our blessed Redeemer are displayed, then divine authority is set forth and it is our duty to listen.[210] Jesus, "our blessed Redeemer," finally comes into the picture. Blair has not gone over completely to the camp of the Enlightenment, but he has gone a long way.

VII. Andrew Thomson (1779-1831)

Andrew Thomson deserves to be considered one of Scotland's major liturgical reformers.[211] He is remembered for his work in the restoration of catechetical instruction, for his work on the Psalter, and for the recovery of systematic expository preaching. These were, of course, all very important features of Scottish Presbyterian worship. It was not that any of them

---

207. Blair, *Sermons,* 4:240.
208. Blair, *Sermons,* 4:241.
209. Blair, *Sermons,* 4:245.
210. Blair, *Sermons,* 4:246.
211. For biographical material on Thomson, see Blaikie, *The Preachers of Scotland,* pp. 272-76; David C. Lachman, "Thomson, Andrew Mitchell," in *Dictionary of Scottish Church History and Theology,* pp. 819-20; and the memoir introducing the volume *Sermons and Sacramental Exhortations by the Late Andrew Thomson, D.D., Minister of St. George's Church Edinburgh* (Edinburgh: Printed for William Whyte & Co., William Collins and M. Ogle, Glasgow; J. Dewar, Perth; and Longman, & Co., London, 1831), hereafter Thomson, *Sacramental Exhortations.*

had completely lapsed by 1800, but more that during the ascendancy of moderatism they had not been cultivated. The Enlightenment wanted nothing to do with catechisms. Ministers no longer devoted themselves to catechetical preaching as they once had, and parents began to neglect teaching the catechism at home. During the age of George Frideric Handel, the Scottish Psalter seemed terribly old-fashioned in more cultivated circles. For the common people, the hymns of the Methodists were much more attractive. The Scots were not yet ready to give up their psalms, but they were ready to try some new tunes, and Thomson is supposed to have provided some music for this purpose. But for us, Thomson's most important liturgical reform was the recovery of classical Reformed expository preaching. As we find it in the memoir which precedes a posthumous volume of his sacramental sermons, he was one of the chief causes of "the revival of taste for the faithful preaching of the Gospel."

Andrew Thomson was a son of the manse. Eventually his father, Dr. John Thomson, became one of the most respected of Edinburgh's pastors, but when Andrew was born his father had just begun his ministry in the village of Sanquhar in Dumfriesshire. Andrew's university studies were done in Edinburgh. In 1802 he was licensed by the Presbytery of Kelso, and a few months later ordained to the church of Sprouston. Eventually he was called to be the first pastor of Saint George's Church in Edinburgh, just constructed on the park at the end of George Street, in a newly built and rather stately quarter of the city. Even today it is an area of the city marked by its handsome regency buildings. When Andrew was pastor of Saint George's, it was the very fashionable, big new church in the new town. He served a congregation of the city's most progressive and enlightened citizens.

Not until he was established at Saint George's did he begin to make considerable departures from moderatism. His departures were in two directions. He had a sincere love for the doctrinal and liturgical traditions of classical Protestantism, and at the same time he had a number of passionate social concerns. Thomson stood very strongly for the abolition of slavery in the British colonies. The issue at the time was the use of slave labor in Jamaica and the West Indies. The plantation owners had argued that they could not make these tropical islands productive without slave labor and should therefore be granted an exception to the usual laws, or at the least, as the discussion of the subject went in those days, a delay in the enforcement of abolition in order to make the necessary adjustments to insure continuous production. The large sugar plantations of the West Indies were extremely profitable at the time, and the use of slave labor in the colonies was hotly debated. Thomson was one who demanded the immediate abolition of slavery. To say the least, he was hardly the delight of Edinburgh's Tories.

Thomson's revival of expository preaching is of particular interest because it recovered a number of significant features which had eroded over the years. He preached the *lectio continua* more rapidly than had become the practice in earlier generations. Under the Puritans, one rarely got through more than a verse or two per sermon, and except for shorter books such as the General Epistles, ministers tended more and more to preach through chapters rather than whole books. This made the *lectio continua* move very slowly, and as we have remarked elsewhere, only too often lead to the ultimate abandonment of the *lectio continua*. Thomson reversed this process and began to go through the various books of the Bible at six to twelve verses per sermon. In 1816 two volumes of his sermons were published, *Lectures, Expository and Practical, on Select Portions of Scripture*.[212] The two volumes contain only twenty-five sermons and are obviously intended to give a sampling of Thomson's preaching.[213] It appears that the collection is made up of sermons from a *lectio continua* series on the Gospel of Luke, another on the Acts of the Apostles, and a third on the Sermon on the Mount. For the series on the Sermon on the Mount we have sermons on:

Matthew 5:13-16
Matthew 6:1-18
Matthew 6:9-15
Matthew 6:25-34
Matthew 7:1-11
Matthew 7:12-20

These sermons are scattered throughout the two volumes. Even at that, one can easily imagine that behind them there was originally a series of

---

212. Andrew Thomson, *Lectures, Expository and Practical, on Select Portions of Scripture*, 2 vols. (Edinburgh: Printed for William Blackwood, Edinburgh; and T. Cadell and W. Davies, London, 1816).

213. There is no introduction to this collection of sermons and no indication why these particular sermons are chosen, or arranged as they are. No dates are given to indicate when they were preached. While the six sermons on Acts are in order, as are the eight sermons on Luke 7, 13, and 14, the six sermons on Matthew's version of the Sermon on the Mount are scattered throughout the two volumes. I can find no explanation for this arrangement.

ten or twenty sermons which treated the whole Sermon on the Mount. For the series on Luke we have the following:

Luke 7:18-23
Luke 7:24-35
Luke 7:36-50
Luke 11:51-54
Luke 13:1-9
Luke 13:10-17
Luke 13:18-30
Luke 13:31-35
Luke 14:1-14
Luke 14:15-24

The first sermon on Luke 13 and the sermon on Luke 11 are out of order; still, one easily gets the impression from this list that these sermons have been taken from a *lectio continua* series of sermons on Luke which must have contained something like a hundred sermons. For the series from Acts we have:

Acts 3:12-16
Acts 3:17-21
Acts 3:22-26
Acts 4:1-12
Acts 4:13-22
Acts 4:23-37

The very least one can say is that there must originally have been a sermon on Acts 3:1-11, which tells the story of the healing of the lame man at the gate of the Temple which began the events recorded in the rest of chapter 3 and chapter 4. One can probably go even further and suggest that these six sermons are taken from a series which continued through the whole of Acts.

A. Sermons on Acts

Let us look briefly at these sermons on Acts, supposing we have here a few of what was a much longer series of expository sermons on the book. We will find a number of significant things. Thomson's use of the *lectio continua* in his expository preaching is much closer to the practice of Chrysostom, Augustine, and Calvin than to the Reformed preachers of the seventeenth and eighteenth centuries. In fact, one wonders if Thomson had not studied the sermons of Chrysostom, Augustine, and Calvin with the intention of recovering classical expository preaching.

One way his sermons show a return to a more classical practice is the type of exposition he uses. Thomson's sermons are classical in their simplicity. Taking his six sermons on Acts 3 and 4, we find many of the methods used by Chrysostom on one hand and Calvin on the other. The introduction to most of them is little more than a summary of what was said in the immediately preceding verses, a very brief explanation of the context of the passage he intends to preach, or perhaps a few words enumerating the subjects treated in the passage before him.

Thomson's sermons are organized on the principle of a running commentary on the text. He reads a verse or two, makes appropriate comments and perhaps an application, then reads another verse or two, makes his commentary or application, and continues in this vein until his passage is covered. In this way he divides his sermon into three to six divisions. This method has been used from the earliest days of Christian preaching. There is no particular attempt to find a unity of theme, although occasionally such a unity does appear. The Scholastic sermon, especially the Protestant scholastic sermon of the seventeenth and eighteenth centuries, was characterized by a concern to maintain a unity of subject throughout.

Thomson's sermons show no particular attempt to develop a conclusion in which all the parts are drawn together, although sometimes the application at the end is appropriate to the whole sermon. This concern for unity of theme is one of those principles of Greek and Roman artistic expression which many Christian preachers have emulated, particularly the Scholastics both of the Middle Ages and of the seventeenth century. Others, however, have ignored it. For Thomson the text itself organizes the sermon. Here again we find him following a practice used by many of the preachers of the patristic and the Reformation periods.

Another method of exposition he uses is to paraphrase the text. In the sermon on Acts 4:13-22 our preacher reads from his text the following two verses: "But Peter and John answered and said unto them, Whether it be right in the sight of God to hearken unto you more than unto God, judge ye. For we cannot but speak the things which we have seen and heard."[214] This is expounded by a long paraphrase put in the mouth of the apostles elaborating the sentiments of the text. The paraphrase makes clear that the apostles intend no disrespect for properly constituted authority and elaborates the basis of divine authority in their preaching. We cannot conscientiously remain silent. They could not refrain from attesting the miracles that Christ had performed before their eyes, or from asserting those doctrines they knew to be divine. "We cannot withhold that message which God has commissioned us to deliver to mankind. . . ."[215] After this long interpretive paraphrase, almost four hundred words, our preacher commends the faithfulness of the apostles and suggests that all Christians are under the obligation to be faithful to God's commands even when the authorities of this world try to dissuade us. This paraphrase both enforces the words of the text and builds toward the application which the preacher finally makes. Calvin, we remember, often used similar paraphrases.

Sometimes Thomson expounds the text by refuting a misunderstanding. In the sermon on the end of chapter 4 he takes up the passage which tells us that the first Christians had all things in common. He tells us that some have claimed that this was the reason the early Church grew so rapidly. The poor figured there was great financial advantage in joining the Church. The rapid growth of the early Church, as they understand it, is to be explained on an economic basis rather than on the power of faith.[216] Thomson goes on at some length refuting this point. Then he points out that there is no reason the Church should always practice a community of goods. He is not too sure why it did this at the time, but the important thing to notice is the overriding devotion to the common good. He concludes by admiring the charitable concern of the early Church and exhorting his congregation to the same charity even if exercised in very different ways.

Thomson is quite sensitive to the need of a Christian apologetic. Apologetic is for him a major dimension of exposition. His text often gives him an opportunity to defend Christian teachings. In the sermon on Acts 4:23-37 he reads from verse 30 the line "that signs and wonders may be done by the name of thy holy child Jesus," and comments, "The great object at which the Apostles aimed, that which engrossed all their

214. Acts 4:19-20, as quoted in Thomson, *Lectures,* 2:28.
215. Thomson, *Lectures,* 2:45.
216. Thomson, *Lectures,* 2:74ff.

attention, and kindled all their zeal, and animated all their prayers, was the propagation of the Gospel."[217] In order to fulfill this purpose, Thomson suggests, they asked God for boldness and that their preaching be confirmed by miraculous signs. This allows Thomson to launch into a long apologetic for miracles. Thomson's apologetic may not be the sort we would raise almost two hundred years later, but our interest here is the way apologetic has become exposition. Thomson takes up his argument: "This shews us the view which the Apostles had of the importance of miracles. Indeed we find, both from their language and from that of Christ before them, that miracles form the grand evidence on which the truth of our holy religion rests. Take away the reality of these, and then, however excellent Christianity may be in itself, and however beneficial in its tendency, it is reduced to a mere human speculation, without authority, and without effect."[218] Not many preachers today would be so daring, but it is certainly true that the New Testament itself understands the miracles as a divine sealing of the apostolic witness.

Thomson goes on to say of miracles, "It becomes us, therefore, to examine them carefully, to meditate upon them frequently, to regard them as the voice of God himself, and to open our minds with all humility and readiness to those convictions which a proper consideration of them is fitted to produce." We cannot help but notice his splendid rhetoric. He has obviously learned the art which had been so carefully cultivated in his native city. "And it becomes us, . . . to be continually on our guard against those insidious attempts which are too often made to undermine that great foundation of our faith, by means of ridicule, and sophistry, and confident assertion, both in the course of conversation, and in the popular productions of literary or scientific genius." Thomson's attack on the promoters of the Enlightenment becomes more obvious. "The subject of miracles has been frequently and laboriously argued; and we do not hesitate to say, that the reasoning which satisfied a Locke, a Newton, and a Boyle, is not to be set aside by the witless sneers or the unsupported opinions of any philosopher in these days, even though he be possessed of the most splendid talents, and the most extensive acquirements."[219]

Thomson's rhetoric sounds at this point more like the law court

217. Thomson, *Lectures,* 2:64.
218. Thomson, *Lectures,* 2:66.
219. Thomson, *Lectures,* 2:67.

503

than the pulpit, but it is eloquent nevertheless. We are tempted to suggest that the forensic tone of his exposition reminds us of Calvin, a preacher trained in the rhetoric of the law courts. Thomson's advocacy of the Christian belief in miracles continues. "It deserves at least to be treated with more respect, and weighed with more fulness, and accuracy, and candour, than infidels have ever yet bestowed upon it, before we give it up as either unsound or inconclusive."[220] The preacher is not intimidated by the intellectuals of his day. He is as well educated and as cultured as any of them. "And surely it will be wise in us not to part with a system so full of purity and of consolation as the Gospel is, till those who would deprive us of it have discovered something of equal excellence to substitute in its place; more particularly as this surrender is required for no other end, than to gratify those who cannot bear the idea, that God should condescend in mercy to reveal his will to man, or that he should so far interfere with his own creation, as to work a miracle for accomplishing the most benevolent of all his purposes."[221]

Thomson has two very significant points here. First, the passage from Acts makes it clear that the earliest Christians considered miracles an essential part of their witness, and our preacher is obviously on guard against any attempt to remove them from Scripture as unnecessary to the gospel.[222] Second, our preacher sees no reason why Christians should accept the thesis that it would be unfitting for God to break the laws of nature when God himself had established the laws.[223] This was an argument frequently advanced against miracles in that day. Thomson simply says it does not really carry that much weight. His apologetic is in the end one of his significant methods of exposition.

Another method of exposition he uses with much skill might be called transparency. On the surface of things the speaker is explaining the historical situation reported by the text, but it is done so transparently that hearers realize he is really talking about the current situation. In the sermon on Acts 4:1-12 our preacher takes up the passage, "And as they spake unto the people, the priests, and the captain of the temple, and the Sadducees came upon them, — being grieved that they taught the people, and preached through Jesus the resurrection from the dead."[224] Thomson

220. Thomson, *Lectures,* 2:68.
221. Thomson, *Lectures,* 2:66-68.
222. Thomson, *Lectures,* 2:67.
223. Thomson, *Lectures,* 2:68.
224. Acts 4:1-2, as in Thomson, *Lectures,* 2:1.

comments at some length on who these priests, the captain, and the Sadducees were. He comes up with quite a bit of historical information, but the longer he goes on the clearer it becomes that these priests, their soldiers, and their lawyers were certain all-too-prominent citizens of Edinburgh.[225] They were the powerful ecclesiastics who with their government functionaries, their theologians, and their lawyers kept a spiritually sluggish and truculent moderatism thoroughly in control of the Church of Scotland. This transparency, as we have called it, is one of the most effective tools used by expository preachers. It is not often recognized for what it is. All too often one thinks the preacher is talking about the long ago and far away. Those who are more poetically inclined realize that with transparency, history is a metaphor for the contemporary.

A very basic sort of commentary Thomson uses frequently is analysis. After reading a few lines of the text, he will say, "Now we see three things happening here," or perhaps, "There are two reasons why the Apostle says this." Then he enumerates. We find this sort of analysis all through his sermons. In the sermon on Acts 4:13-22 he takes verse 16, "What shall we do to these men? for that indeed a notable miracle has been done by them is manifest to all them that dwell in Jerusalem; and we cannot deny it." Then he comments, "It is perfectly clear, that the Jewish rulers had a fixed resolution to bear down the religion of Christ, whatever sacrifices of principle, of feeling, and of consistency, the attempt might cost them. That religion shocked their prejudices, diminished their authority, exposed their hypocrisy, cut up the sources of their temporal emolument, and frustrated all the hopes which they had foolishly, but sanguinely, entertained of the kingdom of the promised Messiah."

Again we cannot help but call attention to Thomson's masterful use of words, to his precise and varied vocabulary. Thomson continues, "For these reasons, he, by whom it was published to the world, became the object of their inveterate enmity and relentless vengeance. They never thought of ascertaining the truth of his mission; into that they were careless of inquiring. They never gave any candid attention to the proofs of it which he daily exhibited to their view."[226]

Thomson's indictment continues: "Even when their gainsaying was confuted, and the demonstration of incontrovertible facts forced upon their minds, they either refused to draw the inferences which reason dic-

225. Thomson, *Lectures,* 2:3-8.
226. Thomson, *Lectures,* 2:28.

tated, or, in spite of these inferences, persevered in their opposition."[227] Then our preacher remarks, "In reflecting on this conduct of the Jewish Sanhedrin, there are two remarks which naturally suggest themselves to our consideration. In the first place, we find here a reluctant but explicit testimony to the truth of our religion given by its bitterest enemies. . . . In the second place, we observe in the procedure of the Sanhedrin what we cannot fail to condemn, and what it becomes us carefully to avoid. How worthless and contemptible does their conduct appear towards the Apostles! The truth is demonstrated to them; yet they shut their eyes and their hearts against its influence."[228] Here, of course, Thomson is giving us an exposition of a passage of Scripture having to do with a trial; only naturally does he argue his case as if it were a trial.

To be sure, Thomson uses such standard expository techniques as suggesting alternative translations to his text and frequently explaining passages of Scripture by other passages of Scripture. These two chapters of Acts include a number of references to the prophecies of the Old Testament, and Thomson is always careful to explain how the apostles understood these prophecies to have been fulfilled by the ministry of Christ and the experience of the early Church. We see this being done again and again in the history of Christian preaching. Thomson makes no attempt to demonstrate his erudition in his preaching. He never shows off his Greek and Hebrew. He is obviously conversant with the Greek text and the usual exegetical aids that one would expect from a Scottish preacher of the period, but one is never astounded by an "original" interpretation or a "brilliant" piece of exegesis. There are no learned gleanings from the authorities of the past. The only thing that impresses us is his thoughtful study of the text itself.

What is surprising is how few metaphors, similes, examples, and illustrations we find. Thomson was a popular preacher who drew a large congregation. We usually imagine that such techniques are essential to popular preaching. Evidently this is not always the case. One thing which seems to have kept people interested was a certain Celtic intensity which so often characterizes the Scottish pulpit. Another thing we notice is that Thomson seems to have had a natural gift for oratory. This sort of thing is not always evident in a published sermon. When we read the printed text, however, the rhythm and flow of his words seem to come without effort

227. Thomson, *Lectures*, 2:37-38.
228. Thomson, *Lectures*, 2:40-41.

or affectation. One often notes parallel constructions in his printed text which suggest that he had an innate sense of the cadences of language.

Surely the one thing above all else that made him a significant preacher was that his preaching called people to faith. His expository preaching was at the same time evangelistic. His approach to preaching is made very clear in his comments on Peter's message of repentance in Acts 3:14-15: "But ye denied the Holy One and the Just, and desired a murderer to be granted unto you; — And killed the Prince of life, whom God hath raised from the dead."[229] Thomson comments, "Such was the conduct of which the Jews had been guilty towards Jesus. And the Apostle presses it upon them with the greater earnestness, because he is going to exhort them to the work of repentance. This was a doctrine peculiarly applicable to them, in reference to the subject on which he had been addressing them. It applies to all men, for all have sinned."[230]

For Thomson, a call to repentance is the basis of a call to faith. He cites the last verse of the passage before him: "Whom God hath raised from the dead, whereof we are witnesses: And his name, through faith in his name, hath made this man strong, whom ye see and know; yea the faith which is by him, hath given him this perfect soundness in the presence of you all."[231] Thomson comments briefly on how faith in the risen Christ had saved the lame man and then concludes the sermon with the following call to faith: "This is the practical conclusion to which the statement of the Apostles inevitably leads. Let us take it home to ourselves. . . . Let it . . . have the effect of establishing, and strengthening, and enlivening that faith in the Redeemer, by which we shall be justified and saved. Christ is, at this moment, 'exalted as a Prince and a Saviour, to give repentance and the forgiveness of sins.'"[232] Thomson would present to all of us Jesus as both Lord and Savior, that we might all receive him by faith. "Let us be constrained by his grace and authority to comply with the call, to forsake the iniquity of our ways, to turn unto the Lord with our whole heart, and to be conformed to the death and resurrection of Jesus, so that, dying unto sin, and living unto righteousness, we may at last be admitted to the joys of heaven."[233]

What makes the preaching of Andrew Thomson worship is that the

229. Thomson, *Lectures,* 1:244.
230. Thomson, *Lectures,* 1:256.
231. Thomson, *Lectures,* 1:262.
232. Thomson, *Lectures,* 1:265.
233. Thomson, *Lectures,* 1:265-66.

gospel proclaimed by the apostles in Jerusalem is heard once more eighteen hundred years later in Edinburgh. When the gospel is proclaimed in faithfulness and heard with faith, God is glorified, and therein worshiped.

B. Communion Sermons

As we have seen several times now, by long tradition in the Church of Scotland the preaching that accompanied the celebration of the Lord's Supper had a particularly evangelistic function. It was at Communion that young people first made the covenant vows. Having learned the catechism, they were admitted to the Lord's Table. They professed their faith implicitly in receiving the bread and wine of Communion. For older members of the congregation each new celebration of the Sacrament was an occasion for renewing the same covenantal vows, the same confession of faith. Covenantal theology was fundamental to the celebration of the Supper. It was appropriate, therefore, that the preaching which preceded the giving of the bread and wine call the people to faith.

Several of Andrew Thomson's communion sermons have been preserved in a posthumous volume, *Sermons and Sacramental Exhortations by the Late Andrew Thomson, D.D., Minister of St. George's Church Edinburgh*.[234] The second sermon in the collection, "Human and Divine Love Contrasted," is a particularly fine example of a Scottish communion sermon. The text is Romans 5:7-8, "For scarcely for a righteous man will one die; yet peradventure for a good man some would even dare to die. But God commendeth his love toward us, in that, while we were yet sinners, Christ died for us." The sermon is an exposition of this text in the formal sense of expository preaching, and yet it is a textual and thematic sermon in that the text is apparently chosen for its suitability to the occasion. It is one of those classic texts which sum up the heart of the Christian message and is therefore, from the Scottish point of view at least, particularly appropriate for the celebration of Communion.

A short introduction sets forth the theme of the sermon. "God's love to men, in its various relations, and in its various expressions, is the great and prevalent theme of the gospel. The gospel, indeed, is altogether a manifestation of that love. . . . It is not only asserted that God loves us, but one principal object of whatever the sacred writers have been

234. For full citational information, see n. 211 above.

prompted to say, appears to be that of magnifying the divine attribute."[235] It is about that divine attribute, the love of God, that Thomson intends to preach. This is the very heart of the gospel, and Thomson intends to do this that he might inspire faith in the hearts of his people. He introduces his subject by making the point that Scripture gives all kinds of figures and analogies for God's love, but as we study them we find that there is no true analogy to it. God's love surpasses any attempt to express it by analogy. Our text makes this very clear. The love of God is without parallel.[236]

The sermon is divided into two parts. First our preacher speaks of the love of God toward our fellow creatures.[237] He tells us that the instances of human beings sacrificing their lives for others are rare. The apostle grants that there might well be some, but he does not seem to have any in mind. This is clear from the indefinite words in the text, *"Scarcely* for a righteous man will one die; yet *peradventure . . ."* (emphasis Thomson's). Even if one finds examples occasionally, one must allow that these acts frequently are motivated by a mixture of desire for glory or other forms of self-interest. To develop his point Thomson suggests a series of hypothetical situations which might inspire one to sacrifice one's life for another. Even with these appealing and appropriate possibilities, one cannot be sure that even the most highly motivated and altruistic of people would be willing to sacrifice their lives. Even when a very strong bond of friendship or family is involved, the giving of one's life for another is seldom observed. Even Jesus made this point: "Greater love hath no man than this, that a man lay down his life for his friends" (John 15:13). As Thomson puts it, "This is the utmost limit to which human affection can go."[238]

Our preacher now makes a magnificent transition. "Now, in all the examples to which we have referred, the sacrifice is made in consideration of motives that arise from worth exhibited, or benefits conferred, or obligations of some kind or other imposed, by them on whose account it has been demanded." One might well imagine that one could give one's life for a good man, or for a man from whom one had received much good, but could one give one's life for one who had been unfriendly and un-

---

235. Thomson, *Sacramental Exhortations,* p. 32.
236. Thomson, *Sacramental Exhortations,* p. 33.
237. Thomson, *Sacramental Exhortations,* p. 34.
238. Thomson, *Sacramental Exhortations,* p. 39.

grateful? Could one die for someone who had been "iniquitous, malevolent, and hostile; . . . guilty of atrocious crimes committed against the comfort, the reputation, the honour, of one who had lavished upon him every token of kind regard, who had treated him with the confidence of a friend, with the affection of a brother, with the tenderness of a parent"?[239]

The tragic tone of Thomson's language is gripping. Even reading it today we are mesmerized. "[A]nd supposing that for all his demerit, he had been condemned to die, and under his sentence of condemnation, cherished as bitter an enmity, and expressed as determined a vengeance, against his benefactor as he had ever done before — would that benefactor, or would any of the children of men, consent to occupy his room, and suffer his judicial fate, in order to send him back again to the life, and the liberty, and the enjoyment, which he had so justly forfeited?"[240] This long rhetorical question finally demands its answer: "Ah! no: that is a height of love, which humanity has never reached, and of which humanity is utterly incapable. Philosophy may conjecture it as possible, and poetry may give it a place in her fictitious delineations. But we observe not the seeds or elements of it in the moral constitution of man."[241]

This brings Thomson to his second point. "But that which man in all his love to his brethren has never felt, or offered, or accomplished, has been realized and manifested in the love which he has experienced from the holy God. 'God commendeth his love toward us, in that, while we were yet sinners, Christ died for us.'"[242] This second point is developed in two respects: Christ died for us, and he died for us while we were yet sinners.

In developing the idea that Christ died for us, Thomson wants to make it clear that the death of Christ demonstrated the love of God, and it did this because Christ is God. With this our preacher brings out a whole series of passages from Scripture to support his point. He then takes up the doctrine of the Trinity and holds forth on that subject at length to show that Christ's sacrifice of himself was an expression of the love of the Father as much as the love of the Son. This is characteristic of Scottish preaching, which never flinches at either long deliberations on

239. Thomson, *Sacramental Exhortations,* p. 40.
240. Thomson, *Sacramental Exhortations,* p. 41.
241. Thomson, *Sacramental Exhortations,* pp. 40-41.
242. Thomson, *Sacramental Exhortations,* pp. 41-42.

the precise meaning of the text nor involved discussions of fine points of theology.

The sermon comes to its climax with the marvelous passage, "But there are resources in the eternal mind, which are equally beyond our reach and our comprehension. There is a power, and a magnitude, and a richness in the love of God towards those upon whom it is set, to which the love of the creature cannot even approximate, of which the imagination of the creature could not have formed any previous idea, and which, even to the experience of the creature, presents a subject of inscrutable mystery — a theme of wondering gratitude and praise." Human love, on the other hand, is something quite different. "Man may love, man should love, man must love his fellows; but he never did, and never can love them like God. His is a love that throws man's into the distance and the shade. Had he only loved us as man loves, there would have been no salvation — no heaven — no felicity for us — no glad tidings to cheer our hearts; — no promised land on which to fix our anticipations — no table of commemoration and of communion spread for us in the wilderness, to refresh us amidst the toils, and the languishings, and the sorrows of our pilgrimage thither."[243]

For Thomson the mystery of God's love is beyond human understanding. "But behold! God is love itself; and his love, in all its workings, and in all its influences, and in all its effects, can stoop to no parallel with the best and most ardent of human affections. Guilt, which forbids and represses man's love, awakens, and kindles, and secures God's. Death for the guilty is too wide a gulf for man's love to pass over. God's love to the guilty is infinitely 'stronger than death,' and spurns at all such limits, and smiles at the agonies and the ignominies of a cross, that it may have its perfect work."[244]

As Thomson presents the love of God, it is surprising, incredibly surprising. Certainly it is beyond the limits of reason alone. It is beyond anything eighteenth-century rationalism would allow. "God, in the exercise of his love towards our sinful and miserable race, is concerned, where man would be unmoved, indifferent, and cold. God is full of pity, where man would frown with stern and relentless aversion. God forgives, where man would condemn and punish. God saves, where man would destroy. 'While we were yet sinners, Christ died for us.'" Having made his essen-

---

243. Thomson, *Sacramental Exhortations,* p. 44.
244. Thomson, *Sacramental Exhortations,* p. 45.

tial point, Thomson relates the sermon to the celebration of Communion which follows. Such a great love of God should be remembered, celebrated, and proclaimed at every possible opportunity. Such love obligates us to devote ourselves to God's service. It demands that we pledge our allegiance to Christ and follow his example in all our ways, that we forsake the ways of this world. It is this, Thomson tells his congregation, which we are to do at this sacred table. "In the good providence of God, that opportunity is now before us. . . . Let us sit down at a communion table with hearts overflowing with love to Him who first loved us, and who loved us in the midst of our unworthiness, and who loved us even to the death. Let us exercise a vigorous and a lively faith in the merit of that great atonement."[245]

It is with love, with faith, and with hope that one approaches the Lord's Table. Hope for the future is just as important as remembering the past. "And having experienced the love of God in giving Christ to the death for us, let us rest upon the promise, that this divine Saviour will come again — that he, whom we commemorate as having once suffered for our transgressions, will appear hereafter, and ere long, to give us complete and eternal redemption, and that, having rescued us from the dishonours of the grave, and clothed us with the robe of immortality, and introduced us into the incorruptible inheritance of his Father's kingdom," will receive us in his heavenly glory. In the end God will transform us in the image of his Son, "and will tune our hearts for pouring forth the rapturous strains of that high anthem, 'Unto him that loved us, and washed us from sins in his own blood, and hath made us kings and priests unto God even his Father; to him be glory and dominion for ever and ever. Amen.'"[246]

Here we see something of the greatest possible importance. We see evangelistic preaching which is integrally related to the sacrament of the Lord's Supper. The call to faith is a call to the Lord's Table.

VIII. Thomas Chalmers (1780-1847)

The majestic monument to Thomas Chalmers which commands the whole length of Princes Street in Edinburgh is testimony to the tremen-

245. Thomson, *Sacramental Exhortations,* pp. 47-48.
246. Thomson, *Sacramental Exhortations,* pp. 51-52.

dous respect lavished on this preacher by a nation which has always loved her preachers. The genius of Chalmers is a gem of many facets.[247] He was a man of science who in younger years taught classes in both mathematics and chemistry at the University of Saint Andrews and candidated for leading professorial chairs in both subjects, although he had already been licensed to preach by the Presbytery of Saint Andrews. He was a political economist who published significant works in the field. As professor of moral philosophy at Saint Andrews, he explored the relation of Christian faith to the new science of economics in his *Christian and Civic Economy of Large Towns*. During his remarkable eight-year pastorate in Glasgow, he revolutionized the pastoral care of the poor and studied the New Testament in order to recover the offices of elder and deacon. He had a passion for diaconal work and sometimes has been called the Abraham Lincoln of Scotland's poor. He was a pioneer of popular education among the underprivileged and an apologist for Christianity among the learned. His remarkable series of sermons on the relation of Christianity and science delivered at the Tron Church in Glasgow in 1817, *Discourses on Astronomy*, went through nine editions, selling twenty thousand copies in the first year. It was Chalmers more than any one else who began to pry the fingers of the state from the reins of the Church of Scotland. The establishment of the Free Church of Scotland successfully challenged the authority of the government in religious matters, and within a century the Free Church and the established Church were reunited in a Church of Scotland free of any government control.

For those who like to speak of stars by their magnitude, Chalmers is easily in the first rank, together with Chrysostom, Spurgeon, Bernard, and not many more. Chalmers was a great preacher, but not in the sense of superb literary style. His sentences are long and lumbering. He commits all kinds of stylistic crimes — crimes Hugh Blair never would have

247. For biographical information on Chalmers, see Blaikie, *The Preachers of Scotland*, pp. 276-90; Stewart J. Brown, *Thomas Chalmers and the Godly Commonwealth in Scotland* (Oxford and New York: Oxford University Press, 1982); A. C. Cheyne, ed., *The Practical and the Pious: Essays on Thomas Chalmers (1780-1847)* (Edinburgh: Saint Andrew Press, 1985); William Hanna, *Life of Thomas Chalmers*, ed. James C. Moffat (Cincinnati: Moore, Anderson, Wilstach & Keys; New York: Newman & Ivison, 1853); Hanna, *Memoirs of the Life and Writings of Thomas Chalmers*, 4 vols. (Edinburgh: Published for T. Constable by Sutherland and Knox, 1849-52); Hugh Watt, *Thomas Chalmers and the Disruption* (Edinburgh and New York: T. Nelson and Sons, 1943); Mrs. Margaret O. W. Oliphant, *Life of Thomas Chalmers* (London: Methuen & Co., [1912]).

committed — and yet there is something compelling about his language. He was more the public speaker than the writer. Stylistically, at least, he comes more from the age of romanticism than the age of classicism. His oratory is powerful, full of authority. The sermons that have come down to us are filled with rich ideas. Peals of thunder and flashes of lightning descend from his pulpit. There is an intellectual intensity and a spiritual depth in his sermons that make them constantly interesting. Chalmers drew great crowds when he preached. Scotsmen realized that in this man the sort of preaching Scotland had known in the days of John Knox and Richard Cameron was with them once more.

A. Apologetic Preaching

There were many facets to the genius of Thomas Chalmers. He was fascinated by the natural sciences just as he was by theology or, as we will show further on, by sociology and economics. Chalmers, as the greatest of preachers most often are, was a well-rounded preacher. That he should preach on some of the subjects he found so interesting was only natural, and yet he did seem to hesitate about doing a series of apologetic sermons. He addresses the subject in the preface to the published sermons.[248]

These are, of course, marvelous sermons. Like the sermons on the six days of creation Saint Basil the Great preached back in the fourth century, these sermons are clearly doxological even if filled with magnificent passages about nature and the natural sciences of the day. One is reminded of the apologetical sermons of Theodoret of Cyr. Apologetical as they may be, they are filled with awe and wonder. Praise and adoration salt every sentence.

When Chalmers preached these sermons, he realized the relation of science and religion needed to be addressed. The natural sciences, the Enlightenment had claimed, showed the foolishness of religious faith, and Chalmers was fully aware of the need to answer this attack. He preached these sermons in 1817, only two years after he was appointed minister of the Tron Church in Glasgow.

---

248. Thomas Chalmers, *Discourses on the Christian Revelation, Viewed in Connection with the Modern Astronomy,* vol. 7 in *The Works of Thomas Chalmers, D.D. & LL.D.,* 25 vols. (Glasgow: William Collins; London: Hamilton, Adams, & Co., [1836-42]), p. ix, hereafter Chalmers, *Discourses on Astronomy.*

Particularly disturbing to Chalmers were a number of assertions concerning the meaning of the discoveries of modern astronomers. As the Enlightenment understood it, the vastness of the universe was beginning to become evident. The earth and those who populated it were too insignificant for God to take any interest in. Deism seemed a much more realistic faith when one became aware of the vastness of the universe. Deism had dispensed with the doctrine of providence and wanted no illusions about God being the least concerned about human problems and predicaments. Modern astronomy, some claimed, made the God of Abraham, Isaac, and Jacob, yes, even the God and Father of our Lord Jesus Christ, ridiculous.

Chalmers begins his series with a sermon on Psalm 8:3-4 (KJV): "When I consider thy heavens, the work of thy fingers, the moon and the stars, which thou hast ordained; What is man, that thou art mindful of him? and the son of man, that thou visitest him?" The psalmist considers the heavens, and

> Instead of a dark and unpeopled solitude, he sees it crowded with splendour, and filled with the energy of the Divine presence. Creation rises in its immensity before him; and the world, with all which it inherits, shrinks into littleness at a contemplation so vast, so overpowering. He wonders that he is not overlooked amid the grandeur and the variety which are on every side of him; and passing upward from the majesty of nature to the majesty of nature's Architect, he exclaims, "What is man, that thou art mindful of him; or the son of man, that thou shouldest deign to visit him?"[249]

Here Chalmers brings out all the eloquence of romanticism. These sermons are almost a pulpit version of the Beethoven symphonies. The two men were almost contemporary, of course. And as to Chalmers's romanticism, we remember that he was only ten years younger than Sir Walter Scott. The variety, animation, and vitality of the heavens were a constant source of wonder!

Starting with Psalm 8, Chalmers begins to wonder about the possibility that other planets in other solar systems might have intelligent life. Perhaps there, too, God has planted life, "worshippers of His glory."[250] Chalmers sees no reason not to believe that the God of Abraham, Isaac,

---

249. Chalmers, *Discourses on Astronomy,* pp. 18-19.
250. Chalmers, *Discourses on Astronomy,* p. 25.

and Jacob is also the God of innumerable creatures planted on innumerable planets over an infinite cosmos. Even today theologians and astrophysicists are asking the same question. Does an infinite God necessarily imply a finite cosmos? Apparently Chalmers, at least, was willing to ask the question.

It may be humiliating to us, but there is more to God's universe than this little world on which we have been placed.[251] At this our preacher descants on the stars beyond our solar system: "Are they only made to shed a feeble glimmering over this little spot in the kingdom of nature? or do they serve a purpose worthier of themselves, to light up other worlds, and give animation to other systems?"[252] What a line! What awe and wonder! Like Basil's famous *Hexaemeron,* the description of the creation gives honor to the Creator.

Our preacher moves on to the subject of sunspots, speculating about other suns having their unique characteristics. One wonders whether they, too, rotate, having brighter and fainter sides.[253] "Worlds roll in these distant regions; and these worlds must be the mansions of life."[254] Chalmers recounts some of the discoveries of astronomers most recent in his day. He is obviously fascinated by them. Certainly one of the charms of these sermons for those who heard them at the beginning of the nineteenth century was the amount of information which poured forth from the pulpit. It had been the same way with Basil's *Hexaemeron.* Chalmers tells us about the recent discovery of nebulae. They are like clusters of stars vast distances away from us.[255] Yet even with all this vastness, Chalmers concludes, still God takes notice of us. About that Psalm 8 is most clear: "What is man, that thou art mindful of him? and the son of man, that thou visitest him?" This should fill us with humility and gratitude.[256]

The second discourse is entitled "The Modesty of True Science." It takes for its text I Corinthians 8:2 (KJV), "And if any man think that he knoweth any thing, he knoweth nothing yet as he ought to know." One of the interesting things about this sermon is that it takes Sir Isaac Newton as an admirable example of the modesty of a man of science. Newton was, of course, a man of profound Christian faith. Chalmers apparently

251. Chalmers, *Discourses on Astronomy,* p. 21.
252. Chalmers, *Discourses on Astronomy,* p. 27.
253. Chalmers, *Discourses on Astronomy,* p. 30.
254. Chalmers, *Discourses on Astronomy,* p. 31.
255. Chalmers, *Discourses on Astronomy,* p. 35.
256. Chalmers, *Discourses on Astronomy,* p. 39.

knew quite a bit about Newton's faith and the criticism Voltaire made of it. Voltaire was offended that Newton, so obviously a true scientist, could take seriously the Bible, even to the point of writing a commentary on Revelation. The problem is that Voltaire lacked the modesty of Newton. This, Chalmers points out, is the whole problem of the science of the Enlightenment. It has too much of the arrogance of Voltaire and not enough of the humility of Newton.

The next discourse takes Psalm 113:5-6 (KJV) as its text: "Who is like unto the LORD our God, who dwelleth on high, Who humbleth himself to behold the things that are in heaven, and in the earth!" Infidels have long bragged that they have a more exalted view of God than do those who claim religious faith. Voltaire was famous for his taunt against the anthropomorphism of religious people. If God made man in his own image, then man has certainly returned the compliment. The charge of anthropomorphism goes back to the skeptic philosophers of ancient Greece and Rome, but the Enlightenment certainly revived it. Chalmers's point is that Scripture is not guilty as charged. That should be perfectly clear from the text. God's self-revelation demands a certain condescension or accommodation on God's part. Who is like God? He is unique and totally other.

The amazing thing about God is that he can hold the vast multitude of creation in his mind all at the same time.[257] Chalmers expatiates on the infinite variety of the creation. To imagine that God cannot be constantly conscious of all this is to force on God an anthropomorphism as vicious as any Voltaire blames believers of committing. The gospel is not as absurd as infidels assert. It rather imparts "to his attribute of compassion the infinity of the Godhead, that, rather than lose the single world which had turned to its own way, He should send the messengers of peace to woo and to welcome it back again; and, if justice demanded so mighty a sacrifice, and the law behoved to be so magnified and made honourable, would it not throw a moral sublime over the goodness of the Deity, should He lay upon His own Son the burden of its atonement, that He might again smile upon the world, and hold out the sceptre of invitation to all its families?"[258]

The infidel view limits God. To imagine that God cannot keep the vast number of people who populate this world in his view and, even

---

257. Chalmers, *Discourses on Astronomy,* pp. 72-73.
258. Chalmers, *Discourses on Astronomy,* p. 74.

more, in his mercy, or that God cannot possibly ensure their well-being, is to subject his providence to our human limitations. According to Scripture, not a sparrow falls unnoticed by God, so extensive is his providence.[259] The Enlightenment, sad to say, dispensed with the doctrine of providence.

The text of the fourth discourse is I Peter 1:12b (KJV), "Which things the angels desire to look into." The sermon takes up the subject of angels, suggesting that what Scripture says about them might imply that there are all kinds of other intelligent forms of life populating the cosmos.[260] There are other forms of intelligent life that apparently live peacefully under God's rule and serve him night and day. Only the barest hint of their existence is given us by revelation; otherwise we know nothing of them. Yet one thing Scripture does tell us is that they have a considerable interest in our salvation. This interest comes from their realization that in God's efforts for our salvation, he reveals his character.[261]

The subject of angels and other heavenly powers is continued in the fifth discourse, whose text is Luke 15:7 (KJV), "I say unto you, that likewise joy shall be in heaven over one sinner that repenteth, more than over ninety and nine just persons, which need no repentance." This text takes a very different position from what the infidels would have us believe.[262] Chalmers gives us some beautiful passages here on the concern of angels and archangels, cherubim and seraphim, for us injured and suffering human beings. These heavenly powers and authorities actually love us in spite of our sin and rebellion. What a subject for the exalted prose of romanticism! Chalmers at his most eloquent is a sort of Presbyterian Berlioz. The marvel and the wonder of the heavenly love is only magnified when we consider the extent of the cosmos.

In the penultimate discourse our preacher takes on the subject of spiritual warfare. What subject would be more fascinating for the romantic poet? Quite appropriately he chooses Colossians 2:15 as his text: "And having spoiled principalities and powers, he made a shew of them openly, triumphing over them in it" (KJV). The salvation of one scrawny race on a minor, handicapped planet might not be so crucial to the harmony of the cosmos if it were not for the matter of spiritual warfare. But perhaps

259. Chalmers, *Discourses on Astronomy,* p. 75.
260. Chalmers, *Discourses on Astronomy,* p. 90.
261. Chalmers, *Discourses on Astronomy,* p. 99.
262. Chalmers, *Discourses on Astronomy,* p. 119.

in the cosmic scheme of things this little planet is the theater of a drama far greater than we can even imagine.[263] This conflict, Chalmers concludes, will one day come to an end, and God's mercy and majesty will be vindicated. "On that day, how vain will this presumption of the infidel astronomy appear, when the affairs of men come to be examined in the presence of an innumerable company."[264]

The final discourse takes a very different turn. It puts apologetic in its place. It warns against overemphasizing theological argumentation. It is not argument that moves the heart.[265] Much more important is a humble acceptance of the authority of the Bible.[266] Our preacher pleads for an evangelical modesty in all such matters. There is a place for theology and a place for philosophy as well, but in the end it is a humble acceptance of the gospel which leads us to true wisdom.

Somehow with these sermons we sense that our preacher has entered into the sphere of sanctified imagination. Chalmers suddenly joins the company of Dante, Milton, and C. S. Lewis. When I was in seminary, thoughts like this were dismissed as mythology in a theological world eager to demythologize the gospel, but now, with my children eagerly watching *Star Wars,* it does not seem quite as far out as I at one time thought.

B. Expository Preaching

In 1842 Chalmers published a series of sermons on Paul's epistle to the Romans that he preached while minister at Saint John's Church in Glasgow some twenty years earlier. In the preface he explains that he began the series in September of 1819 and that by November of 1823 had only gotten as far as the beginning of the tenth chapter. From this we gather that he preached this series through his entire four-year ministry at Saint John's. He tells us, "The following is a record of the Sabbath preparations of many years back — now given without change or improvement."[267] What we have here is expository preaching, but because the exposition

---

263. Chalmers, *Discourses on Astronomy,* p. 139.
264. Chalmers, *Discourses on Astronomy,* p. 150.
265. Chalmers, *Discourses on Astronomy,* p. 159.
266. Chalmers, *Discourses on Astronomy,* pp. 167-69.
267. Thomas Chalmers, *Lectures on Romans,* pt. 1, vol. 22 in *The Works of Thomas Chalmers, D.D. & LL.D.,* p. 5.

treats Romans, it is inevitably evangelistic preaching. This is typical of the Scottish approach to evangelistic preaching. Evangelistic preaching and expository preaching are kept closely together.

While we find this throughout the series, it is especially clear in the six sermons on Romans 5:1-11. Let us focus therefore on these sermons. Chalmers begins with a sermon on the first two verses, "Therefore being justified by faith we have peace with God through our Lord Jesus Christ: by whom also we have access by faith into this grace wherein we stand, and rejoice in hope of the glory of God." Our preacher comments, "To be justified here, is not to be made righteous, but to be counted righteous. To be justified by faith, expresses to us the way in which an imputed righteousness is made ours."[268] A bit further on he says, "[A]nd when we read here that we are justified by faith, one should understand that faith is simply the instrument by which we lay hold of this great privilege — not the light itself, but the window through which it passes — the channel of transmission upon our persons, by which there is attached to them the merit of the righteousness which another has wrought, and of the obedience which another has rendered."[269]

Having spoken of what it means to be justified by faith, Chalmers speaks of what it means to have peace with God. The text makes very clear that peace with God is the effect of faith.[270] In fact, it is the proof of our being justified, and yet we are not assured of our salvation by ascertaining that we have peace in our hearts. Our assurance is in Christ, not in ourselves.[271] With this our preacher passes to the next phrase of his text, "This grace wherein we stand." Chalmers says, "The grace wherein we stand is something more than peace with God. We understand it to signify God's positive kindness or favour to us. You may have no wrath against a man, whom at the same time you have no feeling of positive good-will to. You are at peace with him, though not in friendship with him. It is a great deal that God ceases to be offended with us, and is now to inflict upon us no penalty. But it is still more that God should become pleased with us, and is now to pour blessings upon our heads." Chalmers is so taken by this thought that he wants to reiterate it: "It is a mighty deliverance to our own feelings, when our apprehensions are quieted; and

268. Chalmers, *Lectures on Romans,* p. 271.
269. Chalmers, *Lectures on Romans,* p. 272.
270. Chalmers, *Lectures on Romans,* p. 273.
271. Chalmers, *Lectures on Romans,* p. 276.

we have nothing to fear. But it is a still higher condition to be preferred to, when our hopes are awakened; and we rejoice in the sense of God's regard to us now, and in the prospect of His glory hereafter. It is additional to our peace in believing, that we also have joy in believing."[272]

Finally Chalmers comes to our sharing in the glory of God. "But it will be the glory of His moral perfections, that will minister the most of high rapture and reward to these children of immortality. It will be the holiness that recoils from every taint of impurity. It will be the cloudless lustre of justice unbroken, and truth unchanged and unchangeable."[273] Chalmers's vision of the eternal holiness of heaven is wondrous indeed, but he makes the point that it is merciful and loving as well. It is blended with unsearchable wisdom. "And there, seeing Him as He is, do they become altogether like unto Him; and there are they transformed into a character kindred to His own; and there that assimilating process is perfected, by which every creature who is in Paradise, has the image of glory, that shines upon him from the throne, stamped upon his own person."[274] As our preacher presents it, heaven is where the promises are fulfilled. All God's creation "shall see God, and become like unto God — like Him in His hatred of all iniquity, like Him in the love and in the possession of all righteousness."[275]

Chalmers is at his best when he paints the glories of heaven. It is in the hope of such glory that even here on earth we begin to live the life that is eternal. "You will be at no loss now to understand, how it is that he who hath this hope in him, purifieth himself even as God is pure. It is by progress in holiness, in fact, that he is making ground on that alone way which leads and qualifies for heaven. There is no other heaven truly than a heaven of godliness."[276] Obviously for Chalmers justification by faith leads to sanctification by faith. What concerns him in the end is holiness.

The next sermon treats Romans 5:3-5: "And not only so, but we glory in tribulation also: knowing that tribulation worketh patience; and patience, experience; and experience, hope: and hope maketh not ashamed; because the love of God is shed abroad in our hearts by the Holy Ghost, which is given unto us." In this sermon Chalmers takes the hope mentioned in Romans 5:2, and distinguishes between it and the

272. Chalmers, *Lectures on Romans*, pp. 277-78.
273. Chalmers, *Lectures on Romans*, p. 281.
274. Chalmers, *Lectures on Romans*, pp. 281-82.
275. Chalmers, *Lectures on Romans*, p. 293.
276. Chalmers, *Lectures on Romans*, pp. 281-82.

hope of glory that comes to us by faith when we first hear the promise of the gospel and the hope that comes from experience when we endure tribulation with patience. This latter hope is based on the hope that comes from faith.[277] He presents the story of Abraham as an example.[278] God made a twofold promise to him. The one would be fulfilled many ages later, and the other in his own lifetime. In faith Abraham left his native land and journeyed to the land God showed him. There his son Isaac was born. The fulfillment of the one promise strengthened his faith, and now from experience he had an even greater hope in the promise that would be fulfilled many ages later. "It is quite true, that there is a hope in believing; but from this plain example you will perceive it to be just as true, that experience worketh hope."

With this our preacher turns to his application. "Now it is just so in the gospel. There is a promise addrest in it, the accomplishment of which is far off; and a promise, the accomplishment of which is near at hand. The fulfilment of the one is the pledge or token of the fulfilment of the other. By faith in God we may rejoice in hope of the coming glory; and it will be the confirmation of our hope, if we find in ourselves a present holiness. He who hath promised to translate us into a new heaven hereafter, has also promised to confer on us a new heart here."[279] In his application our preacher issues a warning. As much as one may rejoice in the hope of eternal life, one may not forget the hope of being holy in this life. The two go together. If we would rejoice in the hope of holiness in the life to come, we must expect some realization of that holiness in this life. Chalmers exhorts his congregation to work diligently for holiness in this life. But, then, to make it very clear that sanctification comes by faith just as justification does, Chalmers tells us, "We shall be happy if we succeeded in impressing a clear distinction upon your minds between the hope of faith and the hope of experience; and how if the latter is wanting, the former on that account may come to be darkened and extinguished altogether. But remember you are not to wait for the second hope, till you conceive the first."[280] As Chalmers sees it, the first hope draws the second. The Christian moves from hope to hope just as the Christian moves from faith to faith. "Your experience will be bright just in proportion as

277. Chalmers, *Lectures on Romans,* p. 293.
278. Chalmers, *Lectures on Romans,* pp. 295f.
279. Chalmers, *Lectures on Romans,* p. 297.
280. Chalmers, *Lectures on Romans,* p. 298.

your faith is bright; and it is just if ye continue in the faith grounded and settled, and if ye be not moved away from the hope of the gospel which ye have heard, that you will at length be presented holy and unblamable and unreprovable in the sight of God."[281]

Chalmers devotes yet another sermon to Romans 5:5, "And hope maketh not ashamed; because the love of God is shed abroad in our hearts by the Holy Ghost, which is given unto us."[282] In this sermon our expositor focuses on the doctrine of the Holy Spirit, explaining the sanctifying work of the Holy Spirit in the hearts of Christians. We are told that God sheds abroad his love in our hearts "When he sends the Holy Ghost to take up His residence, and there to rule by His influences."[283] The hope of faith which first responded to the promises of the gospel is wrought in us by the Holy Spirit. It is not of ourselves; it is the gift of God.[284] This first work of the Spirit is followed by others. The Holy Spirit teaches us to look on Christ and see in him the fulfillment of God's promises.[285] The Holy Spirit gives us the impulse to keep the sayings of Christ, and when we fulfill this obedience we come to an even greater understanding of the truth.[286] It is the same Holy Spirit who inspires within us both justifying faith and sanctifying faith. Again we see the indissoluble alliance between the faith of Christianity and the obedience of Christianity. The latter originates in the former. The real faith which is unto salvation inspires and originates all the virtues of the gospel.[287]

The fourth of these sermons takes up Romans 5:6-9: "For when we were yet without strength, in due time Christ died for the ungodly. For scarcely for a righteous man will one die: yet peradventure for a good man some would even dare to die. But God commendeth his love towards us, in that, while we were yet sinners, Christ died for us. Much more then, being now justified by his blood, we shall be saved from wrath through him."[288] We already looked at Andrew Thomson's communion sermon on this text. Chalmers uses it to turn our attention from the subjective experience of Christian faith and hope and the inward work of the Holy

---

281. Chalmers, *Lectures on Romans,* pp. 299-300.
282. Chalmers, *Lectures on Romans,* p. 301.
283. Chalmers, *Lectures on Romans,* p. 303.
284. Chalmers, *Lectures on Romans,* p. 305.
285. Chalmers, *Lectures on Romans,* p. 306.
286. Chalmers, *Lectures on Romans,* p. 307.
287. Chalmers, *Lectures on Romans,* p. 309.
288. Chalmers, *Lectures on Romans,* p. 312.

Spirit to the objective act of God for our salvation in Christ's death and resurrection. Chalmers wants to make the point that God's objective act of atonement in the vicarious death of his Son is fundamental to our salvation. It is no less to be cherished than the inward experiences of the graces of the Spirit and the hope of eternal glory. "It was an expression of love so ardent, that even impiety, in full and open and determined career, could not extinguish it. It was at the time of the world's greatest wickedness, that He descended from on high, not to condemn but to save it. It is true that the first effect of this benevolent undertaking, was simply an acquittal to those who had been guilty; and this was but the prelude of greater things to follow. But this first thing was wrought out in the face of greatest provocation, and at the expense of most painful endurance." As Chalmers sees it, this was the time when God's chosen people rejected the Savior God had sent them. "It was when every man had turned to his own way, that God laid upon His Son the iniquities of us all. Our time of greatest regardlessness was His time of greatest regard."[289]

Chalmers makes the point that the objective death of Christ was more than just a common death and the pain Christ endured was far more than the pain of even a particularly cruel death. Christ's death was vicarious. It was a cosmic struggle with principalities and powers. And not only that, Christ bore the wrath of a holy God against all the sin the millions of redeemed had ever committed.[290] Here we have a long passage in which the themes of both Isaiah 53, the vicarious death of the Servant of the Lord who was taken as a lamb to the slaughter, and Isaiah 66, the vintner who tromps out the vintage where the grapes of wrath are stored, are brought together. It is a long, complicated passage, beautiful nonetheless for its depth of perception. But having made a strong point of the objective death of Christ, Chalmers tells us that what is even more important in the text is that this death is for sinners. That Christ died for sinners is even more amazing than that he suffered the pangs of a vicarious atonement. One might understand that God might make such a sacrifice for good men, but that he should make it for sinners demonstrates a love for us that goes beyond our understanding.[291] Here, of course, what Chalmers says about this text is very close to what Thomson said.

The next sermon takes up Romans 5:10, "For if, when we were ene-

289. Chalmers, *Lectures on Romans*, p. 318.
290. Chalmers, *Lectures on Romans*, pp. 319-20.
291. Chalmers, *Lectures on Romans*, pp. 321-22.

mies, we were reconciled to God by the death of his Son, much more, being reconciled, we shall be saved by his life." Once again Chalmers focuses in on the objectivity of the atonement. As usual, he jumps into his subject without a formal introduction, by a few remarks on the fact that Paul obviously considers argument an important means of evangelism. In this text the apostle uses a particular type of argument logicians call *argumentum a fortiore;* that is, if something is true in adverse circumstances, how much more likely is it to be true in favorable circumstances.[292] Chalmers was indeed a great apologist. His discourses on astronomy are among the most successful apologetic sermons in the history of preaching. We are dealing here with exposition rather than apologetic, but just the same Chalmers, the great apologist, wants to make it clear that for the apostle, at least, argument has its place in preaching.

Here, then, is the argument. First there is the adverse situation: "That point of time in the series of general history at which reconciliation was made, was when our Saviour said that it is finished, and gave up the ghost. God may be said to have then become reconciled to the world, in as far as He was ready to enter into agreement with all who drew nigh in the name of this great propitiation." It was at that point, our preacher maintains, that the atonement was complete. "Now think of the state of matters upon earth, previous to the time when reconciliation in this view was entered upon. Think of the strength of that moving principle in the bosom of the Deity, which so inclined Him towards a world then lying in the depths of ungodliness . . . lifting the cry of rebellion against Him." In the crucifixion of Christ we find the ultimate human rejection of the ways of God. This is Chalmers's point. "There was no movement on the part of the world towards God — no returning sense of allegiance towards Him from whom they had revolted so deeply — no abatement of that profligacy which so rioted at large over a wide scene of lawless and thankless and careless abandonment — no mitigation of that foul and audacious insolence by which the throne of Heaven was assailed."[293] In spite of such an adverse situation, in spite of God having every reason to turn his back on man, nevertheless God was gracious. With this Chalmers delivers one of his infamous long sentences, two hundred words long at least. One has to read it to believe it.

---

292. Chalmers, *Lectures on Romans,* p. 327.
293. Chalmers, *Lectures on Romans,* p. 329.

But for God to have done this very thing, when these sinners were persisting in the full spirit and determination of their unholy warfare — for Him to have done so, when, instead of any returning loyalty rising up to Him like the incense of a sweet-smelling savour, the exhalations of idolatry and vice blackened the whole canopy of heaven, and ascended in a smoke of abomination before Him — for Him to have done so at the very time that all flesh had corrupted its ways, and when, either with or without the law of revelation, God saw that the wickedness of man was great in the earth, and that every imagination of the thoughts of his heart was only evil continually — in these circumstances of deep and unalleviated provocation, and when God might have eased Him of His adversaries, by sweeping the whole of this moral nuisance away from the face of the universe which it deformed — for such a time to have been a time of love, when majesty seemed to call for some solemn vindication, but mercy could not let us go — Surely, if through such a barrier between God and the guilty, He, in the longings of His desire after them, forced a pathway of reconciliation, He never will turn Himself away from any, who, cheered forward by His own entreaties, are walking upon that path.[294]

What a long sentence this is, and yet how powerful it is. Reading the sermons of Chalmers is somewhat like reading Karl Barth's *Church Dogmatics*. The long, complicated sentences never obscure the point; they just pound it home again and again. Finally he clinches his argument: "But if, when enemies He Himself found out an approach by which He might beckon them to enter into peace with Him, how much more, when they are so approaching, will He meet them with the light of His countenance, and bless them with the joys of His salvation."[295]

It is interesting that, living when he did, Chalmers makes such a point of the objective, historical reality of the atonement. One remembers that Chalmers and Friedrich Schleiermacher were contemporaries. Something very different was going on in Scotland than in Germany at that time, and it was not that Scotland was intellectually backwards in comparison. If Schleiermacher was preaching in the wake of Immanuel Kant, Chalmers was preaching in the wake of David Hume and Adam Smith. Goethe had introduced romanticism to Germany no less than Robert Burns and Sir Walter Scott had introduced it in Scotland. Something else

294. Chalmers, *Lectures on Romans*, pp. 330-31.
295. Chalmers, *Lectures on Romans*, p. 331.

was going on in Scotland, something every bit as profound, but infinitely more practical. Having insisted on the historical objectivity of the atonement, Chalmers posits that what is true in history is true in our own spiritual experience. Is it not in the midst of sin that God comes to each of us?

> Is there none here present who remembers such a time of his bygone history, and with such a character of alienation from God and from His Christ, as we have now given to it? And who, we ask, recalled him from this alienation? By whose guidance was he conducted to that demonstration either of the press or of the pulpit, which awakened him? Who sent that afflictive visitation to his door, which weaned his spirit from the world, and wooed it to the deathless friendships, and the everduring felicities of heaven? Who made known to him the extent of his guilt, with the overpassing extent of the redemption that is provided for it?[296]

With this long series of rhetorical questions he makes it inevitable that we human beings do not save ourselves. God might have abandoned mankind to its own ways, and said of the human being, "'I will let him alone, since he will have it so'; and given him up to that judicial blindness, under which the vast majority of the world are now sleeping in profoundest lethargy; and withheld altogether that light of the Spirit, which he had done so much to extinguish." Instead of all this, "God kept by him in the midst of his thankless provocations; and, while he was yet a regardless enemy, made His designs of grace to bear upon him; and, throughout all the mazes of his checkered history, conducted him to the knowledge of Himself as a reconciling God."[297] Chalmers's doctrine of providence comes out very clearly. God "so softened his heart with family bereavements, or so tore it from all its worldly dependencies by the disasters of business, or so shook it with frightful agitation by the terrors of the law, or so shone upon it with the light of His free Spirit, as made it glad to escape from the treachery of nature's joys and nature's promises, into a relying faith on the offers and assurances of the gospel."[298] One notices in this passage the strong sense of God's initiative in our salvation. The same initiative God took in the history of the human race he takes in the history of each Christian. What has happened objectively happens subjectively.

296. Chalmers, *Lectures on Romans,* p. 333.
297. Chalmers, *Lectures on Romans,* p. 334.
298. Chalmers, *Lectures on Romans,* pp. 333-34.

Having made this point about the death of Christ, Chalmers now makes the same point about the resurrection of Christ. "The death of a crucified Savior, when beheld under such a view, is the firm stepping-stone to confidence in a risen Saviour. You may learn from it, that His desire and your salvation are most thoroughly at one. Of His good-will to have you into heaven, He has given the strongest pledge and demonstration, by consecrating, with His own blood, a way of access, through which sinners may draw nigh." Chalmers's insight at this point is certainly arresting. If the crucifixion proves God's good will toward us, how much more the resurrection and the ascension! "And now that, as our forerunner, He is already there — now that He has gone up again to the place . . . which He left to die . . . that the barrier to its entrance from our world may be moved away, He has ascended alive and in glory, without another death to endure, for death has no more the dominion over Him — will ever He do any thing to close that entrance which it has cost Him so much to open?"[299] The Christian has every reason to believe that if while we were yet estranged from God Christ died for us, now that we are reconciled to him God will complete the salvation he began and will bring us into the new life of the kingdom of God.[300]

Before concluding this very long sermon, our preacher makes the point that if a sinner will not be recalled from his sin by this invitation, his heart will be hardened. "There is pardon free as the light of heaven to all who will. There is wrath, accumulated and irretrievable wrath, to all who will not."[301] The sermon ends with a forceful warning to those who will not hear the promise of God and embrace the gospel.

With a sermon on Romans 5:11, "And not only so, but we also joy in God through our Lord Jesus Christ, by whom we have now received the atonement," Chalmers sums up what has been said on this key passage of Romans. The final words of this sermon show his whole approach to evangelism. "Let us therefore sound in your hearing the invitations of the gospel; and make it known to you, that your only chance for being translated into that angelic love of God and joy in Him which obtains in paradise, is simply by believing in their honesty."[302] As Chalmers sees it, faith is catching sight of the faithfulness of God. "You can never be too

---

299. Chalmers, *Lectures on Romans,* p. 341.
300. Chalmers, *Lectures on Romans,* pp. 342-43.
301. Chalmers, *Lectures on Romans,* p. 345.
302. Chalmers, *Lectures on Romans,* p. 350.

sure of God's truth. You can never be too sure of the saving efficacy of the blood of His Son. You can never be too sure of your having received such an abundance of grace, as will exceed the measure of all your abounding iniquities. You can never be too sure of the faithfulness and infinite compassion of your Creator who is in heaven; and the more you cherish all this sureness, the more will you rejoice in Him, the shield of whose protection is over you, and the arms of whose everlasting love are round about you."[303] For Chalmers the faithfulness of God is the surest thing in the world. It is our abundant surety. "This sureness is, in fact, the high road to all that enlargement of sacred and spiritual delight, which in every other way is totally inaccessible. And we are not afraid of spoiling you into indolence by all this proclamation; or of lulling you into a habit of remissness in the exertions of duty by it; or of gendering a deceitful Antinomianism in your hearts."[304] Chalmers is aware that whenever a strong Pauline doctrine of grace is preached, there will be those who will level the charge of antinomianism. Yet true grace, as understood in the New Testament, is free. "It is this freeness, and this alone in fact, which will make new creatures of you; which will usher the love of God into your hearts; which will bring down the Holy Ghost upon you from heaven; which will inspire a taste for spiritual delight that you never before felt; and furnish motive and impulse and affection for bearing you onward in the way of active and persevering duty, on the career of moral and spiritual excellence."[305]

One cannot help but notice how different these sermons are from the evangelistic sermons of Whitefield, Wesley, and the Great Awakening preachers of the previous century. In the first place, they are preached to a settled congregation — a newly established congregation, to be sure — but this is still a very different situation from the peripatetic ministry of Whitefield and Wesley. This series of sermons is clearly expository. It is a sustained attempt to present the gospel as Paul outlined it in the Epistle to the Romans. Chalmers thought it important to preach through the Scriptures in a systematic way at the main service for the Lord's Day. It was the foundation of his preaching ministry. From time to time other approaches to preaching were used, but this sustained interpretation of one book of the Bible after another was the heart of his preaching ministry.

303. Chalmers, *Lectures on Romans,* p. 363.
304. Chalmers, *Lectures on Romans,* p. 364.
305. Chalmers, *Lectures on Romans,* pp. 363-64.

C. Diaconal Preaching

Not surprisingly Thomas Chalmers, like John Chrysostom, was a well-known alms preacher. He had the ability to raise money through preaching, and he frequently used this talent to raise money for the relief of the poor. One such sermon has come down to us, preached for the benefit of the Society for the Relief of the Destitute Sick.[306] The sermon was preached at Saint Andrews Church in Edinburgh, a beautiful church in the recently built New Town.

This society was one of those benevolent societies which the ardent evangelicals of the day so frequently established. It concerned itself with the care of the sick, attending to them both medically and pastorally. It was truly diaconal work in that it was as concerned with the salvation of the poor and the sick as it was with ministering to their material needs.

The sermon takes for its text Psalm 41:1 (KJV), "Blessed is he that considereth the poor: the LORD will deliver him in time of trouble." The text does not do much more than bring up the subject. Expository preaching is hardly what we have here. Much more we have an appeal for alms. This might be regarded as a particular genre of preaching, a small genre to be sure, but a genre which has its place with evangelistic, catechetical, or festal preaching. Alms preaching does not really have to have a text, although alms sermons often use texts very well. What is important to notice here is that this sermon fits so well into the total preaching ministry of one of the greatest preachers the Church has ever known. Chalmers was highly respected for revolutionizing the diaconal ministry of his church in Glasgow, and he was also well known for organizing charitable institutions for the whole of Scotland. It was only natural that he should be an alms preacher as well.

The sermon plays fast and loose with the rules of sermon composition. There is no introduction in the usual sense. The preacher meanders around the subject of benevolence in general, bringing up a number of extraneous subjects along the way. The point he eventually gets around to making is that there is a difference between worldly benevolence and sacred benevolence. The apostle Paul spoke of the differences between worldly

---

306. Thomas Chalmers, *Sermon Preached Before the Society for the Relief of the Destitute Sick, April 18, 1813* (Glasgow: John Smith and Son, 1818), in Chalmers, *Sermons Preached on Public Occasions* (Glasgow: William Collins, s.n.), p. 3, hereafter Chalmers, *Relief of the Destitute.*

wisdom and the wisdom of God in the beginning of I Corinthians, and what he says about wisdom can well be said about benevolence.[307]

One reads several pages into the sermon without finding any division of text, and one begins to wonder what the preacher is getting at. Economy of expression is not one of Chalmers's virtues, but we noticed that in his sermons on Romans.

As the sermon goes on, our preacher satirizes a certain sentimentality with which one commonly regards benevolence. Benevolence "is the burden of every poet's song, and every eloquent and interesting enthusiast gives it his testimony. . . . I speak of that enthusiasm of fine sentiment which embellishes the pages of elegant literature, and is addressed to all her sighing and amiable votaries, in the various forms of novel, and poetry, and dramatic entertainment."[308] As any orator knows, satire is an effective means of getting the attention of one's audience, but in the pulpit it is usually out of place. One is not too sure that the support of benevolence by cultured society is something one should satirize. Our preacher insists that the trouble with the sentimental benevolence so popular in cultured circles is that it neglects the spiritual needs of the poor. It serves the poor with material bread but ignores the bread of life.[309] Chalmers is very critical of worldly philanthropists, especially those who want to keep their philanthropy completely secular. Chalmers would definitely be at odds with the Christian activists of recent mainline American Protestantism.

Chalmers was one of those who had been awakened to the need for foreign missions, and he sees in the work of the missionaries who carry the knowledge of divine revelation into the non-Christian countries of the world an example of a much more profound benevolence than the secular benevolence of Great Britain.[310] He is particularly impressed by the work of the Moravian missionaries among the Indians of North America and the Eskimos of Greenland.[311] Our preacher does not want to get into the controversy of whether one should civilize non-Christians first and then Christianize them or first Christianize them and then civilize them. The plain fact is that when one takes the gospel to non-

307. Chalmers, *Relief of the Destitute*, pp. 4-5.
308. Chalmers, *Relief of the Destitute*, p. 5.
309. Chalmers, *Relief of the Destitute*, p. 9.
310. Chalmers, *Relief of the Destitute*, p. 10.
311. Chalmers, *Relief of the Destitute*, p. 11.

Christian people, civilization follows inevitably. It is the spiritual problem which has to be solved first.[312]

The point Chalmers begins to make clear is that Christian benevolence has to get beyond sentimentality. It has to be "considered," to use the word of the text. The Bible teaches us to "consider" the poor.[313] One has to approach the care of the poor and the sick in an organized, businesslike way.[314] This point is well made, but then our evangelical social activist goes back to satirizing the sentimentality of the casually benevolent. He paints an elaborate word picture of a philanthropist who visits a house in the country where a sick father is dying in a rose-covered cottage surrounded by a dear wife and devoted children. The philanthropist makes his contribution and is blessed by a rosy glow. The modern reader finds it a bit much, but Chalmers is getting his point across. The benevolence work of the Church does have to get beyond sentimentality.

This is a hard point to make. One wonders how Chalmers would make it today. Anyone with a television set knows about the sentimental attempts of Hollywood to speak to the questions of social justice. Certainly here is a good contemporary example of secularized benevolence. But we are all so accustomed to this sentimentality. How does a preacher get through to people so hardened in their sentimentality? Chalmers was a social reformer who succeeded in so much! How would a preacher today get beyond our secularization of charity?

Chalmers was an effective preacher. He accomplished much in the organization of Christian social work with the poor of his day. He exhorts his congregation to give money, to be sure, but as Christians we need to give more than money.[315] Often the poor are poor because they have no idea how to handle money. Chalmers makes his point with a series of rhetorical questions. Will he to whom you give your money "husband your charity with care, or will he squander it away in idleness and dissipation? Will he satisfy himself with the brutal luxury of the moment, and neglect the supply of his more substantial necessities, or suffer his children to be trained in ignorance and depravity? Will charity corrupt him into slothfulness?" It takes considerable skill to administer charity, Chalmers insists, as he continues with his rhetorical questions. What is the peculiar

---

312. Chalmers, *Relief of the Destitute,* p. 13.
313. Chalmers, *Relief of the Destitute,* p. 14.
314. Chalmers, *Relief of the Destitute,* p. 17.
315. Chalmers, *Relief of the Destitute,* p. 23.

necessity of the man or woman we would help? "Is it the want of health, or the want of employment? Is it the pressure of a numerous family? Does he need medicine to administer to the diseases of his children? Does he need fuel or raiment to protect them from the inclemency of winter?"[316] Chalmers does have a sense of the comprehensiveness of the care that needs to be given.

Once one gets beyond the sentimentality of benevolence, it becomes clear that a more realistic approach to charity requires a considerable investment of time and organizational skill.[317] This is why we need organizations such as the Society for the Relief of the Destitute Sick. This society has over the years gained much valuable experience in applying Christian benevolence. It has become "an instrument ready made to our hands."[318]

The sermon could easily have ended here, but the meandering of Chalmers is far from finished. The logical Scholastic sermon outline in either its medieval form or in one of the forms of Protestant scholasticism is completely ignored. Our very modern preacher circles back to the problem of secularization of charity.[319] Chalmers had his finger on something. Here is a sermon that would be prophetic today! Our preacher comes down on his enlightened age. "Your benevolence is too short — it does not shoot far enough a-head — it is like regaling a child with a sweatmeat or a toy, then abandoning the happy unreflecting infant to exposure."[320] Wow! What a simile! With this Chalmers opens up his magazine of rhetorical weaponry. How can one feed the elderly and the dying with a few miserable crumbs of material food when they stand on the shores of eternity and do not yet know how to take the hand of the Savior who will lead them to the throne of God? Now, finally, at the end of the sermon Chalmers brings out his exegesis. Did he never take a course in homiletics? He opens up the New Testament word "salvation." It means at the same time the healing of the bodies of the sick and the saving of the souls of the lost.[321] If we would continue the ministry of Jesus, we must do both.[322] The heart of Chalmers was every bit as great as his voice!

316. Chalmers, *Relief of the Destitute,* p. 24.
317. Chalmers, *Relief of the Destitute,* p. 25.
318. Chalmers, *Relief of the Destitute,* p. 26.
319. Chalmers, *Relief of the Destitute,* pp. 27-29.
320. Chalmers, *Relief of the Destitute,* p. 30.
321. Chalmers, *Relief of the Destitute,* pp. 32-33.
322. Chalmers, *Relief of the Destitute,* p. 36.

If my readers will allow me, I want to step back for a moment so that we might look at Chalmers in another perspective. This last week I spent at least three mornings in the seminary library up at Princeton. I must have looked up at that marvelous etching of Chalmers that dominates the second-floor hallway a dozen times. That etching conveys more about the man than I could ever write. But I realized he is important to the heritage of Princeton. He was at the height of his pulpit eloquence when Princeton Seminary was founded. He was the preacher our founding fathers wanted us all to emulate: an evangelical saint, yes, a preacher above all, but a preacher with a passion for the poor. Concern for the poor did not first appear in the 1960s.

D. Insight, Imagination, and the Art of Oratory

As a preacher Chalmers had authority because he witnessed to the authority of the Word of God. His sense of the authority of the Word of God was transparent. He did not have to argue for it. It was there and people recognized it. It was implicit in his whole approach to preaching. What set Chalmers apart was this profound sense of the authority of Scripture.

One sermon that has often been singled out as an outstanding example of Chalmers's preaching is "The Expulsive Power of a New Affection."[323] Let us look at this sermon and ask why it is so effective. What made it a great sermon? Why is it worship?

To begin we must mention the deep insight Chalmers had into human personality, a characteristic that comes quickly into view in this sermon. Our preacher takes his text from I John 2:15, "Love not the world, neither the things that are in the world. If any man love the world, the love of the Father is not in him." The point he wants to make is that the human heart can turn away from the love of the world and the things of the world only when it discovers the love of God and turns to that instead. The love of God has an expulsive power which chases out the love of the world and the things of the world. Chalmers well understands human nature; it does not give up sin until it discovers grace. That is the way we are: we do not give up one thing until we find something better.

If Chalmers has a deep understanding of human nature, it comes from a profound understanding of the Bible. His preaching gave his con-

323. This sermon is found in Chalmers, *Works*, 6:209-33.

gregation insight into what the Word of God has to say to them. In the end one realizes that the Bible really is speaking to us. In this sermon we discover why we cannot love the world and the things of the world and also love God. The two are at enmity with each other; either one must love God or the world — one cannot love both. That is the reasoning implicit in the text. Nothing draws a congregation to a pulpit quite like the authority of the Word. If the Word is preached with clarity and integrity, the people come. It is the love of God which brings them. The authority of the Word is ultimately attractive.

One thing which makes this sermon outstanding is the freshness of Chalmers's insight into Scripture. These insights are not the same old thing we have heard again and again. There is nothing secondhand about them. The preacher has himself studied the Bible, meditated on it, and thought it through. One reads this sermon and says, "You know, I never thought of this before, but it is true."

Closely related to this is the sermon's imagination. Chalmers is able to come up with hypothetical illustrations which make his point clear. At one point he speaks of a woman who spends hours a day playing cards and other games of chance. Nothing will keep her from this frivolous worldly occupation. No arguments about the waste of time will counter her dedication to this vacuous pleasure unless she suddenly gets invited to a ball and must spend the afternoon with her hairdresser and making herself ready. The greater pleasure of the ball takes the place of the lesser pleasure of the card games.[324] The example here is, of course, all quite hypothetical, made up of the preacher's lively imagination. Or again, our preacher speaks of the way a young man devotes himself to the idol of pleasure, but as he matures he gives up his pleasures because of his love for money and gives himself over to trade. Not satisfied with that, he becomes involved in the whirl of city politics and turns from the idol of money to the idol of power.[325]

There is something about this lively sense of the authority of the Word of God which stimulates the imagination. We noticed in the sermon on astronomy the vastness of divine authority. To know God is to have one's mind set on fire. It is to be inspired by God's Spirit. To listen to the Word of God is to have one's imagination fueled.

To our preacher's artful fancy is added his ability for vivid description.

324. Chalmers, *Works,* 6:211-12.
325. Chalmers, *Works,* 6:213-14.

Toward the end of the sermon we find a highly imaginative description of the kingdom of God as though it were a paradisial island. Filled with the most luminous light, the island offered the inhabitants every virtue and piety. Music flowed through the air, and the whole place was filled with flowers. The preacher brings before the ears of his hearers all the delight of the islands of the South Seas. One can see it all as the parishioners of Saint John's in Glasgow must have imagined it. If the preaching of the gospel were able to present the kingdom of God in this way, then surely those who heard that preaching would quickly leave behind this world and its paltry pleasures. I suppose a good number of us will find this particular word picture overblown. As we have already said, Chalmers is Berlioz in the pulpit. It all sounds a bit like the tale of the Glasgow sailor who had just come back from a voyage to the Fiji Islands and had experienced everything Glasgow with its fog and rain is not. But then, the painting of word pictures has always belonged to the art of popular oratory.

Chalmers's oratory was indeed popular oratory. In the pulpit he was about as different from Hugh Blair as he could be. Blair's rhetoric was more literary than oratorical. Chalmers spoke with a salty Scot's brogue. He was a big man with a vigorous delivery. With dramatic gestures he carved out his sentences in the air. Whereas Blair's rhetoric was delicate and refined, Chalmers's was virile and dynamic. It was addressed to the crofters of the Highlands, the dockworkers of Clydeside, as well as the students of the Scottish universities. While much was undoubtedly lost when the sermons went through the printing press, still the texts which have come down to us give evidence of his picturesque language. He was a popular aristocrat, a Scottish laird.

But the language of Chalmers is not always aimed at the dockworkers, artisans, or shopkeepers in his congregation. It could just as easily be directed to the educated and cultivated. In this sermon, for example, he illustrates his point that the love of the pleasures of this world often deceives those who cultivate them by saying the cultivated upper classes of Paris, in spite of their theaters, their balls, and their receptions, often fall prey to ennui.[326] This French word might not be understood by a good portion of the congregation, but for others it makes the point perfectly.

We find a number of biblical illustrations. Chalmers alludes to the parable of Jesus concerning the exorcism of the demon-possessed in Matthew 12:22-32 and parallels. The heart which has been rid of the de-

---

326. Chalmers, *Works,* 6:215.

monic loves of this world must be filled with an even stronger love for God or else other, even worse demons will repossess it.[327] Again illustrating his point that vice must be driven out by something more powerful, he alludes to the story of Aaron's rod which in his contest with the magicians of Pharaoh became a serpent and swallowed up the serpents Pharaoh's magicians so mysteriously produced.[328]

Again we find a striking biblical illustration when our preacher tells us that the sinner cannot free himself from the love of the world without first experiencing the love of God. To ask him to do so is like asking the children of Israel when they were enslaved in Egypt to make bricks without straw.[329] What a beautiful biblical simile!

Still another characteristic of Chalmers's sermons is his large and rich vocabulary. While churchgoers often complain about preachers using big words, and suggest that they use a simple, limited vocabulary, here is a preacher who uses to good advantage a very broad lexical treasury. This is only natural for someone with such a broad field of interest. It is not that his theological vocabulary is so complicated as that he uses words he has learned from what were then the newly developing sciences and industries, in business and medicine and economics.

Among the secrets of Chalmers's rhetoric is his ability during a sermon to repeat the same truth again and again with great variety. It may be an old principle that repetition is the key to teaching, but in Chalmers's pulpit the repetition always comes in a fascinating variety. Certainly this sermon on the power of a new affection gives us abundant evidence of this. In short, Chalmers was a master of the art of oratory, and our detailed examination of this sermon has shown this.

Having spoken at length about why this greatly admired sermon was so effective, let us consider why it is worship. This sermon is a witness to the power of God's love. Such a witness by its very nature glorifies God and is therefore worship. For Chalmers, in the true preaching of the gospel we so behold God that we love him. Chalmers makes that point especially in this sermon. We have seen Scottish preachers often repeat the principle that the purpose of worship is to glorify God and edify the neighbor. If preaching was an important portion of the regular services of worship, it was obviously thought of as fulfilling this principle just as

327. Chalmers, *Works,* 6:216.
328. Chalmers, *Works,* 6:224.
329. Chalmers, *Works,* 6:227.

much as the singing of the psalms, the reading of the lesson, the prayers, and the celebration of the sacraments. This way of regarding preaching as worship was notably characteristic of those who emphasized the evangelistic function of preaching, such as Thomas Boston, Robert Walker, and Thomas Chalmers.

For Scottish piety the memorizing of the *Westminster Shorter Catechism* was fundamental. The first question of that catechism taught that man's chief end is to glorify God and enjoy him forever. That preaching was to serve God's glory was evident. With all the solemn sincerity that is so characteristic of the Scottish soul, the preaching of the Kirk was worship at its most essential.

IX. Conclusion

Yes, there is something unique about Scottish preaching! And probably what makes it unique is the way it has so consistently been understood as worship. Scottish worship has always had a high sense of holiness. The Lord's Day was observed with the most revered solemnity, a day set aside for prayer, the reading and preaching of the Scriptures, and the singing of psalms. Whether done at family prayers in the home or at church, it always had the same solemnity, the same sacral simplicity. As one reads through Scottish sermons, one discovers the great love serious Christians had for the Sabbath. It was a sacrament of the peace and joy of eternity. Then there were those sacred seasons when Communion was celebrated, and for a week everything else was put aside so that one might properly prepare for the Sacrament. Tables were set up and covered with white linen, and the whole community came together. The ministers of neighboring churches were asked to assist in the feast of the Word that accompanied the sacred meal. In Scotland there was never any question about it: preaching is worship.

If I had another twenty years to work on this subject, I think I could develop a number of ideas in these volumes which at this point I can only advance as theories. But then, a hypothesis is often an important step along the way.

Perhaps the reason one never had to make the point that preaching was worship was that it was always understood that preaching was preaching the Word of God. A sermon was never simply an address on a religious topic. Even if the moderatists made some movements in that direc-

538

tion, popular piety just did not follow suit. Preaching was the exposition of sacred Scripture. The serious business of preaching in Scotland was to take a book of the Bible and to preach through it. It had been that way in the days of John Knox, and it was that way when Alexander Whyte preached his extraordinary three-year series on the Psalms at the beginning of the twentieth century. Toward the end of the seventeenth century, under the influence of the *Westminster Directory for Worship,* the models of the Swiss Reformers were in certain respects overshadowed by what some have called Protestant scholasticism. At each service there was a reading of the Scriptures with an exposition of the lesson, following the *lectio continua.* After prayer and the singing of a psalm there was a sermon on some moral or doctrinal point. In effect, the *Westminster Directory* ushered in the double sermon: one an exposition of Scripture, the other a sermon of moral or doctrinal catechism. In the eighteenth century the exposition of the lesson began to disappear. As much as moderatists such as Hugh Blair and Principal Robertson may have compromised the tradition, and as much as Sir Walter Scott may have misunderstood it, when Thomas M'Crie began to do serious historical research on John Knox, Alexander Henderson, and William Guthrie, the Scottish homiletical tradition quickly reappeared. Andrew Thomson and his followers began to get it back into working order, and for a century Scotland was spiritually nourished by some of the greatest preaching the Christian Church has ever heard. It was the love for expository preaching which gave to preaching its strong doxological character. It was the Word of God which was being preached, and that Word was sacred, to be approached with the greatest of reverence. It was because the Word was holy that their expository preaching had to preach the Word through in an orderly and complete manner. With the *lectio continua* one respected the order of the sacred book. The interpretation of the order was important, too. When Thomas Chalmers began his new church in Glasgow, he did it by preaching through Romans, surely an intentional piece of interpretation in itself. Choosing Romans simply said, here is the heart of the gospel and this is the foundation on which the Church is laid, and it is in the preaching of the gospel that the Church is built.

Evangelistic preaching in Scotland was thoroughly expository. As we have demonstrated, Thomson did evangelism when he preached through Acts, just as Chalmers did evangelism when he preached through Romans. Thomas Guthrie was doing evangelism when he preached his long series on Colossians 1:15-20. John Knox could do evangelism even when he was preaching through Isaiah. But another thing about Scottish evangelistic preaching had perhaps even greater significance, and that is that it was solidly connected to the sacraments. As we have shown, the long tradition of the Church of Scotland was that Communion was the time at which the covenant vows were first made and then repeatedly renewed. To go to Communion was a confession of faith, and therefore the preaching that prepared for Communion was a call to faith. Even when George Whitefield preached at the Cambuslang revival, the revival was consummated by a great celebration of Communion.

It was the same way with prophetic preaching. Prophetic preaching was thoroughly grounded in expository preaching. There was, to be sure, always that time when a prophetic word would suddenly be given at the time and place which God had determined, completely outside the normal processes and procedures of institutionalized worship. Chalmers often had a great word for a great moment. As we shall see, when Thomas Guthrie did his four prophetic sermons, *The City,* there was genuine exposition. Even more, when he did his series on the Epistle of James, he demonstrated how a fresh interpretation of a passage of Scripture can be very prophetic.

The tradition of John Knox did not end with Thomson and Chalmers. It continued through the nineteenth century and even into our day, but we will pick that up further on in our story.

CHAPTER IX

Evangelical Anglicanism

The preaching of the Evangelical Anglicans was significant in that it nourished the Church.[1] Evangelical Anglicanism nourished a large portion of the English church for a long time. While not known for producing great homiletical literature, the Evangelicals did produce preaching which reached the people. Wherever the Church of England produced a solid Evangelical witness, the common people began to return, and yet one has to search out volumes of great Evangelical Anglican sermons. They did not leave many behind. They had no John Donne, no John Tillotson, no John Henry Newman. From a literary standpoint John Newton's sermons are not especially interesting. They are conscientious enough, to be sure, but the primary impact of his ministry was elsewhere than in the pulpit. Charles Simeon was as faithful a preacher of God's Word as the Church has ever known. The fruit of his preaching was rich and abundant, yet it is hard to call him a "great preacher" because for the most part he left only sermon outlines rather than actual sermons. Even

---

1. For more general works on eighteenth-century Anglicanism and its preaching, see Spencer Cecil Carpenter, *Eighteenth Century Church and People* (London: Murray, 1959); Horton Davies, *Worship and Theology in England,* 3 vols. (Grand Rapids: Wm. B. Eerdmans Publishing Co., 1996); James Downey, *The Eighteenth Century Pulpit: A Study of the Sermons of Butler, Berkeley, Secker, Sternas, Whitefield, and Wesley* (Oxford: Clarendon, 1969); Charles Hugh Egerton Smyth, *The Art of Preaching: A Practical Survey of Preaching in the Church of England, 1747-1939* (London: SPCK; New York: Macmillan, [1940]); and Norman Sykes, *From Sheldon to Secker: Aspects of English Church History, 1660-1768* (Cambridge: University Press, 1959).

more significantly, he was not concerned to produce literate homiletical masterpieces. His interest was much more pragmatic. He wanted above all to get the message across. But if we do not study the preaching of the Evangelicals for its literary achievement, we do study it for its pastoral effectiveness.[2]

I. Pietism in an English Context

The awakenings that appeared in America under Edwards and the Tennents, in Germany among the pietists, and in England under George Whitefield and the Wesleys outside the usual structures of the official Church of England, now began to appear in the mainstream of the Anglican establishment. The Great Awakening in America was an all-embracing movement which brought together Congregationalists in the Connecticut Valley, Dutch Reformed in the Raritan Valley of New Jersey, Scotch-Irish Presbyterians on the Appalachian frontier, and Anglicans in the South all the way to Savannah, Georgia. The Great Awakening was the spiritual birth of the American nation.

The Church of England experienced an awakening, too. It came later than elsewhere, and yet it had the usual markings of a pietistic revival. We spoke of Dutch pietism in the early seventeenth century as a deepening of the Protestant Reformation, and even of French Catholic pietism which appeared in protest to the spiritual totalitarianism of Louis XIV. But it was in Germany that pietism achieved its most easily recognized expression. Spener's *Pia Desideria* became a sort of manifesto of the movement. Zinzendorf's utopian community at Herrnhut became the blueprint for a new understanding of Christian society, and the

2. For studies on Evangelical Anglicanism, see George Reginald Balleine, *A History of the Evangelical Party in the Church of England* (London, New York, et al.: Longman Green & Co., 1933); *Evangelicalism: Comparative Studies of Popular Protestantism in North America, the British Isles, and Beyond* (New York: Oxford University Press, 1994); Horton Davies, *Worship and Theology in England;* Kenneth Hylson-Smith, *Evangelicals in the Church of England, 1734-1984* (Edinburgh: T. & T. Clark, 1989); Marcus L. Loane, *Cambridge and the Evangelical Succession* (London: Lutterworth Press, [1952]); John H. Pratt, *The Thought of the Evangelical Leaders* (Edinburgh: Banner of Truth Trust, 1978); John Stewart Reynolds, *The Evangelicals at Oxford, 1735-1871* (Oxford: Blackwell, 1953); John Charles Ryle, *Five Christian Leaders of the Eighteenth Century* (1885; reprint, Edinburgh and Carlisle, Pa.: Banner of Truth Trust, 1979); and Alexander Clinton Zabriskie, *Anglican Evangelicalism* (Philadelphia: Church Historical Society, [1943]).

hymns of Francke and Tersteegen became the theme songs of a deeply Protestant spirituality. Now we must speak of pietism, English style.

Pietism is a sort of spiritual posture which has a way of appearing and reappearing down through the history of the Church. We spoke of Byzantine pietism as manifested in the sermons of Symeon the New Theologian, and of nominalist pietism in the sermons of Jean Gerson, Thomas à Kempis, and Johann Geiler von Kaysersberg. Now we look at a particular form of Anglican pietism. Whenever the formal structure of the Church becomes too insensitive to the movement of the Spirit, or whenever the worship of the Church becomes too conventionalized, there begins to appear a pietistic reaction. That seems to be a sort of rule of spiritual evolution.

Pietism is not the same thing as Puritanism, and particularly not the Puritanism that appeared in England and America in the seventeenth century. Pietism is a very private sort of religion while Puritanism was very public. The Puritans believed in a church sponsored by the magistrate. Pietism retreated into the prayer closet. It emphasized small groups, the *ecclesiola in ecclesia,* the church within the church. The force behind Puritanism was Parliament; the force behind Methodism was the cottage meeting.

But also, pietism is otherworldly while Puritanism is essentially a worldly religion. Puritanism had rejected asceticism quite thoroughly while pietism could be very ascetic. The pietist allowed himself few of the joys of this world. Puritan spirituality was much more robust.

One could go on at some length about the differences between the two, but the pietism of the eighteenth century picked up and reasserted much of seventeenth-century Puritanism. The strong emphasis on the ministry of the Word is a cardinal feature of both movements. We will find that the Evangelical Anglicans reasserted several of the classical genres of preaching. They were particularly effective in recovering evangelistic preaching. Samuel Walker and William Romaine have left us very fine collections of evangelistic sermons. The Evangelicals also did much to recover expository preaching. This had flourished among the fathers of the ancient Church and again at the Reformation, but among the latitudinarians of the early eighteenth century it had floundered. Before the end of the eighteenth century Henry Venn was among the few ministers of the established Church who consistently cultivated it. Only in the 1790s did Charles Simeon begin his ministry of systematic expository preaching. Simeon is, of course, one of the most well known practitioners of expository preaching. Stationed as he was at Holy Trinity Church in Cambridge, his example did much to restore expository preaching to the whole English-speaking Church. As we will see, the Evangelicals had a strong sense of the doxological dimension of preaching.

Evangelical Anglicanism might well be regarded as a pietist reaction to the latitudinarianism of the Church of England during much of the eighteenth century.

A. Latitudinarianism

Latitudinarianism might be defined as a sort of spiritual torpor which descended on England during the early eighteenth century. It was moderatism taken to the extreme. There was something typically English in latitudinarianism. It seemed to prey on some of the worst traits of the national character. If the English are traditionally phlegmatic, latitudinarianism provided a religious temper to match. For several generations the national spirituality was governed by the ancient Greek maxim, Moderation in All Things. That the leadership of the Church quite openly disdained "enthusiasm" was a true sign of the times.

Latitudinarianism spawned a school of preaching which was widely recognized in its day.[3] Latitudinarian preachers were approved by the leaders of society and were duly honored on public occasions, but they did not fill churches or set congregations on fire. The paradigm for latitudinarian preaching was William and Mary's archbishop of Canterbury, John Tillotson. Many preachers followed his example, among the best known being George Berkeley, Joseph Butler, and Thomas Secker.

Latitudinarianism was characteristic of the preaching of the established Church of England from the accession of William and Mary well into the eighteenth century. A few preachers of the period such as George Berkeley (1685-1753) transcended this spiritual torpor. Berkeley, even to this day, is well known as a philosopher. He was also an outstanding and well-received preacher. Educated at Trinity College in Dublin, he was appointed dean of Derry in 1724. For some time he preached in the Anglican church in Rhode Island. He was very popular there, even among Baptists and Quakers. Eventually he was appointed bishop of Cloyne. Even though he preached frequently, few of his sermons have come down to us.

---

3. For a particularly perceptive study of eighteenth-century English preaching, see Downey, *The Eighteenth Century Pulpit*, especially the introductory chapter, pp. 1-29.

Joseph Butler (1692-1752) was the model of the latitudinarian preacher, although his preaching represents the school with its best foot forward. He was logical but unimpassioned. He had little to say about Jesus, and less about salvation. Butler is best known as a moral philosopher. Although brought up Presbyterian, he conformed to the established Church and in 1714 entered Oriel College in Oxford. In 1718 he was appointed preacher at Rolls Chapel in London. For eight years he was the preacher there, and that was where he delivered his famous series of sermons setting forth his moral philosophy. For some time he was the theological confidant of Queen Caroline, and eventually through her support was made bishop of Durham.

Thomas Secker (1693-1768) was an apologist for the good life, a chaplain to the liberal establishment, the consummate church administrator. Rapidly he passed through a series of ecclesiastical preferments. In 1733 he was appointed rector of Saint James Westminster, giving him easy access to the court. As a preacher he was well received, especially by the upper classes. His theology was rather High Church, insisting on the legitimacy of the Church of England, its hierarchy and liturgy. He was forever defending every detail of the religious establishment. It was all very rational and proper, as Secker understood it. Everything was right with the world, especially in England, and it was the job of the preacher to support the commonwealth as it had been so wisely established. There was a problem, however; even if Secker was completely orthodox in his theology, he had no gospel of eternal salvation. Everything was all right the way it was. His reasonable, sensible preaching was a great inspiration to his affluent parishioners.

B. Enthusiasm

But if the nation of shopkeepers, to use Napoleon's "put-down," can at times be characterized as phlegmatic, there are also times when suddenly the ancient Celtic mysticism flames forth. Anglican Evangelicalism was a retrieval of so much that was English.[4] The evangelistic zeal of Celtic Christianity had made the British Isles Christian long before great areas of

---

4. For a perceptive discussion of this subject, see Monsignor Ronald Arbuthnott Knox's work, *Enthusiasm: A Chapter in the History of Religion with Special Reference to the Seventeenth and Eighteenth Centuries* (New York: Oxford University Press, 1950).

the Continent had been touched by the gospel. Patrick, Columba, Columbanus, Aidan, and Cuthbert were among the most enthusiastic evangelists the Church has ever known. The Anglo-Saxons continued the evangelical heritage of Willibrord, Burchart, and above all, Boniface. It was Boniface, a "turned-on" Anglo-Saxon, who was the apostle of Germany. Phlegmatic at times, yes, but when turned on, Anglo-Saxons can be impossible to turn off. Evangelicalism is as English as Parliament. Whether in America or England, there is something about the Anglo-Saxon soul which responds to the missionary challenge. That England has always been a missionary-sending nation hardly needs to be demonstrated. The evangelistic concern of English Christians could not ultimately be repressed.

Hardly less English was the tradition of John Wycliffe. Protestantism sprang from Anglo-Saxon roots as much as from Saxon roots. The independence of the Church of England from the Roman pope had been maintained by Wycliffe long before Luther appeared. Wycliffe had challenged the doctrine of transubstantiation every bit as staunchly as Zwingli. The reason is simple: good Englishmen are too empirical to go along with sacramental magic. Wycliffe's English Bible was both published and preached long before Luther. Even more, the Lollards had exercised an enthusiastic preaching ministry and had sealed their testimony with martyr upon martyr from Wycliffe's time right up to the beginning of the Reformation.

There are those who would have us believe that England embraced Protestantism only because of the dynastic intrigues of the court of Henry VIII, yet the popularity of Protestantism in England has been proven again and again. It was the English people who made England Protestant, not the English king. Henry was far too vacillating, Elizabeth far too opportunistic to bring about as sweeping a reformation as England experienced in the sixteenth century. It was the preaching of the gospel as found in the Book of Homilies that won England. It was "turned-on" preachers like Nicholas Ridley, John Hooper, William Perkins, George Herbert, Richard Sibbes, Richard Rogers, and Thomas Manton who changed the hearts of Englishmen. Anglican Evangelicalism more than anything else was the resurfacing of a long-cherished English tradition of Protestantism.

II. Samuel Walker of Truro (1714-61)

Among those who experienced a spiritual awakening in the eighteenth century was Samuel Walker, a young minister of Cornwall in the far southwest of England. Walker was a few years younger than the Wesleys.[5] In fact, he was born in the same year as George Whitefield. While they were all at Oxford at the same time, there is no evidence that they met, at least not when Walker was a student. Walker's conversion experience came sometime after his student days. In fact, it was well into his pastoral ministry that he experienced his spiritual awakening. In this, of course, he was much like the Wesleys. But there was a big difference between Walker and the early Methodists. Walker stayed very firmly within the usual ministerial patterns of the Church of England. He was spiritually turned on, but he was not a Dissenter. And yet, like the Wesleys, he was more a pietist than a Puritan.

The great-grandson of the highly respected bishop of Norwich, Joseph Hall, he came from a well-connected family. He went to school at Exeter and then in 1732 went on to Oxford. There he pursued his studies in the leisure and comfort usually associated with that well-endowed institution. He enjoyed the innocent genteel pleasures of being a theology student, although he was conscientious enough in his studies. He received his bachelor of arts in 1736 and was appointed curate in Dodescomb Leigh, a small village church near Exeter. As tutor to a young nobleman, he traveled on the Continent. In eighteenth-century England, making the grand tour was considered the final polishing of a proper education. The picture we get of him at this period suggests that he lacked the religious intensity of the Wesleys and other members of their holy club, and in fact was probably the sort of divinity student who steered clear of that kind of enthusiasm.

That, of course, was the issue in the eighteenth century. Government-sponsored religion had become very bland, very conventional, and depressingly halfhearted. Whether in Protestant England or in Catholic France, the king's church had made serious compromises with the world.

---

5. For biographical material on Walker, see George Davies, *Early Cornish Evangelicals, 1735-60: A Study of Walker of Truro and Others* (London: SPCK, 1951); Ryle, "Walker of Truro, and His Ministry," in *Five Christian Leaders of the Eighteenth Century,* pp. 306-27; and Edward Bickersteth, "The Memoirs of Samuel Walker," in Samuel Walker, *Fifty-two Sermons on the Baptismal Covenant, the Creed, and the Ten Commandments* (London: Printed for C. Dilly and T. Browne, 1789).

Returning from his travels on the Continent, Walker was appointed curate and then vicar at Lanlivery in Cornwall. Six years later he was appointed rector of Truro, where he became acquainted with George Conon, the master of Truro Grammar School. Apparently it was under his influence that Walker began to develop his evangelical piety.

It is against this background that we must listen to his sermons. His best-known series of sermons has come down to us under the title *The Christian: A Course of Eleven Practical Sermons,* which was first published in London in 1755.[6] This series went through at least twelve editions. The sermons are clearly evangelistic, with the purpose of bringing Walker's congregation to the same sort of spiritual awakening Walker himself had experienced. The series begins with several sermons outlining the plight of the human race, our sinful rebellion against God, and the threat of eternal judgment. God, in his love for his creation, has nevertheless provided a way of salvation. Sending his Son, Jesus Christ, to offer a perfect sacrifice, God has offered to redeem us from slavery to sin. Through faith in that love of God so clearly proved by the offering of God's very own Son we can enter into a new life. These sermons are particularly strong in their understanding of faith. Faith is trusting in Christ to the extent of following him. At considerable length our evangelist develops the idea that the believer is a new creature (cf. II Cor. 5:17). The grace of God brings about a change in the heart of the believer. Walker contrasts the difference between the "Formalist" and those who have entered into this new life in Christ. The largest and most detailed part of this series is taken up in describing the Christian life. Walker is a preacher of justification by faith, but even more of sanctification by faith.

These are beautifully written sermons. It is a pleasure to read Walker's balanced sentences and carefully developed paragraphs. He uses a rich and precise vocabulary. He was a very logical preacher, and his mastery of formal logic at Oxford contributed to the clarity of his sermons. But Walker was also preaching to an age that admired rationalism. Here was a preacher who understood the language of his day. The variety of his sentence structure makes it easy to listen to these most literate compositions. Apparently he was regarded as an excellent public speaker. He regularly preached to a full church when he was at home, and drew large crowds when he preached abroad as well.

6. For this study an edition published in Glasgow was used: Samuel Walker, *The Christian: A Course of Eleven Practical Sermons* (Glasgow: Chalmers and Collins, 1825).

There is one problem some of us might have with Walker. His view of the Christian life gives the impression that it is terribly severe. Speaking of the life of the new creation, he lays down the rules but somehow communicates less effectively the joy of the Christian life. His Christianity sounds very much like late medieval pietism. One wonders if he had not been schooled by the Brethren of the Common Life or had spent a lot of time reading Thomas à Kempis. There is a big difference between Walker's pietism and the Puritanism of the previous century.

Also popular was a series of catechetical sermons.[7] That there are fifty-two sermons in the collection suggests they were preached on Sunday evenings or at special catechetical services. Several other series have come down to us from Walker. Published posthumously, his ten sermons, *The Refiner, or, God's Method of Purifying his People,* appeared in Hull in 1790. Yet another series, *The Christian Armour: Ten Sermons, now first published from the Author's Remains,* appeared in London in 1841. These make even more clear the picture of Walker as an evangelist and catechist with a passion for holiness. Typical of the eighteenth century, his understanding of holiness was thoroughly pietist.

In a larger view, however, we are perhaps best to understand Walker as a prophetic preacher whom God sent to awaken the Church from a somnolent formality. Superficiality was the weakness of the eighteenth century, and pietism reacted to it with prophetic vigor.

III. William Romaine (1714-95)

Beloved minister of Saint Anne's, Blackfriars, William Romaine was for many years the leading Evangelical Anglican in London.[8] He was a much admired preacher who spoke forth the historic Protestant faith with both passion and learning.

This preacher was the grandson of a French Huguenot merchant

7. Walker, *Fifty-two Sermons on the Baptismal Covenant, the Creed, and the Ten Commandments.*

8. For biographical material on Romaine, see W. B. Cadogan, "The Life of the Rev. William Romaine, A.M.," in *The Whole Works of the Late Reverend William Romaine, A.M.,: comprising the life of Mr. Romaine,* vol. 1 (Edinburgh: T. Nelson, 1840); Peter Toon, *William Romaine, the Life, Walk, and Triumph of Faith with an Account of His Life and Work* (Cambridge and London: James Clarke & Co., 1970); and Ryle, *Five Christian Leaders,* pp. 149-79.

who had fled his native land sometime before the revocation of the Edict of Nantes in 1685. As so many Protestants in France, he saw the persecutions mounting and realized hard days were ahead. He therefore relocated his business at Hartlepool, a port town in the north of England, on the east coast, not too far from Durham. The preacher's father was a devout man who was sufficiently prosperous to have been elected mayor. Young Romaine received a thorough grounding in the Christian faith not only from his home, but from his grammar school as well. Bernard Gilpin's School in Durham had been founded at the time of the Reformation and had served the Protestant cause ever since. From there he went on to Oxford and received both a bachelor's and a master's degree. He was regarded as an accomplished scholar, especially in Hebrew.

Interestingly enough, Romaine was also at Oxford with the Wesleys and Whitefield, just as Walker had been. Even more striking is the fact that Walker, Romaine, and Whitefield were all born in 1714. They were exactly the same age. Romaine, just as Walker, never seems to have crossed paths with the others. At that time Romaine would have shied away from anything that could be called enthusiastic. He was a devout Christian, inclined toward Puritanism, perhaps, but not a pietist.

In 1738 Romaine was installed as curate at Banstead in Surrey. This small country church gave him the opportunity to study the Scriptures very carefully. After a few years he began to work on a revision of the Hebrew dictionary of Marius de Calasio first published in 1620. While in Banstead he made the acquaintance of Sir Daniel Lambert, who in time became the lord mayor of London and appointed him his chaplain. This gave the young preacher entree into the ecclesiastical circles of the capital. In the meantime Romaine had moved into London to supervise the publication of his dictionary. He filled a number of short-term preaching posts in the city until 1749, when he was given the lectureship of Saint Dunstan's in the West.

Romaine's theology began to move away from the latitudinarianism so typical of eighteenth-century Anglicanism. His faith became more and more experiential. Like Whitefield and Jonathan Edwards, he became what some have termed an "evangelical Calvinist." Romaine always stayed on good terms with the Wesleys, but he was not an Arminian, and furthermore he was determined not to leave the established Church.

In 1750 he was given, in addition to his evening lectureship at Saint Dunstan's, the duties of the morning service at Saint George's, Hanover Square. This was a new church in a fashionable quarter of the city. In time his "turned-on" preaching began to bring crowds to the church and the inhabitants of the neighborhood started to complain that the "hoi polloi" were taking up all the seats. The more comfortable and stylish members of the congregation won out, and Romaine was dismissed. The deeper problem, of course, was that latitudinarianism might have satisfied the needs of the upper class, but the common people needed something a bit more substantial. That was what the Evangelicals were supplying, and that in itself discomforted the establishment.

Romaine had every provocation for leaving the established Church, but his belief in providence and his enduring patience prevailed. As his commitment to the Evangelical cause grew and as his popularity increased, so did the opposition of his latitudinarian colleagues. He had to go to court to defend his position as lecturer at Saint Dunstan's. The rector there disapproved of his approach to the preaching of the gospel and refused to give him access to the pulpit. According to the decision of the court, Romaine was confirmed in the lectureship, and it was determined that he would fulfill the terms of it by preaching at seven o'clock on Sunday evenings. The rector, however, did not accept the settlement gracefully. The doors were not opened until exactly on the hour and no lighting was provided, leaving poor Romaine to preach with a candle in his hand. The crowds still came, however. People spilled out into the streets, especially before the service began. All this commotion and the size of the crowd brought the bishop to attend one evening. The bishop was very favorably impressed with Romaine's sermon, and things were finally settled a bit more amicably.

For more than forty-five years Romaine preached at Saint Dunstan's on Sunday evenings. During this time he is said to have preached through the entire Bible once and certain books even more frequently. Apparently preaching the *lectio continua* on Sunday evenings was a widespread practice among Evangelical Anglicans of this period.

During this time he also began to make summer preaching tours. He preached at the fashionable watering stations such as Bath and Brighton, in Buckinghamshire and even as far north as Yorkshire. In the north country his ministry was to simpler country people. In these preaching tours he came to know something of the progress of the Evangelical movement and made the acquaintance of many of its leaders.

The countess of Huntingdon began to take an interest in Romaine's preaching. The "mother in Israel," as John Wesley is supposed to have called her, was a hearty supporter of the Evangelical cause. She maintained a number of chapels about the country and gave her "chaplains" an opportunity to preach in them. Romaine was one of her favorites. As it happened, the parish of Saint Anne's, Blackfriars, in London became vacant, and the countess used her influence to procure the position for Romaine.

In 1766 Romaine entered into his pastorate at Saint Anne's, Blackfriars. For the first time in his thirty-six-year ministry he was a rector of a parish rather than merely a curate or a lecturer. It was something of a milestone for the Evangelical movement, for finally the Evangelicals had a parish of the established Church in the city of London. Romaine continued as an active preacher in London for many years. At the age of eighty-one he was preaching both at Blackfriars and at Saint Dunstan's right down until a few weeks of his death. In those final years he had become such a prominent figure in the religious life of the city that his funeral became a public event attended by notables of both church and state.

Eight volumes of Romaine's works were published in 1801. His most frequently published work was a treatise on the Christian life, *The Life, Walk, and Triumph of Faith*. Some of his occasional sermons had been published separately. By far the most popular of his sermon series, *Twelve Discourses upon the Law and the Gospel* was published in 1760.[9] These sermons came out of his preaching ministry at Saint Dunstan's.

Typical of the preaching of the Evangelical revivals of the eighteenth century, these sermons emphasize the hopelessness of the human situation, the vicarious sacrifice of Christ as God's gracious plan for our salvation, and faith as the key to living a godly life. They are especially eloquent on the subject of love toward God and love toward the neighbor. As the sermons of the eighteenth-century Evangelicals generally, they paint a bright picture of the blessings of God in the life to come. The hope of salvation was what made Evangelical preaching the powerhouse behind social change. This is what the latitudinarians did not have.

The twelve sermons treat the following subjects:

1. The necessity of divine teaching
2. The moral Law

9. William Romaine, *Twelve Discourses upon the Law and the Gospel*. For this study the edition of 1801 has been used: *Works of the Late Reverend William Romaine, A.M., Rector of Saint Andrew by the Wardrobe and Saint Ann, Blackfriars, and Lecturer of Saint Dunstan in the West, London*, 2nd ed., 8 vols. (London: Crosby and Letterman, 1801), 3:31-431.

3. The ceremonial law
4. The law of faith
5. Imputed righteousness
6. Being righteous
7. The right knowledge of God
8. The right love of God
9. The right love of the neighbor
10. The cleansing power of Christ's blood
11. The balm of Gilead
12. The promises of God

They are clearly evangelistic sermons. That was at the heart of the Evangelical Anglican mission. We have here a series of evangelistic sermons, like many we have spoken about in the history of preaching. It is designed to shepherd the congregation through the conversion experience. This is what eighteenth-century Evangelicals meant by preaching the gospel. Here are evangelistic sermons directed not to total pagans who had never heard of Christ, but rather to the latitudinarian, lukewarm Christians of London.

As J. C. Ryle, the famous Anglican bishop of Birmingham, paints Romaine, he was a city preacher, particularly adept at reaching the crowds of the growing metropolis. London was a fashionable city in the middle of the eighteenth century. From India, from the Orient, from the Americas, exotic luxuries were piling into the warehouses of the city. A leisure class had time to discuss the newest sciences and philosophies. The star of the British Empire was beginning to rise. London was a marketplace of exciting ideas. Deism was discussed by everyone, and many of the upper classes felt no need to take traditional Christianity too seriously. Yet London was a city in which the social decay of the Industrial Revolution was becoming a real problem. Romaine preached repentance. He addressed these evangelistic sermons to both the religiously careless and those whose Christian devotion was only a formality.[10] The Formalists, as he calls them, were those who performed the outward devotions of the established religion without inner devotion. Our preacher hoped to stir up his congregation to a more experiential and vital faith.[11] As Romaine saw it, an objective saying of the liturgy was hardly a fulfillment of the first tablet

10. Romaine, *Discourses,* 3:176.
11. Romaine, *Discourses,* 3:52.

of the Law. God commands us in the first and greatest commandment to love him. To attend church without heartfelt devotion hardly fulfills even the first commandment.[12] This is a typically pietistic concern. All the way through these sermons we find this concern for the subjective experience of worship. True worship took place in the movements of the heart, and without it the mere saying of the liturgy had little point. The service of worship, but especially genuine preaching, was true worship when it set forth the abounding love and rich mercy of our divine Redeemer.[13] By pointing the way to salvation the faithful preacher proclaimed the rich mercy and abundant love of the Son of God. When human beings entered into the way of salvation, the glory of God was realized. For Romaine, as for Evangelicals generally, preaching had a strong doxological function.

IV. John Newton (1725-1807)

If we might be allowed a rather wooden pun, there was something very new about John Newton.[14] He was a new sort of Englishman, a very common sort of man, no pedigree, no tradition of learning, no heritage of piety. Here was a minister of the established Church of England who knew neither Cambridge nor Oxford. He was brought up on the docksides of London where his father was a shipmaster. When he was twelve years old, instead of being sent off to school he went to sea with his father. He learned the trade routes of the Mediterranean, a dangerous venture in the days of the Barbary pirates. At eighteen he was impressed

12. Romaine, *Discourses,* 3:255f.

13. Romaine, *Discourses,* 3:167.

14. For biographical material on Newton, see D. Bruce Hindmarsh, "I Am a Sort of Middle-man: The Politically Correct Evangelicalism of John Newton," in *Amazing Grace: Evangelicalism in Australia, Britain, Canada, and the United States,* ed. G. Rowlyk and others (Montreal: McGill-Queen's University Press, 1994), pp. 29-55; Hindmarsh, *John Newton and the English Evangelical Tradition between the Conversions of Wesley and Wilberforce* (Oxford: Clarendon, 1996); Hindmarsh, "The Olney Autobiographers: English Conversion Narrative in the Mid–Eighteenth Century," *Journal of Ecclesiastical History* 49 (January 1998): 61-84; Bernard Martin, *An Ancient Mariner: A Biography of John Newton* (London: Epworth Press, 1960); *John Newton of Olney and St. Mary Woolnoth: An Autobiography and Narrative Compiled Chiefly from His Diary and Other Unpublished Documents* (Edinburgh: Banner of Truth Trust, 1998); and John Charles Pollock, *Amazing Grace: John Newton's Story* (San Francisco: Harper and Row, 1981).

into the Royal Navy. He did well as a seaman and was soon made midshipman. In time his ship called at Plymouth and he tried to escape, but he was apprehended and his servitude made even more severe. Finally he was able to trade posts, but the new position was on a ship involved in the African slave trade. Again he did well and was soon shipmaster as his father before him. In spite of his growing material success he was restless. He obviously had the gift of leadership, but the slave trade disgusted him. This experience gave him a revulsion for slavery, and in later life he supported other Evangelicals in their efforts to end the slave trade.

In his midtwenties, having experienced some of the more brutal realities of life, he began to give himself an education, much in the same way as his American contemporary Benjamin Franklin. As a matter of fact, Franklin was another of these new men — very learned yet self-taught; experiential geniuses they were, scientific and yet quite literary. Just as Franklin taught himself to write for the poor Richards of the eighteenth century, so Newton taught himself both to write and to preach to the people of that new age of social revolution.

Newton, like Franklin, belonged to a world Oxford and Cambridge would never understand. Newton had a conversion experience on 10 March 1748. His religion was experiential in the way it had been for Jonathan Edwards, the Wesleys, and George Whitefield. That was the way cutting-edge religion was in the eighteenth century.

In 1755 Newton landed a position as surveyor of the tides at Liverpool that allowed him a certain amount of leisure time, of which he made good use. He devoted himself to learning Latin, Greek, and Hebrew. In effect he was preparing himself for ordination, without the aid of a theological seminary. Without the patina of the ancient universities so essential to the Anglican establishment, he was determined to prepare himself for a ministry to the ordinary men and women of England who were laying the foundations of a very new society.

A. Ordination of a Self-Taught Man

In 1758 Newton applied to the archbishop of York for ordination. He was turned down. We are not told why, but we can well imagine that with his lack of a formal education he hardly spoke the King's English. Besides that, he resonated with the enthusiasm of George Whitefield and the Wesleys. No doubt he just did not have the air of a proper clergyman.

Perhaps it was because he, like Whitefield, had gone back to the Calvinism of sixteenth-century English Protestantism. Like many young Englishmen, Newton was rediscovering classical Protestantism. The Evangelical Anglicans were looking for something more than they were getting from their parish churches. Latitudinarianism had become just plain boring; Arminianism had spent its force. To the guardians of the established religion these new, enthusiastic types were offensive. Perhaps that is why the archbishop turned Newton down.

Things improved, however. A few years later, in 1764, he was nominated to the parish of Olney, and the bishop of Lincoln ordained him. He was very well received there. He had a way with men. Being a natural leader and having much experience with the roughest sort of seaman made him a kind of pastor who commanded the respect of his congregation. He was no dainty dominie. There was something virile about his simple straightforward piety, and his congregation followed his pastoral leadership.

One of the fruits of his pastorate in Olney was his friendship with the poet William Cowper, who had come to live in the parish in 1767. The two men developed a good working relationship, and in 1779 they published the *Olney Hymns*. Cowper was an accomplished poet, although not a poet of first magnitude. Several of his hymns are still in use. Several of Newton's contributions are still very popular as well. One thinks of "Glorious things of thee are spoken" with its rich biblical typology. "How sweet the name of Jesus sounds" and "One there is above all other" are still sung today, but Newton's hymn "Amazing Grace" is among the all-time favorites of English hymnody.

B. A Democratized Rhetoric

Newton's hymns are only one indication of his literary gifts. Whether in his hymns or sermons, Newton used a simple, direct language. His sermons are well organized. They follow the sort of outline popular in England at the time. There is an introduction, followed by a short division of the text. Two or three, sometimes four points are made, then an application concludes the sermon. His sermons were straightforwardly expository in the sense that he aimed at explaining a specific text. That seems to be typical of the Evangelical Anglicans. Indeed, Newton seems to be quite conscientious about this. Often the strength of his sermons is largely dependent on his clear, simple sermon outlines. It is one of the primary characteristics of his style.

Newton regularly gives us fine similes and metaphors, but he is modest in their use. One never gets the feeling he has searched them out or strained after them. They obviously come out of his rich experience of life, upon which he has reflected with sensitivity and candor. There is nothing immature, hasty, or ill considered in these sermons. His figures of speech come not from his literary culture but from his own insight.

It is the same way with his biblical illustrations. How often we have noticed in the history of preaching that one of the most effective ways of making a point is to give a biblical illustration. Here again the effectiveness of Newton's biblical illustrations comes from the depth of his understanding of the Scriptures. He understands Scripture because he has lived life so fully.

If Newton's sermon cycle *The Messiah* is any indication, he uses typology exceedingly well. He used classic typology in his hymn "Glorious things of thee are spoken," and we notice that his typology sticks to the classic types. That is, he relies on the long-recognized types the Church has repeated down through the centuries. Possibly in such matters either directly or indirectly he is following Matthew Henry, who is about as dependable a guide to biblical interpretation as Newton could have found. As we have often suggested, typology is an integral part of biblical poetry. It is part of the thought rhyming that we often find in Scripture. As every real poet understands, typology is a folk art. One might almost say it is something that comes out of the racial memory of a people. Typology, as poetry, real poetry, is preeminently popular.

The democratizing of rhetoric is evident in his sermons because he sticks so closely to the biblical imagery, which has a universality to it. Somehow it speaks to all classes of people. Korean factory workers, Scottish shepherds, English seamen, and Silicon Valley computer operators all seem to be able to make sense of it.

Although strongly dependent on the biblical imagery, Newton's sermons seem quite free of theological jargon. The vocabulary is very democratic. It is not the vocabulary of the schools. These sermons are not addressed to the theological literati but to the new kind of Englishmen, those who were exploring the world and founding the new sciences and businesses of what today we call the modern world. The rhetoric of Newton's sermons is not the highly mystical religious rhetoric characteristic of the late Middle Ages. The religious experience medieval rhetoric dealt with was much more monastic and ascetic. This experiential religious rhetoric, on the other hand, was much more businesslike, much more scientific, much more middle class. It was the sort of language used in newspapers rather than in prayer books. In short, it was a very democratized sort of rhetoric.

C. The Evangelical Mission

Newton was minister to the church of Olney for some fifteen years. Then in 1779 he was called to London, where he served the congregation of Saint Mary Woolnoth for almost thirty years. There he had a popular ministry in the capital city of the British Empire. What an opportunity! That empire was at the threshold of its greatness. It would provide a good portion of the political context of the missionary movement of Evangelical Protestantism. If Evangelical missionaries went out to every conceivable shore, to the remotest islands of the sea, they were taken there by British ships. That Evangelical missionary movement which would shape the Christian Church for centuries to come would think of London as its home base — not the only home base, to be sure, but certainly one of the most important.

The Evangelical mission was to bear witness to the grace of God in Jesus Christ, yes, to the amazing grace of God in Christ. This grace is to the end of our salvation, and not only our salvation but the salvation of all peoples throughout the earth. It is of its very essence a missionary faith. It is missionary in that it bears witness to every human being on the face of the earth, testifying to the power of God to save us all from our sin. It is in Scripture alone that this grace is revealed to us, and therefore it is through the preaching of the Scriptures that this witness is communicated. The reading and preaching of Scripture is a means of grace. It is by that grace alone that our salvation has been won, and it is by faith alone that we enter into it.

We wish we had from Newton a series of sermons which laid out the Evangelical message. We do not have that exactly. We do, however, have a number of autobiographical writings. For fifty years he kept a journal of his religious experiences, a common practice over the centuries among pietists. Selections from it have been published repeatedly ever since his first attempt in 1764. In these selections we hear Newton's witness to his own conversion. We have a good number of letters which were treasured by the Evangelicals of England in the nineteenth century, in which the Evangelical message is very clear as well, but our concern in this study is preaching. Sad to say, not many of Newton's sermons have come down to us. But we do have one remarkable series of sermons preached in London between 1784 and 1785. It is a particularly interesting series for us because it illustrates how the proclamation of the gospel is worship. It shows us how Evangelical Protestantism understands the doxological dimension of preaching. This series is unusual because it is fifty expository sermons on the biblical texts of George Frideric Handel's oratorio *Messiah*. These sermons were originally published under the title *Messiah: Fifty Expository Discourses on the Series of Scriptural Passages which form the Subject of the Celebrated Oratorio of Handel. Preached in the years 1784 and 1785, in the Parish Church of St. Mary Woolnoth, Lombard-Street.*[15]

There are a number of remarkable things about these sermons. Here we have a year's worth of sermons, and yet they do not follow the liturgical calendar. This seems to have frequently been done in eighteenth-century Anglicanism. Christmas, Epiphany, Good Friday, Easter, and Whitsunday were observed, but not much more. Anglican preachers often followed their own fancy once the prayer book service had been faithfully read — we have very few series of lectionary sermons from the Anglican preachers of this period. Here is a series of sermons which treats the central mysteries of our redemption and yet it does not follow the liturgical calendar.

Equally remarkable is the fact that Handel's oratorio should be based on such a perceptive series of Scripture passages. Almost from the beginning the deep insights of this arrangement of texts were recognized. Our preacher had heard a performance of the oratorio at Westminster Abbey, and apparently the singing left the congregation in awe. Not only did Handel's musical work impress the congregation, but the passages of Scripture behind it left the devout of England equally enthusiastic. That an oratorio should be based on such a powerful anthology of the sacred Scriptures was truly amazing. Almost from the beginning, in English-speaking lands this oratorio has been recognized as a significant musical expression of the Christian faith. For more than two hundred years it has been the primary musical festival of the English-speaking world.

That a course of sermons should be developed on the framework of

---

15. The edition used for this study is found in *The Works of John Newton*, vol. 4 (Edinburgh and Carlisle, Pa.: Banner of Truth Trust, 1988), hereafter Newton, *Messiah.*

an artistic masterpiece may surprise us, but this was not the first time
something like this had been done. In fact, it was done fairly frequently in
the later Middle Ages. We mentioned Johann Geiler von Kaysersberg's series of sermons on Sebastian Brandt's *Ship of Fools.* One would not want
to do this sort of thing too often, but there are times when an imaginative
tactic like this does have its value. One value of Geiler's series, for example, was that it kept Christians in conversation with the artistic and literary culture of the day. *Ship of Fools* was one of the masterpieces of late medieval German literature. Geiler knew Brandt personally. In fact, the two
were good friends, both living in Strasbourg. Geiler had read his friend's
work and as a Christian preacher responded to it. Newton has done the
same thing.

Yet, more should be said. The compelling feature of Handel's *Messiah* is that it helps us see the beauty of Scripture. The sheer beauty of the
texts themselves comes through with such clarity in these glorious musical settings. What is happening here is that the music serves as a witness
to the beauty of God's Word. God's Word, his redemptive, healing Word,
is gracious, and as such is beautiful. Handel's oratorio bears witness to
this, and so do these sermons of Newton's. As Psalm 119 with its 176
verses gives witness to the beauty of the Law, so Newton's sermons witness
to the beauty of the gospel.

D. Worship as Witness to God's Glory

In this series we begin to see how the preaching of Newton and the Evangelicals of the eighteenth century is to be understood as worship, whether
they were Evangelical Anglicans, American Puritans, or German pietists.
For Newton the texts of Scripture Handel put to music were a witness to
God's glory. To hear Handel's anthem, "And the glory, the glory of the
Lord shall be revealed, and all flesh shall see it together," is to hear a definition of the divine glory. The story goes that even the king of England
when he heard the "Hallelujah Chorus" rose to his feet. Yes, even the king
recognized that here was a witness to the highest glory. The royal majesty
was only relative, the divine glory infinite.

The style of music in Handel's work and the style of oratory in
Newton's sermons are very different. Handel, true to his age, wrote in a
rococo style, ornate and florid. The style of Newton, however, is simple
and sober. Strangely enough, the two could not be more opposite, and yet

the expositions of Scripture which Newton brings us reveal a seriousness in the texts of the oratorio which makes them even more magnificent. Handel's *Messiah*, like Mozart's *Requiem*, transcends the style of the age. The texts in each case demand it.

Interestingly enough, the texts of Scripture used in the *Messiah*, taken together, are a cannonade against the Deism that was becoming so popular in the eighteenth century. The Enlightenment had strongly opposed the orthodox doctrine of the Trinity. Unitarianism had become increasingly popular through the course of the century. The texts assembled by the oratorio, on the other hand, are preeminently orthodox. At a number of points in this series of sermons Newton points to the orthodox tendency of these texts. Anglo-Saxon Evangelicalism, as German pietism, had always affirmed classical Christian orthodoxy. In fact, its insistence on orthodoxy is the basis of its doxology. It is orthodox Christianity which glorifies God. Deism, like the Arianism of the fourth century, is an insult to the majesty of the Son of God, and if an insult to the Son, it is an insult to the Father as well. On the other hand, when true doctrine is taught, then God is glorified. That, at least, is the way the orthodox have always looked at it. For Evangelicals true doctrine is the inner presupposition of true worship. It is the faith of the heart that is the essence of worship.

For the Evangelicals, however, the service to which God has called us is much more than simply teaching orthodox doctrine.[16] It is, to be sure, at least that, but it is also the giving of a witness. Two things are involved here. First, we must recognize that the giving of a witness is above all the living of a Christian life. In fact, the latter has to be prior to the former, because the essence of the witness is that it is the grace of God which brought one from darkness to light, from slavery under sin to a new life. There is no witness to give without the transformed life.[17]

Newton is remembered not so much as a good preacher as a good man. He was not so much an athlete of piety as simply a good man. His goodness was the sort other men recognized. Seamen, merchants, and businessmen recognized his simple, straightforward goodness.

The second thing involved here is that the witness was given that those who heard it might be converted. We find several examples of this in several sermons.[18] A witness is given that the truth might become clear,

16. Newton, *Messiah*, sermon XXXI, p. 342.
17. Newton, *Messiah*, sermon XVII, p. 205.
18. Newton, *Messiah*, sermon XIX, p. 229; sermon XXVI, p. 302.

that it might be recognized.[19] The giving of a witness in public worship is important because this witness strengthens the faith of the faithful, encourages the faith of the weak, and inspires the faith of the doubtful. Here we find once again one of the cardinal biblical concepts of worship. This was the motive of so much of the worship of the Temple. This was the theology behind the votive sacrifices. Here was the reason one came to the Temple to tell the story of divine deliverance before the great congregation. The witness told the story of God's saving mercy, and in giving this witness God was glorified.[20] We have often spoken of this theology of worship. It comes particularly to expression in Psalms 22 and 107. Having been saved from some catastrophe, the worshiper comes to the Temple and recounts the story of God's deliverance. Telling this story is a witness. It recounts the story of God's saving acts, gives thanks for that salvation, and confesses the obligation one therefore has toward God. It is both worship and evangelism at the same time.

V. Robert Hawker (1753-1827)

Plymouth is a busy port city in the south of England. It was as minister of one of the parish churches of Plymouth that Robert Hawker exercised his well-rounded and effective ministry.[21] As a preacher Hawker was especially well known for his course of ten sermons defending the doctrine of Christ's divinity. It was so well received that it won him a doctorate from the University of Edinburgh. These sermons are a good example of classic doctrinal preaching. But Hawker was also a gifted communicator with those who had no formal academic training. He was a popular preacher, but he was far more. His pastoral ministry was extensive. Typical of the Evangelicals, he was renowned for his charitable works.

Hawker was, above all, a writer of tracts for the common people. A good part of his published work consists of these tracts. In 1802 he founded the Great Western Society for Dispersing Religious Tracts among the Poor of the Western District. He was concerned about the lit-

19. Newton, *Messiah,* sermon XIX, pp. 227f.

20. Newton, *Messiah,* sermons XXX, XXXI, and XXXII.

21. Very little biographical work has been done on Hawker. Aside from "Hawker, Robert, D.D.," in *Dictionary of National Biography,* 9:201-3, the chief source is the memoir of John Williams found at the beginning of the ten-volume edition of his works, *The Works of the Rev. Robert Hawker, D.D.,* 10 vols. (London: Ebenezer Palmer, 1831).

eracy of the poor and was active in founding schools for underprivileged children. This was why he founded a Sunday school in his parish. Not only was it a school for children who could not pay for an education, but it became an orphanage as well. Medical care for the poor was another of his concerns. This was only natural, of course, because of his experience as a surgeon for the Royal Navy. The more we read about Hawker's ministry, the more it sounds like that of August Hermann Francke, the German pietist.

Hawker was born in Exeter. His father, a surgeon, died before he was two years old, and he was brought up by his widowed mother. In spite of early inclinations toward the ministry, his mother wanted him to follow in his father's footsteps as a surgeon. There was a fine grammar school in Exeter, and there he learned the classical languages in order to qualify for a professional career. Having finished his schoolwork, his mother apprenticed him to a surgeon at Plymouth by the name of White. At the age of nineteen he married Anne Raines and began a family. To support his growing family he became an assistant surgeon in the Royal Marines. In that capacity he served for three years. And yet, more and more he felt the call to the ministry. In 1778 he matriculated in Magdalen Hall, Oxford. He and his wife already had several children, but in spite of the practical problems, he persevered in his ministerial preparations. In the meantime the surgeon to whom he had been apprenticed back in Plymouth had become mayor. As it happened, a church position became vacant and, as mayor, White proposed his apprentice's name. By the end of the year he was back in Plymouth, having been ordained as a deacon. For the next six years he served as curate to the rector of the parish, John Bedford. When Bedford died Hawker became his successor.

We are interested in Hawker's preaching because it shows the serious theological concern of the Evangelical Anglicans. This interest in systematic theology is not what one expects from a more pietistic type of Christianity. Perhaps it surfaced because Deism, so popular in the eighteenth century, had challenged Christian orthodoxy. How or why it may have been, the Evangelicals were consistently orthodox in their theology, just as they were activist in their social concern.

Hawker's *Sermons on the Divinity of Christ* are above all popular sermons.[22] They are not addressed to theologians, nor are they dumbed-

---

22. For the text of these sermons, see Robert Hawker, *Sermons on the Divinity of Christ*, in *The Works of the Rev. Robert Hawker, D.D.*, 1:9-198.

down sermons for the ignorant, but they are addressed to the average English churchgoer of the eighteenth century, to the artisans and shopkeepers of an English town. The common people are treated as intelligent human beings. Hawker argues his case for the divinity of Christ not in heavy theological or philosophical terms but in straightforward biblical terms, and this is, no doubt, one reason he was able to communicate with his congregation.

This series was followed by a similar series, *Sermons on the Divinity and Operation of the Holy Ghost.*[23] Here, of course, in the theological locus of the doctrine of the Holy Spirit, the typical pietist will always have very legitimate insights. Even today the pietism of the neo-Pentecostal movement would have us pay particular attention to the doctrine of the Holy Spirit. In this matter modern Pentecostal theology is following in the footsteps of the Evangelical Anglicans of the eighteenth century. Whether it is the nominalist pietism of the late Middle Ages or the Byzantine pietism of the Eastern Church, pietism always takes an interest in the Holy Spirit. This may come as a surprise to many, but charismatic Anglicans have a long tradition behind them.

VI. Charles Simeon (1759-1836)

Charles Simeon had a tremendous influence on the preaching of the Church of England from the end of the eighteenth century well into the nineteenth century; in fact, that influence spread through the whole English-speaking world.[24] Simeon was not only a major preacher in his

---

23. Robert Hawker, *Sermons on the Divinity and Operation of the Holy Ghost,* in *The Works of the Rev. Robert Hawker, D.D.,* 1:199-575.

24. For works on the life and ministry of Charles Simeon, see Arthur Bennett, "Charles Simeon: Prince of Evangelicals," *Churchman* 102, no. 2 (1988): 122-42; John Bishop, "Charles Simeon: Preaching to Exalt the Savior, Promote Holiness," *Preaching* 10 (November-December 1994): 56-58; John E. Booty, "Reformers and Missionaries: The Bible in the Eighteenth and Early Nineteenth Centuries," in *Anglicanism and the Bible,* ed. F. Borsch (Wilton, Conn.: Morehouse Barlow, 1984), pp. 117-42; William Carus, *Memoirs of the Life of the Rev. Charles Simeon* (London: J. Hatchard; Cambridge: Deightons and Macmillan, 1847); Horton Davies, *Worship and Theology,* 3:232f.; Hugh Evan Hopkins, *Charles Simeon of Cambridge* (Grand Rapids: William B. Eerdmans Publishing Co., 1977); Hopkins, *Charles Simeon, Preacher Extraordinary,* Grove Liturgical Study, vol. 18 (Bramcote, Nottinghamshire: Grove Books, 1979); Russell Jones Levenson, Jr., "To Humble the Sinner, to Exalt the Savior, to Promote Holiness: Reflections on the

time but a teacher of preaching for generations to come. Never was he a professor of homiletics, but rather as minister of Holy Trinity Church in Cambridge he provided an example of a fervent and orthodox exposition of Scripture in the center of that historic university town for something like forty years. In addition, he crowned his preaching ministry with the publication of his eminently useful *Horae Homileticae.*[25] These sermon outlines guided English-speaking preachers of all denominations for generations. The example of Simeon has inspired preacher after preacher right down to our own day, our contemporary John Stott, the distinguished preacher of All Soul's Church in London, being a notable example.

It was from a privileged home that this preacher came. He was the youngest son of a prominent lawyer of Reading. His mother died when he was just a boy, and at the age of seven young Charles was sent off to Eton, the famous English boarding school. Following the traditions of the time, he graduated from Eton and went to Kings College in Cambridge. It was a path often followed.

Simeon's religious training was routine, not much more than the formal Anglicanism required at the schools to which he had been sent. Shortly after he arrived at Kings College he received an official communication that he was to present himself to receive Communion at the college chapel. This was one of those requirements used to maintain conformity to the Anglican religious establishment. For most students this was just something one had to go through to keep up appearances. Somehow, in the providence of God, for young Charles it was a call to serious religious commitment. Conscientiously he prepared himself to receive the Sacrament. He entered into the Anglican formality with Puritan earnestness.

Earnestness in matters of religious experience was not very frequently found among proper English gentlemen at the end of the eighteenth century. Religious enthusiasm was relegated to the lower classes, to Dissenters, Methodists, and Nonconformists. For a proper Anglican it

---

Life, Ministry, and Legacy of Charles Simeon," *Sewanee Theological Review* 41 (Christmas 1998): 47-65; Handley Carr Glyn Moule, *Charles Simeon* (London: Methuen, 1892); Charles Simeon, *Evangelical Preaching,* introduction by John R. W. Stott (Portland, Oreg.: Multnomah, 1986); and Charles Hugh Egerton Smyth, *Simeon and Church Order: A Study of the Origins of the Evangelical Revival in Cambridge in the Eighteenth Century* (Cambridge: University Press, 1940).

25. Charles Simeon, *Horae Homileticae; or, Discourses Digested into One Continued Series and Forming upon Every Book of the Old and New Testament,* 8th ed., 21 vols. (London: Henry G. Bohn, 1848).

was just not good form. Here, however, was a young man of good family who had had a conversion experience. It had come about without the nurture of a devout family, the witness of a fellow student, or even the preaching of a proper minister. It was, amazingly enough, through a conscientious participation in the Lord's Supper. If one might be allowed a pious observation, it seems to have come about through a sovereign act of divine providence.

It was only slowly that this thoroughly converted young man began to find the fellowship of other Christians who had had similar experiences of conversion. Three years later he came into the circle of Henry Venn. John Venn, Henry's son, introduced him to his father, who was a prominent figure in the growing circle of evangelical Anglicans. This circle nourished young Simeon, and he soon became thoroughly evangelical.

In 1783 Simeon was ordained a priest. His first charge was to the parish of Saint Edward's in Cambridge, where he was warmly received by the congregation. It was not an important post, but that did not bother young Simeon. His father, however, being a man of influence, had a connection with the bishop of Ely and wrote to him recommending his son to the pastorate of Holy Trinity Church in the center of the university town. Holy Trinity was a major assignment. That the young minister should be given so important a position was resented by many of the leading parishioners. At first Simeon's pastoral leadership was resisted. It was a number of years before he was well received by his people, but eventually, through conscientious pastoral work, he won them over.

The rather high-handed play of influence by the bishop was not the only factor in the initial unpopularity of our young preacher. The sort of serious preaching Simeon offered was not very popular in the Anglican pulpit of the eighteenth century. In fact, the religious establishment prided itself on a certain carelessness in devotional matters, and religious enthusiasm was regarded with suspicion even among the clergy. The Enlightenment had done much to cool the ardor of faith, and especially among the upper classes, disenchantment with religion was the prevailing mood. This was especially the case with the intellectuals of that university town. The enlightened were not very devout. Even at that, Simeon finally began to fill his church. The young parson had something different about him. He was so obviously a member of the establishment and yet he was so enthusiastic. He provided an alternative to the tedium of latitudinarian conformity.

For the whole course of his ministry Simeon worked at making Anglican preaching a significant means of serving God's glory. He taught a whole new generation a high reverence for God's Word. As we have said, this teaching was done primarily through his example. He was in a perfect position to set an example of doxological preaching to the whole university. Indeed, as we look back at it now, his appointment to that pulpit seems as providential as his conversion. So many of England's brightest minds would sit under that pulpit. Strange as it may seem to us today, homiletics was not taught at either Cambridge or Oxford in the eighteenth century, even though most of the Anglican clergy was trained in these universities. The art of preaching was taught by example. As one heard sermon after sermon, year after year, one was just supposed to pick up the way it was done. As we saw in a previous volume, it had been that way in Paris in the Middle Ages. The university sermon was supposed to set the example. In the university at Cambridge, at the end of the eighteenth century and well into the nineteenth century, Simeon was a particularly prominent example.

But there was another important dimension to Simeon's homiletical leadership. He published twenty-one volumes of sermon outlines, eventually entitled *Horae Homileticae,* with the intention of showing the typical preacher how to open up the Scriptures in order that the sinner be humbled, Christ be exalted, and holiness promoted.[26] These were Simeon's words, and they sum up his ministry quite well.

Simeon wanted to treat the whole of Scripture from Genesis to Revelation. This monumental work was not, however, composed all at the same time. It went through a considerable evolution. The first installment appeared in 1796. It consisted of an English translation of Jean Claude's *Essay on the Composition of a Sermon,* together with Simeon's notes and commentary on Claude's text and 100 sermon outlines illustrating Claude's method.

That Simeon should have reached back to Claude, the last Huguenot preacher of Paris before the revocation of the Edict of Nantes, is significant. Claude's essay, along with the work of Hyperius and William Perkins's *The Art of Prophecying,* has been a classic among the preaching manuals of Protestantism. Claude was heir to the homiletical traditions of French Protestantism. He was the successor to Jean Daillé in the pulpit at Charenton. It was there, outside the walls of Paris, that the Edict of Nantes allowed the Protestants of Paris to worship. Charenton was the

26. Simeon, *Horae Homileticae,* 1:xxi.

great Huguenot pulpit. When the Edict was revoked in 1685, Claude was ordered to leave the country in twenty-four hours. He was the leading voice of French Protestantism, and Louis XIV was determined to silence him. It was he who so skillfully countered the baroque eloquence of Jacques Bossuet, the classic Catholic orator at the court of the Sun King. Here indeed, in Claude's work, was the distilled wisdom of Protestant homiletical theory.[27]

In 1801 the Cambridge University Press published the second edition of Simeon's monumental work, now with the title *Helps to Composition*. This edition contained five hundred sermon outlines and had great success. Eighteen years later, in 1819, a third edition was published. In the meantime the Napoleonic Wars had come to an end and England was launched into the nineteenth century. No longer a curiosity, the Evangelical Revival had swelled to high tide. The social reforms which were so central to Evangelical Protestantism were being realized. By this time the collection of sermon outlines had grown to seventeen volumes. As a publishing venture it was a success. This work which began so modestly now took an imposing title, *Horae Homileticae*. One might translate this rather obscure title with "A Time for Preaching," or more woodenly, "Preaching Hours."

Simeon covered a good part of the Bible in these seventeen volumes of sermon outlines, and then decided to press on and complete the whole Bible from Genesis to Revelation. He reached this goal in 1832; the whole thing was published in twenty-one volumes. At considerable expense Simeon had a number of beautiful presentation copies bound. The first was presented to King William IV, when the preacher was received at court. Copies were presented to the archbishops of Canterbury and York and to all the important theological libraries of Great Britain and the Continent. There is even one treasured in the library of Princeton Theological Seminary, complete with a dedication in Simeon's own hand. This

---

27. In fact, Claude was proposing some distinct reforms in French Protestant preaching. Not realizing that the running commentary on a chapter or a paragraph of Scripture had been a very ancient method of preaching the Scriptures, Claude advocated choosing a single text from a chapter and expounding this shorter text. In this respect Claude moved away from Calvin and many of the earlier French Huguenot preachers whose sermons were a running commentary on longer passages of Scripture. Claude's concern to maintain the Aristotelian unity of theme was foreign to the Protestant Reformers. See Hughes Oliphant Old, *The Reading and Preaching of the Scriptures in the Worship of the Church*, vol. 4, *The Age of the Reformation* (Grand Rapids: Wm. B. Eerdmans Publishing Co., 2002), pp. 444f.

final edition, completed four years before our preacher's death, contains 2,536 sermon outlines covering the entire Bible.

A. The Art of Expository Preaching

This noted homiletical preceptor did not come to his method all at once. He was certain he wanted his preaching to be an exposition of Scripture, but no one had taught him how to do this. After developing some methods through trial and error, he discovered the essay of Jean Claude, who so clearly expressed what he was beginning to realize. Claude's essay gave him the method for which he had been searching.

At the heart of Claude's method was the conviction that a sermon should be an exposition of a text of Scripture. In this Claude and Simeon were in complete agreement. Furthermore, a sermon should be the unfolding of a single message from that text rather than a series of ideas strung together but not essentially related.[28] For Simeon, as for Claude before him, a sermon should unfold a short text rather than comment on a whole chapter. By doing this one could achieve unity of theme, which was very important, as Claude saw it. Here again Simeon followed Claude closely.

Another principle Simeon shared with Claude was that a text should be chosen which expresses the intention of the biblical author. It is the thoughts of Moses, Isaiah, the apostle Paul, and above all Jesus which interest us, not the religious philosophy or pious meditations of the preacher. A text should be chosen which expresses a complete thought of the biblical author, not a few words which give the preacher the excuse to charge forth on some topic which may be of interest to him or his congregation. The text should sum up in a few words a basic teaching of Scripture. Obviously not every phrase or every sentence in the Bible is an appropriate text for a sermon. Sometimes one gets the impression that the texts in Simeon's work are carved out of the Bible as though they were oracles imbedded in the sacred books. These are treated as the oracles of Delphi rather than as a sacred story. The whole Bible seems to be treated as though it were the book of Proverbs. One notices that in preaching through the Abraham cycle in Genesis, for example, Simeon averages

28. No doubt quite unconsciously, it was at this point that Simeon and Claude departed from the practice of both the Reformers and the Fathers.

about one sermon per chapter. Instead of going through the chapter verse by verse as the fathers of the ancient Church or as the Protestant Reformers had done, he chooses as his text one verse which sums up the teaching of the whole chapter.

In preaching through the Gospel of John, however, he gives us eleven sermons for the first chapter, three for the second, and seven for the third.[29] He continues with nine sermons on chapter 4, eleven on chapter 5, and eleven on chapter 6.[30] One gets the impression that he considered the exposition of *a* text of Scripture not the same thing as an exposition of *the* text of Scripture. Somehow "text" has come to mean a sentence of Scripture on which a sermon can be built rather than simply Scripture itself.

As Simeon understood it, preaching was a matter of unfolding or elaborating Scripture. He well understood that this was the way the biblical text was supposed to be handled. The writings themselves had been composed to summarize the ideas of the prophets and apostles so that their disciples could at a later time unpack them. Simeon seems to have understood this to be the nature of the biblical writings. The biblical authors had put down the sayings of Jesus, the apostles, or the prophets in the most concentrated form possible so that they could be memorized or stored in written form. The production and preservation of written texts was a costly matter in the days before the printing press. One did not, therefore, write down and copy out everything the teacher said. One summarized the message of the teacher, then passed it on in concentrated form. It was the job of the preacher to take these concentrated texts and open them up again, unfold them and elaborate them.

The first step the preacher should take after choosing his text is to discern the scope of the text. "What is the principal scope and meaning of the text?" This Simeon underlines, begging every young minister to remember it. One should ask oneself what subject the text treats, what both the extent and the limitations of that subject might be, and then introduce nothing into the sermon which does not in some way throw light on this subject. The next step is to ask of what parts the text consists, or of what parts it can most easily and naturally be resolved.[31] By asking this question one produces the sermon outline, or skeleton, as Simeon liked

29. Simeon, *Horae Homileticae,* 13:186-277.
30. Simeon, *Horae Homileticae,* 13:277-415.
31. Simeon, *Horae Homileticae,* 1:vi.

to call it. The sermon outline was really the key to Simeon's method. It gave both unity and clarity to the sermon. It was what kept the sermon simple. From the standpoint of a Protestant aesthetic, clarity was of the highest value, simplicity the fundamental art.

Again following Claude, Simeon teaches us to develop a sermon in a four-part arrangement. The sermon should begin with an introduction, followed by a division of the text, making clear to the congregation what points will be drawn from it. The main body of the sermon, then, should be the discussion of these points. The sermon should conclude with the application of the text.[32] This application might be the teaching of Christian doctrine or an exhortation to live the Christian life. What is suggested here is a very simple homiletical procedure. Compared to the homiletical system which had gone before, it was not very complicated. Today it sounds rather perfunctory, but that is because this tradition has been adopted by so many homileticians. Simeon's point has been well taken.

In reading through Simeon's sermon briefs, the modern reader cannot help but find the introductions rather bland and colorless. Those of us who were brought up on the typical mainline American sermon have come to expect something more striking or unusual. Simeon, again following Claude, made a point of doing just the opposite. He recommends that the introduction be direct and simple. Its purpose is to prepare the minds of the congregation.[33] It should open up the discussion in a natural and easy way, but should never become so interesting that the body of the sermon becomes anticlimactic. In fact, our homiletician tells us that the introduction should be cool and slow rather than agitated and dramatic.[34] What a contrast to the baroque preaching so popular at the court of Louis XIV.

Indeed, it is in the discussion of the text that we find Simeon's outlines most interesting. Again and again it is his analysis of the text which claims our interest. In this Simeon shows a real sensitivity to Scripture. Claude suggested to him several approaches to the discussion of the text. One can discuss it by explication, that is, by unfolding it, explaining its import, and showing its reasonableness and excellency. Or one can discuss it by observations, drawing out its substance in a series of remarks.

32. Simeon, *Horae Homileticae*, 1:vi.
33. Simeon, *Horae Homileticae*, 21:396.
34. Simeon, *Horae Homileticae*, 21:402f.

Illustrations can be given to support the text. Parallel passages of Scripture can be cited that prove the truths found in the passage. Particularly important for Simeon, as one sees from reading his outlines, are his perpetual applications. He is intent on showing how the teachings of Scripture are to be applied. To be sure, Simeon lived before modern biblical studies had been able to demonstrate their value, but one is constantly impressed by what he is able to do with a simple reading of the text. He seems to have at least some knowledge of the original languages, but one gets the impression that he has done very little with commentaries or the theological treatises of learned biblical scholars. He is supposed to have been very dependent on the Scottish biblical scholar John Brown of Haddington. His *Self-Interpreting Bible with Explanatory Comments* was very popular in the eighteenth century. Otherwise Simeon seems to have relied primarily on the old principle of interpreting Scripture by Scripture. His use of parallel passages is often brilliant, and his best illustrations are biblical illustrations.

In exegesis and hermeneutic Simeon seems a bit naive. We do not get the impression he knows too much about the historical or geographical context of the passages of Scripture he interprets. This will trouble many of us as we read over these sermon outlines. Still, the most recent literary criticism is beginning to recognize the importance of interpreting the text as it has come down to us.

It is in the discussion of the text where Simeon found Claude's essay most helpful. Claude had much to say which Simeon put to very good use, as we can see from Simeon's sermon outlines, but the applications were even more important for the Evangelicals of the eighteenth century. The Evangelical sermon, especially in Simeon's day, was intent on both social reform and personal moral reform.

For Simeon the conclusion of the sermon is the application. If classical rhetoric had taught that a discourse should begin with an introduction and end with a conclusion, Simeon understood that for the sermon the conclusion should be the application. And yet he was a great believer in perpetual application, which apparently meant making applications all the way through the sermon. Even at that, in the conclusion he wrapped it all up in a grand admonition. If the introduction was to be cool and rather slow, the conclusion was supposed to be animated and passionate.

B. Protestant Plain Style

In the preface of the *Horae Homileticae* our preacher gives us a three-point outline of how he understands the Protestant plain style. The Protestant plain style was certainly not invented by Charles Simeon. In fact, he does not use the term, and yet he is a good example of it. By the beginning of the seventeenth century it was a well-established characteristic of the Protestant aesthetic. Whether in Germany, in Huguenot France, in the Netherlands, or in England, Protestants reacted strongly against the baroque style of the Counter-Reformation. Already during the reign of Queen Elizabeth I we find in William Perkins's celebrated homiletical manual *The Art of Prophecying* an attempt to work out the Protestant plain style. As we have said elsewhere, one might trace it back to Philipp Melanchthon, Luther's young colleague in Wittenberg.[35] Simeon's statement of this principle is very simple. As he sees it, a sermon should have unity of design, perspicuity of arrangement, and simplicity of diction.

Unity of design is fundamental to effective communication. A preacher should decide on the subject of his text and stick to it. If the sermon goes back and forth from one subject to another, it runs the risk of confusing the listener. This is a sound principle for any literary composition, or any other work of art, for that matter. One finds it advocated by the rhetoricians of classical antiquity. More importantly, it is just good common sense. The art of the preacher is effectively to communicate the gospel; to maintain unity of design helps achieve effectiveness.

Perspicuity of arrangement is the second principle. The word "perspicuity" is not a common word today. A more contemporary vocabulary might use "clarity." For any kind of public speaking, as for any kind of literary communication, clarity is the highest beauty. That seems very obvious for us today, but in the age of the baroque and the rococo it was not. The great French Catholic preachers of the seventeenth and eighteenth centuries were more concerned with sacred eloquence and ecclesiastical rhetoric. French Protestantism, on the other hand, took an entirely different approach to the art of preaching. For the Huguenots clarity was the soul of beauty. That the Anglican Evangelicals should choose a French Huguenot like Jean Claude to follow in their preaching is of considerable significance. Here again we are dealing with one of the fundamental principles of a Protestant aesthetic.

35. Simeon, *Horae Homileticae,* 1:vi.

Much the same thing could be said about simplicity of diction. Simeon never found it necessary to convince his congregation of the depth of his learning. It would no doubt have been a temptation in a pulpit like that of Holy Trinity Church in Cambridge to make an effort to impress the intellectuals of that university town. But one never suspects our preacher of this sort of thing. There is never any striving for brilliance, let alone wit. For this preacher at least, simplicity in the things of God was of the soul of reverence. However pretentious one might be elsewhere, when one entered into the presence of God, humility was essential; putting on airs was out of place. As men like Simeon saw it, simple honesty demanded a reverent simplicity. Here, too, is a fundamental principle of a Protestant aesthetic — reverent simplicity. The sumptuous ceremonial of Catholic worship, to the traditional Protestant at least, seemed pretentious and therefore irreverent.

By the middle of the eighteenth century, especially in England, the standard practice was for ministers to write out their sermons and then read them to their congregations. For the latitudinarians especially, the production of a complete manuscript, in faultless literary form, was essential. The sermon became more and more literary and less and less oratorical. Wesley, if I am correctly informed, did this to the end of his life. Supposedly Jonathan Edwards did the same thing. George Whitefield was thought of as a real innovator when he departed from the practice. Simeon took a mediating position. He advised young preachers to write out their sermons in the earlier years of their ministry. As they became more mature, they should free themselves from their manuscript and preach from their outline, formulating their thought in the face of the congregation. This he believed a minister could do if he had thoroughly thought through his text, produced his outline, and carefully premeditated his applications. There was much in the preaching of Simeon that was improvised. Especially in later years his preaching apparently had a definite improvisational style.

This improvisational style has often, although not always, been part of the Protestant plain style. There was a real distinction between the *reading* of the Scriptures and the *preaching* of the sermon. The former involved the careful and exact reading of a set canonical text, but the sermon was much freer. It was appropriate that it be spontaneous. It went without saying that the passage to be preached needed to be carefully studied beforehand. But even at that, the sermon made no pretense of being set or canonical. To be sure, the Reformed sermon was understood as the Word of God. The preacher was supposed to preach the Word, but that preaching was not the Word in exactly the same sense as Scripture is the Word of God. The Word of the Lord abideth forever, but the sermons, sad to say, are heard today and forgotten tomorrow. They speak to a particular time, but time passes on.

C. The Excellency of the Liturgy

Thoroughgoing Anglican that he was, Charles Simeon was devoted to the *Book of Common Prayer* and the liturgy found in it. To make this very clear he published a series of sermons entitled *The Excellency of the Liturgy*.[36] It is important to notice that this spokesman of Evangelical Anglicanism makes quite unmistakable that his Evangelical commitments in no way compromise his attachment to the Anglican prayer book. Wesley had felt the same way, but the Methodist people just did not follow his lead in this. It was quite different with Simeon and the Evangelical Anglicans. They were thoroughly committed to the liturgy of the *Book of Common Prayer*. Simeon was able to do what Wesley would have loved to have done a generation before.

This did not, however, imply that Evangelical Anglicans felt bound to the lectionary in the way the High Church movement would develop this in the next generation. As we mentioned, the great Anglican preachers of the seventeenth century had no qualms about departing from the lectionary. Especially at morning or evening prayer, they would read the appointed lessons at the point required in the prayer-book service, but when they got to the sermon, which was normally after the official service had been completed, they would preach on a text of their own choosing. Plenty of the best Anglican preaching had no relation to the lectionary. This was true well into the nineteenth century.

With Simeon we seem to have the use of both the lectionary and the *lectio continua*. Particularly interesting is the fact that in addition to his use of the lectionary for Sundays and holidays, at a number of points he used the Anglican lectionary for daily morning and evening prayer. We wish we knew exactly how he arranged his preaching on the calendar. Sad to say, the sermons in the *Horae Homileticae* are not dated. They have

---

36. Charles Simeon, *The Excellency of the Liturgy, in Four Discourses, Preached before the University of Cambridge, in November, 1811* (Cambridge: Printed by J. Smith, 1812).

been rearranged so that the texts follow the order of the books of the Bible. That does not mean they were always preached that way. One might, with a more intensive study of the records that have come down to us, be able to figure out exactly how Simeon used the liturgical calendar, but even a preliminary study brings several things to light. He preached a certain number of sermons on the lessons appointed in the lectionary for Sundays and holidays. Occasionally he mentions in his introduction the lesson appointed for a particular day.[37] He also must have preached a *lectio continua* at other times, as seems to be the case, for example, with his sermons on Leviticus. Only two lessons from Leviticus are mentioned in the prayer book. Simeon gives us twenty sermons for the twenty-seven chapters in the book, and these sermons seem to follow along rather evenly through the book. It is easy to imagine that these sermons were part of a *lectio continua* series.

But there is another consideration. It may well be that for much of the Bible he followed the *lectio continua* as mapped out in the *Book of Common Prayer* for the order of morning and evening prayer.[38] One notices, for example, that in preaching through the Abraham cycle he provides one sermon for each of the lessons appointed in the prayer book.[39] To be sure, these lessons are appointed for weekdays rather than Sundays. As far as we know, Simeon preached only twice a week, once on Sunday morning and once on Sunday evening. Possibly he followed the list of appointed lessons in the prayer book, but instead of preaching them on weekday mornings five or six days a week he preached them once a week on Sunday evening.[40] He may even have preached his *lectio continua* on Sunday mornings, especially on the Sundays after Epiphany or the Sundays after Trinity. At this point in our research we hesitate to be too precise, but he seems to have sometimes followed the lectionary and sometimes the *lectio continua*.

Let us now ask the question we keep asking in these volumes: How did this preacher understand the reading and preaching of Scripture to be worship? Very interestingly Simeon seems to regard preaching as worship

---

37. Simeon, *Horae Homileticae*, 1:150.

38. As was shown in the previous volume, the *Book of Common Prayer* contains two lectionaries: the traditional lectionary for Sundays and holidays, and the lectionary for the daily service of morning and evening prayer.

39. Simeon, *Horae Homileticae*, 1:96-198.

40. This seems to be similar to the practice of William Romaine when he preached at Saint Dunstan's in the West on Sunday evening. See above.

in much the same way as John Newton. In fact, this seems to be characteristic of Evangelical preaching. The preaching of the gospel as Evangelicals understood it exalts Christ, and because preaching exalts Christ it is worship. Simeon, as Evangelicals in general, had a doxological understanding of his preaching. Others may find their preaching too didactic, but Evangelicals themselves understood it as doxological.

We noted several times that the keys of Simeon's homiletics are found in the preface to the *Horae Homileticae*. On how preaching is to be understood as worship, we once again turn to this preface. There we learn that true preaching should humble the sinner, exalt the Savior, and promote holiness. This is spelled out in capital letters.[41] These are obviously the cardinal principles of Simeon's approach to preaching. Let us consider them for a moment.

For Evangelicals witnessing is at the very center of the Christian life. The High Church emphasis on prayer and sacraments does not give quite the importance to witnessing that the Evangelicals do, and consequently seems to miss the point about witnessing being doxological. But it is very specifically because the proclamation of the gospel exalts the grace, mercy, and loving-kindness of God that it is so clearly worship. The whole missionary thrust is the working out of the universality of God's reign. "Make a joyful noise unto the Lord, all ye lands." It is because God is to be worshiped by all peoples about the earth that the Evangelicals of the Church of England like Simeon founded the Church Missionary Society (CMS). Simeon's work for the support of the CMS was one of his greatest contributions. It was this concern to exalt Christ among all peoples that made the Evangelical social reforms so successful. Both their missionary work and their social reform were an outgrowth of their conviction that all peoples should praise God together. The preaching of the gospel and the demand for social reform exalted the Savior and were therefore worship.

Preaching is also worship if it humiliates the sinner. To humiliate the sinner is to bring the sinner to his or her knees. It is to bring all of us to repentance. The call to repentance is part of worship every bit as much as the call to praise. As we have often said, even the most casual reading through of the psalms makes this clear. A good part of prayer is lamentation. Both Israel and the Christian Church constantly pray the psalms of confession as an integral part of their worship. The best of Christian preaching has always begun with a call for repentance. Patristic preaching,

41. Simeon, *Horae Homileticae,* 1:xxi.

577

medieval preaching, and Reformation preaching all included it. What we saw particularly in Bernardino da Siena and Girolamo Savonarola was also true for the Evangelicals. The call to repentance was essential to the full diet of Christian worship. No course of evangelistic sermons was complete without it. For the latitudinarian congregation it may have been offensive, but it has a legitimate place in classical Christian worship.

Finally Simeon would emphasize that true preaching should promote holiness. Ultimately true worship comes about when the people of God reflect the holiness of God. In ancient Israel that was the constant concern of the prophets. Canaanite worship, by contrast, ignored holiness, and yet the Canaanites loved ceremonial. Like the priests of Baal on Mount Carmel, they pranced around their altars for hours, but they forgot that there is no approaching the holy without being consumed by the refining fire of God's holiness. That was what the worship of Isaiah was all about in the year King Uzziah died (Isa. 6:1-13). To worship God truly is to enter into the refining fire of God's holiness. Simeon did well to write these three points in capital letters: HUMBLE THE SINNER. EXALT THE SAVIOR. PROMOTE HOLINESS. These three principles of Simeon's serve very well as an outline of the Evangelical understanding of worship.

Bibliography

Bibliography for Chapter I

Allmen, Jean-Jacques von. *L'Église et ses fonctions d'après Jean-Frédéric Ostervald.* Neuchâtel: Imprimerie Delachaux et Niestlé, 1947.

Gordon, A. "Howe, John." In *Dictionary of National Biography,* 10 (1891): 85-88. 22 vols. London: Oxford University Press, 1885-1973.

———. "Tillotson, John." In *Dictionary of National Biography,* 19:872f. 22 vols. London: Oxford University Press, 1885-1973.

Henry, Matthew. *The Complete Works of Matthew Henry.* 2 vols. 1855. Reprint, Grand Rapids: Baker, 1978.

———. *The Life of the Rev. Philip Henry, A.M.* First published 1698. Found in John Bickerton Williams, *The Lives of Philip and Matthew Henry,* 2 vols. in 1 (Edinburgh and Carlisle, Pa.: Banner of Truth Trust, 1974).

Horton, Robert Forman. *John Howe.* London: Methuen, 1895.

Howe, John. *The Whole Works of the Rev. John Howe, M.A.* Edited by John Hunt. 8 vols. London: F. Westley, 1822.

———. *The Works of the Late Reverend and Learned John Howe, M.A.* 2 vols. London: Printed for John Clark and Richard Hett, John and Benjamin Sprint, Daniel Midwinter, Ranew Robinson, Richard Ford, Aaron Ward, L. Jackson, and Samuel Chandler, 1724.

———. *The Works of the Late Reverend and Learned John Howe, M.A.* 3 vols. Reprint of the 1724 edition with biography by Rev. J. P. Hewlett. Ligonier, Pa.: Soli Deo Gloria Publications, 1990.

Lavater, Johann Kaspar. *Johann Caspar Lavaters ausgewählte Werke.* Edited by Ernst Staehelin. 4 vols. Zürich: Zwingli-Verlag, 1943.

Locke, Louis Glenn. *Tillotson: A Study in Seventeenth-Century Literature.* Copenhagen: Rosenkilde and Bagger, 1954.

McKim, Donald J., ed. *Historical Handbook of Major Biblical Interpreters.* Downers Grove, Ill.: InterVarsity, 1998.

Ostervald, Jean-Frédéric. *Catéchisme ou instruction dans la religion chrestienne.* Geneva: Compagnie des Libraires, 1702.

————. *A Catechism for Youth, Containing a Brief but Comprehensive Summary of the Doctrines and Duties of Christianity.* Translated by Samuel Bayard. New York: Published by Whiting and Watson for the New Jersey Bible Society, 1812.

————. *Douze sermons sur divers textes de l'écriture sainte.* Geneva: Chez Fabri & Barrillot, 1722.

Rogers, Henry. *The Life and Character of John Howe, M.A.: With an Analysis of His Writings.* London: William Ball, 1836.

La Sainte Bible qui contient le Vieux et le Nouveau Testament, Revuë & corrigée sur le text Hébreu & Grec par les pasteurs & les Professeurs de l'Eglise de Genève. Avec les *Argumens et les Réflections* sur les chapitres de l'Ecriture Sainte & des Notes par Jean-Frédéric Ostervald. Nouvelle edition, revuë, corrigée & augmentée. Neuchâtel: Imprimerie d'Abraham Boyve et Compagnie, 1744.

Sauer, Klaus Martin. *Die Predigttätigkeit Johann Kaspar Lavaters (1741-1801).* Zürich: Theologischer Verlag Zürich, 1988.

Saurin, Jacques. *Sermons of the Rev. James Saurin, late Pastor of the French Church at The Hague.* Translated by R. Robertson, H. Hunter, and J. Sutcliff. 2 vols. Princeton, N.J.: D. A. Borrenstein, 1827.

————. *Sermons sur divers textes de l'Escriture Sainte.* 10 vols. La Haye: Abraham Troyel, 1708-49.

Simon, Irène. *Three Restoration Divines: Barrow, South, Tillotson: Selected Sermons.* 2 vols. Paris: Société l'Editions "Les Belles Lettres," 1976.

Tillotson, John. *The Works of Dr. John Tillotson.* 10 vols. London: Richard Priestley, 1820.

Tong, William. *An Account of the Life and Death of . . . Matthew Henry.* London, 1716.

Vinet, Alexandre Rodolphe. *Histoire de la prédication: parmi les réformés de France au dix-septième siècle.* Paris: Chez les éditeurs, 1860.

Williams, John Bickerton. *The Life of Matthew Henry.* First published 1828. Found in John Bickerton Williams, *The Lives of Philip and Matthew Henry,* 2 vols. in 1 (Edinburgh and Carlisle, Pa.: Banner of Truth Trust, 1974).

————. *The Lives of Philip and Matthew Henry.* 2 vols. in 1. Edinburgh and Carlisle, Pa.: Banner of Truth Trust, 1974.

Bibliography for Chapter II

Aland, Kurt. "Bibel und Bibeltext bei August Hermann Francke und Johann Albrecht Bengel." In *Pietismus und Bible,* edited by Kurt Aland. Wittenberg: Luther Verlag, 1970.

———. "Spener und Luther. Zur Rechtfertigung Wiedergeburt." In Festschrift für Martin Brecht. 1992.

———, ed. *Pietismus und Bible.* Wittenberg: Luther Verlag, 1970.

Alexander, Samuel D., comp. *Sermons and Essays by the Tennents and Their Contemporaries.* Philadelphia: Presbyterian Board of Publication, 1855.

Baker, Frank. *John Wesley and the Church of England.* Nashville: Abingdon, 1970.

Belden, Albert D. *George Whitefield, the Awakener: A Modern Study of the Evangelical Revival.* London: S. Law, Marston and Co., 1930.

Bengel, Johann Albrecht. *Du Wort des Vaters, rede Du!: Ausgewählte Schriften, Predigten und Lieder.* Metzingen, Württemberg: Verlag Ernst Franz, 1962.

Benson, Louis F. "President Davies as a Hymnwriter." *Journal of the Presbyterian Historical Society* 2 (1903): 277-86.

Bowmer, John C. *The Sacrament of the Lord's Supper in Early Methodism.* London: Dacre Press, 1951.

Brecht, Martin. *Der Pietismus vom siebzehnten bis zum frühen achtzehnten Jahrhundert.* 2 vols. Göttingen: Vandenhoeck & Ruprecht, 1993.

Brecht, Martin, Klaus Deppermann, Ulrich Gäbler, and Hartmut Lehmann. *Geschichte des Pietismus.* 2 vols. Göttingen: Vandenhoeck & Ruprecht, 1995.

Brink, Frederick W. "Gilbert Tennent, Dynamic Preacher." *Journal of the Presbyterian Historical Society* 32 (1954): 91-107.

Brown, Dale W. *Understanding Pietism.* Grand Rapids: Wm. B. Eerdmans Publishing Co., 1978.

Cannon, William Ragsdale. *The Theology of John Wesley.* Lanham, Md., New York, and London: University Press of America, 1974.

Cell, George Croft. *The Rediscovery of John Wesley.* New York: Henry Holt, 1935.

Cho, John Chongnahm. "John Wesley's View on Baptism." *Wesleyan Theological Journal* 7, no. 1 (spring 1972).

Coalter, Milton J., Jr. *Gilbert Tennent, Son of Thunder: A Case Study of Continental Pietism's Impact on the First Great Awakening in the Middle Colonies.* New York, Westport, Conn., and London: Greenwood Press, 1986.

Cushman, Robert E. *John Wesley's Experimental Divinity.* Nashville: Abingdon, 1989.

Dallimore, Arnold A. *George Whitefield: The Life and Times of the Great Evangelist of the Eighteenth-Century Revival.* 2 vols. Westchester, Ill.: Cornerstone Books, 1970-79.

Davies, Horton. *Worship and Theology in England.* Vol. 3, *From Watts and Wesley* to Maurice, 1690-1850. Grand Rapids: Wm. B. Eerdmans Publishing Co., 1996.

Davies, Samuel. Sermons of the Rev. Samuel Davies, A.M. 3 vols. Philadelphia: Presbyterian Board of Publication, 1854. Reprint, Morgan, Pa.: Soli Deo Gloria Publications, 1993-95.

Edwards, Maldwyn Lloyd. John Wesley and the Eighteenth Century. London: G. Allen & Unwin, 1933.

Francke, August Hermann. "Of the Most Useful Way of Preaching." In The Christian Preacher; or, Discourses on Preaching by Several Eminent Divines, English and Foreign, edited, revised, and abridged by Edward Williams. Philadelphia: William Woolward, 1810.

Gewehr, Wesley M. The Great Awakening in Virginia, 1740-1790. Durham, N.C.: Duke University Press, 1930.

Gillies, John. Memoirs of the Life of the Reverend George Whitefield, M.A. London: Printed for Edward and Charles Dilly, 1772.

Gledstone, James Paterson. George Whitefield, Field Preacher. New York: American Tract Society, [1901].

Hall, David D. The Faithful Shepherd, a History of the New England Ministry in the Seventeenth Century. New York: Norton, 1972.

Harmelink, Herman. "Another Look at Frelinghuysen and His Awakening." Church History 37 (December 1968): 423-38.

Heimert, Alan, and Perry Miller, eds. The Great Awakening. Indianapolis and New York: Bobbs-Merrill, 1967.

Heitzenrater, Richard P. Wesley and the People Called Methodists. Nashville: Abingdon, 1995.

Hempton, David. The Religion of the People: Methodism and Popular Religion, c. 1750-1900. London and New York: Routledge, 1996.

Henry, Stuart C. George Whitefield: Wayfaring Witness. New York: Abingdon, 1957.

Heppe, Heinrich. Geschichte des Pietismus und der Mystik in der reformierten Kirche. Leiden: Brill, 1879.

Hoffman, John Charles. "Pietism." In New Catholic Encyclopedia, 11:355. 17 vols. Washington, D.C.: Catholic University of America Press, 1968.

Knox, Ronald A. Enthusiasm: A Chapter in the History of Religion. London: Oxford University Press, 1950.

Lindström, Harald. Wesley and Sanctification: A Study in the Doctrine of Salvation. Stockholm: Nya Bokförlage aktiebolaget, Almgvist & Wiksells Boktryckeri A.B., 1946.

Lodge, Martin E. "The Crisis of the Churches in the Middle Colonies, 1720-1750." In Interpreting Colonial America: Selected Readings, edited by James Kirby Martin. New York: Dodd and Mead, 1973.

Maxson, Charles Hartshorn. *The Great Awakening in the Middle Colonies.* Chicago: University of Chicago Press, 1920.

Oden, Thomas C. *Wesley's Scriptural Christianity: A Plain Exposition of His Teaching on Christian Doctrine.* Grand Rapids: Zondervan, 1994.

Outler, Albert C. *John Wesley.* New York: Oxford University Press, 1964.

————. *The Wesleyan Theological Tradition: Essays of Albert Outler.* Edited by Thomas C. Oden and Leicester R. Longden. Grand Rapids: Zondervan, 1991.

Overton, John H. *The Evangelical Revival in the Eighteenth Century.* London: Longmans, Green, & Co., 1900.

Peschke, Erhard. *Die frühen Katechismus Predigten August Hermann Franckes, 1693-1695.* Göttingen: Vandenhoeck & Ruprecht, 1992.

Piette, Maximin. *John Wesley in the Evolution of Protestantism.* New York: Sheed and Ward, 1937.

Pilcher, George William. *Samuel Davies: Apostle of Dissent in Colonial Virginia.* Knoxville: University of Tennessee Press, [1971].

Rattenbury, John Ernest. *The Conversion of the Wesleys: A Critical Study.* London: Epworth Press, 1938.

Reist, Irwin. "John Wesley's View on Baptism." *Wesleyan Theological Journal* 7, no. 1 (spring 1972).

Ritschl, Albrecht. *Die Geschichte des Pietismus.* 3 vols. Bonn: A. Marcus, 1880-86.

Rüttgardt, Jan Olaf. "Zur Entstehung und Bedeutung der Berliner Wiedergeburtspredigten Philipp Jakob Speners." In *Philipp Jakob Spener, Schriften,* edited by Erich Bayreuther, 7/I: 1-112. 16 vols. Hildesheim, Zürich, and New York: Georg Olms Verlag, 1994.

Sattler, Gary R. *God's Glory, Neighbor's Good: A Brief Introduction to the Life and Writings of August Hermann Francke.* Chicago: Covenant Press, 1982.

Schmid, Heinrich. *Die Geschichte des Pietismus.* Nordlingen: C. H. Beck, 1863.

Schmidt, M. "Pietismus." In *Die Religion in Geschichte und Gegenwart,* 5:370-81. 3rd ed. 6 vols. Tübingen: J. C. B. Mohr (Paul Siebeck), 1957-65.

Schmidt, Martin. "Philipp Jakob Spener und die Bible." In *Pietismus und Bible,* edited by Kurt Aland. Witten: Luther-Verlag, 1970.

Semmel, Bernard. *The Methodist Revolution.* New York: Basic Books, 1973.

Snyder, Howard A. *The Radical Wesley.* Downers Grove, Ill.: InterVarsity, 1980.

Spener, Philipp Jakob. *Die Evangelische Glaubens-Lehre 1688, Predigten über die Evangelien.* Photolithographic reproduction with introduction by Dietrich Blaufuss and Erich Beyreuther. Vol. 3, *Philipp Jakob Spener, Schriften.* Hildesheim, Zürich, and New York: Georg Olms Verlag, 1986.

————. *Der hochwichtige Articul von der Wiedergeburt (1696) 1715.* Vol. 7, *Philipp Jakob Spener, Schriften.* Hildesheim, Zürich, and New York: Georg Olms Verlag, 1994.

————. *Philipp Jakob Spener, Schriften.* Edited by Erich Beyreuther. 16 vols. Hildesheim, Zürich, and New York: Georg Olms Verlag, 1979-.

Sprague, William Buell. *Annals of the American Pulpit, or Commemorative Notices of Distinguished American Clergymen of Various Denominations.* New York: Robert Carter & Brothers, 1857-[1869].

Stein, K. James. *Philipp Jakob Spener: Pietist Patriarch.* Chicago: Covenant Press, 1986.

Stoeffler, F. Ernest. *Continental Pietism and Early American Christianity.* Grand Rapids: Wm. B. Eerdmans Publishing Co., 1976.

————. *The Rise of Evangelical Pietism.* Leiden: Brill, 1971.

Strong, Douglas M. "Whitefield, George." In *Historical Dictionary of Methodism,* edited by Charles Yrigoyen, Jr., and Susan E. Warrick. Lanham, Md., and London: Scarecrow Press, 1996.

Stuart, Henry. *George Whitefield, Wayfaring Witness.* New York and Nashville: Abingdon, 1957.

Sykes, Norman. *Church and State in England in the Eighteenth Century.* Cambridge: University Press, 1934.

————. *From Sheldon to Secker: Aspects of English Church History, 1660-1768.* Cambridge: University Press, 1959.

Tanis, James. *Dutch Calvinistsic Pietism in the Middle Colonies: A Study in the Life and Times of Theodorus Jacobus Frelinghuysen.* The Hague: Martinus Nijhoff, 1967.

Tennent, Gilbert. *The Espousals Or a Passionate Perswasive. To a Marriage with the Lamb of God, Wherein the Sinners Misery and the Redeemers Glory is Unvailed in A Sermon upon Gen. 24 49. Preach'd at N. Brunswyck, June the 22d 1735.* New York: J. Peter Zenger, 1735.

Wallmann, Johannes. *Philipp Jakob Spener und die Anfänge des Pietismus.* Tübingen: J. C. B. Mohr (Paul Siebeck), 1986.

Wesley, John. *Wesley's Standard Sermons.* Edited by Edward H. Sugden. 2 vols. London: Epworth Press, 1921.

Whitefield, George. *Select Sermons of George Whitefield.* Edited by J. C. Ryle. London: Banner of Truth Trust, 1959.

————. *Sermons on Important Subjects.* London: Henry Fischer, Son and P. Jackson, 1831.

————. *Works.* 6 vols. London: Printed by Edward and Charles Dilly, 1771.

Yrigoyen, Charles. *John Wesley: Holiness of Heart and Life.* New York: Mission Education and Cultivation Program Dept. for the Women's Division, General Board of Global Ministries, United Methodist Church, 1996.

Bibliography for Chapter III

Albro, John A. *The Life of Thomas Shepard.* Found as the memoir prefacing *The Works of Thomas Shepard, First Pastor of the First Church, Cambridge.* 3 vols. Boston: Boston Tract and Book Society, 1853. Reprint, New York: AMS Press, 1967.

Baxter, Richard. *Some Unpublished Correspondence of the Reverend Richard Baxter and the Reverend John Eliot, the Apostle of the American Indians.* Manchester: Manchester University Press, 1931.

Bercovitch, Sacvan. *The American Jeremiad.* Madison: University of Wisconsin Press, 1978.

Bowden, Henry W., and James P. Ronda. *John Eliot's Indian Dialogues, a Study in Cultural Interaction.* Westport, Conn., and London: Greenwood Press, 1980.

Brand, David C. *Profile of the Last Puritan: Jonathan Edwards, Self-Love, and the Dawn of the Beatific.* Atlanta: Scholars, 1991.

Burroughs, Jeremiah. *The Saints' Happiness.* Photolithographic reproduction. Beaver Falls, Pa.: Soli Deo Gloria Publications, [1989?].

Bush, Sargent, Jr. *The Writings of Thomas Hooker: Spiritual Adventure in Two Worlds.* Madison: University of Wisconsin Press, 1980.

Cherry, Conrad. *The Theology of Jonathan Edwards: A Reappraisal.* Bloomington: Indiana University Press, 1990.

Colman, Benjamin. *The Blessing of Zebulun and Issachar.* Boston: Printed by B. Green, Printer to His Excellency the Governour and Council for Samuel Gerrish, at his shop, 1719.

————. *Case of Satan's Fiery Darts in Blasphemous Suggestions and Hellish Annoyances.* Boston: Printed by Rogers and Fowle, 1744.

————. *Credibility of the Christian Doctrine of the Resurrection.* Boston: Printed for Thos. Hancock, 1729.

————. *A Humble Discourse of the Incomprehensibleness of God.* Boston: Printed by J. Draper, for D. Henchman, 1740.

————. *The Judgments of Providence in the Hand of Christ.* Boston: Printed for J. Phillips . . . and T. Hancock, 1727.

Cotton, John. *Christ the Fountaine of Life; or, Sundry Choyse Sermons on Part of the Fifth Chapter of the First Epistle of St. John.* Boston: Robert Ibbitson, 1651.

————. *The New England Way.* Library of American Puritan Writings, vol. 12. Edited by Sacvan Bercovitch. New York: AMS Press, 1984.

————. *The True Constitution of a particular visible Church, proved by Scripture.* London: Printed for Samuel Satterthwaite, 1642. Reprinted in John Cotton, *The New England Way.* Library of American Puritan Writings, vol. 12. Edited by Sacvan Bercovitch. New York: AMS Press, 1984.

————. *The Way of the Churches of Christ in New-England, Measured and examined by the Golden Reed of the Sanctuary.* London: Printed by Matthew Simmons, 1645. Reprinted in John Cotton, *The New England Way.* Library of American Puritan Writings, vol. 12. Edited by Sacvan Bercovitch. New York: AMS Press, 1984.

Davies, Horton. *The Worship of the American Puritans, 1629-1730.* New York: P. Lang, 1990.

Edwards, Jonathan. *Charity and Its Fruits.* In Edwards, *Ethical Writings,* edited by Paul Ramsey, in *The Works of Jonathan Edwards,* vol. 8. New Haven and London: Yale University Press, 1989.

————. *Charity and Its Fruits, Christian Love as Manifested in the Heart and Life.* London: Banner of Truth, 1969.

————. *Distinguishing Marks of a Work of the Spirit of God.* Boston: S. Kneeland, 1741. In Edwards, *The Great Awakening,* edited by C. C. Goen, in *The Works of Jonathan Edwards,* vol. 4. New Haven and London: Yale University Press, 1972.

————. *A Faithful Narrative.* In Edwards, *The Great Awakening,* edited by C. C. Goen, in *The Works of Jonathan Edwards,* vol. 4. New Haven and London: Yale University Press, 1972.

————. *The Life of David Brainerd.* Edited by Norman Pettit. In *The Works of Jonathan Edwards,* vol. 7. New Haven and London: Yale University Press, 1985.

————. *Sermons and Discourses, 1720-1723.* Edited by Wilson H. Kimnach. In *The Works of Jonathan Edwards,* vol. 10. New Haven and London: Yale University Press, 1992.

————. *The Sermons of Jonathan Edwards: A Reader.* Edited by Wilson H. Kimnach, Kenneth P. Minkema, and Douglas A. Sweeney. New Haven and London: Yale University Press, 1999.

Eliot, John. *A Brief Narrative of the Progress of the Gospel Among the Indians of New England.* Cambridge, Mass., 1670.

————. *Indian Dialogues, for their instruction in that great service of Christ, in calling home their Countrymen to the Knowledge of God, and of themselves, and of Iesus Christ.* Cambridge: Marmaduke Johnson, 1671.

————. *The Indian Primer.* Cambridge, Mass., 1669.

————. *John Eliot and the Indians, being letters addressed to the Rev. Jonathan Hanmer of Barnstable.* New York: [Adams and Grace Press], 1915.

————. *John Eliot's Indian Dialogues.* Westport, Conn.: Greenwood Press, 1980.

Eliot, John, and Thomas Mayhew, Jr. *Tears of Repentance; or, A Further Narrative of the Progress of the Gospel Amongst the Indians in New England.* London, 1663.

Elliott, Emory. *Power and the Pulpit in Puritan New England.* Princeton: Princeton University Press, 1975.

Emerson, Everett H. *John Cotton.* New Haven: College and University Press with Twayne Publishers, 1965.

————. *John Cotton.* Rev. ed. Boston: Twayne Publishers, 1990.

Gerstner, John H. *The Rational Biblical Theology of Jonathan Edwards.* Powhatan, Va.: Berea Publications; Orlando, Fla.: Ligonier Ministries, 1991-92.

Hall, David D. *The Faithful Shepherd: A History of the New England Ministry in the Seventeenth Century.* Chapel Hill: University of North Carolina Press, 1972.

Hall, Michael G. *The Last American Puritan: The Life of Increase Mather, 1639-1723.* Middletown, Conn.: Wesleyan University Press, 1988.

Hambrick-Stowe, Charles E. *The Practice of Piety: Puritan Devotional Disciplines in Seventeenth-Century New England.* Chapel Hill: Published for the Institute of Early American History and Culture, Williamsburg, Virginia, by the University of North Carolina Press, 1982.

Hatch, Nathan O., and Harry S. Stout, eds. *Jonathan Edwards and the American Experience.* New York: Oxford University Press, 1988.

Holifield, E. Brooks. *The Covenant Sealed: The Development of Puritan Sacramental Theology in Old and New England, 1570-1720.* New Haven: Yale University Press, 1974.

Holmes, Thomas James. *Increase Mather: A Bibliography of His Works.* Cleveland: [Printed at the Harvard University Press], 1931.

Hooker, Thomas. *The Application of Redemption by the Effectual Work of the Word and Spirit of Christ.* London: Printed by Peter Cole, 1657.

————. *The Poor Doubting Christian Drawn to Christ.* Photolithographic edition of a collection of five sermons published in 1845. Keyser, W.Va.: Odom Publications, 1991.

————. *Redemption, Three Sermons.* Introduction by Everett H. Emerson. Gainesville, Fla.: Scholars Facsimiles and Reprints, 1956.

Hooker, Thomas, et al. *Salvation in New England: Selections from the Sermons of the First Preachers.* Edited by Phyllis M. Jones and Nicholas R. Jones. Austin and London: University of Texas Press, 1977.

Jenson, Robert W. *America's Theologian: A Recommendation of Jonathan Edwards.* New York: Oxford University Press, 1988.

Levy, Babette May. *Preaching in the First Half Century of New England.* Hartford: American Society of Church History, 1945.

Lowance, Mason I., Jr. *Increase Mather.* New York: Twayne Publishers, [1974].

Mather, Increase. *Sermons Wherein Those Eight Characters of the Blessed Commonly Called the Beatitudes, are Opened and Applyed in Fifteen Discourses. To which is added, a Sermon concerning the Assurance of the Love of Christ.* Boston: Printed by B. Green for Daniel Henchman, 1718.

————. *Testimony against Prophane Customs.* Introduction and notes by William

Peden. 1687. Reprint, Charlottesville: Published by the University of Virginia Press for the Tracy W. McGregor Library, 1953.

Middlekauff, Robert. *The Mathers: Three Generations of Puritan Intellectuals, 1596-1728*. New York: Oxford University Press, 1971.

Miller, Perry. *Errand into the Wilderness*. Cambridge: Harvard University Press, Belknap Press, 1956.

————. *Jonathan Edwards*. Cleveland: World Publishing, 1964.

————. *The New England Mind, the Seventeenth Century*. New York: Macmillan, 1939.

Murray, Iain Hamish. *Jonathan Edwards: A New Biography*. Edinburgh and Carlisle, Pa.: Banner of Truth Trust, 1987.

Norton, John. *Abel being Dead yet Speaketh; or, The Life and Death of that deservedly Famous Man of God Mr. John Cotton, Late Teacher of the Church of Christ, at Boston in New-England*. London: Tho. Newcomb for Lodowick Lloyd, 1658. Found in John Cotton, *The New England Way*, Library of American Puritan Writings, vol. 12, edited by Sacvan Bercovitch. New York: AMS Press, 1984.

Pettit, Norman. *The Heart Prepared: Grace and Conversion in Puritan Spiritual Life*. New Haven: Yale University Press, 1966.

Plumstead, A. W. *The Wall and the Garden: Selected Massachusetts Election Sermons, 1670-1775*. Minneapolis: University of Minnesota Press, 1968.

Shepard, Thomas. *God's Plot: Puritan Spirituality in Thomas Shepard's Cambridge*. Edited by Michael McGiffert. Revised and expanded edition. Amherst: University of Massachusetts Press, 1994.

————. *God's Plot, the Paradoxes of Puritan Piety, Being the Autobiography and Journal of Thomas Shepard*. Edited with an introduction by Michael McGiffert. Amherst: University of Massachusetts Press, 1972.

————. *The Parable of the Ten Virgins Opened and Applied*. In *The Works of Thomas Shepard*, vol. 2. Doctrinal Tract and Book Society, 1853. Reprint, New York: AMS Press, 1967.

————. *A Wholesome Caveat in a Time of Liberty*. In *The Works of Thomas Shepard*, vol. 3. Doctrinal Tract and Book Society, 1853. Reprint, New York: AMS Press, 1967.

————. *The Works of Thomas Shepard*. 3 vols. Doctrinal Tract and Book Society, 1853. Reprint, New York: AMS Press, 1967.

Shuffleton, Frank. *Thomas Hooker, 1586-1647*. Princeton: Princeton University Press, 1977.

Stout, Harry S. *The New England Soul: Preaching and Religious Culture in Colonial New England*. New York and Oxford: Oxford University Press, 1986.

Turell, Ebenezer. *The Life and Character of the Reverend Benjamin Colman, D.D. (1749)*. Facsimile reproduction with introduction by Christopher R. Reaske. Delmar, N.Y.: Scholars' Facsimiles & Reprints, 1972.

Turnbull, Ralph G. *Jonathan Edwards the Preacher.* Grand Rapids: Baker, 1958.

Van Dyken, Seymour. *Samuel Willard: Preacher of Orthodoxy in an Era of Change.* Grand Rapids: Wm. B. Eerdmans Publishing Co., 1971.

Vaughan, Alden T. *The New England Frontier: Puritans and Indians, 1620-1675.* Boston: Little, Brown, 1965.

Walker, Williston. *Ten New England Leaders.* New York and Boston: Silver, Burdett and Co., 1901.

Werge, Thomas. *Thomas Shepard.* Boston: Twayne Publishers, 1987.

Whyte, Alexander. *Thomas Shepard: Pilgrim Father and Founder of Harvard: His Spiritual Experience and Experimental Preaching.* Edinburgh: Oliphant and Ferrier, 1909.

Willard, Samuel. *A Compleat Body of Divinity in Two Hundred and Fifty Expository Lectures on the Assembly's Shorter Catechism.* Boston: Printed by B. Green and S. Kneeland for B. Eliot and D. Henchman, 1726.

———. *The Fiery Tryal No Strange Thing.* Boston, 1682.

———. *Reformation, the Great Duty of an Afflicted People: Setting Forth the Sin and Danger There Is of Neglecting of It, Under the Continued and Repented Judgments of God: Being the Substance of What Was Preached on a Solemn Day of Humiliation Kept by the 3rd Gathered Church in Boston, on Aug. 23, 1694.* Boston: Printed by Barth, 1694.

———. *The Truly Blessed Man, or, the way to be happy here, and for ever: being the substance of divers sermons preached on, Psalm XXXII.* Boston: Printed by B. Green and J. Allen for Michael Perry, 1700.

Winslow, Ola Elizabeth. *John Eliot, Apostle to the Indians.* Boston: Houghton Mifflin, 1968.

Ziff, Larzer. *The Career of John Cotton: Puritanism and the American Experience.* Princeton: Princeton University Press, 1962.

Bibliography for Chapter IV

Abraham a Sancta Clara. *Sämmtliche Werke.* 21 vols. Lindau: Verlag von Johann Thomas Stettner, 1846.

Bianchi, L. *Studien zur Beurteilung des Abraham a Santa Clara.* Heidelberg, 1924.

Chudoba, Bohdan. "Czech Literature." In *New Catholic Encyclopedia,* 4:585-88. 17 vols. Washington, D.C.: Catholic University of America Press, 1968.

Clark, A. J. "Abraham of Sancta Clara." In *New Catholic Encyclopedia,* 1:35. 17 vols. Washington, D.C.: Catholic University of America Press, 1968.

Daniel, David P. "Hungary." In *The Oxford Encyclopedia of the Reformation,* 2:272-76. 4 vols. New York and Oxford: Oxford University Press, 1996.

Egres, Odo Joseph. "Pázmány, Péter." In *New Catholic Encyclopedia,* 11:35. 17 vols. Washington, D.C.: Catholic University of America Press, 1968.

"Eugene of Savoy." In *Encyclopedia Britannica*, 9:882-84. 11th ed. 29 vols. New York: Encyclopedia Britannica, 1910-11.

Felicijan, Joseph. "Klesl, Melchior." In *New Catholic Encyclopedia*, 8:212. 17 vols. Washington, D.C.: Catholic University of America Press, 1968.

Frinta, Mojmír Svatopluk. "Czechoslovakian Art." In *New Catholic Encyclopedia*, 4:598-605. 17 vols. Washington, D.C.: Catholic University of America Press, 1968.

Fudge, Thomas A. "Myth, Heresy and Propaganda in the Radical Hussite Movement." Diss., University of Cambridge, 1992.

Grindly, Anton. *Geschichte der Gegenreformation in Böhmen.* Leipzig: Verlag von Duncker und Humbolt, 1894.

Kaminsky, Harold. *A History of the Hussite Revolution.* Berkeley and Los Angeles: University of California Press, 1967.

Karajan, T. G. von. *Abraham a Sancta Clara.* Vienna, 1867.

Kastl, Maria. *Das Schriftwort in Leopolds predigten des 17. und 18. Jahrhunderts.* Vienna: Braumüller, 1988.

Kornis, J. *Le Cardinal Pázmány, 1570-1637.* Paris, 1937.

Kosáry, Dominic G. *A History of Hungary.* Cleveland and New York: Benjamin Franklin Bibliophile Society, 1941.

Krajcar, John, and Michael Lacko. "Czechoslovakia." In *New Catholic Encyclopedia*, 4:592. 17 vols. Washington, D.C.: Catholic University of America Press, 1968.

Lodi, F. *Menschen im Barock: Abraham a Santa Clara über des religiosesittliche im Österreich 1670-1710.* Vienna, 1938.

Lukinich, Imre. *A History of Hungary in Biographical Sketches.* Translated by Catherine Dallas. Freeport, N.Y.: Books for Libraries Press, 1968.

Medgyesi, Pál. *Erdély romlásának okairól.* Budapest: Magvetö Kiadó, n.d.

Mullet, Michael M. *The Catholic Reformation.* London and New York: Routledge, 1999.

Nemeskürty, István, Lázsló Orosz, Béla G. Németh, and Attila Tomás. *A History of Hungarian Literature.* Edited by Tibor Klaniczay. Budapest: Corvina, 1982.

Olin, John C. *The Catholic Reformation: Savonarola to Ignatius Loyola.* New York, Evanston, and London: Harper and Row, 1969.

Osterhaven, M. Eugene. "Reformed Galley Slaves." *Reformatusok Lapja*, pp. 3-4.

Otter, Jiří. *The Evangelical Church of Czech Brethren.* Prague: Evangelical Publishing House, 1992.

Pázmány, Péter. *Predikácziók.* Budapest: Nyomatott a M. Kir. Tud.-Egyetemi Nyomdában, 1905.

"Peikhart, Franz." Found in Constant von Wurzbach, editor. *Biographisches Lexikon des Öesterreichs*, 21:430-31. 60 volumes. Wien: Druck und Verlag der K. K. Hof — und Staatsdruckerei, 1870.

Pescheck, Christian Adolf. *The Reformation and Anti-Reformation in Bohemia.* 2 vols. London: Houlston and Stoneman, 1845.

Péter, Katalin. "Bornemisza, Péter." In *The Oxford Encyclopedia of the Reformation,* 1:201-2. 4 vols. New York and Oxford: Oxford University Press, 1996.

Ravasz, Lázsló. *A Gyülekezeti Igehirdetés Elmélete (Homiletika).* Pápa, Hungary: Református Fôiskola, 1915.

Reuss, Rodolphe. *La destruction du Protestantisme en Bohème.* 2nd ed. Paris: J. Cherbuliez, 1868.

Revesz, Imre. *History of the Hungarian Reformed Church.* Translated by George A. F. Knight. Washington, D.C.: Hungarian Reformed Federation of America, 1956.

Říčan, Rudolf. *Das Reich Gottes in den Böhmischen Ländern.* Stuttgart: Evangelisches Verlagswerk, 1957.

Schneyer, Johann Baptist. *Geschichte des katholischen Predigt.* Freiburg im Breisgau: Seelsorge Verlag, 1969.

Sinor, Denis. *History of Hungary.* Westport, Conn.: Greenwood Press, 1976.

"Soissons, Counts of." In *Encyclopedia Britannica.* 25:352-53. 11th ed. 32 vols. New York: Encyclopedia Britannica, 1910.

Spinka, Matthew. *John Hus, a Biography.* Princeton: Princeton University Press, 1968.

Toth, William. "Stephen Kis of Szeged, Hungarian Reformer." *Archiv für Reformationsgeschichte* (1953): 86-102.

Unghváry, Alexander Sándor. *The Hungarian Protestant Reformation in the Sixteenth Century under the Ottoman Impact.* Texts and Studies in Religion, vol. 48. Lewiston, Lampeter, and Queenston: Edwin Mellen Press, 1989.

Vooght, Paul de. *L'hérésie de Jean Hus.* Louvain: Publications Universitaires du Louvain, 1960.

Welzig, Werner. *Predigten der Barockzeit: Texte und Kommentar.* Vienna: Österreichischen Akademie der Wissenschaften, 1995.

Williams, George Huntston. *The Radical Reformation.* Philadelphia: Westminster, 1962.

Bibliography for Chapter V

Berger, John A. *The Franciscan Missions of California.* New York: Putnam, [1941].

Bolton, Herbert Eugene. *The Colonization of North America, 1493-1783.* New York: Macmillan, 1920.

———. *The Mission as a Frontier Institution in the Spanish-American Colonies.* El Paso: Printed at Texas Western College Press for Academic Reprints, 1960.

————, trans. and ed. *Fray Juan Crespí, Missionary Explorer on the Pacific Coast, 1769-1774.* Berkeley, 1927. Reprint, New York: AMS Press, 1971.

Couve de Murville, Maurice N. L. *The Man Who Founded California: The Life of Blessed Junípero Serra.* San Francisco: Ignatius, 2000.

Englebert, Omer. *The Last of the Conquistadors, Junípero Serra (1713-1784).* New York: Harcourt, Brace and Co., 1956.

Fogel, Daniel. *Junípero Serra, the Vatican, and Enslavement Theology.* San Francisco, ISM Press, 1988.

Geiger, Maynard. *Franciscan Missionaries in Hispanic California, 1769-1848: A Biographical Dictionary.* San Marino: Huntington Library, 1969.

————, trans. and ed. *Palóu's Life of Fray Junípero Serra.* Washington, D.C.: Academy of American Franciscan History, 1945.

Lasuén, Fermín Francisco de. *Writings.* Translated and edited by Finbar Kenneally. 2 vols. Washington, D.C.: Academy of American Franciscan History, 1965.

Norris, Jim. *After "The Year Eighty": The Demise of Franciscan Power in Spanish New Mexico.* Albuquerque: University of New Mexico Press, 2000.

Palóu, Francisco. *Historical Memoirs of New California by Francisco Palóu, O.F.M.* Translated and edited by Herbert Eugene Bolton. New York: Russel and Russel, 1966.

————. *Relación historica de la Vida . . . del V. P. Fray Junípero Serra.* Mexico, 1787.

Xavier, Adro. *Junípero Serra.* Barcelona: Editorial Casals, 1986.

Bibliography for Chapter VI

Antim of Iveria. *Opere.* Edited by Gabriel Ştrempel. Bucharest: Editora Minerva, 1972.

Comşa, Gheorghe. *Istoria Predicei la Români.* Bucharest: Tipografia Cărţilor Bisericeşti, 1921.

Gaster, Moses. "Anthim the Iberian." In *Encyclopedia Britannica,* 2:94. 11th ed. 29 vols. New York: Encyclopedia Britannica, 1910-11.

————. "Rumania: Literature." In *Encyclopedia Britannica,* 23:844-45. 11th ed. 29 vols. New York: Encyclopedia Britannica, 1910-11.

Pacurariu, Mircea. *Istoria Bisericii Ortodoxe Române.* Bucharest: Institutul Biblic si de Misiune al Bisericii Ortodoxe Române, 1978.

Bibliography for Chapter VII

Cracraft, James. *The Church Reform of Peter the Great.* Palo Alto, Calif.: Stanford University Press, 1971.

Fedotov, George P. *The Russian Religious Mind (I): Kievan Christianity, the Tenth to Thirteenth Centuries.* In *The Collected Works of George P. Fedotov,* vol. 3. Belmont, Mass.: Nordland, 1975.

————. *A Treasury of Russian Spirituality.* Vaduz: Buchervertriebanstalt, 1988.

Fennell, John. *A History of the Russian Church to 1448.* London and New York: Longmans, 1995.

Gorodetzky, Nadejda. *Saint Tikhon of Zadonsk: Inspirer of Dostoevsky.* Crestwood, N.Y.: St. Vladimir's Seminary Press, 1976.

Jugie, Martin. "Philarete Drozdov." In *Dictionnaire de théologie catholique* xii (1933): col. 1378.

Kalinovitch, Paul. "Metropolitan Philaret of Moscow and His Significance for the Russian and Universal Church." Translated by Seraphim Englehardt. *Orthodox Life* 46 (July/August 1996): 43-49; and 46 (September/October 1996): 41-49.

Kataiev, N. *Geschichte der Predigt in der russischen Kirche.* Translated from Russian into German by Alexis Markow. Stuttgart: Verlag von W. Kohlhammer, 1889.

Philaret of Moscow. *Select Sermons by Philaret of Moscow.* London: J. Masters, 1873.

Pospielovsky, Dimitry. *The Orthodox Church in the History of Russia.* Crestwood, N.Y.: St. Vladimir's Seminary Press, 1998.

Sermons and Rhetoric of Kievan Rus'. Translated and with an introduction by Simon Franklin. Cambridge, Mass.: Distributed by Harvard University Press for the Ukrainian Research Institute of Harvard University, 1991.

Ware, Kallistos Timothy. "Metropolitan Philaret of Moscow (1782-1867)." *Eastern Churches Review* 2 (spring 1968): 24-28.

Bibliography for Chapter VIII

Bardgett, Frank D. "Fergusson, David." In *Dictionary of Scottish Church History and Theology,* edited by Nigel M. de S. Cameron. Edinburgh: T. & T. Clark, 1993.

Blaikie, William Garden. *The Preachers of Scotland.* Edinburgh: T. & T. Clark, 1888.

Blair, Hugh. *Lectures on Rhetoric and Belles Lettres.* Edited with a critical introduction by Harold F. Harding. 2 vols. Carbondale and Edwardsville: Southern Illinois University Press, 1965.

593

————. *Sermons.* 5 vols. London: Printed for A. Strahan and T. Cadell in the Strand; Edinburgh: W. Creech, 1792-96.

————. *Sermons.* London: T. Tegg & Son, 1834.

Boston, Thomas. *The Complete Works of the Late Rev. Thomas Boston of Ettrick.* Edited by Samuel M'Millan. 12 vols. London: William Tegg & Co., 1853.

————. *The Complete Works of the Late Rev. Thomas Boston, Ettrick.* Edited by Samuel M'Millan. 12 vols. London, 1853. Reprint, Wheaton, Ill.: Richard Owen Roberts, Publishers, 1980.

————. *A Soliloquy on the Art of Man-Fishing.* Edited by D. D. F. MacDonald. Paisley: Gardner, 1900.

Brown, Stewart J. *Thomas Chalmers and the Godly Commonwealth in Scotland.* Oxford and New York: Oxford University Press, 1982.

Bruce, Robert. *The Mystery of the Lord's Supper.* Edited by Thomas F. Torrance. Richmond: John Knox, 1958.

————. *Sermons by Robert Bruce.* Reprinted from the original edition of MDXC and MDXCI with collections for his life by Robert Wodrow, now first printed from the manuscript in the library of the University of Glasgow. Edited by William Cunningham. Edinburgh: Wodrow Society, 1843.

————. *Sermons Preached in the Kirk of Edinburgh, by M. Robert Bruce, Minister of Christs Evangel there: as they were received from his mouth.* Edinburgh: Robert Waldegrave, 1591.

Burleigh, John H. S. *A Church History of Scotland.* London: Oxford University Press, 1960.

Cameron, Nigel M. de S., ed. *Dictionary of Scottish Church History and Theology.* Edinburgh: T. & T. Clark, 1993.

Chalmers, Thomas. *Discourses on the Christian Revelation, Viewed in Connection with the Modern Astronomy.* Vol. 7 in *The Works of Thomas Chalmers, D.D. & LL.D.* 25 vols. Glasgow: William Collins; London: Hamilton, Adams, & Co., [1836-42].

————. *Lectures on Romans,* pt. 1. Vol. 22 in *The Works of Thomas Chalmers, D.D. & LL.D.* 25 vols. Glasgow: William Collins; London: Hamilton, Adams, & Co., [1836-42].

————. *Sermon Preached Before the Society for the Relief of the Destitute Sick, April 18, 1813.* Glasgow: John Smith and Son, 1818. In Chalmers, *Sermons Preached on Public Occasions.* Glasgow: William Collins, s.n.

————. *The Works of Thomas Chalmers, D.D. & LL.D..* 25 vols. Glasgow: William Collins; London: Hamilton, Adams, & Co., [1836-1842].

Cheyne, A. C., ed. *The Practical and the Pious: Essays on Thomas Chalmers (1780-1847).* Edinburgh: Saint Andrew Press, 1985.

Cowan, Ian B. *The Scottish Covenanters, 1660-1680.* London: Gollancz, 1976.

Donaldson, Gordon. *Faith of the Scots.* London: Batsford, 1990.

————. "Scotland." In *Oxford Encyclopedia of the Reformation,* 4:28-31. 4 vols. New York and Oxford: Oxford University Press, 1996.

————. *Scotland: James V to James VII.* Rev. ed. Edinburgh History of Scotland, vol. 3. Edinburgh: Oliver & Boyd, 1987.

————. *The Scottish Reformation.* Reprint, Cambridge: University Press, 1979.

Douglas, J. D. "Henderson, Alexander." In *Dictionary of Scottish Church History and Theology,* edited by Nigel M. de S. Cameron. Edinburgh: T. & T. Clark, 1993.

Golden, James L., and Edward P. Corbett. *The Rhetoric of Blair, Campbell, and Whately: With Updated Bibliographies.* Carbondale and Edwardsville: Southern Illinois University Press, 1990.

Hanna, William. *Life of Thomas Chalmers.* Edited by James C. Moffat. Cincinnati: Moore, Anderson, Wilstach & Keys; New York: Newman & Ivison, 1853.

————. *Memoirs of the Life and Writings of Thomas Chalmers.* 4 vols. Edinburgh: Published for T. Constable by Sutherland and Knox, 1849-52.

Henderson, Alexander. *Sermons, Prayers and Pulpit Addresses by Alexander Henderson.* Edited by R. Thomson Martin. Edinburgh: John Maclaren, 1867.

Henderson, G. D. *Religious Life in Seventeenth-Century Scotland.* Cambridge: Cambridge University Press, 1937.

Hodges, Louis Igou. "Dickson, David." In *Dictionary of Scottish Church History and Theology,* edited by Nigel M. de S. Cameron. Edinburgh: T. & T. Clark, 1993.

Isbell, Sherman. "Rutherford, Samuel." In *Dictionary of Scottish Church History and Theology,* edited by Nigel M. de S. Cameron. Edinburgh: T. & T. Clark, 1993.

Janton, Pierre. *John Knox (ca. 1513-1572): L'homme and l'oeuvre.* Paris: Didier, 1967.

Kennedy, George A. *Classical Rhetoric and Its Christian and Secular Tradition from Ancient to Modern Times.* Chapel Hill: University of North Carolina Press, 1980.

Kirk, James. *Patterns of Reform.* Edinburgh: T. & T. Clark, 1989.

Knox, John. *John Knox's History of the Reformation in Scotland.* Edited by William Croft Dickinson. London: Nelson; New York: Philosophical Library, 1949.

Lachman, David C. "Blair, Robert." In *Dictionary of Scottish Church History and Theology,* edited by Nigel M. de S. Cameron. Edinburgh: T. & T. Clark, 1993.

————. "Boston, Thomas." In *Dictionary of Scottish Church History and Theology,* edited by Nigel M. de S. Cameron. Edinburgh: T. & T. Clark, 1993.

————. *The Marrow Controversy, 1718-1723: An Historical and Theological Analysis.* Edinburgh: Rutherford House, 1988.

————. "Thomson, Andrew Mitchell." In *Dictionary of Scottish Church History and Theology,* edited by Nigel M. de S. Cameron. Edinburgh: T. & T. Clark, 1993.

Loane, Marcus L. *Makers of Religious Freedom in the Seventeenth Century.* Grand Rapids: Wm. B. Eerdmans Publishing Co., [1961].

Macleod, John. *Scottish Theology in Relation to Church History Since the Reformation.* Edinburgh and Carlisle, Pa.: Banner of Truth Trust, 1974.

Makey, W. *The Church of the Covenant, 1637-1651.* Edinburgh: John Donald, 1979.

McGowan, Andrew T. B. *The Federal Theology of Thomas Boston.* Carlisle: Paternoster, 1997.

McIntosh, John R. *Church and Theology in Enlightenment Scotland: The Popular Party, 1740-1800.* East Lothian, Scotland: Tuckwell Press, 1998.

————. "Willison, John." In *Dictionary of Scottish Church History and Theology,* edited by Nigel M. de S. Cameron. Edinburgh: T. & T. Clark, 1993.

M'Crie, Thomas. *The Life of Alexander Henderson, minister of Edinburgh, and one of the commissioners from the Church of Scotland to the assembly of divines at Westminster.* London: Thomas Nelson, 1847.

————. *Life of John Knox.* Edinburgh, 1812.

————. *Life of John Knox.* Philadelphia: Presbyterian Board of Publication, 1845.

McRoberts, David, ed. *Essays on the Scottish Reformation.* Glasgow: Burns, 1962.

Murray, T. *Life of Samuel Rutherford.* Edinburgh, 1827.

Oliphant, Mrs. Margaret O. W. *Life of Thomas Chalmers.* London: Methuen & Co., [1912].

Percy of Newcastle, Lord Eustace. *John Knox.* Richmond: John Knox, [1965].

Reed, Kevin. "John Knox and the Reformation of Worship in the Scottish Reformation." In *Worship in the Presence of God,* edited by David Lachman and Frank J. Smith. Greenville, S.C.: Greenville Seminary Press, 1992.

Reid, W. Stanford. *Trumpeter of God.* New York: Scribner, 1974.

Ridley, Jasper. *John Knox.* New York: Oxford University Press, 1968.

Rutherford, Samuel. *Quaint Sermons of Samuel Rutherford.* Edited by Andrew A. Bonar. London: Hodder and Stoughton, 1885. Photolithographic reprint, Morgan, Pa.: Soli Deo Gloria, 1999.

Ryken, Philip Graham. *Thomas Boston as Preacher of the Four Fold State.* Rutherford Studies in Historical Theology. Edinburgh: Rutherford House, 1999.

Schmitz, Robert Morell. *Hugh Blair.* New York: King's Crown Press, 1948.

Thomson, Andrew. *Lectures, Expository and Practical, on Select Portions of Scrip-*

ture. 2 vols. Edinburgh: Printed for William Blackwood, Edinburgh; and T. Cadell and W. Davies, London, 1816.

————. *Sermons and Sacramental Exhortations by the Late Andrew Thomson, D.D., Minister of St. George's Church Edinburgh.* Edinburgh: Printed for William Whyte & Co., William Collins and M. Ogle, Glasgow; J. Dewar, Perth; and Longman, & Co., London, 1831.

Thomson, James Pringle. *Alexander Henderson, the Covenanter.* Edinburgh: Oliphant, 1912.

Walker, James. *The Theology and Theologians of Scotland, 1560-1750.* Reprint, Edinburgh: Knox Press, 1982.

Walker, Robert. *Sermons on Practical Subjects.* Trenton, N.J.: J. Justice and A. M'Kean, 1820.

————. *Sermons on Practical Subjects, Late one of the Ministers of the High Church of Edinburgh, to which is prefixed a character of the Author by Hugh Blair, D.D.* 5th ed. 3 vols. Edinburgh: C. Elliot and G. Robinson, 1785.

Watt, Hugh. *Thomas Chalmers and the Disruption.* Edinburgh and New York: T. Nelson and Sons, 1943.

Weir, David A. *The Origins of the Federal Theology in Sixteenth-Century Reformation Thought.* Oxford: Oxford University Press, 1990.

Welch, John. *Forty-eight Select Sermons.* Glasgow: Robert Chapman and Alexander Duncan, 1786.

Whyte, Alexander. *Samuel Rutherford and some of his Correspondents.* Edinburgh and London: Oliphant Anderson and Ferrier, 1894.

Willison, John. *The Practical Works of the Rev. John Willison.* Edited by W. M. Hetherington. London: Blackie and Son, [ca. 1830].

————. *Sacramental Meditations and Advices.* Newark, N.J.: Printed for William Tuttle, 1812.

Wormald, Janny. "Knox, John." In *Oxford Encyclopedia of the Reformation,* 2:380-81. 4 vols. New York and Oxford: Oxford University Press, 1996.

Wright, David F., and Gary D. Badcock, eds. *Disruption to Diversity: Edinburgh Divinity, 1846-1996.* Edinburgh: T. & T. Clark, 1996.

Young, James. "Life of John Welsh." In *Dictionary of Scottish Church History and Theology,* edited by Nigel M. de S. Cameron. Edinburgh: T. & T. Clark, 1993.

Bibliography for Chapter IX

Balleine, George Reginald. *A History of the Evangelical Party in the Church of England.* London, New York, et al.: Longman Green & Co., 1933.

Bennett, Arthur. "Charles Simeon: Prince of Evangelicals." *Churchman* 102, no. 2 (1988): 122-42.

Bishop, John. "Charles Simeon: Preaching to Exalt the Savior, Promote Holiness." *Preaching* 10 (November-December 1994): 56-58.

Booty, John E. "Reformers and Missionaries: The Bible in the Eighteenth and Early Nineteenth Centuries." In *Anglicanism and the Bible,* edited by F. Borsch. Wilton, Conn.: Morehouse Barlow, 1984.

Carpenter, Spencer Cecil. *Eighteenth Century Church and People.* London: Murray, 1959.

Carus, William. *Memoirs of the Life of the Rev. Charles Simeon.* London: J. Hatchard; Cambridge: Deightons and Macmillan, 1847.

Davies, George. *Early Cornish Evangelicals, 1735-60: A Study of Walker of Truro and Others.* London: SPCK, 1951.

Davies, Horton. *Worship and Theology in England.* 3 vols. Grand Rapids: William B. Eerdmans Publishing Co., 1996.

Downey, James. *The Eighteenth Century Pulpit: A Study of the Sermons of Butler, Berkeley, Secker, Sternas, Whitefield, and Wesley.* Oxford: Clarendon, 1969.

Evangelicalism: Comparative Studies of Popular Protestantism in North America, the British Isles, and Beyond. New York: Oxford University Press, 1994.

Hawker, Robert. *Sermons on the Divinity and Operation of the Holy Ghost.* In *The Works of the Rev. Robert Hawker, D.D.* 10 vols. London: Ebenezer Palmer, 1831.

————. *Sermons on the Divinity of Christ.* In *The Works of the Rev. Robert Hawker, D.D.* 10 vols. London: Ebenezer Palmer, 1831.

————. *The Works of the Rev. Robert Hawker, D.D.* 10 vols. London: Ebenezer Palmer, 1831.

Hindmarsh, D. Bruce. "I Am a Sort of Middle-man: The Politically Correct Evangelicalism of John Newton." In *Amazing Grace: Evangelicalism in Australia, Britain, Canada, and the United States,* edited by G. Rowlyk and others. Montreal: McGill-Queen's University Press, 1994.

————. *John Newton and the English Evangelical Tradition between the Conversions of Wesley and Wilberforce.* Oxford: Clarendon, 1996.

————. "The Olney Autobiographers: English Conversion Narrative in the Mid–Eighteenth Century." *Journal of Ecclesiastical History* 49 (January 1998): 61-84.

Hopkins, Hugh Evan. *Charles Simeon of Cambridge.* Grand Rapids: William B. Eerdmans Publishing Co., 1977.

————. *Charles Simeon, Preacher Extraordinary.* Grove Liturgical Study, vol. 18. Bramcote, Nottinghamshire: Grove Books, 1979.

Hylson-Smith, Kenneth. *Evangelicals in the Church of England, 1734-1984.* Edinburgh: T. & T. Clark, 1989.

Knox, Ronald Arbuthnott. *Enthusiasm: A Chapter in the History of Religion with Special Reference to the Seventeenth and Eighteenth Centuries.* New York: Oxford University Press, 1950.

Levenson, Russell Jones, Jr. "To Humble the Sinner, to Exalt the Savior, to Promote Holiness: Reflections on the Life, Ministry, and Legacy of Charles Simeon." *Sewanee Theological Review* 41 (Christmas 1998): 47-65.

Loane, Marcus L. *Cambridge and the Evangelical Succession.* London: Lutterworth Press, [1952].

Martin, Bernard. *An Ancient Mariner: A Biography of John Newton.* London: Epworth Press, 1960.

Moule, Handley Carr Glyn. *Charles Simeon.* London: Methuen, 1892.

Newton, John. *John Newton of Olney and St. Mary Woolnoth: An Autobiography and Narrative Compiled Chiefly from His Diary and Other Unpublished Documents.* Edinburgh: Banner of Truth Trust, 1998.

————. *Messiah: Fifty Expository Discourses on the Series of Scriptural Passages which form the Subject of the Celebrated Oratorio of Handel. Preached in the years 1784 and 1785, in the Parish Church of St. Mary Woolnoth, Lombard-Street.* In *The Works of John Newton,* vol. 4. Edinburgh and Carlisle, Pa.: Banner of Truth Trust, 1988.

————. *The Works of John Newton.* 6 vols. Edinburgh and Carlisle, Pa.: Banner of Truth Trust, 1988.

Pollock, John Charles. *Amazing Grace: John Newton's Story.* San Francisco: Harper and Row, 1981.

Pratt, John H. *The Thought of the Evangelical Leaders.* Edinburgh: Banner of Truth Trust, 1978.

Reynolds, John Stewart. *The Evangelicals at Oxford, 1735-1871.* Oxford: Blackwell, 1953.

Romaine, William. *Twelve Discourses upon the Law and the Gospel.* In *Works of the Late Reverend William Romaine, A.M., Rector of Saint Andrew by the Wardrobe and Saint Ann, Blackfriars, and Lecturer of Saint Dunstan in the West, London.* 2nd ed. 8 vols. London: Crosby and Letterman, 1801.

————. *The Whole Works of the Late Reverend William Romaine, A.M.,: comprising the life of Mr. Romaine.* Edinburgh: T. Nelson, 1840.

————. *Works of the Late Reverend William Romaine, A.M., Rector of Saint Andrew by the Wardrobe and Saint Ann, Blackfriars, and Lecturer of Saint Dunstan in the West, London.* 2nd ed. 8 vols. London: Crosby and Letterman, 1801.

Rowlyk, G., and others, eds. *Amazing Grace: Evangelicalism in Australia, Britain, Canada, and the United States.* Montreal: McGill-Queen's University Press, 1994.

Ryle, John Charles. *Five Christian Leaders of the Eighteenth Century.* 1885. Reprint, Edinburgh and Carlisle, Pa.: Banner of Truth Trust, 1979.

Simeon, Charles. *Evangelical Preaching.* Introduction by John R. W. Stott. Portland, Oreg.: Multnomah, 1986.

————. *The Excellency of the Liturgy, in Four Discourses, Preached before the Uni-*

versity of Cambridge, in November, 1811. Cambridge: Printed by J. Smith, 1812.

—————. *Horae Homileticae; or, Discourses Digested into One Continued Series and Forming upon Every Book of the Old and New Testament.* 8th ed. 21 vols. London: Henry G. Bohn, 1848.

Smyth, Charles Hugh Egerton. *The Art of Preaching: A Practical Survey of Preaching in the Church of England, 1747-1939.* London: SPCK; New York: Macmillan, [1940].

—————. *Simeon and Church Order: A Study of the Origins of the Evangelical Revival in Cambridge in the Eighteenth Century.* Cambridge: University Press, 1940.

Sykes, Norman. *From Sheldon to Secker: Aspects of English Church History, 1660-1768.* Cambridge: University Press, 1959.

Toon, Peter. *William Romaine, the Life, Walk, and Triumph of Faith with an Account of His Life and Work.* Cambridge and London: James Clarke & Co., 1970.

Walker, Samuel. *The Christian: A Course of Eleven Practical Sermons.* Glasgow: Chalmers and Collins, 1825.

—————. *Fifty-two Sermons on the Baptismal Covenant, the Creed, and the Ten Commandments.* London: Printed for C. Dilly and T. Browne, 1789.

Zabriskie, Alexander Clinton. *Anglican Evangelicalism.* Philadelphia: Church Historical Society, [1943].

Index

613